The Oxford Reader

DEBORAH H. HOLDSTEIN
Columbia College Chicago

DANIELLE AQUILINE
Oakton Community College

New York   Oxford
OXFORD UNIVERSITY PRESS

Oxford University Press is a department of the University of Oxford.
It furthers the University's objective of excellence in research, scholarship,
and education by publishing worldwide. Oxford is a registered trademark of
Oxford University Press in the UK and certain other countries.

Published in the United States of America by Oxford University Press
198 Madison Avenue, New York, NY 10016, United States of America.

© 2023 by Oxford University Press

> For titles covered by Section 112 of the US Higher Education
> Opportunity Act, please visit www.oup.com/us/he for the latest
> information about pricing and alternate formats.

All rights reserved. No part of this publication may be reproduced, stored in
a retrieval system, or transmitted, in any form or by any means, without the
prior permission in writing of Oxford University Press, or as expressly permitted
by law, by license, or under terms agreed with the appropriate reproduction
rights organization. Inquiries concerning reproduction outside the scope of the
above should be sent to the Rights Department, Oxford University Press,
at the address above.

You must not circulate this work in any other form
and you must impose this same condition on any acquirer.

Library of Congress Cataloging-in-Publication Data
Names: Holdstein, Deborah H., 1952- editor. | Aquiline, Danielle, editor.
Title: The Oxford reader / [edited by] Deborah H. Holdstein, Danielle
  Aquiline.
Description: New York, NY : Oxford University Press, [2023] | Includes
  bibliographical references and index. | Summary: "A renewed emphasis on
  more traditional forms of literacy that is, sustained reading, writing,
  and thinking comes at a particularly urgent moment. In a world of
  alternative facts and fake news, the importance of a well and deeply
  educated citizenry is reinvigorated. Consequently, even within the
  multimodal classroom, many instructors have continued (or have begun
  anew) to introduce (or reintroduce) the modes to employ readings that
  direct students to read carefully, to respond and argue cogently and
  accountably, and to become nimble and ready writers, no matter the
  occasion for writing. The Oxford Reader aims to distinguish itself by
  offering not only an expected mix of classic and contemporary
  selections, but also a variety of genres to emphasize nonfiction but not
  exclude some literary works as well as prominent pieces from blogs and
  other online sources. This spectrum of voices and genres and time
  periods will illustrate that what is considered contemporary thinking
  often has its roots elsewhere"—Provided by publisher.
Identifiers: LCCN 2021049743 (print) | LCCN 2021049744 (ebook) | ISBN
  9780190856014 (paperback) | ISBN 9780197619360 (epub)
Subjects: LCSH: Literature—Collections.
Classification: LCC PN6014 .O94 2023 (print) | LCC PN6014 (ebook) | DDC
  808.8—dc23/eng/20211105
LC record available at https://lccn.loc.gov/2021049743
LC ebook record available at https://lccn.loc.gov/2021049744

Printed by Sheridan Books, Inc., United States of America

CHRONOLOGICAL CONTENTS

PREFACE   xix

INTRODUCTION   xxi

The Allegory of the Cave   1
Plato
    For Informal Writing   7
    For Discussion   7
    For Writing   7

A Modest Proposal (1729)   9
Jonathan Swift
    For Informal Writing   16
    For Discussion   16
    For Writing   16

The Cask of Amontillado (1846)   17
Edgar Allan Poe
    For Informal Writing   20
    For Discussion   20
    For Writing   21
WHAT'S NEW IS OLD   21

What to the Slave Is the Fourth of July? (1852)   23
Frederick Douglass
    For Informal Writing   43
    For Discussion   43
    For Writing   43

Address to the Legislature of New York (1854)   45
Elizabeth Cady Stanton
> For Informal Writing   59
> For Discussion   59
> For Writing   59

Life Without Principle (1863)   61
Henry David Thoreau
> For Informal Writing   76
> For Discussion   76
> For Writing   76

Advice to Youth (1882)   77
Mark Twain
> For Informal Writing   79
> For Discussion   79
> For Writing   80

The Necklace (1884)   81
Guy de Maupassant
> For Informal Writing   88
> For Discussion   88
> For Writing   88

Shooting an Elephant (1936)   89
George Orwell
> For Informal Writing   95
> For Discussion   95
> For Writing   95

WHAT'S NEW IS OLD   95

The Lottery (1948)   97
Shirley Jackson
> For Informal Writing   104
> For Discussion   104
> For Writing   105

Notes of a Native Son (1955)   107
James Baldwin
> For Informal Writing   123
> For Discussion   124

For Writing   124
WHAT'S NEW IS OLD   124

Letter from a Birmingham Jail, an Excerpt (1963)   125
Martin Luther King, Jr.
    For Informal Writing   137
    For Discussion   137
    For Writing   137

The Ballot or the Bullet (1964)   139
Malcolm X
    For Informal Writing   155
    For Discussion   155
    For Writing   155
WHAT'S NEW IS OLD   156

Trip to Hanoi (1968)   157
Susan Sontag
    For Informal Writing   205
    For Discussion   205
    For Writing   205
WHAT'S NEW IS OLD   205

Speech on Impeachment (We the People) (1974)   207
Barbara Jordan
    For Informal Writing   211
    For Discussion   211
    For Writing   211

Why I Write (1976)   213
Joan Didion
    For Informal Writing   218
    For Discussion   218
    For Writing   218

Split at the Root (1982)   219
Adrienne Rich
    For Informal Writing   229
    For Discussion   229
    For Writing   229

Just Walk on By: A Black Man Ponders His Ability to Alter Public Space (1986) 231
Brent Staples
- For Informal Writing 234
- For Discussion 234
- For Writing 235

Am I Blue? (1986) 237
Alice Walker
- For Informal Writing 241
- For Discussion 241
- For Writing 241

How to Tame a Wild Tongue, an Excerpt (1987) 243
Gloria Anzaldúa
- For Informal Writing 249
- For Discussion 249
- For Writing 249

The Management of Grief (1988) 251
Bharati Mukherjee
- For Informal Writing 264
- For Discussion 264
- For Writing 264

Sh**** First Drafts (1994) 265
Anne Lamott
- For Informal Writing 268
- For Discussion 268
- For Writing 268

The Secret Life of the Love Song (1999) 269
Nick Cave
- For Informal Writing 276
- For Discussion 277
- For Writing 277

The Waiter's Wife (1999) 279
Zadie Smith
- For Informal Writing 291
- For Discussion 291
- For Writing 291

CHRONOLOGICAL CONTENTS   vii

The Perils of Indifference (1999)   293
Elie Wiesel
    For Informal Writing   297
    For Discussion   297
    For Writing   297

Fast Food Nation, an Excerpt (2000)   299
Eric Schlosser
    For Informal Writing   307
    For Discussion   307
    For Writing   307

Why We Travel (2000)   309
Pico Iyer
    For Informal Writing   317
    For Discussion   317
    For Writing   317

The Youth in Asia (2000)   319
David Sedaris
    For Informal Writing   326
    For Discussion   326
    For Writing   326
WHAT'S NEW IS OLD   326

Shooting Dad (2000)   327
Sarah Vowell
    For Informal Writing   332
    For Discussion   333
    For Writing   333

Consider the Lobster (2004)   335
David Foster Wallace
    For Informal Writing   350
    For Discussion   350
    For Writing   350

1918 Influenza: The Mother of All Pandemics (2006)   351
Jeffrey K. Taubenberger and David M. Morens
    For Informal Writing   361
    For Discussion   362

For Writing 362
WHAT'S NEW IS OLD 362

Is Google Making Us Stupid? (2008) 363
Nicholas Carr
    For Informal Writing 372
    For Discussion 372
    For Writing 372

The Matthew Effect (2008) 373
Malcolm Gladwell
    For Informal Writing 385
    For Discussion 385
    For Writing 385

Go Gentle Into That Good Night (2009) 387
Roger Ebert
    For Informal Writing 391
    For Discussion 391
    For Writing 392

Assassins of the Mind (2009) 393
Christopher Hitchens
    For Informal Writing 398
    For Discussion 398
    For Writing 399

Reprieve (2009) 401
Tim Kreider
    For Informal Writing 404
    For Discussion 404
    For Writing 405

A Tale of Three Coming Out Stories (2012) 407
Roxane Gay
    For Informal Writing 413
    For Discussion 413
    For Writing 414

My President Was Black (2017) 415
Ta-Nehisi Coates
    For Informal Writing 449
    For Discussion 449
    For Writing 449

Going It Alone (2017) 451
Rahawa Haile
    For Informal Writing 458
    For Discussion 459
    For Writing 459

To Be, or Not to Be (2018) 461
Masha Gessen
    For Informal Writing 469
    For Discussion 469
    For Writing 470
WHAT'S NEW IS OLD   470

You Owe Me an Apology (2018) 471
Brittany Packnett Cunningham
    For Informal Writing 474
    For Discussion 474
    For Writing 475

Origin Story: Carrying Histories of Protest (2019) 477
Jaquira Díaz
    For Informal Writing 483
    For Discussion 484
    For Writing 484

The American Nightmare (2020) 485
Ibram X. Kendi
    For Informal Writing 491
    For Discussion 491
    For Writing 491

Pandemics Leave Us Forever Altered (2020) 493
Charles C. Mann
    For Informal Writing   499
    For Discussion   499
    For Writing   499
WHAT'S NEW IS OLD   499

Facebook Is a Doomsday Machine (2020) 501
Adrienne LaFrance
    For Informal Writing   510
    For Discussion   510
    For Writing   511
WHAT'S NEW IS OLD   511

INDEX   513

THEMATIC CONTENTS

ART & CULTURE

The Cask of Amontillado (1846) 17
Edgar Allan Poe

The Lottery (1948) 97
Shirley Jackson

The Secret Life of the Love Song (1999) 269
Nick Cave

Why We Travel (2000) 309
Pico Iyer

Why I Write (1976) 213
Joan Didion

Sh**** First Drafts (1994) 265
Anne Lamott

DOING WHAT'S RIGHT

Shooting an Elephant (1936) 89
George Orwell

The Perils of Indifference (1999) 293
Elie Wiesel

Speech on Impeachment (We the People)
(1974) 207
Barbara Jordan

Life Without Principle (1863) 61
Henry David Thoreau

Origin Story: Carrying Histories of Protest
(2019) 477
Jaquira Díaz

Letter from a Birmingham Jail,
an Excerpt (1963) 125
Martin Luther King, Jr.

CULTURAL RECKONINGS

Advice to Youth (1882) 77
Mark Twain

Is Google Making Us Stupid? (2008) 363
Nicholas Carr

The Matthew Effect (2008) 373
Malcolm Gladwell

The Waiter's Wife (1999) 279
Zadie Smith

What to the Slave Is the Fourth of July? (1852) 23
Frederick Douglass

A Modest Proposal (1729) 9
Jonathan Swift

The Youth in Asia (2000) 319
David Sedaris

Shooting Dad (2000) 327
Sarah Vowell

RACE & IDENTITY

Notes of a Native Son (1955) 107
James Baldwin

Split at the Root (1982) 219
Adrienne Rich

Just Walk on By: A Black Man Ponders His Ability to Alter Public Space (1986) 231
Brent Staples

My President Was Black (2017) 415
Ta-Nehisi Coates

The American Nightmare (2020) 485
Ibram X. Kendi

You Owe Me an Apology (2018) 471
Brittany Packnett Cunningham

To Be, or Not to Be (2018) 461
Masha Gessen

A Tale of Three Coming Out Stories (2012) 407
Roxane Gay

THINKING ABOUT THINKING

The Allegory of the Cave 1
Plato

Go Gentle Into That Good Night (2009) 387
Roger Ebert

Assassins of the Mind (2009) 393
Christopher Hitchens

Reprieve (2009) 401
Tim Kreider

The Ballot or the Bullet (1964) 139
Malcolm X

ALTERED PERSPECTIVES

Address to the Legislature of New York (1854) 45
Elizabeth Cady Stanton

The Necklace (1884) 81
Guy de Maupassant

How to Tame a Wild Tongue, an Excerpt (1987) 243
Gloria Anzaldúa

The Management of Grief (1988) 251
Bharati Mukherjee

Am I Blue? (1986) 237
Alice Walker

Trip to Hanoi (1968) 157
Susan Sontag

HEALTH & ENVIRONMENT

Consider the Lobster (2004) 335
David Foster Wallace

1918 Influenza: The Mother of All Pandemics (2006) 351
Jeffrey K. Taubenberger and David M. Morens

Fast Food Nation, an Excerpt (2000) 299
Eric Schlosser

Going It Alone (2017) 451
Rahawa Haile

Pandemics Leave Us Forever Altered (2020) 493
Charles C. Mann

Facebook Is a Doomsday Machine (2020) 501
Adrienne LaFrance

ABOUT THE AUTHORS

Deborah H. Holdstein is Professor of English at Columbia College Chicago. Danielle Aquiline is Professor of English at Oakton Community College.

PREFACE

The first thing instructors may notice about this book is its relative brevity: Unlike our worthy competitors, we believe that a carefully selected group of essays can inform, inspire, and challenge our students toward accountable and worthwhile discussion and writing. While the number of readings may not compare to the vast contents of other, perhaps similar volumes, we are intentional in ensuring that this reader is affordable while being accessible as well as academically and intellectually challenging to our students.

This book is structured as follows: The primary table of contents is chronological and therefore less prescriptive for faculty members who chart their own, respected courses in their classrooms. Nonetheless, we see value in looking across time and cultural milieu for productive comparison; after all, some things never change—for instance, the need for clear and cogent argument. At the same time, we offer a thematic table of contents to pique instructors' and students' curiosity about the directions in which these essays might provoke productive discussion and writing.

Each selection in this volume features an author headnote and extensive apparatus, including questions for informal writing, for discussion, and for more formal (often research-based) writing, along with opportunities for cross-talk between and among different readings, authors, and generations.

INTRODUCTION

WHY READING AND WRITING MATTER

It may seem to some that the metaphorical pendulum has swung entirely and exclusively toward the 280-word tweet, the abbreviated language of tweets and texts (CU ltr), and an overemphasis on anything brief, immediate, or Instagram or Pinterest visual.

Nonetheless, we recognize, as do many others, that a need remains for sustained reading, thinking, and writing. Careful analysis of news, documents, social media posts, and the like requires abilities that are appropriately critical in nature. Reading essays and other writing that are part of a vast, chronological sweep and a variety of perspectives can instruct us in several things, among them that what's old is new and what's new is old, as you'll see by the questions at the end of each selection that make these types of connections.

At the same time, we acknowledge that we all live in a world where we have access to information with varying degrees of merit—perhaps too much—through smart phones, tablets, and other technologies that often limit careful reading and thought but require that careful reading all the more. Living in the digital era, moreover, also can disadvantage the traditional textbook; at this point in time, however, it appears to us that the traditional textbook, carefully curated, is more important than ever for slower reading and more careful thinking and writing.

Writers know that there are many occasions for writing, some brief, some complex, some neither. But why, in the twenty-first century, should students be prepared to write in various ways and to familiarize themselves with various genres? As one of our students succinctly phrased it, "There can never be too much literacy." We agree.

This renewed emphasis on more traditional forms of literacy—that is, sustained reading, writing, and thinking—comes at a particularly urgent moment: In a world of "alternative facts," "fake news," and the like, the importance of a deeply and well-educated citizenry is reinvigorated. Consequently, even within the multimodal classroom, many instructors have continued (or have begun anew) to introduce (or reintroduce) the modes and to employ readings that direct students to read carefully, to respond and argue cogently and accountably, and to become nimble and ready writers, no matter the occasion for writing.

SOME WAYS TO APPROACH THE READINGS IN THIS BOOK

In this volume, you will find selections from several genres and points in history that we hope will challenge you and generate fruitful discussion and writing. We have been intentional in choosing pieces that cross generations, themes, and subjects, pieces that we trust you will also put into conversation with one another. As you read the various essays and works of fiction in the text—we believe that there is much to learn from the literary text as well—ask yourself the following questions, as well as others you will generate in discussion with your instructor and classmates:

- What do I know about this author? How might I learn more?
- What do I know about this subject? How can this reading add to my existing knowledge?
- How is this essay/story similar or different to something I've read in class or read or heard about elsewhere?
- What seems to be the goal of this particular reading? Does the author articulate a clear argument? Is the argument implied?
- Why might the author choose the particular genre and strategy for writing?
- What is my response to the argument or point being made in the selection? How can I use specific information within the piece to bolster (or refute) my initial response?
- How is this reading—or the argument, implied or otherwise—similar or different to other readings in the book? How so?
- What is the context in which this particular reading might have been written? If the essay or story isn't current—say, within the last two or so years—how and why might it still be current?

We hope these questions will be just a start to more questions—leading to fruitful engagement with the text, discussion about the text, and writing about the text.

THE RHETORICAL SITUATION AND THE RHETORICAL MODES

As you read, you will discover that writers choose particular strategies, often called *rhetorical strategies*, in crafting their works. To determine the best rhetorical strategies, writers often assess the *rhetorical situation*.

Part of determining the rhetorical situation is to assess how best to articulate an argument to whatever audience happens to be addressed. To be sure, most audiences are complex—that is, this Introduction is suited for student readers as well as instructors, not for either category alone. And as we all know, "student readers" is not a monolithic, predictable category, so it is a complex audience in and of itself.

Nonetheless, as you read through this volume, you will see a number of different types of "categories" or genres for writing. Some of these will reveal situational contexts—a political address, such as the speech by Elie Wiesel, for instance—while others demonstrate a more intentional attempt on the part of the writer to persuade an audience using a variety of strategies and structures. Description, comparison/contrast, narrative, argument—all examples of "modes" and ways to approach a writing project—can also be mixed within one essay, such as a writer deciding that description or personal narrative is used on the way toward making an effective argument. Brittany Packnett Cunningham's "You Owe Me An Apology" is an example of this kind of modal hybridity, among many others in this volume.

Each of these modes can be considered the same as the tools in a craftperson's toolbelt. That is, it's important to recognize how and why you as a writer might choose to use these tools, as well as when it is useful and appropriate for the writers whose work you are reading to use the modes themselves. The Greek philosopher Aristotle, in fact, is the source by which the factors determined in this decision-making are named "the rhetorical situation."[1]

To Consider Additionally as You Read and Write:

Just as we provided questions that might be useful to think about as you read through the selections in this volume, there are also questions that writers such as the many featured here consider as they craft their work. These are questions you also will want to consider as you draft your own writing:

Consider the Writer—Or, as Aristotle Put It, the Speaker

Who is the speaker? How does she or he convey authority? Does the speaker work to develop ethos (your sense of the credibility, authority, and accountability of the writer)? What is the experience of the speaker and how does that experience award the speaker credibility?

Consider the Audience—Your Readers

Who is the target audience for your argument? What does the audience expect? Does the audience consist of experts in the field of study? Will the audience be evaluating the written text in any way? What is the audience's relationship to the writer?

---

[1] The following discussion is adapted liberally from Holdstein and Aquiline, *Who Says? A Writer's Research,* 3rd Edition, 2021, Oxford University Press.

Consider the Purpose—In Addition to Fulfilling the Assignment
Is the piece of writing meant to convey a message? Make a point? Entertain? Delight? Praise? Criticize? Analyze? Is the writing trying to persuade us of something? What is the goal?

Consider the Topic—Larger Issues
What is the effect of using a particular tone for this writing assignment? What are the specific conventions for the particular discipline in which you are writing? Does the writing provide the necessary context for the argument being made?

Consider the Occasion
Why is this piece of writing being composed? In what context will this writing be presented? What are the expectations and standard conventions of that particular context? What is the setting for this writing (time, place, etc.)?

Possible Approaches to Writing: Using the Modes
As you read the selections in this volume, it may become apparent that the writer has chosen to use a particularly *modal* approach—perhaps comparison and contrast; argument; narrative in the service of argument; and the like.

The traditional modes (or rhetorical strategies) are defined, briefly, as follows:

- *Analysis and Explaining:* This strategy breaks down a complex idea or set of ideas into its component parts to better explain and make sense of it. This is particularly useful when writing about a nuanced, multifaceted concept.
- *Argument and Persuasion:* This strategy expects that the writer will support a claim or argument authoritatively and appropriately so that your audience will agree with your claim.
- *Cause and Effect:* This strategy suggests that the writer will begin with an effect of an action or instance or the reverse—the effects of a particular event or series of events (climate change, for instance) followed by the causes.
- *Classification and Division:* This strategy is similar to analysis and explaining in that the writer attempts to better define a concept by looking at its numerous parts. What sets it apart from the other is that classification is an attempt to better define something, while analysis is an attempt to better understand that something.
- *Comparison and Contrast:* Here, the writer takes two concepts in their relationship to one another—similarities, differences, and coming to an overall conclusion about these similarities and differences.

Definition: This strategy articulates both what something is and what something is not through examples and descriptions, perhaps also looking at how definitions change in various contexts.

Description: Using description as a strategy involves considering all of the senses when writing about a particular person, place, or thing. What does the sun feel like? How would I describe the environment of my favorite room?

Narration: Narration involves telling stories, including genres such as the memoir, personal essays, and fiction. Generally, narratives follow some sort of sequential order, with transitional words that help readers situate themselves in the story. ("In the end . . .," "First . . .")

Process: This strategy can delineate how something works or happens—for instance, how a bill becomes a law or how to raise yeast dough.

Most importantly, however, writers must recognize that *many of these modes are best used in a hybrid fashion:* That is, a narrative about the qualities of one's favorite room might result in a well-argued essay about the essential qualities of a favorite room. Similarly, comparing and contrasting the school lunch menus at a private versus public school might allow an accountable argument about the qualities of one over the other and the reasons for those differences in quality.

Take it upon yourself to determine what mode-based strategies the writers in this volume have chosen to use and why they might have done so. For instance, a number of pieces in the book rely on personal stories—"narration"—with which to craft an overall argument. Look, for instance, at James Baldwin's "Notes of a Native Son" or David Foster Wallace's "Consider the Lobster." These would be examples of the type of "modal hybridity" we are referring to. Is "cause and effect" at work in "Pandemics Leave Us Forever Altered" by Charles C. Mann and "Facebook Is a Doomsday Machine," by Adrienne LaFrance—with the eventual points examples of "argument?"

No matter the approach to reading or the strategy for writing, it's important to understand that some things don't change: for instance, universal, human concerns and themes; the need for a clear and cogent argument; the strategic relevance of acknowledging one's audience and addressing it accordingly; the use of appropriate tone, diction, and the like. Similarly, it's important to understand that the ways in which we address writing tasks remain somewhat constant. That is, technologies may change, but we must still argue effectively, ethically, and accountably. The topics we may choose to write about, the matters we find important to address, can remain constant over decades and centuries—the reason for a primary Table of Contents that is chronological, indicating the vast sweep of time over which various writers approach differing and similar topics.

ACKNOWLEDGMENTS

We appreciate our colleagues at Oxford University Press, USA, notably Sherith Pankratz, in whose capable hands this book was thrust and for whose support and advocacy we are grateful. We also thank Maeve O'Brien, the editorial assistant, and Steve Helba, our past editor, whose enthusiasm for this project and our authorship deserves (and also receives) our gratitude. It is a privilege to work with OUP.

Columbia College Chicago and Oakton Community College also loom large in their support for this book, and we thank the numerous colleagues who directly or indirectly offered access to digital files, photocopiers, scanners, and the like.

Our personal thank-yous are profound and simple: Deborah and Danielle thank Jay Boersma and Sona Patel, respectively, for deep and unyielding support for any and all projects and ventures. We also acknowledge our children: Danielle's Finn Aquiline and Elias Aquiline, and Deborah's David Gilman and Emily Gilman.

As is the custom of a credible publisher, OUP consulted with colleagues at diverse institutions across the United States for their feedback on this project. We, too, would also like to thank the following reviewers whose insights helped guide us through the revision process for *The Oxford Reader*:

- Jaime Armin Mejia, Texas State University
- Deborah M. Coulter-Harris, University of Toledo
- Cheryl Edelson, Chaminade University of Honolulu
- Briallen Hopper, Yale University
- Rochell J Isaac, LaGuardia Community College, CUNY
- Ashmita Khasnabish, Lasell College
- Mark Lanting, Rock Valley College
- Henry J. Lindborg, University of Wisconsin Colleges
- Tonja McCurdy-Jennings, Georgia Northwestern Technical College
- Laura Morrison, College of the Albemarle
- Hilary Parmentier, Florida Keys Community College
- Joseph Pilaro, Nassau Community College
- Loren Qualls, Ventura College
- Katherine Silvester, Indiana University Bloomington
- Marilyn Sue Yamin, Pellissippi State Community College

We are grateful for both our professional and personal forms of support in our ongoing, productive work as co-authors.

The Allegory of the Cave
Plato (428/427–348/347 BCE)

One of the most famous Greek philosophers and a faithful follower of Socrates, Plato is particularly remembered for the founding of his school of thought (the Platonist School) and for founding the Academy, believed to be the Western world's first institution of higher education. His best-known works include "Forms, A Theory of Ideas," which details two different worlds, the concrete and the abstract, ideas we also see in "The Allegory of the Cave." Plato is also known for his extensive influence on a variety of areas of thought, including mathematics, religion, mysticism, and the essence of knowledge.

Next, said I, compare our nature in respect of education and its lack to such an experience as this. Picture men dwelling in a sort of subterranean cavern with a long entrance open to the light on its entire width. Conceive them as having their legs and necks fettered from childhood, so that they remain in the same spot, able to look forward only, and prevented by the fetters from turning their heads. Picture further the light from a fire burning higher up and at a distance behind them, and between the fire and the prisoners and above them a road along which a low wall has been built, as the exhibitors of puppet shows have partitions before the men themselves, above which they show the puppets.

All that I see, he said.

See also, then, men carrying past the wall implements of all kinds that rise above the wall, and human images and shapes of animals as well, wrought in stone and wood and every material, some of these bearers presumably speaking and others silent.

A strange image you speak of, he said, and strange prisoners.

The Republic of Plato, 2 vols., with an English translation by Paul Shorey, Loeb Classical Library, 1937 (1930).

Like to us, I said. For, to begin with, tell me do you think that these men would have seen anything of themselves or of one another except the shadows cast from the fire on the wall of the cave that fronted them?

How could they, he said, if they were compelled to hold their heads unmoved through life?

And again, would not the same be true of the objects carried past them?

Surely.

If then they were able to talk to one another, do you not think that they would suppose that in naming the things that they saw they were naming the passing objects?

Necessarily.

And if their prison had an echo from the wall opposite them, when one of the passers-by uttered a sound, do you think that he would suppose anything else than the passing shadow to be the speaker?

By Zeus, I do not, said he.

Then in every way such prisoners would deem reality to be nothing else than the shadows of the artificial objects.

Quite inevitably, he said.

Consider, then, what would be the manner of the release and healing from these bonds and this folly if in the course of nature something of this sort should happen to them. When one was freed from his fetters and compelled to stand up suddenly and turn his head around and walk and to lift up his eyes to the light, and in doing all this felt pain and, because of the dazzle and glitter of the light, was unable to discern the objects whose shadows he formerly saw, what do you suppose would be his answer if someone told him that what he had seen before was all a cheat and an illusion, but that now, being nearer to reality and turned toward more real things, he saw more truly? And if also one should point out to him each of the passing objects and constrain him by questions to say what it is, do you not think that he would be at a loss and that he would regard what he formerly saw as more real than the things now pointed out to him?

Far more real, he said.

And if he were compelled to look at the light itself, would not that pain his eyes, and would he not turn away and flee to those things which he is able to discern and regard them as in very deed more clear and exact than the objects pointed out?

It is so, he said.

And if, said I, someone should drag him thence by force up the ascent which is rough and steep, and not let him go before he had drawn him out into the light of the sun, do you not think that he would find it painful to be so haled along, and would chafe at it, and when he came out into the light, that his eyes would be filled with its beams so that he would not be able to see even one of the things that we call real?

Why, no, not immediately, he said.

Then there would be need of habituation, I take it, to enable him to see the things higher up. And at first he would most easily discern the shadows and, after that, the likenesses or reflections in water of men and other things, and later, the things themselves, and from these he would go on to contemplate the appearances in the heavens and heaven itself, more easily by night, looking at the light of the stars and the moon, than by day the sun and the sun's light.

Of course.

And so, finally, I suppose, he would be able to look upon the sun itself and see its true nature, not by reflections in water or phantasms of it in an alien setting, but in and by itself in its own place.

Necessarily, he said.

And at this point he would infer and conclude that this it is that provides the seasons and the courses of the year and presides over all things in the visible region, and is in some sort the cause of all these things that they had seen.

Obviously, he said, that would be the next step.

Well then, if he recalled to mind his first habitation and what passed for wisdom there, and his fellow bondsmen, do you not think that he would count himself happy in the change and pity them?

He would indeed.

And if there had been honors and commendations among them which they bestowed on one another and prizes for the man who is quickest to make out the shadows as they pass and best able to remember their customary precedences, sequences, and coexistences, and so most successful in guessing at what was to come, do you think he would be very keen about such rewards, and that he would envy and emulate those who were honored by these prisoners and lorded it among them, or that he would feel with Homer and greatly prefer while living on earth to be serf of another, a landless man, and endure anything rather than opine with them and live that life?

Yes, he said, I think that he would choose to endure anything rather than such a life.

And consider this also, said I. If such a one should go down again and take his old place would he not get his eyes full of darkness, thus suddenly coming out of the sunlight?

He would indeed.

Now if he should be required to contend with these perpetual prisoners in "evaluating" these shadows while his vision was still dim and before his eyes were accustomed to the dark—and this time required for habituation would not be very short—would he not provoke laughter; and would it not be said of him that he had returned from his journey aloft with his eyes ruined and that it was not worthwhile even to attempt the ascent? And if it were possible to lay hands on and to kill the man who tried to release them and lead them up, would they not kill him?

They certainly would, he said.

This image then, dear Glaucon, we must apply as a whole to all that has been said, likening the region revealed through sight to the habitation of the prison, and the light of the fire in it to the power of the sun. And if you assume that the ascent and the contemplation of the things above is the soul's ascension to the intelligible region, you will not miss my surmise, since that is what you desire to hear. But gods knows whether it is true. But, at any rate, my dream as it appears to me is that in the region of the known the last thing to be seen and hardly seen is the idea of good, and that when seen it must needs point us to the conclusion that this is indeed the cause for all things of all that is right and beautiful, giving birth in the visible world the light, and the author of light and itself in the intelligible world being the authentic source of truth and reason, and that anyone who is to act wisely in private or public must have caught sight of this.

I concur, he said, so far as I am able.

Come then, I said, and join me in this further thought, and do not be surprised that those who have attained to this height are not willing to occupy themselves with the affairs of men, but their souls ever feel the upward urge and the yearning for that sojourn above. For this, I take it, is likely if in this point too the likeness of our image holds.

Yes, it is likely.

And again, do you think it at all strange, said I, if a man returning from divine contemplations to the petty miseries of men cuts a sorry figure and appears most ridiculous, if, while still blinking through the gloom, and before he has become sufficiently accustomed to the environing darkness, he is compelled in courtrooms or elsewhere to contend about the shadows of justice or the images that cast the shadows and to wrangle in debate about the notions of these things in the minds of those who have never seen justice itself?

It would be by no means strange, he said.

But a sensible man, I said, would remember that there are two distinct disturbances of the eyes arising from two causes, according as the shift is from light to darkness or from darkness to light, and, believing that the same thing happens to the soul too, whenever he saw a soul perturbed and unable to discern something, he would not laugh unthinkingly, but would observe whether coming from a brighter life its vision was obscured by the unfamiliar darkness, or whether the passage from the deeper dark of ignorance into a more luminous world and the greater brightness had dazzled its vision. And so he would deem the one happy in its experience and way of life and pity the other, and if it pleased him to laugh at it, his laughter would be less laughable than that at the expense of the soul that had come down from the light above.

That is a very fair statement, he said.

Then, if this is true, our view of these matters must be this, that education is not in reality what some people proclaim it to be in their professions. What they aver is that they can put true knowledge into a soul that does not possess it, as if they were inserting vision into blind eyes.

They do indeed, he said.

But our present argument indicates, said I, that the true analogy for this indwelling power in the soul and the instrument whereby each of us apprehends is that of an eye that could not be converted to the light from the darkness except by turning the whole body. Even so this organ of knowledge must be turned around from the world of becoming together with the entire soul, like the scene-shifting periactus in the theater, until the soul is able to endure the contemplation of essence and the brightest region of being. And this, we say, is the good, do we not?

Yes.

Of this very thing, then, I said, there might be an art, an art of the speediest and most effective shifting or conversion of the soul, not an art of producing vision in it, but on the assumption that it possesses vision but does not rightly direct it and does not look where it should, an art of bringing this about.

Yes, that seems likely, he said.

Then the other so-called virtues of the soul do seem akin to those of the body. For it is true that where they do not pre-exist, they are afterward created by habit and practice. But the excellence of thought, it seems, is certainly of a more divine quality, a thing that never loses its potency, but, according to the direction of its conversion, becomes useful and beneficent, or, again, useless and harmful. Have you never observed in those who are popularly spoken of as bad, but smart men how, keen is the vision of the little soul, how quick it is to discern the things that interest it, a proof that it is not a poor vision which it has, but one forcibly enlisted in the service of evil, so that the sharper its sight the more mischief it accomplishes?

I certainly have, he said.

Observe then, said I, that this part of such a soul, if it had been hammered from childhood, and had thus been struck free of the leaden weights, so to speak, of our birth and becoming, which attaching themselves to it by food and similar pleasures and gluttonies turn downward the vision of the soul—if, I say, freed from these, it had suffered a conversion toward the things that are real and true, that same faculty of the same men would have been most keen in its vision of the higher things, just as it is for the things toward which it is now turned.

It is likely, he said.

Well, then, said I, is not this also likely and a necessary consequence of what has been said, that neither could men who are uneducated and inexperienced in truth ever adequately preside over a state, nor could those who had been permitted to linger on to the end in the pursuit of culture—the one because they have no single aim and purpose in life to which all their actions, public and private, must be directed, and the others, because they will not voluntarily engage in action, believing that while still living they have been transported to the Islands of the Blessed?

True, he said.

It is the duty of us, the founders, then, said I, to compel the best natures to attain the knowledge which we pronounced the greatest, and to win to the vision of the good, to scale that ascent, and when they have reached the heights and taken an adequate view, we must not allow what is now permitted.

What is that?

That they should linger there, I said, and refuse to go down again among those bondsmen and share their labors and honors, whether they are of less or of greater worth.

Do you mean to say that we must do them this wrong, and compel them to live an inferior life when the better is in their power?

You have again forgotten, my friend, said I, that the law is not concerned with the special happiness of any class in the state, but is trying to produce this condition in the city as a whole, harmonizing and adapting the citizens to one another by persuasion and compulsion, and requiring them to impart to one another any benefit which they are severally able to bestow upon the community, and that it itself creates such men in the state, not that it may allow each to take what course pleases him, but with a view to using them for the binding together of the commonwealth.

True, he said, I did forget it.

Observe, then, Glaucon, said I, that we shall not be wronging, either, the philosophers who arise among us, but that we can justify our action when we constrain them to take charge of the other citizens and be their guardians. For we will say to them that it is natural that men of similar quality who spring up in other cities should not share in the labors there. For they grow up spontaneously from no volition of the government in the several states, and it is justice that the self-grown, indebted to none for its breeding, should not be zealous either to pay to anyone the price of its nurture. But you we have engendered for yourselves and the rest of the city to be, as it were, king bees and leaders in the hive. You have received a better and more complete education than the others, and you are more capable of sharing both ways of life. Down you must go then, each in his turn, to the habitation of the others and accustom yourselves to the observation of the obscure things there. For once habituated you will discern them infinitely better than the dwellers there, and you will know what each of the "idols" is and whereof it is a semblance, because you have seen the reality of the beautiful, the just and the good. So our city will be governed by us and you with waking minds, and not, as most cities now which are inhabited and ruled darkly as in a dream by men who fight one another for shadows and wrangle for office as if that were a great good, when the truth is that the city in which those who are to rule are least eager to hold office must needs be best administered and most free from dissension, and the state that gets the contrary type of ruler will be the opposite of this.

By all means, he said.

FOR INFORMAL WRITING

What is allegory? How does it operate in "The Allegory of the Cave?" What are the allegories?

FOR DISCUSSION

1. Popular knowledge of this allegory fixates on the shadows. What do they represent? How are they effective?
2. How does Plato's vision of education square with what you believe or see today? How would you characterize his vision?
3. Comment on the symbols of the escaped prisoner and the cave itself.

FOR WRITING

What do you think Plato sees as the aim of education? How do you know? What specific information in the "Allegory" supports your argument?

A Modest Proposal (1729)
Jonathan Swift (1667–1745)

Considered among the greatest writers of clear and direct prose in the English language, Jonathan Swift was born in Dublin, Ireland, to English parents. Swift devoted a good deal of his life to politics and religion: He was Dean of St. Patrick's Cathedral in Dublin, but he is remembered less for his religious interest and more for his writing (especially his satire). Among his other writings is the celebrated novel Gulliver's Travels *(1726). In a letter to poet Alexander Pope, Swift declared that although he could love individuals, he "hated that animal called man." Clearly, Swift's propensity toward satire is the practical manifestation of those sentiments. The response to "A Modest Proposal" was somewhat predictable: some delighting in the satire, but others assuming that Swift was, indeed, serious.*

It is a melancholy object to those, who walk through this great town, or travel in the country, when they see the streets, the roads, and cabbin-doors crowded with beggars of the female sex, followed by three, four, or six children, all in rags, and importuning every passenger for an alms. These mothers, instead of being able to work for their honest livelihood, are forced to employ all their time in strolling to beg sustenance for their helpless infants who, as they grow up, either turn thieves for want of work, or leave their dear native country, to fight for the Pretender in Spain, or sell themselves to the Barbadoes.

I think it is agreed by all parties, that this prodigious number of children in the arms, or on the backs, or at the heels of their mothers, and frequently of their fathers, is in the present deplorable state of the kingdom, a very great additional grievance; and therefore whoever could find out a fair, cheap and easy method of making these children sound and useful members of the commonwealth, would deserve so well of the publick, as to have his statue set up for a preserver of the nation.

But my intention is very far from being confined to provide only for the children of professed beggars: it is of a much greater extent, and shall take in the whole number of infants at a certain age, who are born of parents in effect as little able to support them, as those who demand our charity in the streets.

As to my own part, having turned my thoughts for many years upon this important subject, and maturely weighed the several schemes of our projectors, I have always found them grossly mistaken in their computation. It is true, a child just dropt from its dam, may be supported by her milk, for a solar year, with little other nourishment: at most not above the value of two shillings, which the mother may certainly get, or the value in scraps, by her lawful occupation of begging; and it is exactly at one year old that I propose to provide for them in such a manner, as, instead of being a charge upon their parents, or the parish, or wanting food and raiment for the rest of their lives, they shall, on the contrary, contribute to the feeding, and partly to the clothing of many thousands.

There is likewise another great advantage in my scheme, that it will prevent those voluntary abortions, and that horrid practice of women murdering their bastard children, alas! too frequent among us, sacrificing the poor innocent babes, I doubt, more to avoid the expence than the shame, which would move tears and pity in the most savage and inhuman breast.

The number of souls in this kingdom being usually reckoned one million and a half, of these I calculate there may be about two hundred thousand couple, whose wives are breeders; from which number I subtract thirty thousand couple, who are able to maintain their own children, (although I apprehend there cannot be so many under the present distresses of the kingdom) but this being granted, there will remain a hundred and seventy thousand breeders. I again subtract fifty thousand, for those women who miscarry, or whose children die by accident or disease within the year. There only remain a hundred and twenty thousand children of poor parents annually born. The question therefore is, How this number shall be reared and provided for? which, as I have already said, under the present situation of affairs, is utterly impossible by all the methods hitherto proposed. For we can neither employ them in handicraft or agriculture; they neither build houses, (I mean in the country) nor cultivate land: they can very seldom pick up a livelihood by stealing till they arrive at six years old; except where they are of towardly parts, although I confess they learn the rudiments much earlier; during which time they can however be properly looked upon only as probationers; as I have been informed by a principal gentleman in the county of Cavan, who protested to me, that he never knew above one or two instances under the age of six, even in a part of the kingdom so renowned for the quickest proficiency in that art.

I am assured by our merchants, that a boy or a girl, before twelve years old, is no saleable commodity, and even when they come to this age, they will not yield above three pounds, or three pounds and half a crown at most, on the exchange; which cannot turn to account either to the parents or kingdom, the charge of nutriments and rags having been at least four times that value.

I shall now therefore humbly propose my own thoughts, which I hope will not be liable to the least objection.

I have been assured by a very knowing American of my acquaintance in London, that a young healthy child well nursed, is, at a year old, a most delicious nourishing and wholesome food, whether stewed, roasted, baked, or boiled; and I make no doubt that it will equally serve in a fricasee, or a ragoust.

I do therefore humbly offer it to publick consideration, that of the hundred and twenty thousand children, already computed, twenty thousand may be reserved for breed, whereof only one fourth part to be males; which is more than we allow to sheep, black cattle, or swine, and my reason is, that these children are seldom the fruits of marriage, a circumstance not much regarded by our savages, therefore, one male will be sufficient to serve four females. That the remaining hundred thousand may, at a year old, be offered in sale to the persons of quality and fortune, through the kingdom, always advising the mother to let them suck plentifully in the last month, so as to render them plump, and fat for a good table. A child will make two dishes at an entertainment for friends, and when the family dines alone, the fore or hind quarter will make a reasonable dish, and seasoned with a little pepper or salt, will be very good boiled on the fourth day, especially in winter.

I have reckoned upon a medium, that a child just born will weigh 12 pounds, and in a solar year, if tolerably nursed, encreaseth to 28 pounds.

I grant this food will be somewhat dear, and therefore very proper for landlords, who, as they have already devoured most of the parents, seem to have the best title to the children.

Infant's flesh will be in season throughout the year, but more plentiful in March, and a little before and after; for we are told by a grave author, an eminent French physician, that fish being a prolifick dyet, there are more children born in Roman Catholick countries about nine months after Lent, than at any other season; therefore, reckoning a year after Lent, the markets will be more glutted than usual, because the number of Popish infants, is at least three to one in this kingdom, and therefore it will have one other collateral advantage, by lessening the number of Papists among us.

I have already computed the charge of nursing a beggar's child (in which list I reckon all cottagers, labourers, and four-fifths of the farmers) to be about two shillings per annum, rags included; and I believe no gentleman would repine to give ten shillings for the carcass of a good fat child, which, as I have said, will make four dishes of excellent nutritive meat, when he hath only some particular friend, or his own family to dine with him. Thus the squire will learn to be a good landlord, and grow popular among his tenants, the mother will have eight shillings neat profit, and be fit for work till she produces another child.

Those who are more thrifty (as I must confess the times require) may flay the carcass; the skin of which, artificially dressed, will make admirable gloves for ladies, and summer boots for fine gentlemen.

As to our City of Dublin, shambles may be appointed for this purpose, in the most convenient parts of it, and butchers we may be assured will not be wanting; although I rather recommend buying the children alive, and dressing them hot from the knife, as we do roasting pigs.

A very worthy person, a true lover of his country, and whose virtues I highly esteem, was lately pleased in discoursing on this matter, to offer a refinement upon my scheme. He said, that many gentlemen of this kingdom, having of late destroyed their deer, he conceived that the want of venison might be well supplied by the bodies of young lads and maidens, not exceeding fourteen years of age, nor under twelve; so great a number of both sexes in every county being now ready to starve for want of work and service: and these to be disposed of by their parents if alive, or otherwise by their nearest relations. But with due deference to so excellent a friend, and so deserving a patriot, I cannot be altogether in his sentiments; for as to the males, my American acquaintance assured me from frequent experience, that their flesh was generally tough and lean, like that of our schoolboys, by continual exercise, and their taste disagreeable, and to fatten them would not answer the charge. Then as to the females, it would, I think, with humble submission, be a loss to the publick, because they soon would become breeders themselves: and besides, it is not improbable that some scrupulous people might be apt to censure such a practice, (although indeed very unjustly) as a little bordering upon cruelty, which, I confess, hath always been with me the strongest objection against any project, how well soever intended.

But in order to justify my friend, he confessed, that this expedient was put into his head by the famous Psalmanaazor, a native of the island Formosa, who came from thence to London, above twenty years ago, and in conversation told my friend, that in his country, when any young person happened to be put to death, the executioner sold the carcass to persons of quality, as a prime dainty; and that, in his time, the body of a plump girl of fifteen, who was crucified for an attempt to poison the Emperor, was sold to his imperial majesty's prime minister of state, and other great mandarins of the court in joints from the gibbet, at four hundred crowns. Neither indeed can I deny, that if the same use were made of several plump young girls in this town, who without one single groat to their fortunes, cannot stir abroad without a chair, and appear at a playhouse and assemblies in foreign fineries which they never will pay for, the kingdom would not be the worse.

Some persons of a desponding spirit are in great concern about that vast number of poor people, who are aged, diseased, or maimed; and I have been desired to employ my thoughts what course may be taken, to ease the nation of so grievous an incumbrance. But I am not in the least pain upon that matter, because it is very well known, that they are every day dying, and rotting, by cold and famine, and filth, and vermin, as fast as can be reasonably expected. And as to the young labourers, they are now in almost as hopeful a condition. They cannot get work, and consequently pine away from want of nourishment, to a degree, that if at any time they are accidentally hired to common labour, they have not strength to perform it, and thus the country and themselves are happily delivered from the evils to come.

I have too long digressed, and therefore shall return to my subject. I think the advantages by the proposal which I have made are obvious and many, as well as of the highest importance.

For first, as I have already observed, it would greatly lessen the number of Papists, with whom we are yearly overrun, being the principal breeders of the nation, as well as our most dangerous enemies, and who stay at home on purpose with a design to deliver the kingdom to the Pretender, hoping to take their advantage by the absence of so many good Protestants, who have chosen rather to leave their country, than stay at home and pay tithes against their conscience to an episcopal curate.

Secondly, The poorer tenants will have something valuable of their own, which by law may be made liable to a distress, and help to pay their landlord's rent, their corn and cattle being already seized, and money a thing unknown.

Thirdly, Whereas the maintainance of a hundred thousand children, from two years old, and upwards, cannot be computed at less than ten shillings a piece per annum, the nation's stock will be thereby encreased fifty thousand pounds per annum, besides the profit of a new dish, introduced to the tables of all gentlemen of fortune in the kingdom, who have any refinement in taste. And the money will circulate among our selves, the goods being entirely of our own growth and manufacture.

Fourthly, The constant breeders, besides the gain of eight shillings sterling per annum by the sale of their children, will be rid of the charge of maintaining them after the first year.

Fifthly, This food would likewise bring great custom to taverns, where the vintners will certainly be so prudent as to procure the best receipts for dressing it to perfection; and consequently have their houses frequented by all the fine gentlemen, who justly value themselves upon their knowledge in good eating; and a skilful cook, who understands how to oblige his guests, will contrive to make it as expensive as they please.

Sixthly, This would be a great inducement to marriage, which all wise nations have either encouraged by rewards, or enforced by laws and penalties. It would encrease the care and tenderness of mothers towards their children, when they were sure of a settlement for life to the poor babes, provided in some sort by the publick, to their annual profit instead of expence. We should soon see an honest emulation among the married women, which of them could bring the fattest child to the market. Men would become as fond of their wives, during the time of their pregnancy, as they are now of their mares in foal, their cows in calf, or sows when they are ready to farrow; nor offer to beat or kick them (as is too frequent a practice) for fear of a miscarriage.

Many other advantages might be enumerated. For instance, the addition of some thousand carcasses in our exportation of barrel'd beef: the propagation of swine's flesh, and improvement in the art of making good bacon, so much wanted among us by the great destruction of pigs, too frequent at our tables; which are no way comparable in taste or magnificence to a well grown, fat yearling child, which roasted whole will make a considerable figure at a Lord Mayor's feast, or any other publick entertainment. But this, and many others, I omit, being studious of brevity.

Supposing that one thousand families in this city, would be constant customers for infants flesh, besides others who might have it at merry meetings, particularly at weddings and christenings, I compute that Dublin would take off annually about twenty thousand carcasses; and the rest of the kingdom (where probably they will be sold somewhat cheaper) the remaining eighty thousand.

I can think of no one objection, that will possibly be raised against this proposal, unless it should be urged, that the number of people will be thereby much lessened in the kingdom. This I freely own, and was indeed one principal design in offering it to the world. I desire the reader will observe, that I calculate my remedy for this one individual Kingdom of Ireland, and for no other that ever was, is, or, I think, ever can be upon Earth. Therefore let no man talk to me of other expedients: Of taxing our absentees at five shillings a pound: Of using neither clothes, nor houshold furniture, except what is of our own growth and manufacture: Of utterly rejecting the materials and instruments that promote foreign luxury: Of curing the expensiveness of pride, vanity, idleness, and gaming in our women: Of introducing a vein of parsimony, prudence and temperance: Of learning to love our country, wherein we differ even from Laplanders, and the inhabitants of Topinamboo: Of quitting our animosities and factions, nor acting any longer like the Jews, who were murdering one another at the very moment their city was taken: Of being a little cautious not to sell our country and consciences for nothing: Of teaching landlords to have at least one degree of mercy towards their tenants. Lastly, of putting a spirit of honesty, industry, and skill into our shopkeepers, who, if a resolution could now be taken to buy only our native goods, would immediately unite to cheat and exact upon us in the price, the measure, and the goodness, nor could ever yet be brought to make one fair proposal of just dealing, though often and earnestly invited to it.

Therefore I repeat, let no man talk to me of these and the like expedients, till he hath at least some glympse of hope, that there will ever be some hearty and sincere attempt to put them into practice.

But, as to myself, having been wearied out for many years with offering vain, idle, visionary thoughts, and at length utterly despairing of success, I fortunately fell upon this proposal, which, as it is wholly new, so it hath something solid and real, of no expence and little trouble, full in our own power, and whereby we can incur no danger in disobliging England. For this kind of commodity will not bear exportation, and flesh being of too tender a consistence, to admit a long continuance in salt, although perhaps I could name a country, which would be glad to eat up our whole nation without it.

After all, I am not so violently bent upon my own opinion, as to reject any offer, proposed by wise men, which shall be found equally innocent, cheap, easy, and effectual. But before something of that kind shall be advanced in contradiction to my scheme, and offering a better, I desire the author or authors will be pleased maturely to consider two points. First, As things now stand, how they will be able to find food and raiment for a hundred thousand useless mouths and backs. And secondly, There being a round million of creatures in humane figure throughout this kingdom, whose whole subsistence put into a common stock, would leave them in debt two million of pounds sterling, adding those who are beggars by profession, to the bulk of farmers, cottagers and labourers, with their wives and children, who are beggars in effect; I desire those politicians who dislike my overture, and may perhaps be so bold to attempt an answer, that they will first ask the parents of these mortals, whether they would not at this day think it a great happiness to have been sold for food at a year old, in the manner I prescribe, and thereby have avoided such a perpetual scene of misfortunes, as they have since gone through, by the oppression of landlords, the impossibility of paying rent without money or trade, the want of common sustenance, with neither house nor clothes to cover them from the inclemencies of the weather, and the most inevitable prospect of intailing the like, or greater miseries, upon their breed for ever.

I profess in the sincerity of my heart, that I have not the least personal interest in endeavouring to promote this necessary work, having no other motive than the publick good of my country, by advancing our trade, providing for infants, relieving the poor, and giving some pleasure to the rich. I have no children, by which I can propose to get a single penny; the youngest being nine years old, and my wife past child-bearing.

FOR INFORMAL WRITING

What is satire? What is irony? What are other examples of satire from popular culture?

FOR DISCUSSION

1. What is the character of the person making these proposals—who is, clearly, not Swift himself? How do you know?
2. What seem to be the primary targets for Swift's attacks?
3. At what point do you realize that Swift might not be completely serious in his proposal? How do you know? Why would some people have missed this?

FOR WRITING

Now that you've defined satire and irony, consider some of the historical contexts of the essay (which you may need to research) to understand what might have motivated Swift to write it. What are the truths revealed in the essay—and to what conclusion do you come regarding them—if indeed satire works only when it reveals truth?

The Cask of Amontillado (1846)
Edgar Allan Poe (1809–1849)

One of the most canonized writers of his or any time, Edgar Allan Poe became an orphan at the age of three and was adopted by a rich businessman in Richmond, John Allan. Out of financial need, Poe enlisted in the US Army in 1827, claiming he was 22 years old when he was only 18. That same year, he released his first collection of poetry, Tamerlane and Other Poems. *Only fifty copies of the work were printed. His poem "The Raven" brought Poe celebrity, but he failed to garner as much success as he wished, turning his attention to prose. In 1833, Poe won a prize from the Baltimore Saturday Visitor for his story "MS Found in a Bottle." After his wife died in 1847, Poe was inspired to explore love and beauty lost in writings. As he was an alcoholic, her death caused his deterioration, and he died mysteriously in Baltimore in 1849. "The Cask of Amontillado" was first published in* Godey's Lady's Book, *a well-known women's magazine.*

Fortunato had hurt me a thousand times and I had suffered quietly. But then I learned that he had laughed at my proud name, Montresor, the name of an old and honored family. I promised myself that I would make him pay for this—that I would have revenge. You must not suppose, however, that I spoke of this to anyone. I would make him pay, yes; but I would act only with the greatest care. I must not suffer as a result of taking my revenge. A wrong is not made right in that manner. And also the wrong would not be made right unless Fortunato knew that he was paying and knew who was forcing him to pay.

I gave Fortunato no cause to doubt me. I continued to smile in his face, and he did not understand that I was now smiling at the thought of what I planned for him, at the thought of my revenge.

Fortunato was a strong man, a man to be feared. But he had one great weakness: he liked to drink good wine, and indeed he drank much of it. So he knew a lot about fine wines, and proudly believed that he was a trained judge of them. I, too, knew old wines well, and I bought the best I could find. And wine, I thought, wine would give me my revenge!

It was almost dark, one evening in the spring, when I met Fortunato in the street, alone. He spoke to me more warmly than was usual, for already he had drunk more wine than was good for him. I acted pleased to see him, and I shook his hand, as if he had been my closest friend.

"Fortunato! How are you?"

"Montresor! Good evening, my friend."

"My dear Fortunato! I am indeed glad that I have met you. I was just thinking of you. For I have been tasting my new wine. I have bought a full cask of a fine wine which they tell me is Amontillado. But. . . ."

"Amontillado! Quite impossible."

"I know. It does not seem possible. As I could not find you I was just going to talk to Luchresi. If anyone understands wines it is Luchresi. He will tell me. . . ."

"Luchresi? He does not know one wine from another!"

"But they say he knows as much about wines as you know."

"Ho!—Come. Let us go."

"Go where?"

"To your vaults. To taste the wine."

"No, my friend, no. I can see that you are not well. And the vaults are cold and wet."

"I do not care. Let us go. I'm well enough. The cold is nothing. Amontillado! Someone is playing games with you. And Luchresi! Ha! Luchresi knows nothing about wines, nothing at all."

As he spoke, Fortunato took my arm, and I allowed him to hurry me to my great stone palace, where my family, the Montresors, had lived for centuries. There was no one at home. I had told the servants that they must not leave the palace, as I would not return until the following morning and they must care for the place. This, I knew, was enough to make it certain that they would all leave as soon as my back was turned.

I took down from their places on the wall two brightly burning lights. I gave one of these to Fortunato and led him to a wide doorway. There we could see the stone steps going down into the darkness.

Asking him to be careful as he followed, I went down before him, down under the ground, deep under the old walls of my palace. We came finally to the bottom of the steps and stood there a moment together. The earth which formed the floor was cold and hard. We were entering the last resting place of the dead of the Montresor family. Here too we kept our finest wines, here in the cool, dark, still air under the ground.

Fortunato's step was not sure, because of the wine he had been drinking. He looked uncertainly around him, trying to see through the thick darkness which pushed in around us. Here our brightly burning lights seemed weak indeed. But our eyes soon became used to the darkness. We could see the bones of the dead lying in large piles along the walls. The stones of the walls were wet and cold.

From the long rows of bottles which were lying on the floor, among the bones, I chose one which contained a very good wine. Since I did not have anything to open the bottle with, I struck the stone wall with it and broke off the small end. I offered the bottle to Fortunato.

"Here, Fortunato. Drink some of this fine Medoc. It will help to keep us warm. Drink!"

"Thank you, my friend. I drink to the dead who lie sleeping around us."

"And I, Fortunato—I drink to your long life."

"Ahh! A very fine wine, indeed! But the Amontillado?"

"It is farther on. Come."

We walked on for some time. We were now under the river's bed, and water fell in drops upon us from above. Deeper into the ground we went, past still more bones.

"Your vaults are many, and large. There seems to be no end to them."

"We are a great family, and an old one. It is not far now. But I can see you are trembling with the cold. Come! Let us go back before it is too late."

"It is nothing. Let us go on. But first, another drink of your Medoc!"

I took up from among the bones another bottle. It was another wine of a fine quality, a De Grâve. Again I broke off the neck of the bottle. Fortunato took it and drank it all without stopping for a breath. He laughed, and threw the empty bottle over his shoulder.

We went on, deeper and deeper into the earth. Finally we arrived at a vault in which the air was so old and heavy that our lights almost died. Against three of the walls there were piles of bones higher than our heads. From the fourth wall someone had pulled down all the bones, and they were spread all around us on the ground. In the middle of the wall was an opening into another vault, if I can call it that—a little room about three feet wide, six or seven feet high, and perhaps four feet deep. It was hardly more than a hole in the wall.

"Go on," I said. "Go in; the Amontillado is in there."

Fortunato continued to go forward, uncertainly. I followed him immediately. Soon, of course, he reached the back wall. He stood there a moment, facing the wall, surprised and wondering. In that wall were two heavy iron rings. A short chain was hanging from one of these and a lock from the other.

20 THE OXFORD READER

Before Fortunato could guess what was happening, I closed the lock and chained him tightly to the wall. I stepped back.

"Fortunato," I said. "Put your hand against the wall. You must feel how the water runs over it. Once more I ask you, please, will you not go back? No? If not, then I must leave you. But first I must do everything I can for you."

"But . . . But the Amontillado?"

"Ah, yes, yes indeed; the Amontillado."

As I spoke these words I began to search among the bones.

Throwing them to one side I found the stones which earlier I had taken down from the wall. Quickly I began to build the wall again, covering the hole where Fortunato stood trembling.

"Montresor! What are you doing!?"

I continued working. I could hear him pulling at the chain, shaking it wildly. Only a few stones remained to put in their place.

"Montresor! Ha-ha. This is a very good joke, indeed. Many times will we laugh about it—ha-ha—as we drink our wine together—ha-ha."

"Of course. As we drink the Amontillado."

"But is it not late? Should we not be going back? They will be expecting us. Let us go."

"Yes. Let us go."

As I said this I lifted the last stone from the ground. "Montresor! For the love of God!!"

"Yes. For the love of God!"

I heard no answer. "Fortunato!" I cried. "Fortunato." I heard only a soft, low sound, a half-cry of fear. My heart grew sick; it must have been the cold. I hurried to force the last stone into its position. And I put the old bones again in a pile against the wall. For half a century now no human hand has touched them. May he rest in peace!

FOR INFORMAL WRITING

From what point of view is the story told? Who is the "you" in the first paragraph? What does the narrator's tone tell you about his intention?

FOR DISCUSSION

1. What can you tell about the narrator's social position—and his character?
2. What hints does Poe give about the "thousand" injuries? How do they motivate the character?
3. How does Poe build suspense in the story, even if we know how it will turn out?

FOR WRITING

Research the concept of the "unreliable narrator." Using evidence from the story, how do we know that Montresor is unreliable?

WHAT'S NEW IS OLD

Consider the narrators of "The Cask of Amontillado" by Poe with Bharati Mukherjee's "The Management of Grief." Look carefully at the narrators of each and the assumptions or beliefs behind their words. How would you compare the narrators in these works of fiction? How do the narrators—whether unreliable or reliable—reveal larger truths about each work?

What to the Slave Is the Fourth of July? (1852)

Frederick Douglass (1818–1895)

Frederick Douglass was born into slavery near Chesapeake Bay, Maryland. He taught himself to read and write when he was a child, and he often said, "Knowledge is the pathway from slavery to freedom." Douglass escaped from slavery in 1838 and went on to become one of the country's best-known abolitionists, whose anti-slavery writings were and are considered to be among the most influential and compelling. "What to the Slave Is the Fourth of July?" was a public address in 1852, directed toward "Mr. President, Friends and Fellow Citizens." (The US President at the time was Millard Filmore.)

Mr. President, Friends and Fellow Citizens:

He who could address this audience without a quailing sensation, has stronger nerves than I have. I do not remember ever to have appeared as a speaker before any assembly more shrinkingly, nor with greater distrust of my ability, than I do this day. A feeling has crept over me, quite unfavorable to the exercise of my limited powers of speech. The task before me is one which requires much previous thought and study for its proper performance. I know that apologies of this sort are generally considered flat and unmeaning. I trust, however, that mine will not be so considered. Should I seem at ease, my appearance would much misrepresent me. The little experience I have had in addressing public meetings, in country schoolhouses, avails me nothing on the present occasion.

The papers and placards say, that I am to deliver a 4th [of] July oration. This certainly sounds large, and out of the common way, for it is true that I have often had the privilege to speak in this beautiful Hall, and to address many who now honor me with their presence. But neither their familiar faces, nor the perfect gage I think I have of Corinthian Hall, seems to free me from embarrassment.

The fact is, ladies and gentlemen, the distance between this platform and the slave plantation, from which I escaped, is considerable—and the difficulties to be overcome in getting from the latter to the former, are by no means slight. That I am here to-day is, to me, a matter of astonishment as well as of gratitude. You will not, therefore, be surprised, if in what I have to say I evince no elaborate preparation, nor grace my speech with any high sounding exordium. With little experience and with less learning, I have been able to throw my thoughts hastily and imperfectly together; and trusting to your patient and generous indulgence, I will proceed to lay them before you.

This, for the purpose of this celebration, is the 4th of July. It is the birthday of your National Independence, and of your political freedom. This, to you, is what the Passover was to the emancipated people of God. It carries your minds back to the day, and to the act of your great deliverance; and to the signs, and to the wonders, associated with that act, and that day. This celebration also marks the beginning of another year of your national life; and reminds you that the Republic of America is now 76 years old. I am glad, fellow-citizens, that your nation is so young. Seventy-six years, though a good old age for a man, is but a mere speck in the life of a nation. Three score years and ten is the allotted time for individual men; but nations number their years by thousands. According to this fact, you are, even now, only in the beginning of your national career, still lingering in the period of childhood. I repeat, I am glad this is so. There is hope in the thought, and hope is much needed, under the dark clouds which lower above the horizon. The eye of the reformer is met with angry flashes, portending disastrous times; but his heart may well beat lighter at the thought that America is young, and that she is still in the impressible stage of her existence. May he not hope that high lessons of wisdom, of justice and of truth, will yet give direction to her destiny? Were the nation older, the patriot's heart might be sadder, and the reformer's brow heavier. Its future might be shrouded in gloom, and the hope of its prophets go out in sorrow. There is consolation in the thought that America is young. Great streams are not easily turned from channels, worn deep in the course of ages. They may sometimes rise in quiet and stately majesty, and inundate the land, refreshing and fertilizing the earth with their mysterious properties. They may also rise in wrath and fury, and bear away, on their angry waves, the accumulated wealth of years of toil and hardship. They, however, gradually flow back to the same old channel, and flow on as serenely as ever. But, while the river may not be turned aside, it may dry up, and leave nothing behind but the withered branch, and the unsightly rock, to howl in the abyss-sweeping wind, the sad tale of departed glory. As with rivers so with nations.

Fellow-citizens, I shall not presume to dwell at length on the associations that cluster about this day. The simple story of it is that, 76 years ago, the people of this country were British subjects. The style and title of your "sovereign people" (in which you now glory) was not then born. You were under the British Crown. Your fathers esteemed the English Government as the home government; and England as the fatherland. This home government, you know, although a considerable distance from your home, did, in the exercise of its parental prerogatives, impose upon its colonial children, such restraints, burdens and limitations, as, in its mature judgment, it deemed wise, right and proper.

But, your fathers, who had not adopted the fashionable idea of this day, of the infallibility of government, and the absolute character of its acts, presumed to differ from the home government in respect to the wisdom and the justice of some of those burdens and restraints. They went so far in their excitement as to pronounce the measures of government unjust, unreasonable, and oppressive, and altogether such as ought not to be quietly submitted to. I scarcely need say, fellow-citizens, that my opinion of those measures fully accords with that of your fathers. Such a declaration of agreement on my part would not be worth much to anybody. It would, certainly, prove nothing, as to what part I might have taken, had I lived during the great controversy of 1776. To say now that America was right, and England wrong, is exceedingly easy. Everybody can say it; the dastard, not less than the noble brave, can flippantly discant on the tyranny of England towards the American Colonies. It is fashionable to do so; but there was a time when to pronounce against England, and in favor of the cause of the colonies, tried men's souls. They who did so were accounted in their day, plotters of mischief, agitators and rebels, dangerous men. To side with the right, against the wrong, with the weak against the strong, and with the oppressed against the oppressor! here lies the merit, and the one which, of all others, seems unfashionable in our day. The cause of liberty may be stabbed by the men who glory in the deeds of your fathers. But, to proceed.

Feeling themselves harshly and unjustly treated by the home government, your fathers, like men of honesty, and men of spirit, earnestly sought redress. They petitioned and remonstrated; they did so in a decorous, respectful, and loyal manner. Their conduct was wholly unexceptionable. This, however, did not answer the purpose. They saw themselves treated with sovereign indifference, coldness and scorn. Yet they persevered. They were not the men to look back.

As the sheet anchor takes a firmer hold, when the ship is tossed by the storm, so did the cause of your fathers grow stronger, as it breasted the chilling blasts of kingly displeasure. The greatest and best of British statesmen admitted its justice, and the loftiest eloquence of the British Senate came to its support. But, with that blindness which seems to be the unvarying characteristic of tyrants, since Pharaoh and his hosts were drowned in the Red Sea, the British Government persisted in the exactions complained of.

The madness of this course, we believe, is admitted now, even by England; but we fear the lesson is wholly lost on our present ruler.

Oppression makes a wise man mad. Your fathers were wise men, and if they did not go mad, they became restive under this treatment. They felt themselves the victims of grievous wrongs, wholly incurable in their colonial capacity.

With brave men there is always a remedy for oppression. Just here, the idea of a total separation of the colonies from the crown was born! It was a startling idea, much more so, than we, at this distance of time, regard it. The timid and the prudent (as has been intimated) of that day, were, of course, shocked and alarmed by it.

Such people lived then, had lived before, and will, probably, ever have a place on this planet; and their course, in respect to any great change, (no matter how great the good to be attained, or the wrong to be redressed by it), may be calculated with as much precision as can be the course of the stars. They hate all changes, but silver, gold and copper change! Of this sort of change they are always strongly in favor.

These people were called Tories in the days of your fathers; and the appellation, probably, conveyed the same idea that is meant by a more modern, though a somewhat less euphonious term, which we often find in our papers, applied to some of our old politicians. Their opposition to the then dangerous thought was earnest and powerful; but, amid all their terror and affrighted vociferations against it, the alarming and revolutionary idea moved on, and the country with it.

On the 2nd of July, 1776, the old Continental Congress, to the dismay of the lovers of ease, and the worshipers of property, clothed that dreadful idea with all the authority of national sanction. They did so in the form of a resolution; and as we seldom hit upon resolutions, drawn up in our day whose transparency is at all equal to this, it may refresh your minds and help my story if I read it. "Resolved, That these united colonies are, and of right, ought to be free and Independent States; that they are absolved from all allegiance to the British Crown; and that all political connection between them and the State of Great Britain is, and ought to be, dissolved."

Citizens, your fathers made good that resolution. They succeeded; and to-day you reap the fruits of their success. The freedom gained is yours; and you, therefore, may properly celebrate this anniversary. The 4th of July is the first great fact in your nation's history—the very ring-bolt in the chain of your yet undeveloped destiny.

Pride and patriotism, not less than gratitude, prompt you to celebrate and to hold it in perpetual remembrance. I have said that the Declaration of Independence is the ring-bolt to the chain of your nation's destiny; so, indeed, I regard it. The principles contained in that instrument are saving principles. Stand by those principles, be true to them on all occasions, in all places, against all foes, and at whatever cost.

From the round top of your ship of state, dark and threatening clouds may be seen. Heavy billows, like mountains in the distance, disclose to the leeward huge forms of flinty rocks! That bolt drawn, that chain broken, and all is lost. Cling to this day—cling to it, and to its principles, with the grasp of a storm-tossed mariner to a spar at midnight.

The coming into being of a nation, in any circumstances, is an interesting event. But, besides general considerations, there were peculiar circumstances which make the advent of this republic an event of special attractiveness.

The whole scene, as I look back to it, was simple, dignified and sublime.

The population of the country, at the time, stood at the insignificant number of three millions. The country was poor in the munitions of war. The population was weak and scattered, and the country a wilderness unsubdued. There were then no means of concert and combination, such as exist now. Neither steam nor lightning had then been reduced to order and discipline. From the Potomac to the Delaware was a journey of many days. Under these, and innumerable other disadvantages, your fathers declared for liberty and independence and triumphed.

Fellow Citizens, I am not wanting in respect for the fathers of this republic. The signers of the Declaration of Independence were brave men. They were great men too—great enough to give fame to a great age. It does not often happen to a nation to raise, at one time, such a number of truly great men. The point from which I am compelled to view them is not, certainly, the most favorable; and yet I cannot contemplate their great deeds with less than admiration. They were statesmen, patriots and heroes, and for the good they did, and the principles they contended for, I will unite with you to honor their memory.

They loved their country better than their own private interests; and, though this is not the highest form of human excellence, all will concede that it is a rare virtue, and that when it is exhibited, it ought to command respect. He who will, intelligently, lay down his life for his country, is a man whom it is not in human nature to despise. Your fathers staked their lives, their fortunes, and their sacred honor, on the cause of their country. In their admiration of liberty, they lost sight of all other interests.

They were peace men; but they preferred revolution to peaceful submission to bondage. They were quiet men; but they did not shrink from agitating against oppression. They showed forbearance; but that they knew its limits. They believed in order; but not in the order of tyranny. With them, nothing was "settled" that was not right. With them, justice, liberty and humanity were "final;" not slavery and oppression. You may well cherish the memory of such men. They were great in their day and generation. Their solid manhood stands out the more as we contrast it with these degenerate times.

How circumspect, exact and proportionate were all their movements! How unlike the politicians of an hour! Their statesmanship looked beyond the passing moment, and stretched away in strength into the distant future. They seized upon eternal principles, and set a glorious example in their defense. Mark them!

Fully appreciating the hardship to be encountered, firmly believing in the right of their cause, honorably inviting the scrutiny of an on-looking world, reverently appealing to heaven to attest their sincerity, soundly comprehending the solemn responsibility they were about to assume, wisely measuring the terrible odds against them, your fathers, the fathers of this republic, did, most deliberately, under the inspiration of a glorious patriotism, and with a sublime faith in the great principles of justice and freedom, lay deep the corner-stone of the national superstructure, which has risen and still rises in grandeur around you. =Of this fundamental work, this day is the anniversary. Our eyes are met with demonstrations of joyous enthusiasm. Banners and pennants wave exultingly on the breeze. The din of business, too, is hushed. Even Mammon seems to have quitted his grasp on this day. The ear-piercing fife and the stirring drum unite their accents with the ascending peal of a thousand church bells. Prayers are made, hymns are sung, and sermons are preached in honor of this day; while the quick martial tramp of a great and multitudinous nation, echoed back by all the hills, valleys and mountains of a vast continent, bespeak the occasion one of thrilling and universal interest—a nation's jubilee.

Friends and citizens, I need not enter further into the causes which led to this anniversary. Many of you understand them better than I do. You could instruct me in regard to them. That is a branch of knowledge in which you feel, perhaps, a much deeper interest than your speaker. The causes which led to the separation of the colonies from the British Crown have never lacked for a tongue. They have all been taught in your common schools, narrated at your firesides, unfolded from your pulpits, and thundered from your legislative halls, and are as familiar to you as household words. They form the staple of your national poetry and eloquence.

I remember, also, that, as a people, Americans are remarkably familiar with all facts which make in their own favor. This is esteemed by some as a national trait—perhaps a national weakness. It is a fact, that whatever makes for the wealth or for the reputation of Americans, and can be had cheap! will be found by Americans. I shall not be charged with slandering Americans, if I say I think the American side of any question may be safely left in American hands.

I leave, therefore, the great deeds of your fathers to other gentlemen whose claim to have been regularly descended will be less likely to be disputed than mine!

My business, if I have any here to-day, is with the present. The accepted time with God and his cause is the ever-living now.

Trust no future, however pleasant,
Let the dead past bury its dead;
Act, act in the living present,
Heart within, and God overhead.

We have to do with the past only as we can make it useful to the present and to the future. To all inspiring motives, to noble deeds which can be gained from the past, we are welcome. But now is the time, the important time. Your fathers have lived, died, and have done their work, and have done much of it well. You live and must die, and you must do your work. You have no right to enjoy a child's share in the labor of your fathers, unless your children are to be blest by your labors. You have no right to wear out and waste the hard-earned fame of your fathers to cover your indolence. Sydney Smith tells us that men seldom eulogize the wisdom and virtues of their fathers, but to excuse some folly or wickedness of their own. This truth is not a doubtful one. There are illustrations of it near and remote, ancient and modern. It was fashionable, hundreds of years ago, for the children of Jacob to boast, we have "Abraham to our father," when they had long lost Abraham's faith and spirit. That people contented themselves under the shadow of Abraham's great name, while they repudiated the deeds which made his name great. Need I remind you that a similar thing is being done all over this country to-day? Need I tell you that the Jews are not the only people who built the tombs of the prophets, and garnished the sepulchres of the righteous? Washington could not die till he had broken the chains of his slaves. Yet his monument is built up by the price of human blood, and the traders in the bodies and souls of men shout — "We have Washington to our father."—Alas! that it should be so; yet so it is.

The evil that men do, lives after them,
The good is oft-interred with their bones.

Fellow-citizens, pardon me, allow me to ask, why am I called upon to speak here to-day? What have I, or those I represent, to do with your national independence? Are the great principles of political freedom and of natural justice, embodied in that Declaration of Independence, extended to us? and am I, therefore, called upon to bring our humble offering to the national altar, and to confess the benefits and express devout gratitude for the blessings resulting from your independence to us?

Would to God, both for your sakes and ours, that an affirmative answer could be truthfully returned to these questions! Then would my task be light, and my burden easy and delightful. For who is there so cold, that a nation's sympathy could not warm him? Who so obdurate and dead to the claims of gratitude, that would not thankfully acknowledge such priceless benefits? Who so stolid and selfish, that would not give his voice to swell the hallelujahs of a nation's jubilee, when the chains of servitude had been torn from his limbs? I am not that man. In a case like that, the dumb might eloquently speak, and the "lame man leap as an hart."

But, such is not the state of the case. I say it with a sad sense of the disparity between us. I am not included within the pale of this glorious anniversary!

Your high independence only reveals the immeasurable distance between us. The blessings in which you, this day, rejoice, are not enjoyed in common.—The rich inheritance of justice, liberty, prosperity and independence, bequeathed by your fathers, is shared by you, not by me. The sunlight that brought life and healing to you, has brought stripes and death to me. This Fourth [of] July is yours, not mine. You may rejoice, I must mourn. To drag a man in fetters into the grand illuminated temple of liberty, and call upon him to join you in joyous anthems, were inhuman mockery and sacrilegious irony. Do you mean, citizens, to mock me, by asking me to speak to-day? If so, there is a parallel to your conduct. And let me warn you that it is dangerous to copy the example of a nation whose crimes, lowering up to heaven, were thrown down by the breath of the Almighty, burying that nation in irrecoverable ruin! I can to-day take up the plaintive lament of a peeled and woe-smitten people!

"By the rivers of Babylon, there we sat down. Yea! we wept when we remembered Zion. We hanged our harps upon the willows in the midst thereof. For there, they that carried us away captive, required of us a song; and they who wasted us required of us mirth, saying, Sing us one of the songs of Zion. How can we sing the Lord's song in a strange land? If I forget thee, O Jerusalem, let my right hand forget her cunning. If I do not remember thee, let my tongue cleave to the roof of my mouth."

Fellow-citizens; above your national, tumultuous joy, I hear the mournful wail of millions! whose chains, heavy and grievous yesterday, are, to-day, rendered more intolerable by the jubilee shouts that reach them. If I do forget, if I do not faithfully remember those bleeding children of sorrow this day, "may my right hand forget her cunning, and may my tongue cleave to the roof of my mouth!" To forget them, to pass lightly over their wrongs, and to chime in with the popular theme, would be treason most scandalous and shocking, and would make me a reproach before God and the world. My subject, then fellow-citizens, is AMERICAN SLAVERY. I shall see, this day, and its popular characteristics, from the slave's point of view. Standing, there, identified with the American bondman, making his wrongs mine, I do not hesitate to declare, with all my soul, that the character and conduct of this nation never looked blacker to me than on this 4th of July! Whether we turn to the declarations of the past, or to the professions of the present, the conduct of the nation seems equally hideous and revolting. America is false to the past, false to the present, and solemnly binds herself to be false to the future. Standing with God and the crushed and bleeding slave on this occasion, I will, in the name of humanity which is outraged, in the name of liberty which is fettered, in the name of the constitution and the Bible, which are disregarded and trampled upon, dare to call in question and to denounce, with all the emphasis I can command, everything that serves to perpetuate slavery—the great sin and shame of America! "I will not equivocate; I will not excuse;" I will use the severest language I can command; and yet not one word shall escape me that any man, whose judgment is not blinded by prejudice, or who is not at heart a slaveholder, shall not confess to be right and just.

But I fancy I hear some one of my audience say, it is just in this circumstance that you and your brother abolitionists fail to make a favorable impression on the public mind. Would you argue more, and denounce less, would you persuade more, and rebuke less, your cause would be much more likely to succeed. But, I submit, where all is plain there is nothing to be argued. What point in the anti-slavery creed would you have me argue? On what branch of the subject do the people of this country need light? Must I undertake to prove that the slave is a man? That point is conceded already. Nobody doubts it. The slaveholders themselves acknowledge it in the enactment of laws for their government. They acknowledge it when they punish disobedience on the part of the slave. There are seventy-two crimes in the State of Virginia, which, if committed by a black man, (no matter how ignorant he be), subject him to the punishment of death; while only two of the same crimes will subject a white man to the like punishment. What is this but the acknowledgement that the slave is a moral, intellectual and responsible being? The manhood of the slave is conceded. It is admitted in the fact that Southern statute books are covered with enactments forbidding, under severe fines and penalties, the teaching of the slave to read or to write. When you can point to any such laws, in reference to the beasts of the field, then I may consent to argue the manhood of the slave. When the dogs in your streets, when the fowls of the air, when the cattle on your hills, when the fish of the sea, and the reptiles that crawl, shall be unable to distinguish the slave from a brute, then will I argue with you that the slave is a man!

For the present, it is enough to affirm the equal manhood of the Negro race. Is it not astonishing that, while we are ploughing, planting and reaping, using all kinds of mechanical tools, erecting houses, constructing bridges, building ships, working in metals of brass, iron, copper, silver and gold; that, while we are reading, writing and cyphering, acting as clerks, merchants and secretaries, having among us lawyers, doctors, ministers, poets, authors, editors, orators and teachers; that, while we are engaged in all manner of enterprises common to other men, digging gold in California, capturing the whale in the Pacific, feeding sheep and cattle on the hill-side, living, moving, acting, thinking, planning, living in families as husbands, wives and children, and, above all, confessing and worshipping the Christian's God, and looking hopefully for life and immortality beyond the grave, we are called upon to prove that we are men!

Would you have me argue that man is entitled to liberty? that he is the rightful owner of his own body? You have already declared it. Must I argue the wrongfulness of slavery? Is that a question for Republicans? Is it to be settled by the rules of logic and argumentation, as a matter beset with great difficulty, involving a doubtful application of the principle of justice, hard to be understood? How should I look to-day, in the presence of Americans, dividing, and subdividing a discourse, to show that men have a natural right to freedom? speaking of it relatively, and positively, negatively, and affirmatively. To do so, would be to make myself ridiculous, and to offer an insult to your understanding.—There is not a man beneath the canopy of heaven, that does not know that slavery is wrong for him.

What, am I to argue that it is wrong to make men brutes, to rob them of their liberty, to work them without wages, to keep them ignorant of their relations to their fellow men, to beat them with sticks, to flay their flesh with the lash, to load their limbs with irons, to hunt them with dogs, to sell them at auction, to sunder their families, to knock out their teeth, to burn their flesh, to starve them into obedience and submission to their masters? Must I argue that a system thus marked with blood, and stained with pollution, is wrong? No! I will not. I have better employments for my time and strength than such arguments would imply.

What, then, remains to be argued? Is it that slavery is not divine; that God did not establish it; that our doctors of divinity are mistaken? There is blasphemy in the thought. That which is inhuman, cannot be divine! Who can reason on such a proposition? They that can, may; I cannot. The time for such argument is passed.

At a time like this, scorching irony, not convincing argument, is needed. O! had I the ability, and could I reach the nation's ear, I would, to-day, pour out a fiery stream of biting ridicule, blasting reproach, withering sarcasm, and stern rebuke. For it is not light that is needed, but fire; it is not the gentle shower, but thunder. We need the storm, the whirlwind, and the earthquake. The feeling of the nation must be quickened; the conscience of the nation must be roused; the propriety of the nation must be startled; the hypocrisy of the nation must be exposed; and its crimes against God and man must be proclaimed and denounced.

What, to the American slave, is your 4th of July? I answer: a day that reveals to him, more than all other days in the year, the gross injustice and cruelty to which he is the constant victim. To him, your celebration is a sham; your boasted liberty, an unholy license; your national greatness, swelling vanity; your sounds of rejoicing are empty and heartless; your denunciations of tyrants, brass fronted impudence; your shouts of liberty and equality, hollow mockery; your prayers and hymns, your sermons and thanksgivings, with all your religious parade, and solemnity, are, to him, mere bombast, fraud, deception, impiety, and hypocrisy — a thin veil to cover up crimes which would disgrace a nation of savages. There is not a nation on the earth guilty of practices, more shocking and bloody, than are the people of these United States, at this very hour.

Go where you may, search where you will, roam through all the monarchies and despotisms of the old world, travel through South America, search out every abuse, and when you have found the last, lay your facts by the side of the everyday practices of this nation, and you will say with me, that, for revolting barbarity and shameless hypocrisy, America reigns without a rival.

Take the American slave-trade, which, we are told by the papers, is especially prosperous just now. Ex-Senator Benton tells us that the price of men was never higher than now. He mentions the fact to show that slavery is in no danger. This trade is one of the peculiarities of American institutions. It is carried on in all the large towns and cities in one-half of this confederacy; and millions are pocketed every year, by dealers in this horrid traffic. In several states, this trade is a chief source of wealth. It is called (in contradistinction to the foreign slave-trade) "the internal slave trade." It is, probably, called so, too, in order to divert from it the horror with which the foreign slave-trade is contemplated. That trade has long since been denounced by this government, as piracy. It has been denounced with burning words, from the high places of the nation, as an execrable traffic. To arrest it, to put an end to it, this nation keeps a squadron, at immense cost, on the coast of Africa. Everywhere, in this country, it is safe to speak of this foreign slave-trade, as a most inhuman traffic, opposed alike to the laws of God and of man. The duty to extirpate and destroy it, is admitted even by our DOCTORS OF DIVINITY. In order to put an end to it, some of these last have consented that their colored brethren (nominally free) should leave this country, and establish themselves on the western coast of Africa! It is, however, a notable fact that, while so much execration is poured out by Americans upon those engaged in the foreign slave-trade, the men engaged in the slave-trade between the states pass without condemnation, and their business is deemed honorable.

Behold the practical operation of this internal slave-trade, the American slave-trade, sustained by American politics and America religion. Here you will see men and women reared like swine for the market. You know what is a swine-drover? I will show you a man-drover. They inhabit all our Southern States. They perambulate the country, and crowd the highways of the nation, with droves of human stock. You will see one of these human flesh-jobbers, armed with pistol, whip and bowie-knife, driving a company of a hundred men, women, and children, from the Potomac to the slave market at New Orleans. These wretched people are to be sold singly, or in lots, to suit purchasers. They are food for the cotton-field, and the deadly sugar-mill. Mark the sad procession, as it moves wearily along, and the inhuman wretch who drives them. Hear his savage yells and his blood-chilling oaths, as he hurries on his affrighted captives! There, see the old man, with locks thinned and gray. Cast one glance, if you please, upon that young mother, whose shoulders are bare to the scorching sun, her briny tears falling on the brow of the babe in her arms. See, too, that girl of thirteen, weeping, yes! weeping, as she thinks of the mother from whom she has been torn! The drove moves tardily. Heat and sorrow have nearly consumed their strength; suddenly you hear a quick snap, like the discharge of a rifle; the fetters clank, and the chain rattles simultaneously; your ears are saluted with a scream, that seems to have torn its way to the center of your soul! The crack you heard, was the sound of the slave-whip; the scream you heard, was from the woman you saw with the babe. Her speed had faltered under the weight of her child and her chains! that gash on her shoulder tells her to move on. Follow the drove to New Orleans. Attend the auction; see men examined like horses; see the forms of women rudely and brutally exposed to the shocking gaze of American slave-buyers. See this drove sold and separated forever; and never forget the deep, sad sobs that arose from that scattered multitude. Tell me citizens, WHERE, under the sun, you can witness a spectacle more fiendish and shocking. Yet this is but a glance at the American slave-trade, as it exists, at this moment, in the ruling part of the United States.

I was born amid such sights and scenes. To me the American slave-trade is a terrible reality. When a child, my soul was often pierced with a sense of its horrors. I lived on Philpot Street, Fell's Point, Baltimore, and have watched from the wharves, the slave ships in the Basin, anchored from the shore, with their cargoes of human flesh, waiting for favorable winds to waft them down the Chesapeake. There was, at that time, a grand slave mart kept at the head of Pratt Street, by Austin Woldfolk. His agents were sent into every town and county in Maryland, announcing their arrival, through the papers, and on flaming "hand-bills," headed CASH FOR NEGROES. These men were generally well dressed men, and very captivating in their manners. Ever ready to drink, to treat, and to gamble. The fate of many a slave has depended upon the turn of a single card; and many a child has been snatched from the arms of its mother by bargains arranged in a state of brutal drunkenness.

The flesh-mongers gather up their victims by dozens, and drive them, chained, to the general depot at Baltimore. When a sufficient number have been collected here, a ship is chartered, for the purpose of conveying the forlorn crew to Mobile, or to New Orleans. From the slave prison to the ship, they are usually driven in the darkness of night; for since the antislavery agitation, a certain caution is observed.

In the deep still darkness of midnight, I have been often aroused by the dead heavy footsteps, and the piteous cries of the chained gangs that passed our door. The anguish of my boyish heart was intense; and I was often consoled, when speaking to my mistress in the morning, to hear her say that the custom was very wicked; that she hated to hear the rattle of the chains, and the heartrending cries. I was glad to find one who sympathized with me in my horror.

Fellow-citizens, this murderous traffic is, to-day, in active operation in this boasted republic. In the solitude of my spirit, I see clouds of dust raised on the highways of the South; I see the bleeding footsteps; I hear the doleful wail of fettered humanity, on the way to the slave-markets, where the victims are to be sold like horses, sheep, and swine, knocked off to the highest bidder. There I see the tenderest ties ruthlessly broken, to gratify the lust, caprice and rapacity of the buyers and sellers of men. My soul sickens at the sight.

> *Is this the land your Fathers loved,*
> *The freedom which they toiled to win?*
> *Is this the earth whereon they moved?*
> *Are these the graves they slumber in?*

But a still more inhuman, disgraceful, and scandalous state of things remains to be presented. By an act of the American Congress, not yet two years old, slavery has been nationalized in its most horrible and revolting form. By that act, Mason and Dixon's line has been obliterated; New York has become as Virginia; and the power to hold, hunt, and sell men, women, and children as slaves remains no longer a mere state institution, but is now an institution of the whole United States. The power is co-extensive with the Star-Spangled Banner and American Christianity. Where these go, may also go the merciless slave-hunter. Where these are, man is not sacred. He is a bird for the sportsman's gun. By that most foul and fiendish of all human decrees, the liberty and person of every man are put in peril. Your broad republican domain is hunting ground for men. Not for thieves and robbers, enemies of society, merely, but for men guilty of no crime. Your lawmakers have commanded all good citizens to engage in this hellish sport. Your President, your Secretary of State, our lords, nobles, and ecclesiastics, enforce, as a duty you owe to your free and glorious country, and to your God, that you do this accursed thing. Not fewer than forty Americans have, within the past two years, been hunted down and, without a moment's warning, hurried away in chains, and consigned to slavery and excruciating torture. Some of these have had wives and children, dependent on them for bread; but of this, no account was made. The right of the hunter to his prey stands superior to the right of marriage, and to all rights in this republic, the rights of God included! For black men there are neither law, justice, humanity, not religion. The Fugitive Slave Law makes mercy to them a crime; and bribes the judge who tries them. An American judge gets ten dollars for every victim he consigns to slavery, and five, when he fails to do so. The oath of any two villains is sufficient, under this hell-black enactment, to send the most pious and exemplary black man into the remorseless jaws of slavery! His own testimony is nothing. He can bring no witnesses for himself. The minister of American justice is bound by the law to hear but one side; and that side, is the side of the oppressor. Let this damning fact be perpetually told. Let it be thundered around the world, that, in tyrant-killing, king-hating, people-loving, democratic, Christian America, the seats of justice are filled with judges, who hold their offices under an open and palpable bribe, and are bound, in deciding in the case of a man's liberty, hear only his accusers!

In glaring violation of justice, in shameless disregard of the forms of administering law, in cunning arrangement to entrap the defenseless, and in diabolical intent, this Fugitive Slave Law stands alone in the annals of tyrannical legislation. I doubt if there be another nation on the globe, having the brass and the baseness to put such a law on the statute-book. If any man in this assembly thinks differently from me in this matter, and feels able to disprove my statements, I will gladly confront him at any suitable time and place he may select.

I take this law to be one of the grossest infringements of Christian Liberty, and, if the churches and ministers of our country were not stupidly blind, or most wickedly indifferent, they, too, would so regard it.

At the very moment that they are thanking God for the enjoyment of civil and religious liberty, and for the right to worship God according to the dictates of their own consciences, they are utterly silent in respect to a law which robs religion of its chief significance, and makes it utterly worthless to a world lying in wickedness. Did this law concern the "mint, anise, and cumin"—abridge the right to sing psalms, to partake of the sacrament, or to engage in any of the ceremonies of religion, it would be smitten by the thunder of a thousand pulpits. A general shout would go up from the church, demanding repeal, repeal, instant repeal!—And it would go hard with that politician who presumed to solicit the votes of the people without inscribing this motto on his banner. Further, if this demand were not complied with, another Scotland would be added to the history of religious liberty, and the stern old Covenanters would be thrown into the shade. A John Knox would be seen at every church door, and heard from every pulpit, and Fillmore would have no more quarter than was shown by Knox, to the beautiful, but treacherous queen Mary of Scotland. The fact that the church of our country, (with fractional exceptions), does not esteem "the Fugitive Slave Law" as a declaration of war against religious liberty, implies that that church regards religion simply as a form of worship, an empty ceremony, and not a vital principle, requiring active benevolence, justice, love and good will towards man. It esteems sacrifice above mercy; psalm-singing above right doing; solemn meetings above practical righteousness. A worship that can be conducted by persons who refuse to give shelter to the houseless, to give bread to the hungry, clothing to the naked, and who enjoin obedience to a law forbidding these acts of mercy, is a curse, not a blessing to mankind. The Bible addresses all such persons as "scribes, Pharisees, hypocrites, who pay tithe of mint, anise, and cumin, and have omitted the weightier matters of the law, judgment, mercy and faith."

But the church of this country is not only indifferent to the wrongs of the slave, it actually takes sides with the oppressors. It has made itself the bulwark of

American slavery, and the shield of American slave-hunters. Many of its most eloquent Divines. who stand as the very lights of the church, have shamelessly given the sanction of religion and the Bible to the whole slave system. They have taught that man may, properly, be a slave; that the relation of master and slave is ordained of God; that to send back an escaped bondman to his master is clearly the duty of all the followers of the Lord Jesus Christ; and this horrible blasphemy is palmed off upon the world for Christianity.

For my part, I would say, welcome infidelity! welcome atheism! welcome anything! in preference to the gospel, as preached by those Divines! They convert the very name of religion into an engine of tyranny, and barbarous cruelty, and serve to confirm more infidels, in this age, than all the infidel writings of Thomas Paine, Voltaire, and Bolingbroke, put together, have done! These ministers make religion a cold and flinty-hearted thing, having neither principles of right action, nor bowels of compassion. They strip the love of God of its beauty, and leave the throng of religion a huge, horrible, repulsive form. It is a religion for oppressors, tyrants, man-stealers, and thugs. It is not that "pure and undefiled religion" which is from above, and which is "first pure, then peaceable, easy to be entreated, full of mercy and good fruits, without partiality, and without hypocrisy." But a religion which favors the rich against the poor; which exalts the proud above the humble; which divides mankind into two classes, tyrants and slaves; which says to the man in chains, stay there; and to the oppressor, oppress on; it is a religion which may be professed and enjoyed by all the robbers and enslavers of mankind; it makes God a respecter of persons, denies his fatherhood of the race, and tramples in the dust the great truth of the brotherhood of man. All this we affirm to be true of the popular church, and the popular worship of our land and nation—a religion, a church, and a worship which, on the authority of inspired wisdom, we pronounce to be an abomination in the sight of God. In the language of Isaiah, the American church might be well addressed, "Bring no more vain ablations; incense is an abomination unto me: the new moons and Sabbaths, the calling of assemblies, I cannot away with; it is iniquity even the solemn meeting. Your new moons and your appointed feasts my soul hateth. They are a trouble to me; I am weary to bear them; and when ye spread forth your hands I will hide mine eyes from you. Yea! when ye make many prayers, I will not hear. YOUR HANDS ARE FULL OF BLOOD; cease to do evil, learn to do well; seek judgment; relieve the oppressed; judge for the fatherless; plead for the widow."

The American church is guilty, when viewed in connection with what it is doing to uphold slavery; but it is superlatively guilty when viewed in connection with its ability to abolish slavery. The sin of which it is guilty is one of omission as well as of commission. Albert Barnes but uttered what the common sense of every man at all observant of the actual state of the case will receive as truth, when he declared that "There is no power out of the church that could sustain slavery an hour, if it were not sustained in it."

Let the religious press, the pulpit, the Sunday school, the conference meeting, the great ecclesiastical, missionary, Bible and tract associations of the land array their immense powers against slavery and slave-holding; and the whole system of crime and blood would be scattered to the winds; and that they do not do this involves them in the most awful responsibility of which the mind can conceive.

In prosecuting the anti-slavery enterprise, we have been asked to spare the church, to spare the ministry; but how, we ask, could such a thing be done? We are met on the threshold of our efforts for the redemption of the slave, by the church and ministry of the country, in battle arrayed against us; and we are compelled to fight or flee. From what quarter, I beg to know, has proceeded a fire so deadly upon our ranks, during the last two years, as from the Northern pulpit? As the champions of oppressors, the chosen men of American theology have appeared—men, honored for their so-called piety, and their real learning. The Lords of Buffalo, the Springs of New York, the Lathrops of Auburn, the Coxes and Spencers of Brooklyn, the Gannets and Sharps of Boston, the Deweys of Washington, and other great religious lights of the land have, in utter denial of the authority of Him by whom they professed to be called to the ministry, deliberately taught us, against the example or the Hebrews and against the remonstrance of the Apostles, they teach that we ought to obey man's law before the law of God.

My spirit wearies of such blasphemy; and how such men can be supported, as the "standing types and representatives of Jesus Christ," is a mystery which I leave others to penetrate. In speaking of the American church, however, let it be distinctly understood that I mean the great mass of the religious organizations of our land. There are exceptions, and I thank God that there are. Noble men may be found, scattered all over these Northern States, of whom Henry Ward Beecher of Brooklyn, Samuel J. May of Syracuse, and my esteemed friend (Rev. R. R. Raymond) on the platform, are shining examples; and let me say further, that upon these men lies the duty to inspire our ranks with high religious faith and zeal, and to cheer us on in the great mission of the slave's redemption from his chains.

One is struck with the difference between the attitude of the American church towards the anti-slavery movement, and that occupied by the churches in England towards a similar movement in that country. There, the church, true to its mission of ameliorating, elevating, and improving the condition of mankind, came forward promptly, bound up the wounds of the West Indian slave, and restored him to his liberty. There, the question of emancipation was a high religious question. It was demanded, in the name of humanity, and according to the law of the living God. The Sharps, the Clarksons, the Wilberforces, the Buxtons, and Burchells and the Knibbs, were alike famous for their piety, and for their philanthropy. The anti-slavery movement there was not an anti-church movement, for the reason that the church took its full share in prosecuting that movement: and the anti-slavery movement in this country will cease to be an anti-church movement, when the church of this country shall assume a favorable, instead of a hostile position towards that movement. Americans! your republican politics, not less than your republican religion, are flagrantly inconsistent. You boast of your love of liberty, your superior civilization, and your pure Christianity, while the whole political power of the nation (as embodied in the two great political parties), is solemnly pledged to support and perpetuate the enslavement of three millions of your countrymen. You hurl your anathemas at the crowned headed tyrants of Russia and Austria, and pride yourselves on your Democratic institutions, while you yourselves consent to be the mere tools and body-guards of the tyrants of Virginia and Carolina. You invite to your shores fugitives of oppression from abroad, honor them with banquets, greet them with ovations, cheer them, toast them, salute them, protect them, and pour out your money to them like water; but the fugitives from your own land you advertise, hunt, arrest, shoot and kill. You glory in your refinement and your universal education yet you maintain a system as barbarous and dreadful as ever stained the character of a nation—a system begun in avarice, supported in pride, and perpetuated in cruelty. You shed tears over fallen Hungary, and make the sad story of her wrongs the theme of your poets, statesmen and orators, till your gallant sons are ready to fly to arms to vindicate her cause against her oppressors; but, in regard to the ten thousand wrongs of the American slave, you would enforce the strictest silence, and would hail him as an enemy of the nation who dares to make those wrongs the subject of public discourse! You are all on fire at the mention of liberty for France or for Ireland; but are as cold as an iceberg at the thought of liberty for the enslaved of America. You discourse eloquently on the dignity of labor; yet, you sustain a system which, in its very essence, casts a stigma upon labor. You can bare your bosom to the storm of British artillery to throw off a threepenny tax on tea; and yet wring the last hard-earned farthing from the grasp of the black laborers of your country. You profess to believe "that, of one blood, God made all nations of men to dwell on the face of all the earth," and hath commanded all men, everywhere to love one another; yet you notoriously hate, (and glory in your hatred), all men whose skins are not colored like your own. You declare, before the world, and are understood by the world to declare, that you "hold these truths to be self evident, that all men are created equal; and are endowed by their Creator with certain inalienable rights; and that, among these are, life, liberty, and the pursuit of happiness;" and yet, you hold securely, in a bondage which, according to your own Thomas Jefferson, "is worse than ages of that which your fathers rose in rebellion to oppose," a seventh part of the inhabitants of your country.

Fellow-citizens! I will not enlarge further on your national inconsistencies. The existence of slavery in this country brands your republicanism as a sham, your humanity as a base pretence, and your Christianity as a lie. It destroys your moral power abroad; it corrupts your politicians at home. It saps the foundation of religion; it makes your name a hissing, and a bye-word to a mocking earth. It is the antagonistic force in your government, the only thing that seriously disturbs and endangers your Union. It fetters your progress; it is the enemy of improvement, the deadly foe of education; it fosters pride; it breeds insolence; it promotes vice; it shelters crime; it is a curse to the earth that supports it; and yet, you cling to it, as if it were the sheet anchor of all your hopes. Oh! be warned! be warned! a horrible reptile is coiled up in your nation's bosom; the venomous creature is nursing at the tender breast of your youthful republic; for the love of God, tear away, and fling from you the hideous monster, and let the weight of twenty millions crush and destroy it forever!

But it is answered in reply to all this, that precisely what I have now denounced is, in fact, guaranteed and sanctioned by the Constitution of the United States; that the right to hold and to hunt slaves is a part of that Constitution framed by the illustrious Fathers of this Republic.

Then, I dare to affirm, notwithstanding all I have said before, your fathers stooped, basely stooped

To palter with us in a double sense:
And keep the word of promise to the ear,
But break it to the heart.

And instead of being the honest men I have before declared them to be, they were the veriest imposters that ever practiced on mankind. This is the inevitable conclusion, and from it there is no escape. But I differ from those who charge this baseness on the framers of the Constitution of the United States. It is a slander upon their memory, at least, so I believe. There is not time now to argue the constitutional question at length—nor have I the ability to discuss it as it ought to be discussed. The subject has been handled with masterly power by Lysander Spooner, Esq., by William Goodell, by Samuel E. Sewall, Esq., and last, though not least, by Gerritt Smith, Esq. These gentlemen have, as I think, fully and clearly vindicated the Constitution from any design to support slavery for an hour.

Fellow-citizens! there is no matter in respect to which, the people of the North have allowed themselves to be so ruinously imposed upon, as that of the pro-slavery character of the Constitution. In that instrument I hold there is neither warrant, license, nor sanction of the hateful thing; but, interpreted as it ought to be interpreted, the Constitution is a GLORIOUS LIBERTY DOCUMENT. Read its preamble, consider its purposes. Is slavery among them? Is it at the gateway? or is it in the temple? It is neither. While I do not intend to argue this question on the present occasion, let me ask, if it be not somewhat singular that, if the Constitution were intended to be, by its framers and adopters, a slaveholding instrument, why neither slavery, slaveholding, nor slave can anywhere be found in it. What would be thought of an instrument, drawn up, legally drawn up, for the purpose of entitling the city of Rochester to a track of land, in which no mention of land was made? Now, there are certain rules of interpretation, for the proper understanding of all legal instruments. These rules are well established. They are plain, common-sense rules, such as you and I, and all of us, can understand and apply, without having passed years in the study of law. I scout the idea that the question of the constitutionality or unconstitutionality of slavery is not a question for the people. I hold that every American citizen has a right to form an opinion of the constitution, and to propagate that opinion, and to use all honorable means to make his opinion the prevailing one. Without this right, the liberty of an American citizen would be as insecure as that of a Frenchman. Ex-Vice-President Dallas tells us that the Constitution is an object to which no American mind can be too attentive, and no American heart too devoted. He further says, the Constitution, in its words, is plain and intelligible, and is meant for the home-bred, unsophisticated understandings of our fellow-citizens. Senator Berrien tell us that the Constitution is the fundamental law, that which controls all others. The charter of our liberties, which every citizen has a personal interest in understanding thoroughly. The testimony of Senator Breese, Lewis Cass, and many others that might be named, who are everywhere esteemed as sound lawyers, so regard the constitution. I take it, therefore, that it is not presumption in a private citizen to form an opinion of that instrument.

Now, take the Constitution according to its plain reading, and I defy the presentation of a single pro-slavery clause in it. On the other hand it will be found to contain principles and purposes, entirely hostile to the existence of slavery.

I have detained my audience entirely too long already. At some future period I will gladly avail myself of an opportunity to give this subject a full and fair discussion.

Allow me to say, in conclusion, notwithstanding the dark picture I have this day presented of the state of the nation, I do not despair of this country. There are forces in operation, which must inevitably work the downfall of slavery. "The arm of the Lord is not shortened," and the doom of slavery is certain. I, therefore, leave off where I began, with hope. While drawing encouragement from the Declaration of Independence, the great principles it contains, and the genius of American Institutions, my spirit is also cheered by the obvious tendencies of the age. Nations do not now stand in the same relation to each other that they did ages ago. No nation can now shut itself up from the surrounding world, and trot round in the same old path of its fathers without interference.

The time was when such could be done. Long established customs of hurtful character could formerly fence themselves in, and do their evil work with social impunity. Knowledge was then confined and enjoyed by the privileged few, and the multitude walked on in mental darkness. But a change has now come over the affairs of mankind. Walled cities and empires have become unfashionable. The arm of commerce has borne away the gates of the strong city. Intelligence is penetrating the darkest corners of the globe. It makes its pathway over and under the sea, as well as on the earth. Wind, steam, and lightning are its chartered agents. Oceans no longer divide, but link nations together. From Boston to London is now a holiday excursion. Space is comparatively annihilated. Thoughts expressed on one side of the Atlantic, are distinctly heard on the other. The far off and almost fabulous Pacific rolls in grandeur at our feet. The Celestial Empire, the mystery of ages, is being solved. The fiat of the Almighty, "Let there be Light," has not yet spent its force. No abuse, no outrage whether in taste, sport or avarice, can now hide itself from the all-pervading light. The iron shoe, and crippled foot of China must be seen, in contrast with nature. Africa must rise and put on her yet unwoven garment. "Ethiopia shall stretch out her hand unto God." In the fervent aspirations of William Lloyd Garrison, I say, and let every heart join in saying it:

> *God speed the year of jubilee*
> *The wide world o'er*
> *When from their galling chains set free,*
> *Th' oppress'd shall vilely bend the knee,*
> *And wear the yoke of tyranny*
> *Like brutes no more.*
> *That year will come, and freedom's reign,*
> *To man his plundered fights again*
> *Restore*
> *God speed the day when human blood*
> *Shall cease to flow!*
> *In every clime be understood,*
> *The claims of human brotherhood,*
> *And each return for evil, good,*
> *Not blow for blow;*
> *That day will come all feuds to end.*
> *And change into a faithful friend*
> *Each foe.*
> *God speed the hour, the glorious hour,*
> *When none on earth*

Shall exercise a lordly power,
Nor in a tyrant's presence cower;
But all to manhood's stature tower,
By equal birth!
That hour will come, to each, to all,
And from his prison-house, the thrall
Go forth.
Until that year, day, hour, arrive,
With head, and heart, and hand I'll strive,
To break the rod, and rend the gyve,
The spoiler of his prey deprive—
So witness Heaven!
And never from my chosen post,
Whate'er the peril or the cost,
Be driven.

FOR INFORMAL WRITING

Before you read this essay, how would you have responded to the question posed by the title? Is your response different after reading the essay? Why and how?

FOR DISCUSSION

1. This is one of the oral addresses you will see in this volume. What clues are there in the text that this was written to be delivered as a speech? How do you know? How is it effective as such?
2. Douglass writes, "At a time like this, scorching irony, not convincing argument, is needed." What is irony? What is scorching irony? Why is it necessary here instead of convincing argument?
3. How does Douglass use scorching irony? What about the address is ironic? Is it effective? How so? How not?

FOR WRITING

As we mentioned earlier, the US President at the time was Millard Fillmore, not one of our most remembered commanders-in-chief. Do some research. What do you learn about Fillmore? About his views of slavery? How might those have influenced Douglass's desire to write and give this address?

Address to the Legislature of New York (1854)

Elizabeth Cady Stanton (1815–1902)

Elizabeth Cady Stanton was a leader in both the suffrage and equal rights movements for women. She received her formal education at the Johnstown Academy and the Emma Willard Troy Female Seminary in New York. Her father was an attorney and a member of the New York State Assembly. His legal work influenced Stanton, and it is said that she received an "informal" legal education at a very early age. She married Henry Stanton, a well-known abolitionist, in 1840, and she met Susan B. Anthony in 1851. With Anthony, Elizabeth Cady Stanton formed a partnership that would eventually lead to the establishment of the Women's Loyal National League, which campaigned for the abolition of slavery, and to their leadership within the American Equal Rights Association for Women. Her writings are extensive, including The Woman's Bible *(1895) and multiple volumes regarding the history of women's suffrage.*

ADDRESS
TO THE
Legislature of New-York,
ADOPTED BY THE
STATE WOMAN'S RIGHTS CONVENTION,
HELD AT ALBANY,
Tuesday and Wednesday, February 14 and 15, 1854.
PREPARED BY
ELIZABETH CADY STANTON,
Of Seneca Falls, N. Y.
ALBANY:
WEED, PARSONS AND COMPANY.
1854.

ADDRESS

To the Legislature of the State of New York:

"The thinking minds of all nations call for change. There is a deep-lying struggle in the whole fabric of society; a boundless, grinding collision of the New with the Old."

The tyrant, Custom, has been summoned before the bar of Common Sense. His Majesty no longer awes the multitude—his sceptre is broken—his crown is trampled in the dust—the sentence of death is pronounced upon him. All nations, ranks and classes have, in turn, questioned and repudiated his authority; and now, that the monster is chained and caged, timid woman, on tiptoe, comes to look him in the face, and to demand of her brave sires and sons, who have struck stout blows for liberty, if, in this change of dynasty, she, too, shall find relief.

Yes, gentlemen, in republican America, in the 19th century, we, the daughters of the revolutionary heroes of '76, demand at your hands the redness of our grievances—a revision of your state constitution—a new code of laws. Permit us then, as briefly as possible, to call your attention to the legal disabilities under which we labor.

1st, Look at the position of woman as woman. It is not enough for us that by your laws we are permitted to live and breathe, to claim the necessaries of life from our legal protectors—to pay the penalty of our crimes; we demand the full recognition of all our rights as citizens of the Empire State. We are persons; native, free-born citizens; property-holders, tax-payers; yet are we denied the exercise of our right to the elective franchise. We support ourselves, and, in part, your schools, colleges, churches, your poor-houses, jails, prisons, the army, the navy, the whole machinery of government, and yet we have no voice in your councils. We have every qualification required by the constitution, necessary to the legal voter, but the one of sex. We are moral, virtuous and intelligent, and in all respects quite equal to the proud white man himself, and yet by your laws we are classed with idiots, lunatics and negroes; and though we do not feel honored by the place assigned us, yet, in fact, our legal position is lower than that of either; for the negro can be raised to the dignity of a voter if he possess himself of $250; the lunatic can vote in his moments of sanity, and the idiot, too, if he be a male one, and not more than nine-tenths a fool; but we, who have guided great movements of charity, established missions, edited journals, published works on history, economy and statistics; who have governed nations, led armies, filled the professor's chair, taught philosophy and mathematics to the *savans* of our age, discovered planets, piloted ships across the sea, are denied the most sacred rights of citizens, because, forsooth, we came not into this republic crowned with the dignity of manhood! Woman is theoretically absolved from all allegiance to the laws of the state. Sec. 1, Bill of Rights, 2 R.S., 301, says that no authority can, on any pretence whatever, be exercised over the citizens of this state but such as is or shall be derived from, and *granted by, the people of this state.*

Now, gentlemen, we would fain know by what authority you have disfranchised one-half the people of this state? You who have so boldly taken possession of the bulwarks of this republic, show us your credentials, and thus prove your exclusive right to govern, not only yourselves, but us. Judge Hurlburt, who has long occupied a high place at the bar in this state, and who recently retired with honor from the bench of the Supreme Court, in his profound work on human rights, has pronounced your present position rank usurpation. Can it be that here, where are acknowledged no royal blood, no apostolic descent, that you, who have declared that all men were created equal—that governments derive their just powers from the consent of the governed, would willingly build up an aristocracy that places the ignorant and vulgar above the educated and refine—the alien and the ditch-digger above the authors and poets of the day—an aristocracy that would raise sons above the mothers that bore them? Would that the men who can sanction a constitution so opposed to the genius of this government, who can enact and execute laws so degrading to womankind, had sprung, Minerva-like, from the brains of their fathers, that the matrons of this republic need not blush to own their sons! Woman's position, under our free institutions, is much lower than under the monarchy of England.

"In England the idea of woman holding official station is not so strange as in the United States. The Countess of Pembroke, Dorset and Montgomery held the office of hereditary sheriff of Westmoreland, and exercised it in person. At the assizes at Appleby, she sat with the judges on the bench. In a reported case, it is stated by counsel, and substantially assented to by the court, that a woman is capable of serving in almost all the offices of the kingdom, such as those of queen, marshal, great chamberlain and constable of England, the champion of England, commissioner of sewers, governor of work house, sexton, keeper of the prison, of the gate house of the dean and chapter of Westminister, returning officer for members of parliament, and constable, the latter of which is in some respects judicial. The office of jailor is frequently exercised by a woman. In the United States a woman may administer on the effects of her deceased husband, and she has occasionally held a subordinate place in the post office department. She has therefore a sort of post mortem, post mistress notoriety; but with the exception of handling letters of administration and letters mailed, she is the submissive creature of the old common law."

True, the unmarried woman has a right to the property she inherits and the money she earns, but she is taxed without representation. And here again you place the negro, so unjustly degraded by you, in a superior position to your own wives and mothers; for colored males, if possessed of a certain amount of property and certain other qualifications, can vote, but if they do not have these qualifications *they are not subject to direct taxation;* wherein they have the advantage of woman, she being subject to taxation for whatever amount she may possess. (Constitution of N.Y. article 2, sec. 2.) But, say you, are not all women sufficiently represented by their fathers, husbands and brothers? Let your statute books answer the question.

Again we demand, in criminal cases, that most sacred of all rights, trial by a jury of our own peers. The establishment of trial by jury is of so early a date that its beginning is lost in antiquity; but the right of trial by a jury of one's own peers is a great, progressive step of advanced civilization. No rank of men have ever been satisfied with being tried by jurors higher or lower in the civil or political scale than themselves; for jealousy on the one hand, and contempt on the other, has ever effectually blinded the eyes of justice. Hence, all along the pages of history, we find the king, the noble, the peasant, the cardinal, the priest, the layman, each in turn protesting against the authority of the tribunal before which they were summoned to appear. Charles the First refused to recognized the competency of the tribunal which condemned him: For how, said he, can subjects judge a king? The stern descendants of our Pilgrim Fathers refused to answer for their crimes before an English Parliament. For how, said they, can a king judge rebels? And shall woman here consent to be tried by her liege lord, who has dubbed himself law-maker, judge, juror, and sheriff, too?—whose power, though sanctioned by Church and State, has no foundation in justice and equity, and is a bold assumption of our inalienable rights. In England a parliament-lord could challenge a jury where a knight was not empannelled. An alien could demand a jury composed half of his own countrymen; or, in some special cases, juries were even constituted entirely of women. Having seen that man fails to do justice to woman in her best estate, to the virtuous, the noble, the true of our sex, should we trust to his tender mercies, the weak, the ignorant, the morally insane? It is not to be denied that the interests of man and woman in the present undeveloped state of the race, and under the existing social arrangements, are and must be antagonistic. The nobleman cannot make just laws for the peasant; the slaveholder for the slave; neither can man make and execute just laws for woman, because in each case, the one in power fails to apply the immutable principles of right to any grade but his own. Shall an erring woman be dragged before a bar of grim-visaged judges, lawyers and jurors, there to be grossly questioned in public on subjects which women scarce breathe in secret to one another? Shall the most sacred relations of life be called up and rudely scanned by men who, by their own admission, are so coarse that women could not meet them even at the polls without contamination? and yet shall she find there no woman's face or voice to pity and defend? Shall the frenzied mother who, to save herself and child from exposure and disgrace, ended the life that had but just begun, be dragged before such a tribunal to answer for her crime? How can man enter into the feelings of that mother? How can he judge of the mighty agonies of soul that impelled her to such an outrage of maternal instincts? How can he weigh the mountain of sorrow that crushed that mother's heart when she wildly tossed her helpless babe into the cold waters of the midnight sea? Where is he who by false vows thus blasted this trusting woman? Had that helpless child no claims on his protection? Ah, he is freely abroad in the dignity of manhood, in the pulpit, in the bench, in the professor's chair. The imprisonment of his victim and the death of his child, detract not a tithe from his standing and complacency. His peers made the law, and shall law-makers lay nets for those of their own rank? Shall laws which come from the logical brain of man take cognizance of violence done to the moral and affectional nature which predominates, as is said, in woman? Statesmen of New-York, whose daughters, guarded by your affection, and lapped amidst luxuries which your indulgence spreads, care more for their nodding plumes and velvet trains than for the statute laws by which their persons and properties are held—who, blinded by custom and prejudice to the degraded position which they and their sisters occupy in the civil scale, haughtily claim that they already have all rights they want, how, think ye, you would feel to see a daughter summoned for such a crime—and remember these daughters are but human—before such a tribunal? Would it not, in that hour, be some consolation to see that she was surrounded by the wise and virtuous of her own sex; by those who had known the depth of a mother's love and the misery of a lover's falsehood; to know that to these she could make her confession, and from them receive her sentence? If so, then listen to our just demands and make such a change in your laws as will secure to every woman tried in your courts, an impartial jury. At this moment among the hundreds of women who are shut up in prisons in this state, not one has enjoyed that most sacred of all rights—that right which you would die to defend for yourselves—trial by a jury of one's peers.

2d. Look at the position of woman as wife. Your laws relating to marriage—founded as they are on the old common law of England, a compound of barbarous usages, but partially modified by progressive civilization—are in open violation of our enlightened ideas of justice, and of the holiest feelings of our nature. If you take the highest view of marriage, as a Divine relation, which love alone can constitute and sanctify, then of course human legislation can only recognize it. Man can neither bind or loose its ties, for that prerogative belongs to God alone, who makes man and woman, and the laws of attraction by which they are united. But if you regard marriage as a civil contract, then let it be subject to the same laws which control all other contracts. Do not make it a kind of half-human, half-divine institution, which you may build up but cannot regulate. Do not, by your special legislation for this one kind of contract, involve yourselves in the greatest absurdities and contradictions.

So long as by your laws no man can make a contract for a horse or piece of land until he is twenty-one years of age, and by which contract he is not bound if any deception has been practiced, or if the party contracting has not fulfilled his part of the agreement—so long as the parties in all mere civil contracts retain their identity and all the power and independence they had before contracting, with the full right to dissolve all partnerships and contracts for any reason, at the will and option of the parties themselves, upon what principle of civil jurisprudence do you permit the boy of fourteen and the girl of twelve, in violation of every natural law, to make a contract more momentous in importance than any other, and then hold them to it, come what may, the whole of their natural lives, in spite of disappointment, deception and misery? Then, too, the signing of this contract is instant civil death to one of the parties. The woman who but yesterday was sued on bended knee, who stood so high in the scale of being as to make an agreement on equal terms with a proud Saxon man, to-day has no civil existence, no social freedom. The wife who inherits no property holds about the same legal position that does the slave on the southern plantation. She can own nothing, sell nothing. She has no right even to the wages she earns; her person, her time, her services are the property of another. She cannot testify, in many cases, against her husband. She can get no redress for wrongs in her own name in any court of justice. She can neither sue nor be sued. She is not held morally responsible for any crime committed in the presence of her husband, so completely is her very existence supposed by the law to be merged in that of another. Think of it; your wives may be thieves, libellers, burglars, incendiaries, and for crimes like these they are not held amenable to the laws of the land, if they but commit them in your dread presence. For them, alas! there is no higher law than the will of man. Herein behold the bloated conceit of these Petruchios of the law, who seem to say:

"Nay, look not big, nor stamp, nor stare, nor fret, I will be master of what is mine own; She is my goods, my chattels; she is my house, My household stuff, my field, my barn, My horse, my ox, my ass, my anything; And here she stands, touch her whoever dare; I'll bring my action on the proudest be, That stops my way, in Padua."

How could man ever look thus on woman?—She, at whose feet Socrates learned wisdom—she, who gave to the world a Saviour, and witnessed alike the adoration of the Magi and the agonies of the Cross. How could such a being, so blessed and honored, ever become the ignoble, servile, cringing slave, with whom the fear of man could be paramount to the sacred dictates of conscience and the holy love of Heaven? By the common law of England, the spirit of which has been but too faithfully incorporated into our statute law, a husband has a right to whip his wife with a rod not larger than his thumb, to shut her up in a room, and administer whatever moderate chastisement he may deem necessary to insure obedience to his wishes, and for her healthful moral development! He can forbid all persons harboring or trusting her on his account. He can deprive her of all social intercourse with her nearest and dearest friends. If by great economy she accumulates a small sum, which for future need she deposit, little by little, in a savings bank, the husband has a right to draw it out, at his option, to use it as he may see fit.

"Husband is entitled to wife's credit or business talents (whenever their intermarriage may have occurred); and goods purchased by her on her own credit, with his consent, while cohabiting with him, can be seized and sold in execution against him for his own debts, and this, though she carry on business in her own name."—7 *Howard's Practice, Reports, 105, Levett agt. Robinson and Witbeck, sheriff, &c.*

"No letters of administration shall be granted to a person convicted of infamous crime; nor to any one incapable by law of making a contract; nor to a person not a citizen of the United States, unless such person reside within the state; nor to any one who is under twenty-one years of age; nor to any person who shall be adjudged incompetent by the surrogate to execute duties of such trust, by reason of drunkenness, improvidence, or want of understanding, nor any married woman; but where a married woman is entitled to administration, the same may be granted to her husband in her right and behalf."

There is nothing that an unruly wife might do against which the husband has not sufficient protection in the law. But not so with the wife. If she have a worthless husband, a confirmed drunkard, a villain or a vagrant, he has still all the rights of a man, a husband and a father. Though the whole support of the family be thrown upon the wife, if the wages she earns be paid to her by her employer, the husband can receive them again. If, by unwearied industry and perseverance, she can earn for herself and children a patch of ground and shed to cover them, the husband can strip her of all her hard earnings, turn her and her little ones out in the cold northern blast, take the clothes from their backs, the bread from their mouths; all this by your laws may he do, and has he done, oft and again, to satisfy the rapacity of that monster in human form, the rum-seller.

But the wife who is so fortunate as to have inherited property, has, by the new law in this state, been redeemed from her lost condition. She is no longer a legal nonentity. This property law, if fairly construed, will overturn the whole code relating to woman and property. The right to property implies the right to buy and sell, to will and bequeath, and herein is the dawning of a civil existence for woman, for now the "femme covert" must have the right to make contracts. So, get ready, gentlemen; the "little justice" will be coming to you one day, deed in hand, for your acknowledgment. When he asks you "if you sign without fear or compulsion," say yes, boldly, as we do. Then, too, the right to will is ours. Now what becomes of the "tenant for life?" Shall he, the happy husband of a millionaire, who has lived in yonder princely mansion in the midst of plenty and elegance, be cut down in a day to the use of one-third of this estate and a few hundred a year, as long as he remains her widower? And should he, in spite of this bounty on celibacy, impelled by his affections, marry again, choosing for a wife a woman as poor as himself, shall he be thrown penniless on the cold world—this child of fortune, enervated by ease and luxury, henceforth to be dependent wholly on his own resources? Poor man! He would be rich, though, in the *sympathies* of many women who have passed through just such an ordeal. But what is property without the right to protect that property by law? It is mockery to say a certain estate is mine, if, without my consent, you have the right to tax me when and how you please, while I have no voice in making the tax-gatherer, the legislator or the law. The right to property will, of necessity, compel us in due time to the exercise of our right to the elective franchise, and then naturally follows the right to hold office.

3d. Look at the position of woman as widow. Whenever we attempt to point out the wrongs of the wife, those who would have us believe that the laws cannot be improved, point us to the privileges, powers and claims of the widow. Let us look into these a little. Behold in yonder humble house a married pair, who, for long years, have lived together, childless and alone. Those few acres of well-tilled land, with the small white house that looks so cheerful through its vines and flowers, attest the honest thrift and simple taste of its owners. This man and woman, by their hard days' labor, have made this home their own. Here they live in peace and plenty, happy in the hope that they may dwell together securely under their own vine and fig tree for the few years that remain to them, and that under the shadow of these trees, planted by their own hands, and in the midst of their household gods, so loved and familiar, here may take their last farewell of earth. But, alas for human hopes! the husband dies, and without will, and the stricken widow, at one fell blow, loses the companion of her youth, her house and home, and half the little sum she had in bank. For the law, which takes no cognizance of widows left with twelve children and not one cent, instantly spies out this widow, takes account of her effects, and announces to her the startling intelligence that but one-third of the house and lot, and one-half the personal property, are hers. The law has other favorites with whom she must share the hard-earned savings of years. In this dark hour of grief, the coarse minions of the law gather round the widow's hearthstone, and, in the name of justice, outrage all natural sense of right; mock at the sacredness of human love, and with cold familiarity proceed to place a monied value on the old arm chair, in which, but a few brief hours since, she closed the eyes that had ever beamed on her with kindness and affection; on the solemn clock in the corner, that told the hour he passed away; on every garment with which his form and presence were associated, and on every article of comfort and convenience that the house contained, even down to the knives and forks and spoons—and the widow saw it all—and when the work was done, she gathered up what the law allowed her and went forth to seek her another home! This is the much talked of widow's dower. Behold the magnanimity of the law in allowing the widow to retain a life interest in one-third the landed estate, and one-half the personal property of her husband, and taking the lion's share to itself! Had she died first, the house and land would all have been the husband's still. No one would have dared to intrude upon the privacy of his home or to molest him in his sacred retreat of sorrow.

How, I ask you, can that be called justice, which makes such a distinction as this between man and woman?

By management, economy and industry, our widow is able, in a few years, to redeem her house and home. But the law never loses sight of the purse, no matter how low in the scale of being its owner may be. It sends it officers round every year to gather in the harvest for the public crib, and no widow who owns a piece of land two feet square ever escapes this reckoning. Our widow, too, who has now twice earned her home, has her annual tax to pay also—a tribute of gratitude that she is permitted to breathe the free air of this republic, where "taxation without representation," by such worthies as John Hancock and Samuel Adams, has been declared "intolerable "tyranny." Having glanced at the magnanimity of the law in its dealings with the widow, let us see how the individual man, under the influence of such laws, doles out justice to his helpmate. The husband has the absolute right to will away his property as he may see fit. If he has children, he can divide his property among them, leaving his wife her third only of the landed estate, thus making her a dependent on the bounty of her own children. A man thirty thousand dollars in personal property, may leave his wife but a few hundred a year, as long as she remains his widow.

The cases are without number where women, who have lived in ease and elegance, at the death of their husbands have, by will, been reduced to the bare necessaries of life. The man who leaves his wife the sole guardian of his property and children is an exception to the general rule. Man has ever manifested a wish the world should indeed be a blank to the companion whom he leaves behind him. The Hindoo makes that wish a law, and burns the widow on the funeral pile of her husband; but the civilized man, impressed with a different view of the sacredness of life, takes a less summary mode of drawing his beloved partner after him; he does it by the deprivation and starvation of the flesh, and the humiliation and mortification of the spirit. In bequeathing to the wife just enough to keep soul and body together, man seems to lose sight of the fact that woman, like himself, takes great pleasure in acts of benevolence and charity. It is but just, therefore, that she should have it in her power to give during her life, and to will away at her death, as her benevolence or obligations might prompt her to do.

4th. Look at the position of woman as *mother*. There is no human love so generous, strong and steadfast as that of the mother for her child; yet behold how cruel and ruthless are your laws touching this most sacred relation.

Nature has clearly made the mother the guardian of the child; but man, in his inordinate love of power, does continually set nature and nature's laws at open defiance. The father may apprentice his child, bind him out to a trade or labor, without the mother's consent—yea, in direct opposition to her most earnest entreaties, her prayers and tears.

He may apprentice his son to a gamester or rumseller, and thus cancel his debts of *honor*. By the abuse of this absolute power, he may bind his daughter to the owner of a brothel, and, by the degradation of his child, supply his daily wants; and such things, gentlemen, have been done in our very midst. Moreover, the father, about to die, may bind out all his children wherever and to whomsoever he may see fit, and thus, in fact, will away the guardianship of all his children from the mother. The Revised Statutes of New-York provide that "every father, whether of full age or a minor, of a child to be born, or of any living child under the age of twenty-one years, and unmarried, may be his *deed or last will*, duly executed, dispose of the custody and tuition of such child during its minority, or for any less time, to any person or persons, in possession or remainder." 2 R. S., page 150, sec. 1.

Thus, by your laws, the child is the absolute property of the father, wholly at his disposal in life or at death.

In case of separation, the law gives the children to the father; no matter what his character or condition. At this very time we can point you to noble, virtuous, well educated mothers in this state, who have abandoned their husbands for their profligacy and confirmed drunkenness. All these have been robbed of their children, who are in the custody of the husband, under the care of his relatives, whilst the mothers are permitted to see them but at stated intervals. But, said one of these mothers, with a grandeur of attitude and manner worthy the noble Roman matron in the palmiest days of that republic, I would rather never see my child again, than be the medium to hand down the low, animal nature of its father, to stamp degradation on the brow of another innocent being. It is enough that one child of his shall call me mother. If you are far sighted statesmen, and do wisely judge of the interests of this commonwealth, you will so shape your future laws as to encourage woman to take the high moral ground that the father of her children must be great and good.

Instead of your present laws, which make the mother and her children the victims of vice and license, you might rather pass laws prohibiting to all drunkards, libertines and fools, the rights of husbands and fathers. Do not the hundreds of laughing idiots that are crowding into our asylums, appeal to the wisdom of our statesmen for some new laws on marriage—to the mothers of this day for a higher, purer morality?

Again, as the condition of the child always follows that of the mother, and as by the abuse of your laws the father may best the mother, so may he the child. What mother cannot bear me witness to untold sufferings. Which cruel, vindictive fathers have visited upon their helpless children? Who ever saw a human being that would not abuse unlimited power? Base and ignoble must that man be, who, let the provocation be what it may, would strike a woman; but he who would lacerate a trembling child is unworthy the name of man. A mother's love can be no protection to a child; she cannot appeal to you to save it from a father's cruelty, for the laws take no cognizance of the mother's most grievous wrongs. Neither at home or abroad can a mother protect her son. Look at the temptations that surround the paths of our youth at every step; look at the gambling and drinking saloons, the club rooms, the dens of infamy and abomination that infest all our villages and cities—slowly but surely sapping the very foundations of all virtue and strength.

By your laws, all these abominable resorts are permitted. It is folly to talk of a mother moulding the character of her son, when all mankind, backed up by law and public sentiment, conspire to destroy her influence. But when woman's moral power shall speak through the ballot-box, then shall her influence be seen and felt; then, in our legislative debates, such questions as the canal tools on salt, the improvement of rivers and harbors, and the claims, of Mr. Smith for damages against the states, would be secondary to the consideration of the legal existence of all these public resorts, which lure our youth on to excessive indulgence and destruction.

Many times and oft it has been asked us, with unaffected seriousness, "what do you women want? What are you aiming at?" Many have manifested a laudable curiosity to know what the wives and daughters could complain of in republican America, where their sires and sons have so bravely fought for freedom and gloriously secured their independence, trampling all tyranny, bigotry and caste in the dust, and declaring to a waiting world the divine truth that all men are created equal. What can *woman* want under such a government? Admit a radical differences in sex and you demand different spheres—water for fish, and air for birds.

It is impossible to make the southern planter believe that his slave feels and reasons just as he does—that injustice and subjection are as galling as to him—that the degradation of living by the will of another, the mere dependent on his caprice, at the mercy of his passions, is as keenly felt by him as his master. If you can force on his unwilling vision a vivid picture of the negro's wrongs, and for a moment touch his soul, his logic brings him instant consolation. He says, the slave does not feel this as I would. Here, gentlemen, is our difficulty: When we plead our cause before the law makers and *savans* of the republic, they cannot take in the idea that men and women are alike; and so long as the mass rest in this delusion, the public mind will not be so much startled by the revelation made of the injustice and degradation of woman's position as by the fact that she should at length wake up to a sense of it.

If you, too, are thus deluded, what avails it that we show by your statute books that your laws are unjust—that woman is the victim of avarice and power? What avails it that we point out the wrongs of woman in social life; the victim of passion and lust? You scorn the thought that she has any natural love of freedom burning in her breast, any clear perception of justice urging her on to demand her rights.

Would to God you could know the burning indignation that fills woman's soul when she turns over the pages of your statute books, and sees there how like feudal barons you freemen hold your women. Would that you could know the humiliations she feels for her sex, when she thinks of all the beardless boys in your law offices, learning these ideas of one-sided justice—taking their first lessons in contempt for all womankind—being indoctrinated into the incapacities of their mothers, and the lordly, absolute rights of man over all women, children and property, and to know that these are to be our future Presidents, Judges, Husbands and Fathers; in sorrow we exclaim, alas! for that nation whose sons bow not in loyalty to woman. The mother is the first object of the child's veneration and love, and they who root out this holy sentiment, dream not of the blighting effect, it has on the boy and the man. The impression left on law students, fresh from your statute books, is most unfavorable to woman's influence; hence you see but few lawyers chivalrous and high-toned in their sentiments towards woman. They cannot escape the legal view which, by constant reading, has become familiarized to their minds: "*Femme covert,*" "downer," "widow's claims," "protection," "incapacities," "incumbrance," is written on the brow of every woman they meet.

But if, gentlemen, you take the ground that the sexes are alike, and, therefore, you are our faithful representative—then why all these special laws for woman? Would not one code answer for all of like needs and wants? Christ's golden rule is better than all the special legislation that the ingenuity of man can devise: "Do unto others as you would have others do unto you." This, men and brethren, is all we ask at your hands. We *ask* no better laws than those you have made for yourselves. We need no other protection than that which yourself present law secure to you.

In conclusion, then, let us say, in behalf of the women of this state, we ask for all that you have asked for yourselves in the progress of your development, since the *May Flower* cast anchor side Plymouth rock; and simply on the ground that the rights of every human being are the same and identical. You may say that the mass of the women of this state do not make the demand; it comes from a few sour, disappointed old maids and childless women.

You are mistaken; the mass speak through us. A very large majority of the women of this state support themselves and their children, and many their husbands too. Go into any village you please, of three of four thousand inhabitants, and you will find as many as fifty men or more, whose only business is to discuss religion and politics, as they watch the trains come and go at the depot, or the passage of a canal boat through a lock; to laugh at the vagaries of some drunken brother, or the capers of a monkey, dancing to the music of his master's organ. All these are supported by their mothers, wives or sisters.

Now, do you *candidly* think these wives do not wish to control the wages they earn—to own the land they buy—the houses they build? to have at their disposal their own children, without being subject to the constant interference and tyranny of an idle, worthless profligate? Do you suppose that any woman is such a pattern of devotion and submission that she willingly stitches all day for a small sum of fifty cents, that she may enjoy the unspeakable privilege, in obedience to your laws, of paying for her husband's tobacco and rum? Think you the wife of the confirmed, beastly drunkard would consent to share with him her home and bed, if law and public sentiment would release her from such gross companionship? Verily, no! Think you the wife, with whom endurance has ceased to be a virtue, who through much suffering has lost all faith in the justice of both Heaven and earth, takes the law in her own hand, severs the unholy bond and turns her back forever upon him whom she once called husband, consents to the law that in such an hour tears her child from her—all that she has left on earth to love and cherish? The drunkards' wives speak through us, and they number 50,000. Think you that the woman who has worked hard all her days, in helping her husband to accumulate a large property, consents to the law that places this wholly at his disposal? Would not the mother, whose only child is bound out for a term of years, against her expressed wishes, deprive the father of this absolute power if she could?

For all these, then, we speak. If to this long list you add all the laboring women, who are loudly demanding remuneration for their unending toil—those women who teach in our seminaries, academies and common schools for a miserable pittance; the widows, who are taxed without mercy; the unfortunate ones in our work houses, poor houses and prisons; who are they that we do not now represent? But a small class of fashionable butterflies, who, through the short summer days, seek the sunshine and the flowers; but the cool breezes of autumn and the hoary frosts of winter will soon chase all these away; then, they too will need and seek protection, and through other lips demand, in their turn, justice and equity at your hands.

APPENDIX

This Address was laid upon the member's desks, Monday morning, Feb. 20, 1854.

When the order of petitions was reached, Mr. D. P. Wood, of Onondaga, presented in the Assembly a petition signed by 5931 men and women, praying for the just and equal rights of women, which, after a spicy debate, was referred to the following select committee:

- James L. Angle, of Monroe Co.,
- George W. Thorn, of Washington Co.,
- Derrick L. Boardman, of Oneida Co.,
- George H. Richards, of New-York,
- James M. Munro, of Onondaga,
- Wesley Gleason, of Fulton,
- Alexander P. Sharpe, of New-York.

In the Senate on the same day, Mr. Richards, of Warren county, presented a petition signed by 4164 men and women, praying for the extension of the right of suffrage to women, and on his motion it was referred to following select committee:

- George Yost, of Montgomery Co.,
- Ben Field, of Orleans Co.,
- W.H. Robertson, of Westchester Co.

The following are the forms of the petitions as agreed upon the Convention held at Rochester, November 30 and December 1, 1853. The signatures were obtained in some thirty counties, by a few individuals, during this short period:

Petition for the Just and Equal Rights of Women

The Legislature of the State of New-York have, by the Acts of 1848 and 1849, testified the purpose of the People of this State to place Married Women on an equality with Married Men in regard to the holding conveying and devising of real and personal property.

We, therefore, the undersigned Petitioners, inhabitants of the State of New-York, male and female, having attained to the age of legal majority, believing that Women, alike married and single, do still suffer under *many and grievous* LEGAL

DISABILITIES, do earnestly request the Senate and Assembly of the State of New-York to appoint a joint committee of both Houses to revise the Statutes of New-York, and to propose such amendments as will fully establish the LEGAL EQUALITY of Women with Men; and do hereby ask a hearing before such committee by our accredited Representatives.

Petition for Woman's Right to Suffrage
Whereas, according to the Declaration of our National Independence Governments derive their just powers from the consent of the governed, we earnestly request the Legislature of New-York to propose to the People of the State such amendments of the Constitution of the State as will secure to females an equal right to the Elective Franchise with Males; and we do hereby request a hearing before the Legislature by our accredited Representatives.

FOR INFORMAL WRITING

Based on Stanton's speech, detail what aspects of women's lives you learn could not be taken for granted as we do today.

FOR DISCUSSION

1. Stanton speaks of the "legal disabilities under which [women] labor." What are these "disabilities?" How does this term evoke the conditions Stanton describes?
2. Remembering that this was written to be spoken and not necessarily read, what is the structure of this speech? Why do you think Stanton chose to structure it as she does?
3. What are the demands that Stanton makes on behalf of women? What are the tenets of her desired outcome? (Be sure to review the *Appendix* as well. Why is that important?)

FOR WRITING

Research aspects of the political and cultural contexts in which Stanton delivers this address. Consider this as you do so: "The tyrant, Custom, has been summoned before the bar of Common Sense." What is this tyrannical set of customs to which Stanton responds, and how do they limit and oppress women?

Life Without Principle (1863)
Henry David Thoreau (1817–1862)

Considered a poet, philosopher, essayist, and naturalist, Henry David Thoreau was educated at Harvard. His best-known works include Walden *(1845) and his essay "Civil Disobedience" (1849). About Thoreau, the American author John Updike wrote, "A century and a half after its publication,* Walden *has become such a totem of the back-to-nature, preservationist, anti-business, civil-disobedience mindset, and Thoreau so vivid a protester, so perfect a crank and hermit saint, that the book risks being as revered and unread as the Bible." Fun fact:* Walden *was on the property of Ralph Waldo Emerson, another noted writer of that time, giving the lie, perhaps, to Thoreau as someone who was totally isolated. Thoreau was also an abolitionist. "Life Without Principle" was published the year after his passing.*

At a lyceum, not long since, I felt that the lecturer had chosen a theme too foreign to himself, and so failed to interest me as much as he might have done. He described things not in or near to his heart, but toward his extremities and superficies. There was, in this sense, no truly central or centralizing thought in the lecture. I would have had him deal with his privatest experience, as the poet does. The greatest compliment that was ever paid me was when one asked me what I *thought*, and attended to my answer. I am surprised, as well as delighted, when this happens, it is such a rare use he would make of me, as if he were acquainted with the tool. Commonly, if men want anything of me, it is only to know how many acres I make of their land—since I am a surveyor—or, at most, what trivial news I have burdened myself with. They never will go to law for my meat; they prefer the shell. A man once came a considerable distance to ask me to lecture on Slavery; but on conversing with him, I found that he and his clique expected seven-eighths of the lecture to be theirs, and only one-eighth mine; so I declined. I take it for granted, when I am invited to lecture anywhere—for I have had a little experience in that business—that there is a desire to hear what I *think* on some subject, though I may be the greatest fool in the country—and not that I should say pleasant things merely, or such as the audience will assent to; and I resolve, accordingly, that I will give them a strong dose of myself. They have sent for me, and engaged to pay for me, and I am determined that they shall have me, though I bore them beyond all precedent.

So now I would say something similar to you, my readers. Since *you* are my readers, and I have not been much of a traveller, I will not talk about people a thousand miles off, but come as near home as I can. As the time is short, I will leave out all the flattery, and retain all the criticism.

Let us consider the way in which we spend our lives.

This world is a place of business. What an infinite bustle! I am awaked almost every night by the panting of the locomotive. It interrupts my dreams. There is no sabbath. It would be glorious to see mankind at leisure for once. It is nothing but work, work, work. I cannot easily buy a blank-book to write thoughts in; they are commonly ruled for dollars and cents. An Irishman, seeing me making a minute in the fields, took it for granted that I was calculating my wages. If a man was tossed out of a window when an infant, and so made a cripple for life, or scared out of his wits by the Indians, it is regretted chiefly because he was thus incapacitated for business! I think that there is nothing, not even crime, more opposed to poetry, to philosophy, ay, to life itself, than this incessant business.

There is a coarse and boisterous money-making fellow in the outskirts of our town, who is going to build a bank-wall under the hill along the edge meadow. The powers have put this into his head to keep him out of mischief, and he wishes me to spend three weeks digging there with him. The result will be that he will perhaps get some more money to hoard, and leave for his heirs to spend foolishly. If I do this, most will commend me as an industrious and hardworking man; but if I choose to devote myself to certain labors which yield more real profit, though but little money, they may be inclined to look on me as an idler. Nevertheless, as I do not need the police of meaningless labor to regulate me, and do not see anything absolutely praiseworthy in this fellow's undertaking, any more than in many an enterprise of our own or foreign governments however amusing it may be to him or them, I prefer to finish my education at a different school.

If a man walk in the woods for love of them half of each day, he is in danger of being regarded as a loafer; but if he spends his whole day as a speculator, shearing off those woods and making earth bald before her time, he is esteemed an industrious and enterprising citizen. As if a town had no interest in its forests but to cut them down!

Most men would feel insulted, if it were proposed all and to employ them in throwing stones over a wall, and then in throwing them back, merely that they might earn their wages. But many are no more worthily employed now. For instance: just after sunrise, one summer morning, I noticed one of my neighbors walking beside his team, which was slowly drawing a heavy hewn stone swung under the axle, surrounded by an atmosphere of industry, his day's work begun—his brow commenced to sweat,—a reproach to all sluggards and idlers—pausing a breast the shoulders of his oxen, and half turning round with a flourish of his merciful whip, while they gained their length on him. And I thought, Such is the labor which the American Congress exists to protect—honest manly toil—honest as the day is long—that makes his bread taste sweet, and keeps society sweet—which all men respect and have consecrated; one of the sacred band, doing the needful, but irksome drudgery. Indeed, I felt a slight reproach, because I observed this from the window, and was not abroad and stirring about a similar business. The day went by and at evening I passed the yard of another neighbor, who keeps many servants, and spends much money foolishly, while he adds nothing to the common stock, and there I saw the stone of the morning lying beside a whimsical structure intended to adorn this Lord Timothy Dexter's premises, and the dignity forthwith departed from the teamsters labor, in my eyes. In my opinion, the sun was made to light worthier toil than this. I may add, that his employer has since run off, in debt to a good part of the town, and, after passing through Chancery, has settled somewhere else, there to become once more a patron of the arts.

The ways by which you may get money almost without exception lead downward. To have done anything by which you earned money merely is to have been truly idle or worse. If the laborer gets no more than the wages which his employer pays him, he is cheated, he cheats himself. If you would get money as a writer or lecturer, you must be popular, which is to go down perpendicularly. Those services which the community will most readily pay for it is most disagreeable to render. You are paid for being something less than a man. The State does not commonly reward a genius any more wisely. Even the poet-laureate would rather not have to celebrate the accidents of royalty. He must be bribed with a pipe of wine; and perhaps another poet is called away from his muse to gauge that very pipe. As for my own business, even that kind of surveying which I could do with most satisfaction my employers do not want. They would prefer that I should do my work coarsely and not too well, ay, not well enough. When I observe that there are different ways of surveying, my employer commonly asks which will give him the most land, not which is most correct. I once invented a rule for measuring cord-wood, and tried to introduce it in Boston; but the measurer there told me that the sellers did not wish to have their wood measured correctly—that he was already too accurate for them, and therefore they commonly got their wood measured in Charlestown before crossing the bridge.

The aim of the laborer should be, not to get his living, to get "a good job," but to perform well a certain work; and, even in a pecuniary sense, it would be economy for a town to pay its laborers so well that they would not feel that they were working for low ends, as for a livelihood merely, but for scientific, or even moral ends. Do not hire a man who does your work for money, but him who does it for love of it.

It is remarkable that there are few men so well employed, so much to their minds, but that a little money or fame would commonly buy them off from their present pursuit. I see advertisements for *active* young men, as if activity were the whole of a young man's capital. Yet I have been surprised when one has with confidence proposed to me, a grown man, to embark in some enterprise of his, as if I had absolutely nothing to do, my life having been a complete failure hitherto. What a doubtful compliment this to pay me! As if he had met me half-way across the ocean beating up against the wind, but bound nowhere, and proposed to me to go along with him! If I did, what do you think the underwriters would say? No, no! I am not without employment at this stage of the voyage. To tell the truth, I saw an advertisement for able-bodied seamen, when I was a boy, sauntering in my native port, and as soon as I came of age I embarked.

The community has no bribe that will tempt a wise man. You may raise money enough to tunnel a mountain, but you cannot raise money enough to hire a man who is minding *his own* business. An efficient and valuable man does what he can, whether the community pay him for it or not. The inefficient offer their inefficiency to the highest bidder, and are forever expecting to be put into office. One would suppose that they were rarely disappointed.

Perhaps I am more than usually jealous with respect to my freedom. I feel that my connection with and obligation to society are still very slight and transient. Those slight labors which afford me a livelihood, and by which it is allowed that I am to some extent serviceable to my contemporaries, are as yet commonly a pleasure to me, and I am not often reminded that they are a necessity. So far I am successful. But I foresee, that, if my wants should be much increased, the labor required to supply them would become a drudgery. If I should sell both my forenoons and afternoons to society, as most appear to do, I am sure, that, for me, there would be nothing left worth living for. I trust that I shall never thus sell my birthright for a mess of pottage. I wish to suggest that a man may be very industrious, and yet not spend his time well. There is no more fatal blunderer than he who consumes the greater part of his life getting his living. All great enterprises are self-supporting. The poet, for instance, must sustain his body by his poetry, as a steam planing-mill feeds its boilers with the shavings it makes. You must get your living by loving. But as it is said of the merchants that ninety-seven in a hundred fail, so the life of men generally, tried by this standard, is a failure, and bankruptcy may be surely prophesied.

Merely to come into the world the heir of a fortune is not to be born, but to be still-born, rather. To be supported by the charity of friends, or a government pension—provided you continue to breathe—by whatever fine synonymes you describe these relations, is to go into the almshouse. On Sundays the poor debtor goes to church to take an account of stock, and finds, of course, that his outgoes have been greater than his income. In the Catholic Church, especially, they go into Chancery, make a clean confession, give up all, and think to start again. Thus men will lie on their backs, talking about the fall of man, and never make an effort to get up.

As for the comparative demand which men make on life, it is an important difference between two, that the one is satisfied with a level success, that his marks can all be hit by point-blank shots, but the other, however low and unsuccessful his life may be, constantly elevates his aim, though at a very slight angle to the horizon. I should much rather be the last man—though, as the Orientals say, "Greatness doth not approach him who is forever looking down; and all those who are looking high are growing poor."

It is remarkable that there is little or nothing to be remembered written on the subject of getting a living; how to make getting a living not merely honest and honorable, but altogether inviting and glorious; for if *getting* a living is not so, then living is not. One would think, from looking at literature, that this question had never disturbed a solitary individual's musings. Is it that men are too much disgusted with their experience to speak of it? The lesson of value which money teaches, which the Author of the Universe has taken so much pains to teach us, we are inclined to skip altogether. As for the means of living, it is wonderful how indifferent men of all classes are about it, even reformers, so called—whether they inherit, or earn, or steal it. I think that society has done nothing for us in this respect, or at least has undone what she has done. Cold and hunger seem more friendly to my nature than those methods which men have adopted and advise to ward them off.

The title *wise* is, for the most part, falsely applied. How can one be a wise man, if he does not know any better how to live than other men?—if he is only more cunning and intellectually subtle? Does Wisdom work in a tread-mill? or does she teach how to succeed *by her example*? Is there any such thing as wisdom not applied to life? Is she merely the miller who grinds the finest logic? It is pertinent to ask if Plato got his *living* in a better way or more successfully than his contemporaries—or did he succumb to the difficulties of life like other men? Did he seem to prevail over some of them merely by indifference, or by assuming grand airs? or find it easier to live, because his aunt remembered him in her will? The ways in which most men get their living, that is, live, are mere make-shifts, and a shirking of the real business of life—chiefly because they do not know, but partly because they do not mean, any better.

The rush to California, for instance, and the attitude, not merely of merchants, but of philosophers and prophets, so called, in relation to it, reflect the greatest disgrace on mankind. That so many are ready to live by luck, and so get the means of commanding the labor of others less lucky, without contributing any value to society! And that is called enterprise! I know of no more startling development of the immorality of trade, and all the common modes of getting a living. The philosophy and poetry and religion of such a mankind are not worth the dust of a puff-ball. The hog that gets his living by rooting, stirring up the soil so, would be ashamed of such company. If I could command the wealth of all the worlds by lifting my finger, I would not pay such a price for it. Even Mahomet knew that God did not make this world in jest. It makes God to be a moneyed gentleman who scatters a handful of pennies in order to see mankind scramble for them. The world's raffle! A subsistence in the domains of Nature a thing to be raffled for! What a comment, what a satire on our institutions! The conclusion will be, that mankind will hang itself upon a tree. And have all the precepts in all the Bibles taught men only this? and is the last and most admirable invention of the human race only an improved muck-rake? Is this the ground on which Orientals and Occidentals meet? Did God direct us so to get our living, digging where we never planted—and He would, perchance, reward us with lumps of gold?

God gave the righteous man a certificate entitling him to food and raiment, but the unrighteous man found a facsimile of the same in God's coffers, and appropriated it, and obtained food and raiment like the former. It is one of the most extensive systems of counterfeiting that the world has seen. I did not know that mankind were suffering for want of gold. I have seen a little of it. I know that it is very malleable, but not so malleable as wit. A grain of gold will gild a great surface, but not so much as a grain of wisdom.

The gold-digger in the ravines of the mountains is as much a gambler as his fellow in the saloons of San Francisco. What difference does it make, whether you shake dirt or shake dice? If you win, society is the loser. The gold-digger is the enemy of the honest laborer, whatever checks and compensations there may be. It is not enough to tell me that you worked hard to get your gold. So does the Devil work hard. The way of transgressors may be hard in many respects. The humblest observer who goes to the mines sees and says that gold-digging is of the character of a lottery; the gold thus obtained is not the same thing with the wages of honest toil. But, practically, he forgets what he has seen, for he has seen only the fact, not the principle, and goes into trade there, that is, buys a ticket in what commonly proves another lottery, where the fact is not so obvious.

After reading Howitt's account of the Australian gold-diggings one evening, I had in my mind's eye, all night, the numerous valleys, with their streams, all cut up with foul pits, from ten to one hundred feet deep, and half a dozen feet across, as close as they can be dug, and partly filled with water—the locality to which men furiously rush to probe for their fortunes—uncertain where they shall break ground—not knowing but the gold is under their camp itself—sometimes digging one hundred and sixty feet before they strike the vein, or then missing it by a foot—turned into demons, and regardless of each other's rights, in their thirst for riches—whole valleys, for thirty miles, suddenly honeycombed by the pits of the miners, so that even hundreds are drowned in them—standing in water, and covered with mud and clay, they work night and day, dying of exposure and disease. Having read this, and partly forgotten it, I was thinking, accidentally, of my own unsatisfactory life, doing as others do; and with that vision of the diggings still before me, I asked myself, why I might not be washing sonic gold daily, though it were only the finest particles—why *I* might not sink a shaft down to the gold within me, and work that mine. *There* is a Ballarat, a Bendigo for you—what though it were a Sulky Gully? At any rate, I might pursue some path, however solitary and narrow and crooked, in which I could walk with love and reverence. Wherever a man separates from the multitude, and goes his own way in this mood, there indeed is a fork in the road, though ordinary travellers may see only a gap in the paling. His solitary path across lots will turn out the *higher way* of the two.

Men rush to California and Australia as if the true gold were to be found in that direction; but that is to go to the very opposite extreme to where it lies. They go prospecting farther and farther away from the true lead, and are most unfortunate when they think themselves most successful. Is not our *native* soil auriferous? Does not a stream from the golden mountains flow through our native valley? and has not this for more than geologic ages been bringing down the shining particles and forming the nuggets for us? Yet, strange to tell, if a digger steal away, prospecting for this true gold, into the unexplored solitudes around us, there is no danger that any will dog his steps, and endeavor to supplant him. He may claim and undermine the whole valley even, both the cultivated and the uncultivated portions, his whole life long in peace, for no one will ever dispute his claim. They will not mind his cradles or his toms. He is not confined to a claim twelve feet square, as at Ballarat, but may mine anywhere, and wash the whole wide world in his tom.

Howitt says of the man who found the great nugget which weighed twenty-eight pounds, at the Bendigo diggings in Australia: "He soon began to drink; got a horse and rode all about, generally at full gallop, and when he met people, called out to inquire if they knew who he was, and then kindly informed them that he was 'the bloody wretch that had found the nugget.' At last he rode full speed against a tree, and I think however nearly knocked his brains out." I think, however, there was no danger of that, for he had already knocked his brains out against the nugget. Howitt adds, "He is a hopelessly ruined man." But he is a type of the class. They are all fast men. Hear some of the names of the places where they dig: "Jackass Flat"—"Sheep's-Head Gully"—"Murderer's Bar," etc. Is there no satire in these names? Let them carry their ill-gotten wealth where they will, I am thinking it will still be "Jackass Flat," if not "Murderer's Bar," where they live.

The last resource of our energy has been the robbing of graveyards on the Isthmus of Darien, an enterprise which appears to be but in its infancy; for, according to late accounts, an act has passed its second reading in the legislature of New Granada, regulating this kind of mining; and a correspondent of the "Tribune" writes: "In the dry season, when the weather will permit of the country being properly prospected, no doubt other rich *guacas* [that is, graveyards] will be found." To emigrants he says: "do not come before December; take the Isthmus route in preference to the Boca del Toro one; bring no useless baggage, and do not cumber yourself with a tent; but a good pair of blankets will be necessary; a pick, shovel, and axe of good material will be almost all that is required"; advice which might have been taken from the "Burker's Guide." And he concludes with this line in Italics and small capitals: "*If you are doing well at home*, stay there," which may fairly be interpreted to mean, "If you are getting a good living by robbing graveyards at home, stay there."

But why go to California for a text? She is the child of New England, bred at her own school and church.

It is remarkable that among all the preachers there are so few moral teachers. The prophets are employed in excusing the ways of men. Most reverend seniors, the *illuminati* of the age, tell me, with a gracious, reminiscent smile, betwixt an aspiration and a shudder, not to be too tender about these things—to lump all that, that is, make a lump of gold of it. The highest advice I have heard on these subjects was grovelling. The burden of it was—It is not worth your while to undertake to reform the world in this particular. Do not ask how your bread is buttered; it will make you sick, if you do—and the like. A man had better starve at once than lose his innocence in the process of getting his bread. If within the sophisticated man there is not an unsophisticated one, then he is but one of the devil's angels. As we grow old, we live more coarsely, we relax a little in our disciplines, and, to some extent, cease to obey our finest instincts. But we should be fastidious to the extreme of sanity, disregarding the gibes of those who are more unfortunate than ourselves.

In our science and philosophy, even, there is commonly no true and absolute account of things. The spirit of sect and bigotry has planted its hoof amid the stars. You have only to discuss the problem, whether the stars are inhabited or not, in order to discover it. Why must we daub the heavens as well as the earth? It was an unfortunate discovery that Dr. Kane was a Mason, and that Sir John Franklin was another. But it was a more cruel suggestion that possibly that was the reason why the former went in search of the latter. There is not a popular magazine in this country that would dare to print a child's thought on important subjects without comment. It must be submitted to the D.D.'s. I would it were the chickadee-dees.

You come from attending the funeral of mankind to attend to a natural phenomenon. A little thought is sexton to all the world.

I hardly know an *intellectual* man, even, who is so broad and truly liberal that you can think aloud in his society. Most with whom you endeavor to talk soon come to a stand against some institution in which they appear to hold stock—that is, some particular, not universal, way of viewing things. They will continually thrust their own low roof, with its narrow skylight, between you and the sky, when it is the unobstructed heavens you would view. Get out of the way with your cobwebs, wash your windows, I say! In some lyceums they tell me that they have voted to exclude the subject of religion. But how do I know what their religion is, and when I am near to or far from it? I have walked into such an arena and done my best to make a clean breast of what religion I have experienced, and the audience never suspected what I was about. The lecture was as harmless as moonshine to them. Whereas, if I had read to them the biography of the greatest scamps in history, they might have thought that I had written the lives of the deacons of their church. Ordinarily, the inquiry is, Where did you come from? or, Where are you going? That was a more pertinent question which I overheard one of my auditors put to another one—"What does he lecture for?" It made me quake in my shoes.

To speak impartially, the best men that I know are not serene, a world in themselves. For the most part, they dwell in forms, and flatter and study effect only more finely than the rest. We select granite for the underpinning of our houses and barns; we build fences of stone; but we do not ourselves rest on an underpinning of granitic truth, the lowest primitive rock. Our sills are rotten. What stuff is the man made of who is not coexistent in our thought with the purest and subtilest truth? I often accuse my finest acquaintances of an immense frivolity; for, while there are manners and compliments we do not meet, we do not teach one another the lessons of honesty and sincerity that the brutes do, or of steadiness and solidity that the rocks do. The fault is commonly mutual, however; for we do not habitually demand any more of each other.

That excitement about Kossuth, consider how characteristic, but superficial, it was!—only another kind of politics or dancing. Men were making speeches to him all over the country, but each expressed only the thought, or the want of thought, of the multitude. No man stood on truth. They were merely banded together, as usual, one leaning on another, and all together on nothing; as the Hindoos made the world rest on an elephant, the elephant on a tortoise, and the tortoise on a serpent, and had nothing to put under the serpent. For all fruit of that stir we have the Kossuth hat.

Just so hollow and ineffectual, for the most part, is our ordinary conversation. Surface meets surface. When our life ceases to be inward and private, conversation degenerates into mere gossip. We rarely meet a man who can tell us any news which he has not read in a newspaper, or been told by his neighbor; and, for the most part, the only difference between us and our fellow is, that he has seen the newspaper, or been out to tea, and we have not. In proportion as our inward life fails, we go more constantly and desperately to the post-office. You may depend on it, that the poor fellow who walks away with the greatest number of letters, proud of his extensive correspondence, has not heard from himself this long while.

I do not know but it is too much to read one newspaper a week. I have tried it recently, and for so long it seems to me that I have not dwelt in my native region. The sun, the clouds, the snow, the trees say not so much to me. You cannot serve two masters. It requires more than a day's devotion to know and to possess the wealth of a day.

We may well be ashamed to tell what things we have read or heard in our day. I do not know why my news should be so trivial—considering what one's dreams and expectations are, why the developments should be so paltry. The news we hear, for the most part, is not news to our genius. It is the stalest repetition. You are often tempted to ask why such stress is laid on a particular experience which you have had—that, after twenty-five years, you should meet Hobbins, Registrar of Deeds, again on the sidewalk. Have you not budged an inch, then? Such is the daily news. Its facts appear to float in the atmosphere, insignificant as the sporules of fungi, and impinge on some neglected *thallus*, or surface of our minds, which affords a basis for them, and hence a parasitic growth. We should wash ourselves clean of such news. Of what consequence, though our planet explode, if there is no character involved in the explosion? In health we have not the least curiosity about such events. We do not live for idle amusement. I would not run round a corner to see the world blow up.

All summer, and far into the autumn, perchance, you unconsciously went by the newspapers and the news, and now you find it was because the morning and the evening were full of news to you. Your walks were full of incidents.

You attended, not to the affairs of Europe, but to your own affairs in Massachusetts fields. If you chance to live and move and have your being in that thin stratum in which the events that make the news transpire—thinner than the paper on which it is printed—then these things will fill the world for you; but if you soar above or dive below that plane, you cannot remember nor be reminded of them. Really to see the sun rise or go down every day, so to relate ourselves to a universal fact, would preserve us sane forever. Nations! What are nations? Tartars, and Nuns, and Chinamen! Like insects, they swarm. The historian strives in vain to make them memorable. It is for want of a man that there are so many men. It is individuals that populate the world. Any man thinking may say with the Spirit of Lodin—

> "I look down from my height on nations,
> And they become ashes before me;—
> Calm is dwelling in the clouds;
> Pleasant are the great fields of my rest."

Pray, let us live without being drawn by dogs, Esquimaux-fashion, tearing over hill and dale, and biting each other's ears.

Not without a slight shudder at the danger, I often perceive how near I had come to admitting into my mind the details of some trivial affair—the news of the street; and I am astonished to observe how willing men are to lumber their minds with such rubbish—to permit idle rumors and incidents of the most insignificant kind to intrude on ground which should be sacred to thought. Shall the mind be a public arena, where the affairs of the street and the gossip of the tea-table chiefly are discussed? Or shall it be a quarter of heaven itself—an hypaethral temple, consecrated to the service of the gods? I find it so difficult to dispose of the few facts which to me are significant, that I hesitate to burden my attention with those which are insignificant, which only a divine mind could illustrate. Such is, for the most part, the news in newspapers and conversation. It is important to preserve the mind's chastity in this respect. Think of admitting the details of a single case of the criminal court into our thoughts, to stalk profanely through their very *sanctum sanctorum* for an hour, ay, for many hours! to make a very bar-room of the mind's inmost apartment, as if for so long the dust of the street had occupied us,—the very street itself, with all its travel, its bustle, and filth had passed through our thoughts' shrine! Would it not be an intellectual and moral suicide? When I have been compelled to sit spectator and auditor in a court-room for some hours, and have seen my neighbors, who were not compelled, stealing in from time to time, and tiptoeing about with washed hands and faces, it has appeared to my mind's eye, that, when they took off their hats, their ears suddenly expanded into vast hoppers for sound, between which even their narrow heads were crowded. Like the vanes of windmills, they caught the broad, but shallow stream of sound, which, after a few titillating gyrations in their coggy brains, passed out the other side. I wondered if, when they got home, they were as careful to wash their ears as before their hands and faces. It has seemed to me, at such a time, that the auditors and the witnesses, the jury and the counsel, the judge and the criminal at the bar—if I may presume him guilty before he is convicted—were all equally criminal, and a thunderbolt might be expected to descend and consume them all together.

By all kinds of traps and sign-boards, threatening the extreme penalty of the divine law, exclude such trespassers from the only ground which can be sacred to you. It is so hard to forget what it is worse than useless to remember! If I am to be a thoroughfare, I prefer that it be of the mountain brooks, the Parnassian streams, and not the town sewers. There is inspiration, that gossip which comes to the ear of the attentive mind from the courts of heaven. There is the profane and stale revelation of the barroom and the police court. The same ear is fitted to receive both communications. Only the character of the hearer determines to which it shall be open, and to which closed. I believe that the mind can be permanently profaned by the habit of attending to trivial things, so that all our thoughts shall be tinged with triviality. Our very intellect shall be macadamized as it were—its foundation broken into fragments for the wheels of travel to roll over; and if you would know what will make the most durable pavement, surpassing rolled stones, spruce blocks, and asphaltum, you have only to look into some of our minds which have been subjected to this treatment so long.

If we have thus desecrated ourselves—as who has not?—the remedy will be by wariness and devotion to reconsecrate ourselves, and make once more a fane of the mind. We should treat our minds, that is, ourselves, as innocent and ingenuous children, whose guardians we are, and be careful what objects and what subjects we thrust on their attention. Read not the Times. Read the Eternities. Conventionalities are at length as bad as impurities. Even the facts of science may dust the mind by their dryness, unless they are in a sense effaced each morning, or rather rendered fertile by the dews of fresh and living truth. Knowledge does not come to us by details, but in flashes of light from heaven. Yes, every thought that passes through the mind helps to wear and tear it, and to deepen the ruts, which, as in the streets of Pompeii, evince how much it has been used. How many things there are concerning which we might well deliberate, whether we had better know them—had better let their peddling-carts be driven, even at the slowest trot or walk, over that bridge of glorious span by which we trust to pass at last from the farthest brink of time to the nearest shore of eternity! Have we no culture, no refinement—but skill only to live coarsely and serve the Devil?—to acquire a little worldly wealth, or fame, or liberty, and make a false show with it, as if we were all husk and shell, with no tender and living kernel to us? Shall our institutions be like those chestnut-burs which contain abortive nuts, perfect only to prick the fingers?

America is said to be the arena on which the battle of freedom is to be fought; but surely it cannot be freedom in a merely political sense that is meant. Even if we grant that the American has freed himself from a political tyrant, he is still the slave of an economical and moral tyrant. Now that the republic—the *res-publica*—has been settled, it is time to look after the *res-privata*—the private state—to see, as the Roman senate charged its consuls, "*ne quid res* PRIVATA *detrimenti caperet,*" that the private state receive no detriment.

Do we call this the land of the free? What is it to be free from King George and continue the slaves of King Prejudice? What is it to be born free and not to live free? What is the value of any political freedom, but as a means to moral freedom? Is it a freedom to be slaves, or a freedom to be free, of which we boast? We are a nation of politicians, concerned about the outmost defences only of freedom. It is our children's children who may perchance be really free. We tax ourselves unjustly. There is a part of us which is not represented. It is taxation without representation. We quarter troops, we quarter fools and cattle of all sorts upon ourselves. We quarter our gross bodies on our poor souls, till the former eat up all the latter's substance.

With respect to a true culture and manhood, we are essentially provincial still, not metropolitan—mere Jonathans. We are provincial, because we do not find at home our standards—because we do not worship truth, but the reflection of truth—because we are warped and narrowed by an exclusive devotion to trade and commerce and manufactures and agriculture and the like, which are but means, and not the end.

So is the English Parliament provincial. Mere country bumpkins, they betray themselves, when any more important question arises for them to settle, the Irish question, for instance—the English question why did I not say? Their natures are subdued to what they work in. Their "good breeding" respects only secondary objects. The finest manners in the world are awkwardness and fatuity, when contrasted with a finer intelligence. They appear but as the fashions of past days—mere courtliness, knee-buckles and small-clothes, out of date. It is the vice, but not the excellence of manners, that they are continually being deserted by the character; they are cast-off clothes or shells, claiming the respect which belonged to the living creature. You are presented with the shells instead of the meat, and it is no excuse generally, that, in the case of some fishes, the shells are of more worth than the meat. The man who thrusts his manners upon me does as if he were to insist on introducing me to his cabinet of curiosities, when I wished to see himself. It was not in this sense that the poet Decker called Christ "the first true gentleman that ever breathed." I repeat that in this sense the most splendid court in Christendom is provincial, having authority to consult about Transalpine interests only, and not the affairs of Rome. A praetor or proconsul would suffice to settle the questions which absorb the attention of the English Parliament and the American Congress.

Government and legislation! these I thought were respectable professions. We have heard of heaven-born Numas, Lycurguses, and Solons, in the history of the world, whose *names* at least may stand for ideal legislators; but think of legislating to *regulate* the breeding of slaves, or the exportation of tobacco! What have divine legislators to do with the exportation or the importation of tobacco? what humane ones with the breeding of slaves? Suppose you were to submit the question to any son of God—and has He no children in the Nineteenth Century? is it a family which is extinct?—in what condition would you get it again? What shall a State like Virginia say for itself at the last day, in which these have been the principal, the staple productions? What ground is there for patriotism in such a State? I derive my facts from statistical tables which the States themselves have published.

A commerce that whitens every sea in quest of nuts and raisins, and makes slaves of its sailors for this purpose! I saw, the other day, a vessel which had been wrecked, and many lives lost, and her cargo of rags, juniper-berries, and bitter almonds were strewn along the shore. It seemed hardly worth the while to tempt the dangers of the sea between Leghorn and New York for the sake of a cargo of juniper berries and bitter almonds. America sending to the Old World for her bitters! Is not the sea-brine, is not shipwreck bitter enough to make the cup of life go down here? Yet such, to a great extent, is our boasted commerce; and there are those who style themselves statesmen and philosophers who are so blind as to think that progress and civilization depend on precisely this kind of interchange and activity—the activity of flies about a molasses-hogshead. Very well, observes one, if men were oysters. And very well, answer I, if men were mosquitoes.

Lieutenant Herndon, whom our government sent to explore the Amazon, and, it is said, to extend the area of slavery, observed that there was wanting there "an industrious and active population, who know what the comforts of life are, and who have artificial wants to draw out the great resources of the country." But what are the "artificial wants" to be encouraged? Not the love of luxuries, like the tobacco and slaves of, I believe, his native Virginia, nor the ice and granite and other material wealth of our native New England; nor are "the great resources of a country'" that fertility or barrenness of soil which produces these. The chief want, in every State that I have been into, was a high and earnest purpose in its inhabitants. This alone draws out "the great resources" of Nature, and at last taxes her beyond her resources; for man naturally dies out of her. When we want culture more than potatoes, and illumination more than sugar-plums, then the great resources of a world are taxed and drawn out, and the result, or staple production, is, not slaves, nor operatives, but men—those rare fruits called heroes, saints, poets, philosophers, and redeemers.

In short, as a snow-drift is formed where there is a lull in the wind, so, one would say, where there is a lull of truth, an institution springs up. But the truth blows right on over it, nevertheless, and at length blows it down.

What is called politics is comparatively something so superficial and inhuman, that, practically, I have never fairly recognized that it concerns me at all. The newspapers, I perceive, devote some of their columns specially to politics or government without charge; and this, one would say, is all that saves it; but, as I love literature, and, to some extent, the truth also, I never read those columns at any rate. I do not wish to blunt my sense of right so much. I have not got to answer for having read a single President's Message. A strange age of the world this, when empires, kingdoms, and republics come a-begging to a private man's door, and utter their complaints at his elbow! I cannot take up a newspaper but I find that some wretched government or other, hard pushed, and on its last legs, is interceding with me, the reader, to vote for it—more importunate than an Italian beggar; and if I have a mind to look at its certificate, made, perchance, by some benevolent merchant's clerk, or the skipper that brought it over, for it cannot speak a word of English itself, I shall probably read of the eruption of some Vesuvius, or the overflowing of some Po, true or forged, which brought it into this condition. I do not hesitate, in such a case, to suggest work, or the almshouse; or why not keep its castle in silence, as I do commonly? The poor President, what with preserving his popularity and doing his duty, is completely bewildered. The newspapers are the ruling power. Any other government is reduced to a few marines at Fort Independence. If a man neglects to read the Daily Times, Government will go down on its knees to him, for this is the only treason in these days.

Those things which now most engage the attention of men, as politics and the daily routine, are, it is true, vital functions of human society, but should be unconsciously performed like the corresponding functions of the physical body. They are *infra*-human, a kind of vegetation. I sometimes awake to a half consciousness of them going on about me, as a man may become conscious of some of the processes of digestion in a morbid state, and so have the dyspepsia as it is called. It is as if a thinker submitted himself to be rasped by the great gizzard of creation. Politics is, as it were, the gizzard of society, full of grit and gravel, and the two political parties are its two opposite halves—sometimes split into quarters, it may be, which grind on each other. Not only individuals, but States, have thus a confirmed dyspepsia, which expresses itself, you can imagine by what sort of eloquence. Thus our life is not altogether a forgetting, but also, alas! to a great extent, a remembering of that which we should never have been conscious of, certainly not in our waking hours. Who should we not meet, not always as dyspeptics, to tell our bad dreams, but sometimes as *eu*peptics, to congratulate each other on the ever-glorious morning? I do not make an exorbitant demand, surely.

FOR INFORMAL WRITING

What, according to Thoreau's essay, is a life of principle?

FOR DISCUSSION

1. How would you articulate the themes presented by Thoreau for a principled life?
2. What does this essay reveal about Thoreau's own perceptions of wealth?
3. "A commerce that whitens every sea in quest of nuts and raisins and makes slaves of its sailors for this purpose!" Comment on Thoreau's perspective here. How is it relevant to our time?

FOR WRITING

"What is called politics is comparatively something so superficial and inhuman, that, practically, I have never fairly recognized that it concerns me at all. ... The poor President, what with preserving his popularity and doing his duty, is completely bewildered. The newspapers are the ruling power. Any other government is reduced to a few marines at Fort Independence. If a man neglects to read the Daily Times, Government will go down on its knees to him, for this is the only treason in these days." Do some research to determine the political context of Thoreau's time that would have motivated this statement. (Note that Thoreau seems to have sympathy for the then-President.)

Advice to Youth (1882)
Mark Twain (1835–1910)

Born Samuel Clemens in Missouri, Mark Twain was a humorist, writer, and lecturer best known for The Adventures of Tom Sawyer *(1876) and* The Adventures of Huckleberry Finn *(1884), often considered the "great American novel." Both books—and much of Twain's other writing—were influenced by Twain's own youth and young adulthood near and on the Mississippi River. Twain's satirical essay (and speech) "Advice to Youth" can be considered a type of humorous, nineteenth-century speech for a graduation ceremony. The author had been asked to address the youth of America. This is the result.*

Being told I would be expected to talk here, I inquired what sort of talk I ought to make. They said it should be something suitable to youth—something didactic, instructive, or something in the nature of good advice. Very well. I have a few things in my mind which I have often longed to say for the instruction of the young; for it is in one's tender early years that such things will best take root and be most enduring and most valuable. First, then. I will say to you my young friends—and I say it beseechingly, urgently—

Always obey your parents, when they are present. This is the best policy in the long run, because if you don't, they will make you. Most parents think they know better than you do, and you can generally make more by humoring that superstition than you can by acting on your own better judgment.

Be respectful to your superiors, if you have any, also to strangers, and sometimes to others. If a person offend you, and you are in doubt as to whether it was intentional or not, do not resort to extreme measures; simply watch your chance and hit him with a brick. That will be sufficient. If you shall find that he had not intended any offense, come out frankly and confess yourself in the wrong when you struck him; acknowledge it like a man and say you didn't mean to. Yes, always avoid violence; in this age of charity and kindliness, the time has gone by for such things. Leave dynamite to the low and unrefined.

Go to bed early, get up early—this is wise. Some authorities say get up with the sun; some say get up with one thing, others with another. But a lark is really the best thing to get up with. It gives you a splendid reputation with everybody to know that you get up with the lark; and if you get the right kind of lark, and work at him right, you can easily train him to get up at half past nine, every time—it's no trick at all.

Now as to the matter of lying. You want to be very careful about lying; otherwise you are nearly sure to get caught. Once caught, you can never again be in the eyes to the good and the pure, what you were before. Many a young person has injured himself permanently through a single clumsy and ill finished lie, the result of carelessness born of incomplete training. Some authorities hold that the young ought not to lie at all. That of course, is putting it rather stronger than necessary; still while I cannot go quite so far as that, I do maintain, and I believe I am right, that the young ought to be temperate in the use of this great art until practice and experience shall give them that confidence, elegance, and precision which alone can make the accomplishment graceful and profitable. Patience, diligence, painstaking attention to detail—these are requirements; these in time, will make the student perfect; upon these only, may he rely as the sure foundation for future eminence. Think what tedious years of study, thought, practice, experience, went to the equipment of that peerless old master who was able to impose upon the whole world the lofty and sounding maxim that "Truth is mighty and will prevail"—the most majestic compound fracture of fact which any of woman born has yet achieved. For the history of our race, and each individual's experience, are sewn thick with evidences that a truth is not hard to kill, and that a lie well told is immortal. There is in Boston a monument of the man who discovered anesthesia; many people are aware, in these latter days, that that man didn't discover it at all, but stole the discovery from another man. Is this truth mighty, and will it prevail? Ah no, my hearers, the monument is made of hardy material, but the lie it tells will outlast it a million years. An awkward, feeble, leaky lie is a thing which you ought to make it your unceasing study to avoid; such a lie as that has no more real permanence than an average truth. Why, you might as well tell the truth at once and be done with it. A feeble, stupid, preposterous lie will not live two years—except it be a slander upon somebody. It is indestructible, then of course, but that is no merit of yours. A final word: begin your practice of this gracious and beautiful art early—begin now. If I had begun earlier, I could have learned how.

Never handle firearms carelessly. The sorrow and suffering that have been caused through the innocent but heedless handling of firearms by the young! Only four days ago, right in the next farm house to the one where I am spending the summer, a grandmother, old and gray and sweet, one of the loveliest spirits in the land, was sitting at her work, when her young grandson crept in and got down an old, battered, rusty gun which had not been touched for many years and was supposed not to be loaded, and pointed it at her, laughing and threatening to shoot. In her fright she ran screaming and pleading toward the door on the other side of the room; but as she passed him he placed the gun almost against her very breast and pulled the trigger! He had supposed it was not loaded. And he was right—it wasn't. So there wasn't any harm done. It is the only case of that kind I ever heard of. Therefore, just the same, don't you meddle with old unloaded firearms; they are the most deadly and unerring things that have ever been created by man. You don't have to take any pains at all with them; you don't have to have a rest, you don't have to have any sights on the gun, you don't have to take aim, even. No, you just pick out a relative and bang away, and you are sure to get him. A youth who can't hit a cathedral at thirty yards with a Gatling gun in three quarters of an hour, can take up an old empty musket and bag his grandmother every time, at a hundred. Think what Waterloo would have been if one of the armies had been boys armed with old muskets supposed not to be loaded, and the other army had been composed of their female relations. The very thought of it make one shudder.

There are many sorts of books; but good ones are the sort for the young to read. Remember that. They are a great, an inestimable, and unspeakable means of improvement. Therefore be careful in your selection, my young friends; be very careful; confine yourselves exclusively to Robertson's *Sermons*, Baxter's *Saints' Rest*, *The Innocents Abroad*, and works of that kind.

But I have said enough. I hope you will treasure up the instructions which I have given you, and make them a guide to your feet and a light to your understanding. Build your character thoughtfully and painstakingly upon these precepts, and by and by, when you have got it built, you will be surprised and gratified to see how nicely and sharply it resembles everybody else's.

FOR INFORMAL WRITING

Though it's certainly no longer the nineteenth century (or the twentieth, for that matter), many of you reading this are still considered the "youth of America." Using Twain as your touchstone, how might Twain's advice be the same (or different) now?

FOR DISCUSSION

1. Define satire. What language in the essay lets you know that this essay is satiric? Humorous? What is Twain's tone? How do you know?

2. What does Twain seem to think about his audience? Does he address the audience appropriately, even for a humorous piece? Why or why not?
3. What is Twain's primary piece of advice to youth? Can you take it seriously, even in the midst of this admittedly humorous essay? Explain your response. Use examples from the text to support your points.

FOR WRITING

Twain acknowledges certain cultural truths in this essay; masked in this satirical advice seems to be some real advice. Consider, for example, the final lines: "Build your character thoughtfully and painstakingly . . . and by and by, when you have got it built, you will be surprised and gratified to see how nicely and sharply it resembles everybody else's." What is Twain saying—what in these lines does he seem to be responding to? How do you know? What is his attitude toward characters that resembles "everybody else's?" How might you discern what Twain's real advice to youth might be? Use examples from the essay to support your point of view.

The Necklace (1884)
Guy de Maupassant (1850–1893)

Guy de Maupassant, a French author, was considered to be a virtuoso of the short story. Often placed in the "naturalist" school, his stories many times have an ironic twist at the end. A master also of social commentary, his work occasionally ends with disillusionment or pessimism on the part of the main character. De Maupassant enlisted as a volunteer in the Franco-Prussian War of 1870. After eight years, he was transferred to the Ministry of Public Instruction in Paris, where he became a contributing editor for several newspapers. It was then that he began to write short stories and novels. His first success as a writer came in 1880 with the publication of "Boule de Suif" ("Ball of Lard"). De Maupassant died at the age of 43, having been committed to an institution after attempting suicide. He wrote his own epitaph: "I have coveted everything and taken pleasure in nothing."

She was one of those pretty and charming girls who are sometimes, as if by a mistake of destiny, born in a family of clerks. She had no dowry, no expectations, no means of being known, understood, loved, wedded, by any rich and distinguished man; and she let herself be married to a little clerk at the Ministry of Public Instruction.

She dressed plainly because she could not dress well, but she was as unhappy as though she had really fallen from her proper station; since with women there is neither caste nor rank; and beauty, grace, and charm act instead of family and birth. Natural fineness, instinct for what is elegant, suppleness of wit, are the sole hierarchy, and make from women of the people the equals of the very greatest ladies.

She suffered ceaselessly, feeling herself born for all the delicacies and all the luxuries. She suffered from the poverty of her dwelling, from the wretched look of the walls, from the worn-out chairs, from the ugliness of the curtains.

All those things, of which another woman of her rank would never even have been conscious, tortured her and made her angry. The sight of the little Breton peasant who did her humble house-work aroused in her regrets which were despairing, and distracted dreams. She thought of the silent antechambers hung with Oriental tapestry, lit by tall bronze candelabra, land of the two great footmen in knee-breeches who sleep in the big arm-chairs, made drowsy by the heavy warmth of the hot-air stove. She thought of the long salons fitted up with ancient silk, of the delicate furniture carrying priceless curiosities, and of the coquettish perfumed boudoirs made for talks at five o'clock with intimate friends, with men—famous and sought after, whom all women envy and whose attention they all desire.

When she sat down to dinner, before the round table covered with a table-cloth three days old, opposite her husband, who uncovered the soup-tureen and declared with an enchanted air, "Ah, the good pot-au-feu! I don't know anything better than that," she thought of dainty dinners, of shining silverware, of tapestry which peopled the walls with ancient personages and with strange birds flying in the midst of a fairy forest; and she thought of delicious dishes served on marvellous plates, and of the whispered gallantries which you listen to with a sphinx-like smile, while you are eating the pink flesh of a trout or the wings of a quail.

She had no dresses, no jewels, nothing. And she loved nothing but that; she felt made for that. She would so have liked to please, to be envied, to be charming, to be sought after.

She had a friend, a former school-mate at the convent, who was rich, and whom she did not like to go and see any more becaise she suffered so keenly when she came back.

But, one evening, her husband returned home with a triumphant air, and holding a large envelope in his hand.

"There," said he, "here is something for you."

She tore the paper sharply, and drew out a printed card which bore these words:

"The Minister of Public Instruction and Mme. Georges Ramponneau request the honor of M. and Mme. Loisel's company at the palace of the Ministry on Monday evening, January 18th."

Instead of being delighted, as her husband hoped, she threw the invitation on the table with disdain, murmuring:

"What do you want me to do with that?"

"But, my dear, I thought you would be glad. You never go out, and this is such a fine opportunity. I had awful trouble to get it. Every one wants to go; it is very select, and they are not giving many invitations to clerks. The whole official world will be there."

She looked at him with an irritated eye, and she said, impatiently:

"And what do you want me to put on my back?"

He had not thought of that; he stammered:

"Why, the dress you go to the theatre in. It looks very well, to me."

He stopped, distracted, seeing that his wife was crying. Two great tears descended slowly from the corners of her eyes towards the corners of her mouth. He stuttered:

"What's the matter? What's the matter?"

But, by a violent effort, she had conquered her grief, and she replied, with a calm voice, while she wiped her wet cheeks:

"Nothing. Only I have no dress, and therefore I can't go to this ball. Give your card to some colleague whose wife is better equipped than I."

He was in despair. He resumed:

"Come, let us see, Mathilde. How much would it cost, a suitable dress, which you could use on other occasions, something very simple?"

She reflected several seconds, making her calculations and wondering also what sum she could ask without drawing on herself an immediate refusal and a frightened exclamation from the economical clerk.

Finally, she replied, hesitatingly:

"I don't know exactly, but I think I could manage it with four hundred francs."

He had grown a little pale, because he was laying aside just that amount to buy a gun and treat himself to a little shooting next summer on the plain of Nanterre, with several friends who went to shoot larks down there, of a Sunday.

But he said:

"All right. I will give you four hundred francs. And try to have a pretty dress."

The day of the ball drew near, and Mme. Loisel seemed sad, uneasy, anxious. Her dress was ready, however. Her husband said to her one evening:

"What is the matter? Come, you've been so queer these last three days."

And she answered:

"It annoys me not to have a single jewel, not a single stone, nothing to put on. I shall look like distress. I should almost rather not go at all."

He resumed:

"You might wear natural flowers. It's very stylish at this time of the year. For ten francs you can get two or three magnificent roses."

She was not convinced.

"No; there's nothing more humiliating than to look poor among other women who are rich."

But her husband cried:

"How stupid you are! Go look up your friend Mme. Forestier, and ask her to lend you some jewels. You're quite thick enough with her to do that."

She uttered a cry of joy:

"It's true. I never thought of it." The next day she went to her friend and told of her distress.

Mme. Forestier went to a wardrobe with a glass door, took out a large jewel-box, brought it back, opened it, and said to Mme. Loisel:

"Choose, my dear."

She saw first of all some bracelets, then a pearl necklace, then a Venetian cross, gold and precious stones of admirable workmanship. She tried on the ornaments before the glass, hesitated, could not make up her mind to part with them, to give them back. She kept asking:

"Haven't you any more?"

"Why, yes. Look. I don't know what you like."

All of a sudden she discovered, in a black satin box, a superb necklace of diamonds; and her heart began to beat with an immoderate desire. Her hands trembled as she took it. She fastened it around her throat, outside her high-necked dress, and remained lost in ecstasy at the sight of herself.

Then she asked, hesitating, filled with anguish:
"Can you lend me that, only that?"
"Why, yes, certainly."
She sprang upon the neck of her friend, kissed her passionately, then fled with her treasure.

The day of the ball arrived. Mme. Loisel made a great success. She was prettier than them all, elegant, gracious, smiling, and crazy with joy. All the men looked at her, asked her name, endeavored to be introduced. All the attaches of the Cabinet wanted to waltz with her. She was remarked by the minister himself.

She danced with intoxication, with passion, made drunk by pleasure, forgetting all, in the triumph of her beauty in the glory of her success in a sort of cloud of happiness composed of all this homage, of all this admiration, of all these awakened desires, and of that sense of complete victory which is so sweet to woman's heart.

She went away about four o'clock in the morning. Her husband had been sleeping since midnight, in a little deserted anteroom, with three other gentlemen whose wives were having a very good time.

He threw over her shoulders the wraps which he had brought, modest wraps of common life, whose poverty contrasted with the elegance of the ball dress. She felt this and wanted to escape so as not to be remarked by the other women, who were enveloping themselves in costly furs.

Loisel held her back.

"Wait a bit. You will catch cold outside. I will go and call a cab."

But she did not listen to him, and rapidly descended the stairs. When they were in the street they did not find a carriage; and they began to look for one, shouting after the cabmen whom they saw passing by at a distance.

They went down towards the Seine, in despair, shivering with cold. At last they found on the quay one of those ancient noctambulant coupés which, exactly as if they were ashamed to show their misery during the day, are never seen round Paris until after nightfall.

It took them to their door in the Rue des Martyrs and once more, sadly, they climbed up homeward. All was ended, for her. And as to him, he reflected that he must be at the Ministry at ten o'clock.

She removed the wraps, which covered her shoulders, before the glass, so as once more to see herself in all her glory. But suddenly she uttered a cry. She had no longer the necklace around her neck!

Her husband, already half-undressed, demanded: "What is the matter with you?"

She turned madly towards him:
"I have—I have—I've lost Mme. Forestier's necklace."
He stood up, distracted.
"What!—how?—Impossible!"

And they looked in the folds of her dress, in the folds of her cloak, in her pockets, everywhere. They did not find it. He asked:

"You're sure you had it on when you left the ball?"

"Yes, I felt it in the vestibule of the palace."

"But if you had lost it in the street we should have heard it fall. It must be in the cab."

"Yes. Probably. Did you take his number?"

"No. And you, didn't you notice it?"

"No."

They looked, thunderstruck, at one another. At last Loisel put on his clothes.

"I shall go back on foot," said he, "over the whole route which we have taken, to see if I can't find it."

And he went out. She sat waiting on a chair in her ball dress, without strength to go to bed, overwhelmed, without fire, without a thought.

Her husband came back about seven o'clock. He had found nothing.

He went to Police Headquarters, to the newspaper offices, to offer a reward; he went to the cab companies—everywhere, in fact, whither he was urged by the least suspicion of hope.

She waited all day, in the same condition of mad fear before this terrible calamity.

Loisel returned at night with a hollow, pale face; he had discovered nothing.

"You must write to your friend," said he, "that you have broken the clasp of her necklace and that you are having it mended. That will give us time to turn round."

She wrote at his dictation.

At the end of a week they had lost all hope. And Loisel, who had aged five years, declared:

"We must consider how to replace that ornament."

The next day they took the box which had contained it, and they went to the jeweller whose name was found within. He consulted his books.

"It was not I, madame, who sold that necklace; I must simply have furnished the case."

Then they went from jeweller to jeweller, searching for a necklace like the other, consulting their memories, sick both of them with chagrin and with anguish.

They found in a shop at the Palais Royal, a string of diamonds which seemed to them exactly like the one they looked for. It was worth forty thousand francs. They could have it for thirty-six.

So they begged the jeweller not to sell it for three days yet. And they made a bargain that he should buy it back for thirty-four thousand francs, in case they found the other one before the end of February.

Loisel possessed eighteen thousand francs which his father had left him. He would borrow the rest.

He did borrow, asking a thousand francs of one, five hundred of another, five louis here, three louis there. He gave notes, took up ruinous obligations, dealt with usurers, and all the race of lenders. He compromised all the rest of his life, risked his signature without even knowing if he could meet it; and, frightened by the pains yet to come, by the black misery which was about to fall upon him, by the prospect of all the physical privations and of all the moral tortures which he was to suffer, he went to get the new necklace, putting down upon the merchant's counter thirty-six thousand francs.

When Mme. Loisel took back the necklace, Mme. Forestier said to her, with a chilly manner:

"You should have returned it sooner, I might have needed it."

She did not open the case, as her friend had so much feared. If she had detected the substitution, what would she have thought, what would she have said? Would she not have taken Mme. Loisel for a thief?

Mme. Loisel now knew the horrible existence of the needy. She took her part, moreover, all on a sudden, with heroism. That dreadful debt must be paid. She would pay it. They dismissed their servant; they changed their lodgings; they rented a garret under the roof.

She came to know what heavy housework meant and the odious cares of the kitchen. She washed the dishes, using her rosy nails on the greasy pots and pans. She washed the dirty linen, the shirts, and the dish-cloths, which she dried upon a line; she carried the slops down to the street every morning, and carried up the water, stopping for breath at every landing. And, dressed like a woman of the people, she went to the fruiterer, the grocer, the butcher, her basket on her arm, bargaining, insulted, defending her miserable money sou by sou.

Each month they had to meet some notes, renew others, obtain more time.

Her husband worked in the evening making a fair copy of some tradesman's accounts, and late at night he often copied manuscript for five sous a page.

And this life lasted ten years.

At the end of ten years they had paid everything, everything, with the rates of usury, and the accumulations of the compound interest.

Mme. Loisel looked old now. She had become the woman of impoverished households—strong and hard and rough. With frowsy hair, skirts askew, and red hands, she talked loud while washing the floor with great swishes of water. But sometimes, when her husband was at the office, she sat down near the window, and she thought of that gay evening of long ago, of that ball where she had been so beautiful and so feted.

What would have happened if she had not lost that necklace? Who knows? Who knows? How life is strange and changeful! How little a thing is needed for us to be lost or to be saved!

But, one Sunday, having gone to take a walk in the Champs Elysées to refresh herself from the labors of the week, she suddenly perceived a woman who was leading a child. It was Mme. Forestier, still young, still beautiful, still charming.

Mme. Loisel felt moved. Was she going to speak to her? Yes, certainly. And now that she had paid, she was going to tell her all about it. Why not?

She went up.

"Good-day, Jeanne." The other, astonished to be familiarly addressed by this plain good-wife, did not recognize her at all, and stammered:

"But—madame!—I do not know—You must have mistaken."

"No. I am Mathilde Loisel."

Her friend uttered a cry.

"Oh, my poor Mathilde! How you are changed!"

"Yes, I have had days hard enough, since I have seen you, days wretched enough—and that because of you!"

"Of me! How so?"

"Do you remember that diamond necklace which you lent me to wear at the ministerial ball?"

"Yes. Well?"

"Well, I lost it."

"What do you mean? You brought it back."

"I brought you back another just like it. And for this we have been ten years paying. You can understand that it was not easy for us, us who had nothing. At last it is ended, and I am very glad."

Mme. Forestier had stopped.

"You say that you bought a necklace of diamonds to replace mine?"

"Yes. You never noticed it, then! They were very like."

And she smiled with a joy which was proud and naïve at once. Mme. Forestier, strongly moved, took her two hands.

"Oh, my poor Mathilde! Why, my necklace was paste. It was worth at most five hundred francs!"

FOR INFORMAL WRITING

How is "The Necklace" a morality tale? How do you know? Using evidence from the story, what would you say is its moral?

FOR DISCUSSION

1. What parallels can you draw between de Maupassant's own epitaph, noted above, and the primary theme(s) of "The Necklace?"
2. What is a "naturalist?" (In literature, not in nature.) Using what you determine to be the themes of "The Necklace," discuss how the story fits this movement and de Maupassant's view of social class and social striving.
3. Analyze the main characters. What do you think of them? Why? What in the dialogue and language persuade you of your point of view?

FOR WRITING

Research and define "irony" and "dramatic irony." What is the difference? (Are both at work in this story?) Using specific evidence from the story to support your argument, how is "The Necklace" ironic? Comment on the ending. Where in the story do you begin to suspect the ending? How does this contribute to your perspective?

Shooting an Elephant (1936)
George Orwell (1903-1950)

George Orwell is the pseudonym of Eric Arthur Blair, who was born in Bengal, India. Orwell continues to be a popular and widely read writer, noted for the novels Animal Farm *(1945) and* 1984 *(1949). Orwell decided not to attend university, instead taking the Indian Civil Service exams and becoming a policeman in Burma (now Myanmar), an experience that inspired* Burmese Days *(1934), which undoubtedly led to his interest in satire and the social and political observations of his time. His observations, however, are considered prescient in their emphasis on surveillance, autocracy, and loss of personal freedom. "Shooting an Elephant" was published in 1936 in the literary magazine* New Writing, *and in 1948, it was broadcast by the BBC as a radio program.*

In Moulmein, in Lower Burma, I was hated by large numbers of people—the only time in my life that I have been important enough for this to happen to me. I was sub-divisional police officer of the town, and in an aimless, petty kind of way anti-European feeling was very bitter. No one had the guts to raise a riot, but if a European woman went through the bazaars alone somebody would probably spit betel juice over her dress. As a police officer I was an obvious target and was baited whenever it seemed safe to do so. When a nimble Burman tripped me up on the football field and the referee (another Burman) looked the other way, the crowd yelled with hideous laughter. This happened more than once. In the end the sneering yellow faces of young men that met me everywhere, the insults hooted after me when I was at a safe distance, got badly on my nerves. The young Buddhist priests were the worst of all. There were several thousands of them in the town and none of them seemed to have anything to do except stand on street corners and jeer at Europeans.

"Shooting an Elephant" from A COLLECTION OF ESSAYS by George Orwell. Copyright © 1950 by Sonia Brownell Orwell and renewed 1978 by Sonia Pitt-Rivers. Reprinted by permission of Houghton Mifflin Harcourt Publishing Company. All rights reserved.

All this was perplexing and upsetting. For at that time I had already made up my mind that imperialism was an evil thing and the sooner I chucked up my job and got out of it the better. Theoretically—and secretly, of course—I was all for the Burmese and all against their oppressors, the British. As for the job I was doing, I hated it more bitterly than I can perhaps make clear. In a job like that you see the dirty work of Empire at close quarters. The wretched prisoners huddling in the stinking cages of the lock-ups, the grey, cowed faces of the long-term convicts, the scarred buttocks of the men who had been flogged with bamboos—all these oppressed me with an intolerable sense of guilt. But I could get nothing into perspective. I was young and ill-educated and I had had to think out my problems in the utter silence that is imposed on every Englishman in the East. I did not even know that the British Empire is dying, still less did I know that it is a great deal better than the younger empires that are going to supplant it. All I knew was that I was stuck between my hatred of the empire I served and my rage against the evil-spirited little beasts who tried to make my job impossible. With one part of my mind I thought of the British Raj as an unbreakable tyranny, as something clamped down, in *saecula saeculorum,* upon the will of prostrate peoples; with another part I thought that the greatest joy in the world would be to drive a bayonet into a Buddhist priest's guts. Feelings like these are the normal by-products of imperialism; ask any Anglo-Indian official, if you can catch him off duty.

One day something happened which in a roundabout way was enlightening. It was a tiny incident in itself, but it gave me a better glimpse than I had had before of the real nature of imperialism—the real motives for which despotic governments act. Early one morning the sub-inspector at a police station the other end of the town rang me up on the phone and said that an elephant was ravaging the bazaar. Would I please come and do something about it? I did not know what I could do, but I wanted to see what was happening and I got on to a pony and started out. I took my rifle, an old .44 Winchester and much too small to kill an elephant, but I thought the noise might be useful *in terrorem.* Various Burmans stopped me on the way and told me about the elephant's doings. It was not, of course, a wild elephant, but a tame one which had gone "must." It had been chained up, as tame elephants always are when their attack of "must" is due, but on the previous night it had broken its chain and escaped. Its mahout, the only person who could manage it when it was in that state, had set out in pursuit, but had taken the wrong direction and was now twelve hours' journey away, and in the morning the elephant had suddenly reappeared in the town. The Burmese population had no weapons and were quite helpless against it. It had already destroyed somebody's bamboo hut, killed a cow and raided some fruit-stalls and devoured the stock; also it had met the municipal rubbish van and, when the driver jumped out and took to his heels, had turned the van over and inflicted violences upon it.

The Burmese sub-inspector and some Indian constables were waiting for me in the quarter where the elephant had been seen. It was a very poor quarter, a labyrinth of squalid bamboo huts, thatched with palmleaf, winding all over a steep hillside. I remember that it was a cloudy, stuffy morning at the beginning of the rains. We began questioning the people as to where the elephant had gone and, as usual, failed to get any definite information. That is invariably the case in the East; a story always sounds clear enough at a distance, but the nearer you get to the scene of events the vaguer it becomes. Some of the people said that the elephant had gone in one direction, some said that he had gone in another, some professed not even to have heard of any elephant. I had almost made up my mind that the whole story was a pack of lies, when we heard yells a little distance away. There was a loud, scandalized cry of "Go away, child! Go away this instant!" and an old woman with a switch in her hand came round the corner of a hut, violently shooing away a crowd of naked children. Some more women followed, clicking their tongues and exclaiming; evidently there was something that the children ought not to have seen. I rounded the hut and saw a man's dead body sprawling in the mud. He was an Indian, a black Dravidian coolie, almost naked, and he could not have been dead many minutes. The people said that the elephant had come suddenly upon him round the corner of the hut, caught him with its trunk, put its foot on his back and ground him into the earth. This was the rainy season and the ground was soft, and his face had scored a trench a foot deep and a couple of yards long. He was lying on his belly with arms crucified and head sharply twisted to one side. His face was coated with mud, the eyes wide open, the teeth bared and grinning with an expression of unendurable agony. (Never tell me, by the way, that the dead look peaceful. Most of the corpses I have seen looked devilish.) The friction of the great beast's foot had stripped the skin from his back as neatly as one skins a rabbit. As soon as I saw the dead man I sent an orderly to a friend's house nearby to borrow an elephant rifle. I had already sent back the pony, not wanting it to go mad with fright and throw me if it smelt the elephant.

The orderly came back in a few minutes with a rifle and five cartridges, and meanwhile some Burmans had arrived and told us that the elephant was in the paddy fields below, only a few hundred yards away. As I started forward practically the whole population of the quarter flocked out of the houses and followed me. They had seen the rifle and were all shouting excitedly that I was going to shoot the elephant. They had not shown much interest in the elephant when he was merely ravaging their homes, but it was different now that he was going to be shot. It was a bit of fun to them, as it would be to an English crowd; besides they wanted the meat. It made me vaguely uneasy. I had no intention of shooting the elephant—I had merely sent for the rifle to defend myself if necessary—and it is always unnerving to have a crowd following you. I marched down the hill, looking and feeling a fool, with the rifle over my shoulder and an ever-growing army of people jostling at my heels. At the bottom, when you got away from the huts, there was a metalled road and beyond that a miry waste of paddy fields a thousand yards across, not yet ploughed but soggy from the first rains and dotted with coarse grass. The elephant was standing eight yards from the road, his left side towards us. He took not the slightest notice of the crowd's approach. He was tearing up bunches of grass, beating them against his knees to clean them and stuffing them into his mouth.

I had halted on the road. As soon as I saw the elephant I knew with perfect certainty that I ought not to shoot him. It is a serious matter to shoot a working elephant—it is comparable to destroying a huge and costly piece of machinery—and obviously one ought not to do it if it can possibly be avoided. And at that distance, peacefully eating, the elephant looked no more dangerous than a cow. I thought then and I think now that his attack of "must" was already passing off; in which case he would merely wander harmlessly about until the mahout came back and caught him. Moreover, I did not in the least want to shoot him. I decided that I would watch him for a little while to make sure that he did not turn savage again, and then go home.

But at that moment I glanced round at the crowd that had followed me. It was an immense crowd, two thousand at the least and growing every minute. It blocked the road for a long distance on either side. I looked at the sea of yellow faces above the garish clothes—faces all happy and excited over this bit of fun, all certain that the elephant was going to be shot. They were watching me as they would watch a conjurer about to perform a trick. They did not like me, but with the magical rifle in my hands I was momentarily worth watching. And suddenly I realized that I should have to shoot the elephant after all. The people expected it of me and I had got to do it; I could feel their two thousand wills pressing me forward, irresistibly. And it was at this moment, as I stood there with the rifle in my hands, that I first grasped the hollowness, the futility of the white man's dominion in the East. Here was I, the white man with his gun, standing in front of the unarmed native crowd—seemingly the leading actor of the piece; but in reality I was only an absurd puppet pushed to and fro by the will of those yellow faces behind. I perceived in this moment that when the white man turns tyrant it is his own freedom that he destroys. He becomes a sort of hollow, posing dummy, the conventionalized figure of a sahib.

For it is the condition of his rule that he shall spend his life in trying to impress the "natives," and so in every crisis he has got to do what the "natives" expect of him. He wears a mask, and his face grows to fit it. I had got to shoot the elephant. I had committed myself to doing it when I sent for the rifle. A sahib has got to act like a sahib; he has got to appear resolute, to know his own mind and do definite things. To come all that way, rifle in hand, with two thousand people marching at my heels, and then to trail feebly away, having done nothing—no, that was impossible. The crowd would laugh at me. And my whole life, every white man's life in the East, was one long struggle not to be laughed at.

But I did not want to shoot the elephant. I watched him beating his bunch of grass against his knees, with that preoccupied grandmotherly air that elephants have. It seemed to me that it would be murder to shoot him. At that age I was not squeamish about killing animals, but I had never shot an elephant and never wanted to. (Somehow it always seems worse to kill a *large* animal.) Besides, there was the beast's owner to be considered. Alive, the elephant was worth at least a hundred pounds; dead, he would only be worth the value of his tusks, five pounds, possibly. But I had got to act quickly. I turned to some experienced-looking Burmans who had been there when we arrived, and asked them how the elephant had been behaving. They all said the same thing: he took no notice of you if you left him alone, but he might charge if you went too close to him.

It was perfectly clear to me what I ought to do. I ought to walk up to within, say, twenty-five yards of the elephant and test his behavior. If he charged, I could shoot; if he took no notice of me, it would be safe to leave him until the mahout came back. But also I knew that I was going to do no such thing. I was a poor shot with a rifle and the ground was soft mud into which one would sink at every step. If the elephant charged and I missed him, I should have about as much chance as a toad under a steam-roller. But even then I was not thinking particularly of my own skin, only of the watchful yellow faces behind. For at that moment, with the crowd watching me, I was not afraid in the ordinary sense, as I would have been if I had been alone. A white man mustn't be frightened in front of "natives"; and so, in general, he isn't frightened. The sole thought in my mind was that if anything went wrong those two thousand Burmans would see me pursued, caught, trampled on and reduced to a grinning corpse like that Indian up the hill. And if that happened it was quite probable that some of them would laugh. That would never do.

There was only one alternative. I shoved the cartridges into the magazine and lay down on the road to get a better aim. The crowd grew very still, and a deep, low, happy sigh, as of people who see the theatre curtain go up at last, breathed from innumerable throats. They were going to have their bit of fun after all. The rifle was a beautiful German thing with cross-hair sights. I did not then know that in shooting an elephant one would shoot to cut an imaginary bar running from ear-hole to ear-hole. I ought, therefore, as the elephant was sideways on, to have aimed straight at his ear-hole, actually I aimed several inches in front of this, thinking the brain would be further forward.

When I pulled the trigger I did not hear the bang or feel the kick—one never does when a shot goes home—but I heard the devilish roar of glee that went up from the crowd. In that instant, in too short a time, one would have thought, even for the bullet to get there, a mysterious, terrible change had come over the elephant. He neither stirred nor fell, but every line of his body had altered. He looked suddenly stricken, shrunken, immensely old, as though the frightful impact of the bullet had paralysed him without knocking him down. At last, after what seemed a long time—it might have been five seconds, I dare say—he sagged flabbily to his knees. His mouth slobbered. An enormous senility seemed to have settled upon him. One could have imagined him thousands of years old. I fired again into the same spot. At the second shot he did not collapse but climbed with desperate slowness to his feet and stood weakly upright, with legs sagging and head drooping. I fired a third time. That was the shot that did for him. You could see the agony of it jolt his whole body and knock the last remnant of strength from his legs. But in falling he seemed for a moment to rise, for as his hind legs collapsed beneath him he seemed to tower upward like a huge rock toppling, his trunk reaching skyward like a tree. He trumpeted, for the first and only time. And then down he came, his belly towards me, with a crash that seemed to shake the ground even where I lay.

I got up. The Burmans were already racing past me across the mud. It was obvious that the elephant would never rise again, but he was not dead. He was breathing very rhythmically with long rattling gasps, his great mound of a side painfully rising and falling. His mouth was wide open—I could see far down into caverns of pale pink throat. I waited a long time for him to die, but his breathing did not weaken. Finally I fired my two remaining shots into the spot where I thought his heart must be. The thick blood welled out of him like red velvet, but still he did not die. His body did not even jerk when the shots hit him, the tortured breathing continued without a pause. He was dying, very slowly and in great agony, but in some world remote from me where not even a bullet could damage him further. I felt that I had got to put an end to that dreadful noise. It seemed dreadful to see the great beast lying there, powerless to move and yet powerless to die, and not even to be able to finish him. I sent back for my small rifle and poured shot after shot into his heart and down his throat. They seemed to make no impression. The tortured gasps continued as steadily as the ticking of a clock.

In the end I could not stand it any longer and went away. I heard later that it took him half an hour to die. Burmans were bringing dahs and baskets even before I left, and I was told they had stripped his body almost to the bones by the afternoon.

Afterwards, of course, there were endless discussions about the shooting of the elephant. The owner was furious, but he was only an Indian and could do nothing. Besides, legally I had done the right thing, for a mad elephant has to be killed, like a mad dog, if its owner fails to control it. Among the Europeans opinion was divided. The older men said I was right, the younger men said it was a damn shame to shoot an elephant for killing a coolie, because an elephant was worth more than any damn Coringhee coolie. And afterwards I was very glad that the coolie had been killed; it put me legally in the right and it gave me a sufficient pretext for shooting the elephant. I often wondered whether any of the others grasped that I had done it solely to avoid looking a fool.

FOR INFORMAL WRITING

How does this essay weigh the narrator's own misgivings with the desires of the people in the town? In a larger sense, in what ways does Orwell attempt to reconcile these two competing positions?

FOR DISCUSSION

1. What in your life—and in the lives of others you know—can be described as "Orwellian"? How do you define this, a term that is bandied about quite frequently in response to conditions that curtail privacy and personal initiative?
2. Why do you think the narrative is told in both present and past tense? What effect does this have? Look specifically at the story.
3. Comment on Orwell's use of language and the details of this narrative. For instance, look at the use of Latin phrases. Why would Orwell choose to do this?

FOR WRITING

Orwell is viewed as an "anti-imperialist," and this story is often used as a metaphor for the downfall of the British Empire. Research imperialism and the British Empire of the late 19th and early 20th centuries. How does this information challenge or alter your original reading of this narrative? How does it confirm it?

WHAT'S NEW IS OLD

Read this essay along with David Foster Wallace's "Consider the Lobster." While at face value both seem to be about types of animal cruelty, they both involve ethical considerations. How is this so? How does each raise ethical concerns differently?

The Lottery (1948)
Shirley Jackson (1916–1965)

Shirley Jackson was known as a writer specializing in mystery and horror. Her best-known novel, The Haunting of Hill House *(1959), is considered a quintessential horror tale. Jackson received the National Book Award and the Edgar Allan Poe Award;* Time *magazine called* We Have Always Lived in the Castle *(1962) "one of 1962's ten best novels." In addition to several memoirs, Jackson also wrote stories for children, including* The Witchcraft of Salem Village *(1956),* The Bad Children *(1958), and* Nine Magic Wishes *(1966). "The Lottery" is perhaps Jackson's most famous work, and it continues to be widely anthologized, read, and taught.*

The morning of June 27th was clear and sunny, with the fresh warmth of a full-summer day; the flowers were blossoming profusely and the grass was richly green. The people of the village began to gather in the square, between the post office and the bank, around ten o'clock; in some towns there were so many people that the lottery took two days and had to be started on June 26th, but in this village, where there were only about three hundred people, the whole lottery took less than two hours, so it could begin at ten o'clock in the morning and still be through in time to allow the villagers to get home for noon dinner.

The children assembled first, of course. School was recently over for the summer, and the feeling of liberty sat uneasily on most of them; they tended to gather together quietly for a while before they broke into boisterous play, and their talk was still of the classroom and the teacher, of books and reprimands. Bobby Martin had already stuffed his pockets full of stones, and the other boys

---

THE LOTTERY by Shirley Jackson. Copyright © 1948, 1949 by Shirley Jackson. Copyright renewed 1976, 1977 by Laurence Hyman, Barry Hyman, Mrs. Sarah Webster and Mrs. Joanne Schnurer. Reprinted by permission of Farrar, Straus and Giroux. All rights Reserved.

soon followed his example, selecting the smoothest and roundest stones; Bobby and Harry Jones and Dickie Delacroix—the villagers pronounced this name "Dellacroy"—eventually made a great pile of stones in one corner of the square and guarded it against the raids of the other boys. The girls stood aside, talking among themselves, looking over their shoulders at the boys, and the very small children rolled in the dust or clung to the hands of their older brothers or sisters.

Soon the men began to gather, surveying their own children, speaking of planting and rain, tractors and taxes. They stood together, away from the pile of stones in the corner, and their jokes were quiet and they smiled rather than laughed. The women, wearing faded house dresses and sweaters, came shortly after their menfolk. They greeted one another and exchanged bits of gossip as they went to join their husbands. Soon the women, standing by their husbands, began to call to their children, and the children came reluctantly, having to be called four or five times. Bobby Martin ducked under his mother's grasping hand and ran, laughing, back to the pile of stones. His father spoke up sharply, and Bobby came quickly and took his place between his father and his oldest brother.

The lottery was conducted—as were the square dances, the teen club, the Halloween program—by Mr. Summers, who had time and energy to devote to civic activities. He was a round-faced, jovial man and he ran the coal business, and people were sorry for him because he had no children and his wife was a scold. When he arrived in the square, carrying the black wooden box, there was a murmur of conversation among the villagers, and he waved and called, "Little late today, folks." The postmaster, Mr. Graves, followed him, carrying a three-legged stool, and the stool was put in the center of the square and Mr. Summers set the black box down on it. The villagers kept their distance, leaving a space between themselves and the stool, and when Mr. Summers said, "Some of you fellows want to give me a hand?" there was a hesitation before two men, Mr. Martin and his oldest son, Baxter, came forward to hold the box steady on the stool while Mr. Summers stirred up the papers inside it.

The original paraphernalia for the lottery had been lost long ago, and the black box now resting on the stool had been put into use even before Old Man Warner, the oldest man in town, was born. Mr. Summers spoke frequently to the villagers about making a new box, but no one liked to upset even as much tradition as was represented by the black box. There was a story that the present box had been made with some pieces of the box that had preceded it, the one that had been constructed when the first people settled down to make a village here. Every year, after the lottery, Mr. Summers began talking again about a new box, but every year the subject was allowed to fade off without anything being done. The black box grew shabbier each year: by now it was no longer completely black but splintered badly along one side to show the original wood color, and in some places faded or stained.

Mr. Martin and his oldest son, Baxter, held the black box securely on the stool until Mr. Summers had stirred the papers thoroughly with his hand. Because so much of the ritual had been forgotten or discarded, Mr. Summers had been successful in having slips of paper substituted for the chips of wood that had been used for generations. Chips of wood, Mr. Summers had argued, had been all very well when the village was tiny, but now that the population was more than three hundred and likely to keep on growing, it was necessary to use something that would fit more easily into the black box. The night before the lottery, Mr. Summers and Mr. Graves made up the slips of paper and put them in the box, and it was then taken to the safe of Mr. Summers' coal company and locked up until Mr. Summers was ready to take it to the square next morning. The rest of the year, the box was put way, sometimes one place, sometimes another; it had spent one year in Mr. Graves' barn and another year underfoot in the post office, and sometimes it was set on a shelf in the Martin grocery and left there.

There was a great deal of fussing to be done before Mr. Summers declared the lottery open. There were the lists to make up—of heads of families, heads of households in each family, members of each household in each family. There was the proper swearing-in of Mr. Summers by the postmaster, as the official of the lottery; at one time, some people remembered, there had been a recital of some sort, performed by the official of the lottery, a perfunctory, tuneless chant that had been rattled off duly each year; some people believed that the official of the lottery used to stand just so when he said or sang it, others believed that he was supposed to walk among the people, but years and years ago this part of the ritual had been allowed to lapse. There had been, also, a ritual salute, which the official of the lottery had had to use in addressing each person who came up to draw from the box, but this also had changed with time, until now it was felt necessary only for the official to speak to each person approaching. Mr. Summers was very good at all this; in his clean white shirt and blue jeans, with one hand resting carelessly on the black box, he seemed very proper and important as he talked interminably to Mr. Graves and the Martins.

Just as Mr. Summers finally left off talking and turned to the assembled villagers, Mrs. Hutchinson came hurriedly along the path to the square, her sweater thrown over her shoulders, and slid into place in the back of the crowd. "Clean forgot what day it was," she said to Mrs. Delacroix, who stood next to her, and they both laughed softly. "Thought my old man was out back stacking wood," Mrs. Hutchinson went on, "and then I looked out the window and the kids was gone, and then I remembered it was the twenty-seventh and came a-running."

She dried her hands on her apron, and Mrs. Delacroix said, "You're in time, though. They're still talking away up there."

Mrs. Hutchinson craned her neck to see through the crowd and found her husband and children standing near the front. She tapped Mrs. Delacroix on the arm as a farewell and began to make her way through the crowd. The people separated good-humoredly to let her through: two or three people said, in voices just loud enough to be heard across the crowd, "Here comes your Missus, Hutchinson," and "Bill, she made it after all." Mrs. Hutchinson reached her husband, and Mr. Summers, who had been waiting, said cheerfully, "Thought we were going to have to get on without you, Tessie." Mrs. Hutchinson said, grinning, "Wouldn't have me leave m'dishes in the sink, now, would you. Joe?," and soft laughter ran through the crowd as the people stirred back into position after Mrs. Hutchinson's arrival.

"Well, now," Mr. Summers said soberly, "guess we better get started, get this over with, so's we can go back to work. Anybody ain't here?"

"Dunbar," several people said. "Dunbar, Dunbar."

Mr. Summers consulted his list. "Clyde Dunbar," he said. "That's right. He's broke his leg, hasn't he? Who's drawing for him?"

"Me, I guess," a woman said, and Mr. Summers turned to look at her. "Wife draws for her husband," Mr. Summers said. "Don't you have a grown boy to do it for you, Janey?" Although Mr. Summers and everyone else in the village knew the answer perfectly well, it was the business of the official of the lottery to ask such questions formally. Mr. Summers waited with an expression of polite interest while Mrs. Dunbar answered.

"Horace's not but sixteen yet," Mrs. Dunbar said regretfully. "Guess I gotta fill in for the old man this year."

"Right," Mr. Summers said. He made a note on the list he was holding. Then he asked, "Watson boy drawing this year?"

A tall boy in the crowd raised his hand. "Here," he said. "I'm drawing for my mother and me." He blinked his eyes nervously and ducked his head as several voices in the crowd said things like, "Good fellow, lad," and "Glad to see your mother's got a man to do it."

"Well," Mr. Summers said, "guess that's everyone. Old Man Warner make it?"

"Here," a voice said, and Mr. Summers nodded.

A sudden hush fell on the crowd as Mr. Summers cleared his throat and looked at the list. "All ready?" he called. "Now, I'll read the names—heads of families first—and the men come up and take a paper out of the box. Keep the paper folded in your hand without looking at it until everyone has had a turn. Everything clear?"

The people had done it so many times that they only half listened to the directions: most of them were quiet, wetting their lips, not looking around. Then Mr. Summers raised one hand high and said, "Adams." A man disengaged himself from the crowd and came forward. "Hi, Steve," Mr. Summers said, and Mr. Adams said, "Hi, Joe." They grinned at one another humorlessly and nervously. Then Mr. Adams reached into the black box and took out a folded paper. He held it firmly by one corner as he turned and went hastily back to his place in the crowd, where he stood a little apart from his family, not looking down at his hand.

"Allen," Mr. Summers said. "Anderson. . . . Bentham."

"Seems like there's no time at all between lotteries any more," Mrs. Delacroix said to Mrs. Graves in the back row. "Seems like we got through with the last one only last week."

"Time sure goes fast," Mrs. Graves said.

"Clark. . . . Delacroix."

"There goes my old man," Mrs. Delacroix said. She held her breath while her husband went forward.

"Dunbar," Mr. Summers said, and Mrs. Dunbar went steadily to the box while one of the women said, "Go on, Janey," and another said, "There she goes."

"We're next," Mrs. Graves said. She watched while Mr. Graves came around from the side of the box, greeted Mr. Summers gravely and selected a slip of paper from the box. By now, all through the crowd, there were men holding the small folded papers in their large hand, turning them over and over nervously. Mrs. Dunbar and her two sons stood together, Mrs. Dunbar holding the slip of paper.

"Harburt. . . . Hutchinson."

"Get up there, Bill," Mrs. Hutchinson said, and the people near her laughed.

"Jones."

"They do say," Mr. Adams said to Old Man Warner, who stood next to him, "that over in the north village they're talking of giving up the lottery."

Old Man Warner snorted. "Pack of crazy fools," he said. "Listening to the young folks, nothing's good enough for them. Next thing you know, they'll be wanting to go back to living in caves, nobody work any more, live that way for a while. Used to be a saying about 'Lottery in June, corn be heavy soon.' First thing you know, we'd all be eating stewed chickweed and acorns. There's always been a lottery," he added petulantly. "Bad enough to see young Joe Summers up there joking with everybody."

"Some places have already quit lotteries," Mrs. Adams said.

"Nothing but trouble in that," Old Man Warner said stoutly. "Pack of young fools."

"Martin." And Bobby Martin watched his father go forward. "Overdyke. . . . Percy."

"I wish they'd hurry," Mrs. Dunbar said to her older son. "I wish they'd hurry."

"They're almost through," her son said.

"You get ready to run tell Dad," Mrs. Dunbar said.

Mr. Summers called his own name and then stepped forward precisely and selected a slip from the box. Then he called, "Warner."

"Seventy-seventh year I been in the lottery," Old Man Warner said as he went through the crowd. "Seventy-seventh time."

"Watson." The tall boy came awkwardly through the crowd. Someone said, "Don't be nervous, Jack," and Mr. Summers said, "Take your time, son."

"Zanini."

After that, there was a long pause, a breathless pause, until Mr. Summers, holding his slip of paper in the air, said, "All right, fellows." For a minute, no one moved, and then all the slips of paper were opened. Suddenly, all the women began to speak at once, saying, "Who is it?," "Who's got it?," "Is it the Dunbars?," "Is it the Watsons?" Then the voices began to say, "It's Hutchinson. It's Bill," "Bill Hutchinson's got it."

"Go tell your father," Mrs. Dunbar said to her older son.

People began to look around to see the Hutchinsons. Bill Hutchinson was standing quietly, staring down at the paper in his hand. Suddenly, Tessie Hutchinson shouted to Mr. Summers, "You didn't give him time enough to take any paper he wanted. I saw you. It wasn't fair!"

"Be a good sport, Tessie," Mrs. Delacroix called, and Mrs. Graves said, "All of us took the same chance."

"Shut up, Tessie," Bill Hutchinson said.

"Well, everyone," Mr. Summers said, "that was done pretty fast, and now we've got to be hurrying a little more to get done in time." He consulted his next list. "Bill," he said, "you draw for the Hutchinson family. You got any other households in the Hutchinsons?"

"There's Don and Eva," Mrs. Hutchinson yelled. "Make them take their chance!"

"Daughters draw with their husbands' families, Tessie," Mr. Summers said gently. "You know that as well as anyone else."

"It wasn't fair," Tessie said.

"I guess not, Joe," Bill Hutchinson said regretfully. "My daughter draws with her husband's family; that's only fair. And I've got no other family except the kids."

"Then, as far as drawing for families is concerned, it's you," Mr. Summers said in explanation, "and as far as drawing for households is concerned, that's you, too, right?"

"Right," Bill Hutchinson said.

"How many kids, Bill?" Mr. Summers asked formally.

"Three," Bill Hutchinson said.

"There's Bill, Jr., and Nancy, and little Dave. And Tessie and me." "All right, then," Mr. Summers said. "Harry, you got their tickets back?"

Mr. Graves nodded and held up the slips of paper. "Put them in the box, then," Mr. Summers directed. "Take Bill's and put it in."

"I think we ought to start over," Mrs. Hutchinson said, as quietly as she could. "I tell you it wasn't fair. You didn't give him time enough to choose. Everybody saw that."

Mr. Graves had selected the five slips and put them in the box. and he dropped all the papers but those onto the ground, where the breeze caught them and lifted them off.

"Listen, everybody," Mrs. Hutchinson was saying to the people around her.

"Ready, Bill?" Mr. Summers asked, and Bill Hutchinson, with one quick glance around at his wife and children, nodded.

"Remember," Mr. Summers said, "take the slips and keep them folded until each person has taken one. Harry, you help little Dave." Mr. Graves took the hand of the little boy, who came willingly with him up to the box. "Take a paper out of the box, Davy," Mr. Summers said. Davy put his hand into the box and laughed. "Take just one paper," Mr. Summers said. "Harry, you hold it for him." Mr. Graves took the child's hand and removed the folded paper from the tight fist and held it while little Dave stood next to him and looked up at him wonderingly.

"Nancy next," Mr. Summers said. Nancy was twelve, and her school friends breathed heavily as she went forward switching her skirt and took a slip daintily from the box. "Bill, Jr.," Mr. Summers said, and Billy, his face red and his feet overlarge, near knocked the box over as he got a paper out. "Tessie," Mr. Summers said. She hesitated for a minute, looking around defiantly, and then set her lips and went up to the box. She snatched a paper out and held it behind her.

"Bill," Mr. Summers said, and Bill Hutchinson reached into the box and felt around, bringing his hand out at last with the slip of paper in it.

The crowd was quiet. A girl whispered, "I hope it's not Nancy," and the sound of the whisper reached the edges of the crowd.

"It's not the way it used to be," Old Man Warner said clearly. "People ain't the way they used to be."

"All right," Mr. Summers said. "Open the papers. Harry, you open little Dave's."

Mr. Graves opened the slip of paper, and there was a general sigh through the crowd as he held it up and everyone could see that it was blank. Nancy and Bill,

Jr., opened theirs at the same time and both beamed and laughed, turning around to the crowd and holding their slips of paper above their heads.

"Tessie," Mr. Summers said. There was a pause, and then Mr. Summers looked at Bill Hutchinson, and Bill unfolded his paper and showed it. It was blank.

"It's Tessie," Mr. Summers said, and his voice was hushed. "Show us her paper, Bill."

Bill Hutchinson went over to his wife and forced the slip of paper out of her hand. It had a black spot on it, the black spot Mr. Summers had made the night before with the heavy pencil in the coal company office. Bill Hutchinson held it up, and there was a stir in the crowd.

"All right, folks." Mr. Summers said. "Let's finish quickly."

Although the villagers had forgotten the ritual and lost the original black box, they still remembered to use stones. The pile of stones the boys had made earlier was ready; there were stones on the ground with the blowing scraps of paper that had come out of the box. Delacroix selected a stone so large she had to pick it up with both hands and turned to Mrs. Dunbar. "Come on," she said. "Hurry up."

Mr. Dunbar had large stones in both hands, and she said, gasping for breath. "I can't run at all. You'll have to go ahead, and I'll catch up with you."

The children had stones already. And someone gave little Davy Hutchinson few pebbles.

Tessie Hutchinson was in the center of a cleared space by now, and she held her hands out desperately as the villagers moved in on her. "It isn't fair," she said. A stone hit her on the side of the head. Old Man Warner was saying, "Come on, come on, everyone." Steve Adams was in the front of the crowd of villagers, with Mrs. Graves beside him.

"It isn't fair, it isn't right," Mrs. Hutchinson screamed, and then they were upon her.

FOR INFORMAL WRITING

This story might be considered a dystopian narrative. To what does that refer? Where have you seen or read other examples of dystopian stories?

FOR DISCUSSION

1. What is foreshadowing? How do you see this in "The Lottery?" How does it contribute to the mood and outcome of the story?
2. What is the framing of the story? How does the story begin? How does it set up and then defy your expectations?

3. Look at Jackson's language in the story. Why does it matter that Mr. Graves, for instance, is "round-faced" and "jovial?" At what point do things seem to turn? How do you know?

FOR WRITING

"The Lottery" falls into a tradition we acknowledge elsewhere in this volume, one called "gothic." Find another story that is considered a good example of gothic fiction, and compare it to "The Lottery". How do these represent the gothic in different ways? In what ways are they similar? After you define "gothic," look at each story specifically to argue your perspective.

Notes of a Native Son (1955)
James Baldwin (1924–1987)

James Baldwin, the eldest of nine children, grew up in Harlem, New York City. Baldwin left New York City for Paris in 1948, where he began to focus on his writing, specifically fiction, nonfiction, and playwriting. He returned to the United States nine years later to become an active participant in the civil rights movement. According to a review in The New York Times, *Baldwin's writing grappled with "his insistence on removing, layer by layer, the hardened skin with which Americans shield themselves from their country." His' essays are perhaps most notable, and his collections, such as* Nobody Knows My Name *(1961) and* Notes of a Native Son *(1955), intersect Baldwin's own biography with his politics. This excerpt forms the first chapter of* Notes.

On the Twenty-Ninth of July, in 1943, my father died. On the same day, a few hours later, his last child was born.

Over a month before this, while all our energies were concentrated in waiting for these events, there had been, in Detroit, one of the bloodiest race riots of the century. A few hours after my father's funeral, while he lay in state in the undertaker's chapel, a race riot broke out in Harlem. On the morning of the third of August, we drove my father to the graveyard through a wilderness of smashed plate glass.

The day of my father's funeral had also been my nineteenth birthday. As we drove him to the graveyard, the spoils of injustice, anarchy, discontent, and hatred were all around us. It seemed to me that God himself had devised, to mark my father's end, the most sustained and brutally dissonant of codas. And it seemed to me, too, that the violence which rose all about us as my father left the

---

Notes of a Native Son Copyright © 1949, 1950, 1951, 1953, 1954, 1955 by James Baldwin Reprinted with permission from Beacon Press, Boston Massachusetts.

world had been devised as a corrective for the pride of his eldest son. I had declined to believe in that apocalypse which had been central to my father's vision; very well, life seemed to be saying, here is something that will certainly pass for an apocalypse until the real thing comes along. I had inclined to be contemptuous of my father for the conditions of his life, for the conditions of our lives. When his life had ended I began to wonder about that life and also, in a new way, to be apprehensive about my own.

I had not known my father very well. We had got on badly, partly because we share, in our different fashions, the vice of stubborn pride.

When he was dead I realized that I had hardly ever spoken to him. When he had been dead a long time I began to wish I had. It seems to be typical of life in America, where opportunities, real and fancied, are thicker than anywhere else on the globe, that the second generation has no time to talk to the first. No one, including my father, seems to have known exactly how old he was, but his mother had been born during slavery. He was of the first generation of free men. He, along with thousands of other Negroes, came North after 1919 and I was part of that generation which had never seen the landscape of what Negroes sometimes call the Old Country.

He had been born in New Orleans and had been a quite young man there during the time that Louis Armstrong, a boy, was running errands for the dives and honky-tonks of what was always presented to me as one of the most wicked of cities—to this day, whenever I think of New Orleans, I also helplessly think of Sodom and Gomorrah. My father never mentioned Louis Armstrong, except to forbid us to play his records; but there was a picture of him on our wall for a long time. One of my father's strong-willed female relatives had placed it there and forbade my father to take it down. He never did, but he eventually maneuvered her out of the house and when, some years later, she was in trouble and near death, he refused to do anything to help her.

He was, I think, very handsome. I gather this from photographs and from my own memories of him, dressed in his Sunday best and on his way to preach a sermon somewhere, when I was little. Handsome, proud, and ingrown, "like a toenail," somebody said. But he looked to me, as I grew older, like pictures I had seen of African tribal chieftains: he really should have been naked, with warpaint on and barbaric mementos, standing among spears. He could be chilling in the pulpit and indescribably cruel in his personal life and he was certainly the most bitter man I have ever met; yet it must be said that there was something else in him, buried in him, which lent him his tremendous power and, even, a rather crushing charm. It had something to do with his blackness, I think—he was very black—with his blackness and his beauty, and with the fact that he knew that he was black but did not know that he was beautiful. He claimed to be proud of his blackness but it had also been the cause of much humiliation and it had fixed bleak boundaries to his life. He was not a young man when we were growing up and he had already suffered many kinds of ruin; in his outrageously demanding and protective way he loved his children, who were black like him and menaced, like him; and all these things sometimes showed in his face when he tried, never to my knowledge with any success, to establish contact with any of us. When he took one of his children on his knee to play, the child always became fretful and began to cry; when he tried to help one of us with our homework the absolutely unabating tension which emanated from him caused our minds and our tongues to become paralyzed, so that he, scarcely knowing why, flew into a rage and the child, not knowing why, was punished. If it ever entered his head to bring a surprise home for his children, it was, almost unfailingly, the wrong surprise and even the big watermelons he often brought home on his back in the summertime led to the most appalling scenes. I do not remember, in all those years, that one of his children was ever glad to see him come home. From what I was able to gather of his early life, it seemed that this inability to establish contact with other people had always marked him and had been one of the things which had driven him out of New Orleans. There was something in him, therefore, groping and tentative, which was never expressed and which was buried with him. One saw it most clearly when he was facing new people and hoping to impress them. But he never did, not for long. We went from church to smaller and more improbable church, he found himself in less and less demand as a minister, and by the time he died none of his friends had come to see him for a long time. He had lived and died in an intolerable bitterness of spirit and it frightened me, as we drove him to the graveyard through those unquiet, ruined streets, to see how powerful and overflowing this bitterness could be and to realize that this bitterness now was mine.

When he died I had been away from home for a little over a year. In that year I had had time to become aware of the meaning of all my father's bitter warnings, had discovered the secret of his proudly pursed lips and rigid carriage: I had discovered the weight of white people in the world. I saw that this had been for my ancestors and now would be for me an awful thing to live with and that the bitterness which had helped to kill my father could also kill me.

He had been ill a long time—in the mind, as we now realized, reliving instances of his fantastic intransigence in the new light of his affliction and endeavoring to feel a sorrow for him which never, quite, came true. We had not known that he was being eaten up by paranoia, and the discovery that his cruelty, to our bodies and our minds, had been one of the symptoms of his illness was not, then, enough to enable us to forgive him. The younger children felt, quite simply, relief that he would not be coming home anymore. My mother's observation that it was he, after all, who had kept them alive all these years meant nothing because the problems of keeping children alive are not real for children. The older children felt, with my father gone, that they could invite their friends to the house without fear that their friends would be insulted or, as had sometimes happened with me, being told that their friends were in league with the devil and intended to rob our family of everything we owned. (I didn't fail to wonder, and it made me hate him, what on earth we owned that anybody else would want.)

His illness was beyond all hope of healing before anyone realized that he was ill. He had always been so strange and had lived, like a prophet, in such unimaginably close communion with the Lord that his long silences which were punctuated by moans and hallelujahs and snatches of old songs while he sat at the living-room window never seemed odd to us. It was not until he refused to eat because, he said, his family was trying to poison him that my mother was forced to accept as a fact what had, until then, been only an unwilling suspicion. When he was committed, it was discovered that he had tuberculosis and, as it turned out, the disease of his mind allowed the disease of his body to destroy him. For the doctors could not force him to eat, either, and, though he was fed intravenously, it was clear from the beginning that there was no hope for him. In my mind's eye I could see him, sitting at the window, locked up in his terrors; hating and fearing every living soul including his children who had betrayed him, too, by reaching toward the world which had despised him. There were nine of us. I began to wonder what it could have felt like for such a man to have had nine children whom he could barely feed. He used to make little jokes about our poverty, which never, of course, seemed very funny to us; they could not have seemed very funny to him, either, or else our all too feeble response to them would never have caused such rages. He spent great energy and achieved, to our chagrin, no small amount of success in keeping us away from the people who surrounded us, people who had all-night rent parties to which we listened when we should have been sleeping, people who cursed and drank and flashed razor blades on Lenox Avenue. He could not understand why, if they had so much energy to spare, they could not use it to make their lives better. He treated almost everybody on our block with a most uncharitable asperity and neither they, nor, of course, their children were slow to reciprocate.

The only white people who came to our house were welfare workers and bill collectors. It was almost always my mother who dealt with them, for my father's temper, which was at the mercy of his pride, was never to be trusted. It was clear that he felt their very presence in his home to be a violation: this was conveyed by his carriage, almost ludicrously stiff, and by his voice, harsh and vindictively polite. When I was around nine or ten I wrote a play which was directed by a young, white schoolteacher, a woman, who then took an interest in me, and gave me books to read and, in order to corroborate my theatrical bent, decided to take me to see what she somewhat tactlessly referred to as "real" plays. Theater-going was forbidden in our house, but, with the really cruel intuitiveness of a child, I suspected that the color of this woman's skin would carry the day for me. When, at school, she suggested taking me to the theater, I did not, as I might have done if she had been a Negro, find a way of discouraging her, but agreed that she should pick me up at my house one evening. I then, very cleverly, left all the rest to my mother, who suggested to my father, as I knew she would, that it would not be very nice to let such a kind woman make the trip for nothing. Also, since it was a schoolteacher, I imagine that my mother countered the idea of sin with the idea of "education," which word, even with my father, carried a kind of bitter weight.

Before the teacher came my father took me aside to ask why she was coming, what interest she could possibly have in our house, in a boy like me. I said I didn't know but I, too, suggested that it had something to do with education. And I understood that my father was waiting for me to say something—I didn't quite know what; perhaps that I wanted his protection against this teacher and her "education." I said none of these things and the teacher came and we went out. It was clear, during the brief interview in our living room, that my father was agreeing very much against his will and that he would have refused permission if he had dared. The fact that he did not dare caused me to despise him: I had no way of knowing that he was facing in that living room a wholly unprecedented and frightening situation.

Later, when my father had been laid off from his job, this woman became very important to us. She was really a very sweet and generous woman and went to a great deal of trouble to be of help to us, particularly during one awful winter. My mother called her by the highest name she knew: she said she was a "christian." My father could scarcely disagree but during the four or five years of our relatively close association he never trusted her and was always trying to surprise in her open, Midwestern face the genuine, cunningly hidden, and hideous motivation. In later years, particularly when it began to be clear that this "education" of mine was going to lead me to perdition, he became more explicit and warned me that my white friends in high school were not really my friends and that I would see, when I was older, how white people would do anything to keep a Negro down. Some of them could be nice, he admitted, but none of them were to be trusted and most of them were not even nice. The best thing was to have as little to do with them as possible. I did not feel this way and I was certain, in my innocence, that I never would.

But the year which preceded my father's death had made a great change in my life. I had been living in New Jersey, working in defense plants, working and living among southerners, white and black. I knew about the south, of course, and about how southerners treated Negroes and how they expected them to behave, but it had never entered my mind that anyone would look at me and expect me to behave that way. I learned in New Jersey that to be a Negro meant, precisely, that one was never looked at but was simply at the mercy of the reflexes the color of one's skin caused in other people. I acted in New Jersey as I had always acted, that is as though I thought a great deal of myself—I had to act that way—with results that were, simply, unbelievable. I had scarcely arrived before I had earned the enmity, which was extraordinarily ingenious, of all my superiors and nearly all my co-workers. In the beginning, to make matters worse, I simply did not know what was happening. I did not know what I had done, and I shortly began to wonder what anyone could possibly do, to bring about such unanimous, active, and unbearably vocal hostility. I knew about Jim Crow but I had never experienced it. I went to the same self-service restaurant three times and stood with all the Princeton boys before the counter, waiting for a hamburger and coffee; it was always an extraordinarily long time before anything was set before me; but it was not until the fourth visit that I learned that, in fact, nothing had ever been set before me: I had simply picked something up. Negroes were not served there, I was told, and they had been waiting for me to realize that I was always the only Negro present. Once I was told this, I determined to go there all the time. But now they were ready for me and, though some dreadful scenes were subsequently enacted in that restaurant, I never ate there again.

It was the same story all over New Jersey, in bars, bowling alleys, diners, places to live. I was always being forced to leave, silently, or with mutual imprecations. I very shortly became notorious and children giggled behind me when I passed and their elders whispered or shouted—they really believed that I was mad. And it did begin to work on my mind, of course; I began to be afraid to go anywhere and to compensate for this I went places to which I really should not have gone and where, God knows, I had no desire to be. My reputation in town naturally enhanced my reputation at work and my working day became one long series of acrobatics designed to keep me out of trouble. I cannot say that these acrobatics succeeded. It began to seem that the machinery of the organization I worked for was turning over, day and night, with but one aim: to eject me. I was fired once, and contrived, with the aid of a friend from New York, to get back on the payroll; was fired again and bounced back again. It took a while to fire me for the third time, but the third time took. There were no loopholes anywhere. There was not even any way of getting back inside the gates.

That year in New Jersey lives in my mind as though it were the year during which, having an unsuspected predilection for it, I first contracted some dread, chronic disease, the unfailing symptom of which is a kind of blind fever, a pounding in the skull and fire in the bowels. Once this disease is contracted, one can never be really carefree again, for the fever, without an instant's warning, can recur at any moment. It can wreck more important things than race relations. There is not a Negro alive who does not have this rage in his blood—one has the choice, merely, of living with it consciously or surrendering to it. As for me, this fever has recurred in me, and does, and will until the day I die.

My last night in New Jersey, a white friend from New York took me to the nearest big town, Trenton, to go to the movies and have a few drinks. As it turned out, he also saved me from, at the very least, a violent whipping. Almost every detail of that night stands out very clearly in my memory. I even remember the name of the movie we saw because its title impressed me as being so patly ironical. It was a movie about the German occupation of France, starring Maureen O'Hara and Charles Laughton and called *This Land Is Mine*. I remember the name of the diner we walked into when the movie ended: it was the "American Diner." When we walked in the counterman asked what we wanted and I remember answering with the casual sharpness which had become my habit: "We want a hamburger and a cup of coffee, what do you think we want?" I do not know why, after a year of such rebuffs, I so completely failed to anticipate his answer, which was, of course, "We don't serve Negroes here." This reply failed to discompose me, at least for the moment. I made some sardonic comment about the name of the diner and we walked out into the streets.

This was the time of what was called the "brownout," when the lights in all American cities were very dim. When we reentered the streets something happened to me which had the force of an optical illusion, or a nightmare. The streets were very crowded and I was facing north. People were moving in every direction but it seemed to me, in that instant, that all of the people I could see, and many more than that, were moving toward me, against me, and that everyone was white. I remember how their faces gleamed. And I felt, like a physical sensation, a click at the nape of my neck as though some interior string connecting my head to my body had been cut. I began to walk. I heard my friend call after me, but I ignored him. Heaven only knows what was going on in his mind, but he had the good sense not to touch me—I don't know what would have happened if he had—and to keep me in sight. I don't know what was going on in my mind, either; I certainly had no conscious plan. I wanted to do something to crush these white faces, which were crushing me. I walked for perhaps a block or two until I came to an enormous, glittering, and fashionable restaurant in which I knew not even the intercession of the Virgin would cause me to be served. I pushed through the doors and took the first vacant seat I saw, at a table for two, and waited.

I do not know how long I waited and I rather wonder, until today, what I could possibly have looked like. Whatever I looked like, I frightened the waitress who shortly appeared, and the moment she appeared all of my fury flowed toward her. I hated her for her white face, and for her great, astounded, frightened eyes.

I felt that if she found a black man so frightening I would make her fright worthwhile.

She did not ask me what I wanted, but repeated, as though she had learned it somewhere, "We don't serve Negroes here." She did not say it with the blunt, derisive hostility to which I had grown so accustomed, but, rather, with a note of apology in her voice, and fear. This made me colder and more murderous than ever. I felt I had to do something with my hands. I wanted her to come close enough for me to get her neck between my hands.

So I pretended not to have understood her, hoping to draw her closer. And she did step a very short step closer, with her pencil poised incongruously over her pad, and repeated the formula: "... don't serve Negroes here."

Somehow, with the repetition of that phrase, which was already ringing in my head like a thousand bells of a nightmare, I realized that she would never come any closer and that I would have to strike from a distance. There was nothing on the table but an ordinary water-mug half full of water, and I picked this up and hurled it with all my strength at her. She ducked and it missed her and shattered against the mirror behind the bar. And, with that sound, my frozen blood abruptly thawed, I returned from wherever I had been, I saw, for the first time, the restaurant, the people with their mouths open, already, as it seemed to me, rising as one man, and I realized what I had done, and where I was, and I was frightened. I rose and began running for the door. A round, potbellied man grabbed me by the nape of the neck just as I reached the doors and began to beat me about the face. I kicked him and got loose and ran into the streets. My friend whispered, "Run!" and I ran.

My friend stayed outside the restaurant long enough to misdirect my pursuers and the police, who arrived, he told me, at once. I do not know what I said to him when he came to my room that night. I could not have said much. I felt, in the oddest, most awful way, that I had somehow betrayed him. I lived it over and over and over again, the way one relives an automobile accident after it has happened and one finds oneself alone and safe. I could not get over two facts, both equally difficult for the imagination to grasp, and one was that I could have been murdered. But the other was that I had been ready to commit murder. I saw nothing very clearly but I did see this: that my life, my real life, was in danger, and not from anything other people might do but from the hatred I carried in my own heart.

I had returned home around the second week in June in great haste because it seemed that my father's death and my mother's confinement were both but a matter of hours. In the case of my mother, it soon became clear that she had simply made a miscalculation. This had always been her tendency and I don't believe that a single one of us arrived in the world, or has since arrived anywhere else, on time. But none of us dawdled so intolerably about the business of being born as did my baby sister. We sometimes amused ourselves, during those endless, stifling weeks, by picturing the baby sitting within in the safe, warm dark, bitterly regretting the necessity of becoming a part of our chaos and stubbornly putting it off as long as possible. I understood her perfectly and congratulated her on showing such good sense so soon. Death, however, sat as purposefully at my father's bedside as life stirred within my mother's womb and it was harder to understand why he so lingered in that long shadow. It seemed that he had bent, and for a long time, too, all of his energies toward dying. Now death was ready for him but my father held back.

All of Harlem, indeed, seemed to be infected by waiting. I had never before known it to be so violently still. Racial tensions throughout this country were exacerbated during the early years of the war, partly because the labor market brought together hundreds of thousands of ill-prepared people and partly because Negro soldiers, regardless of where they were born, received their military training in the south. What happened in defense plants and army camps had repercussions, naturally, in every Negro ghetto. The situation in Harlem had grown bad enough for clergymen, policemen, educators, politicians, and social workers to assert in one breath that there was no "crime wave" and to offer, in the very next breath, suggestions as to how to combat it. These suggestions always seemed to involve playgrounds, despite the fact that racial skirmishes were occurring in the playgrounds, too. Playground or not, crime wave or not, the Harlem police force had been augmented in March, and the unrest grew—perhaps, in fact, partly as a result of the ghetto's instinctive hatred of policemen. Perhaps the most revealing news item, out of the steady parade of reports of muggings, stabbings, shootings, assaults, gang wars, and accusations of police brutality, is the item concerning six Negro girls who set upon a white girl in the subway because, as they all too accurately put it, she was stepping on their toes. Indeed she was, all over the nation. I had never before been so aware of policemen, on foot, on horseback, on corners, everywhere, always two by two. Nor had I ever been so aware of small knots of people. They were on stoops and on corners and in doorways, and what was striking about them, I think, was that they did not seem to be talking. Never, when I passed these groups, did the usual sound of a curse or a laugh ring out and neither did there seem to be any hum of gossip. There was certainly, on the other hand, occurring between them communication extraordinarily intense. Another thing that was striking was the unexpected diversity of the people who made up these groups. Usually, for example, one would see a group of sharpies standing on the street corner, jiving the passing chicks; or a group of older men, usually, for some reason, in the vicinity of a barber shop, discussing baseball scores, or the numbers, or making rather chilling observations about women they had known.

Women, in a general way, tended to be seen less often together—unless they were church women, or very young girls, or prostitutes met together for an unprofessional instant. But that summer I saw the strangest combinations: large, respectable, churchly matrons standing on the stoops or the corners with their hair tied up, together with a girl in sleazy satin whose face bore the marks of gin and the razor, or heavy-set, abrupt, no-nonsense older men, in company with the most disreputable and fanatical "race" men, or these same "race" men with the sharpies, or these sharpies with the churchly women. Seventh Day Adventists and Methodists and Spiritualists seemed to be hobnobbing with Holyrollers and they were all, alike, entangled with the most flagrant disbelievers; something heavy in their stance seemed to indicate that they had all, incredibly, seen a common vision, and on each face there seemed to be the same strange, bitter shadow.

The churchly women and the matter-of-fact, no-nonsense men had children in the Army. The sleazy girls they talked to had lovers there, the sharpies and the "race" men had friends and brothers there. It would have demanded an unquestioning patriotism, happily as uncommon in this country as it is undesirable, for these people not to have been disturbed by the bitter letters they received, by the newspaper stories they read, not to have been enraged by the posters, then to be found all over New York, which described the Japanese as "yellow-bellied Japs." It was only the "race" men, to be sure, who spoke ceaselessly of being revenged— how this vengeance was to be exacted was not clear—for the indignities and dangers suffered by Negro boys in uniform; but everybody felt a directionless, hopeless bitterness, as well as that panic which can scarcely be suppressed when one knows that a human being one loves is beyond one's reach, and in danger. This helplessness and this gnawing uneasiness does something, at length, to even the toughest mind. Perhaps the best way to sum all this up is to say that the people I knew felt, mainly, a peculiar kind of relief when they knew that their boys were being shipped out of the south, to do battle overseas. It was, perhaps, like feeling that the most dangerous part of a dangerous journey had been passed and that now, even if death should come, it would come with honor and without the complicity of their countrymen. Such a death would be, in short, a fact with which one could hope to live.

It was on the twenty-eighth of July, which I believe was a Wednesday, that I visited my father for the first time during his illness and for the last time in his life. The moment I saw him I knew why I had put off this visit so long. I had told my mother that I did not want to see him because I hated him. But this was not true. It was only that I had hated him and I wanted to hold on to this hatred. I did not want to look on him as a ruin: it was not a ruin I had hated. I imagine that one of the reasons people cling to their hates so stubbornly is because they sense, once hate is gone, that they will be forced to deal with pain.

We traveled out to him, his older sister and myself, to what seemed to be the very end of a very Long Island. It was hot and dusty and we wrangled, my aunt and I, all the way out, over the fact that I had recently begun to smoke and, as she said, to give myself airs. But I knew that she wrangled with me because she could not bear to face the fact of her brother's dying. Neither could I endure the reality of her despair, her unstated bafflement as to what had happened to her brother's life, and her own. So we wrangled and I smoked and from time to time she fell into a heavy reverie. Covertly, I watched her face, which was the face of an old woman; it had fallen in, the eyes were sunken arid lightless; soon she would be dying, too.

In my childhood—it had not been so long ago—I had thought her beautiful. She had been quick-witted and quick-moving and very generous with all the children and each of her visits had been an event. At one time one of my brothers and myself had thought of running away to live with her. Now she could no longer produce out of her handbag some unexpected and yet familiar delight. She made me feel pity and revulsion and fear. It was awful to realize that she no longer caused me to feel affection. The closer we came to the hospital the more querulous she became and at the same time, naturally, grew more dependent on me. Between pity and guilt and fear I began to feel that there was another me trapped in my skull like a jack-in-the-box who might escape my control at any moment and fill the air with screaming.

She began to cry the moment we entered the room and she saw him lying there, all shriveled and still, like a little black monkey. The great, gleaming apparatus which fed him and would have compelled him to be still even if he had been able to move brought to mind, not beneficence, but torture; the tubes entering his arm made me think of pictures I had seen when a child, of Gulliver, tied down by the pygmies on that island. My aunt wept and wept, there was a whistling sound in my father's throat; nothing was said; he could not speak. I wanted to take his hand, to say something. But I do not know what I could have said, even if he could have heard me. He was not really in that room with us, he had at last really embarked on his journey; and though my aunt told me that he said he was going to meet Jesus, I did not hear anything except that whistling in his throat. The doctor came back and we left, into that unbearable train again, and home. In the morning came the telegram saying that he was dead. Then the house was suddenly full of relatives, friends, hysteria, and confusion and I quickly left my mother and the children to the care of those impressive women, who, in Negro communities at least, automatically appear at times of bereavement armed with lotions, proverbs, and patience, and an ability to cook. I went downtown. By the time I returned, later the same day, my mother had been carried to the hospital and the baby had been born.

For my father's funeral I had nothing black to wear and this posed a nagging problem all day long. It was one of those problems, simple, or impossible of solution, to which the mind insanely clings in order to avoid the mind's real trouble. I spent most of that day at the downtown apartment of a girl I knew, celebrating my birthday with whisky and wondering what to wear that night. When planning a birthday celebration one naturally does not expect that it will be up against competition from a funeral and this girl had anticipated taking me out that night, for a big dinner and a nightclub afterwards. Sometime during the course of that long day we decided that we would go out anyway, when my father's funeral service was over. I imagine I decided it, since, as the funeral hour approached, it became clearer and clearer to me that I would not know what to do with myself when it was over. The girl, stifling her very lively concern as to the possible effects of the whisky on one of my father's chief mourners, concentrated on being conciliatory and practically helpful. She found a black shirt for me somewhere and ironed it and, dressed in the darkest pants and jacket I owned, and slightly drunk, I made my way to my father's funeral.

The chapel was full, but not packed, and very quiet. There were, mainly, my father's relatives, and his children, and here and there I saw faces I had not seen since childhood, the faces of my father's one-time friends. They were very dark and solemn now, seeming somehow to suggest that they had known all along that something like this would happen. Chief among the mourners was my aunt, who had quarreled with my father all his life; by which I do not mean to suggest that her mourning was insincere or that she had not loved him. I suppose that she was one of the few people in the world who had, and their incessant quarreling proved precisely the strength of the tie that bound them. The only other person in the world, as far as I knew, whose relationship to my father rivaled my aunt's in depth was my mother, who was not there.

It seemed to me, of course, that it was a very long funeral. But it was, if anything, a rather shorter funeral than most, nor, since there were no overwhelming, uncontrollable expressions of grief, could it be called—if I dare to use the word—successful. The minister who preached my father's funeral sermon was one of the few my father had still been seeing as he neared his end. He presented to us in his sermon a man whom none of us had ever seen—a man thoughtful, patient, and forbearing, a Christian inspiration to all who knew him; and a model for his children. And no doubt the children, in their disturbed and guilty state, were almost ready to believe this; he had been remote enough to be anything and, anyway, the shock of the incontrovertible, that it was really our father lying up there in that casket, prepared the mind for anything. His sister moaned and this grief-stricken moaning was taken as corroboration. The other faces held a dark, noncommittal thoughtfulness. This was not the man they had known, but they had scarcely expected to be confronted with him; this was, in a sense deeper than questions of fact, the man they had not known, and the man they had not known may have been the real one. The real man, whoever he had been, had suffered and now he was dead: this was all that was sure and all that mattered now. Every man in the chapel hoped that when his hour came he, too, would be eulogized, which is to say forgiven, and that all of his lapses, greeds, errors, and strayings from the truth would be invested with coherence and looked upon with charity. This was perhaps the last thing human beings could give each other and it was what they demanded, after all, of the Lord. Only the Lord saw the midnight tears, only He was present when one of His children, moaning and wringing hands, paced up and down the room. When one slapped one's child in anger the recoil in the heart reverberated through heaven and became part of the pain of the universe. And when the children were hungry and sullen and distrustful and one watched them, daily, growing wilder, and further away, and running headlong into danger, it was the Lord who knew what the charged heart endured as the strap was laid to the backside; the Lord alone who knew what one would have said if one had had, like the Lord, the gift of the living word. It was the Lord who knew of the impossibility every parent in that room faced: how to prepare the child for the day when the child would be despised and how to create in the child—by what means?—a stronger antidote to this poison than one had found for oneself. The avenues, side streets, bars, billiard halls, hospitals, police stations, and even the playgrounds of Harlem—not to mention the houses of correction, the jails, and the morgue—testified to the potency of the poison while remaining silent as to the efficacy of whatever antidote, irresistibly raising the question of whether or not such an antidote existed; raising, which was worse, the question of whether or not an antidote was desirable; perhaps poison should be fought with poison. With these several schisms in the mind and with more terrors in the heart than could be named, it was better not to judge the man who had gone down under an impossible burden. It was better to remember: Thou knowest this man's fall; but thou knowest not his wrassling.

While the preacher talked and I watched the children—years of changing their diapers, scrubbing them, slapping them, taking them to school, and scolding them had had the perhaps inevitable result of making me love them, though I am not sure I knew this then—my mind was busily breaking out with a rash of disconnected impressions. Snatches of popular songs, indecent jokes, bits of books I had read, movie sequences, faces, voices, political issues—I thought I was going mad; all these impressions suspended, as it were, in the solution of the faint nausea produced in me by the heat and liquor. For a moment I had the impression that my alcoholic breath, inefficiently disguised with chewing gum, filled the entire chapel. Then someone began singing one of my father's favorite songs and, abruptly, I was with him, sitting on his knee, in the hot, enormous, crowded church which was the first church we attended. It was the Abyssinian Baptist Church on 138th Street. We had not gone there long. With this image, a host of others came. I had forgotten, in the rage of my growing up, how proud my father had been of me when I was little. Apparently, I had had a voice and my father had liked to show me off before the members of the church. I had forgotten what he had looked like when he was pleased but now I remembered that he had always been grinning with pleasure when my solos ended. I even remembered certain expressions on his face when he teased my mother—had he loved her? I would never know. And when had it all begun to change? For now it seemed that he had not always been cruel. I remembered being taken for a haircut and scraping my knee on the footrest of the barber's chair and I remembered my father's face as he soothed my crying and applied the stinging iodine. Then I remembered our fights, fights which had been of the worst possible kind because my technique had been silence.

I remembered the one time in all our life together when we had really spoken to each other.

It was on a Sunday and it must have been shortly before I left home. We were walking, just the two of us, in our usual silence, to or from church. I was in high school and had been doing a lot of writing and I was, at about this time, the editor of the high school magazine. But I had also been a Young Minister and had been preaching from the pulpit. Lately, I had been taking fewer engagements and preached as rarely as possible. It was said in the church, quite truthfully, that I was "cooling off."

My father asked me abruptly, "You'd rather write than preach, wouldn't you?"

I was astonished at his question—because it was a real question. I answered, "Yes."

That was all we said. It was awful to remember that that was all we had ever said.

The casket now was opened and the mourners were being led up the aisle to look for the last time on the deceased. The assumption was that the family was too overcome with grief to be allowed to make this journey alone and I watched while my aunt was led to the casket and, muffled in black, and shaking, led back to her seat. I disapproved of forcing the children to look on their dead father, considering that the shock of his death, or, more truthfully, the shock of death as a reality, was already a little more than a child could bear, but my judgment in this matter had been overruled and there they were, bewildered and frightened and very small, being led, one by one, to the casket. But there is also something very gallant about children at such moments. It has something to do with their silence and gravity and with the fact that one cannot help them. Their legs, somehow, seem exposed, so that it is at once incredible and terribly clear that their legs are all they have to hold them up.

I had not wanted to go to the casket myself and I certainly had not wished to be led there, but there was no way of avoiding either of these forms. One of the deacons led me up and I looked on my father's face. I cannot say that it looked like him at all. His blackness had been equivocated by powder and there was no suggestion in that casket of what his power had or could have been. He was simply an old man dead, and it was hard to believe that he had ever given anyone either joy or pain. Yet, his life filled that room. Further up the avenue his wife was holding his newborn child. Life and death so close together, and love and hatred, and right and wrong, said something to me which I did not want to hear concerning man, concerning the life of man.

After the funeral, while I was downtown desperately celebrating my birthday, a Negro soldier, in the lobby of the Hotel Braddock, got into a fight with a white policeman over a Negro girl. Negro girls, white policemen, in or out of uniform, and Negro males—in or out of uniform—were part of the furniture of the lobby of the Hotel Braddock and this was certainly not the first time such an incident had occurred. It was destined, however, to receive an unprecedented publicity, for the fight between the policeman and the soldier ended with the shooting of the soldier. Rumor, flowing immediately to the streets outside, stated that the soldier had been shot in the back, an instantaneous and revealing invention, and that the soldier had died protecting a Negro woman. The facts were somewhat different—for example, the soldier had not been shot in the back, and was not dead, and the girl seems to have been as dubious a symbol of womanhood as her white counterpart in Georgia usually is, but no one was interested in the facts. They preferred the invention because this invention expressed and corroborated their hates and fears so perfectly. It is just as well to remember that people are always doing this. Perhaps many of those legends, including Christianity, to which the world clings began their conquest of the world with just some such concerted surrender to distortion. The effect, in Harlem, of this particular legend was like the effect of a lit match in a tin of gasoline. The mob gathered before the doors of the Hotel Braddock simply began to swell and to spread in every direction, and Harlem exploded.

The mob did not cross the ghetto lines. It would have been easy, for example, to have gone over Morningside Park on the west side or to have crossed the Grand Central railroad tracks at 125th Street on the east side, to wreak havoc in white neighborhoods. The mob seems to have been mainly interested in something more potent and real than the white face, that is, in white power, and the principal damage done during the riot of the summer of 1943 was to white business establishments in Harlem. It might have been a far bloodier story, of course, if, at the hour the riot began, these establishments had still been open. From the Hotel Braddock the mob fanned out, east and west along 125th Street, and for the entire length of Lenox, Seventh, and Eighth Avenues. Along each of the avenues, and along each major side street—116th, 125th, 135th, and so on—bars, stores, pawnshops, restaurants, even little luncheonettes had been smashed open and entered and looted—looted, it might be added, with more haste than efficiency. The shelves really looked as though a bomb had struck them. Cans of beans and soup and dog food, along with toilet paper, corn flakes, sardines and milk tumbled every which way, and abandoned cash registers and cases of beer leaned crazily out of the splintered windows and were strewn along the avenues. Sheets, blankets, and clothing of every description formed a kind of path, as though people had dropped them while running. I truly had not realized that Harlem had so many stores until I saw them all smashed open; the first time the word wealth ever entered my mind in relation to Harlem was when I saw it scattered in the streets. But one's first, incongruous impression of plenty was countered immediately by an impression of waste. None of this was doing anybody any good. It would have been better to have left the plate glass as it had been and the goods lying in the stores.

It would have been better, but it would also have been intolerable, for Harlem had needed something to smash. To smash something is the ghetto's chronic need. Most of the time it is the members of the ghetto who smash each other, and themselves. But as long as the ghetto walls are standing there will always come a moment when these outlets do not work. That summer, for example, it was not enough to get into a fight on Lenox Avenue, or curse out one's cronies in the barber shops. If ever, indeed, the violence which fills Harlem's churches, pool halls, and bars erupts outward in a more direct fashion, Harlem and its citizens are likely to vanish in an apocalyptic flood. That this is not likely to happen is due to a great many reasons, most hidden and powerful among them the Negro's real relation to the white American. This relation prohibits, simply, anything as uncomplicated and satisfactory as pure hatred. In order really to hate white people, one has to blot so much out of the mind—and the heart—that this hatred itself becomes an exhausting and self-destructive pose. But this does not mean, on the other hand, that love comes easily: the white world is too powerful, too complacent, too ready with gratuitous humiliation, and, above all, too ignorant and too innocent for that. One is absolutely forced to make perpetual qualifications and one's own reactions are always canceling each other out. It is this, really, which has driven so many people mad, both white and black. One is always in the position of having to decide between amputation and gangrene. Amputation is swift but time may prove that the amputation was not necessary—or one may delay the amputation too long. Gangrene is slow, but it is impossible to be sure that one is reading one's symptoms right. The idea of going through life as a cripple is more than one can bear, and equally unbearable is the risk of swelling up slowly, in agony, with poison. And the trouble, finally, is that the risks are real even if the choices do not exist.

"But as for me and my house," my father had said, "we will serve the Lord." I wondered, as we drove him to his resting place, what this line had meant for him. I had heard him preach it many times. I had preached it once myself, proudly giving it an interpretation different from my father's. Now the whole thing came back to me, as though my father and I were on our way to Sunday school and I were memorizing the golden text: And if it seem evil unto you to serve the Lord, choose you this day whom you will serve; whether the gods which your fathers served that were on the other side of the flood, or the gods of the "Amorites, in whose land ye dwell: but as for me and my house, we will serve the Lord. I suspected in these familiar lines a meaning which had never been there for me before. All of my father's texts and songs, which I had decided were meaningless, were arranged before me at his death like empty bottles, waiting to hold the meaning which life would give them for me. This was his legacy: nothing is ever escaped. That bleakly memorable morning I hated the unbelievable streets and the Negroes and whites who had, equally, made them that way. But I knew that it was folly, as my father would have said, this bitterness was folly. It was necessary to hold on to the things that mattered. The dead man mattered, the new life mattered; blackness and whiteness did not matter; to believe that they did was to acquiesce in one's own destruction. Hatred, which could destroy so much, never failed to destroy the man who hated and this was an immutable law.

It began to seem that one would have to hold in the mind forever two ideas which seemed to be in opposition. The first idea was acceptance, the acceptance, totally without rancor, of life as it is, and men as they are: in the light of this idea, it goes without saying that injustice is a commonplace. But this did not mean that one could be complacent, for the second idea was of equal power: that one must never, in one's own life, accept these injustices as commonplace but must fight them with all one's strength. This fight begins, however, in the heart and it now had been laid to my charge to keep my own heart free of hatred and despair. This intimation made my heart heavy and, now that my father was irrecoverable, I wished that he had been beside me so that I could have searched his face for the answers which only the future would give me now.

FOR INFORMAL WRITING

Baldwin's essay, like many in this volume, examines politics through the lens of personal experience. How does this kind of personal narrative make the political aspects of Baldwin's work more persuasive than it might be otherwise? Reference specific passages from the text that might support the personal-as-political aspects of this work.

FOR DISCUSSION

1. How does Baldwin use the birth of a sibling and the death of his father as frames for the narrative? Comment on the effectiveness of these frames.
2. How does Baldwin's personal essay characterize life in Harlem? What is your sense of his experience? How do you know?
3. Baldwin writes, "Hatred, which could destroy so much, never failed to destroy the man who hated and this was an immutable law." What does Baldwin mean by this? What evidence backs up your perspective?

FOR WRITING

Much has been written about Harlem, New York, as a political and cultural space that evoked the African American experience in twentieth-century United States. Research literary depictions of Harlem from one or two well-known writers of the Harlem Renaissance and after. Using specific details from your reading, compare and contrast these characterizations; to what conclusion do you come?

> ### WHAT'S NEW IS OLD
>
> Look at Baldwin's essay alongside a more current essay about race and politics in the United States—for instance, "The American Nightmare" by Ibram X. Kendi or "My President Was Black" by Ta-Nehisi Coates. What are the similarities? Differences? To what conclusion do you come after reviewing the two essays on similar subjects?

Letter from a Birmingham Jail, an Excerpt (1963)

Martin Luther King, Jr. (1929–1968)

An icon (if not the icon) of the modern civil rights movement, and best-known for this essay as well as his "I Have a Dream" speech, the Rev. Dr. Martin Luther King, Jr., earned his doctorate at Boston University in 1955. In 1959, King visited the birthplace of Mahatma Gandhi, a trip that inspired King's commitment to nonviolent activism. In 1960, King was arrested after refusing to leave a lunch counter at a department store in Raleigh, North Carolina. In response, President John F. Kennedy called Coretta Scott King to express his support, helping to recognize Martin Luther King, Jr., as a preeminent activist. He delivered the "I Have a Dream" speech at the Lincoln Memorial in 1963, and he received the Nobel Peace Prize in 1964. Dr. King was assassinated in 1968. "Letter From a Birmingham Jail" was written in longhand after King and supporters were arrested after a peaceful demonstration in downtown Birmingham, Alabama.

My Dear Fellow Clergyman:

While confined here in the Birmingham city jail, I came across your recent statement calling our present activities "unwise and untimely." Seldom, if ever, do I pause to answer criticism of my work and ideas. If I sought to answer all of the criticisms that cross my desk, my secretaries would be engaged in little else in the course of the day, and I would have no time for constructive work. But since I feel that you are men of genuine good will and your criticisms are sincerely set forth, I would like to answer your statement in what I hope will be patient and reasonable terms.

Reprinted by arrangement with The Heirs to the Estate of Martin Luther King Jr., c/o Writers House as agent for the proprietor New York, NY. Copyright © 1963 by Dr. Martin Luther King, Jr. Renewed © 1991 by Coretta Scott King.

I think I should give the reason for my being in Birmingham, since you have been influenced by the argument of "outsiders coming in." I have the honor of serving as president of the Southern Christian Leadership Conference, an organization operating in every southern state, with headquarters in Atlanta, Georgia. We have some eighty-five affiliate organizations all across the South, one being the Alabama Christian Movement for Human Rights. Whenever necessary and possible, we share staff, educational and financial resources with our affiliates. Several months ago our local affiliate here in Birmingham invited us to be on call to engage in a nonviolent direct-action program if such were deemed necessary. We readily consented, and when the hour came we lived up to our promises. So I am here, along with several members of my staff, because we were invited here. I am here because I have basic organizational ties here.

Beyond this, I am in Birmingham because injustice is here. Just as the eighth-century prophets left their little villages and carried their "thus saith the Lord" far beyond the boundaries of their hometowns; and just as the Apostle Paul left his little village of Tarsus and carried the gospel of Jesus Christ to practically every hamlet and city of the Greco-Roman world, I too am compelled to carry the gospel of freedom beyond my particular hometown. Like Paul, I must constantly respond to the Macedonian call for aid.

Moreover, I am cognizant of the interrelatedness of all communities and states. I cannot sit idly by in Atlanta and not be concerned about what happens in Birmingham. Injustice anywhere is a threat to justice everywhere. We are caught in an inescapable network of mutuality, tied in a single garment of destiny. Whatever affects one directly affects all indirectly. Never again can we afford to live with the narrow, provincial "outside agitator" idea. Anyone who lives inside the United States can never be considered an outsider.

You deplore the demonstrations that are presently taking place in Birmingham. But I am sorry that your statement did not express a similar concern for the conditions that brought the demonstrations into being. I am sure that each of you would want to go beyond the superficial social analyst who looks merely at effects and does not grapple with underlying causes. I would not hesitate to say that it is unfortunate that so-called demonstrations are taking place in Birmingham at this time, but I would say in more emphatic terms that it is even more unfortunate that the white power structure of this city left the Negro community with no other alternative.

In any nonviolent campaign there are four basic steps: collection of the facts to determine whether injustices are alive, negotiation, self-purification, and direct action. We have gone through all of these steps in Birmingham. There can be no gainsaying of the fact that racial injustice engulfs this community. Birmingham is probably the most thoroughly segregated city in the United States. Its ugly record of police brutality is known in every section of this country. Its unjust treatment of Negroes in the courts is a notorious reality. There have been more unsolved bombings of Negro homes and churches in Birmingham than in any other city in this nation. These are the hard, brutal, and unbelievable facts. On the basis of them, Negro leaders sought to negotiate with the city fathers. But the political leaders consistently refused to engage in good-faith negotiation.

Then came the opportunity last September to talk with some of the leaders of the economic community. In these negotiating sessions certain promises were made by the merchants, such as the promise to remove the humiliating racial signs from the stores. On the basis of these promises, Reverend Shuttlesworth and the leaders of the Alabama Christian Movement for Human Rights agreed to call a moratorium on any type of demonstration. As the weeks and months unfolded, we realized that we were the victims of a broken promise. The signs remained. As in so many experiences of the past, we were confronted with blasted hopes, and the dark shadow of a deep disappointment settled upon us. So we had no alternative except that of preparing for direct action, whereby we would present our very bodies as a means of laying our case before the conscience of the local and national community. We were not unmindful of the difficulties involved. So we decided to go through a process of self-purification. We started having workshops on nonviolence and repeatedly asked ourselves the questions, "Are you able to accept blows without retaliating?" and "Are you able to endure the ordeals of jail?" We decided to set our direct-action program around the Easter season, realizing that, with exception of Christmas, this was the largest shopping period of the year. Knowing that a strong economic withdrawal program would be the by-product of direct action, we felt that this was the best time to bring pressure on the merchants for the needed changes. Then it occurred to us that the March election was ahead, and so we speedily decided to postpone action until after election day. When we discovered that Mr. Conner was in the runoff, we decided again to postpone action so that the demonstration could not be used to cloud the issues. At this time we agreed to begin our nonviolent witness the day after the runoff.

This reveals that we did not move irresponsibly into direct action. We, too, wanted to see Mr. Conner defeated, so we went through postponement after postponement to aid in this community need. After this we felt that direct action could be delayed no longer.

You may well ask, "Why direct action, why sit-ins, marches, and so forth? Isn't negotiation a better path?" You are exactly right in your call for negotiation. Indeed, this is the purpose of direct action. Nonviolent direct action seeks to create such a crisis and establish such creative tension that a community that has consistently refused to negotiate is forced to confront the issue. It seeks so to dramatize the issue that it can no longer be ignored. I just referred to the creation of tension as a part of the work of the nonviolent resister. This may sound rather shocking. But I must confess that I am not afraid of the word "tension." I have earnestly worked and preached against violent tension, but there is a type of constructive nonviolent tension that is necessary for growth. Just as Socrates felt that it was necessary to create a tension in the mind so that individuals could rise from the bondage of myths and half-truths to the unfettered realm of creative analysis and objective appraisal, we must see the need of having nonviolent gadflies to create the kind of tension in society that will help men to rise from the dark depths of prejudice and racism to the majestic heights of understanding and brotherhood.

So, the purpose of direct action is to create a situation so crisis-packed that it will inevitably open the door to negotiation. We therefore concur with you in your call for negotiation. Too long has our beloved Southland been bogged down in the tragic attempt to live in monologue rather than dialogue.

One of the basic points in your statement is that our acts are untimely. Some have asked, "Why didn't you give the new administration time to act?" The only answer that I can give to this inquiry is that the new administration must be prodded about as much as the outgoing one before it acts. We will be sadly mistaken if we feel that the election of Mr. Boutwell will bring the millennium to Birmingham. While Mr. Boutwell is much more articulate and gentle than Mr. Conner, they are both segregationists, dedicated to the task of maintaining the status quo. The hope I see in Mr. Boutwell is that he will be reasonable enough to see the futility of massive resistance to desegregation. But he will not see this without pressure from the devotees of civil rights. My friends, I must say to you that we have not made a single gain in civil rights without determined legal and nonviolent pressure. History is the long and tragic story of the fact that privileged groups seldom give up their privileges voluntarily. Individuals may see the moral light and voluntarily give up their unjust posture; but, as Reinhold Niebuhr has reminded us, groups are more immoral than individuals.

We know through painful experience that freedom is never voluntarily given by the oppressor; it must be demanded by the oppressed. Frankly, I have never yet engaged in a direct-action movement that was "well timed" according to the timetable of those who have not suffered unduly from the disease of segregation. For years now I have heard the word "wait." It rings in the ear of every Negro with a piercing familiarity. This "wait" has almost always meant "never." It has been a tranquilizing thalidomide, relieving the emotional stress for a moment, only to give birth to an ill-formed infant of frustration. We must come to see with the distinguished jurist of yesterday that "justice too long delayed is justice denied."

We have waited for more than three hundred and forty years for our God-given and constitutional rights. The nations of Asia and Africa are moving with jetlike speed toward the goal of political independence, and we still creep at horse-and-buggy pace toward the gaining of a cup of coffee at a lunch counter. I guess it is easy for those who have never felt the stinging darts of segregation to say "wait." But when you have seen vicious mobs lynch your mothers and fathers at will and drown your sisters and brothers at whim; when you have seen hate-filled policemen curse, kick, brutalize, and even kill your black brothers and sisters with impunity; when you see the vast majority of your twenty million Negro brothers smothering in an airtight cage of poverty in the midst of an affluent society; when you suddenly find your tongue twisted and your speech stammering as you seek to explain to your six-year-old daughter why she cannot go to the public amusement park that has just been advertised on television, and see tears welling up in her little eyes when she is told that Funtown is closed to colored children, and see the depressing clouds of inferiority begin to form in her little mental sky, and see her begin to distort her little personality by unconsciously developing a bitterness toward white people; when you have to concoct an answer for a five-year-old son asking in agonizing pathos, "Daddy, why do white people treat colored people so mean?"; when you take a cross-country drive and find it necessary to sleep night after night in the uncomfortable corners of your automobile because no motel will accept you; when you are humiliated day in and day out by nagging signs reading "white" and "colored"; when your first name becomes "nigger" and your middle name becomes "boy" (however old you are) and your last name becomes "John," and when your wife and mother are never given the respected title "Mrs."; when you are harried by day and haunted by night by the fact that you are a Negro, living constantly at tiptoe stance, never knowing what to expect next, and plagued with inner fears and outer resentments; when you are forever fighting a degenerating sense of "nobodyness"—then you will understand why we find it difficult to wait. There comes a time when the cup of endurance runs over and men are no longer willing to be plunged into an abyss of injustice where they experience the bleakness of corroding despair. I hope, sirs, you can understand our legitimate and unavoidable impatience.

You express a great deal of anxiety over our willingness to break laws. This is certainly a legitimate concern. Since we so diligently urge people to obey the Supreme Court's decision of 1954 outlawing segregation in the public schools, it is rather strange and paradoxical to find us consciously breaking laws. One may well ask, "How can you advocate breaking some laws and obeying others?" The answer is found in the fact that there are two types of laws: there are just laws, and there are unjust laws. I would agree with St. Augustine that "an unjust law is no law at all."

Now, what is the difference between the two? How does one determine when a law is just or unjust? A just law is a man-made code that squares with the moral law, or the law of God. An unjust law is a code that is out of harmony with the moral law. To put it in the terms of St. Thomas Aquinas, an unjust law is a human law that is not rooted in eternal and natural law. Any law that uplifts human personality is just. Any law that degrades human personality is unjust. All segregation statutes are unjust because segregation distorts the soul and damages the personality. It gives the segregator a false sense of superiority and the segregated a false sense of inferiority. To use the words of Martin Buber, the great Jewish philosopher, segregation substitutes an "I-it" relationship for the "I-thou" relationship and ends up relegating persons to the status of things. So segregation is not only politically, economically, and sociologically unsound, but it is morally wrong and sinful. Paul Tillich has said that sin is separation. Isn't segregation an existential expression of man's tragic separation, an expression of his awful estrangement, his terrible sinfulness? So I can urge men to obey the 1954 decision of the Supreme Court because it is morally right, and I can urge them to disobey segregation ordinances because they are morally wrong.

Let us turn to a more concrete example of just and unjust laws. An unjust law is a code that a majority inflicts on a minority that is not binding on itself. This is difference made legal. On the other hand, a just law is a code that a majority compels a minority to follow, and that it is willing to follow itself. This is sameness made legal.

Let me give another explanation. An unjust law is a code inflicted upon a minority which that minority had no part in enacting or creating because it did not have the unhampered right to vote. Who can say that the legislature of Alabama which set up the segregation laws was democratically elected? Throughout the state of Alabama all types of conniving methods are used to prevent Negroes from becoming registered voters, and there are some counties without a single Negro registered to vote, despite the fact that the Negroes constitute a majority of the population. Can any law set up in such a state be considered democratically structured?

These are just a few examples of unjust and just laws. There are some instances when a law is just on its face and unjust in its application. For instance, I was arrested Friday on a charge of parading without a permit. Now, there is nothing wrong with an ordinance which requires a permit for a parade, but when the ordinance is used to preserve segregation and to deny citizens the First Amendment privilege of peaceful assembly and peaceful protest, then it becomes unjust.

Of course, there is nothing new about this kind of civil disobedience. It was seen sublimely in the refusal of Shadrach, Meshach, and Abednego to obey the laws of Nebuchadnezzar because a higher moral law was involved. It was practiced superbly by the early Christians, who were willing to face hungry lions and the excruciating pain of chopping blocks before submitting to certain unjust laws of the Roman Empire. To a degree, academic freedom is a reality today because Socrates practiced civil disobedience.

We can never forget that everything Hitler did in Germany was "legal" and everything the Hungarian freedom fighters did in Hungary was "illegal." It was "illegal" to aid and comfort a Jew in Hitler's Germany. But I am sure that if I had lived in Germany during that time, I would have aided and comforted my Jewish brothers even though it was illegal. If I lived in a Communist country today where certain principles dear to the Christian faith are suppressed, I believe I would openly advocate disobeying these anti-religious laws.

I must make two honest confessions to you, my Christian and Jewish brothers. First, I must confess that over the last few years I have been gravely disappointed with the white moderate. I have almost reached the regrettable conclusion that the Negro's great stumbling block in the stride toward freedom is not the White Citizens Councillor or the Ku Klux Klanner but the white moderate who is more devoted to order than to justice; who prefers a negative peace which is the absence of tension to a positive peace which is the presence of justice; who constantly says, "I agree with you in the goal you seek, but I can't agree with your methods of direct action"; who paternalistically feels that he can set the timetable for another man's freedom; who lives by the myth of time; and who constantly advises the Negro to wait until a "more convenient season." Shallow understanding from people of good will is more frustrating than absolute misunderstanding from people of ill will. Lukewarm acceptance is much more bewildering than outright rejection.

In your statement you asserted that our actions, even though peaceful, must be condemned because they precipitate violence. But can this assertion be logically made? Isn't this like condemning the robbed man because his possession of money precipitated the evil act of robbery? Isn't this like condemning Socrates because his unswerving commitment to truth and his philosophical delvings precipitated the misguided popular mind to make him drink the hemlock? Isn't this like condemning Jesus because His unique God-consciousness and never-ceasing devotion to His will precipitated the evil act of crucifixion? We must come to see, as federal courts have consistently affirmed, that it is immoral to urge an individual to withdraw his efforts to gain his basic constitutional rights because the quest precipitates violence. Society must protect the robbed and punish the robber.

I had also hoped that the white moderate would reject the myth of time. I received a letter this morning from a white brother in Texas which said, "All Christians know that the colored people will receive equal rights eventually, but is it possible that you are in too great of a religious hurry? It has taken Christianity almost 2000 years to accomplish what it has. The teachings of Christ take time to come to earth." All that is said here grows out of a tragic misconception of time. It is the strangely irrational notion that there is something in the very flow of time that will inevitably cure all ills. Actually, time is neutral. It can be used either destructively or constructively. I am coming to feel that the people of ill will have used time much more effectively than the people of good will. We will have to repent in this generation not merely for the vitriolic words and actions of the bad people but for the appalling silence of the good people. We must come to see that human progress never rolls in on wheels of inevitability. It comes through the tireless efforts and persistent work of men willing to be coworkers with God, and without this hard work time itself becomes an ally of the forces of social stagnation.

You spoke of our activity in Birmingham as extreme. At first I was rather disappointed that fellow clergymen would see my nonviolent efforts as those of an extremist. I started thinking about the fact that I stand in the middle of two opposing forces in the Negro community. One is a force of complacency made up of Negroes who, as a result of long years of oppression, have been so completely drained of self-respect and a sense of "somebodyness" that they have adjusted to segregation, and, on the other hand, of a few Negroes in the middle class who, because of a degree of academic and economic security and because at points they profit by segregation, have unconsciously become insensitive to the problems of the masses. The other force is one of bitterness and hatred and comes perilously close to advocating violence. It is expressed in the various black nationalist groups that are springing up over the nation, the largest and best known being Elijah Muhammad's Muslim movement. This movement is nourished by the contemporary frustration over the continued existence of racial discrimination. It is made up of people who have lost faith in America, who have absolutely repudiated Christianity, and who have concluded that the white man is an incurable devil.

I have tried to stand between these two forces, saying that we need not follow the do-nothingism of the complacent or the hatred and despair of the black nationalist. There is a more excellent way, of love and nonviolent protest. I'm grateful to God that, through the Negro church, the dimension of nonviolence entered our struggle.

If this philosophy had not emerged, I am convinced that by now many streets of the South would be flowing with floods of blood. And I am further convinced that if our white brothers dismiss as "rabble-rousers" and "outside agitators" those of us who are working through the channels of nonviolent direct action and refuse to support our nonviolent efforts, millions of Negroes, out of frustration and despair, will seek solace and security in black nationalist ideologies, a development that will lead inevitably to a frightening racial nightmare.

Oppressed people cannot remain oppressed forever. The urge for freedom will eventually come. This is what has happened to the American Negro.

Something within has reminded him of his birthright of freedom; something without has reminded him that he can gain it. Consciously and unconsciously, he has been swept in by what the Germans call the *Zeitgeist,* and with his black brothers of Africa and his brown and yellow brothers of Asia, South America, and the Caribbean, he is moving with a sense of cosmic urgency toward the promised land of racial justice. Recognizing this vital urge that has engulfed the Negro community, one should readily understand public demonstrations. The Negro has many pent-up resentments and latent frustrations. He has to get them out. So let him march sometime; let him have his prayer pilgrimages to the city hall; understand why he must have sit-ins and freedom rides. If his repressed emotions do not come out in these nonviolent ways, they will come out in ominous expressions of violence. This is not a threat; it is a fact of history. So I have not said to my people, "Get rid of your discontent." But I have tried to say that this normal and healthy discontent can be channeled through the creative outlet of nonviolent direct action. Now this approach is being dismissed as extremist. I must admit that I was initially disappointed in being so categorized.

But as I continued to think about the matter, I gradually gained a bit of satisfaction from being considered an extremist. Was not Jesus an extremist in love?—"Love your enemies, bless them that curse you, pray for them that despitefully use you." Was not Amos an extremist for justice?—"Let justice roll down like waters and righteousness like a mighty stream." Was not Paul an extremist for the gospel of Jesus Christ?—"I bear in my body the marks of the Lord Jesus." Was not Martin Luther an extremist?—"Here I stand; I can do no other so help me God." Was not John Bunyan an extremist?—"I will stay in jail to the end of my days before I make a mockery of my conscience." Was not Abraham Lincoln an extremist?—"This nation cannot survive half slave and half free." Was not Thomas Jefferson an extremist?—"We hold these truths to be self-evident, that all men are created equal." So the question is not whether we will be extremist, but what kind of extremists we will be. Will we be extremists for hate, or will we be extremists for love? Will we be extremists for the preservation of injustice, or will we be extremists for the cause of justice?

I had hoped that the white moderate would see this. Maybe I was too optimistic. Maybe I expected too much. I guess I should have realized that few members of a race that has oppressed another race can understand or appreciate the deep groans and passionate yearnings of those that have been oppressed, and still fewer have the vision to see that injustice must be rooted out by strong, persistent, and determined action. I am thankful, however, that some of our white brothers have grasped the meaning of this social revolution and committed themselves to it. They are still all too small in quantity, but they are big in quality. Some, like Ralph McGill, Lillian Smith, Harry Golden, and James Dabbs, have written about our struggle in eloquent, prophetic, and understanding terms. Others have marched with us down nameless streets of the South. They sat in with us at lunch counters and rode in with us on the freedom rides. They have languished in filthy roach-infested jails, suffering the abuse and brutality of angry policemen who see them as "dirty nigger lovers." They, unlike many of their moderate brothers, have recognized the urgency of the moment and sensed the need for powerful "action" antidotes to combat the disease of segregation.

Let me rush on to mention my other disappointment. I have been disappointed with the white church and its leadership. Of course, there are some notable exceptions. I am not unmindful of the fact that each of you has taken some significant stands on this issue. I commend you, Reverend Stallings, for your Christian stand this past Sunday in welcoming Negroes to your Baptist Church worship service on a nonsegregated basis. I commend the Catholic leaders of this state for integrating Springhill College several years ago.

But despite these notable exceptions, I must honestly reiterate that I have been disappointed with the church. I do not say that as one of those negative critics who can always find something wrong with the church. I say it as a minister of the gospel who loves the church, who was nurtured in its bosom, who has been sustained by its Spiritual blessings, and who will remain true to it as long as the cord of life shall lengthen.

I had the strange feeling when I was suddenly catapulted into the leadership of the bus protest in Montgomery several years ago that we would have the support of the white church. I felt that the white ministers, priests, and rabbis of the South would be some of our strongest allies. Instead, some few have been outright opponents, refusing to understand the freedom movement and misrepresenting its leaders; all too many others have been more cautious than courageous and have remained silent behind the anesthetizing security of stained-glass windows.

In spite of my shattered dreams of the past, I came to Birmingham with the hope that the white religious leadership of this community would see the justice of our cause and with deep moral concern serve as the channel through which our just grievances could get to the power structure. I had hoped that each of you would understand. But again I have been disappointed.

I have heard numerous religious leaders of the South call upon their worshipers to comply with a desegregation decision because it is the law, but I have longed to hear white ministers say, follow this decree because integration is morally right and the Negro is your brother. In the midst of blatant injustices inflicted upon the Negro, I have watched white churches stand on the sidelines and merely mouth pious irrelevancies and sanctimonious trivialities. In the midst of a mighty struggle to rid our nation of racial and economic injustice, I have heard so many ministers say, "Those are social issues which the gospel has nothing to do with," and I have watched so many churches commit themselves to a completely otherworldly religion which made a strange distinction between bodies and souls, the sacred and the secular.

There was a time when the church was very powerful. It was during that period that the early Christians rejoiced when they were deemed worthy to suffer for what they believed. In those days the church was not merely a thermometer that recorded the ideas and principles of popular opinion; it was the thermostat that transformed the mores of society. Wherever the early Christians entered a town the power structure got disturbed and immediately sought to convict them for being "disturbers of the peace" and "outside agitators." But they went on with the conviction that they were "a colony of heaven" and had to obey God rather than man. They were small in number but big in commitment. They were too God-intoxicated to be "astronomically intimidated." They brought an end to such ancient evils as infanticide and gladiatorial contest.

Things are different now. The contemporary church is so often a weak, ineffectual voice with an uncertain sound. It is so often the arch supporter of the status quo. Far from being disturbed by the presence of the church, the power structure of the average community is consoled by the church's often vocal sanction of things as they are.

But the judgment of God is upon the church as never before. If the church of today does not recapture the sacrificial spirit of the early church, it will lose its authentic ring, forfeit the loyalty of millions, and be dismissed as an irrelevant social club with no meaning for the twentieth century. I meet young people every day whose disappointment with the church has risen to outright disgust.

I hope the church as a whole will meet the challenge of this decisive hour. But even if the church does not come to the aid of justice, I have no despair about the future. I have no fear about the outcome of our struggle in Birmingham, even if our motives are presently misunderstood. We will reach the goal of freedom in Birmingham and all over the nation, because the goal of America is freedom. Abused and scorned though we may be, our destiny is tied up with the destiny of America. Before the Pilgrims landed at Plymouth, we were here. Before the pen of Jefferson scratched across the pages of history the majestic words of the Declaration of Independence, we were here. For more than two centuries our forepar-ents labored here without wages; they made cotton king; and they built the homes of their masters in the midst of brutal injustice and shameful humiliation—and yet out of a bottomless vitality our people continue to thrive and develop. If the inexpressible cruelties of slavery could not stop us, the opposition we now face will surely fail. We will win our freedom because the sacred heritage of our nation and the eternal will of God are embodied in our echoing demands.

I must close now. But before closing I am impelled to mention one other point in your statement that troubled me profoundly. You warmly commended the Birmingham police force for keeping "order" and "preventing violence." I don't believe you would have so warmly commended the police force if you had seen its angry violent dogs literally biting six unarmed, nonviolent Negroes. I don't believe you would so quickly commend the policemen if you would observe their ugly and inhuman treatment of Negroes here in the city jail; if you would watch them push and curse old Negro women and young Negro girls; if you would see them slap and kick old Negro men and young boys, if you would observe them, as they did on two occasions, refusing to give us food because we wanted to sing our grace together. I'm sorry that I can't join you in your praise for the police department.

It is true that they have been rather disciplined in their public handling of the demonstrators. In this sense they have been publicly "nonviolent." But for what purpose? To preserve the evil system of segregation. Over the last few years I have consistently preached that nonviolence demands that the means we use must be as pure as the ends we seek. So I have tried to make it clear that it is wrong to use immoral means to attain moral ends. But now I must affirm that it is just as wrong, or even more, to use moral means to preserve immoral ends.

I wish you had commended the Negro demonstrators of Birmingham for their sublime courage, their willingness to suffer, and their amazing discipline in the midst of the most inhuman provocation. One day the South will recognize its real heroes. They will be the James Merediths, courageously and with a majestic sense of purpose facing jeering and hostile mobs and the agonizing loneliness that characterizes the life of the pioneer. They will be old, oppressed, battered Negro women, symbolized in a seventy-two-year-old woman of Montgomery, Alabama, who rose up with a sense of dignity and with her people decided not to ride the segregated buses, and responded to one who inquired about her tiredness with ungrammatical profundity, "My feets is tired, but my soul is rested." They will be young high school and college students, young ministers of the gospel and a host of their elders courageously and nonviolently sitting in at lunch counters and willingly going to jail for conscience's sake. One day the South will know that when these disinherited children of God sat down at lunch counters they were in reality standing up for the best in the American dream and the most sacred values in our Judeo-Christian heritage.

Never before have I written a letter this long—or should I say a book? I'm afraid that it is much too long to take your precious time. I can assure you that it would have been much shorter if I had been writing from a comfortable desk, but what else is there to do when you are alone for days in the dull monotony of a narrow jail cell other than write long letters, think strange thoughts, and pray long prayers?

If I have said anything in this letter that is an understatement of the truth and is indicative of an unreasonable impatience, I beg you to forgive me. If I have said anything in this letter that is an overstatement of the truth and is indicative of my having a patience that makes me patient with anything less than brotherhood, I beg God to forgive me.

Yours for the cause of Peace and Brotherhood,
MARTIN LUTHER KING, JR.

FOR INFORMAL WRITING

Is this essay about justice or reconciliation—or both? What evidence in the text persuades you one way or another? Why?

FOR DISCUSSION

1. With your class, analyze King's use of language. What do you notice about it? What effect does it have on you? Why?
2. In the letter, King offers justifications for the demonstrations that led to his imprisonment specifically and for political demonstrations more generally. Which of these justifications is the most powerful, and why?
3. One of the reasons that instructors like to assign this essay—and like to see it in books such as this—is its rhetorical structure. First, what does that mean? Consider examples such as this: "You spoke of our activity in Birmingham as extreme." Who is "you," and what is gained by addressing this audience directly? How does King follow up this assertion? In addition, King uses a rhetorical strategy called "call and response." What is it? How does he use it?

FOR WRITING

Throughout "Letter from a Birmingham Jail," King employs religious allusion, also addressing the letter to "My Dear Fellow Clergymen." How do biblical and other religious references work in this essay? (For instance, "Of course, there is nothing new about this kind of civil disobedience. It was seen sublimely in the refusal of Shadrach, Meshach, and Abednego to obey the laws of Nebuchadnezzar because a higher moral law was involved. It was practiced superbly by the early Christians, who were willing to face hungry lions and the excruciating pain of chopping blocks before submitting to certain unjust laws of the Roman Empire.") Why do you think King employed references such as this? What is the (hoped for) result of this strategy?

The Ballot or the Bullet (1964)
Malcolm X (1925–1965)

Well-known civil rights and Muslim activist Malcolm X was born Malcom Little. He spent six years in prison after an arrest for robbery, and during that time, he educated himself, also becoming a Muslim and a disciple of Elijah Muhammad, who founded the Nation of Islam. Malcolm X became the spokesperson for Black separatism, encouraging Black Americans to sever economic, social, and political connections to whites. Though often considered alongside the Rev. Dr. Martin Luther King, Jr., as a civil rights activist, King and Malcolm X met only once, when on March 26, 1964, the two attended the US Senate's debate on the Civil Rights Bill. Malcolm X was assassinated in 1965. The following speech was delivered on April 3, 1964, in Cleveland, Ohio, on the occasion of President Lyndon B. Johnson's campaign for election.

Mr. Moderator, Brother Lomax, brothers and sisters, friends and enemies: I just can't believe everyone in here is a friend, and I don't want to leave anybody out. The question tonight, as I understand it, is "The Negro Revolt, and Where Do We Go From Here?" or What Next?" In my little humble way of understanding it, it points toward either the ballot or the bullet.

Before we try and explain what is meant by the ballot or the bullet, I would like to clarify something concerning myself. I'm still a Muslim; my religion is still Islam. That's my personal belief. Just as Adam Clayton Powell is a Christian minister who heads the Abyssinian Baptist Church in New York, but at the same time takes part in the political struggles to try and bring about rights to the black people in this country; and Dr. Martin Luther King is a Christian minister down in Atlanta, Georgia, who heads another organization fighting for the civil rights

---

"The Ballot or the Bullet" by Malcolm X Copyright © 1965 by Betty Shabazz Used with permission of X Legacy, LLC. Copyright © 1965, 1989 by Betty Shabazz and Pathfinder Press. Reprinted by permission.

of black people in this country; and Reverend Galamison, I guess you've heard of him, is another Christian minister in New York who has been deeply involved in the school boycotts to eliminate segregated education; well, I myself am a minister, not a Christian minister, but a Muslim minister; and I believe in action on all fronts by whatever means necessary.

Although I'm still a Muslim, I'm not here tonight to discuss my religion. I'm not here to try and change your religion. I'm not here to argue or discuss anything that we differ about, because it's time for us to submerge our differences and realize that it is best for us to first see that we have the same problem, a common problem, a problem that will make you catch hell whether you're a Baptist, or a Methodist, or a Muslim, or a nationalist. Whether you're educated or illiterate, whether you live on the boulevard or in the alley, you're going to catch hell just like I am. We're all in the same boat and we all are going to catch the same hell from the same man. He just happens to be a white man. All of us have suffered here, in this country, political oppression at the hands of the white man, economic exploitation at the hands of the white man, and social degradation at the hands of the white man.

Now in speaking like this, it doesn't mean that we're anti-white, but it does mean we're anti-exploitation, we're anti-degradation, we're anti-oppression. And if the white man doesn't want us to be anti-him, let him stop oppressing and exploiting and degrading us. Whether we are Christians or Muslims or nationalists or agnostics or atheists, we must first learn to forget our differences. If we have differences, let us differ in the closet; when we come out in front, let us not have anything to argue about until we get finished arguing with the man. If the late President Kennedy could get together with Khrushchev and exchange some wheat, we certainly have more in common with each other than Kennedy and Khrushchev had with each other.

If we don't do something real soon, I think you'll have to agree that we're going to be forced either to use the ballot or the bullet. It's one or the other in 1964. It isn't that time is running out—time has run out!

1964 threatens to be the most explosive year America has ever witnessed. The most explosive year. Why? It's also a political year. It's the year when all of the white politicians will be back in the so-called Negro community jiving you and me for some votes. The year when all of the white political crooks will be right back in your and my community with their false promises, building up our hopes for a letdown, with their trickery and their treachery, with their false promises which they don't intend to keep. As they nourish these dissatisfactions, it can only lead to one thing, an explosion; and now we have the type of black man on the scene in America today—I'm sorry, Brother Lomax—who just doesn't intend to turn the other cheek any longer.

Don't let anybody tell you anything about the odds are against you. If they draft you, they send you to Korea and make you face 800 million Chinese. If you can be brave over there, you can be brave right here. These odds aren't as great as those odds. And if you fight here, you will at least know what you're fighting for.

I'm not a politician, not even a student of politics; in fact, I'm not a student of much of anything. I'm not a Democrat. I'm not a Republican, and I don't even consider myself an American. If you and I were Americans, there'd be no problem. Those Honkies that just got off the boat, they're already Americans; Polacks are already Americans; the Italian refugees are already Americans. Everything that came out of Europe, every blue-eyed thing, is already an American. And as long as you and I have been over here, we aren't Americans yet.

Well, I am one who doesn't believe in deluding myself. I'm not going to sit at your table and watch you eat, with nothing on my plate, and call myself a diner. Sitting at the table doesn't make you a diner, unless you eat some of what's on that plate. Being here in America doesn't make you an American. Being born here in America doesn't make you an American. Why, if birth made you American, you wouldn't need any legislation; you wouldn't need any amendments to the Constitution; you wouldn't be faced with civil-rights filibustering in Washington, DC, right now. They don't have to pass civil-rights legislation to make a Polack an American.

No, I'm not an American. I'm one of the 22 million black people who are the victims of Americanism. One of the 22 million black people who are the victims of democracy, nothing but disguised hypocrisy. So, I'm not standing here speaking to you as an American, or a patriot, or a flag-saluter, or a flag-waver—no, not I. I'm speaking as a victim of this American system. And I see America through the eyes of the victim. I don't see any American dream; I see an American nightmare.

These 22 million victims are waking up. Their eyes are coming open. They're beginning to see what they used to only look at. They're becoming politically mature. They are realizing that there are new political trends from coast to coast. As they see these new political trends, it's possible for them to see that every time there's an election the races are so close that they have to have a recount. They had to recount in Massachusetts to see who was going to be governor, it was so close. It was the same way in Rhode Island, in Minnesota, and in many other parts of the country. And the same with Kennedy and Nixon when they ran for president. It was so close they had to count all over again. Well, what does this mean? It means that when white people are evenly divided, and black people have a bloc of votes of their own, it is left up to them to determine who's going to sit in the White House and who's going to be in the dog house.

It was the black man's vote that put the present administration in Washington, DC. Your vote, your dumb vote, your ignorant vote, your wasted vote put in an administration in Washington, DC, that has seen fit to pass every kind of legislation imaginable, saving you until last, then filibustering on top of that. And your and my leaders have the audacity to run around clapping their hands and talk about how much progress we're making. And what a good president we have. If he wasn't good in Texas, he sure can't be good in Washington, DC. Because Texas is a lynch state. It is in the same breath as Mississippi, no different; only they lynch you in Texas with a Texas accent and lynch you in Mississippi with a Mississippi accent. And these Negro leaders have the audacity to go and have some coffee in the White House with a Texan, a Southern cracker—that's all he is—and then come out and tell you and me that he's going to be better for us because, since he's from the South, he knows how to deal with the Southerners. What kind of logic is that? Let Eastland be president, he's from the South too. He should be better able to deal with them than Johnson.

In this present administration they have in the House of Representatives 257 Democrats to only 177 Republicans. They control two-thirds of the House vote. Why can't they pass something that will help you and me? In the Senate, there are 67 senators who are of the Democratic Party. Only 33 of them are Republicans. Why, the Democrats have got the government sewed up, and you're the one who sewed it up for them. And what have they given you for it? Four years in office, and just now getting around to some civil-rights legislation. Just now, after everything else is gone, out of the way, they're going to sit down now and play with you all summer long—the same old giant con game that they call filibuster. All those are in cahoots together. Don't you ever think they're not in cahoots together, for the man that is heading the civil-rights filibuster is a man from Georgia named Richard Russell. When Johnson became president, the first man he asked for when he got back to Washington, DC, was "Dicky"—that's how tight they are. That's his boy, that's his pal, that's his buddy. But they're playing that old con game. One of them makes believe he's for you, and he's got it fixed where the other one is so tight against you, he never has to keep his promise.

So it's time in 1964 to wake up. And when you see them coming up with that kind of conspiracy, let them know your eyes are open. And let them know you—something else that's wide open too. It's got to be the ballot or the bullet. The ballot or the bullet. If you're afraid to use an expression like that, you should get on out of the country; you should get back in the cotton patch; you should get back in the alley. They get all the Negro vote, and after they get it, the Negro gets nothing in return. All they did when they got to Washington was give a few big Negroes big jobs. Those big Negroes didn't need big jobs, they already had jobs. That's camouflage, that's trickery, that's treachery, window-dressing. I'm not trying to knock out the Democrats for the Republicans. We'll get to them in a minute. But it is true; you put the Democrats first and the Democrats put you last.

Look at it the way it is. What alibis do they use, since they control Congress and the Senate? What alibi do they use when you and I ask, "Well, when are you going to keep your promise?" They blame the Dixiecrats. What is a Dixiecrat? A Democrat. A Dixiecrat is nothing but a Democrat in disguise. The titular head of the Democrats is also the head of the Dixiecrats, because the Dixiecrats are a part of the Democratic Party. The Democrats have never kicked the Dixiecrats out of the party. The Dixiecrats bolted themselves once, but the Democrats didn't put them out. Imagine, these lowdown Southern segregationists put the Northern Democrats down. But the Northern Democrats have never put the Dixiecrats down. No, look at that thing the way it is. They have got a con game going on, a political con game, and you and I are in the middle. It's time for you and me to wake up and start looking at it like it is, and trying to understand it like it is; and then we can deal with it like it is.

The Dixiecrats in Washington, DC, control the key committees that run the government. The only reason the Dixiecrats control these committees is because they have seniority. The only reason they have seniority is because they come from states where Negroes can't vote. This is not even a government that's based on democracy. It is not a government that is made up of representatives of the people. Half of the people in the South can't even vote. Eastland is not even supposed to be in Washington. Half of the senators and congressmen who occupy these key positions in Washington, DC, are there illegally, are there unconstitutionally.

I was in Washington, DC, a week ago Thursday, when they were debating whether or not they should let the bill come onto the floor. And in the back of the room where the Senate meets, there's a huge map of the United States, and on that map it shows the location of Negroes throughout the country. And it shows that the Southern section of the country, the states that are most heavily concentrated with Negroes, are the ones that have senators and congressmen standing up filibustering and doing all other kinds of trickery to keep the Negro from being able to vote. This is pitiful. But it's not pitiful for us any longer; it's actually pitiful for the white man, because soon now, as the Negro awakens a little more and sees the vise that he's in, sees the bag that he's in, sees the real game that he's in, then the Negro's going to develop a new tactic.

These senators and congressmen actually violate the constitutional amendments that guarantee the people of that particular state or county the right to vote. And the Constitution itself has within it the machinery to expel any representative from a state where the voting rights of the people are violated. You don't even need new legislation. Any person in Congress right now, who is there from a state or a district where the voting rights of the people are violated, that particular person should be expelled from Congress. And when you expel him, you've removed one of the obstacles in the path of any real meaningful legislation in this country. In fact, when you expel them, you don't need new legislation, because they will be replaced by black representatives from counties and districts where the black man is in the majority, not in the minority.

If the black man in these Southern states had his full voting rights, the key Dixiecrats in Washington, DC, which means the key Democrats in Washington, DC, would lose their seats. The Democratic Party itself would lose its power. It would cease to be powerful as a party. When you see the amount of power that would be lost by the Democratic Party if it were to lose the Dixiecrat wing, or branch, or element, you can see where it's against the interests of the Democrats to give voting rights to Negroes in states where the Democrats have been in complete power and authority ever since the Civil War. You just can't belong to that Party without analyzing it.

I say again, I'm not anti-Democrat, I'm not anti-Republican, I'm not anti-anything. I'm just questioning their sincerity, and some of the strategy that they've been using on our people by promising them promises that they don't intend to keep. When you keep the Democrats in power, you're keeping the Dixiecrats in power. I doubt that my good Brother Lomax will deny that. A vote for a Democrat is a vote for a Dixiecrat. That's why, in 1964, it's time now for you and me to become more politically mature and realize what the ballot is for; what we're supposed to get when we cast a ballot; and that if we don't cast a ballot, it's going to end up in a situation where we're going to have to cast a bullet. It's either a ballot or a bullet.

In the North, they do it a different way. They have a system that's known as gerrymandering, whatever that means. It means when Negroes become too heavily concentrated in a certain area, and begin to gain too much political power, the white man comes along and changes the district lines. You may say, "Why do you keep saying white man?" Because it's the white man who does it. I haven't ever seen any Negro changing any lines. They don't let him get near the line. It's the white man who does this. And usually, it's the white man who grins at you the most, and pats you on the back, and is supposed to be your friend. He may be friendly, but he's not your friend.

So, what I'm trying to impress upon you, in essence, is this: You and I in America are faced not with a segregationist conspiracy, we're faced with a government conspiracy. Everyone who's filibustering is a senator—that's the government. Everyone who's finagling in Washington, DC, is a congressman—that's the government. You don't have anybody putting blocks in your path but people who are a part of the government. The same government that you go abroad to fight for and die for is the government that is in a conspiracy to deprive you of your voting rights, deprive you of your economic opportunities, deprive you of decent housing, deprive you of decent education. You don't need to go to the employer alone, it is the government itself, the government of America, that is responsible for the oppression and exploitation and degradation of black people in this country. And you should drop it in their lap. This government has failed the Negro. This so-called democracy has failed the Negro. And all these white liberals have definitely failed the Negro.

So, where do we go from here? First, we need some friends. We need some new allies. The entire civil-rights struggle needs a new interpretation, a broader interpretation. We need to look at this civil-rights thing from another angle—from the inside as well as from the outside. To those of us whose philosophy is black nationalism, the only way you can get involved in the civil-rights struggle is give it a new interpretation. That old interpretation excluded us. It kept us out. So, we're giving a new interpretation to the civil-rights struggle, an interpretation that will enable us to come into it, take part in it. And these handkerchief-heads who have been dillydallying and pussy footing and compromising—we don't intend to let them pussyfoot and dillydally and compromise any longer.

How can you thank a man for giving you what's already yours? How then can you thank him for giving you only part of what's already yours? You haven't even made progress, if what's being given to you, you should have had already. That's not progress. And I love my Brother Lomax, the way he pointed out we're right back where we were in 1954. We're not even as far up as we were in 1954. We're behind where we were in 1954. There's more segregation now than there was in 1954. There's more racial animosity, more racial hatred, more racial violence today in 1964, than there was in 1954. Where is the progress?

And now you're facing a situation where the young Negro's coming up. They don't want to hear that "turn-the-other-cheek" stuff, no. In Jacksonville, those were teenagers, they were throwing Molotov cocktails. Negroes have never done that before. But it shows you there's a new deal coming in. There's new thinking coming in. There's new strategy coming in. It'll be Molotov cocktails this month, hand grenades next month, and something else next month. It'll be ballots, or it'll be bullets. It'll be liberty, or it will be death. The only difference about this kind of death—it'll be reciprocal. You know what is meant by "reciprocal"? That's one of Brother Lomax's words. I stole it from him. I don't usually deal with those big words because I don't usually deal with big people. I deal with small people. I find you can get a whole lot of small people and whip hell out of a whole lot of big people. They haven't got anything to lose, and they've got everything to gain. And they'll let you know in a minute: "It takes two to tango; when I go, you go."

The black nationalists, those whose philosophy is black nationalism, in bringing about this new interpretation of the entire meaning of civil rights, look upon it as meaning, as Brother Lomax has pointed out, equality of opportunity. Well, we're justified in seeking civil rights, if it means equality of opportunity, because all we're doing there is trying to collect for our investment. Our mothers and fathers invested sweat and blood. Three hundred and ten years we worked in this country without a dime in return—I mean without a dime in return. You let the white man walk around here talking about how rich this country is, but you never stop to think how it got rich so quick. It got rich because you made it rich.

You take the people who are in this audience right now. They're poor. We're all poor as individuals. Our weekly salary individually amounts to hardly anything. But if you take the salary of everyone in here collectively, it'll fill up a whole lot of baskets. It's a lot of wealth. If you can collect the wages of just these people right here for a year, you'll be rich—richer than rich. When you look at it like that, think how rich Uncle Sam had to become, not with this handful, but millions of black people. Your and my mother and father, who didn't work an eight-hour shift, but worked from "can't see" in the morning until "can't see" at night, and worked for nothing, making the white man rich, making Uncle Sam rich. This is our investment. This is our contribution, our blood.

Not only did we give of our free labor, we gave of our blood. Every time he had a call to arms, we were the first ones in uniform. We died on every battlefield the white man had. We have made a greater sacrifice than anybody who's standing up in America today. We have made a greater contribution and have collected less. Civil rights, for those of us whose philosophy is black nationalism, means: "Give it to us now. Don't wait for next year. Give it to us yesterday, and that's not fast enough."

I might stop right here to point out one thing. Whenever you're going after something that belongs to you, anyone who's depriving you of the right to have it is a criminal. Understand that. Whenever you are going after something that is yours, you are within your legal rights to lay claim to it. And anyone who puts forth any effort to deprive you of that which is yours, is breaking the law, is a criminal. And this was pointed out by the Supreme Court decision. It outlawed segregation.

Which means segregation is against the law. Which means a segregationist is breaking the law. A segregationist is a criminal. You can't label him as anything other than that. And when you demonstrate against segregation, the law is on your side. The Supreme Court is on your side.

Now, who is it that opposes you in carrying out the law? The police department itself. With police dogs and clubs. Whenever you demonstrate against segregation, whether it is segregated education, segregated housing, or anything else, the law is on your side, and anyone who stands in the way is not the law any longer. They are breaking the law; they are not representatives of the law. Any time you demonstrate against segregation and a man has the audacity to put a police dog on you, kill that dog, kill him, I'm telling you, kill that dog. I say it, if they put me in jail tomorrow, kill that dog. Then you'll put a stop to it. Now, if these white people in here don't want to see that kind of action, get down and tell the mayor to tell the police department to pull the dogs in. That's all you have to do. If you don't do it, someone else will.

If you don't take this kind of stand, your little children will grow up and look at you and think "shame." If you don't take an uncompromising stand, I don't mean go out and get violent; but at the same time you should never be nonviolent unless you run into some nonviolence. I'm nonviolent with those who are nonviolent with me. But when you drop that violence on me, then you've made me go insane, and I'm not responsible for what I do. And that's the way every Negro should get. Any time you know you're within the law, within your legal rights, within your moral rights, in accord with justice, then die for what you believe in. But don't die alone. Let your dying be reciprocal. This is what is meant by equality. What's good for the goose is good for the gander.

When we begin to get in this area, we need new friends, we need new allies. We need to expand the civil-rights struggle to a higher level—to the level of human rights. Whenever you are in a civil-rights struggle, whether you know it or not, you are confining yourself to the jurisdiction of Uncle Sam. No one from the outside world can speak out in your behalf as long as your struggle is a civil-rights struggle. Civil rights comes within the domestic affairs of this country. All of our African brothers and our Asian brothers and our Latin-American brothers cannot open their mouths and interfere in the domestic affairs of the United States. And as long as it's civil rights, this comes under the jurisdiction of Uncle Sam.

But the United Nations has what's known as the charter of human rights; it has a committee that deals in human rights. You may wonder why all of the atrocities that have been committed in Africa and in Hungary and in Asia, and in Latin America are brought before the UN, and the Negro problem is never brought before the UN. This is part of the conspiracy. This old, tricky blue-eyed liberal who is supposed to be your and my friend, supposed to be in our corner, supposed to be subsidizing our struggle, and supposed to be acting in the capacity of an adviser, never tells you anything about human rights. They keep you wrapped up in civil rights. And you spend so much time barking up the civil-rights tree, you don't even know there's a human-rights tree on the same floor.

When you expand the civil-rights struggle to the level of human rights, you can then take the case of the black man in this country before the nations in the

UN. You can take it before the General Assembly. You can take Uncle Sam before a world court. But the only level you can do it on is the level of human rights. Civil rights keeps you under his restrictions, under his jurisdiction. Civil rights keeps you in his pocket. Civil rights means you're asking Uncle Sam to treat you right. Human rights are something you were born with. Human rights are your God-given rights. Human rights are the rights that are recognized by all nations of this earth. And any time any one violates your human rights, you can take them to the world court.

Uncle Sam's hands are dripping with blood, dripping with the blood of the black man in this country. He's the earth's number-one hypocrite. He has the audacity—yes, he has—imagine him posing as the leader of the free world. The free world! And you over here singing "We Shall Overcome." Expand the civil-rights struggle to the level of human rights. Take it into the United Nations, where our African brothers can throw their weight on our side, where our Asian brothers can throw their weight on our side, where our Latin-American brothers can throw their weight on our side, and where 800 million Chinamen are sitting there waiting to throw their weight on our side.

Let the world know how bloody his hands are. Let the world know the hypocrisy that's practiced over here. Let it be the ballot or the bullet. Let him know that it must be the ballot or the bullet.

When you take your case to Washington, DC, you're taking it to the criminal who's responsible; it's like running from the wolf to the fox. They're all in cahoots together. They all work political chicanery and make you look like a chump before the eyes of the world. Here you are walking around in America, getting ready to be drafted and sent abroad, like a tin soldier, and when you get over there, people ask you what are you fighting for, and you have to stick your tongue in your cheek. No, take Uncle Sam to court, take him before the world.

By ballot I only mean freedom. Don't you know—I disagree with Lomax on this issue—that the ballot is more important than the dollar? Can I prove it? Yes. Look in the UN. There are poor nations in the UN; yet those poor nations can get together with their voting power and keep the rich nations from making a move. They have one nation–one vote, everyone has an equal vote. And when those brothers from Asia, and Africa and the darker parts of this earth get together, their voting power is sufficient to hold Sam in check. Or Russia in check. Or some other section of the earth in check. So, the ballot is most important.

Right now, in this country, if you and I, 22 million African-Americans—that's what we are—Africans who are in America. You're nothing but Africans. Nothing but Africans. In fact, you'd get farther calling yourself African instead of Negro. Africans don't catch hell. You're the only one catching hell. They don't have to pass civil-rights bills for Africans. An African can go anywhere he wants right now. All you've got to do is tie your head up. That's right, go anywhere you want. Just stop being a Negro. Change your name to Hoogagagooba. That'll show you how silly the white man is. You're dealing with a silly man. A friend of mine who's very dark put a turban on his head and went into a restaurant in Atlanta before they called themselves desegregated. He went into a white restaurant, he sat down, they served him, and he said, "What would happen if a Negro came in here?" And there he's sitting, black as night, but because he had his head wrapped up the waitress looked back at him and says, "Why, there wouldn't no nigger dare come in here."

So, you're dealing with a man whose bias and prejudice are making him lose his mind, his intelligence, every day. He's frightened. He looks around and sees what's taking place on this earth, and he sees that the pendulum of time is swinging in your direction. The dark people are waking up. They're losing their fear of the white man. No place where he's fighting right now is he winning. Everywhere he's fighting, he's fighting someone your and my complexion. And they're beating him. He can't win any more. He's won his last battle. He failed to win the Korean War. He couldn't win it. He had to sign a truce. That's a loss.

Any time Uncle Sam, with all his machinery for warfare, is held to a draw by some rice eaters, he's lost the battle. He had to sign a truce. America's not supposed to sign a truce. She's supposed to be bad. But she's not bad any more. She's bad as long as she can use her hydrogen bomb, but she can't use hers for fear Russia might use hers. Russia can't use hers, for fear that Sam might use his. So, both of them are weapon-less. They can't use the weapon because each's weapon nullifies the other's. So the only place where action can take place is on the ground. And the white man can't win another war fighting on the ground. Those days are over. The black man knows it, the brown man knows it, the red man knows it, and the yellow man knows it. So they engage him in guerrilla warfare. That's not his style. You've got to have heart to be a guerrilla warrior, and he hasn't got any heart. I'm telling you now.

I just want to give you a little briefing on guerrilla warfare because, before you know it, before you know it. It takes heart to be a guerrilla warrior because you're on your own. In conventional warfare you have tanks and a whole lot of other people with you to back you up—planes over your head and all that kind of stuff. But a guerrilla is on his own. All you have is a rifle, some sneakers and a bowl of rice, and that's all you need—and a lot of heart. The Japanese on some of those islands in the Pacific, when the American soldiers landed, one Japanese sometimes could hold the whole army off. He'd just wait until the sun went down, and when the sun went down they were all equal. He would take his little blade and slip from bush to bush, and from American to American. The white soldiers couldn't cope with that. Whenever you see a white soldier that fought in the Pacific, he has the shakes, he has a nervous condition, because they scared him to death.

The same thing happened to the French up in French Indochina. People who just a few years previously were rice farmers got together and ran the heavily-mechanized French army out of Indochina. You don't need it—modern warfare today won't work. This is the day of the guerrilla. They did the same thing in Algeria. Algerians, who were nothing but Bedouins, took a rine and sneaked off to the hills, and de Gaulle and all of his highfalutin' war machinery couldn't defeat those guerrillas. Nowhere on this earth does the white man win in a guerrilla warfare. It's not his speed. Just as guerrilla warfare is prevailing in Asia and in parts of Africa and in parts of Latin America, you've got to be mighty naive, or you've got to play the black man cheap, if you don't think some day he's going to wake up and find that it's got to be the ballot or the bullet.

l would like to say, in closing, a few things concerning the Muslim Mosque, Inc., which we established recently in New York City. It's true we're Muslims and our religion is Islam, but we don't mix our religion with our politics and our economics and our social and civil activities—not any more. We keep our religion in our mosque. After our religious services are over, then as Muslims we become involved in political action, economic action and social and civic action. We become involved with anybody, anywhere, any time and in any manner that's designed to eliminate the evils, the political, economic and social evils that are afflicting the people of our community.

The political philosophy of black nationalism means that the black man should control the politics and the politicians in his own community; no more. The black man in the black community has to be re-educated into the science of politics so he will know what politics is supposed to bring him in return. Don't be throwing out any ballots. A ballot is like a bullet. You don't throw your ballots until you see a target, and if that target is not within your reach, keep your ballot in your pocket.

The political philosophy of black nationalism is being taught in the Christian church. It's being taught in the NAACP. It's being taught in CORE meetings. It's being taught in SNCC Student Nonviolent Coordinating Committee meetings. It's being taught in Muslim meetings. It's being taught where nothing but atheists and agnostics come together. It's being taught everywhere. Black people are fed up with the dillydallying, pussyfooting, compromising approach that we've been using toward getting our freedom. We want freedom now, but we're not going to get it saying "We Shall Overcome." We've got to fight until we overcome.

The economic philosophy of black nationalism is pure and simple. It only means that we should control the economy of our community. Why should white people be running all the stores in our community? Why should white people be running the banks of our community? Why should the economy of our community be in the hands of the white man? Why? If a black man can't move his store into a white community, you tell me why a white man should move his store into a black community. The philosophy of black nationalism involves a re-education program in the black community in regards to economics. Our people have to be made to see that any time you take your dollar out of your community and spend it in a community where you don't live, the community where you live will get poorer and poorer, and the community where you spend your money will get richer and richer.

Then you wonder why where you live is always a ghetto or a slum area. And where you and I are concerned, not only do we lose it when we spend it out of the community, but the white man has got all our stores in the community tied up; so that though we spend it in the community, at sundown the man who runs the store takes it over across town somewhere. He's got us in a vise. So the economic philosophy of black nationalism means in every church, in every civic organization, in every fraternal order, it's time now for our people to become conscious of the importance of controlling the economy of our community. If we own the stores, if we operate the businesses, if we try and establish some industry in our own community, then we're developing to the position where we are creating employment for our own kind. Once you gain control of the economy of your own community, then you don't have to picket and boycott and beg some cracker downtown for a job in his business.

The social philosophy of black nationalism only means that we have to get together and remove the evils, the vices, alcoholism, drug addiction, and other evils that are destroying the moral fiber of our community. We ourselves have to lift the level of our community, the standard of our community to a higher level, make our own society beautiful so that we will be satisfied in our own social circles and won't be running around here trying to knock our way into a social circle where we're not wanted. So I say, in spreading a gospel such as black nationalism, it is not designed to make the black man re-evaluate the white man—you know him already—but to make the black man re-evaluate himself. Don't change the white man's mind—you can't change his mind, and that whole thing about appealing to the moral conscience of America—America's conscience is bankrupt. She lost all conscience a long time ago. Uncle Sam has no conscience.

They don't know what morals are. They don't try and eliminate an evil because it's evil, or because it's illegal, or because it's immoral; they eliminate it only when it threatens their existence. So you're wasting your time appealing to the moral conscience of a bankrupt man like Uncle Sam. If he had a conscience, he'd straighten this thing out with no more pressure being put upon him. So it is not necessary to change the white man's mind. We have to change our own mind. You can't change his mind about us. We've got to change our own minds about each other. We have to see each other with new eyes. We have to see each other as brothers and sisters. We have to come together with warmth so we can develop unity and harmony that's necessary to get this problem solved ourselves. How can we do this? How can we avoid jealousy? How can we avoid the suspicion and the divisions that exist in the community? I'll tell you how.

I have watched how Billy Graham comes into a city, spreading what he calls the gospel of Christ, which is only white nationalism. That's what he is. Billy Graham is a white nationalist; I'm a black nationalist. But since it's the natural tendency for leaders to be jealous and look upon a powerful figure like Graham with suspicion and envy, how is it possible for him to come into a city and get all the cooperation of the church leaders? Don't think because they're church leaders that they don't have weaknesses that make them envious and jealous—no, everybody's got it. It's not an accident that when they want to choose a cardinal, as Pope I over there in Rome, they get in a closet so you can't hear them cussing and fighting and carrying on.

Billy Graham comes in preaching the gospel of Christ. He evangelizes the gospel. He stirs everybody up, but he never tries to start a church. If he came in trying to start a church, all the churches would be against him. So, he just comes in talking about Christ and tells everybody who gets Christ to go to any church where Christ is; and in this way the church cooperates with him. So we're going to take a page from his book.

Our gospel is black nationalism. We're not trying to threaten the existence of any organization, but we're spreading the gospel of black nationalism. Anywhere there's a church that is also preaching and practicing the gospel of black nationalism, join that church. If the NAACP is preaching and practicing the gospel of black nationalism, join the NAACP. If CORE is spreading and practicing the gospel of black nationalism, join CORE. Join any organization that has a gospel that's for the uplift of the black man. And when you get into it and see them pussyfooting or compromising, pull out of it because that's not black nationalism. We'll find another one.

And in this manner, the organizations will increase in number and in quantity and in quality, and by August, it is then our intention to have a black nationalist convention which will consist of delegates from all over the country who are interested in the political, economic and social philosophy of black nationalism. After these delegates convene, we will hold a seminar; we will hold discussions; we will listen to everyone. We want to hear new ideas and new solutions and new answers. And at that time, if we see fit then to form a black nationalist party, we'll form a black nationalist party. If it's necessary to form a black nationalist army, we'll form a black nationalist army. It'll be the ballot or the bullet. It'll be liberty or it'll be death.

It's time for you and me to stop sitting in this country, letting some cracker senators, Northern crackers and Southern crackers, sit there in Washington, DC, and come to a conclusion in their mind that you and I are supposed to have civil rights. There's no white man going to tell me anything about my rights. Brothers and sisters, always remember, if it doesn't take senators and congressmen and presidential proclamations to give freedom to the white man, it is not necessary for legislation or proclamation or Supreme Court decisions to give freedom to the black man. You let that white man know, if this is a country of freedom, let it be a country of freedom; and if it's not a country of freedom, change it.

We will work with anybody, anywhere, at any time, who is genuinely interested in tackling the problem head-on, nonviolently as long as the enemy is nonviolent, but violent when the enemy gets violent. We'll work with you on the voter-registration drive, we'll work with you on rent strikes, we'll work with you on school boycotts; I don't believe in any kind of integration; I'm not even worried about it, because I know you're not going to get it anyway; you're not going to get it because you're afraid to die; you've got to be ready to die if you try and force yourself on the white man, because he'll get just as violent as those crackers in Mississippi, right here in Cleveland. But we will still work with you on the school boycotts because we're against a segregated school system. A segregated school system produces children who, when they graduate, graduate with crippled minds. But this does not mean that a school is segregated because it's all black. A segregated school means a school that is controlled by people who have no real interest in it whatsoever.

Let me explain what I mean. A segregated district or community is a community in which people live, but outsiders control the politics and the economy of that community. They never refer to the white section as a segregated community. It's the all-Negro section that's a segregated community. Why? The white man controls his own school, his own bank, his own economy, his own politics, his own everything, his own community; but he also controls yours. When you're under someone else's control, you're segregated. They'll always give you the lowest or the worst that there is to offer, but it doesn't mean you're segregated just because you have your own. You've got to control your own. Just like the white man has control of his, you need to control yours.

You know the best way to get rid of segregation? The white man is more afraid of separation than he is of integration. Segregation means that he puts you away from him, but not far enough for you to be out of his jurisdiction; separation means you're gone. And the white man will integrate faster than he'll let you separate. So we will work with you against the segregated school system because it's criminal, because it is absolutely destructive, in every way imaginable, to the minds of the children who have to be exposed to that type of crippling education.

Last but not least, I must say this concerning the great controversy over rifles and shotguns. The only thing that I've ever said is that in areas where the government has proven itself either unwilling or unable to defend the lives and the property of Negroes, it's time for Negroes to defend themselves. Article number two of the constitutional amendments provides you and me the right to own a rifle or a shotgun. It is constitutionally legal to own a shotgun or a rifle. This doesn't mean you're going to get a rifle and form battalions and go out looking for white folks, although you'd be within your rights—I mean, you'd be justified; but that would be illegal and we don't do anything illegal. If the white man doesn't want the black man buying rifles and shotguns, then let the government do its job.

That's all. And don't let the white man come to you and ask you what you think about what Malcolm says—why, you old Uncle Tom. He would never ask you if he thought you were going to say, "Amen!" No, he is making a Tom out of you." So, this doesn't mean forming rifle clubs and going out looking for people, but it is time, in 1964, if you are a man, to let that man know. If he's not going to do his job in running the government and providing you and me with the protection that our taxes are supposed to be for, since he spends all those billions for his defense budget, he certainly can't begrudge you and me spending $12 or $15 for a single-shot, or double-action. I hope you understand. Don't go out shooting people, but any time—brothers and sisters, and especially the men in this audience; some of you wearing Congressional Medals of Honor, with shoulders this wide, chests this big, muscles that big—any time you and I sit around and read where they bomb a church and murder in cold blood, not some grownups, but four little girls while they were praying to the same God the white man taught them to pray to, and you and I see the government go down and can't find who did it.

Why, this man—he can find Eichmann hiding down in Argentina somewhere. Let two or three American soldiers, who are minding somebody else's business way over in South Vietnam, get killed, and he'll send battleships, sticking his nose in their business. He wanted to send troops down to Cuba and make them have what he calls free elections—this old cracker who doesn't have free elections in his own country.

No, if you never see me another time in your life, if I die in the morning, I'll die saying one thing: the ballot or the bullet, the ballot or the bullet.

If a Negro in 1964 has to sit around and wait for some cracker senator to filibuster when it comes to the rights of black people, why, you and I should hang our heads in shame. You talk about a march on Washington in 1963, you haven't seen anything. There's some more going down in '64.

And this time they're not going like they went last year. They're not going singing "We Shall Overcome." They're not going with white friends. They're not going with placards already painted for them. They're not going with round-trip tickets. They're going with one-way tickets. And if they don't want that non-nonviolent army going down there, tell them to bring the filibuster to a halt.

The black nationalists aren't going to wait. Lyndon B. Johnson is the head of the Democratic Party. If he's for civil rights, let him go into the Senate next week and declare himself. Let him go in there right now and declare himself. Let him go in there and denounce the Southern branch of his party. Let him go in there right now and take a moral stand—right now, not later. Tell him, don't wait until election time. If he waits too long, brothers and sisters, he will be responsible for letting a condition develop in this country which will create a climate that will bring seeds up out of the ground with vegetation on the end of them looking like something these people never dreamed of. In 1964, it's the ballot or the bullet.

Thank you.

FOR INFORMAL WRITING

In another version of this speech, Malcolm X says, "Why does it look like it might be the year of the ballot or the bullet?" After you read the text of the speech, how might you answer this question?

FOR DISCUSSION

1. How would you characterize Malcolm X's sense of the "economic exploitation" of Black Americans?
2. In another work, Malcom X writes, "Not long ago, an English writer telephoned me from London, asking questions. One was, 'What's your alma mater?' I told him, 'Books.'" What's an alma mater? How do you respond to Malcom X's statement? What in this speech indicates his learning?
3. Malcolm X invokes Black nationalism as the answer to the problems faced by African Americans. How does he articulate this in the speech? How is it the nexus at the intersection of politics and religion?

FOR WRITING

Consider this alongside other speeches and writings by Malcolm X. Using examples from this work, discuss his views on the relationships among social activism, self-empowerment, personal and social responsibility, and the importance, by implication, of being an educated citizen.

WHAT'S NEW IS OLD

Compare the text of this speech by Malcolm X with the excerpt from Eric Schlosser's *Fast Food Nation*. How might a reading of the Malcolm X speech inform some of your sense of Schlosser's arguments, particularly as they pertain to low-wage workers?

Trip to Hanoi (1968)
Susan Sontag (1933–2004)

Susan Sontag was a prominent critic, filmmaker, teacher, and philosopher. While she primarily is credited as an essayist, she also wrote and published novels. Born in New York City and educated at the University of Chicago, the University of California at Berkeley, and Harvard University, Sontag was also a lifelong human rights activist. She served as President of the American Center of PEN, a prominent writers' organization. Sontag was also a MacArthur Fellow. Her books—on subjects ranging from the arts, human rights, and other subjects—have been translated into thirty-two languages. "A Trip to Hanoi" was originally published in Esquire *magazine and represents work by Sontag that did not shy away from controversy.*

Though I have been and am passionately opposed to the American aggression in Vietnam, I accepted the unexpected invitation to go to Hanoi that came in mid-April with the pretty firm idea that I wouldn't write about the trip upon my return. Being neither a journalist nor a political activist (though a veteran signer of petitions and anti-war demonstrator) nor an Asian specialist, but rather a stubbornly unspecialized writer who has so far been largely unable to incorporate into either novels or essays my evolving radical political convictions and sense of moral dilemma at being a citizen of the American empire, I doubted that my account of such a trip could add anything new to the already eloquent opposition to the war. And contributing to the anti-war polemic seemed to me the only worthwhile reason for an American to be writing about Vietnam now.

Perhaps the difficulty started there, with the lack of a purpose that really justified in my own mind my being invited to North Vietnam. Had I brought

---

From "Trip to Hanoi" from STYLES OF RADICAL WILL by Susan Sontag. Copyright © 1967, 1969 by Susan Sontag. Reprinted by permission of Farrar, Straus and Giroux. All Rights Reserved.

some clear intentions about the usefulness (to me or to anyone else) of my visit, I probably would have found it easier to sort out and assimilate what I saw. If occasionally I could have reminded myself that I was a writer and Vietnam was "material," I might have fended off some of the confusions that beset me. As it was, the first days of my stay were profoundly discouraging, with most of my energies going toward trying to keep my gloom within tolerable limits. But now that I'm back, and since returning want after all to write about North Vietnam, I don't regret that early decision. By denying myself a role that could have shielded me from my ignorance and spared me a lot of personal discomfort, I unwittingly assisted what discoveries I eventually did make during the trip.

Of course, it wasn't only this original refusal to envisage the trip as a professional task that opened the way to my confusion. In part, my bewilderment was direct and unavoidable: the honest reflex of being culturally dislocated. Also, I should mention that few Americans who visit Hanoi at this time go alone, the usual practice being, for the convenience of the Vietnamese, to assemble groups of sometimes two, usually three, four, or five people who often don't know each other before the trip. I traveled to North Vietnam as one of three. And I had met neither of the two other Americans in whose company I made the trip—Andrew Kopkind, the journalist, and Robert Greenblatt, a mathematician from Cornell now working full time for the anti-war movement—before our rendezvous in Cambodia in late April. Yet this trip involves unremitting and not wholly voluntary proximity, the kind befitting a romance or a dangerous emergency, lasting without pause for at least a month. (We were invited for two weeks. It took us ten days, because of delays and missed connections, to go from New York via Paris and Phnom Penh to Hanoi, and just under a week to make the return trip.) Naturally, the situation with my companions claimed a sizable part of the attention that, had I traveled alone, would have gone to the Vietnamese: sometimes in the form of an obligation, most often as a pleasure. There was the practical necessity of learning to live amicably and intelligently with two strangers in circumstances of instant intimacy, strangers even if, or perhaps especially since, they were people already known to me by reputation and, in the case of Andy Kopkind, by his writing, which I admired. We were further drawn together by being in what was to all three of us an alien part of the world (neither Bob Greenblatt nor I had ever been to Asia before; Andy Kopkind had made one trip five years ago, visiting Saigon, Bangkok, the Philippines, and Japan), and meeting no one whose native language was English (except a USIS official and an American journalist in Laos, where we were stuck for four days on our way "in," and four American college students sponsored by SDS who arrived in Hanoi at the beginning of our second week). All this added together, it seems inevitable that we spent a great deal of time talking—gratefully, often feverishly—to each other.

Still, I don't mean to suggest that these elements of my situation account for the wistfully negative tone of my early impressions of Vietnam. The serious explanation for that I would locate not in the distractions and pressures of being one of an arbitrarily assembled yet inseparable trio in a new land, but in the demands and limitations of the approach to Vietnam I myself was capable of. Made miserable and angry for four years by knowledge of the excruciating suffering of the Vietnamese people at the hands of my government, now that I was actually there and being plied with gifts and flowers and rhetoric and tea and seemingly exaggerated kindness, I didn't feel any more than I already had ten thousand miles away. But being in Hanoi was far more mysterious, more puzzling intellectually, than I expected. I found that I couldn't avoid worrying and wondering how well I understood the Vietnamese, and they me and my country.

Yet this problem I posed for myself, frustrating as it proved, was perhaps the most important and fruitful one, at least to me. For it was not information (at least in the ordinary sense) that I'd come to find. Like anyone who cared about Vietnam in the last years, I already knew a great deal; and I could not hope to collect more or significantly better information in a mere two weeks than was already available. Ranging from the early reports in *The New York Times* by Harrison Salisbury of his visit in December and January of 1965–66 (later expanded into a book, *Behind the Lines—Hanoi*) and *The Other Side*, the book written jointly by Staughton Lynd and Tom Hayden, the first Americans from the antiwar movement to visit North Vietnam, to the analyses of Philippe Devillers and Jean Lacouture in the French press, to the recent articles by Mary McCarthy which I've been reading since my return to the United States, a multiple account has accumulated which conveys in vivid detail how Hanoi and large parts of North Vietnam appear to a sympathetic or at least reasonably objective outsider looking on. Anyone who wants to can get information on the achievements of the country since the French left in 1954: the expansion of medical services, the reorganization of education, the creation of a modest industrial base, and the beginnings of diversified agriculture. Even easier to obtain are the facts about the years of merciless bombing by the United States of all the population centers of North Vietnam— with the exception of downtown Hanoi (which has, however, been doused with "anti-personnel" or fragmentation bombs, those that don't harm buildings but only kill people)—and the destruction of virtually all the new schools and hospitals and factories built since 1954, as well as most bridges, theatres, pagodas, and Catholic churches and cathedrals. In my own case, several years of reading and of viewing newsreels had furnished a large portfolio of miscellaneous images of Vietnam: napalmed corpses, live citizens on bicycles, the hamlets of thatched huts, the razed cities like Nam Dinh and Phu Ly, the cylindrical, one-person bomb shelters spaced along the sidewalks of Hanoi, the thick yellow straw hats worn by schoolchildren as protection against fragmentation bombs. (Indelible horrors, pictorial and statistical, supplied by courtesy of television and *The New York Times* and *Life*, without one's even having to bestir oneself to consult the frankly partisan books of Wilfred Burchett or the documentation assembled by the Russell Foundation's International War Crimes Tribunal.) But the confrontation with the originals of these images didn't prove to be a simple experience; actually to see and touch them produced an effect both exhilarating and numbing. Matching concrete reality with mental image was at best a mechanical or merely additive process, while prying new facts from the Vietnamese officials and ordinary citizens I was meeting was a task for which I'm not particularly well equipped. Unless I could effect in myself some change of awareness, of consciousness, it would scarcely matter that I'd actually been to Vietnam. But that was exactly what was so hard, since I had only my own culture-bound, disoriented sensibility for an instrument.

Indeed, the problem was that Vietnam had become so much a fact of my consciousness as an American that I was having enormous difficulty getting it outside my head. The first experience of being there absurdly resembled meeting a favorite movie star, one who for years has played a role in one's fantasy life, and finding the actual person so much smaller, less vivid, less erotically charged, and mainly different. Most convincing were the experiences that were least real, like the evening of our arrival. I was nervous throughout the flight in the small International Control Commission plane that had belatedly taken off from Vientiane; and landing in Hanoi's Gia Lam airport at night several hours later, I was mainly relieved just to be alive and on the ground, and hardly bothered that I knew neither where I was nor whom I was with. Hugging my flowers, I crossed the dark landing area, trying to keep straight the names of the four smiling men from the Peace Committee who had come to meet us. And if our flight and landing had the quality of a hallucination, the rest of that night seemed like one vast back projection, with overvivid extensions and fore-shortenings of time, scale, and movement. First, there were either the few minutes or the hour spent waiting for our luggage in the bleak airport building, awkwardly chatting with the Vietnamese. Then, when we were distributed in three cars and started into the darkness, there was the rhythm of the ride into Hanoi. A little way from the airport, the cars lurched down a bumpy dirt road onto the narrow, shuddering pontoon bridge over the Red River that has replaced the bombed-out iron one, and inched across that; but once on the other side, the cars seemed to go too fast and, entering Hanoi, passing through dim streets, opened a rude swathe in the stream of indistinguishable figures on bicycles, until we halted in front of our hotel. Its name, Thong Nhat, means Reunification, someone said: a huge building, and indeterminate in style. A dozen people were sitting about the very plain lobby, mostly non-Orientals but at that point otherwise unidentifiable. After we were taken upstairs and shown to our large rooms, there was a late supper for us in a stark, deserted dining room with rows of propeller fans slowly turning overhead. "Our" Vietnamese waited for us in the lobby. When we joined them, we asked if, late as it was, they would mind going out with us for a walk. So out we went, weak with excitement. Along the streets, now almost empty of people, we passed clusters of trucks parked between tents which, they told us, sheltered all-night "mobile workshops" or "dispersed factories." We went as far as the Mot Cot pagoda in the Petit Lac, and lingering there, heard some—to me, barely intelligible—tales of ancient Vietnamese history. Once back in the hotel lobby, Oanh, evidently the leader of the group from the Peace Committee, gently urged us to go to bed. People in Hanoi, he explained, rise and eat breakfast very early (since the bombing started, most stores open at 5 AM and close a few hours later), and they would be coming by for us at 8 AM the next day, which happened to be Buddha's birthday, to take us to a pagoda. I remember reluctantly saying good night to the Vietnamese and to my two companions; in my room, spending a quarter of an hour trying to cope with the high vault of white mosquito netting covering the bed; and finally sinking into a difficult, agitated, but happy sleep.

Of course, North Vietnam was unreal that first night. But it continued to seem unreal, or at least incomprehensible, for days afterwards. To be sure, that initial haunting vision of wartime Hanoi at night was corrected by more mundane daytime experiences. The Thong Nhat Hotel shrank to ordinary size (one could even visualize it in its former incarnation, the Metropole of French colonial days); individuals of varying age and character emerged out of the silent collective traffic of bicyclists and pedestrians; and the Petit Lac and the nearby tree-shaded streets became places of daily resort, where we walked casually, without our guides, whenever it wasn't too hot and one or two or all three of us had a spare hour. Though so far from and so unlike the only cities I knew, those of America and Europe, Hanoi quickly gained an eerie familiarity. Yet when I was honest with myself I had to admit that the place was simply too foreign, that I really understood nothing at all, except at a "distance."

In his brilliant episode in the film *Far from Vietnam*, Godard reflects (as we hear his voice, we see him sitting behind an idle movie camera) that it would be good if we each made a Vietnam inside ourselves, especially if we cannot actually go there (Godard had wanted to shoot his episode in North Vietnam, but was denied a visa). Godard's point—a variant on Che's maxim that, in order to crack the American hegemony, revolutionaries have the duty to create "two, three, many Vietnams"—had seemed to me exactly right. What I'd been creating and enduring for the last four years was a Vietnam inside my head, under my skin, in the pit of my stomach. But the Vietnam I'd been thinking about for years was scarcely filled out at all. It was really only the mold into which the American seal was cutting. My problem was not to try to feel more inside myself. My problem was that I (luckier than Godard) was now actually in Vietnam for a brief time, yet somehow was unable to make the full intellectual and emotional connections that my political and moral solidarity with Vietnam implied.

The most economical way, I think, of conveying these early difficulties is to transcribe from journal entries I made during the first week after our arrival on the third of May.

May 5.

The cultural difference is the hardest thing to estimate, to overcome. A difference of manners, style, therefore of substance. (And how much of what I'm struck by is Asian, how much specifically Vietnamese, I am unlikely to find out on my first trip to Asia.) Clearly, they have a different way here of treating the guest, the stranger, the foreigner, not to mention the enemy. Also, I'm convinced, the Vietnamese have a different relation to language. The difference can't just be due to the fact that my sentences, already slowed down and simplified, more often than not have to be mediated by a translator. For even when I'm in conversation with someone who speaks English or French, it seems to me we're both talking baby talk.

To all this add the constraint of being reduced to the status of a child: scheduled, led about, explained to, fussed over, pampered, kept under benign surveillance. Not only a child individually but, even more exasperating, one of a group of children. The four Vietnamese from the Peace Committee who are seeing us around act as our nurses, our teachers. I try to discover the differences between each of them, but can't; and I worry that they don't see what's different or special about me. All too often I catch myself trying to please them, to make a good impression—to get the best mark of the class. I present myself as an intelligent, well-mannered, cooperative, uncomplicated person. So not only do I feel like a rather corrupt child but, being neither a child nor in fact as simple and easy to know as the way I'm coming on would indicate, I feel somewhat of a fraud. (It's no extenuation that this open, legible person is perhaps who I would like to be.)

Maybe, if I'm cheating, with the best intentions, trying to make it easier for them, they're doing the same for us. Is that why, though I know they must be different from each other, I can't get beyond the surface markings? Oanh has the most personal authority, walks and sits with that charming "American" slouch, and sometimes seems moody or distracted. (We've learned that his wife has been ill ever since she was captured and tortured for a year by the French in the early 1950's; and he has several small children.) Hieu alternates between boyishness— he giggles—and the pointed composure of a junior bureaucrat. Phan has the most affable manners; he usually seems out of breath when he talks, which he loves doing; he's also one of the very few plump Vietnamese I've seen. Toan generally looks eager and slightly intimidated, and never speaks unless you ask him a question. But what else? Phan is the oldest, I think. Today we learned, to our great surprise, that Oanh is forty-six. It doesn't help that every Vietnamese (especially the men, who rarely go bald or even gray) looks at least ten years younger than he is.

What makes it especially hard to see people as individuals is that everybody here seems to talk in the same style and to have the same things to say. This impression is reinforced by the exact repetition of the ritual of hospitality at each place we visit. A bare room, a low table, wooden chairs, perhaps a couch. We all shake hands, then sit around the table, which holds several plates of overripe green bananas, Vietnamese cigarettes, damp cookies, a dish of paper-wrapped candies made in China, cups for tea. We are introduced. They tell us their names. We shake hands again. Pause. The spokesman of their group, wherever we are visiting (a factory, a school, a government ministry, a museum), gazes at us benignly, smiles, "*Cac ban* ..." ("Friends ...") He has started his speech of welcome. Someone comes through a curtain and begins serving tea.

May 6.

Of course, I'm not sorry to have come. Being in Hanoi is at the very least a duty, for me an important act of personal and political affirmation. What I'm not yet reconciled to is that it's also a piece of political theatre. They are playing their roles, we (I) must play ours (mine). The heaviness of it all comes from the fact that the script is written entirely by them; and they're directing the play, too. Though this is how it has to be—it's their country, their life-and-death struggle, while we are volunteers, extras, figurants who retain the option of getting off the stage and sitting safely in the audience—it makes my acts here appear to me largely dutiful, and the whole performance a little sad.

We have a role: American friends of the Vietnamese struggle. (About forty Americans in some way connected with the anti-war movement in the States have made this trip before us.) The trip to Hanoi is a kind of reward or patronage. We are being given a treat, being thanked for our unsolicited efforts; and then we are to return home with a reinforced sense of solidarity, to continue our separate ways of opposing the current American policy.

There is, of course, an exquisite politeness in this corporate identity. We are not asked, separately or collectively, to say why we merit this trip. Our being recommended (by Americans who were invited earlier and retain the confidence of the Vietnamese) and our willingness to come (all this way, at our own expense, and facing the risk of prosecution when we return to the States) seem to put

Bob's, Andy's, and my efforts on the same level. Nobody here poses questions about what we specifically do for the anti-war movement, or asks us to justify the quality of our activities; it seems to be assumed that we each do what we can. Though our Vietnamese hosts evidently know we are not Communists, and indeed seem to have no illusions about the American Communist Party—"We know our Communist friends in the United States are not in great number," a government official remarked dryly—nobody inquires into our political beliefs. We are *cac ban* all.

Everybody says, "We know the American people are our friends. Only the present American government is our enemy." A journalist we met commended our efforts to "safeguard the freedom and prestige of the United States." Though I honor the nobility of this attitude, I'm exasperated by their naïveté. Do they really believe what they're saying? Don't they understand anything about America? Part of me can't help regarding them as children—beautiful, patient, heroic, martyred, stubborn children. And I know that I'm not a child, though the theatre of this visit requires that I play the role of one. The same shy, tender smile appears on the face of the soldier we pass in the park, the elderly Buddhist scholar, and the waitress in the hotel dining room as on the faces of the children lined up to greet us at the evacuated primary school we visited today just outside Hanoi; and we're smiling at them like that, too. We get little presents and souvenirs wherever we go, and at the end of each visit Bob distributes a handful of anti-war buttons (how lucky that he thought to bring a bagful of them). The most impressive of his random collection are the jumbo blue and white buttons from last October's March on the Pentagon, which we save for special occasions. How could we not be moved at the moment we are pinning on their tiny red and gold badges while they are adorning themselves with our big anti-war buttons? How could we not also be in bad faith?

The root of my bad faith: that I long for the three-dimensional, textured, "adult" world in which I live in America—even as I go about my (their) business in this two-dimensional world of the ethical fairy tale where I am paying a visit, and in which I do believe.

Part of the role (theirs and mine) is the stylizing of language: speaking mostly in simple declarative sentences, making all discourse either expository or interrogative. Everything is on one level here. All the words belong to the same vocabulary: struggle, bombings, friend, aggressor, imperialist, patriot, victory, brother, freedom, unity, peace. Though my strong impulse is to resist their flattening out of language, I've realized that I must talk this way—with moderation—if I'm to say anything that's useful to them. That even includes using the more loaded local epithets like "the puppet troops" (for the forces of the Saigon government) and "the American movement" (they mean *us*!). Luckily, I'm already comfortable with some of the key words. Within the last year, back in the States, I had started saying "the Front" (instead of Viet Cong) and "black people" (instead of Negroes) and "liberated zones" (for territory controlled by the National Liberation Front). But I'm far from getting it right, from their point of view. I notice that when I say "Marxism," it's usually rendered by our translator as "Marxism-Leninism." And while they may speak of "the socialist camp," it's hardly possible for me to say anything other than "Communist countries."

It's not that I judge their words to be false. For once, I think, the political and moral reality is as simple as the Communist rhetoric would have it. The French *were* "the French colonialists"; the Americans *are* "imperialist aggressors"; the Thieu-Ky regime *is* a "puppet government." Then what finicky private standard or bad vibrations make me balk? Is it just the old conviction of the inadequacy of that language, to which I was first introduced during my precociously political childhood when I read *PM* and Corliss Lamont and the Webbs on Russia, and later, by the time I was a junior at North Hollywood High School, worked in the Wallace campaign and attended screenings of Eisenstein films at the American-Soviet Friendship Society? But surely neither the philistine fraud of the American CP [Communist Party] nor the special pathos of fellow-traveling in the 1940's is relevant here: North Vietnam, spring 1968. Yet how difficult it is, once words have been betrayed, to take them seriously again. Only within the last two years (and that very much because of the impact of the Vietnam war) have I been able to pronounce the words "capitalism" and "imperialism" again. For more than fifteen years, though capitalism and imperialism hardly ceased to be facts in the world, the words themselves had seemed to me simply unusable, dead, dishonest (because a tool in the hands of dishonest people). A great deal is involved in these recent linguistic decisions: a new connection with my historical memory, my aesthetic sensibility, my very idea of the future. That I've begun to use some elements of Marxist or neo-Marxist language again seems almost a miracle, an unexpected remission of historical muteness, a new chance to address problems that I'd renounced ever understanding.

Still, when I hear these tag words here, spoken by the Vietnamese, I can't help experiencing them as elements of an *official* language, and they become again an alien way of talking. I'm not referring now to the truth of this language (the realities that the words point to), which I do acknowledge, but to the context and range of sensibility it presupposes. What's painfully exposed for me, by the way the Vietnamese talk, is the gap between ethics and aesthetics. As far as I can tell, the Vietnamese possess—even within the terribly austere and materially deprived existence they are forced to lead now—a lively, even passionate aesthetic sense. More than once, for instance, people have quite unaffectedly expressed their indignation and sadness at the disfigurement of the *beauty* of the Vietnamese countryside by the American bombing. Someone even commented on the "many beautiful names," like Cedar Falls and Junction City, that the Americans have given their "savage operations in the south." But the leading way of thinking and speaking in Vietnam is unreservedly moralistic. (I suspect this is quite natural to the Vietnamese, a cultural trait that precedes any grafting on of the moralizing framework of Communist language.) And perhaps it's the general tendency of aesthetic consciousness, when developed, to make judgments more complex and more highly qualified, while it's in the very nature of moral consciousness to be simplifying, even simplistic, and to sound—in translation at least—stiff and old-fashioned. There's a committee here (someone had left a piece of stationery in the hotel lobby) for maintaining contact with South Vietnamese intellectuals, called "Committee of Struggle Against US Imperialists and Henchmen's Persecution of Intellectuals in South Vietnam." Henchmen! But aren't they? In today's Vietnam News Agency bulletin the American soldiers are called "cruel thugs." Although again the quaintness of phrase makes me smile, that is just what they are—from the vantage point of helpless peasants being napalmed by swooping diving metal birds. Still, quite apart from the quaintness of particular words, such language does make me uncomfortable. Whether because I am laggard or maybe just dissociated, I both assent to the unreserved moral judgment and shy away from it, too. I believe they are right. At the same time, nothing here can make me forget that events are much more complicated than the Vietnamese represent them. But exactly what complexities would I have them acknowledge? Isn't it enough that their struggle is, objectively, just? Can they ever afford subtleties when they need to mobilize every bit of energy to continue standing up to the American Goliath? . . . Whatever I conclude, it seems to me I end up patronizing them.

Perhaps all I'm expressing is the difference between being an actor (them) and being a spectator (me). But that's a big difference, and I don't see how I can bridge it. My sense of solidarity with the Vietnamese, however genuine and felt, is a moral abstraction developed (and meant to be lived out) at a great distance from them. Since my arrival in Hanoi, I must maintain that sense of solidarity alongside new unexpected feelings which indicate that, unhappily, it will always remain a moral abstraction. For me—a spectator?—it's monochromatic here, and I feel oppressed by that.

May 7.

Now, I think, I really understand—for the first time—the difference between history and psychology. It's the world of psychology that I miss. (What I meant yesterday by the "adult" world.) They live exclusively in the world of history.

And not only in history, but in a monothematic history that people allude to in more or less the same terms wherever we go. Today we got it in full, during a long, guided tour of the Historical Museum: four thousand years of continuous history, more than two thousand years of being overrun by foreign aggressors. The first successful Vietnamese uprising against foreign rule, in AD 40, was led by two women generals, the Trung sisters. That was over a thousand years before Joan of Arc, our woman guide at the museum added, as if to indicate we hadn't registered the proper surprise at the idea of a woman general. And you also have two of them, I joked back. She smiled slightly, then went on: "The tradition of the two sisters remains until now. In the present struggle many ladies have shown themselves worthwhile." No pleasantry, that. Oanh, who we've learned is one of the leading composers in North Vietnam, has written a song about the two sisters, and many temples in Hanoi and nearby are dedicated to them.... As the Vietnamese understand their history, it consists essentially of one scenario, which has been played out over and over again. Particular historical identities dissolve into instructive equivalences. The Americans = the French (who first entered Vietnam in 1787 with missionaries, and officially invaded the country in 1858) = the Japanese (in World War II) = the "Northern feudalists" (our guide's usual way of referring to the millennia of invading Chinese, I suppose out of politeness to the nominal ally of today). The general who repelled the Chinese invasion of 1075–76, Ly Thuong Kiet, was a poet as well and used his poems to rouse the Vietnamese people to take up arms—just like Ho Chi Minh, the guide pointed out. She told us the generals who defended the country against three invasions by "the Mongols" (another euphemism for the Chinese?) in the thirteenth century—in 1257, 1284–85, and 1287–88—originated the basic techniques of guerrilla warfare that General Giap successfully employed against the French between 1946 and 1954 and now uses against the Americans. In one room, examining a terrain map of the battle site, we learned that the turning point in a struggle against an invasion by two hundred thousand Manchu dynasty troops in 1789 was a surprise Tet offensive. As she relates, with the aid of maps and dioramas, the great sea battles on the Bach Dang River in 938 and 1288 which successfully terminated other wars of resistance, I detect unmistakable parallels to the strategies used at Dien Bien Phu. (The other night we saw an hour film on the Dien Bien Phu campaign, part original footage and part reconstruction. Today, by the way, is the anniversary of that victory, though I've seen no signs in Hanoi of any festivities.)

My first reaction to the didactically positive way the Vietnamese have of recounting their history is to find it simpleminded ("childish" again). I have to remind myself that historical understanding can have other purposes than the ones I take for granted: objectivity and completeness. This is history for use—for survival, to be precise—and it is an entirely *felt* history, not the preserve of detached intellectual concern. The past continues in the form of the present, and the present extends backwards in time. I see that there's nothing arbitrary or merely quaint (as I'd thought) in the standard epithet for Americans which I've seen on billboards and wall posters: *giac My xam luoc,* "pirate American aggressors." The very first foreign invaders were pirates. So the Chinese, the French, the Japanese, now the Americans, and anybody else who invades Vietnam will always be pirates, too.

Even more than the Jews, the Vietnamese seem to suffer from an appalling lack of variety in their collective existence. History is one long martyrdom: in the case of Vietnam, the chain of episodes of victimization at the hands of great powers. And one of their proudest boasts is that people here have succeeded in retaining "Vietnamese characteristics, though we live close to the Chinese superpower and were under complete French domination for eighty years," in the words of our guide today. Perhaps only a martyr people, one which has managed to survive against crushing odds, develops so acute and personal a historical concern. And this extraordinarily vivid sense of history—of living simultaneously in the past, the present, and the future—must be one of the great sources of Vietnamese strength.

But the decision to survive at all costs in suffering obviously imposes its own aesthetic, its own peculiar and (to people not consciously driven by the imperative of survival) maddening sensibility. The Vietnamese historical sense, being, above all, a sense of the sameness of history, is reflected, naturally, in the sameness of what they say—what they feel we ought to listen to. I've become aware here of how greatly prized, and taken for granted, the value of *variety* is in Western culture. In Vietnam, apparently, something doesn't become less valuable or useful because it has been done (or said) before. On the contrary, repetition confers value on something. It is a positive moral style. Hence, the capsule summaries of Vietnamese history we get from most people we visit, almost as much a part of the ritual as the tea and green bananas and expressions of friendship for the American people whom we're supposed to represent.

But further, these speeches of historical recital that we hear almost daily are just one symptom of the general predilection of the Vietnamese for putting all information into a historical narrative. I've noticed that when we're discussing or asking questions about the country today, each account given to us is formulated around a pivotal date; usually either August 1945 (victory of the Vietnamese revolution, the founding of the state by Ho Chi Minh) or 1954 (expulsion of the French colonialists) or 1965 (beginning of "the escalation," as they call the American bombing). Everything is either before or after something else.

Their framework is chronological. Mine is both chronological and geographical. I am continually reaching toward cross-cultural comparisons, and these are the context of most of my questions. But because they don't share this context, they seem mildly puzzled by many things I ask. How hard it was yesterday, for instance, to get the affable, French-educated Minister of Higher Education, Professor Ta Quang Buu, to explore the differences between the French lycée curriculum used until 1954 and the program the Vietnamese have devised to replace it. Though he heard my question, for a while he simply didn't see the point of it. All he wanted was to outline the Vietnamese system (kindergarten plus ten grades), report how few schools of any kind existed before 1954 and how many have been opened since (except for a good medical school inherited from the French, almost all university-level facilities have had to be developed from scratch), cite figures on rising literacy, tell how increasing numbers of teachers have been trained and young people given access to higher education and older people enrolled in adult-education courses since that date. The same thing happened when we talked to the Minister of Public Health, Dr. Pham Ngoc Thach, in his office in Hanoi, and when we met the young doctor of the tiny hamlet of Vy Ban in Hoa Binh province. After explaining that most of the Vietnamese population had no medical services of any kind under the French, they were eager to tell us how many hospitals and infirmaries have been built and how many doctors have been trained and to describe the programs undertaken since 1954 that have brought malaria under control and virtually eliminated opium addiction, but were quite taken aback when we wanted to know whether Vietnamese medicine was entirely Western in orientation or whether, as we suspected, Western techniques were mixed with Chinese methods such as herbal medicines and acupuncture. They must find us dilettantish, and may even regard such questions as a means of refusing full emotional solidarity with the unity and urgency of their struggle. Perhaps. It's still true that since Andy, Bob, and I don't share a history with the Vietnamese the historical view does narrow our understanding. To gain insight into what the Vietnamese are trying to build we must relate what they tell us to knowledge and perspectives we already have. But what we know, of course, is just what they don't know. And so most of our questions are a kind of rudeness, to which they respond with unfailing courtesy and patience, but sometimes obtusely.

May 8.

Judging from these first days, I think it's hopeless. There is a barrier I can't cross. I'm overcome by how exotic the Vietnamese are—impossible for us to understand them, clearly impossible for them to understand us. No, I'm hedging here. The truth is: I feel I *can* in fact understand them (if not relate to them, except on their simplistic terms). But it seems to me that while my consciousness does include theirs, or could, theirs could never include mine. They may be nobler, more heroic, more generous than I am, but I have more on my mind than they do—probably just what precludes my ever being that virtuous. Despite my admiration for the Vietnamese and my shame over the deeds of my country, I still feel like someone from a "big" culture visiting a "little" culture. My consciousness, reared in that "big" culture, is a creature with many organs, accustomed to being fed by a stream of cultural goods, and infected by irony. While I don't think I'm lacking in moral seriousness, I shrink from having my seriousness ironed out; I know I'd feel reduced if there were no place for its contradictions and paradoxes, not to mention its diversions and distractions. Thus, the gluttonous habits of my consciousness prevent me from being at home with what I most admire, and—for all my raging against America—firmly unite me to what I condemn. "American friend" indeed!

Of course, I *could* live in Vietnam, or an ethical society like this one—but not without the loss of a big part of myself. Though I believe incorporation into such a society will greatly improve the lives of most people in the world (and therefore support the advent of such societies), I imagine it will in many ways impoverish mine. I live in an unethical society that coarsens the sensibilities and thwarts the capacities for goodness of most people but makes available for minority consumption an astonishing array of intellectual and aesthetic pleasures. Those who don't enjoy (in both senses) my pleasures have every right, from their side, to regard my consciousness as spoiled, corrupt, decadent. I, from my side, can't deny the immense richness of these pleasures, or my addiction to them. What came to mind this afternoon was the sentence of Talleyrand that Bertolucci used as the motto of his sad, beautiful film: "He who has not lived before the revolution has never known the sweetness of life." I told Andy, who knows the film, what I'd been thinking, and he confessed to similar feelings. We were walking alone in a quarter of Hanoi far from the hotel and, like truants, began talking—nostalgically?—about San Francisco rock groups and *The New York Review of Books*.

Does all this mental appetitiveness and lust for variety disqualify me from entering, at least partially, into the singular reality of North Vietnam? I suspect it does, that it already has, as indicated by my baffled, frustrated reactions to the Vietnamese so far. Maybe I'm only fit to share a people's revolutionary aspirations at a comfortable distance from them and their struggle—one more volunteer in the armchair army of bourgeois intellectuals with radical sympathies in the head. Before I give up, though, I must make sure I've read these feelings correctly. My impulse is to follow the old, severe rule: if you can't put your life where your head (heart) is, then what you think (feel) is a fraud. But it's premature to talk of fraud and hypocrisy. If the test is whether I can put my life (even imaginatively) in Vietnam, the time to take it isn't now but when I have a somewhat less meager grasp of the country.

Even if I fail the test of being able to identify myself with the Vietnamese, what have I actually proven? Perhaps I haven't experienced the constraints, real or imaginary, of ethical—or revolutionary—societies in general, only of this one. Maybe I'm only saying I find something uncongenial about North Vietnam.... And yet I do like the Vietnamese, respond to them, feel good with them, sometimes really happy here. Doesn't it all come down to the absurd complaint—the complaint of a real child, me—that people here aren't making it easier for me to perceive them, the wish that the Vietnamese "show" themselves to me clearly so that I can't find them opaque, simple-minded, naïve? Now I'm back where I started. The sense of the barrier between them and me. My not understanding them, their not understanding me. No judgments now (at least none I really believe).

May 9.

How odd to feel estranged from Vietnam here, when Vietnam has been present in my thoughts every day in America. But if the Vietnam I've carried around like a wound in my heart and mind is not invalidated by what I see in Hanoi, it doesn't seem particularly related to this place at this time either. Having arrived after March 31, we are not under bombardment, though along with everyone else in Hanoi we take shelter at least once a day when the American reconnaissance planes come over. Where civilians are being slaughtered, villages burned, and crops poisoned, we aren't permitted to go. (Not for reasons of military security, since earlier American visitors were taken to areas under bombardment, but out of concern for our safety: where there's American bombing now, it goes on almost round the clock. The average daily tonnage of bombs being dropped on North Vietnam since March 31, though confined to the area below the 19th parallel, *exceeds* the daily average unloaded on the whole country before the "limited bombing pause.") We see only a handsome, evenly impoverished, clean Asian City; we see charming, dignified people living amid bleak material scarcity and the most rigorous demands on their energies and patience. The leveled towns and villages in the countryside to which we drive on short trips already constitute a tableau from the past, a thoroughly *accepted* environment in which people go on functioning, working toward their victory, making their revolution. I wasn't prepared for all this calm. Thinking about Vietnam in America, it seems natural to dwell on destruction and suffering. But not here. In Vietnam, there is also a peaceful, fiercely industrious present with which a visitor must be connected; and I'm not. I want their victory. But I don't understand their revolution.

It's all around me, of course, but I feel I'm in a glass box. We're supposed to be learning about it through the "activities" Oanh & Co. have set up in consultation with us since our arrival. In principle, we wanted to see anything and everything, and that's what's happening—though individual interests are swiftly catered to. (It was at my request that we spent an afternoon watching a movie being shot at the principal film studio in Hanoi; because Bob wanted to meet some mathematicians, a meeting with six math professors from the University of Hanoi was arranged, to which we all ended up going.) We are truly seeing and doing a great deal: at least one visit or meeting is planned for every morning and afternoon, and often in the evening as well, though we have an hour and a half each for lunch and dinner and are encouraged to rest after lunch until three o'clock, when the worst heat of the day is over. In other words, we're in the hands of skilled bureaucrats specializing in relations with foreigners. (Yes, even Oanh—whom I like more and more. Especially he.) All right, I see the inevitability of that. Who else could possibly take charge of us? But even within that framework, shouldn't we be able to go beyond it? I don't think I can. I'm obsessed by the protocol of our situation, which leaves me unable to believe I'm seeing a genuine sample of what this country is like. That suggests the trip isn't going to teach me something usable about revolutionary societies, as I'd assumed it would—unless I count getting so shaken up, as I was yesterday, that I question my right to profess a radical politics at all.

But perhaps there isn't much an American radical *can* learn from the Vietnamese revolution, because the Vietnamese themselves are too alien, in contrast to the considerable amount I think one can learn from the Cuban revolution, because—especially from this perspective—the Cubans are pretty much like us. Though it's probably an error, I can't help comparing the Vietnamese with the Cuban revolution: that is, my experience of it during a three-month stay in Cuba in 1960, plus accounts of how it has developed from friends who've visited more recently. (I probably won't understand anything here until I put Cuba out of my mind. But I can't ignore an experience that seems to me comparable to this one which I felt I did understand and do have imaginative access to.) And almost all my comparisons turn out favorable to the Cubans, unfavorable to the Vietnamese—by the standard of what's useful, instructive, imitable, relevant to American radicalism.

Take, for instance, the populist manners of the Cuban revolution. The Cubans, as I remember well, are informal, impulsive, easily intimate, and manic, even marathon talkers. These may not always be virtues, but they seem so in the context of a successful, entrenched revolutionary society. In Vietnam, everything seems formal, measured, controlled, planned. I long for someone to be indiscreet here. To talk about his personal life, his emotions. To be carried away by "feeling." Instead, everyone is exquisitely polite, yet somehow bland. It fits with the impression Vietnam gives of being an almost sexless culture, from all that I've observed, and from the evidence of the three movies I've seen so far in Hanoi this week and the novel I read last night in English translation. (Hieu confirmed, when I asked him, that there is no kissing in Vietnamese plays and films; obviously there's none in the streets or parks. I haven't seen people touching each other even in a casual way.) As Cuba has proved, a country doesn't have to adopt the puritan style when it goes Communist. And, probably, the Vietnamese attitudes toward sex and the expression of private feeling formed part of this culture long before the advent of revolutionary Marxist idealism. Nevertheless, they do discomfort a Western neo-radical like myself for whom revolution means not only creating political and economic justice but releasing and validating personal (as well as social) energies of all kinds, including erotic ones. And this is what revolution has meant in Cuba—despite waves of interference mainly by old-style orthodox Communist bureaucrats, who have been contested by Fidel precisely on this point.

I can't help contrasting the casual egalitarianism I observed among Cubans, whatever their rank or degree of responsibility, with the strongly hierarchical features of this society. No one is in the least servile here, but people know their place. While the deference I notice given to some by others is always graceful, there is clearly the feeling that certain people are more important or valuable than others and deserve a bigger share of the pitifully few comforts available. Hence, the store to which we were taken the third day to get tire sandals and have us each fitted for a pair of Vietnamese trousers. Hieu and Phan told us, with an almost proprietary pride, that this was a special store, reserved for foreigners (diplomatic personnel, guests) and important government people. I thought they should recognize that the existence of such facilities is "un-Communist." But maybe I'm showing here how "American" I am.

I'm troubled, too, by the meals at the Thong Nhat. While every lunch and dinner consists of several delicious meat and fish courses (we're eating only Vietnamese food) and whenever we eat everything in one of the large serving bowls a waitress instantly appears to put another one on our table, ninety-nine percent of the Vietnamese will have rice and bean curd for dinner tonight and are lucky to eat meat or fish once a month. Of course I haven't said anything. They'd probably be mystified, even insulted, if I suggested that we shouldn't be eating so much more than the average citizen's rations. It's well known that lavish and (what would be to us) self-sacrificing hospitality to guests is a staple of Oriental culture. Do I really expect them to violate their own sense of decorum? Still, it bothers me.... It also exasperates me that we're driven even very short distances; the Peace Committee has rented two cars, in fact—Volgas—that wait with their drivers in front of the hotel whenever we're due to go anywhere. The office of the NLF [National Liberation Front] delegation in Hanoi, which we visited the other day, was all of two blocks from the hotel. And some of our destinations proved to be no more than fifteen or twenty blocks away. Why don't they let us walk, as Bob, Andy, and I have agreed among ourselves we'd feel more comfortable doing? Do they have a rule: only the best for the guests? But that kind of politeness, it seems to me, could well be abolished in a Communist society. Or must we go by car because they think we're weak, effete foreigners (Westerners? Americans?) who also need to be reminded to get out of the sun? It disquiets me to think that Vietnamese might regard walking as beneath our dignity (as official guests, celebrities, or something). Whatever their reason, there's no budging them on this. We roll through the crowded streets in our big ugly black cars—the chauffeurs blasting away on their horns to make people on foot and on bicycles watch out, give way.... Best, of course, would be if they would lend us, or let us rent, bicycles. But though we've dropped hints to Oanh more than once, it's clear they don't or won't take the request seriously. When we broach it, are they at least amused? Or do they just think we're being silly or impolite or dumb?

All I seem to have figured out about this place is that it's a very complex self that an American brings to Hanoi. At least this American! I sometimes have the miserable feeling that my being here (I won't speak for Andy and Bob) is a big waste of our Vietnamese hosts' time. Oanh should be spending these days writing music. Phan could reread Moliere (he taught literature before he started working full-time for the Peace Committee) or visit his teenage daughters, who have been evacuated to the countryside. Hieu, whose profession turns out to be journalism, could be usefully composing articles in the dreadful prose of the North Vietnamese press. Only Toan, who apparently has some clerical job, might lose out; tagging along with the three others to entertain and keep busy the overgrown obtuse foreign guests is probably more amusing than that. What do the Vietnamese imagine is happening to us here? Do they grasp when we understand and when we don't? I'm thinking particularly of Oanh, who is obviously very shrewd and has traveled a lot in Europe, but also of all the smiling people who talk to us, flatter us ("We know your struggle is hard," someone said today), explain things to us. I fear they don't know the difference. They are simply too generous, too credulous.

But I'm also drawn to that kindly credulity. I like how people stare, often gape at us wherever we go in Hanoi. I feel they are enjoying us, that it's a pleasant experience for them to see us. I asked Oanh today if he thought people in the streets realized that we are Americans. He said that most wouldn't. Then who do they think we are, I asked. Probably Russians, was his answer; and indeed, several people have called out *tovarich* and some other Russian word at us. Most people, though, don't say anything in our direction. They stare calmly, point, then discuss us with their neighbors. Hieu says the comment most frequently made about us when we stroll or go to the movies is—delivered with good-natured amazement—how tall we are.

I go out for walks more often by myself now, whenever it's not too hot—trying to relate to the looks people give me, enjoying the ambiguities of my identity, protected by the fact that I don't speak Vietnamese and can only look back and smile. I'm no longer even surprised, as I first was, at how comfortable I am walking alone, even when I get lost in obscure neighborhoods far from the hotel. Though I'm aware of the possibility of an unpleasant incident occurring when I'm in another part of the city, unable to explain who I am or even read signs, I still feel entirely safe. There must be very few foreigners in Hanoi—except within a few blocks of the Thong Nhat, I've seen no one on the streets who isn't Vietnamese; yet here I walk unescorted among these people as if I had a perfect right to be prowling around Hanoi and to expect them all, down to the last old man squatting by the curb selling wooden flutes, to understand that and to ignore me in their amiable way. The impression of civility and lack of violence Hanoi gives is astounding, not just in comparison with any big American city but with Phnom Penh and Vientiane as well. People here are animated, plainly gregarious, but notably unquarrelsome among themselves. Even when the streets are most crowded, there's scarcely any strident noise. Though I see many small but not too well-nourished children and babies, I've yet to hear one cry.

Perhaps I feel so secure because I don't take the Vietnamese altogether seriously as "real people," according to the grim view popular where I come from that "real people" are dangerous, volatile; one is never altogether safe with them. I hope it's not that. I know I wouldn't prefer the Vietnamese to be mean or ill-tempered. But as much as I love the deep, sweet silence of Hanoi, I do miss among the Vietnamese a certain element of abrasiveness, a bigger—it doesn't have to be louder—range in their feelings.

For instance, it seems to me a defect that the North Vietnamese aren't good enough haters. How else to explain the odd fact that they actually appear to be quite fond of America? One of the recurrent themes of Dr. Thach's conversation with us was his fervent admiration for America's eminence in technology and science. (This from a cabinet minister of the country being ravaged by the cruelly perfect weapons produced by that very science and technology.) And I suspect that the extent to which the Vietnamese are so interested in and well informed about American politics—as I learned answering some questions put to me in the last days about the Nebraska primary, about Lindsay's influence in Harlem, and about American student radicalism—isn't mere expediency, part of the policy of knowing your enemy, but springs from just plain fascination with the United States. The government and professional people here who have radios listen regularly to the Voice of America and, to be sure, chuckle away at the American version of the war: this week, it's the VOA's denial that any serious military engagements are taking place in Saigon. But at the same time they seem quite respectful of American political processes and even a little sympathetic to the problems America faces as the leading world power. Poets read us verses about "your Walt Whitman" and "your Edgar Allan Poe." At the Writers Union tonight someone asked me if I knew Arthur Miller and flushed with shy pleasure when I said I did and could pass on to him the copy of the Vietnamese translation of *Death of a Salesman* I'd just been shown. "Tell us about your Norman Mailer," a young novelist asked me, and then apologized because Mailer hasn't yet been translated into Vietnamese. And they all wanted to know what kind of books I write, and made me promise to send them copies when I got back to the States. "We are very interested in American literature," someone repeated. Few translations of fiction are being published in Hanoi now, but one of the few this year was an anthology of American short stories: Mark Twain, Jack London, Hemingway, Dorothy Parker, plus some of the "progressive" writers from the 1930's favored in Eastern Europe. When I mentioned that Americans didn't consider Howard Fast and Albert Maltz in the same class as most others in the collection, one Vietnamese writer assured me they knew that. The trouble was that they actually had very few books—their main library, at the University of Hanoi, was bombed—and most of the volumes of American literature in Hanoi are the choices, and editions, of the Foreign Languages Press in Moscow. "In socialist countries with whom we have normal relations, we can't find modern American writers," he added with a laugh. Another writer who was listening to our conversation grinned.

Of course, I'm delighted to learn that some Vietnamese are not unaware that belonging to the "socialist camp" has its disadvantages—among them, cultural isolation and intellectual provincialism. But it's also sad to think of them carrying the burden of that awareness as well, when they're so acutely conscious of Vietnam as an isolated, provincial country in its own right. Doctors, writers, academics we've talked to speak of feeling desperately cut off. As one professor said, after describing the growth of the science faculties since 1954: "But we still fail to grasp the main tendencies of work going on in the rest of the world. The material we receive is late and not adequate." For all their pride in the progress made since the French were expelled, people often mention to us, apologetically, what a "backward" country Vietnam still is. And then I realize how aware they are that we come from the world's most "advanced" country; their respect for the United States is there, whether voiced or not.

It's at these moments that I also feel like the visitor from America, though in another way. It must be because I'm so American after all, too profoundly a citizen of the nation that thinks itself the greatest in everything, that I feel actually embarrassed by the modest (if proud) self-affirmation of citizens of a small, weak nation. Their cordial interest in America is so evidently sincere that it would be boorish not to respond to it. Yet somehow it chills me, for it seems a little indecent. I'm aware now how their unexpectedly complex, yet ingenuous, relation to the United States overlays every situation between individual Vietnamese and Bob, Andy, and me. But I don't have the insight or the moral authority to strip us down to our "real" situation, beyond pathos. My political sympathies being what they are, perhaps there's no way for me or someone like me to be here except in some stereotyped capacity (as an "American friend"), no way to avoid being either self-effacing or passive or sentimental or patronizing— just as there's no way for Americans, myself included, not to measure a good six inches taller than the average Vietnamese.

There are pages more of the same in the first half of the journal I kept during my stay, interspersed with pages and pages of detailed notes on each of our visits and encounters. The strictly reportorial body of my journal, full of factual information and physical descriptions and summaries of conversations, conveys an attitude of intense, uncomplicatedly attentive concentration. But the subjective interludes, which I have partly transcribed, convey something else—the callowness and stinginess of my response.

It wasn't that I'd expected to feel at ease in North Vietnam, or to find the Vietnamese as a people exactly like Europeans and Americans. But neither had I expected to be so baffled, so mistrustful of my experiences there—and unable to subdue the backlash of my ignorance. My understanding of the country was limited to Vietnam's election as the target of what's most ugly in America: the principle of "will," the self-righteous taste for violence, the insensate prestige of technological solutions to human problems. I had some knowledge of the style of American will, from living at various times in the Southwest, in California, in the Midwest, in New England, and in recent years in New York, and from observing its impact on Western Europe during the last decade. What I didn't understand, hadn't even a clue to, was the nature of Vietnamese will—its styles, its range, its nuances. Breton has distinguished two forms of the will in authentic revolutionary struggle: "revolutionary patience" and "the cry." But these can't be confronted without grasping something of the specific quality of a people—just what I was finding so difficult in North Vietnam. Whether I concluded that my limitations, or theirs, were being exposed by my inability to have a satisfactory contact with the Vietnamese, the impasse was the same. By around the fifth day, as the extracts from my journal indicate, I was ready to give up—on myself, which meant on the Vietnamese as well.

And then, suddenly, my experience started changing. The psychic cramp with which I was afflicted in the early part of my stay began to ease and the Vietnamese as real people, and North Vietnam as a real place, came into view.

The first sign was that I became more comfortable in talking to people: not only to Oanh, our chief guide—I talked to him more than to any other Vietnamese during my stay—but also to a militia girl or factory worker or schoolteacher or doctor or village leader whom we'd spend an hour with and never see again. I became less preoccupied with the constrictions of their language (a great deal of which I knew must be put down to that "abstractness" or "vagueness" of speech remarked on by Western visitors to every Oriental country) and with the reduction of my own resources of expression, and more sensitive to distinctions in the way the Vietnamese talked. For a start, I could distinguish between a propagandistic level of language (which still may convey the truth, but nevertheless sounds oppressive and wrong) and a merely simple kind of language. I learned, too, to pay more rather than less attention to whatever was constantly reiterated, and discovered the standard words and phrases to be richer than I'd thought.

Take, for instance, the notion of respect. "We respect your Norman Morrison" was a phrase often used in the ceremonial speeches of greeting made to us at each of our visits in Hanoi and in the countryside. We learned that Oanh had written a popular "Song to Emily"—Norman Morrison's youngest daughter, whom he took along with him when he went to immolate himself in front of the Pentagon. At the Writers Union, someone chanted for us a beautiful poem (which I'd read beforehand in English and French translation) called "The Flame of Morrison." Truck drivers taking supplies along the perilous route down to the 17th parallel are likely to have a picture of Norman Morrison pasted on their sun visors, perhaps alongside a photograph of Nguyen Van Troi, the Saigonaise youth who was executed several years ago for plotting to assassinate McNamara during his visit to South Vietnam. At first a visitor is likely to be both moved by this cult of Norman Morrison and made uncomfortable by it. Although the emotion of individuals is plainly unfeigned, it seems excessive, sentimental, and redolent of the hagiography of exemplary cardboard heroes that has been a regular feature of Stalinist and Maoist culture. But after the twentieth time that Norman Morrison's name was invoked (often shyly, always affectionately, with an evident desire to be friendly and gracious to us, who were Americans), I started understanding the very specific relation the Vietnamese have with Norman Morrison. The Vietnamese believe that the life of a people, its very will, is nourished and sustained by heroes. And Norman Morrison really is a hero, in a precise sense. (The Vietnamese don't, as I suspected at first, overestimate the actual impact of his sacrifice upon the conscience of America; far more than its practical efficacy, what matters to them is the moral success of his deed, its *completeness* as an act of self-transcendence.) Therefore, they're speaking quite accurately when they declare their "respect" for him and when they call him, as they often do, their "benefactor." Norman Morrison has become genuinely important for the Vietnamese, so much so that they can't comprehend that he mightn't be an equally important element of consciousness to us, three of their "American friends."

That very definition of us as friends, initially a source of some embarrassment and malaise, now seemed—another sign of the change in me—more comprehensible. Whereas at first I'd felt both moved, sometimes to tears, and constrained by the friendliness shown to us, eventually I could simply appreciate it, becoming more genuine and flexible in my own response. I surely had no grounds for suspecting the Vietnamese of duplicity, or for dismissing their attitude as naïve. Since, after all, I was a friend, why was it naïve or gullible of them to know that? Instead of being so amazed at their ability to transcend their situation as America's victims and our identity as citizens of the enemy nation, I began to imagine concretely how it was indeed possible for the Vietnamese, at this moment in their history, to welcome American citizens as friends. It was important, I realized, not to be abashed by all the small gifts and flowers thrust on us wherever we went. I'd minded that we weren't allowed to pay for anything during our stay— not even the numerous books I asked for or the cables I sent my son in New York every few days to let him know I was all right (despite my insistence that at least I be allowed to pay for these). Gradually, I could see it was just stingy of me to resist, or feel oppressed by, the material generosity of our hosts.

But the change didn't consist only in my becoming a more graceful recipient of Vietnamese generosity, a better audience for their elaborate courtesy. Here, too, there was something further to be understood; and through more contact with people in Vietnam, I discovered their politeness to be quite unlike "ours," and not only because there was so much more of it. In America and Europe, being polite (whether in large or small doses) always carries a latent hint of insincerity, a mild imputation of coercion. For us, politeness means conventions of amiable behavior people have agreed to practice, whether or not they "really" feel like it, because their "real" feelings aren't consistently civil or generous enough to guarantee a working social order. By definition, politeness is never truly honest; it testifies to the disparity between social behavior and authentic feeling. Perhaps this disparity, accepted in this part of the world as an article of faith concerning the human condition, is what gives us our taste for irony. Irony becomes essential as a mode of indicating the truth, a whole life-truth: namely, that we both mean and don't mean what we're saying or doing. I had originally been disconcerted by the absence of irony among the Vietnamese. But if I could renounce, at least imaginatively, my conviction of the inevitability of irony, the Vietnamese suddenly looked far less undecipherable. Their language didn't seem quite so imprisoning and simplistic, either. (For the development of ironic truths, one needs lots of words. Without irony, not so many words are required.)

The Vietnamese operate by another notion of civility than the one we're accustomed to, and that implies a shift in the meaning of honesty and sincerity. Honesty as it is understood in Vietnam bears little resemblance to the sense of honesty that has been elevated by secular Western culture virtually above all other values. In Vietnam, honesty and sincerity are functions of the dignity of the individual. A Vietnamese, by being sincere, reinforces and enhances his personal dignity. In this society, being sincere often means precisely forfeiting one's claim to dignity, to an attractive appearance; it means the willingness to be shameless. The difference is acute. This culture subscribes to an empirical or descriptive notion of sincerity, which measures whether a man is sincere by how fully and accurately his words mirror his hidden thoughts and feelings. The Vietnamese have a normative or prescriptive notion of sincerity. While our aim is to make the right alignment—correspondence—between one's words and behavior and one's inner life (on the assumption that the truth voiced by the speaker is ethically neutral, or rather is rendered ethically neutral or even praiseworthy by the speaker's willingness to avow it), theirs is to construct an appropriate relation between the speaker's words and behavior and his social identity. Sincerity, in Vietnam, means behaving in a manner *worthy* of one's role; sincerity is a mode of ethical aspiration.

Thus, it's off the point to speculate whether the warmth of Pham Van Dong during the hour conversation Bob, Andy, and I had with him in the late afternoon of May 16 was sincere in our sense, or whether the Prime Minister "really" wanted to embrace us as we left his office, before walking us out the front door and across the gravel driveway to our waiting cars. He was sincere in the Vietnamese sense: his behavior was attractive, it was becoming, it intended good. Nor is it quite right to ask whether the Vietnamese "really" hate the Americans, even though they say they don't; or to wonder why they don't hate Americans, if indeed they do not. One basic unit of Vietnamese culture is the extraordinary, beautiful gesture. But gesture mustn't be interpreted in our sense—something put on, theatrical. The gestures a Vietnamese makes aren't a performance external to his real personality. By means of gestures, those acts brought off according to whatever standards he affirms, his self is constituted. And in certain cases, personality can be wholly redefined by a single, unique gesture: for a person to do something finer than he ever has done may promote him, without residue, to a new level on which such acts are regularly possible. (In Vietnam, moral ambition is a truth—an already confirmed reality—in a way it isn't among us, because of our psychological criteria of "the typical" and "the consistent." This contrast sheds light on the quite different role political and moral exhortation plays in a society like Vietnam. Much of the discourse we would dismiss as propagandistic or manipulative possesses a depth for the Vietnamese to which we are insensitive.)

Vietnam—at least in its official view of itself—may strike the secular Western eye as a society tremendously overextended ethically, that is, psychologically. But such a judgment depends entirely on our current, modest standards of how much virtue human beings are capable of. And Vietnam is, in many ways, an affront to these standards. I remember feeling just so affronted when, during the first afternoon of a two-day drive into mountainous Hoa Binh province north of Hanoi, we stopped briefly somewhere in the countryside to visit the grave of an American pilot. As we got out of our cars and walked off the road about fifty yards through the high grass, Oanh told us that it was the pilot of an F-105 brought down by a farmer with a rifle about a year ago. The pilot had failed to eject and crashed with his plane on this very spot; some villagers recovered his body from the wreckage. Coming into a clearing, we saw not a simple grave but an elevated mound decorated with chunks of the plane's engine and a crumpled piece of wing, like a Chamberlain sculpture, and with flowers, and topped by a wooden marker on which was written the pilot's name and the date of his death. I stood there some minutes feeling haunted, barely able to comprehend that initial act of burial, astonished by the look of the site and the evidence that it was still being looked after. And afterwards, when the vice-chairman of the province's administrative council, who was traveling in my car, explained that the pilot had been buried, and in "a coffin of good wood," so that his family in America could come after the war and take his body home, I felt almost undone. What is one to make of this amazing act? How could these people, who have had spouses and parents and children murdered by this pilot and his comrades (the load of one F-105, four canisters of CBU's, kills every unsheltered living creature within an area of one square kilometer), quietly take up their shovels and tastefully arrange his grave? What did they feel? Did they realize that whatever his objective guilt, he, just as much as their dead, was a precious, irreplaceable human being who should not have died? Could they pity him? Did they forgive him? But maybe these questions are misleading. What's likely is that the villagers thought burying the pilot was a beautiful (they would probably say "humane") thing to do—a standard that both overrides and transforms their personal feelings, so far as these might enter the matter.

Such transpersonal gestures are hard for a visitor to credit on their own terms. Certainly, I wasn't entirely able to put aside my own habitual understanding of how people function. Throughout the two weeks, I was continually tempted to frame psychological questions about the Vietnamese—all the while knowing how loaded such questions are with arbitrary, Western ethical assumptions. If it even makes sense to inquire, for instance, what "ego" is for the Vietnamese, I could observe that it doesn't take many of the expressive forms familiar to us. People in North Vietnam seem astonishingly calm, and though they talk of little else but the war, their discourse is singularly unmarked by hate. Even when they use the melodramatic Communist language of denunciation, it comes out sounding dutiful and a little flat. They talk of atrocities, the marrow of their history, with an almost gentle sorrow, and still with amazement. Can these things really have happened, their manner says. Did the French really disembowel that row of handcuffed plantation workers who had gone on strike, as the photograph we saw in the Revolutionary Museum shows? How can the Americans not be *ashamed* of what they're doing here? was the unspoken question that echoed throughout our tour of another, smaller "museum" in Hanoi devoted to a display of the various genocidal weapons used by the Americans on North Vietnam in the last three years. Indeed, I think, they don't quite understand—which, after all, is just the failure of understanding one might expect to find in a culture built on shame that's currently under attack by a culture whose energies come from deploying huge increments of guilt.

That Vietnam is a culture founded on shame probably accounts for much of what one sees (and does not see) there in the range of people's expressiveness. And my formation in a culture founded on guilt is surely one reason I found it hard to understand them. I would guess that guilt-cultures are typically prone to intellectual doubt and moral convolutedness, so that, from the point of view of guilt, all cultures founded on shame are indeed "naïve." The relation to moral demands tends to be much less ambivalently felt in shame-cultures, and collective action and the existence of public standards have an inherent validity they do not possess for us.

Prominent among these public standards in Vietnam is decorum—more generally, the concern for maintaining in all exchanges between people an exacting moral tone. I might have imagined this concern to be simply Asian if I hadn't already seen something of Cambodians and Laotians, in contrast with whom the Vietnamese are much more dignified and reserved, even prudish in their manner, and also more discreet in their dress. No matter how fiercely hot it gets, nowhere does one see in Vietnam (as one does throughout Cambodia and Laos) a man in shorts or without a shirt. Everyone is neatly, if shabbily, dressed from neck to ankles—women as well as men wear long trousers—and great value is placed on being clean. The pride of people in Na Phon when they showed us their two-stall brick and cement public latrine, the first such facility in the hamlet and completed just a day earlier, had to do with more than hygiene or convenience. The new latrine was a kind of moral victory. "All the water of the Eastern Sea could not wash away the dirt left by the enemy" is a saying that dates from one of the innumerable Vietnamese struggles against the Chinese, a war which began in 1418 and ended victoriously in 1427. No doubt the North Vietnamese regard with a similar anguish the three years of American assault: once again, and most horrendously, their country has been defiled. The moral metaphor of cleanliness and dirt is, of course, found almost universally, in all cultures; still, I felt it to be especially strong in Vietnam. Its strength is strikingly expressed in the eighteenth-century epic *Kieu*, the most famous work of Vietnamese literature. (The poem is studied in detail in the schools and recited often on the radio; practically every Vietnamese knows long passages from it by heart.) When the story begins, the heroine, *Kieu*, is a young girl. A young man sees her, falls in love with her, secretly, and patiently courts her, but family duties suddenly call him away before he can explain. Believing herself abandoned and faced by a family crisis of her own, *Kieu* sells herself as a concubine to a rich man, to save her father from debtors' prison. Only after twenty years of mistreatment and degradation, in which she ends up in a brothel and from there escapes to become a bonze, is *Kieu* able to return home, where she meets again the man she loved. He asks her to marry him. In the long final scene, which takes place on their wedding night, *Kieu* tells her husband that, although she loves him deeply and has never enjoyed sexual relations with any other man, their marriage can't be consummated. He protests that her unfortunate life during their long separation means nothing to him; but she insists that she is not clean. Precisely as they love each other, she argues, they must make this sacrifice.

Eventually, out of respect and love for her, he agrees. The poem ends with a description of the harmony and joy of their married life. To a Western sensibility, such a happy ending is hardly happy at all. We would rather have *Kieu* die of tuberculosis in the arms of her true love, just after they are reunited, than award them a lifetime together of renunciation. But to the Vietnamese, even today, the resolution of the story is both satisfying and just. What may appear to us as their being "closed," secretive, or unexpressive, I think, is partly that they are a remarkably fastidious people.

Needless to say, the standards of today are not the same as those proposed in *Kieu*. Sexual self-control, however, is still much admired. In present-day Vietnam, women and men work, eat, fight, and sleep together without raising any issue of sexual temptation. By now the Vietnamese understand that Westerners don't have the same standards of sexual propriety. Oanh, when he told me that it's very unusual for Vietnamese husbands and wives to be unfaithful to each other, even in circumstances of lengthy separation caused by war, said he knew marital fidelity was "not common" in the West. With an edge of self-mockery, he mentioned how shocked he was on one of his first trips to Europe—it was to Russia—to hear people at parties telling "indecent" jokes to each other. Now, he assured me, it bothers him less. With their incorrigible politeness, the Vietnamese have concluded that we arrange such matters differently. Thus, whenever Andy Kopkind, Bob Greenblatt, and I traveled in the countryside, no matter how primitive and small the sleeping accommodations, we were always given separate rooms (or something that passed for rooms); but on one of these trips, when we were accompanied by a nurse because Bob had become slightly ill in Hanoi the day before our departure, I noticed that the young, pretty nurse slept in the same room as our guides and drivers, who were all men. . . . Sexual self-discipline, I imagine, must be taken for granted in Vietnam. It's only a single aspect of the general demand made on the individual to maintain his dignity and to put himself at the disposal of others for the common good. In contrast to Laos and Cambodia, with their "Indian" or "southern" atmosphere that derives from an eclectic blend of Hindu and Buddhist influences, Vietnam presents the paradox of a country sharing the same severely tropical climate but living by the classical values—hard work, discipline, seriousness—of a country with a temperate or cold climate. This "northern" atmosphere is undoubtedly the legacy of those hordes of "Northern feudalists." (I also gathered that it is more attenuated in the southern region of the country. People in Hanoi describe the Saigonese as more easygoing, more emotional, more charming, but also less honest and sexually looser—in short, the conventional northern clichés about southerners.)

Thus, while the exacting demands the Vietnamese make upon themselves, in their present form, are undoubtedly reinforced by the paramilitary ethos of a left-revolutionary society under invasion, their basic form has deep historical roots, particularly in the Confucian as distinct from the Buddhist strands in Vietnamese culture. In some societies, notably Chinese, these two traditions have been experienced as sharply antagonistic. But in Vietnam, I suspect, they have not. Most Vietnamese, of course, apart from a large Catholic minority, are Buddhists. Even though we saw mostly old people praying in the pagodas, a good deal of domestic ritual still takes place (we saw altars in many homes); beyond that, there appears to be a considerable secular continuity with Buddhist values. Nevertheless, whatever in Vietnam persists of the Buddhist ethos—with its fatalism, its intellectual playfulness, its stress on charity—seems quite compatible with the ethos of discipline characteristic of Confucianism. The behavior of the Vietnamese reflects the Confucian idea that both the body politic and an individual's well-being depend on cultivating the rules of appropriate and just behavior. Also intact is the Confucian view expressed by Hsün Tzu: "All rules of decorum and righteousness are the product of the acquired virtue of the sage and not the products of the nature of man." This Confucian idea of a people's dependence on its sages partly explains the veneration felt by the Vietnamese for Ho Chi Minh, their sage-poet-leader. But only partly. As indeed the Vietnamese often insist, their regard for Ho has nothing in common with the mindless adulation surrounding Mao today. Ho's birthday is mainly an annual occasion for the North Vietnamese to show their good taste, the delicacy of their feeling toward him. "We love and respect our leader," commented the monthly journal *Hoc Tap* on Ho's birthday last year, "but we do not deify him." Far from treating him like the usual bigger-than-life, heroic, all-wise leader, people I met spoke of Ho as if they knew him personally, and what fascinates and stirs them is their sense of him as a real man. Humorous anecdotes illustrating his modesty and shyness are legion. People find him charming, even a little eccentric. And they are moved when they speak of him, reminiscing about his years of privation in exile and his sufferings in Chinese jails throughout the 1930's, and worrying over his physical frailty. *Bac Ho*, Uncle Ho, is no special title, with Orwellian Big Brother overtones, but ordinary courtesy; a Vietnamese of any age addresses someone of an older generation to whom he's not related as "Uncle" or "Aunt." (Swedish has the same usage, except that *tant* and *farbror* are used only by children or young people to address adults who are strangers, and wouldn't be said by a middle-aged person to a seventy-year-old.) The feeling for Ho Chi Minh, an intimate affection and gratitude, is only the apex of the feeling that exists between people in a small, beleaguered nation who are able to regard each other as members of one big family. Indeed, almost all the virtues admired by the Vietnamese—such as frugality, loyalty, self-sacrifice, and sexual fidelity—have, as their basic supporting metaphor, the authority of family life. Here is still another feature pointing back to Confucianism—as distinct from Buddhism, which attaches the highest prestige to monastic separation from society and the renunciation of family ties—and away from the austerity and "puritanism" of Vietnamese culture considered as something relatively new, the graft of revolutionary ideology. (Considered as "Marxist-Leninist *thought*," Vietnamese Communism seems conveniently vague and outstandingly platitudinous.) Though a visitor is tempted to attribute the extraordinary discipline of the country in large measure to the influence of Communist ideology, it's probably the other way around: that the influence of Communist moral demands derived its authority from the indigenous Vietnamese respect for a highly moralized social and personal order.

But I am making the Vietnamese sound more solemn than they are, when actually what is particularly noticeable is the grace with which these ends are pursued. In conversation, the Vietnamese are low-keyed; even in public meetings, they are laconic and not particularly hortatory. It is hard to recognize the passionate consciousness when it lacks the signs of passion as we know them— such as agitation and pathos. One realizes that these are people living through the most exalted moment of their consciousness, the climax of more than a quarter of a century of continuous struggle. They have already beaten the French against incredible odds. (The French first brought napalm to Vietnam. Between 1950 and 1954, eighty percent of the French budget for the war was paid for by the United States.) Now, even more incredibly, they've demonstrated they can endure whatever punishment the Americans can inflict on them, and still cohere and prosper as a people, while in the South the National Liberation Front is steadily extending its support and control of territory. Yet most of the time this mood of exaltation has to be inferred by the sympathetic observer—not because the Vietnamese are unemotional, but because of their habitual emotional tact, a cultural principle of the conservation of emotional energy. We were told that in heavily bombed places in the countryside it's common for the farmers to take their coffins with them each day when they go to the rice fields, so that if someone dies, he can be buried right then while the others continue working. In the evacuated schools, children pack up their personal belongings and bedding before they leave the dormitory hut each morning for classes and pile the tiny bundles neatly in the nearest dirt shelter, in case there is a bombing raid during the day and the hut bums down; each evening they take their bundles out of the shelter, unpack them, and set up the dormitory again. . . . More than once, observing the incredible matter-of-factness of the Vietnamese, I thought of the Jews' more wasteful and more brilliant style of meeting their historical destiny of chronic suffering and struggle. One advantage of the Vietnamese over the Jews as a martyr people, perhaps, is simply that of any culture dominated by the peasant type over a culture that has crystallized into an urban bourgeoisie. Unlike the Jews, the Vietnamese belong to a culture whose various psychic types have not yet reached a high degree of articulation (forcing them to reflect upon each other). It is also the advantage of having a history, albeit mainly of cruel persecution, that is anchored to a land with which people identify themselves, rather than simply (and, therefore, complicatedly) to an "identity."

The Jews' manner of experiencing their suffering was direct, emotional, persuasive. It ran the gamut from stark declamation to ironic self-mockery. It attempted to engage the sympathy of others. At the same time, it projected a despair over the difficulties of engaging others. The source of the Jewish stubbornness, of their miraculous talent for survival, is their surrender to a complex kind of pessimism. Perhaps something like the Jewish (and also "Western") style of overt expressive suffering was what I unconsciously expected to find when I came to Vietnam. That would explain why at first I took for opaqueness and naïveté the quite different way the Vietnamese have of experiencing a comparably tragic history.

It took me a while, for instance, to realize that the Vietnamese were genuinely constrained by a kind of modesty about showing us the unspeakable sufferings they have endured. Even when describing the American atrocities, they hastened to emphasize—almost as if it would be bad taste not to—that the full horror of America's war on Vietnam couldn't be seen anywhere in the North. For that, they said, one must see "what is happening to our brothers in the South."

We heard the statistics of civilian casualties since February 7, 1965: sixty percent of all people killed are women and children; twenty percent of those killed and seriously wounded are elderly people. We were taken to see towns where formerly no fewer than twenty thousand and as many as eighty thousand people lived, in which not a single building was standing. We saw photographs of bodies riddled with pellets from fragmentation bombs or charred by incendiary weapons (besides napalm, the Americans also drop white phosphorus, Thermit, and magnesium on the Vietnamese). We met briefly with some forlorn victims of "the escalation," among them a girl of twenty-four whose husband and mother-in-law and children had been killed in a single raid, and an elderly Mother Superior and two young nuns who were the only survivors of the bombing of a Catholic convent located just south of Hanoi. Nevertheless, our North Vietnamese hosts seemed anything but eager to ply us with atrocities. They seemed more pleased to tell us, as we visited ruin after ruin, when there had been no casualties—as was the case when the new 170-bed hospital outside of Hoa Binh City was destroyed. (The hospital had been evacuated just before the first raid in September 1967; it was bombed several times afterwards and of course has never been reoccupied.) The impression the Vietnamese prefer to give, and do, is of a peaceful, viable, optimistic society. Ho Chi Minh has even given, in a speech after August 1945, a five-point recipe "for making life optimistic": each person must (1) be good in politics, (2) be able to draw or paint, (3) know music, (4) practice some sport, and (5) know at least one foreign language. Thus, by optimism among the Vietnamese, I mean not only their implacable conviction that they are going to win, but their espousal of optimism as a form of understanding, the emphasis placed throughout the whole society on continuous improvement.

Indeed, one of the most striking aspects of Vietnam is the positiveness of their approach to almost any problem. As Professor Buu, the Minister of Higher Education, remarked without a trace of irony: "The Americans have taught us a lot. For instance, we see that what's necessary for education is not beautiful buildings, like the brand-new Polytechnic School in Hanoi which we had to abandon in 1965 with the start of the escalation. When we went into the jungle and built the decentralized schools, education improved. We'd like better food and more colorful clothes, of course, but in these three years we've learned one can do many things without them. We don't regard them as fundamental, though very important all the same." Among the advantages, he said, in having been forced to evacuate the colleges of Hanoi into the countryside were that the college students had to put up their new school buildings themselves and learn how to grow their own food (every evacuated school or factory forms a new community and is asked not to be parasitic on the nearest village but to become self-sufficient on the level of a subsistence economy). Through these ordeals, "a new man" is being formed. Somehow, incredibly, the Vietnamese appreciate the assets of their situation, particularly its effect on character. When Ho Chi Minh said that bombing heightens the "spirit" of people, he meant more than a stiffening of morale. There is the belief that the war has effected a permanent improvement in the moral level of people. For instance, for a family to be uprooted and have all its possessions destroyed (many families have relics going back ten centuries) has always been considered in Vietnam the worst possible fate, but now that just this has happened to so many tens of thousands of families, people have discovered the positive advantages of being stripped of everything: that one becomes more generous, less attached to "things." (This is the theme of a movie I saw, *The Forest of Miss Tham*, in which at the end, to facilitate the repair of a truck route after bombing, an old peasant volunteers to cut down the two trees he has spent his whole life growing.) The bombing has also been, for instance, an occasion for developing people's poise and articulateness and administrative talents. Each village or hamlet, through an elected team, does its own reporting on the bombing; in Hanoi and Haiphong, several residents from each street are delegated to make out detailed reports. I remember, on our inspection of the bombed areas of Hanoi, receiving such a report from the leader of the "investigation team" of Quan Than Street (two kilometers from our hotel), an elderly uneducated worker who, since he was elected to this job by his neighbors, had learned a whole new set of skills. The war has made people cleverer and also democratized the use of intelligence, since everybody has essentially the same task: protecting the country, repelling the aggressors. Throughout North Vietnam, self-help plus cooperation has become the regular form of social and economic life. This may sound like the conventional code of a socialist economy applied in an underdeveloped country. But North Vietnam is not just one more small, economically backward member of the Third World, afflicted with the standard handicaps of an overspecialized economy (imposed by colonial rule), illiteracy, disease, and hard-to-assimilate tribal peoples culturally anterior to the majority population. (Vietnam has sixty "ethnic minorities.") It is a country that has literally been gashed and poisoned and leveled by steel, toxic chemicals, and fire. Under these circumstances, self-sufficiency would hardly be enough—were it not for the remarkable ability of the Vietnamese somehow to nourish themselves on disaster.

People there put it much more simply: it's just a question of being sufficiently ingenious. The overwhelming superiority of the United States in manpower, weapons, and resources and the extent of the devastation already wrought on their country pose a definite "problem," as the Vietnamese often said, but one they fully expect to solve by their unlimited and "creative" devotion to work. Everywhere we went, we saw evidence of the tremendous output of toil needed to keep North Vietnam going. Work is, as it were, evenly distributed over the whole surface of the country—like the huge wooden crates lying, unguarded, on the edges of sidewalks on many streets in Hanoi ("dour evacuated warehouses," Oanh said) and on country roads, or the piles of tools and other material left in the open alongside the railroad tracks so that repair of the track can start within minutes after a bombing. Nevertheless, willing as the Vietnamese are to rebuild the country inch by inch with shovel and hammer, they have a rather elegant sense of priorities. For instance, it was usual for the craters blasted in rice fields by the B-52's to be filled in by the farmers within days after the raid. But we saw several craters, made by 2,000- and 3,000-pound bombs, so big it had been judged that the time and labor needed to fill them would be prohibitive; these had been converted into fish-breeding ponds. Though the ongoing and endless work of repairing bomb-damaged sites and facilities or constructing new, better-protected ones consumes most of their energies now, the Vietnamese think a great deal about the future. Mindful of their postwar need for people with sophisticated skills, the Vietnamese have not mobilized teachers and professors or any of the 200,000 students in colleges and vocational schools; indeed, the number of students enrolled in programs of higher education has steadily risen since 1965. Architects have already drawn up plans for the completely new cities (including Hanoi, which the North Vietnamese fully expect to be razed before the Americans finally withdraw) that must be built after the war.

A visitor may conclude that this work, for all its ingenuity, is mainly conservative in purpose—the means whereby the society can survive—and only secondarily expresses a revolutionary vision—the instrument of a society bent on radical change. But the two purposes, I think, cannot be separated. The war seems to have democratized North Vietnam more profoundly, and radically, than any of the socialist economic reforms undertaken between 1954 and 1965. For instance, the war has broken down one of the few strong articulations in Vietnamese society: between the city and the country. (Peasants still make up eighty percent of the North Vietnamese population.) When the American bombing started, over a million and a half people left Hanoi, Haiphong, and other smaller cities and scattered throughout the countryside, where they have been living now for several years; the population of Hanoi alone dropped from around one million before 1985 to less than 200,000. And this migration, several Vietnamese told me, has already effected a marked change in manners and sensibility, both among peasants who have had to absorb a colony of motley refugees with urban habits and tastes, and among people from Hanoi or Haiphong, many of whom knew nothing about the starkly primitive conditions of daily existence that still prevail in the villages and hamlets but find themselves thriving psychically on physical austerity and the community-mindedness of rural life.

The war has also democratized the society by destroying most of the modest physical means as well as restricting the social space Vietnam had at its disposal for differentiated kinds of production (I include everything from industry to the arts). Thus, more and more people are working at all kinds of activities at the same level—with their bare hands. Each small, low building in the complexes of evacuated schools that have been set up throughout the countryside had to be made in the simplest way: mud walls and a straw roof. All those kilometers of neat trenches connecting and leading away from every building, to get the children out in case of attack, had to be painstakingly dug out of the red clay. The omnipresent bomb shelters—throughout Hanoi, in each village and hamlet, at intervals on the side of every road, in every tilled field—had to be put up, one by one, by people living nearby, in their spare time. (Since 1965, the Vietnamese have dug more than 50,000 kilometers of trenches and constructed, for a population of 17,000,000, more than 21,000,000 bomb shelters.) Late one night, on our way back to Hanoi from a trip to the north, we visited a decentralized factory housed in crude sheds at the foot of a mountain. While several hundred women and young boys were operating the machines by the light of kerosene lamps, a dozen men using only hammers were widening the walls of a small adjacent cave to make a shelter safe from bombing for the biggest machinery. Almost everything in North Vietnam has to be done manually, with a minimum of tools. Time enough to wonder what the vaunted aid from Russia and China amounts to: however much there is of it, it's scarcely enough. The country is pitifully lacking in such elementary hospital equipment as sterilizers and X-ray machines, in typewriters, in basic tools like lathes and pneumatic drills and welding machines; there seem to be plenty of bicycles and quite a few transistor radios, but books of all kinds, paper, pens, phonographs, clocks, and cameras are very scarce; the most modest consumer goods are virtually nonexistent. Clothing, too, exists only in a limited supply. A Vietnamese is lucky if he owns two sets of clothes and one pair of shoes; rationing allows each person six meters of cotton fabric a year. (The cotton comes in only a few colors and most garments are almost identically cut: black trousers and white blouses for the women; tan, gray, or beige trousers and tan or white shirts for the men. Ties are never worn, and jackets only rarely.) Even the clothes of very high officials are frayed, dully stained, shiny from repeated washings. Dr. Thach, cousin of the former puppet emperor Bao Dai and, before throwing in his lot with the revolution, one of the richest landowners in Vietnam, mentioned that he hasn't had any new clothes in two years. Food is very short, too, though no one starves. Industrial workers get a monthly ration of 24 kilos of rice; everyone else, including the highest government officials, gets 13.5 kilos a month.

Lacking almost everything, the Vietnamese are forced to put everything they do have to use, sometimes multiple use. Part of this ingenuity is traditional; for example, the Vietnamese make an astonishing number of things out of bamboo—houses, bridges, irrigation devices, scaffolding, carrying poles, cups, tobacco pipes, furniture. But there are many new inventions. Thus, American planes have become virtual mines in the sky. (The supply is still far from cut off. During our stay in Hanoi, the Vietnamese bagged a dozen of the unmanned reconnaissance planes that have been flying over several times a day since March 31; and they get more planes below the 19th parallel, where the air attack is more intense now than at any time before the "limited bombing pause.") Each plane that's shot down is methodically taken apart. The tires are cut up to make the rubber sandals that most people wear. Any component of the engine that's still intact is modified to be reused as part of a truck motor. The body of the plane is dismantled, and the metal is melted down to be made into tools, small machine parts, surgical instruments, wire, spokes for bicycle wheels, combs, ashtrays, and of course the famous numbered rings given as presents to visitors. Every last nut, bolt, and screw from the plane is used. The same holds for anything else the Americans drop. In several hamlets we visited, the bell hanging from a tree which summoned people to meetings or sounded the air-raid alert was the casing of an unexploded bomb. Being shown through the infirmary of a Thai hamlet, we saw that the protective canopy of the operating room, relocated, since the bombing, in a rock grotto, was a flare parachute.

In these circumstances, the notion of a "people's war" is no mere propagandistic slogan but takes on a real concreteness, as does that favorite hope of modem social planners, decentralization. A people's war means the total, voluntary, generous mobilization of every able-bodied person in the country, so that everyone is available for any task. It also means the division of the country into an indefinite number of small, self-sufficient communities which can survive isolation, make decisions, and continue contributing to production. People on a local level are expected, for instance, to solve any kind of problem put to them as the aftermath of enemy bombing.

To observe in some of its day-to-day functioning a society based on the principle of total use is particularly impressive to someone who comes from a society based on maximal waste. An unholy dialectic is at work here, in which the big wasteful society dumps its garbage, its partly unemployable proletarian conscripts, its poisons, and its bombs upon a small, virtually defenseless, frugal society whose citizens, those fortunate enough to survive, then go about picking up the debris, out of which they fashion materials for daily use and self-defense.

The principle of total use applies not only to things but to thoughts as well, and grasping this helped me to stop mechanically chafing at the intellectual flatness of Vietnamese discourse. As each material object must be made to go a long way, so must each idea. Vietnamese leaders specialize in an economical, laconic wisdom. Take the saying of Ho, repeated to us often: "Nothing is more precious than independence and liberty." Not until I'd heard the quote many many times did I actually consider it. But when I did, I thought, yes, it really does say a great deal. One could indeed, as the Vietnamese have, live spiritually from that simple sentence for a long time. The Vietnamese regard Ho not as a thinker but as a man of action; his words are for use. The same standard applies to the iconography of the Vietnamese struggle, which is hardly outstanding for either visual or ideological subtlety. (Of course, the utilitarian principle doesn't work equally well in all contexts, as evidenced by the rather low level of Vietnamese visual art, with the exception of posters. In contrast to the poor development not only of painting but of film, prose fiction, and dance as well, poetry and theatre seemed to me the only arts in a sophisticated condition, as arts, in Vietnam now.) The principle of getting maximal use from everything may partly explain why there are still quite a few pictures of Stalin in North Vietnam, hanging on the wall in some but hardly all government offices, factories, and schools. Stalin is the traditional figure on the right in the tintype pantheon Marx-Engels-Lenin-Stalin, and the Vietnamese lack both time and incentive for symbolic controversy. The composition of that quartet represents a form of politeness to the leading country and titular head of the "socialist camp" which was installed when the present government came to power in 1954. People in North Vietnam are perfectly well aware that the picture is out of date in 1968, and many North Vietnamese appeared to me to have grave reservations about the Soviet Union's domestic and foreign policies, even the character of its people. (Ho Chi Minh, whose picture is rarely to be seen in public buildings, pointedly refused the Lenin Prize a few years ago.) But whatever the Vietnamese, especially in Hanoi, might think, or even express privately, about the Russians—that they are collaborating with the Americans, that they don't genuinely back Vietnam's struggle, that they've abandoned the ideals of genuine Communism and of world revolution, that they're prone to be drunks and boors—does not yet invalidate the old icon. It remains, at least for the present, as a polite tribute to the idea of unity and solidarity among the Communist countries.

It's all part of the Vietnamese style, which seems guided by an almost principled avoidance of "heaviness," of making more complications than are necessary. No one can fail to credit the Vietnamese with subtlety in planning large-scale actions, as evidenced in the fabulous strategic sense of General Giap. But directness and plainness remain the rule when it comes to expressing something or making a gesture, and not out of any deeper artfulness. It was my impression that the Vietnamese, as a culture, genuinely believe that life is simple. They also believe, incredible as it may seem considering their present situation, that life is full of joy. Joy is to be discerned behind what is already so remarkable: the ease and total lack of self-pity with which people worked a backbreaking number of hours, or daily faced the possibility of their own death and the death of those they love. The phenomena of existential agony, of alienation, just don't appear among the Vietnamese—probably in part because they lack our kind of "ego" and our endowment of free-floating guilt. Of course, it's hard for a visitor to take all this at face value. I spent much of my early time in Vietnam wondering what lay "behind" the Vietnamese's apparent psychic equilibrium. The kind of seriousness—identified, Confucian-style, with unselfishness—that is deeply ingrained in Vietnamese culture is something which visitors from the Western capitalist world, equipped with their tools of psychological debunking, can hardly recognize, much less fully credit. Right away, the delicate build of the Vietnamese and their sheer physical gracefulness can set a gawky, big-boned American on edge. The Vietnamese behave with an unfaltering personal dignity that we tend to find suspect, either naïve or sham. And they appear so singularly and straightforwardly involved with the virtue of courage, and with the ideal of a noble, brave life. We live in an age marked by the discrediting of the heroic effort; hence, the awareness most people in this society have of their lives, whether they are appalled by it or not, as stale and flat. But in Vietnam one is confronted by a whole people possessed by a belief in what Lawrence called "the subtle, lifelong validity of the heroic impulse." Educated urban Americans, imbued with a sense of the decline of the heroic spirit, must find it especially difficult to perceive what animates the Vietnamese, to correlate the "known" historical dossier of their long, patient struggle to liberate their country with what can really be "believed" about people.

Ultimately, the difficulty encountered visiting North Vietnam reflects the crisis of credulity that is endemic in Western post-industrial society. Not only do the Vietnamese have virtues that thoughtful people in this part of the world simply don't believe in any more. They also mix virtues that we consider incompatible. For instance, we think war to be by its very nature "dehumanizing." But North Vietnam is simultaneously a martial society, completely mobilized for armed struggle, and a deeply civil society which places great value on gentleness and the demands of the heart. One of the more astonishing instances of Vietnamese concern for the heart, related to me by Phan, is the treatment accorded the thousands of prostitutes rounded up after the liberation of Hanoi from the French in 1954. They were put in charge of the Women's Union, which set up rehabilitation centers for them in the countryside, where they first passed months being elaborately pampered. Fairy tales were read to them; they were taught children's games and sent out to play. "That," Phan explained, "was to restore their innocence and give them faith again in man. You see, they had seen such a terrible side of human nature. The only way for them to forget that was to become little children again." Only after this period of mothering were they taught to read and write, instructed in a trade by which they could support themselves, and given dowries to improve their chances of eventually marrying. There seems no doubt that people who can think up such therapy really have a different moral imagination than we have. And as the quality of Vietnamese love differs from ours, so does the nature of their hate. Of course, the Vietnamese hate the Americans in some sense—but not as Americans would, if we had been subjected to equivalent punishment at the hands of a superior power. The North Vietnamese genuinely care about the welfare of the hundreds of captured American pilots and give them bigger rations than the Vietnamese population gets, "because they're bigger than we are," as a Vietnamese army officer told me, "and they're used to more meat than we are." People in North Vietnam really do believe in the goodness of man ("People in every country are good," Ho said in 1945, "only the governments are bad"), and in the perennial possibility of rehabilitating the morally fallen, among whom they include implacable enemies, even the Americans. In spite of all the stiff words disseminated by the Vietnamese, it's impossible not to be convinced by the genuineness of these concerns.

Still, apart from the general problem of credulity a Western visitor brings to a society like Vietnam, one may be doubly wary of any deeply positive reaction to the Vietnamese. The moment one begins to be affected by the moral beauty of the Vietnamese, not to mention their physical grace, a derisive inner voice starts calling it phony sentimentality. Understandably, one fears succumbing to that cut-rate sympathy for places like Vietnam which, lacking any real historical or psychological understanding, becomes another instance of the ideology of primitivism. The revolutionary politics of many people in capitalist countries is only a new guise for the old conservative culture-criticism: posing against overcomplex, hypocritical, devitalized, urban society choking on affluence the idea of a simple people living the simple life in a decentralized, uncoercive, passionate society with modest material means. As eighteenth-century *philosophes* pictured such a pastoral ideal in the Pacific islands or among the American Indians, and German romantic poets supposed it to have existed in ancient Greece, late twentieth-century intellectuals in New York and Paris are likely to locate it in the exotic revolutionary societies of the Third World. If some of what I've written evokes the very cliché of the Western left-wing intellectual idealizing an agrarian revolution that I was so set on not being, I must reply that a cliché is a cliché, truth is truth, and direct experience is—well—something one repudiates at one's peril. In the end I can only avow that armed with these very self-suspicions, I found, through direct experience, North Vietnam to be a place which, in many respects, *deserves* to be idealized.

But having stated my admiration for the Vietnamese (people society) as bluntly and vulnerably as I can, I should emphasize that none of this amounts to a claim that North Vietnam is a model of a just state. One has only to recall the more notorious enemies committed by the present government for example, the persecution of the Trotskyist faction and the execution of its leaders in 1946, and the forcible collectivization of agriculture in1956, the brutalities and injustices of which high officials have recently admitted. Still, a foreigner should try to avoid padding out the lamentable facts with a reflex reaction to words. Upon learning that in North Vietnam today everyone belongs to at least one "organization" (usually several), a non-Communist visitor is likely to assume that the Vietnamese must be regimented and deprived of personal liberty. With the rise to dominance of the ideology of the bourgeoisie in the last two centuries, people in Europe and America have learned to associate membership in public organizations with becoming "depersonalized," and to identify achievement of the most valuable human goals with the autonomy of private life. But this apparently isn't how the threat of depersonalization arises in Vietnam; there, people rather experience themselves as dehumanized or depersonalized when they are not bound to each other in regular forms of collectivity. Again, a visitor of the independent Left will probably wince each time the Vietnamese mention "the Party." (The 1946 constitution does allow for a plurality of political groupings, and there is a Socialist Party and a Democratic Party, both of which publish weekly newspapers and have some representation in the government. But *Lao Dong*, the Workers Party, with nearly a hundred members on its Central Committee, is "the Party"; it runs the country, and the candidates it proposes are overwhelmingly favored by the electoral system.) But the preference for government by a single party of newly independent countries which have never known multiparty democracy is a fact that merits a more discriminating response than automatic disapproval. Several Vietnamese I met themselves brought up the dangers of single-party rule and claimed that in spite of these dangers the Workers Party had proved it deserves to hold power by being responsive to the concrete local demands of people. For the Vietnamese, "the Party" simply means the effective leadership of the country—from Ho Chi Minh, founder of the independent nation and of the Party (in 1930), to the young cadre just out of the Party School who comes to a village under bombardment to show its inhabitants how to build shelters or volunteers to live in the high mountains, among the Meo or Muong minorities, and teach them how to read and write. Of course, this conception of the Party as a vast corps of skilled, ethically impeccable, mostly unpaid public servants, tutoring and working alongside people in all their activities, sharing their hardships, doesn't exempt the Vietnamese system from terrible abuses. But neither does it preclude the possibility that the present system functions humanely, with genuine substantive democracy, much of the time.

In any case, I noticed that the word "democracy" was frequently invoked in Vietnam, far more often than in any other Communist country I've visited, including Cuba. The Vietnamese claim that democracy has deep roots in their culture, specifically in the customs of a fiercely independent peasantry. ("The law of the king must be subordinate to the law of the village," runs an old proverb.) Even in the past, Dr. Thach said, the form of the regime—kings and mandarins—was authoritarian, but its content—the traditions of village life—was democratic. Whether or not this account stands up to objective scrutiny, it's interesting that the Vietnamese *think* it true that their country is, and always has been, democratic. North Vietnam is the only Communist country I know in which people regularly praise the United States for being, after all and despite everything, "a great democracy." (As I've suggested, the Vietnamese don't show a very advanced command of Marxist thinking and critical analysis.) All this, myth as well as reality, must be taken into consideration when evaluating the nature of public institutions in North Vietnam and their role in promoting or discouraging individuality. The life of an institution cannot be appraised by examining a blueprint of its structure; run under the auspices of different feelings, similar structures can have a quite different quality. For instance, when love enters into the substance of social relations, the connection of people to a single party need not be dehumanizing. Though it's second nature for me to suspect the government of a Communist country of being oppressive and rigid, if not worse, most of my preconceptions about the misuses of state power in North Vietnam were really an abstraction. Against that abstract suspiciousness I must set (and be overruled by) what I actually saw when I was there—that the North Vietnamese genuinely love and admire their leaders; and, even more inconceivable to us, that the government loves the people. I remember the poignant, intimate tones in Pham Van Dong's voice as he described the sufferings the Vietnamese have endured in the last quarter of a century and theft heroism, decency, and essential innocence. Seeing for the first time in my life a prime minister praising the moral character of his country's people with tears in his eyes has modified my ideas about the conceivable relations between rulers and ruled, and given me a more complex reaction to what I would ordinarily dismiss as mere propaganda.

For while no dearth of propaganda is put out by the North Vietnamese, what makes one despair is that this propaganda conveys so poorly, insensitively, and unconvincingly the most admirable qualities of the society built since 1954. Anyone who consults the publications about North Vietnam (on education, public health, the new role of women, literature, war crimes, etc.) issued in English and French by the Foreign Languages Press in Hanoi will not only get virtually nothing of the delicate texture of North Vietnamese society but be positively misled by the bombastic, shrill, and overly general character of these texts. Toward the close of my stay I mentioned to several government people that foreigners, reading these books and press releases, couldn't possibly form an idea of what North Vietnam is like, and explained my general impression that their revolution is being betrayed by its language. Though the Vietnamese I talked to seemed aware of the problem—they indicated I wasn't the first foreign visitor to tell them this—I felt they're far from knowing how to solve it. (I learned that Pham Van Dong had made a speech three years ago criticizing "the disease of rhetoric" that he charged was rife among the political cadres and appealing for an "improvement" of the Vietnamese language. But the only concrete advice he gave was that people spend less time talking about politics and more time reading classical Vietnamese literature.)

Can North Vietnam really be such an exceptional place? That's a question I have no way of answering. But I do know that North Vietnam, while definitely no Shangri-La, is a truly remarkable country; that the North Vietnamese is an extraordinary human being, and in ways not accounted for by the well-known fact that any keen struggle, a really desperate crisis, usually brings out the best (if not the worst) in people and promotes a euphoria of comradeship. What is admirable in the Vietnamese goes deeper than that. The Vietnamese are "whole" human beings, not "split" as we are. Inevitably, such people are likely to give outsiders the impression of great "simplicity." But while the Vietnamese are stripped down, they are hardly simple in any sense that grants us the right to patronize them.

It is *not* simple to be able to love calmly, to trust without ambivalence, to hope without self-mockery, to act courageously, to perform arduous tasks with unlimited resources of energy. In this society, a few people are able just faintly to imagine all these as achievable goals—though only in their private life. But in Vietnam the very distinction taken for granted here between the public and the private has not been strongly developed. This indistinct separation between public and private among the Vietnamese also informs their pragmatic, verbally and conceptually meager style of making their revolution. By way of contrast, the acute sense of the discontinuity of private and public in the West may partly explain the amount of talk, often very interesting talk, that accompanies every revolutionary gesture.* In our society, talk is perhaps the most intricately developed expression of private individuality. Conducted at this high pitch of development, talking becomes a double-edged activity: both an aggressive act and an attempted embrace. Thus talk often testifies to the poverty or inhibition of our feelings; it flourishes as a substitute for more organic connections between people. (When people really love, or are genuinely in touch with themselves, they tend to shut up.) But Vietnam is a culture in which people have not got the final devastating point about talking, have not gauged the subtle, ambivalent resources of language—because they don't experience as we do the isolation of a "private self." Talk is still a rather plain instrumentality for them, a less important means of being connected with their environment than direct feeling, love.

The absence of the sharp distinction between public and private spheres also allows the Vietnamese a relation to their country that must seem exotic to us. It is open to the Vietnamese to love their country passionately, every inch of it. One can't exaggerate the fervor of their patriotic passion and their intense attachment to particular places. Most people, I noticed, volunteer quickly where they are from, with a special melancholy if they were born in the South and have therefore been prevented from returning there for many years. And I remember Oanh describing his childhood on his uncle's fishing boat in Ha Long Bay, a famous resort area during the French colonial period. (Oanh recalled the excitement he felt as a small boy in the late 1920's when Paulette Goddard spent a holiday there.) But when Oanh had gone on for a while about the splendors of the rock formations in the bay, now heavily bombed, he stopped, almost apologetically, to say something like: Of course your Rocky Mountains must be very beautiful, too.

But is it possible to feel like that about America now? That was something I often debated with the Vietnamese. They assured me that I must love America

---

*What brings about genuine revolutionary change is the shared experience of revolutionary feelings—not rhetoric, not the discovery of social injustice, not even intelligent analysis, and not any action considered in itself. And one can indeed "talk" revolutions away, by a disproportion between consciousness and verbalization, on the one hand, and the amount of practical will, on the other. (Hence the failure of the recent revolution in France. The French students talked—and very beautifully, too—instead of reorganizing the administration of the captured universities. Their staging of street demonstrations and confrontations with the police was conceived as a rhetorical or symbolic, rather than a practical, act; it too was a kind of talking.)

In our society, "idealistic" tends to mean "disorganized"; "militant" tends to mean merely "emotional." Most of the people in Europe and the Americas who are quite vociferous in their denunciations of the society in which they live are profoundly confused and thoughtless not only about what they would prefer instead but about any plan for actually taking power, so radical change might be effected. Indeed, revolution in the Western capitalist countries seems, more often than not, to be an activity expressly designed never to succeed. For many people, it is an asocial activity, a form of action designed for the assertion of individuality against the body politic. It is the ritual activity of outsiders, rather than of people united by a passionate bond to their country.

just as much as they love Vietnam. It's my patriotism that makes me oppose my country's foreign policy; I want to preserve the honor of the country I cherish above all others. There was some truth in what they said: all Americans—alas—believe that America is special, or ought to be. But I knew I didn't feel the positive emotion that Vietnamese attributed to me. Outrage and disappointment, yes. Love, no. Putting it in the baby language they and I shared (which I'd become rather skillful at), I explained: it's hard to love America right now, because of the violence which America is exporting all over the world; and given that the interests of humanity come before those of any particular people, a decent American today must be an internationalist first and a patriot second. Once at the Writers Union, when I had made this point (and not for the first time, so my voice may have been a little plaintive), a young poet answered me soothingly in English: "We are patriots, but in a happy way. You have more suffering in your patriotism." Sometimes they seemed to understand, but more often they didn't. Perhaps the difficulty is that, as I've already mentioned, they're quite fond of America themselves. People in Vietnam appear to take for granted that the United States is in many ways the greatest country in the world: the richest, the most advanced technologically, the most alive culturally, the most powerful, even the most free. They are not only endlessly curious about America—Oanh said several times how much he longs to visit the States as soon as the war is over—but genuinely admiring. I have described earlier the avidity of the poets and novelists for American literature. Pham Van Dong mentioned respectfully "your Declaration of Independence," from which Ho Chi Minh quoted when he declared the independence of Vietnam from the French on September 2, 1945. Hoang Tung, the editor of the principal daily paper, *Nhan Dan*, spoke of his "love" for the United States and praised to us "your tradition of freedom" which makes possible such creative political acts as the sit-in and the teach-in. The United States, he said, disposes of possibilities of good unmatched by any other country in the world.

If their view of the United States seemed at first improbable, then innocent and touching, the emotion the Vietnamese have for their own country seemed utterly alien, and even dangerous. But by the end of my visit I began to feel less estranged. Discovering the essential purity of their own patriotism showed me that such an emotion need not be identical with chauvinism. (How sensitive the Vietnamese are to the difference was clear in the only slightly concealed distaste of people I met in Hanoi for recent developments in China, like the cult of Mao and the cultural revolution.) If the Vietnamese could make such distinctions, so could I. Of course, I knew perfectly well why the attitude the Vietnamese expected of me was in fact so difficult. Ever since World War II, the rhetoric of patriotism in the United States has been in the hands of reactionaries and yahoos;

by monopolizing it, they have succeeded in rendering the idea of loving America synonymous with bigotry, provincialism, and selfishness. But perhaps one shouldn't give up so easily. When the chairman of the Writers Union, Dang Thai Mai, said in his speech of welcome to Bob, Andy, and myself, "You are the very picture of the genuine American," why should I have slightly flinched?

If what I feel is that flag-waving Legionnaires and Irish cops and small-town car salesmen who will vote for George Wallace are the genuine Americans, not I—which I fear part of me does feel—isn't that cowardly, shallow, and simply untrue? Why should I (we) not think of myself (ourselves) as a genuine American? With a little more purity of vision—but one would have to close the seepage of private despair into public grievances—maybe an intelligent American who cares for the other ninety-six percent of the human population and for the bio-ecological future of the planet could love America, too. Probably no serious radical movement has any future in America unless it can revalidate the tarnished idea of patriotism. One of my thoughts in the closing days of my stay in North Vietnam was that I would like to try.

Unfortunately, the first test of my vow came much sooner than I expected, almost immediately, in the first hours after leaving Hanoi the evening of May 17, and I failed right off. I wish something could be arranged to insure a proper "coming down" for visitors to North Vietnam in the first days after their departure. Unprepared, the ex-guest of the Democratic Republic of North Vietnam is in for a series of brutal assaults. Thirty minutes out of Hanoi, it was the spectacle of the drunken Polish members of the International Control Commission sitting around a table in the forward part of the plane dealing out a deck of pornographic playing cards. As we made our first touchdown, in the small airfield of Vientiane, it was seeing the landing area crowded with planes marked Air America (the CIA's private airline) which leave daily from here to drop napalm on villages in Northern Laos held by the Pathet Lao. Then came the taxi ride into Vientiane itself, River City USA (as Andy dubbed it), sordid outpost of the American empire. Servile, aggressive Laotian pedicab drivers trying to hustle a fare, an elderly lady tourist or a freaked-out hippie or an American soldier, weaved in and out of Cadillacs driven by American businessmen and Laotian government personnel. We passed the movie theatres showing skin flicks for the GI's, the "American" bars, the strip joints, stores selling paperbacks and picture magazines that could have been transplanted directly from Times Square, the American Embassy, Air France, signs for the weekly meeting of the Rotary Club. In the lobby of the Lane Xang, the one "modern" hotel in Vientiane, we bought copies of *Newsweek* and *Time* to catch up on what had been going on, during our absence of two weeks, in our world. Minutes later, Bob, Andy, and I were sitting on benches covered with thick red plastic in the hotel's air-conditioned cocktail lounge, getting drunk, soaking up Muzak, and poring helplessly, incredulously, and eagerly through the magazines. We began cracking hysterical jokes, with Andy further amplifying on his running gag about the Lone Ranger and Tonto that had been Bob's and my delight since the beginning of the trip—only it wasn't funny now. We debated going out and buying some grass (what else could one do here?) but decided against it, mainly because we were reluctant to go into the street and get even more depressed. By midnight we were all feeling positively sick. When dawn came four insomniac hours later, I could see out the window of my room across the flat, almost dry Mekong River. The river bed is an unguarded frontier, for what lies on the far side is Thailand, another, much more important American colony, home of the bases from which most planes take off daily to bomb the country we had just left.... And so on, out and out, further away from North Vietnam.

Due to one of the misadventures typical of the ICC flights, we had already spent four days in Vientiane before we went to Hanoi, staying at this very hotel, walking all over the town we'd just driven through. And though we had been jolted by its sordidness then, it seemed now that we couldn't have taken its full measure. And yet, of course, it had all been there before, and we'd seen it. In contrast to her subtler dealings with Western Europe, America exports to Southeast Asia only the most degraded aspects of her culture. And in that part of the world there is no dressing up or concealing the visible signs of American might. Though it could be helpful anyway to abstain from *Time* and *Newsweek* for at least ten days after a visit to North Vietnam, an American must brace himself for a big cultural shock—reverse cultural dislocation, I suppose—when the first environment he sees after leaving Hanoi is a place like Vientiane.

Remembering the intimations I'd had in North Vietnam of the possibility of loving my own country, I wanted very much not to react crudely, moralistically, not to slip back into the old posture of alienation. And after a while the keenest part of my outrage did subside. For the anger an American is likely to direct toward the emblems of his country's imperial dominance isn't founded simply upon their inherent repulsiveness, which permits no reaction other than aversion, but rather upon the despairing conviction that American power in its present form and guided by its present purposes is *invincible*. But this may not be, probably isn't, the case. The Vietnamese, for one, don't think so. And their wilder judgments do, by this time, have a claim to be taken seriously. After all, who—except the Vietnamese themselves—would have predicted on February 7, 1965, that this small, poor nation could hold out against the awesome cruelty and thoroughness of American military force? But they have. Three years ago, enlightened world opinion pitied the Vietnamese, knowing that they couldn't possibly stand up to the United States; and the slogan of people protesting against the war was "Peace in Vietnam." Three years later, "Victory for Vietnam" is the only credible slogan. The Vietnamese don't want anybody's pity, as people in Hanoi told me; they want solidarity. The "tragedy" is Johnson's and the American government's, for continuing the war, Hoang Tung said. "There are many difficulties until the war ends," he added, "but we remain optimistic." For the Vietnamese, their victory is a "necessary fact."

The consequences for Vietnam of the eventual defeat of the American invasion are not hard to envisage. They will consist, for the most part, in unqualified improvements over the present situation: cessation of all bombing, withdrawal of American troops from the South, the collapse of the Thieu-Ky government, and the accession to power of a government dominated by the National Liberation Front, which some day, but not in the near future (according to the present leadership of the NLF), will unite with the Hanoi government so that at long last the divided country will be reunified. But one can only speculate about the consequences of this defeat for the United States. It could be a turning point in our national history, for good or bad. Or it could mean virtually nothing—just the liquidation of a bad investment that leaves the military-industrial establishment free for other adventures with more favorable odds. To believe that things in America could move either way doesn't seem to me overly optimistic. But then, if there's at least some hope for America, 1968 would be the wrong time for people in this country who look toward radical change to lose heart.

As Hegel said, the problem of history is the problem of consciousness. The interior journey I made during my recent stay in Hanoi made the truth of this grandiose maxim sharp and concrete for me. There, in North Vietnam, what was ostensibly a somewhat passive experience of historical education became, as I think now it had to, an active confrontation with the limits of my own thinking.

The Vietnam that, before my trip to Hanoi, I supposed myself imaginatively connected with, proved when I was there to have lacked reality. During these last years, Vietnam has been stationed inside my consciousness as a quintessential image of the suffering and heroism of "the weak." But it was really America "the strong" that obsessed me—the contours of American power, of American cruelty, of American self-righteousness. In order eventually to encounter what was there in Vietnam, I had to forget about America; even more ambitiously, to push against the boundaries of the overall Western sensibility from which my American one derives. But I always knew I hadn't made more than a brief, amateurish foray into the Vietnamese reality. And anything really serious I'd gotten from my trip would return me to my starting point: the dilemmas of being an American, an unaffiliated radical American, an American writer.

For in the end, of course, an American has no way of incorporating Vietnam into his consciousness. It can glow in the remote distance like a navigator's star, it can be the seat of geological tremors that make the political ground shake under our own feet. But the virtues of the Vietnamese are certainly not directly emulatable by Americans; they're even hard to describe plausibly. And the revolution that remains to be made in this country must be made in American terms, not those of an Asian peasant society. Radical Americans have profited from the war in Vietnam, profited from having a clear-cut moral issue on which to mobilize discontent and expose the camouflaged contradictions in the system. Beyond isolated private disenchantment or despair over America's betrayal of its ideals, Vietnam offered the key to a systematic criticism of America. In this scheme of use, Vietnam becomes an ideal Other. But such a status only makes Vietnam, already so alien culturally, even further removed from this country. Hence the task awaiting any sympathetic person who goes there: to understand what one is nevertheless barred from understanding. When American radicals visit North Vietnam, all things are thrown into question—their necessarily American attitudes to Communism, to revolution, to patriotism, to violence, to language, to courtesy, to eros, not to mention the more general Western features of their identity. I can testify that, at the very least, the world seems much bigger since I went to North Vietnam than it did before.

I came back from Hanoi considerably chastened. Life here looks both uglier and more promising. To describe what is promising, it's perhaps imprudent to invoke the promiscuous ideal of revolution. Still, it would be a mistake to underestimate the amount of diffuse yearning for radical change pulsing through this society. Increasing numbers of people do realize that we must have a more generous, more humane way of being with each other; and great, probably convulsive, social changes are needed to create these psychic changes. To prepare intelligently for radical change requires not only lucid and truthful social analysis: for instance, understanding better the realities of the distribution of political and economic power in the world which have secured for America its present hegemony. An equally relevant weapon is the analysis of psychic geography and history: for instance, getting more perspective on the human type that gradually became ascendant in the West from the time of the Reformation to the industrial revolution to modern post-industrial society. Almost everyone would agree that this isn't the only way human beings could have evolved, but very few people in Europe and America really, organically *believe* that there is any other way for a person to be or can *imagine* what they might be like. How can they when, after all, that's what they are, more or less? It's hard to step over one's own feet.

And yet, I think, the path isn't altogether blocked. Of course, most people are unlikely to come to a direct awareness of how local is the human type they embody, and even less likely to appreciate how arbitrary, drastically impoverished, and in urgent need of replacement it is. But they do know something else: that they are unhappy and that their lives are cramped and savorless and embittered. If that discontent isn't channeled off to be repaired by the kind of psycho-therapeutic awareness which robs it of social and political, of historical, dimension, the wide prevalence of unfocused unhappiness in modern Western culture could be the beginning of real knowledge—by which I mean the knowing that leads simultaneously to action and to self-transcendence, the knowing that would lead to a new version of human nature in this part of the world.

Ordinarily, changes in the human type (which is to say, in the quality of human relations) evolve very slowly, almost imperceptibly. Unfortunately, the exigencies of modern history being what they are, we can't be content to wait for the course of natural deliverance. There may not be enough time, given this society's strong taste for self-destructiveness. And even if Western man refrains from blowing himself up, his continuing as he is makes it so awfully hard, perhaps soon intolerably so, on the rest of the world—that is, most of the world, the more than two billion people who are neither white nor rich nor as expansionist as we are. Just possibly, the process of recasting the particular historical form of our human nature prevalent in Europe and America can be hurried a little, by more people becoming aware of capacities for sentiments and behavior that this culture's values have obscured and slandered.

An event that makes new feelings conscious is always the most important experience a person can have. These days, it's a pressing moral imperative as well. I was very lucky, I think: my ignorance, my empathic talents, and the habit of being dissatisfied with myself worked together to allow just such an experience by the end of my trip to North Vietnam in May. (Though the new feelings that were revealed to me are undoubtedly quite old in a historical sense, I personally had never experienced them before, or been able to name them, or been hitherto capable of believing in them.) Now, once again, I am far from Vietnam, trying to make these feelings live here in an appropriate and authentic form. That sounds difficult. Still, I doubt that what's required is a great effort of "holding on." In and by itself, such an experience is transformative. It is indelible.

I recognized a limited analogy to my present state in Paris in early July when, talking to acquaintances who had been on the barricades in May, I discovered they don't really accept the failure of their revolution. The reason for their lack of "realism," I think, is that they're still possessed by the new feelings revealed to them during those weeks—those precious weeks in which vast numbers of ordinarily suspicious, cynical urban people, workers and students, behaved with an unprecedented generosity and warmth and spontaneity toward each other. In a way, then, the young veterans of the barricades are right in not altogether

acknowledging their defeat, in being unable fully to believe that things have returned to pre-May normality, if not worse. Actually it is they who are being realistic. Someone who has enjoyed new feelings of that kind—a reprieve, however brief, from the inhibitions on love and trust this society enforces—is never the same again. In him, the "revolution" has just started, and it continues. So I discover that what happened to me in North Vietnam did not end with my return to America, but is still going on.
(June–July 1968)

FOR INFORMAL WRITING

How does Sontag—a respected intellectual and celebrated writer—seem to discount her authority in this piece? Why would she do that, and to what effect?

FOR DISCUSSION

1. Examine and comment on Sontag's journal entries. How is she "reduced to the status of a child?"
2. "Even if I fail the test of being able to identify myself with the Vietnamese, what have I actually proven? Perhaps I haven't experienced the constraints, real or imaginary, of ethical—or revolutionary—societies in general, only of this one." What does Sontag mean by this? How is she trying to navigate her understanding of culture in Vietnam, and how are they trying to understand her? What in the essay points to these issues?
3. What does Sontag find most surprising about her time in Hanoi? Why? What assumptions underlie this surprise?

FOR WRITING

"We know the American people are our friends. Only the present American government is our enemy." Research the historical contexts that would provoke these statements. What about the American government would have made it seem an enemy to the North Vietnamese at that time?

WHAT'S NEW IS OLD

Consider this piece alongside Pico Iyer's "Why We Travel." Although Iyer's article was published about thirty years after Sontag's, how might you examine Iyer's more focused experience through Sontag's more philosophical lens on the importance of travel?

Speech on Impeachment (We the People) (1974)
Barbara Jordan (1936–1996)

Barbara Jordan was a member of the Texas Senate and of the US House of Representatives. Known as a compelling and thoughtful thinker and speaker, she was the first African American woman to give a keynote address at the Democratic National Convention (1976). She chaired the first US Commission on Immigration Reform (1994 until her death), and in 1994, President Bill Clinton awarded her the Presidential Medal of Freedom. She had honorary degrees from over twenty institutions, including Harvard and Princeton. This speech was delivered to remind colleagues on the House Judiciary Committee of the grounds for impeachment—in this instance, of President Richard Nixon.

Thank you, Mr. Chairman.

Mr. Chairman, I join my colleague Mr. Rangel in thanking you for giving the junior members of this committee the glorious opportunity of sharing the pain of this inquiry. Mr. Chairman, you are a strong man, and it has not been easy but we have tried as best we can to give you as much assistance as possible.

Earlier today, we heard the beginning of the Preamble to the Constitution of the United States: "We the people." It's a very eloquent beginning. But when that document was completed on the seventeenth of September in 1787, I was not included in that "We the people." I felt somehow for many years that George Washington and Alexander Hamilton just left me out by mistake. But through the process of amendment, interpretation, and court decision, I have finally been included in "We the people."

Today I am an inquisitor. An hyperbole would not be fictional and would not overstate the solemnness that I feel right now. My faith in the Constitution is whole; it is complete; it is total. And I am not going to sit here and be an idle spectator to the diminution, the subversion, the destruction, of the Constitution.

"Who can so properly be the inquisitors for the nation as the representatives of the nation themselves?" "The subjects of its jurisdiction are those offenses which proceed from the misconduct of public men." And that's what we're talking about. In other words, [the jurisdiction comes] from the abuse or violation of some public trust.

It is wrong, I suggest, it is a misreading of the Constitution for any member here to assert that for a member to vote for an article of impeachment means that that member must be convinced that the President should be removed from office. The Constitution doesn't say that. The powers relating to impeachment are an essential check in the hands of the body of the Legislature against and upon the encroachments of the Executive. The division between the two branches of the Legislature, the House and the Senate, assigning to the one the right to accuse and to the other the right to judge, the Framers of this Constitution were very astute. They did not make the accusers and the judgers—and the judges the same person.

We know the nature of impeachment. We've been talking about it awhile now. It is chiefly designed for the President and his high ministers to somehow be called into account. It is designed to "bridle" the Executive if he engages in excesses. "It is designed as a method of national inquest into the conduct of public men." The Framers confided in the Congress the power if need be, to remove the President in order to strike a delicate balance between a President swollen with power and grown tyrannical, and preservation of the independence of the Executive.

The nature of impeachment: a narrowly channeled exception to the separation-of-powers maxim. The Federal Convention of 1787 said that. It limited impeachment to high crimes and misdemeanors and discounted and opposed the term "maladministration." "It is to be used only for great misdemeanors," so it was said in the North Carolina ratification convention. And in the Virginia ratification convention: "We do not trust our liberty to a particular branch. We need one branch to check the other."

"No one need be afraid"—the North Carolina ratification convention—"No one need be afraid that officers who commit oppression will pass with immunity." "Prosecutions of impeachments will seldom fail to agitate the passions of the whole community," said Hamilton in the Federalist Papers, number 65. "We divide into parties more or less friendly or inimical to the accused." I do not mean political parties in that sense.

The drawing of political lines goes to the motivation behind impeachment; but impeachment must proceed within the confines of the constitutional term "high crime[s] and misdemeanors." Of the impeachment process, it was Woodrow Wilson who said that "Nothing short of the grossest offenses against the plain law of the land will suffice to give them speed and effectiveness. Indignation so great as to overgrow party interest may secure a conviction; but nothing else can."

Common sense would be revolted if we engaged upon this process for petty reasons. Congress has a lot to do: Appropriations, Tax Reform, Health Insurance, Campaign Finance Reform, Housing, Environmental Protection, Energy Sufficiency, Mass Transportation. Pettiness cannot be allowed to stand in the face of such overwhelming problems. So today we are not being petty. We are trying to be big, because the task we have before us is a big one.

This morning, in a discussion of the evidence, we were told that the evidence which purports to support the allegations of misuse of the CIA by the President is thin. We're told that that evidence is insufficient. What that recital of the evidence this morning did not include is what the President did know on June the 23rd, 1972.

The President did know that it was Republican money, that it was money from the Committee for the Re-Election of the President, which was found in the possession of one of the burglars arrested on June the 17th. What the President did know on the 23rd of June was the prior activities of E. Howard Hunt, which included his participation in the break-in of Daniel Ellsberg's psychiatrist, which included Howard Hunt's participation in the Dita Beard ITT affair, which included Howard Hunt's fabrication of cables designed to discredit the Kennedy administration.

We were further cautioned today that perhaps these proceedings ought to be delayed because certainly there would be new evidence forthcoming from the President of the United States. There has not even been an obfuscated indication that this committee would receive any additional materials from the President. The committee subpoena is outstanding, and if the President wants to supply that material, the committee sits here. The fact is that on yesterday, the American people waited with great anxiety for eight hours, not knowing whether their President would obey an order of the Supreme Court of the United States.

At this point, I would like to juxtapose a few of the impeachment criteria with some of the actions the President has engaged in. Impeachment criteria: James Madison, from the Virginia ratification convention. "If the President be connected in any suspicious manner with any person and there be grounds to believe that he will shelter him, he may be impeached."

We have heard time and time again that the evidence reflects the payment to defendants money. The President had knowledge that these funds were being paid and these were funds collected for the 1972 presidential campaign. We know that the President met with Mr. Henry Petersen 27 times to discuss matters related to Watergate, and immediately thereafter met with the very persons who were implicated in the information Mr. Petersen was receiving. The words are: "If the President is connected in any suspicious manner with any person and there be grounds to believe that he will shelter that person, he may be impeached."

Justice Story: "Impeachment" is attended—"is intended for occasional and extraordinary cases where a superior power acting for the whole people is put into operation to protect their rights and rescue their liberties from violations." We know about the Huston plan. We know about the break-in of the psychiatrist's office. We know that there was absolute complete direction on September 3rd when the President indicated that a surreptitious entry had been made in Dr. Fielding's office, after having met with Mr. Ehrlichman and Mr. Young. "Protect their rights." "Rescue their liberties from violation."

The Carolina ratification convention impeachment criteria: those are impeachable "who behave amiss or betray their public trust." Beginning shortly after the Watergate break-in and continuing to the present time, the President has engaged in a series of public statements and actions designed to thwart the lawful investigation by government prosecutors. Moreover, the President has made public announcements and assertions bearing on the Watergate case, which the evidence will show he knew to be false. These assertions, false assertions, impeachable, those who misbehave. Those who "behave amiss or betray the public trust."

James Madison again at the Constitutional Convention: "A President is impeachable if he attempts to subvert the Constitution." The Constitution charges the President with the task of taking care that the laws be faithfully executed, and yet the President has counseled his aides to commit perjury, willfully disregard the secrecy of grand jury proceedings, conceal surreptitious entry, attempt to compromise a federal judge, while publicly displaying his cooperation with the processes of criminal justice. "A President is impeachable if he attempts to subvert the Constitution."

If the impeachment provision in the Constitution of the United States will not reach the offenses charged here, then perhaps that 18th-century Constitution should be abandoned to a 20th-century paper shredder!

Has the President committed offenses, and planned, and directed, and acquiesced in a course of conduct which the Constitution will not tolerate? That's the question. We know that. We know the question. We should now forthwith proceed to answer the question. It is reason, and not passion, which must guide our deliberations, guide our debate, and guide our decision.

I yield back the balance of my time, Mr. Chairman.

FOR INFORMAL WRITING

Barbara Jordan quotes President James Madison in noting, "A President is impeachable if he attempts to subvert the Constitution." How does Jordan argue that President Nixon may have subverted the Constitution?

FOR DISCUSSION

1. Find the video clip of Barbara Jordan delivering this speech, and read along with it. What differences do you note between the two ways of "reading" her words?
2. What is the opening tone of the speech—"the glorious opportunity of sharing the pain of this inquiry"? What does Jordan mean? Why would she put it that way?
3. How does she juxtapose the Constitution with the President's actions? What is the effect?

FOR WRITING

With research, consider the following: There have been other impeachment inquiries since Nixon's. How does Nixon's compare with, say, the impeachment inquiries against Presidents Bill Clinton and Donald Trump? Be specific.

Why I Write (1976)
Joan Didion (1934–)

One of the preeminent writers and thinkers of the twentieth century, Joan Didion received a degree in English from the University of California, Berkeley. While she was still in college, she landed a job at Vogue *after winning an essay contest hosted by the magazine. Didion eventually became features editor for there. She has published numerous novels, screenplays, and essays, some of which she co-wrote with her husband and fellow writer, John Gregory Dunne. Her book* The Year of Magical Thinking *(2005), chronicles her grief over her husband's sudden death; it received the National Book Award. The essay that follows, one of many Didion wrote about being a writer, hints not only at her own career but also her philosophy of what it means to spend one's life writing.*

Of course I stole the title for this talk, from George Orwell. One reason I stole it was that I like the sound of the words: Why I Write. There you have three short unambiguous words that share a sound, and the sound they share is this:

I

I

I

In many ways writing is the act of saying *I*, of imposing oneself upon other people, of saying *listen to me, see it my way, change your mind.* It's an aggressive, even a hostile act. You can disguise its qualifiers and tentative subjunctives, with ellipses and evasions—with the whole manner of intimating rather than claiming, of alluding rather than stating—but there's no getting around the fact that setting words on paper is the tactic of a secret bully, an invasion, an imposition of the writer's sensibility on the reader's most private space.

I stole the title not only because the words sounded right but because they seemed to sum up, in a no-nonsense way, all I have to tell you. Like many writers

---

First published in the New York Times Book Review 5 December 1976. © Joan Didion.

I have only this one "subject," this one "area": the act of writing. I can bring you no reports from any other front. I may have other interests: I am "interested," for example, in marine biology, but I don't flatter myself that you would come out to hear me talk about it. I am not a scholar. I am not in the least an intellectual, which is not to say that when I hear the word "intellectual" I reach for my gun, but only to say that I do not think in abstracts. During the years when I was an undergraduate at Berkeley I tried, with a kind of hopeless late-adolescent energy, to buy some temporary visa into the world of ideas, to forge for myself a mind that could deal with the abstract.

In short I tried to think. I failed. My attention veered inexorably back to the specific, to the tangible, to what was generally considered, by everyone I knew then and for that matter have known since, the peripheral. I would try to contemplate the Hegelian dialectic and would find myself concentrating instead on a flowering pear tree outside my window and the particular way the petals fell on my floor. I would try to read linguistic theory and would find myself wondering instead if the lights were on in the Bevatron up the hill. When I say that I was wondering if the lights were on in the Bevatron you might immediately suspect, if you deal in ideas at all, that I was registering the Bevatron as a political symbol, thinking in shorthand about the military-industrial complex and its role in the university community, but you would be wrong. I was only wondering if the lights were on in the Bevatron, and how they looked. A physical fact.

I had trouble graduating from Berkeley, not because of this inability to deal with ideas—I was majoring in English, and I could locate the house-and-garden imagery in *The Portrait of a Lady* as well as the next person, "imagery" being by definition the kind of specific that got my attention—but simply because I had neglected to take a course in Milton. I did this. For reasons which now sound baroque I needed a degree by the end of that summer, and the English department finally agreed, if I would come down from Sacramento every Friday and talk about the cosmology of *Paradise Lost*, to certify me proficient in Milton. I did this. Some Fridays I took the Greyhound bus, other Fridays I caught the Southern Pacific's City of San Francisco on the last leg of its transcontinental trip. I can no longer tell you whether Milton put the sun or the earth at the center of his universe in *Paradise Lost*, the central question of at least one century and a topic about which I wrote 10,000 words that summer, but I can still recall the exact rancidity of the butter in the City of San Francisco's dining car, and the way the tinted windows on the Greyhound bus cast the oil refineries around Carquinez Straits into a grayed and obscurely sinister light. In short my attention was always on the periphery, on what I could see and taste and touch, on the butter, and the Greyhound bus. During those years I was traveling on what I knew to be a very shaky passport, forged papers: I knew that I was no legitimate resident in any world of ideas. I knew I couldn't think. All I knew then was what I couldn't do. All I knew then was what I wasn't, and it took me some years to discover what I was.

Which was a writer.

By which I mean not a "good" writer or a "bad" writer but simply a writer, a person whose most absorbed and passionate hours are spent arranging words on pieces of paper. Had my credentials been in order I would never have become a writer. Had I been blessed with even limited access to my own mind there would have been no reason to write. I write entirely to find out what I'm thinking, what I'm looking at, what I see and what it means. What I want and what I fear. Why did the oil refineries around Carquinez Straits seem sinister to me in the summer of 1956? Why have the night lights in the Bevatron burned in my mind for twenty years? *What is going on in these pictures in my mind?*

When I talk about pictures in my mind I am talking, quite specifically, about images that shimmer around the edges. There used to be an illustration in every elementary psychology book showing a cat drawn by a patient in varying stages of schizophrenia. This cat had a shimmer around it. You could see the molecular structure breaking down at the very edges of the cat: the cat became the background and the background the cat, everything interacting, exchanging ions. People on hallucinogens describe the same perception of objects. I'm not a schizophrenic, nor do I take hallucinogens, but certain images do shimmer for me. Look hard enough, and you can't miss the shimmer. It's there. You can't think too much about these pictures that shimmer. You just lie low and let them develop. You stay quiet. You don't talk to many people and you keep your nervous system from shorting out and you try to locate the cat in the shimmer, the grammar in the picture.

Just as I meant "shimmer" literally I mean "grammar" literally. Grammar is a piano I play by ear, since I seem to have been out of school the year the rules were mentioned. All I know about grammar is its infinite power. To shift the structure of a sentence alters the meaning of that sentence, as definitely and inflexibly as the position of a camera alters the meaning of the object photographed. Many people know about camera angles now, but not so many know about sentences. The arrangement of the words matters, and the arrangement you want can be found in the picture in your mind. The picture dictates the arrangement. The picture dictates whether this will be a sentence with or without clauses, a sentence that ends hard or a dying-fall sentence, long or short, active or passive. The picture tells you how to arrange the words and the arrangement of the words tells you, or tells me, what's going on in the picture. *Nota bene:*

It tells you.

You don't tell it.

Let me show you what I mean by pictures in the mind. I began *Play It as It Lays* just as I have begun each of my novels, with no notion of "character" or "plot" or even "incident." I had only two pictures in my mind, more about which later, and a technical intention, which was to write a novel so elliptical and fast that it would be over before you noticed it, a novel so fast that it would scarcely exist on the page at all. About the picture: the first was of white space. Empty space. This was clearly the picture that dictated the narrative intention of the book—a book in which anything that happened would happen off the page, a "white" book to which the reader would have to bring his or her own bad dreams—and yet this picture told me no "story," suggested no situation. The second picture did. This second picture was of something actually witnessed. A young woman with long hair and a short white halter walks through the casino at the Riviera in Las Vegas at one in the morning. She crosses the casino alone and picks up a house telephone. I watch her because I have heard her paged, and recognize her name: she is a minor actress I see around Los Angeles from time to time, in places like Jax and once in a gynecologist's office in the Beverly Hills Clinic, but have never met. I know nothing about her. Who is paging her? Why is she here to be paged? How exactly did she come to this? It was precisely this moment in Las Vegas that made *Play It as It Lays* begin to tell itself to me, but the moment appears in the novel only obliquely, in a chapter which begins:

> Maria made a list of things she would never do. She would never: walk through the Sands or Caesar's alone after midnight. She would never: ball at a party, do S-M unless she wanted to, borrow furs from Abe Lipsey, deal. She would never: carry a Yorkshire in Beverly Hills.

That is the beginning of the chapter and that is also the end of the chapter, which may suggest what I meant by "white space."

I recall having a number of pictures in my mind when I began the novel I just finished, *A Book of Common Prayer*. As a matter of fact one of these pictures was of that Bevatron I mentioned, although I would be hard put to tell you a story in which nuclear energy figures. Another was a newspaper photograph of a hijacked 707 burning on the desert in the Middle East. Another was the night view from a room in which I once spent a week with paratyphoid, a hotel room on the Colombian coast. My husband and I seemed to be on the Colombian coast representing the United States of America at a film festival (I recall invoking the name "Jack Valenti" a lot, as if its reiteration could make me well), and it was a bad place to have fever, not only because my indisposition offended our hosts but because every night in this hotel the generator failed. The lights went out. The elevator stopped. My husband would go to the event of the evening and make excuses for me and I would stay alone in this hotel room, in the dark. I remember standing at the window trying to call Bogotá (the telephone seemed to work on the same principle as the generator) and watching the night wind come up and wondering what I was doing eleven degrees off the equator with a fever of 103. The view from that window definitely figures in *A Book of Common Prayer*, as does the burning 707, and yet none of these pictures told me the story I needed.

The picture that did, the picture that shimmered and made these other images coalesce, was the Panama airport at 6 AM. I was in this airport only once, on a plane to Bogotá that stopped for an hour to refuel, but the way it looked that morning remained superimposed on everything I saw until the day I finished *A Book of Common Prayer*. I lived in that airport for several years. I can still feel the hot air when I step off the plane, can see the heat already rising off the tarmac at 6 AM. I can feel my skirt damp and wrinkled on my legs. I can feel the asphalt stick to my sandals. I remember the big tail of a Pan American plane floating motionless down at the end of the tarmac. I remember the sound of a slot machine in the waiting room. I could tell you that I remember a particular woman in the airport, an American woman, a *norteamericana*, a thin *norteamericana* about forty who wore a big square emerald in lieu of a wedding ring, but there was no such woman there.

I put this woman in the airport later. I made this woman up, just as I later made up a country to put the airport in, and a family to run the country. This woman in the airport is neither catching a plane nor meeting one. She is ordering tea in the airport coffee shop. In fact she is not simply "ordering" tea but insisting that the water be boiled, in front of her, for twenty minutes. Why is this woman in this airport? Why is she going nowhere, where has she been? Where did she get that big emerald? What derangement, or disassociation, makes her believe that her will to see the water boiled can possibly prevail?

> She had been going to one airport or another for four months, one could see it, looking at the visas on her passport. All those airports where Charlotte Douglas's passport had been stamped would have looked alike. Sometimes the sign on the tower would say "Bienvenidos" and sometimes the sign on the tower would say "Bienvenue," some places were wet and hot and others dry and hot, but at each of these airports the pastel concrete walls would rust and stain and the swamp off the runway would be littered with the fuselages of cannibalized Fairchild F-227's and the water would need boiling.
> I knew why Charlotte went to the airport even if Victor did not.
> I knew about airports.

These lines appear about halfway through *A Book of Common Prayer*, but I wrote them during the second week I worked on the book, long before I had any idea where Charlotte Douglas had been or why she went to airports. Until I wrote these lines I had no character called "Victor" in mind: the necessity for mentioning a name, and the name "Victor," occurred to me as I wrote the sentence. *I knew why Charlotte went to the airport* sounded incomplete. *I knew why Charlotte went to the airport even if Victor did not* carried a little more narrative drive. Most important of all, until I wrote these lines I did not know who "I" was, who was telling the story. I had intended until then that the "I" be no more than the voice of the author, a nineteenth-century omniscient narrator. But there it was:

218 THE OXFORD READER

> I knew why Charlotte went to the airport even if Victor did not.
> I knew about airports.

This "I" was the voice of no author in my house. This "I" was someone who not only knew why Charlotte went to the airport but also knew someone called "Victor." Who was Victor? Who was this narrator? Why was this narrator telling me this story? Let me tell you one thing about why writers write: had I known the answer to any of these questions I would never have needed to write a novel.

FOR INFORMAL WRITING

What does this essay reveal about Joan Didion's craft—about being a writer? How might Didion define "creative inspiration?" Look specifically at the essay to support your point of view.

FOR DISCUSSION

1. "All I knew then was what I wasn't, and it took me some years to discover what I was. Which was a writer." How does Didion's path to becoming a writer appear to have gone along with her own self-discovery?
2. "[T]here's no getting around the fact that setting words on paper is the tactic of a secret bully, an invasion, an imposition of the writer's sensibility on the reader's most private space." What does she mean by this? How might Didion characterize the relationship between a writer and a reader?
3. How does conceiving of her plot lines visually, crafting images in her mind, become part of Didion's writing process? How do you know? In what ways do you sometimes "think visually?" To what effect?

FOR WRITING

Research Joan Didion's biography and aspects of her autobiographical work, such as *The White Album* (1979), and examine the ways in which her writing was inspired by pop culture and, for instance, the various rock bands with whom she used to "run." Consider the ways in which cultural references pepper her work, allusions or facts the reader is supposed to "get." For instance, in this essay, she quotes *Play It as It Lays* (1970):

> Maria made a list of things she would never do. She would never: walk through the Sands or Caesar's alone after midnight. She would never: ball at a party, do S-M unless she wanted to, borrow furs from Abe Lipsey, deal. She would never: carry a Yorkshire in Beverly Hills.

What is the effect of these references on the reader? Why would a writer choose to include such culturally specific descriptors?

Split at the Root (1982)
Adrienne Rich (1929–2012)

An influential lesbian writer and activist, Adrienne Rich graduated from Radcliffe College (now part of Harvard University) in 1951, the same year she was selected by noted poet W. H. Auden for the Yale Series of Younger Poets Prize. The 1960s were her most prolific time, as she was inspired by and explored themes of women's rights and the Vietnam War. She won the National Book Award in 1974 for Diving Into the Wreck. *Rich also received awards that include a MacArthur Fellowship, the Lannan Lifetime Achievement Award, and the Ruth Lilly Poetry Prize. In 1997, Rich refused an award from the Clinton administration, the National Medal of Arts, saying, "Art means nothing if it simply decorates the dinner table of the power that holds it hostage." This essay was originally published in one of Rich's six prose collections,* Blood, Bread, and Poetry: Selected Prose, 1979–1985.

For or about fifteen minutes I have been sitting chin in hand in front of the typewriter, staring out at the snow. Trying to be honest with myself, trying to figure out why writing this seems to be so dangerous an act, filled with fear and shame, and why it seems so necessary. It comes to me that in order to write this I have to be willing to do two things: I have to claim my father, for I have my Jewishness from him and not from my gentile mother; and I have to break his silence, his taboos; in order to claim him I have in a sense to expose him.

And there is, of course, the third thing: I have to face the sources and the flickering presence of my own ambivalence as a Jew; the daily, mundane anti-Semitisms of my entire life.

Adrienne Rich, "Split at the Root," Adrienne Rich's Poetry and Prose: A Norton Critical Edition (Norton, 1993), 224–239.

These are stories I have never tried to tell before. Why now? Why, I asked myself sometime last year, does this question of Jewish identity float so impalpably, so ungraspably around me, a cloud I can't quite see the outlines of, which feels to me to be without definition?

And yet I've been on the track of this longer than I think.
In a long poem written in 1960, when I was thirty-one years old, I described myself as "Split at the root, neither Gentile nor Jew, / Yankee nor Rebel." I was still trying to have it both ways: to be neither/nor, trying to live (with my Jewish husband and three children more Jewish in ancestry than I) in the predominantly gentile Yankee academic world of Cambridge, Massachusetts.

But this begins, for me, in Baltimore, where I was born in my father's workplace, a hospital in the Black ghetto, whose lobby contained an immense white marble statue of Christ.

My father was then a young teacher and researcher in the department of pathology at the Johns Hopkins Medical School, one of the very few Jews to attend or teach at that institution. He was from Birmingham, Alabama; his father, Samuel, was Ashkenazic, an immigrant from Austria-Hungary, and his mother, Hattie Rice, a Sephardic Jew from Vicksburg, Mississippi. My grandfather had had a shoe store in Birmingham, which did well enough to allow him to retire comfortably and to leave my grandmother income on his death. The only souvenirs of my grandfather, Samuel Rich, were his ivory flute, which lay on our living-room mantel and was not to be played with; his thin gold pocket watch, which my father wore; and his Hebrew prayer book, which I discovered among my father's books in the course of reading my way through his library. In this prayer book there was a newspaper clipping about my grandparents' wedding, which took place in a synagogue.

My father, Arnold, was sent in adolescence to a military school in the North Carolina mountains, a place for training white southern Christian gentlemen. I suspect that there were few, if any, other Jewish boys at Colonel Bingham's, or at "Mr. Jefferson's university" in Charlottesville, where he studied as an undergraduate. With whatever conscious forethought, Samuel and Hattie sent their son into the dominant southern WASP culture to become an "exception," to enter the professional class. Never, in describing these experiences, did he speak of having suffered from loneliness, cultural alienation, or outsiderhood. Never did I hear him use the word *anti-Semitism*.

It was only in college, when I read a poem by Karl Shapiro beginning "To hate the Negro and avoid the Jew / is the curriculum," that it flashed on me that there was an untold side to my father's story of his student years. He looked recognizably Jewish, was short and slender in build with dark wiry hair and deep-set eyes, high forehead and curved nose.

My mother is a gentile. In Jewish law I cannot count myself a Jew. If it is true that "we think back through our mothers if we are women" (Virginia Woolf)—and I myself have affirmed this—then even according to lesbian theory, I cannot (or need not?) count myself a Jew.

The white southern Protestant woman, the gentile, has always been there for me to peel back into. That's a whole piece of history in itself, for my gentile grandmother and my mother were also frustrated artists and intellectuals, a lost writer and a lost composer between them. Readers and annotators of books, note takers, my mother a good pianist still, in her eighties. But there was also the obsession with ancestry, with "background," the southern talk of family, not as people you would necessarily know and depend on, but as heritage, the guarantee of "good breeding." There was the inveterate romantic heterosexual fantasy, the mother telling the daughter how to attract men (my mother often used the word "fascinate"); the assumption that relations between the sexes could only be romantic, that it was in the woman's interest to cultivate "mystery", conceal her actual feelings. Survival tactics of a kind, I think today; knowing what I know about the white woman's sexual role in the southern racist scenario. Heterosexuality as protection, but also drawing white women deeper into collusion with white men.

It would be easy to push away and deny the gentile in me—that white southern woman, that social christian. At different times in my life I have wanted to push away one or the other burden of inheritance, to say merely I am a woman; I am a lesbian. If I call myself a Jewish lesbian, do I thereby try to shed some of my southern gentile white woman's culpability? If I call myself only through my mother, is it because I pass more easily through a world where being a lesbian often seems like outsiderhood enough?

According to Nazi logic, my two Jewish grandparents would have made me a *Mischling, first-degree*–nonexempt from the Final Solution.

The social world in which I grew up was Christian virtually without needing to say so—christian imagery, music, language, symbols, assumptions everywhere. It was also a genteel, white, middle-class world in which "common" was a term of deep opprobrium. "Common" white people might speak of "niggers"; we were taught never to use that word—*we* said "Negroes" (even as we accepted segregation, the eating taboo, the assumption that Black people were simply of a separate species). Our language was more polite, distinguishing us from the "rednecks" or the lynch-mob mentality. But so charged with negative meaning was even the word "Negro" that as children we were taught never to use it in front of Black people. We were taught that any mention of skin color in the presence of colored people was treacherous, forbidden ground. In a parallel way, the word "Jew" was not used by polite gentiles. I sometimes heard my best friend's father, a Presbyterian minister, allude to "the Hebrew people" or "people of the Jewish faith."

The world of acceptable folk was white, gentile (christian, really), and had "ideals" (which colored people, white "common" people, were not supposed to have). "Ideals" and "manners" included not hurting someone's feelings by calling her or him a Negro or a Jew—naming the hated identity. This is the mental framework of the 1930s and 1940s in which I was raised.

(Writing this, I feel dimly like the betrayer; of my father, who did not speak the word; of my mother, who must have trained me in the messages; of my caste and class; of my whiteness itself.)

Two memories: I am in a play reading at school of *The Merchant of Venice*. Whatever Jewish law says, I am quite sure I was seen as Jewish (with a reassuringly gentile mother) in that double vision that bigotry allows. I am the only Jewish girl in the class, and I am playing Portia. As always, I read my part aloud for my father the night before, and he tells me to convey, with my voice, more scorn and contempt with the word "Jew": "Therefore, Jew. . ." I have to say the word out, and say it loudly. I was encouraged to pretend to be a non-Jewish child acting a non-Jewish character who has to speak the word "Jew" emphatically. Such a child would not have had trouble with the part. But I must have had trouble with the part, if only because the word itself was really taboo. I can see that there was a kind of terrible, bitter bravado about my father's way of handling this. And who would not dissociate from Shylock in order to identify with Portia? As a Jewish child who was also a female, I loved Portia—and, like every other Shakespearean heroine, she proved a treacherous role model.

A year or so later I am in another play, *The School for Scandal*, in which a notorious spendthrift is described as having "many excellent friends among the Jews." In neither case was anything explained, either to me or to the class at large, about this scorn for Jews and the disgust surrounding Jews and money. Money, when Jews wanted it, had it, or lent it to others, seemed to take on a peculiar nastiness; Jews and money had some peculiar and unspeakable relation.

At this same school—in which we had Episcopalian hymns and prayers, and read aloud through the Bible morning after morning—I gained the impression that Jews were in the Bible and mentioned in English literature, that they had been persecuted centuries ago by the wicked Inquisition, but that they seemed not to exist in everyday life. These were the 1940s, and we were told a great deal about the Battle of Britain, the noble French Resistance fighters, the brave, starving Dutch—but I did not learn of the resistance of the Warsaw ghetto until I left home.

I was sent to the Episcopal church, baptized and confirmed, and attended it for about five years, though without belief. That religion seemed to have little to do with belief or commitment; it was liturgy that mattered, not spiritual passion. Neither of my parents ever entered that church, and my father would not enter any church for any reason—wedding or funeral. Nor did I enter a synagogue until I left Baltimore. When I came home from church, for a while, my father insisted on reading aloud to me from Thomas Paine's *The Age of Reason*—a diatribe against institutional religion. Thus, he explained, I would have a balanced view of these things, a choice. He—they—did not give me the choice to be a Jew. My mother explained to me when I was filling out forms for college that if any question was asked about "religion," I should put down "Episcopalian" rather than "none"—to seem to have no religion was, she implied, dangerous.

But it was white social Christianity, rather than any particular christian sect, that the world was founded on. The very word *Christian* was used as a synonym for virtuous, just, peace-loving, generous, etc., etc. The norm was christian: "religion: none" was indeed not acceptable. Anti-Semitism was so intrinsic as not to have a name. I don't recall exactly being taught that the Jews killed Jesus—"Christ killer" seems too strong a term for the bland Episcopal vocabulary—but certainly we got the impression that the Jews had been caught out in a terrible mistake, failing to recognize the true Messiah, and were thereby less advanced in moral and spiritual sensibility. The Jews had actually allowed moneylenders in the Temple (again, the unexplained obsession with Jews and money). They were of the past, archaic, primitive, as older (and darker) cultures are supposed to be primitive; christianity was lightness, fairness, peace on earth, and combined the feminine appeal of "The meek shall inherit the earth" with the masculine stride of "Onward, Christian Soldiers."

Sometime in 1946, while still in high school, I read in the newspaper that a theater in Baltimore was showing films of the Allied liberation of the Nazi concentration camps. Alone, I went downtown after school one afternoon and watched the stark, blurry, but unmistakable newsreels. When I try to go back and touch the pulse of that girl of sixteen, growing up in many ways so precocious and so ignorant, I am overwhelmed by a memory of despair, a sense of inevitability more enveloping than any I had ever known. Anne Frank's diary and many other personal narratives of the Holocaust were still unknown or unwritten. But it came to me, that every one of those piles of corpses, mountains of shoes and clothing had contained, simply, individuals, who had believed, as I now believed of myself, that they were intended to live out a life of some kind of meaning, that the world possessed some kind of sense and order; yet this had happened to them. And I, who believed my life was intended to be so interesting and meaningful, was connected to those dead by something—not just mortality but a taboo name, a hated identity. Or was I—did I really have to be? Writing this now, I feel belated rage that I was so impoverished by the family and social worlds I lived in, that I had to try to figure out by myself what this did indeed mean for me. That I had never been taught about resistance, only about passing. That I had no language for anti-Semitism itself.

When I went home and told my parents where I had been, they were not pleased. I felt accused of being morbidly curious, not healthy, sniffing around death for the thrill of it. And since, at sixteen, I was often not sure of the sources of my feelings or of my motives for doing what I did, I probably accused myself as well. One thing was clear: there was nobody in my world with whom I could discuss those films. Probably at the same time, I was reading accounts of the camps in magazines and newspapers; what I remember were the films and having questions that I could not even phrase, such as *Are those men and women "them" or "us"?*

To be able to ask even the child's astonished question *Why do they hate us so?* means knowing how to say "we." The guilt of not knowing, the guilt of perhaps having betrayed my parents or even those victims, those survivors, through mere curiosity—these also froze in me for years the impulse to find out more about the Holocaust.

1947: I left Baltimore to go to college in Cambridge, Massachusetts, left (I thought) the backward, enervating South for the intellectual, vital North. New England also had for me some vibration of higher moral rectitude, of moral passion even, with its seventeenth-century Puritan self-scrutiny, its nineteenth-century literary "flowering," its abolitionist righteousness, Colonel Shaw and his Black Civil War regiment depicted in granite on Boston Common. At the same time, I found myself, at Radcliffe, among Jewish women. I used to sit for hours over coffee with what I thought of as the "real" Jewish students, who told me about middle-class Jewish culture in America. I described my background—for the first time to strangers—and they took me on, some with amusement at my illiteracy, some arguing that I could never marry into a strict Jewish family, some convinced I didn't "look Jewish," others that I did. I learned the names of holidays and foods, which surnames are Jewish and which are "changed names"; about girls who had had their noses "fixed," their hair straightened. For these young Jewish women, students in the late 1940s, it was acceptable, perhaps even necessary, to strive to look as gentile as possible; but they stuck proudly to being Jewish, expected to marry a Jew, have children, keep the holidays, carry on the culture.

I felt I was testing a forbidden current, that there was danger in these revelations. I bought a reproduction of a Chagall portrait of a rabbi in striped prayer shawl and hung it on the wall of my room. I was admittedly young and trying to educate myself, but I was also doing something that is dangerous: I was flirting with identity.

One day that year I was in a small shop where I had bought a dress with a too-long skirt. The shop employed a seamstress who did alterations, and she came in to pin up the skirt on me. I am sure that she was a recent immigrant, a survivor.

I remember a short, dark woman wearing heavy glasses, with an accent so foreign I could not understand her words. Something about her presence was very powerful and disturbing to me. After marking and pinning up the skirt, she sat back on her knees, looked up at me, and asked in a hurried whisper: "You Jewish?" Eighteen years of training in assimilation sprang into the reflex by which I shook my head, rejecting her, and muttered, "No."

What was I actually saying "no" to? She was poor, older, struggling with a foreign tongue, anxious; she had escaped the death that had been intended for her, but I had no imagination of her possible courage and foresight, her resistance—I did not see in her a heroine who had perhaps saved many lives, including her own. I saw the frightened immigrant, the seamstress hemming the skirts of college girls, the wandering Jew. But I was an American college girl having her skirt hemmed. And I was frightened myself, I think, because she had recognized me ("It takes one to know one," my friend Edie at Radcliffe had said) even if I refused to recognize myself or her, even if her recognition was sharpened by loneliness or the need to feel safe with me.

But why should she have felt safe with me? I myself was living with a false sense of safety.

There are betrayals in my life that I have known at the very moment were betrayals: this was one of them. There are other betrayals committed so repeatedly, so mundanely, that they leave no memory trace behind, only a growing residue of misery, of dull, accreted self-hatred. Often these take the form not of words but of silence. Silence before the joke at which everyone is laughing; the anti-woman joke, the racist joke, the anti-Semitic joke. Silence and then amnesia. Blocking it out when the oppressor's language starts coming from the lips of one we admire, whose courage and eloquence have touched us: *She didn't really mean that; he didn't really say that.* But the accretions build up out of sight, like scale inside a kettle.

1948: I come home from my freshman year at college, flaming with new insights, new information. I am the daughter who has gone out into the world, to the pinnacle of intellectual prestige, Harvard, fulfilling my father's hopes for me, but also exposed to dangerous influences. I have already been reproved for attending a rally for Henry Wallace and the Progressive Party. I challenge my father: "Why haven't you told me that I am Jewish? Why do you never talk about being a Jew?" He answers measuredly, "You know that I have never denied that I am a Jew. But it's not important to me. I am a scientist, a deist. I have no use for organized religion. I choose to live in a world of many kinds of people. There are Jews I admire and others who I despise. I am a person, not simply a Jew." The words are as I remember them, not perhaps exactly as spoken. But that was the message. And it contained enough truth—as all denial drugs itself on partial truth—so that it remained for the time being unanswerable, leaving me high and dry, split at the root, gasping for clarity, for air.

At that time Arnold Rich was living in suspension, waiting to be appointed to the professorship of pathology at Johns Hopkins. The appointment was delayed for years, no Jew ever having held a professional chair in that medical school. And he wanted it badly. It must have been a very bitter time for him, since he had believed so greatly in the redeeming power of excellence, of being the most brilliant, inspired man for the job. With enough excellence, you could presumably make it stop mattering that you were Jewish; you could become the only Jew in the gentile world, a Jew so "civilized," so far from "common," so attractively combining southern gentility with European cultural values that no one would ever confuse you with the raw, "pushy" Jew of New York, the "loud, hysterical" refugees from eastern Europe, the "overdressed" Jews of the urban South.

We—my sister, mother, and I—were constantly urged to speak quietly in public, to dress without ostentation, to repress all vividness or spontaneity, to assimilate with a world which might see us as too flamboyant. I suppose that my mother, pure gentile though she was, could be seen as acting "common" or "Jewish" if she laughed too loudly or spoke aggressively. My father's mother, who lived with us half the year, was a model of circumspect behavior, dressed in dark blue or lavender, retiring in company, ladylike to an extreme, wearing no jewelry except a good gold chain, a narrow brooch, or a string of pearls. A few times, within the family, I saw her anger flare, felt the passion she was repressing. But when Arnold took us out to a restaurant or on a trip, the Rich women were always tuned down to some WASP level my father believed, surely, would protect us all—maybe also make us unrecognizable to the "real Jews" who wanted to seize us, drag us back to the *shtetl*, the ghetto, in its many manifestations.

For, yes, that was a message-that some Jews would be after you, once they "knew," to rejoin them, to re-enter a world that was messy, noisy, unpredictable, maybe poor—"even though," as my mother once wrote me, criticizing my largely Jewish choice of friends in college, "some of them will be the most brilliant, fascinating people you'll ever meet." I wonder if that isn't one message of assimilation—of America—that the unlucky or the unachieving want to pull you backward, that to identify with them is to court downward mobility, lose the precious chance of passing, of token existence. There was always within this sense of Jewish identity a strong class discrimination. Jews might be "fascinating" as individuals but came with huge unruly families who "poured chicken soup over everyone's head" (in the phrase of a white southern male poet). Anti-Semitism could thus be justified by the bad behavior of certain Jews; and if you did not effectively deny family and community, there would always be a remote cousin claiming kinship with you who was the "wrong kind" of Jew.

I have always believed his attitude toward other Jews depended on who they were.... It was my impression that Jews of this background looked down on Eastern European Jews, including Polish Jews and Russian Jews, who generally were not as well educated. This from a letter written to me recently by a gentile who had worked in my father's department, whom I had asked about anti-Semitism there and in particular regarding my father. This informant also wrote me that it was hard to perceive anti-Semitism in Baltimore because the racism made so much more intense an impression: *I would almost have to think that blacks went to a different heaven than the whites, because the bodies were kept in a separate morgue, and some white persons did not even want blood transfusions from black donors.* My father's mind was predictably racist and misogynist; yet as a medical student he noted in his journal that southern male chivalry stopped at the point of any white man in a streetcar giving his seat to an old, weary Black woman standing in the aisle. Was this a Jewish insight—an outsider's insight, even though the outsider was striving to be on the inside?

Because what isn't named is often more permeating than what is, I believe that my father's Jewishness profoundly shaped my own identity and our family existence. They were shaped both by external anti-Semitism and my father's self-hatred, and by his Jewish pride. What Arnold did, I think, was call his Jewish pride something else: achievement, aspiration, genius, idealism. Whatever was unacceptable got left back under the rubric of Jewishness or the "wrong kind" of Jews—uneducated, aggressive, loud. The message I got was that we were really superior: nobody else's father had collected so many books, had traveled so far, knew so many languages. Baltimore was a musical city, but for the most part, in the families of my school friends, culture was for women. My father was an amateur musician, read poetry, adored encyclopedic knowledge. He prowled and pounced over my school papers, insisting I use "grownup" sources; he criticized my poems for faulty technique and gave me books on rhyme and meter and form. His investment in my intellect and talent was egotistical, tyrannical, opinionated, and terribly wearing. He taught me, nevertheless, to believe in hard work, to mistrust easy inspiration, to write and rewrite; to fee l that I was a person of the book, even though a woman; to take ideas seriously. He made me feel, at a very young age, the power of language and that I could share in it.

The Riches were proud, but we also had to be very careful. Our behavior had to be more impeccable than other people's. Strangers were not to be trusted, nor even friends; family issues must never go beyond the family; the world was full of potential slanderers, betrayers, people who could not understand. Even within the family, I realize that I never in my whole life knew what my father was really feeling. Yet he spoke—monologued—with driving intensity. You could grow up in such a house mesmerized by the local electricity, the crucial meanings assumed by the merest things. This used to seem to me a sign that we were all living on some high emotional plane. It was a difficult force field for a favored daughter to disengage from.

Easy to call that intensity Jewish; and I have no doubt that passion is one of the qualities required for survival over generations of persecution. But what happens when passion is rent from its original base, when the white gentile world is softly saying "Be more like us and you can be almost one of us"? What happens when survival seems to mean closing off one emotional artery after another? His forebears in Europe had been forbidden to travel or expelled from one country after another, had special taxes levied on them if they left the city walls, had been forced to wear special clothes and badges, restricted to the poorest neighborhoods. He had wanted to be a "free spirit," to travel widely, among "all kinds of people." Yet in his prime of life he lived in an increasingly withdrawn world, in his house up on a hill in a neighborhood where Jews were not supposed to be able to buy property, depending almost exclusively on interactions with his wife and daughters to provide emotional connectedness. In his home, he created a private defense system so elaborate that even as he was dying, my mother felt unable to talk freely with his colleagues or others who might have helped her. Of course, she acquiesced in this.

The loneliness of the "only," the token, often doesn't feel like loneliness but like a kind of dead echo chamber. Certain things that ought to don't resonate. Somewhere Beverly Smith writes of women of color "inspiring the behavior" in each other. When there's nobody to "inspire the behavior," act out of the culture, there is an atrophy, a dwindling, which is partly invisible. . . .

Sometimes I feel I have seen too long from too many disconnected angles: white, Jewish, anti-Semite, racist, anti-racist, once-married, lesbian, middle-class, feminist, exmatriate southerner, *split at the root*—that I will never bring them whole. I would have liked, in this essay, to bring together the meanings of anti-Semitism and racism as I have experienced them and as I believe they intersect in the world beyond my life. But I'm not able to do this yet. I feel the tension as I think, make notes: *If you really look at the one reality, the other will waver and disperse.* Trying in one week to read Angela Davis and Lucy Davidowicz; trying to hold throughout to a feminist, a lesbian, perspective—what does this mean? Nothing has trained me for this. And sometimes I feel inadequate to make any statement as a Jew; I feel the history of denial within me like an injury, a scar. For assimilation has affected my perceptions; those early lapses in meaning, those blanks, are with me still. My ignorance can be dangerous to me and to others.

Yet we can't wait for the undamaged to make our connections for us; we can't wait to speak until we are perfectly clear and righteous. There is no purity and, in our lifetimes, no end to this process.

This essay, then, has no conclusions: it is another beginning for me. Not just a way of saying, in 1982 Right Wing America, *I too, will wear the yellow star.* It's a moving into accountability, enlarging the range of accountability. I know that in the rest of my life, the next half century or so, every aspect of my identity will have to be engaged. The middle-class white girl taught to trade obedience for privilege. The Jewish lesbian raised to be a heterosexual gentile. The woman who first heard oppression named and analyzed in the Black Civil Rights struggle. The woman with three sons, the feminist who hates male violence. The woman limping with a cane, the woman who has stopped bleeding are also accountable. The poet who knows that beautiful language can lie, that the oppressor's language sometimes sounds beautiful. The woman trying, as part of her resistance, to clean up her act.

FOR INFORMAL WRITING

Think about your own multiple identities, something Rich grapples with in "Split at the Root." How do these influence your view of yourself/yourselves? Like Rich, do you have any identities ascribed to you with which you struggle or that you reject?

FOR DISCUSSION

1. "And yet I've been on the track of this longer than I think." What does Rich mean by that?
2. Rich adamantly prefers to call herself a gentile rather than a Jew. Why? What do you infer from this choice? What does this mean about prejudice and oppression—in a larger sense?
3. "Writing this, I feel dimly like the betrayer." Why? Patrilineal descent is honored in some branches of Judaism. Had this been available to Rich, would her attitude be different? Would she still feel the need to call herself a "gentile?" Why?

FOR WRITING

What was the cultural and political landscape of Rich's upbringing? How does the anti-Semitism that Rich experiences (and that her father experienced) contextualize her own conflicted sense of identity? Given this context, why might her father have rejected his own cultural and religious background? What are the costs of that rejection, both for Rich and her father?

Just Walk on By
A Black Man Ponders His Ability to Alter Public Space (1986)
Brent Staples (1951–)

Brent Staples grew up in a small town outside of Philadelphia. He earned the MA and PhD in psychology from the University of Chicago. An editorial writer for The New York Times *and the author of numerous articles, Staples's books include* Parallel Time: Growing Up in Black and White *(2000) and* An American Love Story *(1999). This essay appeared in* Ms. Magazine *in 1986 as "Just Walk on By" and in* Harper's Magazine *in 1987 as "Black Men and Public Space." Staples won a Pulitzer Prize in 2019 for his work appearing in* The New York Times.

My first victim was a woman—white, well dressed, probably in her early twenties. I came upon her late one evening on a deserted street in Hyde Park, a relatively affluent neighborhood in an otherwise mean, impoverished section of Chicago. As I swung onto the avenue behind her, there seemed to be a discreet, uninflammatory distance between us. Not so. She cast back a worried glance. To her, the youngish black man—a broad six feet two inches with a beard and billowing hair, both hands shoved into the pockets of a bulky military jacket—seemed menacingly close. After a few more quick glimpses, she picked up her pace and was soon running in earnest. Within seconds she disappeared into a cross street.

That was more than a decade ago. I was 23 years old, a graduate student newly arrived at the University of Chicago. It was in the echo of that terrified woman's footfalls that I first began to know the unwieldy inheritance I'd come into—the ability to alter public space in ugly ways. It was clear that she thought herself the quarry of a mugger, a rapist, or worse. Suffering a bout of insomnia, however, I was stalking sleep, not defenseless wayfarers. As a softy who is scarcely able to take a knife to raw chicken—let alone hold it to a person's throat—I was

© Brent Staples

surprised, embarrassed, and dismayed all at once. Her flight made me feel like an accomplice in tyranny. It also made it clear that I was indistinguishable from the muggers who occasionally seeped into the area from the surrounding ghetto. That first encounter, and those that followed signified that a vast unnerving gulf lay between nighttime pedestrians—particularly women—and me. And I soon gathered that being perceived as dangerous is a hazard in itself. I only needed to turn a corner into a dicey situation, or crowd some frightened, armed person in a foyer somewhere, or make an errant move after being pulled over by a policeman. Where fear and weapons meet—and they often do in urban America—there is always the possibility of death.

In that first year, my first away from my hometown, I was to become thoroughly familiar with the language of fear. At dark, shadowy intersections in Chicago, I could cross in front of a car stopped at a traffic light and elicit the *thunk, thunk, thunk, thunk* of the driver—black, white, male, or female—hammering down the door locks. On less traveled streets after dark, I grew accustomed to but never comfortable with people who crossed to the other side of the street rather than pass me. Then there were the standard unpleasantries with police, doormen, bouncers, cab drivers, and others whose business it is to screen out troublesome individuals before there is any nastiness.

I moved to New York nearly two years ago and I have remained an avid night walker. In central Manhattan, the near-constant crowd cover minimizes tense one-on-one street encounters. Elsewhere—visiting friends in SoHo, where sidewalks are narrow and tightly spaced buildings shut out the sky—things can get very taut indeed.

Black men have a firm place in New York mugging literature. Norman Podhoretz in his famed (or infamous) 1963 essay, "My Negro Problem—and Ours," recalls growing up in terror of black males; they were "tougher than we were, more ruthless," he writes—and as an adult on the Upper West Side of Manhattan, he continues, he cannot constrain his nervousness when he meets black men on certain streets. Similarly, a decade later, the essayist and novelist Edward Hoagland extols a New York where once "Negro bitterness bore down mainly on other Negroes." Where some see mere panhandlers, Hoagland sees "a mugger who is clearly screwing up his nerve to do more than just ask for money." But Hoagland has "the New Yorker's quickhunch posture for broken-field maneuvering," and the bad guy swerves away.

I often witness that "hunch posture," from women after dark on the warrenlike streets of Brooklyn where I live. They seem to set their faces on neutral and, with their purse straps strung across their chests bandolier style, they forge ahead as though bracing themselves against being tackled. I understand, of course, that the danger they perceive is not a hallucination. Women are particularly vulnerable to street violence, and young black males are drastically overrepresented among the perpetrators of that violence. Yet these truths are no solace against the kind of alienation that comes of being ever the suspect, against being set apart, a fearsome entity with whom pedestrians avoid making eye contact

It is not altogether clear to me how I reached the ripe old age of 22 without being conscious of the lethality nighttime pedestrians attributed to me. Perhaps it was because in Chester, Pennsylvania, the small, angry industrial town where I came of age in the 1960s, I was scarcely noticeable against a backdrop of gang warfare, street knifings, and murders. I grew up one of the good boys, had perhaps a half-dozen fist fights. In retrospect, my shyness of combat has clear sources.

Many things go into the making of a young thug. One of those things is the consummation of the male romance with the power to intimidate. An infant discovers that random flailings send the baby bottle flying out of the crib and crashing to the floor. Delighted, the joyful babe repeats those motions again and again, seeking to duplicate the feat. Just so, I recall the points at which some of my boyhood friends were finally seduced by the perception of themselves as tough guys. When a mark cowered and surrendered his money without resistance, myth and reality merged—and paid off. It is, after all, only manly to embrace the power to frighten and intimidate. We, as men, are not supposed to give an inch of our lane on the highway; we are to seize the fighter's edge in work and in play and even in love; we are to be valiant in the face of hostile forces.

Unfortunately, poor and powerless young men seem to take all this nonsense literally. As a boy, I saw countless tough guys locked away; I have since buried several, too. They were babies, really—a teenage cousin, a brother of 22, a childhood friend in his mid-twenties—all gone down in episodes of bravado played out in the streets. I came to doubt the virtues of intimidation early on. I chose, perhaps even unconsciously, to remain a shadow—timid, but a survivor.

The fearsomeness mistakenly attributed to me in public places often has a perilous flavor. The most frightening of these confusions occurred in the late 1970s and early 1980s when I worked as a journalist in Chicago. One day, rushing into the office of a magazine I was writing for with a deadline story in hand, I was mistaken for a burglar. The office manager called security and, with an ad hoc posse, pursued me through the labyrinthine halls, nearly to my editor's door. I had no way of proving who I was. I could only move briskly toward the company of someone who knew me.

Another time I was on assignment for a local paper and killing time before an interview. I entered a jewelry store on the city's affluent Near North Side. The proprietor excused herself and returned with an enormous red Doberman pinscher straining at the end of a leash. She stood, the dog extended toward me, silent to my questions, her eyes bulging nearly out of her head. I took a cursory look around, nodded, and bade her good night. Relatively speaking, however, I never fared as badly as another black male journalist. He went to nearby Waukegan, Illinois, a couple of summers ago to work on a story about a murderer who was born there. Mistaking the reporter for the killer, police hauled him from his car at gunpoint and but for his press credentials would probably have tried to book him. Such episodes are not uncommon. Black men trade talks like this all the time.

In "My Negro Problem—And Ours," Podhoretz writes that the hatred he feels for blacks makes itself known to him through a variety of avenues—one being taken for a criminal. Not to do so would surely have led to madness—via that special "paranoid touchiness" that so annoyed Podhoretz at the time he wrote the essay.

I began to take precautions to make myself less threatening. I move about with care, particularly late in the evening. I give a wide berth to nervous people on subway platforms during the wee hours, particularly when I have exchanged business clothes for jeans. If I happened to be entering a building behind some people who appear skittish, I may walk by, letting them clear the lobby before I return, so as not to seem to be following them. I have been calm and extremely congenial on those rare occasions when I've been pulled over by the police.

And on late-evening constitutionals along streets less traveled by, I employ what has proved to be an excellent tension-reducing measure: I whistle melodies from Beethoven and Vivaldi and the more popular classical composers. Even steely New Yorkers hunching toward nighttime destinations seem to relax and occasionally they even join in the tune. Virtually everybody seems to sense that a mugger wouldn't be warbling bright, sunny selections from Vivaldi's *Four Seasons*. It is my equivalent to the cowbell that hikers wear when they know they are in bear country.

FOR INFORMAL WRITING

Why does Staples start the essay the way he does? Is there any irony in his language? How do you know? When do you know?

FOR DISCUSSION

1. How has this essay taken on additional relevance given current concerns in the United States and in the media?
2. Discuss Staples's use of the term "thug." What is its relevance here?

3. "It is not altogether clear to me how I reached the ripe old age of 22 without being conscious of the lethality nighttime pedestrians attributed to me." Discuss.

FOR WRITING

What dynamic does Staples present between "victims" and "predators?" Do these dynamics ever change? In what ways does his use of the terms subvert our assumptions? How effective is this?

Am I Blue? (1986)
Alice Walker (1944–)

Alice Walker is an American writer whose genres include poetry, short stories, and novels; she is also known as a social activist. Her novel The Color Purple *(1982) won the National Book Award and the Pulitzer Prize. She earned her BA at Sarah Lawrence College in 1965, and she wrote her first novel,* The Third Life of Grange Copeland, *in 1969. Walker has taught African American Women's Studies at Yale, Wellesley, The University of Massachusetts–Boston, and at Berkeley. Emory University has acquired her personal archives. Walker writes primarily about race, reconciliation, and female empowerment (or lack of it). The following essay appeared in her 1988 collection* Living By the Word: Selected Essays, 1983–1987.

"Ain't these tears in these eyes tellin' you?"

For about three years my companion and I rented a small house in the country that stood on the edge of a large meadow that appeared to run from the end of our deck straight into the mountains. The mountains, however, were quite far away, and between us and them there was, in fact, a town. It was one of the many pleasant aspects of the house that you never really were aware of this.

It was a house of many windows, low, wide, nearly floor to ceiling in the living room, which faced the meadow, and it was from one of these that I first saw our closest neighbor, a large white horse, cropping grass, flipping its mane, and ambling about—not over the entire meadow, which stretched well out of sight of the house, but over the five or so fenced-in acres that were next to the twenty-odd

---

"Am I Blue?" from LIVING BY THE WORD: Selected Writings 1973-1987 by Alice Walker. Copyright © 1986 by Alice Walker. Reprinted by permission of HarperCollins Publishers. All rights reserved.

that we had rented. I soon learned that the horse, whose name was Blue, belonged to a man who lived in another town, but was boarded by our neighbors next door. Occasionally, one of the children, usually a stocky teenager, but sometimes a much younger girl or boy, could be seen riding Blue. They would appear in the meadow, climb up on his back, ride furiously for ten or fifteen minutes, then get off, slap Blue on the flanks, and not be seen again for a month or more.

There were many apple trees in our yard, and one by the fence that Blue could almost reach. We were soon in the habit of feeding him apples, which he relished, especially because by the middle of summer the meadow grasses—so green and succulent since January—had dried out from lack of rain, and Blue stumbled about munching the dried stalks half-heartedly. Sometimes he would stand very still just by the apple tree, and when one of us came out he would whinny, snort loudly, or stamp the ground. This meant, of course: I want an apple.

It was quite wonderful to pick a few apples or collect those that had fallen to the ground overnight, and patiently hold them, one by one, up to his large, toothy mouth. I remained as thrilled as a child by his flexible dark lips, huge, cubelike teeth that crunched the apples, core and all, with such finality, and his high, broad-breasted enormity; beside which, I felt small indeed. When I was a child, I used to ride horses, and was especially friendly with one named Nan until the day I was riding and my brother deliberately spooked her and I was thrown, head first, against the trunk of a tree. When I came to, I was in bed and my mother was bending worriedly over me; we silently agreed that perhaps horseback riding was not the safest sport for me. Since then I have walked and prefer walking to horseback riding—but I had forgotten the depth of feeling one could see in horses' eyes.

I was therefore unprepared for the expression in Blue's. Blue was lonely. Blue was horribly lonely and bored. I was not shocked that this should be the case; five acres to tramp by yourself, endlessly, even in the most beautiful of meadows—and his was—cannot provide many interesting events, and once the rainy season turned to dry that was about it. No, I was shocked that I had forgotten that human animals and nonhuman animals can communicate quite well; if we are brought up around animals as children we take this for granted. By the time we are adults we no longer remember. However, the animals have not changed. They are in fact completed creations (at least they seem to be, so much more than we) who are not likely to change; it is their nature to express themselves. What else are they going to express? And they do. And, generally speaking, they are ignored.

After giving Blue the apples, I would wander back to the house, aware that he was observing me. Were more apples not forthcoming then? Was that to be his sole entertainment for the day? My partner's small son had decided he wanted to learn how to piece a quilt; we worked in silence on our respective squares as I thought....

Well, about slavery: about white children, who were raised by black people, who knew their first all-accepting love from black women, and then, when they were twelve or so, were told they must "forget" the deep levels of communication between themselves and "mammy" that they knew. Later they would be able to relate quite calmly, "My old mammy was sold to another good family." "My old mammy was—" Fill in the blank. Many more years later a white woman would say: "I can't understand these Negroes, these blacks. What do they want? They're so different from us."

And about the Indians, considered to be "like animals" by the "settlers" (a very benign euphemism for what they actually were), who did not understand their description as a compliment.

And about the thousands of American men who marry Japanese, Korean, Filipina, and other non-English-speaking women and of how happy they report they are, "blissfully," until their brides learn to speak English, at which point the marriages tend to fall apart. What then did the men see, when they looked into the eyes of the women they married, before they could speak English? Apparently only their own reflections.

I thought of society's impatience with the young. "Why are they playing the music so loud?" Perhaps the children have listened to much of the music of oppressed people their parents danced to before they were born, with its passionate but soft cries for acceptance and love, and they have wondered why their parents failed to hear.

I do not know how long Blue had inhabited his five beautiful, boring acres before we moved into our house; a year after we had arrived—and had also traveled to other valleys, other cities, other worlds—he was still there.

But then, in our second year at the house, something happened in Blue's life. One morning, looking out the window at the fog that lay like a ribbon over the meadow, I saw another horse, a brown one, at the other end of Blue's field. Blue appeared to be afraid of it, and for several days made no attempt to go near. We went away for a week. When we returned, Blue had decided to make friends and the two horses ambled or galloped along together, and Blue did not come nearly as often to the fence underneath the apple tree.

When he did, bringing his new friend with him, there was a different look in his eyes. A look of independence, of self-possession, of inalienable horseness. His friend eventually became pregnant. For months and months there was, it seemed to me, a mutual feeling between me and the horses of justice, of peace. I fed apples to them both. The look in Blue's eyes was one of unabashed "this is *itness.*"

It did not, however, last forever. One day, after a visit to the city, I went out to give Blue some apples. He stood waiting, or so I thought, though not beneath the tree. When I shook the tree and jumped back from the shower of apples, he made no move. I carried some over to him. He managed to half-crunch one. The rest he let fall to the ground. I dreaded looking into his eyes—because I had of course noticed that Brown, his partner, had gone—but I did look. If I had been born into slavery, and my partner had been sold or killed, my eyes would have looked like that. The children next door explained that Blue's partner had been "put with him" (the same expression that old people used, I had noticed, when speaking of an ancestor during slavery who had been impregnated by her owner) so that they could mate and she conceive. Since that was accomplished, she had been taken back by her owner, who lived somewhere else.

Will she be back? I asked.

They didn't know.

Blue was like a crazed person. Blue *was*, to me, a crazed person. He galloped furiously, as if he were being ridden, around and around his five beautiful acres. He whinnied until he couldn't. He tore at the ground with his hooves. He butted himself against his single shade tree. He looked always and always toward the road down which his partner had gone. And then, occasionally, when he came up for apples, or I took apples to him, he looked at me. It was a look so piercing, so full of grief, a look so *human*, I almost laughed (I felt too sad to cry) to think there are people who do not know that animals suffer. People like me who have forgotten, and daily forget, all that animals try to tell us. "Everything you do to us will happen to you; we are your teachers, as you are ours. We are one lesson" is essentially it, I think. There are those who never once have even considered animals' rights: those who have been taught that animals actually want to be used and abused by us, as small children "love" to be frightened, or women "love" to be mutilated and raped. . . . They are the great-grandchildren of those who honestly thought, because someone taught them this: "Woman can't think" and "niggers can't faint." But most disturbing of all, in Blue's large brown eyes was a new look, more painful than the look of despair: the look of disgust with human beings, with life; the look of hatred. And it was odd what the look of hatred did. It gave him, for the first time, the look of a beast. And what that meant was that he had put up a barrier within to protect himself from further violence; all the apples in the world wouldn't change that fact.

And so Blue remained, a beautiful part of our landscape, very peaceful to look at from the window, white against the grass. Once a friend came to visit and said, looking out on the soothing view: "And it would have to be a white horse; the very image of freedom." And I thought, yes, the animals are forced to become for us merely "images" of what they once so beautifully expressed. And we are used to drinking milk from containers showing "contented" cows, whose real lives we want to hear nothing about, eating eggs and drumsticks from "happy" hens, and munching hamburgers advertised by bulls of integrity who seem to command their fate.

As we talked of freedom and justice one day for all, we sat down to steaks. I am eating misery, I thought, as I took the first bite. And spit it out.

FOR INFORMAL WRITING

"Ain't these tears in these eyes tellin' you?" Examine these lyrics to the song "Am I Blue?" within the context of this essay. What might they mean?

FOR DISCUSSION

1. How would you describe the relationship between Blue and the narrator?
2. What does Walker have to say about slavery here? How does it relate to Blue?
3. How does the "character" of Blue elicit sympathy and connect with similar feelings in and about humans? To what effect?

FOR WRITING

"As we talked of freedom and justice one day for all, we sat down to steaks. I am eating misery, I thought, as I took the first bite. And spit it out." What are the parallels between inhumane treatment of animals and inhumane treatment more generally? Use examples from Walker's essay to back up your argument.

How to Tame a Wild Tongue, an Excerpt (1987)
Gloria Anzaldúa (1942–2004)

Gloria Anzaldúa was born in the Rio Grande Valley of Texas. A well-known Latinx scholar and writer of work that intersects feminism, culture, and queer theory, Anzaldúa is a self-described "Chicana, dyke-feminist." Anzaldúa became well-known when co-editing The Bridge Called My Back: Writings of Radical Women of Color *(1981). Prior to her death, she had begun working on her dissertation toward a PhD at Duke University. This excerpt from her celebrated book* Borderlands *grapples with the sociocultural complexities of growing up on the Texas-Mexico border, which is loosely autobiographical.*

"We're going to have to control your tongue," the dentist says, pulling out all the metal from my mouth. Silver bits plop and tinkle into the basin. My mouth is a motherlode.

The dentist is cleaning out my roots. I get a whiff of the stench when I gasp. "I can't cap that tooth yet, you're still draining, "he says.

'We're going to have to do something about your tongue," I hear the anger rising in his voice. My tongue keeps pushing out the wads of cotton, pushing back the drills, the long thin needles. "I've never seen anything as strong or as stubborn," he says. And I think, how do you tame a wild tongue, train it to be quiet, how do you bridle and saddle it? How do you make it lie down?

> "Who is to say that robbing a people of its language is less violent than war?"
>
> —Ray Gwyn Smith

Excerpted from Borderlands/La Frontera: The New Mestiza. © 1987, 1999, 2007, 2012 by Gloria Anzaldua. Reprinted by permission of Aunt Lute Books.

I remember being caught speaking Spanish at recess—that was good for three licks on the knuckles with a sharp ruler. I remember being sent to the corner of the classroom for "talking back" to the Anglo teacher when all I was trying to do was tell her how to pronounce my name. "If you want to be American, speak 'American.' If you don't like it, go back to Mexico, where you belong."

"I want you to speak English. *Pa' hallar buen trabajo tienes que vaber hablar el inglés bien. Qué vale toda tu educación si todavía hablas inglés con un* 'accent,'" my mother would say, mortified that I spoke English like a Mexican. At Pan American University, I and all Chicano students were required to take two speech classes. Their purpose: to get rid of our accents.

Attacks on one's form of expression with the intent to censor are a violation of the First Amendment. *El Anglo con cara de inocente nos arrancó la lengua.* Wild tongues can't be tamed, they can only be cut out.

OVERCOMING THE TRADITION OF SILENCE

Ahogadas, escupimos el oscuro.
Peleando con nuestra propia sombra
el silencio nos sepulta.

En boca cerrada no entran moscas. "Flies don't enter a closed mouth" is a saying I kept hearing when I was a child. *Ser habladora* was to be a gossip and a liar, to talk *too* much. *Muchachitas bien criadas*, well-bred girls don't answer back. *Es una falta de respeto* to talk back to one's mother or father. I remember one of the sins I'd recite to the priest in the confession box the few times I went to confession: talking back to my mother, *hablar pa' 'tras, repelar. Hocicona, repelona, chismosa*, having a big mouth, questioning, carrying tales are all signs of being *mal/criada*. In my culture they are all words that are derogatory if applied to women—I've never heard them applied to men.

The first time I heard two women, a Puerto Rican and a Cuban, say the word "*nosotras*," I was shocked. I had not known the word existed. Chicanas use *nosotros* whether we're male or female. We are robbed of our female being by the masculine plural. Language is a male discourse.

> And our tongues have become
> dry the wilderness has
> dried out our tongues and
> we have forgotten speech.
>
> —Irena Klepfisz

Even our own people, other Spanish speakers *nos quieren poner candados en la boca*. They would hold us back with their bag of *reglas de academia*.

OYÉ COMO ZADRA: EL LENGUAJE DE LA FRONTERA

Quien tiene boca se equivoca.
—Mexican saying

"*Pacho*, cultural traitor, you're speaking the oppressor's language by speaking English, you're ruining the Spanish language," I have been accused by various Latinos and Latinas. Chicano Spanish is considered by the purist and by most Latinos deficient, a mutilation of Spanish.

But Chicano Spanish is a border tongue which developed naturally. Change, *evolución, enriquecimiento de palabras nuevas par invención o adopción* have created variants of Chicano Spanish, *un nuevo lenguaje. Un lenguaje que corresponde a un modo de vivir.* Chicano Spanish is not incorrect, it is a living language.

For a people who are neither Spanish nor live in a country in which Spanish is the first language; for a people who live in a country in which English is the reigning tongue but who are not Anglo; for a people who cannot entirely identify with either standard (formal, Castillian) Spanish nor standard English, what recourse is left to them but to create their own language? A language which they can connect their identity to, one capable of communicating the realities and values true to themselves—a language with terms that are neither *español ni inglés*, but both. We speak a patois, a forked tongue, a variation of two languages.

Chicano Spanish sprang out of the Chicanos' need to identify ourselves as a distinct people. We needed a language, with which we could communicate with ourselves, a secret language. For some of us, language is a homeland closer than the Southwest—for many Chicanos today live in the Midwest and the East. And because we are a complex, heterogeneous people, we speak many languages. Some of the languages we speak are:

1. Standard English
2. Working class and slang English
3. Standard Spanish
4. Standard Mexican Spanish
5. North Mexican Spanish dialect
6. Chicano Spanish (Texas, New Mexico, Arizona, and California have regional variations)
7. Tex-Mex
8. *Pachuco* (called caló)

My "home" tongues are the languages I speak with my sister and brothers, with my friends. They are the last five listed, with 6 and 7 being closest to my heart. From school, the media, and job situations, I've picked up standard and working-class English. From Mamagrande Locha and from reading Spanish and Mexican literature, I've picked up Standard Spanish and Standard Mexican Spanish. From *los recién llegados*, Mexican immigrants, and *braceros*, I learned the North Mexican dialect. With Mexicans I'll try to speak either Standard Mexican Spanish or the North Mexican dialect. From my parents and Chicanos living in the Valley, I picked up Chicano Texas Spanish, and I speak it with my mom, younger brother (who married a Mexican and who rarely mixes Spanish with English), aunts, and older relatives.

With Chicanas from *Nuevo Mexico* or *Arizona* I will speak Chicano Spanish a little, but often they don't understand what I'm saying. With most California Chicanas I speak entirely in English (unless I forget). When I first moved to San Francisco, I'd rattle off something in Spanish, unintentionally embarrassing them. Often it is only with another Chicana *tejana* that I can talk freely.

Words distorted by English are known as anglicisms *or pochismos*. The *pocho* is an anglicized Mexican or American of Mexican origin who speaks Spanish with an accent characteristic of North Americans and who distorts and reconstructs the language according to the influence of English. Tex-Mex, or Spanglish, comes most naturally to me. I may switch back and forth from English to Spanish in the same sentence or in the same word. With my sister and my brother Nune and with Chicano *tejano* contemporaries I speak in Tex-Mex.

From kids and people my own age I picked up *Pachuco*. Pachuco (the language of the zoot suiters) is a language of rebellion, both against Standard Spanish and Standard English. It is a secret language. Adults of the culture and outsiders cannot understand it. It is made up of slang words from both English and Spanish. *Ruca* means girl or woman, *vato* means guy or dude, *chale* means no, *simon* means yes, *churro* is sure, talk is *periquiar, pigionear* means petting, *que gacho* means how nerdy, *ponte águila* means watch out, death is called *la pelona*. Through lack of practice and not having others who can speak it, I've lost most of the *Pachuco* tongue.

CHICANO SPANISH

Chicanos, after 250 years of Spanish/Anglo colonization, have developed significant differences in the Spanish we speak. We collapse two adjacent vowels into a single syllable and sometimes shift the stress in certain words such as *maíz/maiz, cohete/cuete*. We leave out certain consonants when they appear between vowels: *lado/lao, mojado/mojao*. Chicanos from South Texas pronounce *f* as *j* as in *jue* (*fue*). Chicanos use "archaisms," words that are no longer in the Spanish language, words that have been evolved out. We say *semos, truje, haiga, ansina*, and *naiden*. We retain the "archaic" *j*, as in *jalar*, that derives from an earlier *h* (the

French *halar* or the Germanic *halon* which was lost to standard Spanish in the 16th century), but which is still found in several regional dialects such as the one spoken in South Texas. (Due to geography, Chicanos from the Valley of South Texas were cut off linguistically from other Spanish speakers. We tend to use words that the Spaniards brought over from Medieval Spain. The majority of the Spanish colonizers in Mexico and the Southwest came from Extremadura—Hernan Cortes was one of them—and Andalucía. Andalusians pronounce *ll* like a *y*, and their *d*'s tend to be absorbed by adjacent vowels: *tirado* becomes *tirao*. They brought *el lenguaje popular, dialectos y regionalismos*.

Chicanos and other Spanish speakers also shift *ll* to *y* and *z* to *s*. We leave out initial syllables, saying *tar* for *estar*, *toy* for *estoy*, *hora* for *ahora* (*cubanos* and puertorriqueños also leave out initial letters of some words). We also leave out the final syllable such as *pa* for *para*. The intervocalic *y*, the *ll* as in *tortilla, ella, botella*, gets replaced by *tortia* or *tortiya*, *ea, botea*. We add an additional syllable at the beginning of certain words: *atocar* for *tocar*, *agastar* for *gastar*. Sometimes we'll say *lavaste las vacijas*, other times *lavates* (substituting the *ates* verb endings for the *aste*).

We use anglicisms, words borrowed from English: *bola* from ball, *carpeta* from carpet, *máchina de lavar* (instead of *lavadora*) from washing machine. Tex-Mex argot, created by adding a Spanish sound at the beginning or end of an English word such as *cookiar* for cook, *watchar* for watch, *parkiar* for park, and *rapiar* for rape, is the result of the pressures on Spanish speakers to adapt to English.

We don't use the word *vosotroslas* or its accompanying verb form. We don't say *claro* (lo mean yes), *imagínate*, or *me emociona*, unless we picked up Spanish from Latinas, out of a book, or in a classroom. Other Spanish-speaking groups are going through the same, or similar, development in their Spanish.

LINGUISTIC TERRORISM

Deslenguadas. Somos Los del español deficiente. We are your linguistic nightmare, your linguistic aberration, your linguistic *mestisaje*, the subject of your *burla*. Because we speak with tongues of fire we are culturally crucified. Racially, culturally, and linguistically *somos huérfanos*—we speak an orphan longue.

Chicanas who grew up speaking Chicano Spanish have internalized the belief that we speak poor Spanish. It is illegitimate, a bastard language. And because we internalize how our language has been used against us by the dominant culture, we use our language differences against each other.

Chicana feminists often skirt around each other with suspicion and hesitation. For the longest time I couldn't figure it out. Then it dawned on me. To be close to another Chicana is like looking into the mirror. We are afraid of what we'll see there. *Pena.* Shame. Low estimation of self. In childhood we are told that our language is wrong. Repeated attacks on our native tongue diminish our sense of self. The attacks continue throughout our lives.

Chicanas feel uncomfortable talking in Spanish to Latinas, afraid of their censure. Their language was not outlawed in their countries. They had a whole lifetime of being immersed in their native tongue; generations, centuries in which Spanish was a first language, taught in school, heard on radio and TV, and read in the newspaper.

If a person, Chicana or Latina, has a low estimation of my native tongue, she also has a low estimation of me. Often with *mexicanas y latinas* we'll speak English as a neutral language. Even among Chicanas we tend to speak English at parties or conferences. Yet, at the same time, we're afraid the other will think we're *agringadas* because we don't speak Chicano Spanish. We oppress each other trying to out-Chicano each other, vying to be the "real" Chicanas, to speak like Chicanos. There is no one Chicano language just as there is no one Chicano experience. A monolingual Chicana whose first language is English or Spanish is just as much a Chicana as one who speaks several variants of Spanish. A Chicana from Michigan or Chicago or Detroit is just as much a Chicana as one from the Southwest. Chicano Spanish is as diverse linguistically as it is regionally.

By the end of this century, Spanish speakers will comprise the biggest minority group in the US, a country where students in high schools and colleges are encouraged to take French classes because French is considered more "cultured." But for a language to remain alive it must be used. By the end of this century English, and not Spanish, will be the mother tongue of most Chicanos and Latinos.

So, if you want to really hurt me, talk badly about my language. Ethnic identity is twin skin to linguistic identity—I am my language. Until I can take pride in my language, I cannot take pride in myself. Until I can accept as legitimate Chicano Texas Spanish, Tex-Mex, and all the other languages I speak, I cannot accept the legitimacy of myself. Until I am free to write bilingually and to switch codes without having always to translate, while I still have to speak English or Spanish when I would rather speak Spanglish, and as long as I have to accommodate the English speakers rather than having them accommodate me, my tongue will be illegitimate.

I will no longer be made to feel ashamed of existing. I will have my voice: Indian, Spanish, white. I will have my serpent's tongue—my woman's voice, my sexual voice, my poet's voice. I will overcome the tradition of silence.

My fingers
move sly against your palm
Like women everywhere, we speak in code. . . .

—Melanie Kaye/Kantrowitz

FOR INFORMAL WRITING

Even though this excerpt is part of a book published in 1987, Anzaldúa's argument still has a good deal of relevance for today's America. Do you agree? Why or why not? What specifically in the text prompts your response?

FOR DISCUSSION

1. The excerpt is about Anzaldúa's "Chicana Spanish" and how it both represented and made her somewhat hesitant about her multicultural identity. In what ways did she have to navigate these various cultures of her life? In a country that is increasingly multicultural (or at least a country that has begun to acknowledge it), does your life at all resonate with Anzaldúa's experience, even if your "cultures" are different? What aspects of the essay prompt this reaction in you?
2. Anzaldúa argues that language can be an act or symbol of rebellion. Looking again to the excerpt, in what ways does Anzaldúaa feel that her language, her very being, is a form of resistance? Against what might she be resisting? How do you know?
3. Look up the definition of "persona." What aspects of Anzaldua's language create a certain tone, and how would you describe her persona? Use specific examples from the text in order to support your point.

FOR WRITING

Find more recent arguments about immigrants' rights to their own language. Using what you find and Anzaldúa's excerpt, construct an argument either for or against "English only" movements. Is it possible to retain one's cultural and linguistic heritage and identities while participating in "larger" culture(s)? Why or why not? What are the benefits of either stance?

The Management of Grief (1988)
Bharati Mukherjee (1940–2017)

Born in Kolkata, formerly Calcutta, Bharati Mukherjee was raised in a household that included fifty extended members of her family. Much of her primary education took place abroad, in England and Switzerland. She eventually earned her PhD and MFA from the University of Iowa. Often considered to be a pioneer of the intercultural novel, Mukherjee is nonetheless known for saying "I am an American, not an Asian American." Much of her work focuses on race, gender, and caste—along with the immigrant experience, much of which is part of "The Management of Grief." Mukherjee was awarded the National Book Critics' Circle Award for The Middleman and Other Stories *(1988).*

A woman I don't know is boiling tea the Indian way in my kitchen. There are a lot of women I don't know in my kitchen, whispering, and moving tactfully. They open doors, rummage through the pantry, and try not to ask me where things are kept. They remind me of when my sons were small, on Mother's Day or when Vikram and I were tired, and they would make big, sloppy omelets. I would lie in bed pretending I didn't hear them.

Dr. Sharma, the treasurer of the Indo-Canada Society, pulls me into the hallway. He wants to know if I am worried about money. His wife, who has just come up from the basement with a tray of empty cups and glasses, scolds him. "Don't bother Mrs. Behave with mundane details." She looks so monstrously pregnant her baby must be days overdue. I tell her she shouldn't he carrying heavy things. "Shaila, "she says, smiling, "this is the fifth." Then she grabs a teenager by his shirttails. He slips his Walkman off his head. He has to be one of her four chil-

---

"The Management of Grief" from THE MIDDLEMAN AND OTHER STORIES copyright © 1988 by Bharati Mukherjee. Used by permission of Grove/Atlantic, Inc. Any third-party use of this material, outside of this publication, is prohibited.

dren, they have the same domed and dented foreheads. "What's the official word now?" she demands. The boy slips the headphones back on. "They're acting evasive, Ma. They're saying it could be an accident or a terrorist bomb."

All morning, the boys have been muttering, Sikh Bomb, Sikh Bomb. The men, not using the word, bow their heads in agreement. Mrs. Sharma touches her forehead at such a word. At least they've stopped talking about space debris and Russian lasers.

Two radios are going in the dining room. They are tuned to different stations. Someone must have brought the radios down from my boys' bedrooms. I haven't gone into their rooms since Kusum came running across the front lawn in her bathrobe. She looked so funny, I was laughing when I opened the door.

The big TV in the den is being whizzed through American networks and cable channels.

"Damn!" some man swears bitterly. "How can these preachers carry on like nothing's happened?" I want to tell him we're not that important. You look at the audience, and at the preacher in his blue robe with his beautiful white hair, the potted palm trees under a blue sky, and you know they care about nothing.

The phone rings and rings. Dr. Sharma's taken charge. "We're with her," he keeps saying. "Yes, yes, the doctor has given calming pills. Yes, yes, pills are having necessary effect." I wonder if pills alone explain this calm. Not peace, just a deadening quiet. I was always controlled, but never repressed. Sound can reach me, but my body is tensed, ready to scream. I hear their voices all around me. I hear my boys and Vikram cry, "Mommy, Shaila!" and their screams insulate me, like headphones.

The woman boiling water tells her story again and again. "I got the news first. My cousin called from Halifax before six A.M., can you imagine? He'd gotten up for prayers and his son was studying for medical exams and he heard on a rock channel that something had happened to a plane. They said first it had disappeared from the radar, like a giant eraser just reached out. His father called me, so I said to him, what do you mean, 'something bad'? You mean a hijacking? And he said, *behn.* there is no confirmation of anything yet, but check with your neighbors because a lot of them must be on that plane. So I called poor Kusum straightaway. I knew Kusum's husband and daughter were booked to go yesterday."

Kusum lives across the street from me. She and Satish had moved in less than a month ago. They said they needed a bigger place. All these people, the Sharmas and friends from the Indo-Canada Society, had been there for the housewarming. Satish and Kusum made homemade tandoori on their big gas grill and even the white neighbors piled their plates high with that luridly red, charred, juicy chicken. Their younger daughter had danced, and even our boys had broken away from the Stanley Cup telecast to put in a reluctant appearance. Everyone took pictures for their albums and for the community newspapers—another of our families had made it big in Toronto—and now I wonder how many of those happy faces are gone. "Why does God give us so much if all along He intends to take it away?" Kusum asks me.

I nod. We sit on carpeted stairs, holding hands like children. "I never once told him that I loved him," I say. I was too much the well brought up woman. I was so well brought up I never felt comfortable calling my husband by his first name.

"It's all right," Kusum says. "He knew. My husband knew. They felt it. Modern young girls have to say it because what they feel is fake."

Kusum's daughter, Pam, runs in with an overnight case. Pam's in her McDonald's uniform. "Mummy! You have to get dressed!" Panic makes her cranky. "A reporter's on his way here."

"Why?"

"You want to talk to him in your bathrobe?" She starts to brush her mother's long hair. She's the daughter who's always in trouble. She dates Canadian boys and hangs out in the mall, shopping for tight sweaters. The younger one, the goody-goody one according to Pam, the one with a voice so sweet that when she sang *bhajans* for Ethiopian relief even a frugal man like my husband wrote out a hundred dollar check, *she* was on that plane. She was going to spend July and August with grandparents because Pam wouldn't go. Pam said she'd rather waitress at McDonald's. "If it's a choice between Bombay and Wonderland, I'm picking Wonderland," she'd said.

"Leave me alone," Kusum yells. "You know what I want to do? If I didn't have to look after you now, I'd hang myself."

Pam's young face goes blotchy with pain. "Thanks," she says, "don't let me stop you."

"Hush," pregnant Mrs. Sharma scolds Pam. "Leave your mother alone. Mr. Sharma will tackle the reporters and fill out the forms. He'll say what has to be said."

Pam stands her ground. "You think I don't know what Mummy's thinking? *Why her?* that's what. That's sick! Mummy wishes my little sister were alive and I were dead."

Kusum's hand in mines trembly hot. We continue to sit on the stairs.

She calls before she arrives, wondering if there's anything I need. Her name is Judith Templeton and she's an appointee of the provincial government. "Multiculturalism?" I ask, and she says, "partially," but that her mandate is bigger. "I've been told you knew many of the people on the flight," she says. "Perhaps if you'd agree to help us reach the others . . . ?"

She gives me time at least to put on tea water and pick up the mess in the front room. I have a few *samosas* from Kusum's housewarming that I could fry up, but then I think, Why prolong this visit?

Judith Templeton is much younger than she sounded. She wears a blue suit with a white blouse and a polka dot tie. Her blond hair is cut short, her only jewelry is pearl drop earrings. Her briefcase is new and expensive looking, a gleaming cordovan leather. She sits with it across her lap. When she looks out the front windows onto the street, her contact lenses seem to float in front of her light blue eyes.

"What sort of help do you want from me?" I ask. She has refused the tea, out of politeness, but I insist, along with some slightly stale biscuits.

"I have no experience," she admits. "That is, I have an MSW and I've worked in liaison with accident victims, but I mean I have no experience with a tragedy of this scale—"

"Who could?" I ask.

"—and with the complications of culture, language, and customs. Someone mentioned that Mrs. Bhave is a pillar—because you've taken it more calmly."

At this, perhaps, I frown, for she reaches forward, almost to take my hand. "I hope you understand my meaning, Mrs. Bhave. There are hundreds of people in Metro directly affected, like you, and some of them speak no English. There are some widows who've never handled money or gone on a bus, and there are old parents who still haven't eaten or gone outside their bedrooms. Some houses and apartments have been looted. Some wives are still hysterical. Some husbands are in shock and profound depression. We want to help, but our hands are tied in so many ways. We have to distribute money to some people, and there are legal documents—these things can be done. We have interpreters, but we don't always have the human touch, or maybe the right human touch. We don't want to make mistakes, Mrs. Bhave, and that's why we'd like to ask you to help us."

"More mistakes, you mean," I say.

"Police matters are not in my hands," she answers.

"Nothing I can do will make any difference," I say. "We must all grieve in our own way."

"But you are coping very well. All the people said, Mrs. Bhave the strongest person of all. Perhaps if the others could see you, talk with you, it would help them."

"By the standards of the people you call hysterical, I am behaving very oddly and very badly, Miss Templeton." I want to say to her, *I wish I could scream, starve, walk into Lake Ontario, jump from a bridge.* "They would not see me as a model. I do not see myself as a model."

I am a freak. No one who has ever known me would think of me reacting this way. This terrible calm will not go away.

She asks me if she may call again, after I get back from a long trip that we all must make. "Of course," I say. "Feel free to call, anytime."

Four days later, I find Kusum squatting on a rock overlooking a bay in Ireland. It isn't a big rock, but it juts sharply out over water. This is as close as we'll ever get to them. June breezes balloon out her sari and unpin her knee-length hair. She has this bewildered look of a sea creature whom the tides have stranded.

It's been one hundred hours since Kusum came stumbling and screaming across my lawn. Waiting around the hospital, we've heard many stories. The police, the diplomats, they tell us things thinking that we're strong, that knowledge is helpful to the grieving, and maybe it is. Some, I know, prefer ignorance, or their own versions. The plane broke into two, they say. Unconsciousness was instantaneous. No one suffered. My boys must have just finished their breakfasts. They loved eating on planes, they loved the smallness of plates, knives, and forks. Last year they saved the airline salt and pepper shakers. Half an hour more and they would have made it to Heathrow.

Kusum says that we can't escape our fate. She says that all those people—our husbands, my boys, her girl with the nightingale voice, all those Hindus, Christians, Sikhs, Muslims, Parsis, and atheists on that plane—were fated to die together off this beautiful bay. She learned this from a swami in Toronto.

I have my Valium.

Six of us "relatives"—two widows and four widowers—choose to spend the day today by the waters instead of sitting in a hospital room and scanning photographs of the dead. That's what they call us now: relatives. I've looked through twenty-seven photos in two days. They're very kind to us, the Irish are very understanding. Sometimes understanding means freeing a tourist bus for this trip to the bay, so we can pretend to spy our loved ones through the glassiness of waves or in sun-speckled cloud shapes.

I could die here, too, and be content.

"What is that, out there?" She's standing and flapping her hands and for a moment I see a head shape bobbing in the waves. She's standing in the water, I, on the boulder. The tide is low, and a round, black, head-sized rock has just risen from the waves. She returns, her sari end dripping and ruined and her face is a twisted remnant of hope, the way mine was a hundred hours ago, still laughing but inwardly knowing that nothing but the ultimate tragedy could bring two women together at six o'clock on a Sunday morning. I watch her face sag into blankness.

"That water felt warm, Shaila," she says at length.

"You can't," I say. "We have to wait for our turn to come."

I haven't eaten in four days, haven't brushed my teeth.

"I know," she says. "I tell myself I have no right to grieve. They are in a better place than we are. My swami says I should be thrilled for them. My swami says depression is a sign of our selfishness."

Maybe I'm selfish. Selfishly I break away from Kusum and run, sandals slapping against stones, to the water's edge. What if my boys aren't lying pinned under the debris? What if they aren't stuck a mile below that innocent blue chop? What if, given the strong currents....

Now I've ruined my sari, one of my best. Kusum has joined me, knee-deep in water that feels to me like a swimming pool. I could settle in the water, and my husband would take my hand and the boys would slap water in my face just to see me scream. "Do you remember what good swimmers my boys were, Kusum?"

"I saw the medals," she says.

One of the widowers, Dr. Ranganathan from Montreal, walks out to us, carrying his shoes in one hand. He's an electrical engineer. Someone at the hotel mentioned his work is famous around the world, something about the place where physics and electricity come together. He has lost a huge family, something indescribable. "With some luck," Dr. Ranganathan suggests to me, "a good swimmer could make it safely to some island. It is quite possible that there may be many, many microscopic islets scattered around."

"You're not just saying that?" I tell Dr. Ranganathan about Vinod, my elder son. Last year he took diving as well.

"It's a parent's duty to hope," he says. "It is foolish to rule out possibilities that have not been tested. I myself have not surrendered hope."

Kusum is sobbing once again. "Dear lady," he says, laying his free hand on her arm, and she calms down.

"Vinod is how old?" he asks me. He's very careful, as we all are. Is, not was.

"Fourteen. Yesterday he was fourteen. His father and uncle were going to take him down to the Taj and give him a big birthday party. I couldn't go with them because I couldn't get two weeks off from my stupid job in June." I process bills for a travel agent. June is a big travel month.

Dr. Ranganathan whips the pockets of his suit jacket inside out. Squashed roses, in darkening shades of pink, float on the water. He tore the roses off creepers in somebody's garden. He didn't ask anyone if he could pluck the roses, but now there's been an article about it in the local papers. When you see an Indian person, it says, please give him or her flowers.

"A strong youth of fourteen," he says, "can very likely pull to safety a younger one."

My sons, though four years apart, were very close. Vinod wouldn't let Mithun drown. Electrical engineering, I think, foolishly perhaps: this man knows important secrets of the universe, things closed to me. Relief spins me lightheaded. No wonder my boys' photographs haven't turned up in the gallery of photos of the recovered dead. "Such pretty roses," I say.

"My wife loved pink roses. Every Friday I had to bring a bunch home. I used to say, Why? After twenty odd years of marriage you're still needing proof positive of my love?" He has identified his wife and three of his children. Then others from Montreal, the lucky ones, intact families with no survivors. He chuckles as he wades back to shore. Then he swings around to ask me a question. "Mrs. Bhave, you are wanting to throw in some roses for your loved ones? I have two big ones left."

But I have other things to float: Vinod's pocket calculator; a half-painted model B-52 for my Mithun. They'd want them on their island. And for my husband? For him I let fall into the calm, glassy waters a poem I wrote in the hospital yesterday. Finally he'll know my feelings for him.

"Don't tumble, the rocks are slippery," Dr. Ranganathan cautions. He holds out a hand for me to grab.

Then it's time to get back on the bus, time to rush back to our waiting posts on hospital benches.

Kusum is one of the lucky ones. The lucky ones flew here, identified in multiplicate their loved ones, then will fly to India with the bodies for proper ceremonies. Satish is one of the few males who surfaced. The photos of faces we saw on the walls in an office at Heathrow and here in the hospital are mostly of women. Women have more body fat, a nun said to me matter-of-factly. They float better.

Today I was stopped by a young sailor on the street. He had loaded bodies, he'd gone into the water when—he checks my face for signs of strength—when the sharks were first spotted. I don't blush, and he breaks down. "It's all right," I say. "Thank you." I had heard about the sharks from Dr. Ranganathan. In his orderly mind, science brings understanding, it holds no terror. It is the shark's duty. For every deer there is a hunter, for every fish a fisherman.

The Irish are not shy; they rush to me and give me hugs and some are crying. I cannot imagine reactions like that on the streets of Toronto. Just strangers, and I am touched. Some carry flowers with them and give them to any Indian they see.

After lunch, a policeman I have gotten to know quite well catches hold of me. He says he thinks he has a match for Vinod. I explain what a good swimmer Vinod is.

"You want me with you when you look at photos?" Dr. Ranganathan walks ahead of me into the picture gallery. In these matters, he is a scientist, and I am grateful. It is a new perspective. "They have performed miracles," he says. "We are indebted to them."

The first day or two the policemen showed us relatives only one picture at a time; now they're in a hurry, they're eager to lay out the possibles, and even the probables.

The face on the photo is of a boy much like Vinod; the same intelligent eyes, the same thick brows dipping into a V. But this boy's features, even his cheeks, are puffier, wider, mushier.

"No." My gaze is pulled by other pictures. There are five other boys who look like Vinod.

The nun assigned to console me rubs the first picture with a fingertip. "When they've been in the water for a while, love, they look a little heavier." The bones under the skin are broken, they said on the first day try to adjust your memories. It's important.

"It's not him. I'm his mother. I'd know."

"I know this one!" Dr. Ranganathan cries out suddenly from the back of the gallery. "And this one!" I think he senses that I don't want to find my boys. "They are the Kutty brothers. They were also from Montreal." I don't mean to be crying. On the contrary, I am ecstatic. My suitcase in the hotel is packed heavy with dry clothes for my boys.

The policeman starts to cry. "I am so sorry, I am so sorry, ma'am. I really thought we had a match."

With the nun ahead of us and the policeman behind, we, the unlucky ones without our children's bodies, file out of the makeshift gallery.

From Ireland most of us go on to India. Kusum and I take the same direct flight to Bombay, so I can help her clear customs quickly. But we have to argue with a man in uniform. He has large boils on his face. The boils swell and glow with sweat as we argue with him. He wants Kusum to wait in line and he refuses to take authority because his boss is on a tea break. But Kusum won't let her coffins out of sight, and I shan't desert her though I know that my parents, elderly and diabetic, must be waiting in a stuffy car in a scorching lot.

"You bastard!" I scream at the man with the popping boils. Other passengers press closer. "You think we're smuggling contraband in those coffins!"

One upon a time we were well brought up women; we were dutiful wives who kept our heads veiled, our voices shy and sweet.

In India, I become, once again, an only child of rich, ailing parents. Old friends of the family come to pay their respects. Some are Sikh, and inwardly, involuntarily, I cringe. My parents are progressive people; they do not blame communities for a few individuals.

In Canada it is a different story now.

"Stay longer," my mother pleads. "Canada is a cold place. Why would you want to be all by yourself?" I stay.

Three months pass. Then another.

"Vikram wouldn't have wanted you to give up things!" they protest. They call my husband by the name he was born with. In Toronto he'd changed to Vik so the men he worked with at his office would find his name as easy as Rod or Chris. "You know, the dead aren't cut off from us!"

My grandmother, the spoiled daughter of a rich *zamindar*, shaved her head with rusty razor blades when she was widowed at sixteen. My grandfather died of childhood diabetes when he was nineteen, and she saw herself as the harbinger of bad luck. My mother grew up without parents, raised indifferently by an uncle, while her true mother slept in a hut behind the main estate house and took her food with the servants. She grew up a rationalist. My parents abhor mindless mortification.

The *zamindar*'s daughter kept stubborn faith in Vedic rituals; my parents rebelled. I am trapped between two modes of knowledge. At thirty-six, I am too old to start over and too young to give up. Like my husband's spirit, I flutter between worlds.

Courting aphasia, we travel. We travel with our phalanx of servants and poor relatives. To hill stations and to beach resorts. We play contract bridge in dusty gymkhana clubs. We ride stubby ponies up crumbly mountain trails. At tea dances, we let ourselves be twirled twice round the ballroom. We hit the holy spots we hadn't made time for before. In Varanasi, Kalighat, Rishikesh, Hardwar, astrologers and palmists seek me out and for a fee offer me cosmic consolations.

Already the widowers among us are being shown new bride candidates. They cannot resist the call of custom, the authority of their parents and older brothers. They must marry; it is the duty of a man to look after a wife. The new wives will be young widows with children, destitute but of good family. They will make loving wives, but the men will shun them. I've had calls from the men over crackling Indian telephone lines. "Save me," they say, these substantial, educated, successful men of forty. "My parents are arranging a marriage for me." In a month they will have buried one family and returned to Canada with a new bride and partial family.

I am comparatively lucky. No one here thinks of arranging a husband for an unlucky widow.

Then, on the third day of the sixth month into this odyssey, in an abandoned temple in a tiny Himalayan village, as I make my offering of flowers and sweetmeats to the god of a tribe of animists, my husband descends to me. He is squatting next to a scrawny *sadhu* in moth-eaten robes. Vikram wears the vanilla suit he wore the last time I hugged him. The *sadhu* tosses petals on a butter-fed flame, reciting Sanskrit mantras and sweeps his face of flies. My husband takes my hands in his.

You're beautiful, he starts. Then, *What are you doing here?*

Shall I stay? I ask. He only smiles, but already the image is fading. *You must finish alone what we started together.* No seaweed wreathes his mouth. He speaks too fast just as he used to when we were an envied family in our pink split-level. He is gone.

In the windowless altar room, smoky with joss sticks and clarified butter lamps, a sweaty hand gropes for my blouse. I do not shriek. The *sadhu* arranges his robe. The lamps hiss and sputter out.

When we come out of the temple, my mother says, "Did you feel something weird in there?"

My mother has no patience with ghosts, prophetic dreams, holy men, and cults.

"No," I lie. "Nothing."

But she knows that she's lost me. She knows that in days I shall be leaving. Kusum's put her house up for sale. She wants to live in an ashram in Hardwar. Moving to Hardwar was her swami's idea. Her swami runs two ashrams, the one in Hardwar and another here in Toronto.

"Don't run away," I tell her.

"I'm not running away," she says. "I'm pursuing inner peace. You think you or that Ranganathan fellow are better off?"

Pam's left for California. She wants to do some modelling, she says. She says when she comes into her share of the insurance money she'll open a yoga-cum-aerobics studio in Hollywood. She sends me postcards so naughty I daren't leave them on the coffee table. Her mother has withdrawn from her and the world.

The rest of us don't lose touch, that's the point. Talk is all we have, says Dr. Ranganathan, who has also resisted his relatives and returned to Montreal and to his job, alone. He says, whom better to talk with than other relatives? We've been melted down and recast as a new tribe.

He calls me twice a week from Montreal. Every Wednesday night and every Saturday afternoon. He is changing jobs, going to Ottawa. But Ottawa is over a hundred miles away, and he is forced to drive two hundred and twenty miles a day. He can't bring himself to sell his house. The house is a temple, he says; the king-sized bed in the master bedroom is a shrine. He sleeps on a folding cot. A devotee.

There are still some hysterical relatives. Judith Templeton's list of those needing help and those who've "accepted" is in nearly perfect balance. Acceptance means you speak of your family in the past tense and you make active plans for moving ahead with your life. There are courses at Seneca and Ryerson we could be taking. Her gleaming leather briefcase is full of college catalogues and lists of cultural societies that need our help. She has done impressive work, I tell her.

"In the text books on grief management," she replies—I am her confidante, I realize, one of the few whose grief has not sprung bizarre obsessions—"there are stages to pass through: rejection, depression, acceptance, reconstruction." She has compiled a chart and finds that six months after the tragedy, none of us still reject reality, but only a handful are reconstructing. "Depressed Acceptance" is the plateau we've reached. Remarriage is a major step in reconstruction (though she's a little surprised, even shocked, over how quickly some of the men have taken on new families). Selling one house and changing jobs and cities is healthy.

How do I tell Judith Templeton that my family surrounds me, and that like creatures in epics, they've changed shapes? She sees me as calm and accepting but worries that I have no job, no career. My closest friends are worse off than I. I cannot tell her my days, even my nights, are thrilling.

She asks me to help with families she can't reach at all. An elderly couple in Agincourt whose sons were killed just weeks after they had brought their parents over from a village in Punjab. From their names, I know they are Sikh. Judith Templeton and a translator have visited them twice with offers of money for air fare to Ireland, with bank forms, power-of-attorney forms, but they have refused to sign, or to leave their tiny apartment. Their sons' money is frozen in the bank. Their sons' investment apartments have been trashed by tenants, the furnishings sold off. The parents fear that anything they sign or any money they receive will end the company's or the country's obligations to them. They fear they are selling their sons for two airline tickets to a place they've never seen.

The high-rise apartment is a tower of Indians and West Indians, with a sprinkling of Orientals. The nearest bus stop kiosk is lined with women in saris. Boys practice cricket in the parking lot. Inside the building, even I wince a bit from the ferocity of onion fumes, the distinctive and immediate Indianness of frying *ghee*, but Judith Templeton maintains a steady flow of information. These poor old people are in imminent danger of losing their place and all their services.

I say to her, "They are Sikh. They will not open up to a Hindu woman." And what I want to add is, as much as I try not to, I stiffen now at the sight of beards and turbans. I remember a time when we all trusted each other in this new country, it was only the new country we worried about.

The two rooms are dark and stuffy. The lights are off, and an oil lamp sputters on the coffee table. The bent old lady has let us in, and her husband is wrapping a white turban over his oiled, hip-length hair. She immediately goes to the kitchen, and I hear the most familiar sound of an Indian home, tap water hitting and filling a teapot.

They have not paid their utility bills, out of fear and the inability to write a check. The telephone is gone; electricity and gas and water are soon to follow. They have told Judith their sons will provide. They are good boys, and they have always earned and looked after their parents.

We converse a bit in Hindi. They do not ask about the crash and I wonder if I should bring it up. If they think I am here merely as a translator, then they may feel insulted. There are thousands of Punjabi speakers, Sikhs, in Toronto to do a better job. And so I say to the old lady, "I too have lost my sons, and my husband, in the crash."

Her eyes immediately fill with tears. The man mutters a few words which sound like a blessing. "God provides and God takes away," he says.

I want to say, But only men destroy and give back nothing.

"My boys and my husband are not coming back," I say. "We have to understand that."

Now the old woman responds. "But who is to say? Man alone does not decide these things." To this her husband adds his agreement.

Judith asks about the bank papers, the release forms. With a stroke of the pen, they will have a provincial trustee to pay their bills, invest their money, send them a monthly pension.

"Do you know this woman?" I ask them.

The man raises his hand from the table, turns it over and seems to regard each finger separately before he answers. "This young lady is always coming here; we make tea for her and she leaves papers for us to sign." His eyes scan a pile of paper in the corner of the room. "Soon we will be out of tea, then will she go away?"

The old lady adds, "I have asked my neighbors and no else gets *angrezi* visitors. What have we done?"

"It's her job," I try to explain. "The government is worried. Soon you will have no place to stay, no lights, no gas, no water."

"Government will get its money. Tell her not to worry, we are honorable people."

I try to explain the government wishes to give money, not take. He raises his hand. "Let them take," he says. "We are accustomed to that. That is no problem."

"We are strong people," says the wife. "Tell her that."

"Who needs all this machinery?" demands the husband. "It is unhealthy, the bright lights, the cold air on a hot day, the cold food, the four gas rings. God will provide, not government."

"When our boys return," the mother says. Her husband sucks his teeth. "Enough talk," he says.

Judith breaks in. "Have you convinced them?" The snaps on her cordovan briefcase go off like firecrackers in that quiet apartment. She lays the sheaf of legal papers on the coffee table.

"If they can't write their names, an X will do—I've told them that."

Now the old lady has shuffled to the kitchen and soon emerges with a pot of tea and two cups. "I think my bladder will go first on a job like this," Judith says to me, smiling. "If only there was some way of reaching them. Please thank her for the tea. Tell her she's very kind."

I nod in Judith's direction and tell them in Hindi, "She thanks you for the tea. She thinks you are being very hospitable but she doesn't have the slightest idea what it means."

I want to say, Humor her. I want to say, My boys and my husband are with me too, more than ever. I look in the old man's eyes and I can read his stubborn, peasant's message: *I have protected this woman as best as I can. She is the only person I have left. Give to me or take from me what you will, but I will not sign for it. I will not pretend that I accept.*

In the car, Judith says. "You see what I'm up against? I'm sure they're lovely people, but their stubbornness and ignorance are driving me crazy. They think signing a paper is signing their son's death warrants, don't they?"

I am looking out the window. I want to say, *In our culture, it is a parent's duty to hope.*

"Now Shaila, this next woman is a real mess. She cries day and night, and she refuses all medical help. We may have to—"

"—Let me out at the subway," I say.

"I beg your pardon?" I can feel those blue eyes staring at me.

It would not be like her to disobey. She merely disapproves, and slows at the corner to let me out. Her voice is plaintive. "Is there anything I said? Anything I did?"

I could answer her suddenly in a dozen ways, but I choose not to. "Shaila? Let's talk about it," I hear, then slam the door.

A wife and mother begins her new life in a new country, and that life is cut short. Yet her husband tells her: Complete what we have started. We who stayed out of politics and came halfway around the world to avoid religious and political feuding have been the first in the New World to die from it. I no longer know what we have started, nor how to complete it. I write letters to the editors of local papers and to members of Parliament. Now at least they admit it was a bomb. One MP answers back, with sympathy, but with a challenge. You want to make a difference? Work on a campaign. Work on mine. Politicize the Indian voter.

My husband's old lawyer helps me set up a trust. Vikram was a saver and a careful investor. He had saved the boys' boarding school and college fees. I sell the pink house at four times what we paid for it and take a small apartment downtown. I am looking for a charity to support.

We are deep in the Toronto winter, gray skies, icy pavements. I stay indoors, watching television. I have tried to assess my situation, how best to live my life, to complete what we began so many years ago. Kusum has written me from Hardwar that her life is now serene. She has seen Satish and has heard her daughter sing again. Kusum was on a pilgrimage, passing through a village when she heard a young girl's voice singing one of her daughter's favorite *bhajans*. She followed the music through the squalor of a Himalayan village, to a hut where a young girl, an exact replica of her daughter, was fanning coals under the kitchen fire. When she appeared, the girl cried out, "Ma!" and ran away. What did I think of that?

I think I can only envy her.

Pam didn't make it to California, but writes me from Vancouver. She works in a department store, giving make-up hints to Indian and Oriental girls. Dr. Ranganathan has given up his commute, given up his house and job, and accepted an academic position in Texas where no one knows his story and he has vowed not to tell it. He calls me now once a week.

I wait, I listen, and I pray, but Vikram has not returned to me. The voices and the shapes and the nights filled with visions ended abruptly several weeks ago.

I take it as a sign.

One rare, beautiful, sunny day last week, returning from a small errand on Yonge Street, I was walking through the park from the subway to my apartment. I live equidistant from the Ontario Houses of Parliament and the University of Toronto. The day was not cold, but something in the bare trees caught my attention. I looked up from the gravel, into the branches and the clear blue sky beyond. I thought I heard the rustling of larger forms, and I waited a moment for voices. Nothing.

"What?" I asked.

Then as I stood in the path looking north to Queen's Park and west to the university, I heard the voices of my family one last time. *Your time has come*, they said. *Go, be brave.*

I do not know where this voyage I have begun will end. I do not know which direction I will take. I dropped the package on a park bench and started walking.

FOR INFORMAL WRITING

Describe the setting of the story. How does it set the tone for the rest of the narrative?

FOR DISCUSSION

1. Why would Mukherjee have chosen to title the story "The Management of Grief"? Is there any irony to this choice? Why or why not?
2. Which characters represent the collision between the "old" country and the "new" country? Why do you think so?
3. How does the story reveal mistaken perceptions on the part of the characters? What are they? Are these inevitable when different aspects of cultures come together or clash? Why or why not?

FOR WRITING

Much of this story grapples with the differences in ways of grieving in Western and Hindu cultures. How does each character deal with grief? What do these differing reactions say about culture and custom? Use examples from the story as support for your perspective.

Sh**** First Drafts (1994)
Anne Lamott (1954–)

Anne Lamott is a novelist, public speaker, writer of nonfiction, and political activist. She is the subject of a 1999 documentary, Bird by Bird with Annie: A Film Portrait of Writer Anne Lamott. *Lamott was awarded a Guggenheim Fellowship in 1995 and has written over a dozen books, including numerous nonfiction titles that are largely autobiographical. A* New York Times *best-selling author, she was born in San Francisco, and she continues to make her home in Marin County, California.*

Now, practically even better news than that of short assignments is the idea of shitty first drafts. All good writers write them. This is how they end up with good second drafts and terrific third drafts. People tend to look at successful writers who are getting their books published and maybe even doing well financially and think that they sit down at their desks every morning feeling like a million dollars, feeling great about who they are and how much talent they have and what a great story they have to tell; that they take in a few deep breaths, push back their sleeves, roll their necks a few times to get all the cricks out, and dive in, typing fully formed passages as fast as a court reporter. But this is just the fantasy of the uninitiated. I know some very great writers, writers you love who write beautifully and have made a great deal of money, and not one of them sits down routinely feeling wildly enthusiastic and confident. Not one of them writes elegant first drafts. All right, one of them does, but we do not like her very much. We do not think that she has a rich inner life or that God likes her or can even stand her. (Although when I mentioned this to my priest friend Tom, he said you can safely assume you've created God in your own image when it turns out that God hates all the same people you do.)

"Shitty First Drafts" from BIRD BY BIRD: SOME INSTRUCTIONS ON WRITING AND LIFE by Anne Lamott, copyright © 1994 by Anne Lamott. Used by permission of Pantheon Books, an imprint of the Knopf Doubleday Publishing Group, a division of Penguin Random House LLC. All rights reserved.

Very few writers really know what they are doing until they've done it. Nor do they go about their business feeling dewy and thrilled. They do not type a few stiff warm-up sentences and then find themselves bounding along like huskies across the snow. One writer I know tells me that he sits down every morning and says to himself nicely, "It's not like you don't have a choice, because you do—you can either type, or kill yourself." We all often feel like we are pulling teeth, even those writers whose prose ends up being the most natural and fluid. The right words and sentences just do not come pouring out like ticker tape most of the time. Now, Muriel Spark is said to have felt that she was taking dictation from God every morning—sitting there, one supposes, plugged into a Dictaphone, typing away, humming. But this is a very hostile and aggressive position. One might hope for bad things to rain down on a person like this.

For me and most of the other writers I know, writing is not rapturous. In fact, the only way I can get anything written at all is to write really, really shitty first drafts.

The first draft is the child's draft, where you let it all pour out and then let it romp all over the place, knowing that no one is going to see it and that you can shape it later. You just let this childlike part of you channel whatever voices and visions come through and onto the page. If one of the characters wants to say, "Well, so what, Mr. Poopy Pants?," you let her. No one is going to see it. If the kid wants to get into really sentimental, weepy, emotional territory, you let him. Just get it all down on paper because there may be something great in those six crazy pages that you would never have gotten to by more rational, grown-up means. There may be something in the very last line of the very last paragraph on page six that you just love, that is so beautiful or wild that you now know what you're supposed to be writing about, more or less, or in what direction you might go—but there was no way to get to this without first getting through the first five and a half pages.

I used to write food reviews for *California* magazine before it folded. (My writing food reviews had nothing to do with the magazine folding, although every single review did cause a couple of canceled subscriptions. Some readers took umbrage at my comparing mounds of vegetable puree with various ex-presidents' brains.) These reviews always took two days to write. First I'd go to a restaurant several times with a few opinionated, articulate friends in tow. I'd sit there writing down everything anyone said that was at all interesting or funny. Then on the following Monday I'd sit down at my desk with my notes and try to write the review. Even after I'd been doing this for years, panic would set in. I'd try to write a lead, but instead I'd write a couple of dreadful sentences, XX them out, try again, XX everything out, and then feel despair and worry settle on my chest like an x-ray apron. It's over, I'd think calmly. I'm not going to be able to get the magic to work this time. I'm ruined. I'm through. I'm toast. Maybe, I'd think, I can get my old job back as a clerk-typist. But probably not. I'd get up and study my teeth in the mirror for a while. Then I'd stop, remember to breathe, make a few phone calls, hit the kitchen and chow down. Eventually I'd go back and sit down at my desk, and sigh for the next ten minutes. Finally I would pick up my one-inch picture frame, stare into it as if for the answer, and every time the answer would come: all I had to do was to write a really shitty first draft of, say, the opening paragraph. And no one was going to see it.

So I'd start writing without reining myself in. It was almost just typing, just making my fingers move. And the writing would be terrible. I'd write a lead paragraph that was a whole page, even though the entire review could only be three pages long, and then I'd start writing up descriptions of the food, one dish at a time, bird by bird, and the critics would be sitting on my shoulders, commenting like cartoon characters. They'd be pretending to snore, or rolling their eyes at my overwrought descriptions, no matter how hard I tried to tone those descriptions down, no matter how conscious I was of what a friend said to me gently in my early days of restaurant reviewing. "Annie," she said, "it is just a piece of *chicken*. It is just a bit of *cake*."

But because by then I had been writing for so long, I would eventually let myself trust the process—sort of, more or less. I'd write a first draft that was maybe twice as long as it should be, with a self-indulgent and boring beginning, stupefying descriptions of the meal, lots of quotes from my black-humored friends that made them sound more like the Manson girls than food lovers, and no ending to speak of. The whole thing would be so long and incoherent and hideous that for the rest of the day I'd obsess about getting creamed by a car before I could write a decent second draft. I'd worry that people would read what I'd written and believe that the accident had really been a suicide, that I had panicked because my talent was waning and my mind was shot.

The next day, I'd sit down, go through it all with a colored pen, take out everything I possibly could, find a new lead somewhere on the second page, figure out a kicky place to end it, and then write a second draft. It always turned out fine, sometimes even funny and weird and helpful. I'd go over it one more time and mail it in.

Then, a month later, when it was time for another review, the whole process would start again, complete with the fears that people would find my first draft before I could rewrite it.

Almost all good writing begins with terrible first efforts. You need to start somewhere. Start by getting something—anything—down on paper. A friend of mine says that the first draft is the down draft—you just get it down. The second draft is the up draft—you fix it up. You try to say what you have to say more accurately. And the third draft is the dental draft, where you check every tooth, to see if it's loose or cramped or decayed, or even, God help us, healthy.

FOR INFORMAL WRITING

Anne Lamott starts her piece with the assumptions people make about how writers work. She writes, "But this is just the fantasy of the uninitiated." Reflect on your own writing process, whether for academic or creative writing. How does your writing process compare with Lamott's? Be specific.

FOR DISCUSSION

1. What does Lamott mean when she says, "For me and most of the other writers I know, writing is not rapturous." How does this statement confirm—or deny—your assumptions about "professional" writers? Why?
2. According to Lamott's writer friend, what is the difference between the "down draft" and the "up draft?"
3. What is the distinction between "process" and "product?" Your instructor may have said that writing is more about the process than the product. What do you think?

FOR WRITING

Read Joan Didion's "Why I Write," included in this anthology. In that essay, Didion, another prominent writer, also concerns herself with the writing process. Compare and contrast the two essays, arguing how they are similar and how they differ. Writers writing about writing is a familiar subgenre. Research another writer who takes this as his/her/their subject. How might that writer's perspective contrast or complement Lamott and Didion?

The Secret Life of the Love Song (1999)

Nick Cave (1957–)

Nick Cave is an Australian singer, composer, author, and screenwriter whose work reveals his preoccupation with themes of love and death. In 1988, Cave published his first book, King Ink, *which was a collection of poems, lyrics, and plays. Ten years later, Cave taught a series of classes on song writing at the Vienna Poetry Academy, before which he delivered the first iteration of this speech. What follows is a revised version of that original speech, which he delivered in 1999 at London's Royal Festival Hall.*

Ladies and gentlemen,
To be invited to come here and teach, to lecture, to impart what knowledge I have collected about poetry, about songwriting has left me with a whole host of conflicting feelings. The strongest, most insistent of these concerns my late father who was an English Literature teacher at the high school I attended back in Australia. I have very clear memories of being about 12 years old and sitting, as you are now, in a classroom or school hall, watching my father, who would be standing, up here, where I am standing, and thinking to myself, gloomily and miserably, for, in the main, I was a gloomy and miserable child: "It doesn't really matter what I do with my life as long as I don't end up like my father." At 40 years old it would appear that there is virtually no action I can take that does not draw me closer to him, that does not make me more like him. At 40 years old I have become my father. And here I am. Teaching.

What I wanted to do here was to talk a bit about the Love Song, to speak about my own personal approach to this genre of songwriting which I believe has been at the very heart of my particular artistic quest. I want to look at some other

---

By permission of Nick Cave

works, that, for whatever reason, I think are sublime achievements in this most noble of artistic pursuits: the creation of the great Love Song.

Looking back at these 20 years, a certain clarity prevails. Amidst the madness and the mayhem, it would seem I have been banging on one particular drum. I see that my artistic life has centred around an attempt to articulate the nature of an almost palpable sense of loss that has laid claim to my life. A great gaping hole was blasted out of my world by the unexpected death of my father when I was 19 years old. The way I learned to fill this hole, this void, was to write. My father taught me this as if to prepare me for his own passing. To write allowed me direct access to my imagination, to inspiration and ultimately to God. I found through the use of language, that I wrote God into existence. Language became the blanket that I threw over the invisible man, that gave him shape and form. The actualising of God through the medium of the Love Song remains my prime motivation as an artist. The Love Song is perhaps the truest and most distinctive human gift for recognising God and a gift that God himself needs. God gave us this gift in order that we speak and sing Him alive because God lives within communication. If the world were to suddenly fall silent God would deconstruct and die. Jesus Christ himself said, in one of His most beautiful quotes, "Where ever two or more are gathered together, I am in your midst." He said this because wherever two or more are gathered together there is language. I found that language became a poultice to the wounds incurred by the death of my father. Language became a salve to longing.

Though the Love Song comes in many guises—songs of exultation and praise, songs of rage and of despair, erotic songs, songs of abandonment and loss—they all address God, for it is the haunted premises of longing that the true Love Song inhabits. It is a howl in the void, for Love and for comfort and it lives on the lips of the child crying for his mother. It is the song of the lover in need of her loved one, the raving of the lunatic, supplicant petitioning his God. It is the cry of one chained to the earth, to the ordinary and to the mundane, craving flight; a flight into inspiration and imagination and divinity. The Love Song is the sound of our endeavours to become God-like, to rise up and above the earthbound and the mediocre.

The loss of my father, I found, created in my life a vacuum, a space in which my words began to float and collect and find their purpose. The great W. H. Auden said: "The so-called traumatic experience is not an accident, but the opportunity for which the child has been patiently waiting—had it not occurred, it would have found another—in order that its life become a serious matter." The death of my father was the "traumatic experience" Auden talks about that left the hole for God to fill. How beautiful the notion that we create our own personal catastrophes and that it is the creative forces within us that are instrumental in doing this. We each have a need to create and sorrow is a creative act.

The Love Song is a sad song, it is the sound of sorrow itself. We all experience within us what the Portuguese call Saudade, which translates as an inexplicable sense of longing, an unnamed and enigmatic yearning of the soul. And it is this feeling that lives in the realms of imagination and inspiration and is the breeding ground for the sad song, for the Love Song is the light of God, deep down, blasting through our wounds.

In his brilliant lecture entitled *The Theory and Function of Duende*, Frederico Garcia Lorca attempts to shed some light on the eerie and inexplicable sadness that lives in the heart of certain works of art. "All that has dark sounds has duende," he says, "that mysterious power that everyone feels but no philosopher can explain." In contemporary rock music, the area in which I operate, music seems less inclined to have in its soul, restless and quivering, the sadness that Lorca talks about. Excitement, often; anger, sometimes: but true sadness, rarely. Bob Dylan has always had it. Leonard Cohen deals specifically in it. It pursues Van Morrison like a black dog and though he tries to he cannot escape it. Tom Waits and Neil Young can summon it. It haunts Polly Harvey. My friends in the Dirty 3 have it by the bucket load. The band Spiritualized are excited by it. Tindersticks desperately want it, but all in all it would appear that duende is too fragile to survive the brutality of technology and the ever increasing acceleration of the music industry. Perhaps there is just no money in sadness, no dollars in duende. Sadness or duende needs space to breathe. Melancholy hates haste and floats in silence. It must be handled with care.

All Love Songs must contain duende. For the Love Song is never truly happy. It must first embrace the potential for pain. Those songs that speak of Love without having within their lines an ache or a sigh are not Love Songs at all but rather Hate Songs disguised as Love Songs, and are not to be trusted. These songs deny us our humanness and our God-given right to be sad and the airwaves are littered with them. The Love Song must resonate with the susurration of sorrow, the tintinnabulation of grief. The writer who refuses to explore the darker regions of the heart will never be able to write convincingly about the wonder, the magic and the joy of love, for just as goodness cannot be trusted unless it has breathed the same air as evil—the enduring metaphor of Christ crucified between two criminals comes to mind here—so within the fabric of the Love Song, within its melody, its lyric, one must sense an acknowledgement of its capacity for suffering.

In Lou Reed's remarkable song "Perfect Day," he writes in near diary form the events that combine to make a perfect day. It is a day that resonates with the bold beauty of love, where he and his lover sit in the park and drink Sangria, feed animals in the zoo, go to a movie show etc. But it is the lines that lurk darkly in the third verse, "I thought I was someone else, someone good" that transforms this otherwise sentimental song into the masterpiece of melancholia that it is.

Not only do these lines ache with failure and shame, but they remind us in more general terms of the transient nature of love itself—that he will have his day "in the park" but, like Cinderella, who must return at midnight to the soot and ash of her disenchanted world, so must he return to his old self, his bad self. It is out of the void that this song springs, clothed in loss and longing.

Around the age of 20, I started reading the Bible and I found in the brutal prose of the Old Testament, in the feel of its words and its imagery an endless source of inspiration. "The Song of Solomon," perhaps the greatest Love Song ever written, had a massive impact upon me. Its openly erotic nature, the metaphoric journey taken around the lovers' bodies—breasts compared to bunches of grapes and young deer, hair and teeth compared to flocks of goats and sheep, legs like pillars of marble, the navel, a round goblet, the belly, a heap of wheat—its staggering imagery rockets us into the world of pure imagination. Although the two lovers are physically separate—Solomon is excluded from the garden where his beloved sings—it is the wild, obsessive projections of one lover on to another that dissolve them into a single being, constructed from a series of rapturous love-metaphors.

"The Song of Solomon" is an extraordinary Love Song but it was the remarkable series of love song/poems known as the Psalms that truly held me. I found the Psalms, which deal directly with the relationship between man and God, teeming with all the clamorous desperation, longing, exultation, erotic violence and brutality that I could hope for. The Psalms are soaked in saudade, drenched in duende and bathed in bloody minded violence. In many ways these songs became the blueprint for many of my more sadistic love songs. Psalm 137, a particular favourite of mine which was turned into a chart hit by the fab little band Boney M is a perfect example of all I have been talking about.

Psalm 137
By the rivers of Babylon, there we sat down / Yea, we wept when we remembered Zion / We hanged our harps upon the willows in the midst thereof / For there they that carried us away captive required of us a song / And they that wasted us required of us mirth saying / Sing us one of the songs of Zion / How shall we sing the Lord's song in a strange land? / If I forget thee, O Jerusalem / Let my right hand forget her cunning / If I do not remember thee, let my tongue cleave to the roof of my mouth / If I prefer not Jerusalem above my chief joy / Remember, O lord, the children of Edom in the day of Jerusalem / Who said Rase it, rase it, even to the foundation thereof / O daughter of Babylon, who art to be destroyed / Happy shall he be, that rewardeth thee as thou hast served us / Happy shall he be, that taketh and dasheth thy little ones against the stones.

The Love Song must be born into the realm of the irrational, absurd, the distracted, the melancholic, the obsessive, the insane for the Love Song is the noise of love itself and love is, of course, a form of madness. Whether it be the love of God, or romantic, erotic love—these are manifestations of our need to be torn away from the rational, to take leave of our senses, so to speak. Love Songs come in many guises and are seemingly written for many reasons—as declarations or to wound—I have written songs for all of these reasons—but ultimately the Love Song exists to fill, with language, the silence between ourselves and God, to decrease the distance between the temporal and the divine.

In Psalm 137 the poet finds himself captive in "a strange land" and is forced to sing a song of Zion. He swears his love to his homeland and dreams of revenge. The Psalm is ghastly in its violent sentiments, as he sings for love of his homeland and his God and that he may be made happy by murdering the children of his enemies. What I found, time and time again in the Bible, especially the Old Testament, was that verses of rapture, of ecstasy and love could hold within them apparently opposite sentiments—hate, revenge, bloody-mindedness etc, that they were not mutually exclusive. This idea has left an enduring impression on my songwriting.

Within the world of modern pop music, a world that deals ostensibly with the Love Song, but in actuality does little more than hurl dollops of warm, custard-coloured baby-vomit down the air waves, true sorrow is not welcome. But occasionally a song comes along that hides behind its disposable, plastic beat a love lyric of truly devastating proportions. "Better The Devil You Know" written by the hitmakers Stock, Aitken and Waterman and sung by the Australian pop sensation Kylie Minogue is such a song. The disclosing of the terror of Love in a piece of mindless, innocuous pop music is an intriguing concept. "Better The Devil You Know" is one of pop music's most violent and distressing love lyrics.

Better The Devil You Know
Say you won't leave me no more / I'll take you back again / No more excuses, no, no / Cause I've heard them all before / A hundred times or more / I'll forgive and forget / If you say you'll never go / Cause it's true what they say / Better the devil you know. / Our love wasn't perfect, I know / I think I know the score / You say you love me, O boy / I can't ask for more / I'll come if you should call / I'll be here every day / Waiting for your love to show / Cause it's true what they say / It's better the devil you know / I'll take you back / I'll take you back again

When Kylie Minogue sings these words there is an innocence to her voice that makes the horror of this chilling lyric all the more compelling. The idea presented within this song, dark and sinister and sad—that all love relationships are by nature abusive and that this abuse, be it physical or psychological, is welcomed and encouraged—shows how even the most innocuous of Love Songs has the potential to hide terrible human truths. Like Prometheus chained to his rock, so that the eagle can eat his liver each night, Kylie becomes love's sacrificial lamb bleating an earnest invitation to the drooling, ravenous wolf that he may devour her time and time again, all to a groovy techno beat. "I'll take you back. I'll take you back again." Indeed. Here the Love Song becomes a vehicle for a harrowing portrait of humanity not dissimilar to that of the Old Testament's Psalms. Both are messages to God that cry out into the yawning void, in anguish and self-loathing, for deliverance.

As I said earlier, my artistic life has centred around the desire, or more accurately, the need to articulate the various feelings of loss and longing that have whistled through my bones and hummed in my blood, throughout my life. In the process I have written about 200 songs, the bulk of which I would say were Love Songs. Love Songs, and therefore, by my definition, sad songs: Out of this considerable mass of material, a handful of them rise above the others as true examples of all I have talked about. "Sad Waters," "Black Hair," "I Let Love In," "Deanna," "From Her to Eternity," "Nobody's Baby Now," "Into My Arms," "Lime Tree Arbour," "Lucy," "Straight To You." I am proud of these songs. They are my gloomy, violent, dark-eyed children. They sit grimly on their own and do not play with the other songs. Mostly they were offspring of complicated pregnancies and difficult and painful births. Most of them are rooted in direct personal experience and were conceived for a variety of reasons but this rag-tag group of Love Songs are, at the death, all the same thing—life lines thrown into the galaxies of the divine by a drowning man.

The reasons why I feel compelled to sit down and write Love Songs are legion. Some of these became clearer to me when I sat down with a friend of mine, who for the sake of his anonymity I will refer to as J. J., and we admitted to each other that we both suffer from psychological disorder that the medical profession call erotographomania. Erotographomania is the obsessive desire to write Love Letters. My friend shared what he had written and sent, over the last five years, more than 7,000 Love Letters to his wife. My friend looked exhausted and his shame was almost palpable. I suffer from the same disease but happily have yet to reach such an advanced stage as my poor friend J. J. We discussed the power of the Love Letter and found that it was, not surprisingly, very similar to the Love Song. Both served as extended meditations on one's beloved. Both served to shorten the distance between the writer and the recipient. Both held within them a permanence and power that the spoken word did not. Both were erotic exercises in themselves. Both had the potential to reinvent, through words, like Pygmalion with his self-created lover of stone, one's beloved. But more than that, both had the insidious power to imprison one's beloved, to bind their hands with love lines, to gag them, to blind them; for words became the defining parameter that keeps the loved one imprisoned in a bondage of poetry. Alas, the most endearing form of correspondence, the Love Letter, like the Love Song has suffered at the hands of the cold speed of technology, at the carelessness and soullessness of our age. I would like to look, finally, at one of my own songs that I recorded for *The Boatmen's Call* album. This song, I feel, exemplifies much of what I've been talking about today. The song is called "Far From Me."

Far From Me
For you dear, I was born / For you I was raised up / For you I've lived and for you I will die / For you I am dying now / You were my mad little lover / In a world where everybody fucks everybody else over / You who are so far from me / Far from me / So far from me / Way across some cold neurotic sea / Far from me / I would talk to you of all matter of things / With a smile you would reply / Then the sun would leave your pretty face / And you'd retreat from the front of your eyes / I keep hearing that you're doing best / I hope your heart beats happy in your infant breast / You are so far from me / Far from me / Far from me / There is no knowledge but I know it / There's nothing to learn from that vacant voice / That sails to me across the line / From the ridiculous to the sublime / It's good to hear you're doing so well / But really can't you find somebody else that you can ring and tell / Did you ever / Care for me? / Were you ever / There for me? / So far from me / You told me you'd stick by me / Through the thick and through the thin / Those were your very words / My fair-weather friend / You were my brave-hearted lover / At the first taste of trouble went running back to mother / So far from me / Far from me / Suspended in your bleak and fishless sea / Far from me / Far from me

"Far From Me" took four months to write, which was the duration of the relationship it describes. The first verse was written in the first week of the affair and is full of all the heroic drama of new love as it describes the totality of feeling whilst acknowledging the potential for pain, "For you I'm dying now." It sets the two lovers it describes against an uncaring world – a world that fucks everybody over—and brings in the notion of the physical distance suggested in the title. Strangely, though, the song, as if awaiting the "traumatic experience" that I spoke of earlier to happen, would not allow itself to be completed until the catastrophe had occurred. Some songs are tricky like that and it is wise to keep your wits about you when dealing with them. I find quite often that the songs I write seem to know more about what is going on in my life than I do. I have pages and pages of fourth verses for this song written while the relationship was still sailing happily along. One such verse went:

> *The Camellia, The Magnolia / Have such a pretty flower / And the bells of St. Marys / Inform us of the hour*

Pretty words, innocent words, unaware that any day the bottom would drop out of the whole thing. Love Songs that attach themselves to actual experiences, that are a poeticising of real events have a peculiar beauty unto themselves. They stay alive in the same way that memories do and being alive, they grow up and undergo changes and develop. A Love Song such as "Far From Me" has found a personality beyond the one that I originally gave it. With the power to influence my own feelings around the actual event itself. This is an extraordinary thing and one of the truly wondrous benefits of songwriting. The songs that I have written that deal with past relationships have become the relationships themselves. Through these songs I have been able to mythologise the ordinary events of my life, lifting them from the temporal plane and hurling them way into the stars. The relationship described in "Far From Me" has been and gone but the song itself lives on, keeping a pulse running through my past. Such is the singular beauty of songwriting.

Twenty years of songwriting has now passed and still the void gapes wide. Still that inexplicable sadness, the duende, the saudade, the divine discontent persists and perhaps it will continue until I see the face of God himself. But when Moses desired to see the face of God, Exodus 33, 188, he was answered that he may not endure it, no man could see His face and live. Well, me, I don't mind. I'm happy to be sad. For the residue, cast off in this search, the songs themselves, my crooked brood of sad-eyed children, rally round and in their way, protect me, comfort me and keep me alive. They are the companions of the soul that lead it into exile, that save the overpowering yearning for that which is not of this world. The imagination desires an alternate and through the writing of the Love Song, one sits and dines with loss and longing, madness and melancholy, ecstasy, magic, joy and love with equal measures of respect and gratitude. The spiritual quest has many faces—religion, art, drugs, work, money, sex—but rarely does the search serve God so directly and rarely are the rewards so great in doing.

Thank you.

FOR INFORMAL WRITING

Think about the love songs you have on your own playlists. Why are you drawn to them, and how do they conform (or not) to Cave's ideal?

FOR DISCUSSION

1. Much of the speech seems to suggest that "all Love Songs must contain duende" because "the Love Song is never truly happy." How would you agree with or refute this notion? What contemporary examples support your point of view?
2. "The Secret Life of the Love Song," while a speech, is very much a piece of art/music criticism. Based on your reading, how would you characterize this genre of writing? What differentiates it from other types of writing that you see in this volume?
3. Look up the term "intertextual." What about this text is intertextual, and how does this intertextuality substantiate Cave's central argument or make it more (or less) compelling?

FOR WRITING

In his speech, Nick Cave characterizes love songs in very particular ways. Identify these characteristics. Then, analyze a contemporary love song through the lens of Cave's speech and his criteria, using specific examples from the song and Cave's speech to back up your point of view.

The Waiter's Wife (1999)
Zadie Smith (1975–)

Zadie Smith's first novel, White Teeth *(2000), brought her prominence. The daughter of a Jamaican mother and an English father, Smith was born in London and changed her name from Sadie to Zadie. She studied English literature at Cambridge University.* White Teeth *was a finalist for the prestigious National Book Critics' Circle Award, and it introduces her focus on race, assimilation, and culture. Smith is currently a tenured professor of creative writing at New York University and has published five novels, two essay collections, and most recently, a play. "The Waiter's Wife" originally appeared in* Granta.

In the spring of 1975, Samad and Alsana Iqbal left Bangladesh and came to live in Whitechapel, London, the other side of town from Archie and Clara Jones. Samad and Archie had a friendship dating back to the Second World War, back to the hot and claustrophobic Churchill tank in which they sat side by side for three months, close enough to smell each other and to recognize those scents thirty years later when Samad emerged from Gate 12, Heathrow, with a young wife and a paisley patterned luggage set in tow. "Long time no see," Archie had said, reaching out to grasp his old friend's palm, but Samad converted the handshake into a hug almost immediately, "Archibald Jones. Long time no bloody *smell*."

They fell back into easy conversation, two old boys slipping swiftly into an acquaintance as comfortable as slippers while their wives stood either side of the bags noting they had this thing in common and no more: that they were young, much younger than the men they stood awkwardly beside. They looked an unlikely pair. Alsana was small and rotund, moon-faced and with thick fingers she

---

"The Waiter's Wife (as it appeared in Granta 67, December 1, 1999)" from WHITE TEETH: A NOVEL by Zadie Smith, copyright © 2000 by Zadie Smith. Used by permission of Random House, an imprint and division of Penguin Random House LLC. All rights reserved.

hid in the folds of her cardigan. Clara was tall, striking, a black girl with a winning smile, wearing red shorts of a shortness that Alsana had never imagined possible, even in this country.

"Hot pants," said Clara, shyly, in response to Alsana's wide eyes, "I made dem myself."

"I sew also," Alsana replied, and they had a pleasant enough chat about seams and bobbins, materials and prices per yard, in a motorway service station over an indigestible lunch. "The wives get on like a house on fire," Archie had said merrily, giving Samad a nudge in the ribs. But this made them nervous, the two young wives, and after the ice-cream sundaes they sat in silence.

So some black people *are* friendly, thought Alsana after that first meeting was over. It was her habit to single one shining exception out of every minority she disliked; certain dentists, certain singers, certain film stars had been granted specialist treatment in the past and now Clara Jones was to be given Alsana's golden reprieve. Their relations were hesitant in the beginning—a few lunch dates here and there, the occasional coffee; neither wished to admit how much time they had on their hands though newly wed, or that Archie and Samad were always together. It wasn't until the Iqbals moved north, two minutes from Archie and his favourite watering hole, that the women truly resigned themselves to their husbands' mutual appreciation society and started something of a rearguard action. Picnics, the movies, museums, swimming pools—just the two of them. But even when they became fairly close, it was impossible to forget what a peculiar couple they made on the bus, in the park.

It took the Iqbals a year to get to Willesden High Road: a year of mercilessly hard graft to make the momentous move from the wrong side of Whitechapel to the wrong side of Willesden. A year's worth of Alsana banging away at the old Singer machine that sat in the kitchen, sewing together pieces of black plastic for a shop called Domination in Soho (many were the nights Alsana would hold up a piece of clothing she had just made—following the plans she was given—and wonder what on earth it was). A year's worth of Samad softly inclining his head at exactly the correct deferential angle, pencil in his right hand, notepad in his left, listening to the appalling pronunciation of the British, Spanish, American, French, Australian:

Go Bye Ello Sag, Please.

Chicken Jail Fret See Wiv Chips, Fanks.

From six in the evening until four in the morning was work and the rest was sleep, sleep without pause, until daylight was as rare as a decent tip. For what is the point, Samad would think, pushing aside two mints and a receipt to find fifteen pence, what is the point of tipping a man the same amount you would throw in a fountain to chase a wish? But before the illegal thought of folding the fifteen pence discreetly in his napkin hand had a chance to give itself form, Mukhul,

Ardashir Mukhul, who ran The Palace and whose wiry frame paced the restaurant, one benevolent eye on the customers, one ever-watchful eye on the staff—Ardashir Mukhul was upon him.

"Saaamaad," he said in his cloying, oleaginous way, "did you kiss the necessary backside this evening, Cousin?"

Samad and Ardashir were distant cousins, Samad the elder by six years. With what joy (pure bliss!) had Ardashir opened the letter last January, to find his older, cleverer, handsomer cousin could get no work as a food inspector in England and could he possibly . . .

"Fifteen pence, Cousin," said Samad lifting his palm.

"Well, every little helps, every little helps," said Ardashir, his dead-fish lips stretching into a stringy smile. "Into the Piss-Pot with it."

The Piss-Pot was a black cooking pot that sat on a plinth outside the staff toilets into which all tips were pooled and then split at the end of the night. For the younger, good-looking waiters like Shiva this was a great injustice. Shiva was the only Hindu on the staff, a tribute to his waitering skills that had triumphed over religious difference. He could make fifteen pounds in tips in an evening if the blubberous white divorcee in the corner was lonely enough, and he batted his long lashes at her effectively. He also made money from the polo-necked directors and producers (The Palace sat in the centre of London's Theatreland) who flattered the boy, watched his ass wiggle provocatively to the bar and back, and swore that the next time someone put *A Passage to India* on the stage, the casting couch would be his. For Shiva then, the Piss-Pot system was simply daylight robbery. But for men like Samad, in his forties, and for the even older, like the white-haired Mohammed (Ardashir's great-uncle), who was eighty if he was a day, who had deep pathways dug into the sides of his mouth where he had smiled when he was young—for men like this the Piss-Pot could not be complained about. It was a boon if anything, and it made more sense to join the collective than pocket fifteen pence and risk being caught (and docked a week's tips).

"You're all on my back!" Shiva would snarl, when he had to relinquish five pounds at the end of the night and drop it into the pot. "You all live off my back! Somebody get these losers off my back! That was my fiver and now it's going to be split sixty-five-fucking-million ways as a hand out to these losers! What is this, communism?"

And the rest would avoid his glare, and busy themselves quietly with other things until one evening, one fifteen-pence evening, Samad said, "Shut up, boy," quietly, almost underneath his breath.

"You!" Shiva swung round to where Samad stood crushing a great tub of lentils for tomorrow's dhal. "You're the worst of them! You're the worst fucking waiter I've ever seen! You couldn't get a tip if you mugged the bastards! I hear you trying to talk to the customer about biology this, politics that—just serve the food, you idiot—you're a waiter, for fuck's sake, you're not Michael Parkinson. *Did I hear you say Delhi—*" Shiva put his apron over his arm and began posturing around the kitchen (he was a pitiful mimic) "*—I was there myself, you know, Delhi University, it was most fascinating, yes—and I fought in the war, for England, yes—yes, yes, charming, charming—*" round and round the kitchen he went, bending his head and rubbing his hands over and over like Uriah Heep, bowing and genuflecting to the head cook, to the old man arranging great hunks of meat in the walk-in freezer, to the young boy scrubbing the inside of the oven. "Samad, Samad . . ." he said with what seemed infinite pity, then stopped abruptly, pulled the apron off and wrapped it round his waist, "you're a sad bastard."

Mohammed looked up from his pot-scrubbing and shook his head again and again. To no one in particular he said, "These young people—what kind of talk? What happened to respect? What kind of talk is this?"

"And you, you can fuck off too—" said Shiva, brandishing a ladle in his direction, "—You old fool! You're not my father."

"Second cousin of your mother's uncle," a voice muttered from the back.

"Bollocks," said Shiva. "Bollocks to that."

He grabbed the mop and was heading off for the toilets, when he stopped by Samad and placed the broom inches from Samad's mouth.

"Kiss it," he sneered: and then impersonating Ardashir's sluggish drawl, "Who knows, Cousin, you might get a raise!"

And that's what it was like most nights; abuse from Shiva and others; condescension from Ardashir; never seeing Alsana; never seeing the sun; clutching fifteen pence and then releasing it; wanting desperately to be wearing a sign, a large white placard that said:

> I AM NOT A WAITER. THAT IS, I AM A WAITER, BUT NOT JUST A WAITER. I HAVE BEEN A STUDENT, A SCIENTIST, A SOLDIER. MY WIFE IS CALLED ALSANA. WE LIVE IN EAST LONDON BUT WE WOULD LIKE TO MOVE NORTH. I AM A MUSLIM BUT ALLAH HAS FORSAKEN ME OR I HAVE FORSAKEN ALLAH. I'M NOT SURE. I HAVE AN ENGLISH FRIEND—ARCHIE—AND OTHERS. I AM FORTY-NINE BUT WOMEN STILL TURN IN THE STREET. SOMETIMES.

But no such placard existing, he had instead the urge, the need, to speak to every man, and like the Ancient Mariner to explain, always to explain, to reassert something, anything. Wasn't that important? But then the heartbreaking disappointment—to find out that the inclining of one's head, poising of one's pen, these were important, so important. It was important to be a good waiter, to listen when someone said:

Lamb Dawn Sock and Rice. Please. With Chips. Thank you.

And fifteen pence clinked on china. Thank you Sir. Thank you so very much.

One evening, shortly after he had put the down payment on the Willesden flat, Samad had waited till everyone left and then climbed the loudly carpeted stairs to Ardashir's office, for he had something to ask him.

"Cousin!" said Ardashir with a friendly grimace at the sight of Samad's body curling cautiously round the door. He knew that Samad had come to enquire about a pay increase, and he wanted his cousin to feel that he had at least considered the case in all his friendly judiciousness before he declined.

"Cousin, come in!"

"Good evening, Ardashir Mukhul," said Samad, stepping fully into the room.

"Sit down, sit down," said Ardashir warmly. "No point standing on ceremony now, is there?"

Samad was glad this was so. He said as much. He took a moment to look with the necessary admiration around the room with its relentless flashes of gold, its thick pile carpet, its furnishings in various shades of yellow and green. One had to admire Ardashir's business sense. He had taken the simple idea of an Indian restaurant (small room, pink tablecloth, loud music, atrocious wallpaper, meals) and just made it bigger. He hadn't improved anything; it was the same old crap but bigger in a bigger building in the biggest tourist trap in London. Leicester Square. You had to admire it and admire the man, who now sat like a benign locust, his slender insectile body swamped in a black leather chair, leaning over the desk, all smiles, a parasite disguised as a philanthropist.

"Cousin, what can I do for you?"

Samad took a deep breath. The matter was . . . what was the matter? The house was the matter. Samad was moving out of East London (where one couldn't bring up children, indeed, one couldn't, not if one didn't wish them to come to bodily harm), from East London, with its National Front gangs, to North London, north-west in fact, where things were more . . . more . . . liberal. Ardashir's eyes glazed over a little as Samad explained his situation. His skinny legs twitched beneath the desk, and in his fingers he manipulated a paperclip until it looked reasonably like an *A*. *A* for Ardashir.

"I need only a small wage increase to help me finance the move. To make things a little easier as we settle in. And Alsana, well, she is pregnant."

Pregnant. Difficult. Ardashir realized the case called for extreme diplomacy.

"Don't mistake me, Samad, we are both intelligent, frank men and I think I can speak frankly . . . I know you're not a *fucking* waiter—" he whispered the expletive and smiled indulgently after it, as if it were a naughty, private thing that brought them closer together, "I see your position . . . of course I do . . . but you must understand mine . . . If I made allowances for every relative I employ I'd be walking around like bloody Mr. Gandhi. Without a pot to piss in. Spinning my thread by the light of the moon. An example: at this very moment that wastrel Fat Elvis brother-in-law of mine, Hussein Ishmael—"

"The butcher?"

"The butcher, demands that I should raise the price I pay for his stinking meat! 'But Ardashir, we are brothers-in-law!' he is saying to me. And I am saying to him, but Mohammed, this is *retail*..."

It was Samad's turn to glaze over. He thought of his wife, Alsana, who was not as meek as he had assumed when they married, to whom he must deliver the bad news: Alsana, who was prone to moments, even fits—yes, fits was not too strong a word—of rage. Cousins, aunts, brothers thought it a bad sign. They wondered if there wasn't some "funny mental history" in Alsana's family, they sympathized with him the way you sympathize with a man who has bought a stolen car with more mileage on it than first thought. In his naivety Samad had simply assumed a woman so young would be . . . easy. But Alsana was not . . . no, she was not easy. It was, he supposed, the way with young women these days.

Ardashir came to the end of what he felt was his perfectly worded speech, sat back satisfied, and laid the *M* for Mukhul he had moulded next to the *A* for Ardashir that sat on his lap.

"Thank you, Sir," said Samad. "Thank you so very much."

That evening there was an awful row. Alsana slung the sewing machine, with the black studded hot pants she was working on, to the floor.

"Useless! Tell me, Samad Miah, what is the point of moving here—nice house, yes very nice, very nice—but where is the food?"

"It is a nice area, we have friends here . . ."

"Who are they?" she slammed her little fist on to the kitchen table, sending the salt and pepper flying to collide spectacularly with each other in the air. "I don't know them! You fight in an old, forgotten war with some Englishman . . . married to a black! Whose friends are they? These are the people my child will grow up around? Their children—half blacky-white? But tell me," she shouted, returning to her favoured topic, "where is our food?"

Theatrically, she threw open every cupboard in the kitchen, "Where is it? Can we eat china?"

Two plates smashed to the floor. She patted her stomach to indicate her unborn child and pointed to the pieces, "Hungry?"

Samad, who had an equally melodramatic nature when prompted, yanked open the freezer and pulled out a mountain of meat which he piled in the middle of the room. His mother worked through the night preparing meals for her family, he said. His mother did not, he said, spend the household money, as Alsana did, on prepared meals, yogurts and tinned spaghetti. Alsana punched him full square in the stomach.

"Samad Iqbal the traditionalist! Why don't I just squat in the street over a bucket and wash clothes? Eh? In fact, what about my clothes? Edible?"

As Samad clutched his winded belly, there in the kitchen she ripped to shreds every stitch she had on and added them to the pile of frozen lamb, spare cuts from the restaurant. She stood naked before him for a moment, the as yet small mound of her pregnancy in full view, then put on a long, brown coat and left the house.

But all the same, she reflected, slamming the door behind her, it was a nice area; she couldn't deny it as she stormed towards the high street, avoiding pavement trees where previously, in Whitechapel, she had avoided flung-out mattresses and the homeless. It would be good for the child. Alsana had a deep-seated belief that living near green spaces was morally beneficial to the young and there to her right was Gladstone Park, a sweeping horizon of green named after the Liberal prime minister (Alsana was from a respected old Bengal family and had read her English History), and in the Liberal tradition it was a park without fences, unlike the more affluent Queen's Park (Victoria's) with its pointed metal railings. Willesden was not as pretty as Queen's Park but it was a nice area. No denying it. No NF kids breaking the basement windows with their steel-capped boots like in Whitechapel. Now she was pregnant she needed a little bit of peace and quiet. Though it was the same here in a way; they all looked at her strangely, this tiny Indian woman stalking the high street in a mackintosh, her plentiful hair flying every which way. *Mali's Kebabs, Mr. Cheungs, Raj's, Malkovich Bakeries*—she read the new, unfamiliar signs as she passed. She was shrewd. She saw what this was. "Liberal? Hosh-kosh nonsense!" No one was more liberal than anyone else anywhere anyway. It was only that here, in Willesden, there wasn't enough of any one thing to gang up against any other thing and send it running to the cellars while windows were smashed.

"Survival is what it is about!" she concluded out loud (she spoke to her baby: she liked to give it one sensible thought a day), making the bell above Crazy Shoes tinkle as she opened the door. Her niece Neena worked here. It was an old-fashioned cobbler's. Neena fixed heels back on to stilettos.

"Alsana, you look like dog shit," Neena called over in Bengali. "What is that horrible coat?"

"It's none of your business is what it is," replied Alsana in English. "I came to collect my husband's shoes not to chit-chat with Niece-Of-Shame."

Neena was used to this, and now Alsana had moved to Willesden there would only be more of it. It used to come in longer sentences (such as, "Niece, you have brought nothing but shame . . ."), but now because Alsana no longer had the time or energy to summon up the necessary shock each time, it had become abridged to Niece-Of-Shame, an all-purpose tag that summed up the general feeling.

"See these soles?" said Neena, taking Samad's shoes off the shelf and handing Alsana the little blue ticket. "They were so worn through, Aunty Alsi, I had to reconstruct them from the very base. From the base! What does he do in them? Run marathons?"

"He works," replied Alsana tersely. "And prays," she added, for she liked to make a point of her respectability, and besides she was really very traditional, very religious, lacking nothing except the faith.

"And don't call me Aunty, I am only two years older than you."

Alsana swept the shoes into a plastic carrier bag and turned to leave.

"I thought that praying was done on people's knees," said Neena, laughing lightly.

"Both, both, asleep, waking, walking," snapped Alsana, as she passed under the tinkly bell once more. "We are never out of sight of the Creator."

"How's the new house, then?" Neena called after her.

But she had gone. Neena shook her head and sighed as she watched her young aunt disappear down the road like a little brown bullet. Alsana. She was young and old at the same time, Neena reflected. She acted so sensible, so straight-down-the-line in her long sensible coat, but you got the feeling—

"Oi! Miss! There's shoes back here that need your attention!" came a voice from the storeroom.

"Keep your tits on," said Neena.

At the corner of the road, Alsana popped behind the post office and removed her pinchy sandals in favour of Samad's shoes. (It was an oddity about Alsana. She was small but her feet were enormous, as if she had more growing to do.) In seconds she whipped her hair into an efficient bun, and wrapped her coat tighter around her to keep out the wind. Then she set off, past the library and up a long green road she had never walked along before. "Survival is all, Little Iqbal," she said to her bump once more. "Survival."

Clara was also pregnant. When their bumps became too large and cinema seats no longer accommodated them, the two women began to meet up for lunch in Kilburn Park, often with the Niece-Of-Shame, the three of them squeezed on to a generous bench, Alsana pressing a thermos of PG Tips into Clara's hand, without milk, with lemon. Unwrapping several layers of cling film to reveal today's peculiar delight: savoury dough-like balls, crumbly Indian sweets shot through with the colours of the kaleidoscope, thin pastry with spiced beef inside, salad with onion, she says to Clara: "Eat up! Stuff yourself silly! They're in there, wallowing around in your belly, waiting for the menu. Woman, don't torture them! You want to starve the bumps?" for, despite appearances, there are six people on that bench (three living, three coming); one girl for Clara, two boys for Alsana.

Alsana says: "Nobody's complaining, let's get that straight. A boy is good and two boys is bloody good. But I tell you, when I turned my head and saw the ultra-business thingummybob—"

"Ultrasound," corrects Clara, through a mouthful of rice.

"—Yes, I almost had the heart attack to finish me off! Two! Feeding one is enough!"

Clara laughs and says she can imagine Samad's face when he saw it.

"No dearie,"—Alsana is reproving, tucking her large feet underneath the folds of her sari, "he didn't see anything. He wasn't there. I am not letting him see things like that. A woman has to have the private things—a husband needn't be involved in body-business, in a lady's . . . *parts*."

Niece-Of-Shame, who is sat between them, sucks her teeth.

"Bloody Hell, Alsi, he must have been involved in your parts sometime, or is this the immaculate bloody conception?"

"So rude," says Alsana to Clara in a snooty, English way. "Too old to be so rude and too young to know any better." And then Clara and Alsana, with the accidental mirroring that happens when two people are sharing the same experience, both lay their hands on their bulges.

Neena, to redeem herself: "Yeah, well how are you doing on names? Any ideas?"

Alsana is decisive. "*Magid* and *Millat*. Ems are good. Ems are strong. Mahatma, Mohammed, that funny Mr. Morecambe, from Morecambe and Wise—letter you can trust."

But Clara is more cautious, because naming seems to her a fearful responsibility, a godlike task for a mere mortal: "I tink I like *Irie*. It patois. Means everyting OK, cool, peaceful, you know?"

Alsana is mock-horrified before the sentence is finished, "'OK'? This is a name for a child? You might as well call her 'Wouldsirlikeanypopadumswiththat?' or 'Niceweatherwearehaving'—"

". . . and Archie likes *Sarah*. Well, dere not much you can argue wid Sarah, but dere's not much to get happy bout either. I suppose if it was good enough for the wife of Abraham . . ."

"Ibrahim," Alsana corrects, out of instinct more than Koranic pedantry. "Popping out babies when she was a hundred years old, by the grace of Allah."

And then Neena, groaning at the turn the conversation is taking: "Well I *like* Irie. It's funky. It's different."

Alsana loves this: "For pity's sake, what does Archibald know about *funky* and *different*? If I were you, dearie," she says patting Clara's knee, "I'd choose Sarah and let that be an end to it. Sometimes you have to let these men have it their way. Anything for a little—how do you say it in the English? For a little—" she puts her finger over tightly pursed lips, like a guard at the gate, "—*shush*."

But in response Niece-Of-Shame bats her voluminous eyelashes, wraps her college scarf round her head like purdah, and says, "Oh yes, Auntie, yes, the little submissive Indian woman. You don't talk to him, he talks at you. You scream and shout at each other, but there's no communication. And in the end he wins anyway because he does whatever he likes when he likes. You don't even know where he is, what he does, what he *feels*, half the time. It's 1975, Alsi. You can't conduct relationships like that any more. It's not like back home. There has to be communication between men and women in the West, they've got to listen to each other, otherwise . . ." Neena mimes a small mushroom cloud going off in her hand.

"What a load of the codswallop," says Alsana sonorously, closing her eyes, shaking her head. "It is you who do not listen. By Allah, I will always give as good as I get. But you presume I *care* what he does. You presume I want to *know*. The truth is, for a marriage to survive you don't need all this talk, talk, talk; all this 'I am this' and 'I am really like this' like on the television, all this revelation—especially when your husband is old, when he is wrinkly and falling apart—you do not *want* to know what is slimy underneath the bed and rattling in the wardrobe."

Neena frowns. Clara cannot raise serious objection, and the rice is handed around once more.

"Moreover," says Alsana after a pause, folding her dimpled arms underneath her breasts, pleased to be holding forth on a subject close to this formidable bosom, "when you are from families such as ours you should have learned that *silence*, what is *not* said, is the very *best* recipe for family life."

"So let me get this straight," says Neena, derisively. "You're saying that a good dose of repression keeps a marriage healthy?"

And as if someone had pressed a button, Alsana is outraged: "Repression! Nonsense silly-billy word! I'm just talking about common sense. What is my husband? What is yours?" she says pointing to Clara. "Twenty-five years they live before we are even born. What are they? What are they capable of? What blood do they have on their hands? What is sticky and smelly in their private areas? Who knows?" She throws her hands up, releasing the questions into the unhealthy Kilburn air, sending a troupe of sparrows up with them.

"What you don't understand, my Niece-Of-Shame, what none of your generation understand—"

"But Auntie," begs Neena, raising her voice, because this is what she really wants to argue about—the largest sticking point between the two of them—Alsana's arranged marriage, "how could you bear to marry someone you didn't know from Adam?"

In response, an infuriating wink. Alsana always likes to appear jovial at the very moment that her interlocutor becomes hot under the collar. "Because, *Miss*

Smarty-pants, it is by far the easier option. It was exactly because Eve did not know Adam from Adam that they got on so A-OK. Let me explain. Yes, I was married to Samad Iqbal the same evening of the very day I met him. Yes, I didn't know him from Adam. But I liked him well enough. We met in the breakfast room on a steaming Dhaka day and he fanned me with *The Times*. I thought he had a good face, a sweet voice, and his backside was high and well formed for a man of his age. Very good. Now every time I learn something more about him *I like him less*. So you see, we were better off the way we were."

Neena stamps her foot in exasperation at the skewed logic.

"—Besides, I will never know him well. Getting anything out of my husband is like trying to squeeze water out when you're stoned."

Neena laughs despite herself, "Water out of a stone."

"Yes, yes. You think I'm so stupid. But I am wise about things like men. I tell you," Alsana prepares to deliver her summation as she has seen it done many years previously by the young Dhaka lawyers with their slick side-partings, "men are the last mystery. God is easy compared with men. Now, enough of the philosophy. Sarnosa?"

She peels the lid off the plastic tub and sits fat, pretty and satisfied on her conclusion.

"Shame that you're having them," says Neena to her aunt, lighting a fag. "Boys, I mean. Shame that you're going to have boys."

"What do you mean?"

This is Clara, who has secretly subscribed (a secret from Alsana and Archie) to a lending library of Neena's through which she has read, in a few short months, *The Female Eunuch* by Greer, *Sex, Race and Class* by Selma James and Jong's *Fear of Flying* all in a clandestine attempt, on Neena's part, to rid Clara of her "false consciousness."

"I mean, I just think men have caused enough chaos this century. There's enough bloody men in the world. If I knew I was going to have a boy . . ." she pauses to prepare her two falsely conscious friends for this new concept, "I'd have to seriously consider abortion."

Alsana screams, claps her hands over one of her own ears and one of Clara's, and then almost chokes on a piece of aubergine with the physical exertion. For some reason the remark simultaneously strikes Clara as funny: hysterically, desperately funny, miserably funny; and the Niece-Of-Shame sits between them, nonplussed, while the two egg-shaped women bend over themselves, one in laughter, the other in horror and near asphyxiation.

"Are you all right, ladies?" It is Sol Jozefowicz, the park keeper, standing in front of them, ready as always to be of aid.

"We are all going to burn in hell, Mr. Jozefowicz, if you call that being all right . . ." explains Alsana, pulling herself together.

Niece-Of-Shame rolls her eyes: "Speak for yourself."

But Alsana is faster than any sniper when it comes to firing back: "I do, I do—thankfully Allah has arranged it that way."

"Good afternoon, Neena, good afternoon, Mrs. Jones," says Sol, offering a neat bow to each. "Are you sure you are all right? Mrs. Jones?"

Clara cannot stop the tears from squeezing out of the corners of her eyes. She cannot work out, at this moment, whether she is crying or laughing; the two states suddenly seem only a stone's throw from each other.

"I'm fine, fine. Sorry to have worried you, Mr. Jozefowicz. Really, I'm fine."

"I do not see what so very funny-funny," mutters Alsana. "The murder of innocents—is this funny?"

"Not in my experience, Mrs. Iqbal, no," says Sol Jozefowicz in the collected manner in which he says everything, passing his handkerchief to Clara. It strikes all three women—the way history will: embarrassingly, without warning, like a blush—what the park keeper's experience might have been. They fall silent.

"Well, as long as you ladies are fine, I'll be getting on," says Sol, motioning that Clara can keep the handkerchief and replacing the hat he had removed in the old fashion. He bows his neat little bow once more, and sets off slowly anticlockwise round the park.

Once Sol is out of earshot Neena says: "OK, Aunty Alsi. I apologize. I apologize . . . What more do you want?"

"Oh, every-bloody-thing," says Alsana, her voice losing the fight, becoming vulnerable. "The whole bloody universe made clear—in a little nutshell. I cannot understand a thing any more, and I am just beginning. You understand?"

She sighs, not waiting for an answer, not looking at Neena, but across the way at the hunched, disappearing figure of Sol winding in and out of the yew trees. "You may be right about Samad . . . about many things . . . maybe there are no good men, not even the two in this belly . . . and maybe I do not talk enough with mine, maybe I have married a stranger . . . you might see the truth better than I . . . what do I know, a barefoot country girl who never went to the universities . . ."

"Oh, Alsi," Neena keeps saying, weaving her regret in and out of Alsana's words like tapestry, feeling bad, "you know I didn't mean it like that."

"But I cannot be worrying-worrying all the time about the truth. I have to worry about the truth that can be lived with. And that is the difference between losing your marbles drinking the salty sea, or swallowing the stuff from the streams. My Niece-Of-Shame believes in the talking cure, eh?" says Alsana, with something of a grin. "Talk, talk, talk and it will be better. Be honest, slice open your heart and spread the red stuff around. But the past is made of more than words, dearie. We married old men, you see? These bumps," Alsana pats them both, "they will always have Daddy-long-legs for fathers. One leg in the present, one in the past. No talking will change this. Their roots will always be tangled."

Just as he reaches the far gate, Sol Jozefowicz turns round to wave, and the three women wave back. And Clara feels a little theatrical, flying the park keeper's cream handkerchief above her head. As if she is seeing someone off on a train journey which crosses the border of two countries.

FOR INFORMAL WRITING

In what ways do aspects of the characters' experience ring true, based on your observations or experience? Why?

FOR DISCUSSION

1. "In his naivety Samad had simply assumed a woman so young would be . . . easy." What are Samad's assumptions? What are his conclusions?
2. How does Alsana try to follow her culture's traditional roles? What is her conflict?
3. How does the following passage speak to the larger themes and issues of this story?

> I am not a waiter. That is, I am a waiter, but not just a waiter. I have been a student, a scientist, a soldier. My wife is called Alsana. We live in East London but we would like to move north. I am a muslim but Allah has forsaken me or i have forsaken Allah. I'm not sure. I have an English friend—Archie—and others. I am forty-nine but women still turn in the street. Sometimes.

What is the significance of this passage? Why do you think so?

FOR WRITING

How does Smith use instances of language and gender to explore issues of assimilation and culture? For instance, consider the character of Alsana, and Samad's observations about her.

The Perils of Indifference (1999)
Elie Wiesel (1928–2016)

Auschwitz survivor, author, activist, teacher, and recipient of the Nobel Peace Prize, the Presidential Medal of Freedom, the Congressional Gold Medal, and numerous other awards, Elie Wiesel was born in Romania. Wiesel lost his mother, father, and younger sister in Nazi concentration camps during World War II and learned much later that his two older sisters had survived. He swore never to write about his experiences in the camps because he felt he could never accurately depict their horrors; however, he had a chance of heart in the 1950s when French novelist François Mauriac convinced him to tell his story. The result was Night *(1960), about a teenage boy who survived the camps. In all, he wrote more than forty books, many depicting the horrible and inhumane treatment suffered during the Holocaust. When Wiesel received the Nobel Peace Prize in 1986, the Nobel Committee called him "a messenger to mankind." This speech was delivered in Washington, DC, in 1999.*

Mr. President, Mrs. Clinton, members of Congress, Ambassador Holbrooke, Excellencies, friends:

Fifty-four years ago to the day, a young Jewish boy from a small town in the Carpathian Mountains woke up, not far from Goethe's beloved Weimar, in a place of eternal infamy called Buchenwald. He was finally free, but there was no joy in his heart. He thought there never would be again.

Liberated a day earlier by American soldiers, he remembers their rage at what they saw. And even if he lives to be a very old man, he will always be grateful to them for that rage, and also for their compassion. Though he did not understand their language, their eyes told him what he needed to know— that they, too, would remember, and bear witness.

By permission of The Elie Wiesel Foundation For Humanity.

And now, I stand before you, Mr. President—Commander-in-Chief of the army that freed me, and tens of thousands of others—and I am filled with a profound and abiding gratitude to the American people.

Gratitude is a word that I cherish. Gratitude is what defines the humanity of the human being. And I am grateful to you, Hillary—or Mrs. Clinton—for what you said, and for what you are doing for children in the world, for the homeless, for the victims of injustice, the victims of destiny and society. And I thank all of you for being here.

We are on the threshold of a new century, a new millennium. What will the legacy of this vanishing century be? How will it be remembered in the new millennium? Surely it will be judged, and judged severely, in both moral and metaphysical terms. These failures have cast a dark shadow over humanity: two World Wars, countless civil wars, the senseless chain of assassinations—Gandhi, the Kennedys, Martin Luther King, Sadat, Rabin—bloodbaths in Cambodia and Nigeria, India and Pakistan, Ireland and Rwanda, Eritrea and Ethiopia, Sarajevo and Kosovo; the inhumanity in the gulag and the tragedy of Hiroshima. And, on a different level, of course, Auschwitz and Treblinka. So much violence, so much indifference.

What is indifference? Etymologically, the word means "no difference." A strange and unnatural state in which the lines blur between light and darkness, dusk and dawn, crime and punishment, cruelty and compassion, good and evil.

What are its courses and inescapable consequences? Is it a philosophy? Is there a philosophy of indifference conceivable? Can one possibly view indifference as a virtue? Is it necessary at times to practice it simply to keep one's sanity, live normally, enjoy a fine meal and a glass of wine, as the world around us experiences harrowing upheavals?

Of course, indifference can be tempting—more than that, seductive. It is so much easier to look away from victims. It is so much easier to avoid such rude interruptions to our work, our dreams, our hopes. It is, after all, awkward, troublesome, to be involved in another person's pain and despair. Yet, for the person who is indifferent, his or her neighbor are of no consequence. And, therefore, their lives are meaningless. Their hidden or even visible anguish is of no interest. Indifference reduces the other to an abstraction.

Over there, behind the black gates of Auschwitz, the most tragic of all prisoners were the "Muselmanner," as they were called. Wrapped in their torn blankets, they would sit or lie on the ground, staring vacantly into space, unaware of who or where they were, strangers to their surroundings. They no longer felt pain, hunger, thirst. They feared nothing. They felt nothing. They were dead and did not know it.

Rooted in our tradition, some of us felt that to be abandoned by humanity then was not the ultimate. We felt that to be abandoned by God was worse than to be punished by Him. Better an unjust God than an indifferent one. For us to be ignored by God was a harsher punishment than to be a victim of His anger. Man can live far from God—not outside God. God is wherever we are. Even in suffering? Even in suffering.

In a way, to be indifferent to that suffering is what makes the human being inhuman. Indifference, after all, is more dangerous than anger and hatred. Anger can at times be creative. One writes a great poem, a great symphony, one does something special for the sake of humanity because one is angry at the injustice that one witnesses. But indifference is never creative. Even hatred at times may elicit a response. You fight it. You denounce it. You disarm it. Indifference elicits no response. Indifference is not a response.

Indifference is not a beginning, it is an end. And, therefore, indifference is always the friend of the enemy, for it benefits the aggressor—never his victim, whose pain is magnified when he or she feels forgotten. The political prisoner in his cell, the hungry children, the homeless refugees—not to respond to their plight, not to relieve their solitude by offering them a spark of hope is to exile them from human memory. And in denying their humanity we betray our own.

Indifference, then, is not only a sin, it is a punishment. And this is one of the most important lessons of this outgoing century's wide-ranging experiments in good and evil.

In the place that I come from, society was composed of three simple categories: the killers, the victims, and the bystanders. During the darkest of times, inside the ghettoes and death camps—and I'm glad that Mrs. Clinton mentioned that we are now commemorating that event, that period, that we are now in the Days of Remembrance—but then, we felt abandoned, forgotten. All of us did.

And our only miserable consolation was that we believed that Auschwitz and Treblinka were closely guarded secrets; that the leaders of the free world did not know what was going on behind those black gates and barbed wire; that they had no knowledge of the war against the Jews that Hitler's armies and their accomplices waged as part of the war against the Allies.

If they knew, we thought, surely those leaders would have moved heaven and earth to intervene. They would have spoken out with great outrage and conviction. They would have bombed the railways leading to Birkenau, just the railways, just once.

And now we knew, we learned, we discovered that the Pentagon knew, the State Department knew. And the illustrious occupant of the White House then, who was a great leader—and I say it with some anguish and pain, because, today is exactly 54 years marking his death—Franklin Delano Roosevelt died on April the 12th, 1945, so he is very much present to me and to us.

No doubt, he was a great leader. He mobilized the American people and the world, going into battle, bringing hundreds and thousands of valiant and brave soldiers in America to fight fascism, to fight dictatorship, to fight Hitler. And so many of the young people fell in battle. And, nevertheless, his image in Jewish history—I must say it—his image in Jewish history is flawed.

The depressing tale of the *St. Louis* is a case in point. Sixty years ago, its human cargo—maybe 1,000 Jews—was turned back to Nazi Germany. And that happened after the Kristallnacht, after the first state-sponsored pogrom, with hundreds of Jewish shops destroyed, synagogues burned, thousands of people put in concentration camps. And that ship, which was already on the shores of the United States, was sent back.

I don't understand. Roosevelt was a good man, with a heart. He understood those who needed help. Why didn't he allow these refugees to disembark? A thousand people—in America, a great country, the greatest democracy, the most generous of all new nations in modern history. What happened? I don't understand. Why the indifference, on the highest level, to the suffering of the victims?

But then, there were human beings who were sensitive to our tragedy. Those non-Jews, those Christians, that we called the "Righteous Gentiles," whose selfless acts of heroism saved the honor of their faith. Why were they so few? Why was there a greater effort to save SS murderers after the war than to save their victims during the war?

Why did some of America's largest corporations continue to do business with Hitler's Germany until 1942? It has been suggested, and it was documented, that the Wehrmacht could not have conducted its invasion of France without oil obtained from American sources. How is one to explain their indifference?

And yet, my friends, good things have also happened in this traumatic century: the defeat of Nazism, the collapse of communism, the rebirth of Israel on its ancestral soil, the demise of apartheid, Israel's peace treaty with Egypt, the peace accord in Ireland. And let us remember the meeting, filled with drama and emotion, between Rabin and Arafat that you, Mr. President, convened in this very place. I was here and I will never forget it.

And then, of course, the joint decision of the United States and NATO to intervene in Kosovo and save those victims, those refugees, those who were uprooted by a man whom I believe that because of his crimes, should be charged with crimes against humanity. But this time, the world was not silent. This time, we do respond. This time, we intervene.

Does it mean that we have learned from the past? Does it mean that society has changed? Has the human being become less indifferent and more human?

Have we really learned from our experiences? Are we less insensitive to the plight of victims of ethnic cleansing and other forms of injustices in places near and far? Is today's justified intervention in Kosovo, led by you, Mr. President, a lasting warning that never again will the deportation, the terrorization of children and their parents be allowed anywhere in the world? Will it discourage other dictators in other lands to do the same?

What about the children? Oh, we see them on television, we read about them in the papers, and we do so with a broken heart. Their fate is always the most tragic, inevitably. When adults wage war, children perish. We see their faces, their eyes. Do we hear their pleas? Do we feel their pain, their agony? Every minute one of them dies of disease, violence, famine. Some of them—so many of them—could be saved.

And so, once again, I think of the young Jewish boy from the Carpathian Mountains. He has accompanied the old man I have become throughout these years of quest and struggle. And together we walk towards the new millennium, carried by profound fear and extraordinary hope.

FOR INFORMAL WRITING

At one point, Wiesel asks, "What is indifference?" How might you answer this question, looking to the speech for guidance?

FOR DISCUSSION

1. How does Wiesel's personal tragedy inform his humanitarian view?
2. Look carefully at the language of this speech. What in the language and tone lets you know that this is a speech?
3. At one point in the speech, Wiesel asks whether we have learned from the past. Have we?

FOR WRITING

Research the contradictory ethical attributes of President Franklin Delano Roosevelt, considered overall and for many good reasons to be among our greatest presidents. What does Wiesel say about him, generally? Why does Wiesel conclude that "nevertheless, his image in Jewish history—I must say it—his image in Jewish history is flawed."

Fast Food Nation, an Excerpt (2000)
Eric Schlosser (1959–)

A journalist, Eric Schlosser has investigated everything from fast food to the drug market to nuclear weapons. He is also a documentary filmmaker and a playwright. Schlosser was a finalist for the Pulitzer Prize for journalism for Command and Control *(2013), about the nuclear arsenal during the Cold War between the United States and the Soviet Union. He served as co-executive producer of a feature documentary,* There Will be Blood *(2014), and as co-producer of* Food, Inc. *(2008). The following excerpt is the introduction to* Fast Food Nation, *the project that brought Schlosser national attention.*

Cheyenne Mountain sits on the eastern slope of Colorado's Front Range, rising steeply from the prairie and overlooking the city of Colorado Springs. From a distance, the mountain appears beautiful and serene, dotted with rocky outcroppings, scrub oak, and ponderosa pine. It looks like the backdrop of an old Hollywood western, just another gorgeous Rocky Mountain vista. And yet Cheyenne Mountain is hardly pristine. One of the nation's most important military installations lies deep within it, housing units of the North American Aerospace Command, the Air Force Space Command, and the United States Space Command. During the mid-1950s, high-level officials at the Pentagon worried that America's air defenses had become vulnerable to sabotage and attack. Cheyenne Mountain was chosen as the site for a top-secret, underground combat operations center. The mountain was hollowed out, and fifteen buildings, most of them three stories high, were erected amid a maze of tunnels and passageways extending for miles. The four-and-a-half-acre underground complex was designed to survive a direct hit by an atomic bomb. Now officially

---

"Introduction" and "What We Eat" from FAST FOOD NATION: The Dark Side of the All-American Meal by Eric Schlosser. Copyright © 2001 by Eric Schlosser. Reprinted by permission of Houghton Mifflin Harcourt Publishing Company. All rights reserved.

called the Cheyenne Mountain Air Force Station, the facility is entered through steel blast doors that are three feet thick and weigh twenty-five tons each; they automatically swing shut in less than twenty seconds. The base is closed to the public, and a heavily armed quick response team guards against intruders. Pressurized air within the complex prevents contamination by radioactive fallout and biological weapons. The buildings are mounted on gigantic steel springs to ride out an earthquake or the blast wave of a thermonuclear strike. The hallways and staircases are painted slate gray, the ceilings are low, and there are combination locks on many of the doors. A narrow escape tunnel, entered through a metal hatch, twists and turns its way out of the mountain through solid rock. The place feels like the set of an early James Bond movie, with men in jumpsuits driving little electric vans from one brightly lit cavern to another.

Fifteen hundred people work inside the mountain, maintaining the facility and collecting information from a worldwide network of radars, spy satellites, ground-based sensors, airplanes, and blimps. The Cheyenne Mountain Operations Center tracks every man-made object that enters North American airspace or that orbits the earth. It is the heart of the nation's early warning system. It can detect the firing of a long-range missile, anywhere in the world, before that missile has left the launch pad.

This futuristic military base inside a mountain has the capability to be self-sustaining for at least one month. Its generators can produce enough electricity to power a city the size of Tampa, Florida. Its underground reservoirs hold millions of gallons of water; workers sometimes traverse them in rowboats. The complex has its own underground fitness center, a medical clinic, a dentist's office, a barbershop, a chapel, and a cafeteria. When the men and women stationed at Cheyenne Mountain get tired of the food in the cafeteria, they often send somebody over to the Burger King at Fort Carson, a nearby army base. Or they call Domino's.

Almost every night, a Domino's deliveryman winds his way up the lonely Cheyenne Mountain Road, past the ominous DEADLY FORCE AUTHORIZED signs, past the security checkpoint at the entrance of the base, driving toward the heavily guarded North Portal, tucked behind chain link and barbed wire. Near the spot where the road heads straight into the mountainside, the delivery man drops off his pizzas and collects his tip. And should Armageddon come, should a foreign enemy someday shower the United States with nuclear warheads, laying waste to the whole continent, entombed within Cheyenne Mountain, along with the high-tech marvels, the pale blue jumpsuits, comic books, and Bibles, future archeologists may find other clues to the nature of our civilization—Big King wrappers, hardened crusts of Cheesy Bread, Barbeque Wing bones, and the red, white, and blue of a Domino's pizza box.

WHAT WE EAT

Over the last three decades, fast food has infiltrated every nook and cranny of American society. An industry that began with a handful of modest hot dog and hamburger stands in southern California has spread to every corner of the nation, selling a broad range of foods wherever paying customers may be found. Fast food is now served at restaurants and drive-throughs, at stadiums, airports, zoos, high schools, elementary schools, and universities, on cruise ships, trains, and airplanes, at K-Marts, Wal-Marts, gas stations, and even at hospital cafeterias. In 1970, Americans spent about $6 billion on fast food; in 2000, they spent more than $110 billion. Americans now spend more money on fast food than on higher education, personal computers, computer software, or new cars. They spend more on fast food than on movies, books, magazines, newspapers, videos, and recorded music—combined.

Pull open the glass door, feel the rush of cool air, walk in, get on line, study the backlit color photographs above the counter, place your order, hand over a few dollars, watch teenagers in uniforms pushing various buttons, and moments later take hold of a plastic tray full of food wrapped in colored paper and cardboard. The whole experience of buying fast food has become so routine, so thoroughly unexceptional and mundane, that it is now taken for granted, like brushing your teeth or stopping for a red light. It has become a social custom as American as a small, rectangular, hand-held, frozen, and reheated apple pie.

This is a book about fast food, the values it embodies, and the world it has made. Fast food has proven to be a revolutionary force in American life; I am interested in it both as a commodity and as a metaphor. What people eat (or don't eat) has always been determined by a complex interplay of social, economic, and technological forces. The early Roman Republic was fed by its citizen-farmers; the Roman Empire, by its slaves. A nation's diet can be more revealing than its art or literature. On any given day in the United States about one-quarter of the adult population visits a fast food restaurant. During a relatively brief period of time, the fast food industry has helped to transform not only the American diet, but also our landscape, economy, workforce, and popular culture. Fast food and its consequences have become inescapable, regardless of whether you eat it twice a day, try to avoid it, or have never taken a single bite.

The extraordinary growth of the fast food industry has been driven by fundamental changes in American society. Adjusted for inflation, the hourly wage of the average US worker peaked in 1973 and then steadily declined for the next twenty-five years. During that period, women entered the workforce in record numbers, often motivated less by a feminist perspective than by a need to pay the bills. In 1975, about one-third of American mothers with young children worked outside the home; today almost two-thirds of such mothers are employed. As the sociologists Cameron Lynne Macdonald and Carmen Sirianni have noted, the entry of so many women into the workforce has greatly increased demand for the types of services that housewives traditionally perform: cooking, cleaning, and child care. A generation ago, three-quarters of the money used to buy food in the United States was spent to prepare meals at home. Today about half of the money used to buy food is spent at restaurants—mainly at fast food restaurants.

The McDonald's Corporation has become a powerful symbol of America's service economy, which is now responsible for 90 percent of the country's new jobs. In 1968, McDonald's operated about one thousand restaurants. Today it has about twenty-eight thousand restaurants worldwide and opens almost two thousand new ones each year. An estimated one out of every eight workers in the United States has at some point been employed by McDonald's. The company annually hires about one million people, more than any other American organization, public or private. McDonald's is the nation's largest purchaser of beef, pork, and potatoes—and the second largest purchaser of chicken. The McDonald's Corporation is the largest owner of retail property in the world. Indeed, the company earns the majority of its profits not from selling food but from collecting rent. McDonald's spends more money on advertising and marketing than any other brand. As a result it has replaced Coca-Cola as the world's most famous brand. McDonald's operates more playgrounds than any other private entity in the United States. It is one of the nation's largest distributors of toys. A survey of American schoolchildren found that 96 percent could identify Ronald McDonald. The only fictional character with a higher degree of recognition was Santa Claus. The impact of McDonald's on the way we live today is hard to overstate. The Golden Arches are now more widely recognized than the Christian cross.

In the early 1970s, the farm activist Jim Hightower warned of the McDonaldization of America. He viewed the emerging fast food industry as a threat to independent businesses, as a step toward a food economy dominated by giant corporations, and as a homogenizing influence on American life. In *Eat Your Heart Out* (1975), he argued that bigger is not better. Much of what Hightower feared has come to pass. The centralized purchasing decisions of the large restaurant chains and their demand for standardized products have given a handful of corporations an unprecedented degree of power over the nation's food supply. Moreover, the tremendous success of the fast food industry has encouraged other industries to adopt similar business methods. The basic thinking behind fast food has become the operating system of today's retail economy, wiping out small businesses, obliterating regional differences, and spreading identical stores throughout the country like a self-replicating code.

America's main streets and malls now boast the same Pizza Huts and Taco Bells, Gaps and Banana Republics, Starbucks and Jiffy-Lubes, Foot Lockers, Snip N' Clips, Sunglass Huts, and Hobbytown USAs. Almost every facet of American life has now been franchised or chained. From the maternity ward at a Columbia/HCA hospital to an embalming room owned by Service Corporation International—the world's largest provider of death care services, based in Houston, Texas, which since 1968 has grown to include 3,823 funeral homes, 523 cemeteries, and 198 crematoriums, and which today handles the final remains of one out of every nine Americans—a person can now go from the cradle to the grave without spending a nickel at an independently owned business.

The key to a successful franchise, according to many texts on the subject, can be expressed in one word: uniformity. Franchises and chain stores strive to offer exactly the same product or service at numerous locations. Customers are drawn to familiar brands by an instinct to avoid the unknown. A brand offers a feeling of reassurance when its products are always and everywhere the same. "We have found out ... that we cannot trust some people who are nonconformists," declared Ray Kroc, one of the founders of McDonald's, angered by some of his franchisees. "We will make conformists out of them in a hurry ... The organization cannot trust the individual; the individual must trust the organization."

One of the ironies of America's fast food industry is that a business so dedicated to conformity was founded by iconoclasts and self-made men, by entrepreneurs willing to defy conventional opinion. Few of the people who built fast food empires ever attended college, let alone business school. They worked hard, took risks, and followed their own paths. In many respects, the fast food industry embodies the best and the worst of American capitalism at the start of the twenty-first century—its constant stream of new products and innovations, its widening gulf between rich and poor. The industrialization of the restaurant kitchen has enabled the fast food chains to rely upon a low-paid and unskilled workforce. While a handful of workers manage to rise up the corporate ladder, the vast majority lack full-time employment, receive no benefits, learn few skills, exercise little control over their workplace, quit after a few months, and float from job to job. The restaurant industry is now America's largest private employer, and it pays some of the lowest wages. During the economic boom of the 1990s, when many American workers enjoyed their first pay raises in a generation, the real value of wages in the restaurant industry continued to fall. The roughly 3.5 million fast food workers are by far the largest group of minimum wage earners in the United States. The only Americans who consistently earn a lower hourly wage are migrant farm workers.

A hamburger and french fries became the quintessential American meal in the 1950s, thanks to the promotional efforts of the fast food chains. The typical

American now consumes approximately three hamburgers and four orders of french fries every week. But the steady barrage of fast food ads, full of thick juicy burgers and long golden fries, rarely mentions where these foods come from nowadays or what ingredients they contain. The birth of the fast food industry coincided with Eisenhower-era glorifications of technology, with optimistic slogans like "Better Living through Chemistry" and "Our Friend the Atom." The sort of technological wizardry that Walt Disney promoted on television and at Disneyland eventually reached its fulfillment in the kitchens of fast food restaurants. Indeed, the corporate culture of McDonald's seems inextricably linked to that of the Disney empire, sharing a reverence for sleek machinery, electronics, and automation. The leading fast food chains still embrace a boundless faith in science—and as a result have changed not just what Americans eat, but also how their food is made.

The current methods for preparing fast food are less likely to be found in cookbooks than in trade journals such as *Food Technologist* and *Food Engineering*. Aside from the salad greens and tomatoes, most fast food is delivered to the restaurant already frozen, canned, dehydrated, or freeze-dried. A fast food kitchen is merely the final stage in a vast and highly complex system of mass production. Foods that may look familiar have in fact been completely reformulated. What we eat has changed more in the last forty years than in the previous forty thousand. Like Cheyenne Mountain, today's fast food conceals remarkable technological advances behind an ordinary-looking façade. Much of the taste and aroma of American fast food, for example, is now manufactured at a series of large chemical plants off the New Jersey Turnpike.

In the fast food restaurants of Colorado Springs, behind the counters, amid the plastic seats, in the changing landscape outside the window, you can see all the virtues and destructiveness of our fast food nation. I chose Colorado Springs as a focal point for this book because the changes that have recently swept through the city are emblematic of those that fast food—and the fast food mentality—have encouraged throughout the United States. Countless other suburban communities, in every part of the country, could have been used to illustrate the same points. The extraordinary growth of Colorado Springs neatly parallels that of the fast food industry: during the last few decades, the city's population has more than doubled. Subdivisions, shopping malls, and chain restaurants are appearing in the foothills of Cheyenne Mountain and the plains rolling to the east. The Rocky Mountain region as a whole has the fastest-growing economy in the United States, mixing high-tech and service industries in a way that may define America's workforce for years to come. And new restaurants are opening there at a faster pace than anywhere else in the nation.

Fast food is now so commonplace that it has acquired an air of inevitability, as though it were somehow unavoidable, a fact of modern life. And yet the dominance of the fast food giants was no more preordained than the march of colonial split-levels, golf courses, and man-made lakes across the deserts of the American West. The political philosophy that now prevails in so much of the West—with its demand for lower taxes, smaller government, an unbridled free market—stands in total contradiction to the region's true economic underpinnings. No other region of the United States has been so dependent on government subsidies for so long, from the nineteenth-century construction of its railroads to the twentieth-century financing of its military bases and dams. One historian has described the federal government's 1950s highway-building binge as a case study in interstate socialism—a phrase that aptly describes how the West was really won. The fast food industry took root alongside that interstate highway system, as a new form of restaurant sprang up beside the new off-ramps. Moreover, the extraordinary growth of this industry over the past quarter-century did not occur in a political vacuum. It took place during a period when the inflation-adjusted value of the minimum wage declined by about 40 percent, when sophisticated mass marketing techniques were for the first time directed at small children, and when federal agencies created to protect workers and consumers too often behaved like branch offices of the companies that were supposed to be regulated. Ever since the administration of President Richard Nixon, the fast food industry has worked closely with its allies in Congress and the White House to oppose new worker safety, food safety, and minimum wage laws. While publicly espousing support for the free market, the fast food chains have quietly pursued and greatly benefited from a wide variety of government subsidies. Far from being inevitable, America's fast food industry in its present form is the logical outcome of certain political and economic choices.

In the potato fields and processing plants of Idaho, in the ranchlands east of Colorado Springs, in the feedlots and slaughterhouses of the High Plains, you can see the effects of fast food on the nation's rural life, its environment, its workers, and its health. The fast food chains now stand atop a huge food-industrial complex that has gained control of American agriculture. During the 1980s, large multinationals—such as Cargill, ConAgra, and IBP—were allowed to dominate one commodity market after another. Farmers and cattle ranchers are losing their independence, essentially becoming hired hands for the agribusiness giants or being forced off the land. Family farms are now being replaced by gigantic corporate farms with absentee owners. Rural communities are losing their middle class and becoming socially stratified, divided between a small, wealthy elite and large numbers of the working poor. Small towns that seemingly belong in a Norman Rockwell painting are being turned into rural ghettos. The hardy, independent farmers whom Thomas Jefferson considered the bedrock of American democracy are a truly vanishing breed. The United States now has more prison inmates than full-time farmers.

The fast food chains' vast purchasing power and their demand for a uniform product have encouraged fundamental changes in how cattle are raised, slaughtered, and processed into ground beef. These changes have made meatpacking—once a highly skilled, highly paid occupation—into the most dangerous job in the United States, performed by armies of poor, transient immigrants whose injuries often go unrecorded and uncompensated. And the same meat industry practices that endanger these workers have facilitated the introduction of deadly pathogens, such as *E. coli* 0157:H7, into America's hamburger meat, a food aggressively marketed to children. Again and again, efforts to prevent the sale of tainted ground beef have been thwarted by meat industry lobbyists and their allies in Congress. The federal government has the legal authority to recall a defective toaster oven or stuffed animal—but still lacks the power to recall tons of contaminated, potentially lethal meat.

I do not mean to suggest that fast food is solely responsible for every social problem now haunting the United States. In some cases (such as the malling and sprawling of the West) the fast food industry has been a catalyst and a symptom of larger economic trends. In other cases (such as the rise of franchising and the spread of obesity) fast food has played a more central role. By tracing the diverse influences of fast food I hope to shed light not only on the workings of an important industry, but also on a distinctively American way of viewing the world.

Elitists have always looked down at fast food, criticizing how it tastes and regarding it as another tacky manifestation of American popular culture. The aesthetics of fast food are of much less concern to me than its impact upon the lives of ordinary Americans, both as workers and consumers. Most of all, I am concerned about its impact on the nation's children. Fast food is heavily marketed to children and prepared by people who are barely older than children. This is an industry that both feeds and feeds off the young. During the two years spent researching this book, I ate an enormous amount of fast food. Most of it tasted pretty good. That is one of the main reasons people buy fast food; it has been carefully designed to taste good. It's also inexpensive and convenient. But the value meals, two-for-one deals, and free refills of soda give a distorted sense of how much fast food actually costs. The real price never appears on the menu.

The sociologist George Ritzer has attacked the fast food industry for celebrating a narrow measure of efficiency over every other human value, calling the triumph of McDonald's the irrationality of rationality. Others consider the fast food industry proof of the nation's great economic vitality, a beloved American institution that appeals overseas to millions who admire our way of life. Indeed, the values, the culture, and the industrial arrangements of our fast food nation are now being exported to the rest of the world. Fast food has joined Hollywood movies, blue jeans, and pop music as one of America's most prominent cultural exports. Unlike other commodities, however, fast food isn't viewed, read, played, or worn. It enters the body and becomes part of the consumer. No other industry offers, both literally and figuratively, so much insight into the nature of mass consumption.

Hundreds of millions of people buy fast food every day without giving it much thought, unaware of the subtle and not so subtle ramifications of their purchases. They rarely consider where this food came from, how it was made, what it is doing to the community around them. They just grab their tray off the counter, find a table, take a seat, unwrap the paper, and dig in. The whole experience is transitory and soon forgotten. I've written this book out of a belief that people should know what lies behind the shiny, happy surface of every fast food transaction. They should know what really lurks between those sesame-seed buns. As the old saying goes: You are what you eat.

FOR INFORMAL WRITING

This book first appeared over twenty years ago. In what ways might the arguments in this excerpt still resonate? Is the United States still a "fast food nation?" Why or why not?

FOR DISCUSSION

1. According to Schlosser, how did industrialization and standardization enable fast food chains to become so commonplace in the United States?
2. What are the "values" embodied by fast food? How might you challenge these "values?"
3. How does the fast food industry transform our "landscape" and our "popular culture?" How might you imagine a time when there was no fast food?

FOR WRITING

In this excerpt, Schlosser alludes to the many cultural, economic, and social implications of the fast food industry, such as the low wages of workers, the influence of government lobbyists on what we eat, the culinary division between classes regarding food, and of course, the implications for our health. Choose one of these topics mentioned by Schlosser and research it more deeply, crafting an argument based on the information you find.

Why We Travel (2000)
Pico Iyer (1957–)

Pico Iyer is a travel writer, novelist, and blogger. His publishing agency says he is a "chronicler of the desire to seek new frontiers." Regarded as one of the greatest living travel writers by publications such as Outside *magazine, Iyer has written over a dozen works of creative nonfiction and has published several books, including* The Open Road *(2008),* The Art of Stillness: Adventures in Going Nowhere *(2014), and* Autumn Light: Season of Fire and Farewells *(2019). "Why We Travel" first appeared in* Salon *and is often considered to be a love letter to travel and travelers.*

We travel, initially, to lose ourselves; and we travel, next, to find ourselves. We travel to open our hearts and eyes and learn more about the world than our newspapers will accommodate. We travel to bring what little we can, in our ignorance and knowledge, to those parts of the globe whose riches are differently dispersed. And we travel, in essence, to become young fools again—to slow time down and get taken in, and fall in love once more. The beauty of this whole process was best described, perhaps, before people even took to frequent flying, by George Santayana in his lapidary essay, "The Philosophy of Travel." We "need sometimes," the Harvard philosopher wrote, "to escape into open solitudes, into aimlessness, into the moral holiday of running some pure hazard, in order to sharpen the edge of life, to taste hardship, and to be compelled to work desperately for a moment at no matter what."

I like that stress on work, since never more than on the road are we shown how proportional our blessings are to the difficulty that precedes them; and I like the stress on a holiday that's "moral" since we fall into our ethical habits as easily as into our beds at night. Few of us ever forget the connection between "travel"

By permission of Pico Iyer

and "travail," and I know that I travel in large part in search of hardship—both my own, which I want to feel, and others', which I need to see. Travel in that sense guides us toward a better balance of wisdom and compassion—of seeing the world clearly, and yet feeling it truly. For seeing without feeling can obviously be uncaring; while feeling without seeing can be blind.

Yet for me the first great joy of traveling is simply the luxury of leaving all my beliefs and certainties at home, and seeing everything I thought I knew in a different light, and from a crooked angle. In that regard, even a Kentucky Fried Chicken outlet (in Beijing) or a scratchy revival showing of *Wild Orchids* (on the Champs-Elysees) can be both novelty and revelation: In China, after all, people will pay a whole week's wages to eat with Colonel Sanders, and in Paris, Mickey Rourke is regarded as the greatest actor since Jerry Lewis.

If a Mongolian restaurant seems exotic to us in Evanston, Ill., it only follows that a McDonald's would seem equally exotic in Ulan Bator—or, at least, equally far from everything expected. Though it's fashionable nowadays to draw a distinction between the "tourist" and the "traveler," perhaps the real distinction lies between those who leave their assumptions at home, and those who don't: Among those who don't, a tourist is just someone who complains, "Nothing here is the way it is at home," while a traveler is one who grumbles, "Everything here is the same as it is in Cairo—or Cuzco or Kathmandu." It's all very much the same.

But for the rest of us, the sovereign freedom of traveling comes from the fact that it whirls you around and turns you upside down, and stands everything you took for granted on its head. If a diploma can famously be a passport (to a journey through hard realism), a passport can be a diploma (for a crash course in cultural relativism). And the first lesson we learn on the road, whether we like it or not, is how provisional and provincial are the things we imagine to be universal. When you go to North Korea, for example, you really do feel as if you've landed on a different planet—and the North Koreans doubtless feel that they're being visited by an extra-terrestrial, too (or else they simply assume that you, as they do, receive orders every morning from the Central Committee on what clothes to wear and what route to use when walking to work, and you, as they do, have loudspeakers in your bedroom broadcasting propaganda every morning at dawn, and you, as they do, have your radios fixed so as to receive only a single channel).

We travel, then, in part just to shake up our complacencies by seeing all the moral and political urgencies, the life-and-death dilemmas, that we seldom have to face at home. And we travel to fill in the gaps left by tomorrow's headlines: When you drive down the streets of Port-au-Prince, for example, where there is almost no paving and women relieve themselves next to mountains of trash, your notions of the Internet and a "one world order" grow usefully revised. Travel is the best way we have of rescuing the humanity of places, and saving them from abstraction and ideology.

And in the process, we also get saved from abstraction ourselves, and come to see how much we can bring to the places we visit, and how much we can become a kind of carrier pigeon—an anti-Federal Express, if you like—in transporting back and forth what every culture needs. I find that I always take Michael Jordan posters to Kyoto, and bring woven ikebana baskets back to California; I invariably travel to Cuba with a suitcase piled high with bottles of Tylenol and bars of soap, and come back with one piled high with salsa tapes, and hopes, and letters to long-lost brothers.

But more significantly, we carry values and beliefs and news to the places we go, and in many parts of the world, we become walking video screens and living newspapers, the only channels that can take people out of the censored limits of their homelands. In closed or impoverished places, like Pagan or Lhasa or Havana, we are the eyes and ears of the people we meet, their only contact with the world outside and, very often, the closest, quite literally, they will ever come to Michael Jackson or Bill Clinton. Not the least of the challenges of travel, therefore, is learning how to import—and export—dreams with tenderness.

By now all of us have heard (too often) the old Proust line about how the real voyage of discovery consists not in seeing new places but in seeing with new eyes. Yet one of the subtler beauties of travel is that it enables you to bring new eyes to the people you encounter. Thus even as holidays help you appreciate your own home more—not least by seeing it through a distant admirer's eyes—they help you bring newly appreciative—distant—eyes to the places you visit. You can teach them what they have to celebrate as much as you celebrate what they have to teach. This, I think, is how tourism, which so obviously destroys cultures, can also resuscitate or revive them, how it has created new "traditional" dances in Bali, and caused craftsmen in India to pay new attention to their works. If the first thing we can bring the Cubans is a real and balanced sense of what contemporary America is like, the second—and perhaps more important—thing we can bring them is a fresh and renewed sense of how special are the warmth and beauty of their country, for those who can compare it with other places around the globe.

Thus travel spins us round in two ways at once: It shows us the sights and values and issues that we might ordinarily ignore; but it also, and more deeply, shows us all the parts of ourselves that might otherwise grow rusty. For in traveling to a truly foreign place, we inevitably travel to moods and states of mind and hidden inward passages that we'd otherwise seldom have cause to visit.

On the most basic level, when I'm in Thailand, though a teetotaler who usually goes to bed at 9 p.m., I stay up till dawn in the local bars; and in Tibet, though not a real Buddhist, I spend days on end in temples, listening to the chants of sutras. I go to Iceland to visit the lunar spaces within me, and, in the uncanny quietude and emptiness of that vast and treeless world, to tap parts of myself generally obscured by chatter and routine.

We travel, then, in search of both self and anonymity—and, of course, in finding the one we apprehend the other. Abroad, we are wonderfully free of caste and job and standing; we are, as Hazlitt puts it, just the "gentlemen in the parlour," and people cannot put a name or tag to us. And precisely because we are clarified in this way, and freed of inessential labels, we have the opportunity to come into contact with more essential parts of ourselves (which may begin to explain why we may feel most alive when far from home).

Abroad is the place where we stay up late, follow impulse and find ourselves as wide open as when we are in love. We live without a past or future, for a moment at least, and are ourselves up for grabs and open to interpretation. We even may become mysterious—to others, at first, and sometimes to ourselves—and, as no less a dignitary than Oliver Cromwell once noted, "A man never goes so far as when he doesn't know where he is going."

There are, of course, great dangers to this, as to every kind of freedom, but the great promise of it is that, traveling, we are born again, and able to return at moments to a younger and a more open kind of self. Traveling is a way to reverse time, to a small extent, and make a day last a year—or at least 45 hours—and traveling is an easy way of surrounding ourselves, as in childhood, with what we cannot understand. Language facilitates this cracking open, for when we go to France, we often migrate to French, and the more childlike self, simple and polite, that speaking a foreign language educes. Even when I'm not speaking pidgin English in Hanoi, I'm simplified in a positive way, and concerned not with expressing myself, but simply making sense.

So travel, for many of us, is a quest for not just the unknown, but the unknowing; I, at least, travel in search of an innocent eye that can return me to a more innocent self. I tend to believe more abroad than I do at home (which, though treacherous again, can at least help me to extend my vision), and I tend to be more easily excited abroad, and even kinder. And since no one I meet can "place" me—no one can fix me in my risumi—I can remake myself for better, as well as, of course, for worse (if travel is notoriously a cradle for false identities, it can also, at its best, be a crucible for truer ones). In this way, travel can be a kind of monasticism on the move: On the road, we often live more simply (even when staying in a luxury hotel), with no more possessions than we can carry, and surrendering ourselves to chance.

This is what Camus meant when he said that "what gives value to travel is fear"—disruption, in other words, (or emancipation) from circumstance, and all the habits behind which we hide. And that is why many of us travel not in search of answers, but of better questions. I, like many people, tend to ask questions of the places I visit, and relish most the ones that ask the most searching questions back of me: In Paraguay, for example, where one car in every two is stolen, and two-thirds of the goods on sale are smuggled, I have to rethink my every Californian assumption. And in Thailand, where many young women give up their bodies in order to protect their families—to become better Buddhists—I have to question my own too-ready judgments. "The ideal travel book," Christopher Isherwood once said, "should be perhaps a little like a crime story in which you're in search of something." And it's the best kind of something, I would add, if it's one that you can never quite find.

I remember, in fact, after my first trips to Southeast Asia, more than a decade ago, how I would come back to my apartment in New York, and lie in my bed, kept up by something more than jet lag, playing back, in my memory, over and over, all that I had experienced, and paging wistfully though my photographs and reading and re-reading my diaries, as if to extract some mystery from them. Anyone witnessing this strange scene would have drawn the right conclusion: I was in love.

For if every true love affair can feel like a journey to a foreign country, where you can't quite speak the language, and you don't know where you're going, and you're pulled ever deeper into the inviting darkness, every trip to a foreign country can be a love affair, where you're left puzzling over who you are and whom you've fallen in love with. All the great travel books are love stories, by some reckoning—from the Odyssey and the Aeneid to the Divine Comedy and the New Testament—and all good trips are, like love, about being carried out of yourself and deposited in the midst of terror and wonder.

And what this metaphor also brings home to us is that all travel is a two-way transaction, as we too easily forget, and if warfare is one model of the meeting of nations, romance is another. For what we all too often ignore when we go abroad is that we are objects of scrutiny as much as the people we scrutinize, and we are being consumed by the cultures we consume, as much on the road as when we are at home. At the very least, we are objects of speculation (and even desire) who can seem as exotic to the people around us as they do to us.

We are the comic props in Japanese home-movies, the oddities in Maliese anecdotes and the fall-guys in Chinese jokes; we are the moving postcards or bizarre *objets trouves* that villagers in Peru will later tell their friends about. If travel is about the meeting of realities, it is no less about the mating of illusions: You give me my dreamed-of vision of Tibet, and I'll give you your wished-for California. And in truth, many of us, even (or especially) the ones who are fleeing America abroad, will get taken, willy-nilly, as symbols of the American Dream.

That, in fact, is perhaps the most central and most wrenching of the questions travel proposes to us: how to respond to the dream that people tender to you? Do you encourage their notions of a Land of Milk and Honey across the horizon, even if it is the same land you've abandoned? Or do you try to dampen their enthusiasm for a place that exists only in the mind? To quicken their dreams may, after all, be to match-make them with an illusion; yet to dash them may be to strip them of the one possession that sustains them in adversity.

That whole complex interaction—not unlike the dilemmas we face with those we love (how do we balance truthfulness and tact?)—is partly the reason why so many of the great travel writers, by nature, are enthusiasts: not just Pierre Loti, who famously, infamously, fell in love wherever he alighted (an archetypal sailor leaving offspring in the form of Madame Butterfly myths), but also Henry Miller, D. H. Lawrence or Graham Greene, all of whom bore out the hidden truth that we are optimists abroad as readily as pessimists as home. None of them was by any means blind to the deficiencies of the places around them, but all, having chosen to go there, chose to find something to admire.

All, in that sense, believed in "being moved" as one of the points of taking trips, and "being transported" by private as well as public means; all saw that "ecstasy" ("ex-stasis") tells us that our highest moments come when we're not stationary, and that epiphany can follow movement as much as it precipitates it. I remember once asking the great travel writer Norman Lewis if he'd ever be interested in writing on apartheid South Africa. He looked at me astonished. "To write well about a thing," he said, "I've got to like it!"

At the same time, as all this is intrinsic to travel, from Ovid to O'Rourke, travel itself is changing as the world does, and with it, the mandate of the travel writer. It's not enough to go to the ends of the earth these days (not least because the ends of the earth are often coming to you); and where a writer like Jan Morris could, a few years ago, achieve something miraculous simply by voyaging to all the great cities of the globe, now anyone with a Visa card can do that. So where Morris, in effect, was chronicling the last days of the Empire, a younger travel writer is in a better position to chart the first days of a new Empire, post-national, global, mobile and yet as diligent as the Raj in transporting its props and its values around the world.

In the mid-19th century, the British famously sent the Bible and Shakespeare and cricket round the world; now a more international kind of Empire is sending Madonna and the Simpsons and Brad Pitt. And the way in which each culture takes in this common pool of references tells you as much about them as their indigenous products might. Madonna in an Islamic country, after all, sounds radically different from Madonna in a Confucian one, and neither begins to mean the same as Madonna on East 14th Street. When you go to a McDonald's outlet in Kyoto, you will find Teriyaki McBurgers and Bacon Potato Pies. The placemats offer maps of the great temples of the city, and the posters all around broadcast the wonders of San Francisco. And—most crucial of all—the young people eating their Big Macs, with baseball caps worn backwards, and tight 501 jeans, are still utterly and inalienably Japanese in the way they move, they nod, they sip their Oolong teas—and never to be mistaken for the patrons of a McDonald's outlet in Rio, Morocco or Managua. These days a whole new realm of exotica arises out of the way one culture colors and appropriates the products of another.

The other factor complicating and exciting all of this is people, who are, more and more, themselves as many-tongued and mongrel as cities like Sydney or Toronto or Hong Kong. I am, in many ways, an increasingly typical specimen, if only because I was born, as the son of Indian parents, in England, moved to America at 7 and cannot really call myself an Indian, an American or an Englishman. I was, in short, a traveler at birth, for whom even a visit to the candy store was a trip through a foreign world where no one I saw quite matched my parents' inheritance, or my own. And though some of this is involuntary and tragic—the number of refugees in the world, which came to just 2.5 million in 1970, is now at least 27.4 million—it does involve, for some of us, the chance to be transnational in a happier sense, able to adapt anywhere, used to being outsiders everywhere and forced to fashion our own rigorous sense of home. (And if nowhere is quite home, we can be optimists everywhere.)

Besides, even those who don't move around the world find the world moving more and more around them. Walk just six blocks, in Queens or Berkeley, and you're traveling through several cultures in as many minutes; get into a cab outside the White House, and you're often in a piece of Addis Ababa. And technology, too, compounds this (sometimes deceptive) sense of availability, so that many people feel they can travel around the world without leaving the room—through cyberspace or CD-ROMs, videos and virtual travel. There are many challenges in this, of course, in what it says about essential notions of family and community and loyalty, and in the worry that air-conditioned, purely synthetic versions of places may replace the real thing—not to mention the fact that the world seems increasingly in flux, a moving target quicker than our notions of it. But there is, for the traveler at least, the sense that learning about home and learning about a foreign world can be one and the same thing.

All of us feel this from the cradle, and know, in some sense, that all the significant movement we ever take is internal. We travel when we see a movie, strike up a new friendship, get held up. Novels are often journeys as much as travel books are fictions; and though this has been true since at least as long ago as Sir John Mandeville's colorful 14th-century accounts of a Far East he'd never visited, it's an even more shadowy distinction now, as genre distinctions join other borders in collapsing.

In Mary Morris's *House Arrest*, a thinly disguised account of Castro's Cuba, the novelist reiterates, on the copyright page, "All dialogue is invented. Isabella, her family, the inhabitants and even *la isla* itself are creations of the author's imagination." On Page 172, however, we read, "*La isla*, of course, does exist. Don't let anyone fool you about that. It just feels as if it doesn't. But it does." No wonder the travel-writer narrator—a fictional construct (or not)?—confesses to devoting her travel magazine column to places that never existed. "Erewhon," after all, the undiscovered land in Samuel Butler's great travel novel, is just "nowhere" rearranged.

Travel, then, is a voyage into that famously subjective zone, the imagination, and what the traveler brings back is—and has to be—an ineffable compound of himself and the place, what's really there and what's only in him. Thus Bruce Chatwin's books seem to dance around the distinction between fact and fancy. V.S. Naipaul's recent book, *A Way in the World*, was published as a non-fictional "series" in England and a "novel" in the United States. And when some of the stories in Paul Theroux's half-invented memoir, *My Other Life*, were published in *The New Yorker*, they were slyly categorized as "Fact and Fiction."

And since travel is, in a sense, about the conspiracy of perception and imagination, the two great travel writers, for me, to whom I constantly return are Emerson and Thoreau (the one who famously advised that "traveling is a fool's paradise," and the other who "traveled a good deal in Concord"). Both of them insist on the fact that reality is our creation, and that we invent the places we see as much as we do the books that we read. What we find outside ourselves has to be inside ourselves for us to find it. Or, as Sir Thomas Browne sagely put it, "We carry within us the wonders we seek without us. There is Africa and her prodigies in us."

So, if more and more of us have to carry our sense of home inside us, we also—Emerson and Thoreau remind us—have to carry with us our sense of destination. The most valuable Pacifics we explore will always be the vast expanses within us, and the most important Northwest Crossings the thresholds we cross in the heart. The virtue of finding a gilded pavilion in Kyoto is that it allows you to take back a more lasting, private Golden Temple to your office in Rockefeller Center.

And even as the world seems to grow more exhausted, our travels do not, and some of the finest travel books in recent years have been those that undertake a parallel journey, matching the physical steps of a pilgrimage with the metaphysical steps of a questioning (as in Peter Matthiessen's great *The Snow Leopard*), or chronicling a trip to the farthest reaches of human strangeness (as in Oliver Sack's *Island of the Color-Blind*, which features a journey not just to a remote atoll in the Pacific, but to a realm where people actually see light differently). The most distant shores, we are constantly reminded, lie within the person asleep at our side.

So travel, at heart, is just a quick way to keeping our minds mobile and awake. As Santayana, the heir to Emerson and Thoreau with whom I began, wrote, "There is wisdom in turning as often as possible from the familiar to the unfamiliar; it keeps the mind nimble; it kills prejudice, and it fosters humor." Romantic poets inaugurated an era of travel because they were the great apostles of open eyes. Buddhist monks are often vagabonds, in part because they believe in wakefulness. And if travel is like love, it is, in the end, mostly because it's a heightened state of awareness, in which we are mindful, receptive, undimmed by familiarity and ready to be transformed. That is why the best trips, like the best love affairs, never really end.

FOR INFORMAL WRITING

What are the various reasons, according to Iyer, that we travel? Looking at the specific examples in Iyer's essay, how do his beliefs about travel reflect your own? How do they not?

FOR DISCUSSION

1. Iyer asserts the following: "We travel, initially, to lose ourselves; and we travel, next, to find ourselves." Explore this paradox. What impact does travel have on us as travelers? What impact should it have?
2. What do you think when Iyer says, "the first great joy of traveling is simply the luxury of leaving all my beliefs and certainties at home and seeing everything I thought I knew in a different light." If you've traveled at all, do you find this to be true? Do you think it's true of most people who travel?
3. Iyer says that for good or ill, American travelers are seen as representatives of the American dream, as if the United States is one, monolithic culture. What do you think of this assertion? More globally, how does Iyer feel that people are in some ways representatives of whatever culture(s) with which they are identified?

FOR WRITING

Throughout the essay, Iyer makes many references to figures of literary and philosophical repute. First, look up each of these writers. (Who are the Romantic poets, anyway?) Choose one of the writers he mentions and research that person's views on travel, crafting an argument that articulates the differences between their writing and Iyer's. How are they similar? Different? To what effect?

The Youth in Asia (2000)
David Sedaris (1956–)

David Sedaris became prominent in 1992 with the broadcast of his "Santaland Diaries" on National Public Radio. Celebrated as a humorist and author, he has single-handedly popularized the contemporary, humorous nonfiction essay. Following the publication of one of his most popular books, Me Talk Pretty One Day *(2000),* Time *magazine named Sedaris "humorist of the year" in 2001. Sedaris has been nominated for numerous Grammy Awards for his many audio books, and he has to a good extent reached "rock star status" based on his ability to sell out arenas during his reading tours. "The Youth in Asia" was originally published in* Esquire *and later appeared in* Me Talk Pretty One Day.

In the early sixties, during what my mother referred to as the "tail end of the Lassie years," my parents were given two collies they named Rastus and Duchess. We were living in upstate New York, out in the country, and the dogs were free to race through the forest. They napped in meadows and stood knee-deep in frigid streams, costars in their own private dog-food commercial. According to our father, anyone could tell that the two of them were in love.

Late one evening, while lying on a blanket in the garage, Duchess gave birth to a litter of slick, potato-sized puppies. When it looked as though one of them had died, our mother placed the creature in a casserole dish and popped it into the oven, like the witch in "Hänsel and Gretel."

"Oh, keep your shirts on," she said. "It's only set on 200. I'm not baking anyone; this is just to keep him warm." The heat revived the sick puppy and left us believing our mother was capable of resurrecting the dead.

Faced with the responsibilities of fatherhood, Rastus took off. The puppies were given away, and we moved south, where the heat and humidity worked

---

Reprinted by permission of Don Congdon Associates, Inc. Copyright (c) 2000 by David Sedaris.

against a collie's best interests. Duchess's once beautiful coat now hung in ragged patches. Age set in and she limped about the house, clearing rooms with her suffocating farts. When finally, full of worms, she collapsed in the ravine beside our house, we reevaluated our mother's healing powers. The entire animal kingdom was beyond her scope; apparently, she could resurrect only the cute dead.

The oven trick was performed on half a dozen peakish hamsters but failed to work on my first guinea pig, who died after eating a couple of cigarettes and an entire pack of matches.

"Don't take it too hard," my mother said, removing her oven mitts. "The world is full of guinea pigs. You can get another one tomorrow."

Eulogies always tended to be brief, our motto being "Another day, another collar."

A short time after Duchess died, our father came home with a German shepherd puppy. For reasons that were never explained, the privilege of naming the dog went to a friend of my older sister's, a fourteen-year-old girl named Cindy. She was studying German at the time, and after carefully examining the puppy and weighing it with her hands, she announced it would be called Mädchen, which apparently meant "girl" to the Volks back in the Vaterland. We weren't wild about the name but considered ourselves lucky that Cindy wasn't studying one of the harder- to- pronounce Asian languages.

When she was six, Mädchen was killed by a car. Her food was still in the bowl when our father brought home an identical German shepherd, whom the same Cindy thoughtfully christened Mädchen Two. This tag-team progression was disconcerting, especially for the new dog, who was expected to possess both the knowledge and the personality of her predecessor.

"Mädchen One would never have wet the floor like that," my father would scold, and the dog would sigh, knowing she was the canine equivalent of a rebound.

Mädchen Two never accompanied us to the beach and rarely posed in any of the family photographs. Once her puppyhood was spent, we more or less lost interest. "We ought to get a dog," we'd sometimes say, completely forgetting that we already had one. She came inside to eat, but most of her time was spent out in the pen, slumped in the A- frame doghouse my father had designed and crafted from scrap pieces of redwood.

"Hey," he'd ask, "how many dogs can say they live in a redwood house?" This always led to my mother's exhausted "Oh, Lou, how many dogs can say that they don't live in a goddamned redwood house?"

Throughout the collie and shepherd years, we had a succession of drowsy, secretive cats who seemed to share a unique bond with our mother. "It's because I open their cans," she said, though we all knew it ran deeper than that. What they had in common was their claws. That and a deep-seated need to destroy my father's golf bag.

The first cat ran away, and the second was hit by a car. The third passed into a disagreeable old age and died hissing at the kitten who had prematurely arrived to replace her. When, at the age of seven, the fourth cat was diagnosed with feline leukemia, my mother was devastated.

"I'm going to have Sadie put to sleep," she said. "It's for her own good, and I don't want to hear a word about it from any of you. This is hard enough as it is."

The cat was put down, and then came the anonymous postcards and crank phone calls orchestrated by my sisters and me. The cards announced a miraculous new cure for feline leukemia, while the callers identified themselves as representatives of *Cat Fancy* magazine. "We'd like to use Sadie as our cover story and were hoping to schedule a photo shoot. Can you have her ready by tomorrow?"

We thought a kitten might lift our mother's spirits, but she declined all offers. "That's it," she said. "My cat days are over."

When Mädchen Two developed splenic tumors, our father dropped everything and ran to her side. Evenings were spent at the animal hospital, lying on a mat outside of her cage and adjusting her IV. He'd never afforded her much attention, but her impending death alerted in him a great sense of duty. He was holding her paw when she died, and he spent the next several weeks asking us how many dogs could say they'd lived in a redwood house.

Our mother, in turn, frequently paused beside my father's tattered, urine-stained golf bag and relived memories of her own.

After spending a petless year with only one child still living at home, my parents visited a breeder and returned with a Great Dane they named Melina. They loved this dog in proportion to her size, and soon their hearts had no room for anyone else. The house was given over to the dog, rooms redecorated to suit her fancy. Enter your former bedroom and you'd be told, "You'd better not let Melina catch you in here," or, "This is where we come to pee-pee when there's nobody home to let us outside, right, girl?"

The dog was my parents' first true common interest, and they loved her equally, each in their own way. My mother's love tended toward the horizontal, a pet being little more than a napping companion, something she could look at and say, "That looks like a good idea. Scoot over, why don't you." A stranger peeking through the window might think that the two of them had entered a suicide pact. She and the dog sprawled like corpses, their limbs arranged into an eternal embrace. "God, that felt good," my mom would say, the two of them waking f or a brief stretch. "Now let's go try it on the living-room floor."

My father loved the Great Dane for her size, and frequently took her on long, aimless drives during which she'd stick her heavy, anvil-sized head out the window and leak great quantities of foamy saliva. Other drivers pointed and stared, rolling down their windows to shout, "Hey, you got a saddle for that thing?" When they went out for a walk, there was the inevitable "Are you walking her, or is it the other way around?"

"Ha, ha," our father always laughed, as if it were the first time he'd heard it. The attention was addictive, and he enjoyed a pride of accomplishment he'd never felt with any of his children. It was as if he were somehow responsible for her size and stature, as if he'd personally designed her spots and trained her to grow to the size of a pony.

When out with the dog, he carried a leash in one hand and a shovel in the other. "Just in case," he said.

"Just in case what? She dies of a heart attack and you need to bury her?" I didn't get it.

"No," he'd say. "It's for her, you know, her ... business."

My father was retired, but the dog had business.

I was living in Chicago when they first got Melina, and every time I came home, the animal was bigger. Every time there were more Marmaduke cartoons on the refrigerator, and every time my voice grew louder as I asked myself, "Who are these people?"

"Down, girl," my parents would chuckle as the dog jumped up, panting for my attention. Her great padded paws reached my waist, then my chest and shoulders, until eventually, her arms wrapped around my neck and her head towering above my own, she came to resemble a dance partner scouting the room for a better offer.

"That's just her way of saying hello," my mother would say, handing me a towel to wipe off the dog's bubbling seepage. "Here, you missed a spot on the back of your head."

Among us children, Melina's diploma from obedience school was seen as the biggest joke since our brother's graduation from Sanderson High School. "So she's not book smart," our mother said. "Big deal. I can fetch my own goddamned newspaper."

The dog's growth was monitored on a daily basis, and every small accomplishment was captured on film. One could find few pictures of my sister Tiffany, while Melina had entire albums devoted to her terrible twos.

"Hit me," my mother said on one of my return visits from Chicago. "No, wait, let me get my camera." She left the room and returned a few moments later. "Okay," she said. "Now hit me. Better yet, why don't you just pretend to hit me?"

I raised my hand and my mother cried out in pain. "Ow!" she yelled. "Somebody help me! This stranger is trying to hurt me, and I don't know why."

I caught an advancing blur moving in from the left, and the next thing I knew, I was down on the ground, the Great Dane ripping holes in the neck of my sweater. The camera flashed, and my mother roared, "God, I love that trick."

I rolled over to protect my face. "It's not a trick."

She snapped another picture. "Oh, don't be so critical. It's close enough."

With us grown and out of the house, my sisters and I reasonably expected our parents' lives to stand still. Their assignment was to stagnate and live in the past. We were supposed to be the center of their lives, but instead they constructed a new family, consisting of Melina and the founding members of her fan club.

Someone who obviously didn't know her too well had given my mother a cheerful stuffed bear with a calico heart stitched onto its chest. According to the manufacturer, the bear's name was Mumbles, and all it needed in order to thrive was two double-A batteries and a regular diet of hugs.

"Where Mumbles?" my mother would ask, and the dog would jump up and snatch the bear from its hiding place on top of the refrigerator, yanking its body this way and that in hopes of breaking its neck. Occasionally, her teeth would press the on switch and the doomed thing would flail its arms, whispering one of its five messages of goodwill.

"That's my girl," my mother would say. "We don't like Mumbles, do we?"

"We?"

During the final years of Mädchen Two and the first half of the Melina epoch, I lived with a female cat named Neil who'd been abandoned by a scary alcoholic with long fingernails and a large collection of kimonos. He was a hateful man, and after he moved, the cat was taken in and renamed by my sister Gretchen, who later passed the animal on to me. My mother looked after the cat when I moved from Raleigh, and she flew her to Chicago once I'd found a place and settled in. I'd taken the cheapest apartment I could find, and it showed.

Though they were nice, my new neighbors could see no connection between their personal habits and the armies of pests aggressively occupying the building.

Neil caught fourteen mice, and scores of others escaped with missing limbs and tails. In Raleigh, she'd just lain around the house doing nothing, but now she had a real job to do.

Her interests broadened, and she listened intently to the radio, captivated by the political and financial stories that failed to interest me. "One more word about the Iran-contra hearings and you'll be sleeping next door with the aliens," I'd say, though we both knew that I didn't really mean it.

Neil was old when she moved to Chicago, and then she got older. The Oliver North testimony now behind her, she started leaving teeth in her bowl and developed the sort of breath that could remove paint. She stopped cleaning herself, and

I took to bathing her in the sink. When she was soaking wet, I could see just how thin and brittle she really was. Her kidneys shrank to the size of raisins, and while I wanted what was best for her, I naturally assumed the vet was joking when he suggested dialysis.

In addition to being old, toothless, and incontinent, it seemed that for the cost of a few thousand dollars, she could also spend three days a week hooked up to a machine. "Sounds awfully tempting," I said. "Just give us a few days to think it over." I took her for a second opinion. Vet number two tested her blood and phoned me a few days later suggesting I consider euthanasia.

I hadn't heard that word since childhood, and immediately recalled a mismatched pair of Japanese schoolboys standing alone in a deserted schoolyard. One of the boys, grossly obese, was attempting to climb the flagpole that towered high above him. Silhouetted against the darkening sky, he hoisted himself a few feet off the ground and clung there, trembling and out of breath. "I can't do it," he said. "This is too hard f or me."

His friend, a gaunt and serious boy named Komatsu, stood below him, offering encouragement. "Oh, but you can do it. You must," he said. "It is required."

This was a scene I had long forgotten, and thinking of it made me unbearably sad. The boys were characters from *Fatty and Skinny*, a Japanese movie regularly presented on *The CBS Children's Film Festival*, a weekly TV series hosted by two puppets and a very patient woman who pretended to laugh at their jokes. My sisters and I watched the program every Saturday afternoon, our gasbag of a collie imposing frequent intermissions.

Having shimmied a few more inches up the pole, Fatty lost his grip and fell down. As he brushed himself off, Skinny ran down the mountain toward the fragile, papery house he shared with his family. This had been Fatty's last chance to prove himself. He'd thought his friend's patience was unlimited, but now he knew that he was wrong. "Komatsuuuuuuuu!" he yelled. "Komatsu, please give me one more chance."

The doctor's voice called me back from the Japanese schoolyard. "So. The euthanasia," he said. "Are you giving it some thought?"

"Yes," I said. "As a matter of fact, I am."

In the end, I returned to the animal hospital and had her put to sleep. When the vet injected the sodium pentobarbital, Neil fluttered her eyes, assumed a nap position, and died. My then-boyfriend stayed to make arrangements, and I ran outside to blubber beside the parked and, unfortunately, locked car. Neil had gotten into the car believing she would live to experience the return trip, and that tore me up. Someone had finally been naive enough to trust me, and I'd rewarded her with death. Racked by guilt, the Youth in Asia sat at their desks and wept bitter tears.

A week after putting her to sleep, I received Neil's ashes in a forest-green can. She'd never expressed any great interest in the outdoors, so I scattered her remains on the carpet and then vacuumed them up. The cat's death struck me as the end of an era. The end of my safe college life, the last of my thirty-inch waist, my faltering relationship with my first real boyfriend— I cried for it all and spent the next several months wondering why so few songs were written about cats.

My mother sent a consoling letter along with a check to cover the cost of the cremation. In the lower-left corner, on the line marked memo, she'd written, "Pet burning." I had it coming.

When my mother died and was cremated herself, we worried that, acting on instinct, our father might run out and immediately replace her. Returning from the funeral, my brother, sisters, and I half expected to find Sharon Two standing at the kitchen counter, working the puzzle from *TV Guide*. "Sharon One would have gotten five-across," our father would have scolded. "Come on, baby, get with it!"

With my mother gone, my father and Melina had each other all to themselves. Though she now occupied the side of the bed left vacant by her former mistress, the dog knew she could never pass as a viable replacement. Her love was too fierce and simple, and she had no talent for argument. Yet she and my father honored their pledge to adore and protect each other. They celebrated anniversaries, regularly renewed their vows, and growled when challenged by outside forces.

"You want me to go where?" When invited to visit one of his children, my father would beg off, saying, "I can't leave town. Who'd take care of Melina?"

Due to their size, Great Danes generally don't live very long. There are cheeses that last longer. At the age of eleven, gray-bearded and teetering, Melina was a wonder of science. My father massaged her arthritic legs, carried her up the stairs, and lifted her in and out of bed. He treated her the way men in movies treat their ailing wives, the way he might have treated my mother had she allowed such naked displays of helplessness and affection. Melina's era had spanned the final ten years of his married life. The dog had ridden in the family's last station wagon. She'd attended my father's retirement party, lived through my sister's wedding, and celebrated the election of two Republican presidents. She grew weaker and lost her appetite, but against all advice, my father simply could not bear to let go.

The Youth in Asia begged him to end her life.

"I can't do it," he said. "This is too hard for me."

"Oh, but you must do it," said Komatsu. "It is required."

A month after Melina was put to sleep, my father returned to the breeder and came home with another Great Dane. A female like Melina, gray spots like Melina, only this one is named Sophie. He tries to love her but readily admits that he may have made a mistake. She's a nice enough dog, but the timing is off.

When walking Sophie through the neighborhood, my father feels not unlike a newly married senior citizen stumbling behind his apathetic young bride. The puppy's stamina embarrasses him, as does her blatant interest in younger men. Passing drivers slow to a stop and roll down their windows. "Hey," they yell. "Are you walking her, or is it the other way around?"

Their words remind him of a more gracious era, of milder forces straining against the well-worn leash. He still gets the attention, but now, in response, he just lifts his shovel and continues on his way.

FOR INFORMAL WRITING

What is the tone of this essay? How do you know? Comment on Sedaris's choice of language, for instance, in making your claim.

FOR DISCUSSION

1. How does Sedaris characterize his mother? What does this characterization reveal about their relationship?
2. The title is obviously a play on words. What is Sedaris getting at with this title? How does it relate to what happens in the essay?
3. Some might argue that this essay is as much about mortality as it is about having pets. Why? What in the essay might suggest this?

FOR WRITING

Sedaris's essays are widely available. Find another of your liking and compare it with "The Youth in Asia." How does Sedaris use humor to approach (often) dark topics? How does he do so, and to what effect?

WHAT'S NEW IS OLD

Read "The Youth in Asia" by David Sedaris alongside "Advice to Youth" by Mark Twain. While each author has "youth" in the title, the subjects are different, and the styles are worthy of comparison. How might you compare the humor—the tone, the language, the intention—of each author? To what conclusion do you come? Are the forms of humor similar? Different? To what purpose and to what effect?

Shooting Dad (2000)
Sarah Vowell (1969–)

As a successful radio personality, Sarah Vowell has a voice that is as well-known as her writing. In fact, she is the voice of the character Violet in the animated film The Incredibles. *Vowell is a long-time contributor to prominent Public Radio programs such as* This American Life, *and she has written for* McSweeney's, Time, Esquire, *and other major publications. She is the author of several nonfiction books that include* The Partly Cloudy Patriot *(2002)*, Assassination Vacation *(2005), and* Take the Cannoli *(2000), from which this essay comes.*

If you were passing by the house where I grew up during my teenage years and it happened to be before Election Day, you wouldn't have needed to come inside to see that it was a house divided. You could have looked at the Democratic campaign poster in the upstairs window and the Republican one in the downstairs window and seen our home for the Civil War battleground it was. I'm not saying who was the Democrat or who was the Republican—my father or I—but I will tell you that I have never subscribed to *Guns & Ammo*, that I did not plaster the family vehicle with National Rifle Association stickers, and that hunter's orange was never my color.

About the only thing my father and I agree on is the Constitution, though I'm partial to the First Amendment, while he's always favored the Second.

I am a gunsmith's daughter. I like to call my parents' house, located on a quiet residential street in Bozeman, Montana, the United States of Firearms. Guns were everywhere, the so-called pretty ones like the circa 1850 walnut muzzleloader hanging on the wall, Dad's clients' fixer-uppers leaning into corners, an entire rack right next to the TV. I had to move revolvers out of my way to make room for a bowl of Rice Krispies on the kitchen table.

From TAKE THE CANNOLI by Sarah Vowell. Copyright © 2000 by Sarah Vowell. Reprinted with the permission of Simon & Schuster, Inc. All rights reserved.

I was eleven when we moved into that Bozeman house. We had never lived in town before, and this was a college town at that. We came from Oklahoma—a dusty little Muskogee County nowhere called Braggs. My parents' property there included an orchard, a horse pasture, and a couple of acres of woods. I knew our lives had changed one morning not long after we moved to Montana when, during breakfast, my father heard a noise and jumped out of his chair. Grabbing a BB gun, he rushed out the front door. Standing in the yard, he started shooting at crows. My mother sprinted after him screaming, "Pat, you might ought to check, but I don't think they do that up here!" From the look on his face, she might as well have told him that his American citizenship had been revoked. He shook his head, mumbling, "Why, shooting crows is a national pastime, like baseball and apple pie." Personally, I preferred baseball and apple pie. I looked up at those crows flying away and thought, I'm going to like it here.

Dad and I started bickering in earnest when I was fourteen, after the 1984 Democratic National Convention. I was so excited when Walter Mondale chose Geraldine Ferraro as his running mate that I taped the front page of the newspaper with her picture on it to the refrigerator door. But there was some sort of mysterious gravity surge in the kitchen. Somehow, that picture ended up in the trash all the way across the room.

Nowadays, I giggle when Dad calls me on Election Day to cheerfully inform me that he has once again canceled out my vote, but I was not always so mature. There were times when I found the fact that he was a gunsmith horrifying. And just weird. All he ever cared about were guns. All I ever cared about was art. There were years and years when he hid out by himself in the garage making rifle barrels and I holed up in my room reading Allen Ginsberg poems, and we were incapable of having a conversation that didn't end in an argument.

Our house was partitioned off into territories. While the kitchen and the living room were well within the DMZ, the respective workspaces governed by my father and me were jealously guarded totalitarian states in which each of us declared ourselves dictator. Dad's shop was a messy disaster area, a labyrinth of lathes. Its walls were hung with the mounted antlers of deer he'd bagged, forming a makeshift museum of death. The available flat surfaces were buried under a million scraps of paper on which he sketched his mechanical inventions in blue ballpoint pen. And the floor, carpeted with spiky metal shavings, was a tetanus shot waiting to happen. My domain was the cramped, cold space known as the music room. It was also a messy disaster area, an obstacle course of musical instruments—piano, trumpet, baritone horn, valve trombone, various percussion doodads (bells!), and recorders. A framed portrait of the French composer Claude Debussy was nailed to the wall. The available flat surfaces were buried under piles of staff paper, on which I penciled in the pompous orchestra music given titles like "Prelude to the Green Door" (named after an O. Henry short story by the way, not the watershed porn flick *Behind the Green Door*) I started writing in junior high.

It has been my experience that in order to impress potential suitors, skip the teen Debussy anecdotes and stick with the always attention-getting line "My dad makes guns." Though it won't cause the guy to like me any better, it will make him handle the inevitable breakup with diplomacy—just in case I happen to have any loaded family heirlooms lying around the house.

But the fact is, I have only shot a gun once and once was plenty. My twin sister, Amy, and I were six years old—six—when Dad decided that it was high time we learned how to shoot. Amy remembers the day he handed us the gun for the first time differently. She liked it.

Amy shared our father's enthusiasm for firearms and the quick-draw cowboy mythology surrounding them. I tended to daydream through Dad's activities—the car trip to Dodge City's Boot Hill, his beloved John Wayne Westerns on TV. My sister, on the other hand, turned into Rooster Cogburn Jr., devouring Duke movies with Dad. In fact, she named her teddy bear Duke, hung a colossal John Wayne portrait next to her bed, and took to wearing one of those John Wayne shirts that button on the side. So when Dad led us out to the backyard when we were six and, to Amy's delight, put the gun in her hand, she says she felt it meant that Daddy trusted us and that he thought of us as "big girls."

But I remember holding the pistol only made me feel small. It was so heavy in my hand. I stretched out my arm and pointed it away and winced. It was a very long time before I had the nerve to pull the trigger and I was so scared I had to close my eyes. It felt like it just went off by itself, as if I had no say in the matter, as if the gun just had this need. The sound it made was as big as God. It kicked little me back to the ground like a bully, like a foe. It hurt. I don't know if I dropped it or just handed it back over to my dad, but I do know that I never wanted to touch another one again. And, because I believed in the devil, I did what my mother told me to do every time I felt an evil presence. I looked at the smoke and whispered under my breath, "Satan, I rebuke thee."

It's not like I'm saying I was traumatized. It's more like I was decided. Guns: Not For Me. Luckily, both my parents grew up in exasperating households where children were considered puppets and/or slaves. My mom and dad were hell-bent on letting my sister and me make our own choices. So if I decided that I didn't want my father's little death sticks to kick me to the ground again, that was fine with him. He would go hunting with my sister, who started calling herself "the loneliest twin in history" because of my reluctance to engage in family activities.

Of course, the fact that I was allowed to voice my opinions did not mean that my father would silence his own. Some things were said during the Reagan administration that cannot be taken back. Let's just say that I blamed Dad for nuclear proliferation and Contra aid. He believed that if I had my way, all the guns would be confiscated and it would take the commies about fifteen minutes to parachute in and assume control.

We're older now, my dad and I. The older I get, the more I'm interested in becoming a better daughter. First on my list: Figure out the whole gun thing.

Not long ago, my dad finished his most elaborate tool of death yet. A cannon. He built a nineteenth-century cannon. From scratch. It took two years.

My father's cannon is a smaller replica of a cannon called the Big Horn Gun in front of Bozeman's Pioneer Museum. The barrel of the original has been filled with concrete ever since some high school kids in the '50s pointed it at the school across the street and shot out its windows one night as a prank. According to Dad's historical source, a man known to scholars as A Guy at the Museum, the cannon was brought to Bozeman around 1870, and was used by local white merchants to fire at the Sioux and Cheyenne Indians who blocked their trade access to the East in 1874.

"Bozeman was founded on greed," Dad says. The courthouse cannon, he continues, "definitely killed Indians. The merchants filled it full of nuts, bolts, and chopped-up horseshoes. Sitting Bull could have been part of these engagements. They definitely ticked off the Indians, because a couple of years later, Custer wanders into them at Little Bighorn. The Bozeman merchants were out to cause trouble. They left fresh baked bread with cyanide in it on the trail to poison a few Indians."

Because my father's sarcastic American history yarns rarely go on for long before he trots out some nefarious ancestor of ours—I come from a long line of moonshiners, Confederate soldiers, murderers, even Democrats—he cracks that the merchants hired some "community-minded Southern soldiers from North Texas." These soldiers had, like my great-great-grandfather John Vowell, fought under pro-slavery guerrilla William C. Quantrill. Quantrill is most famous for riding into Lawrence, Kansas, in 1863 flying a black flag and commanding his men pharaohlike to "kill every male and burn down every house."

"John Vowell," Dad says, "had a little rep for killing people." And since he abandoned my great-grandfather Charles, whose mother died giving birth to him in 1870, and wasn't seen again until 1912, Dad doesn't rule out the possibility that John Vowell could have been one of the hired guns on the Bozeman Trail. So the cannon isn't just another gun to my dad. It's a map of all his obsessions—firearms, certainly, but also American history and family history, subjects he's never bothered separating from each other.

After tooling a million guns, after inventing and building a rifle barrel boring machine, after setting up that complicated shop filled with lathes and blueing tanks and outmoded blacksmithing tools, the cannon is his most ambitious project ever. I thought that if I was ever going to understand the ballistic bee in his bonnet, this was my chance. It was the biggest gun he ever made and I could experience it and spend time with it with the added bonus of not having to actually pull a trigger myself.

I called Dad and said that I wanted to come to Montana and watch him shoot off the cannon. He was immediately suspicious. But I had never taken much interest in his work before and he would take what he could get. He loaded the cannon into the back of his truck and we drove up into the Bridger Mountains. I was a little worried that the National Forest Service would object to us lobbing fiery balls of metal onto its property. Dad laughed, assuring me that "you cannot shoot fireworks, but this is considered a fire*arm*."

It is a small cannon, about as long as a baseball bat and as wide as a coffee can. But it's heavy—110 pounds. We park near the side of the hill. Dad takes his gunpowder and other tools out of this adorable wooden box on which he has stenciled "PAT G. VOWELL CANNONWORKS." Cannonworks: So that's what NRA members call a metal-strewn garage.

Dad plunges his homemade bullets into the barrel, points it at an embankment just to be safe, and lights the fuse. When the fuse is lit, it resembles a cartoon. So does the sound, which warrants Ben Day dot words along the lines of *ker-pow!* There's so much Fourth of July smoke everywhere I feel compelled to sing the national anthem.

I've given this a lot of thought—how to convey the giddiness I felt when the cannon shot off. But there isn't a sophisticated way to say this. It's just really, really cool. My dad thought so, too.

Sometimes, I put together stories about the more eccentric corners of the American experience for public radio. So I happen to have my tape recorder with me, and I've never seen levels like these. Every time the cannon goes off, the delicate needles which keep track of the sound quality lurch into the bad, red zone so fast and so hard I'm surprised they don't break.

The cannon was so loud and so painful, I had to touch my head to make sure my skull hadn't cracked open. One thing that my dad and I share is that we're both a little hard of hearing—me from Aerosmith, him from gunsmith.

He lights the fuse again. The bullet knocks over the log he was aiming at. I instantly utter a sentence I never in my entire life thought I would say. I tell him, "Good shot, Dad."

Just as I'm wondering what's coming over me, two hikers walk by. Apparently, they have never seen a man set off a homemade cannon in the middle of the wilderness while his daughter holds a foot-long microphone up into the air recording its terrorist boom. One hiker gives me a puzzled look and asks, "So you work for the radio and that's your dad?"

Dad shoots the cannon again so that they can see how it works. The other hiker says, "That's quite the machine you got there." But he isn't talking about the cannon. He's talking about my tape recorder and my microphone—which is called a *shotgun* mike. I stare back at him, then I look over at my father's cannon, then down at my microphone, and I think. Oh. My. God. My dad and I are the same person. We're both smart-alecky loners with goofy projects and weird equipment. And since this whole target practice outing was my idea, I was no longer his adversary. I was his accomplice. What's worse, I was liking it.

I haven't changed my mind about guns. I can get behind the cannon because it is a completely ceremonial object. It's unwieldy and impractical, just like everything else I care about. To rob a convenience store with this 110-pound Saturday night special, you'd still be dragging it in the door Sunday afternoon.

I love noise. As a music fan, I'm always waiting for that moment in a song when something just flies out of it and explodes in the air. My dad is a one-man garage band, the kind of rock 'n' roller who slaves away at his art for no reason other than to make his own sound. My dad is an artist—a pretty driven, idiosyncratic one, too. He's got his last *Gesamtkunstwerk* all planned out. It's a performance piece. We're all in it—my mom, the loneliest twin in history, and me.

When my father dies, take a wild guess what he wants done with his ashes. Here's a hint: It requires a cannon.

"You guys are going to love this," he smirks, eyeballing the cannon. "You get to drag this thing up on top of the Gravellies on opening day of hunting season. And looking off at Sphinx Mountain, you get to put me in little paper bags. I can take my last hunting trip on opening morning."

I'll do it, too. I will have my father's body burned into ashes. I will pack these ashes into paper bags. I will go to the mountains with my mother, my sister, and the cannon. I will plunge his remains into the barrel and point it into a hill so that he doesn't take anyone with him. I will light the fuse. But I will not cover my ears. Because when I blow what used to be my dad into the earth, I want it to hurt.

FOR INFORMAL WRITING

The narrative evokes a sense that guns, the National Rifle Association, and the ways that guns represent identity were paramount to Vowell's upbringing. How does Vowell use guns as a metaphor?

FOR DISCUSSION

1. Examine the language in this essay. How would you characterize it? What is the effect?
2. "If you were passing by the house where I grew up in my teenage years and it happened to be before Election Day, you wouldn't have needed to come inside to see that it was a house divided." In what ways was her house divided?
3. Can you identify with Vowell's disassociation from her family? Why or why not?

FOR WRITING

Although the primary theme of the essay focuses on the various ways that Vowell feels like the black sheep of her family, ultimately she realizes that she and her father are more alike than she'd assumed. In what ways does Vowell acknowledge their similarities? What are they?

Consider the Lobster (2004)
David Foster Wallace (1962–2008)

Essayist and novelist David Foster Wallace was known as something of a dark, sardonic commentator on American culture. Called "influential" and "innovative" by The New York Times, *Wallace had a degree in creative writing from the University of Arizona and received a MacArthur "Genius" Grant in 1997. His best-known novel,* Infinite Jest, *was published in 1996; a signature of his style, as seen in this essay, is a (to some) excessive use of footnote and endnotes. Wallace was public about his battles with depression and mental illness and took his own life in September of 2008. This essay was originally published in* Gourmet *magazine and was motivated by a trip to the Maine Lobster Festival.*

The enormous, pungent, and extremely well-marketed Maine Lobster Festival is held every late July in the state's midcoast region, meaning the western side of Penobscot Bay, the nerve stem of Maine's lobster industry. What's called the midcoast runs from Owl's Head and Thomaston in the south to Belfast in the north. (Actually, it might extend all the way up to Bucksport, but we were never able to get farther north than Belfast on Route 1, whose summer traffic is, as you can imagine, unimaginable.) The region's two main communities are Camden, with its very old money and yachty harbor and five-star restaurants and phenomenal B&Bs, and Rockland, a serious old fishing town that hosts the festival every summer in historic Harbor Park, right along the water.[1]

Tourism and lobster are the midcoast region's two main industries, and they're both warm-weather enterprises, and the Maine Lobster Festival represents less an intersection of the industries than a deliberate collision, joyful and lucrative and loud. The assigned subject of this *Gourmet* article is the 56th Annual

---

© David Foster Wallace
[1] There's a comprehensive native apothegm: "Camden by the sea, Rockland by the smell."

MLF, 30 July–3 August 2003, whose official theme this year was "Lighthouses, Laughter, and Lobster." Total paid attendance was over 100,000, due partly to a national CNN spot in June during which a senior editor of *Food & Wine* magazine hailed the MLF as one of the best food-themed galas in the world. 2003 festival highlights: con-certs by Lee Ann Womack and Orleans, annual Maine Sea Goddess beauty pageant, Saturday's big parade, Sunday's William G. Atwood Memorial Crate Race, annual Amateur Cooking Competition, carnival rides and midway attractions and food booths, and the MLF's Main Eating Tent, where something over 25,000 pounds of fresh-caught Maine lobster is consumed after preparation in the World's Largest Lobster Cooker near the grounds' north entrance. Also available are lobster rolls, lobster turnovers, lobster saute, Down East lobster salad, lobster bisque, lobster ravioli, and deep-fried lobster dumplings. Lobster thermidor is obtainable at a sit-down restaurant called the Black Pearl on Harbor Park's northwest wharf. A large all-pine booth sponsored by the Maine Lobster Promotion Council has free pamphlets with recipes, eating tips, and Lobster Fun Facts. The winner of Friday's Amateur Cooking Competition prepares Saffron Lobster Ramekins, the recipe for which is now available for public downloading at www.mainelobsterfestival.com. There are lobster T-shirts and lobster bobblehead dolls and inflatable lobster pool toys and clamp-on lobster hats with big scarlet claws that wobble on springs. Your assigned correspondent saw it all, accompanied by one girlfriend and both his own parents—one of which parents was actually born and raised in Maine, albeit in the extreme northern inland part, which is potato country and a world away from the touristic midcoast.[2]

For practical purposes, everyone knows what a lobster is. As usual, though, there's much more to know than most of us care about—it's all a matter of what your interests are. Taxonomically speaking, a lobster is a marine crustacean of the family Homaridae, characterized by five pairs of jointed legs, the first pair terminating in large pincerish claws used for subduing prey. Like many other species of benthic carnivore, lobsters are both hunters and scavengers. They have stalked eyes, gills on their legs, and antennae. There are a dozen or so different kinds worldwide, of which the relevant species here is the Maine lobster, *Homarus americanus*. The name "lobster" comes from the Old English *loppestre*, which is thought to be a corrupt form of the Latin word for locust combined with the Old English *loppe*, which meant spider.

Moreover, a crustacean is an aquatic arthropod of the class Crustacea, which comprises crabs, shrimp, barnacles, lobsters, and freshwater crayfish. All this is

---

[2] N.B. All personally connected parties have made it clear from the start that they do not want to be talked about in this article.

right there in the encyclopedia. And arthropods are members of the phylum Arthropoda, which phylum covers insects, spiders, crustaceans, and centipedes/millipedes, all of whose main commonality, besides the absence of a centralized brain-spine assembly, is a chitinous exoskeleton composed of segments, to which appendages are articulated in pairs.

The point is that lobsters are basically giant sea insects.[3] Like most arthropods, they date from the Jurassic period, biologically so much older than mammalia that they might as well be from another planet. And they are—particularly in their natural brown-green state, brandishing their claws like weapons and with thick antennae awhip—not nice to look at. And it's true that they are garbagemen of the sea, eaters of dead stuff,[4] although they'll also eat some live shellfish, certain kinds of injured fish, and sometimes one another.

But they are themselves good eating. Or so we think now. Up until sometime in the 1800s, though, lobster was literally low-class food, eaten only by the poor and institutionalized. Even in the harsh penal environment of early America, some colonies had laws against feeding lobsters to inmates more than once a week because it was thought to be cruel and unusual, like making people eat rats. One reason for their low status was how plentiful lobsters, were in old New England. "Unbelievable abundance" is how one source describes the situation, including accounts of Plymouth Pilgrims wading out and capturing all they wanted by hand, and of early Boston's seashore being littered with lobsters after hard storms—these latter were treated as a smelly nuisance and ground up for fertilizer. There is also the fact that premodern lobster was cooked dead and then preserved, usually packed in salt or crude hermetic containers. Maine's earliest lobster industry was based around a dozen such seaside canneries in the 1840s, from which lobster was shipped as far away as California, in demand only because it was cheap and high in protein, basically chewable fuel.

Now, of course, lobster is posh, a delicacy, only a step or two down from caviar. The meat is richer and more substantial than most fish, its taste subtle compared to the marine-gaminess of mussels and clams. In the US pop-food imagination, lobster is now the seafood analog to steak, with which it's so often twinned as Surf 'n' Turf on the really expensive part of the chain steakhouse menu.

In fact, one obvious project of the MLF, and of its omnipresently sponsorial Maine Lobster Promotion Council, is to counter the idea that lobster is unusually luxe or unhealthy or expensive, suitable only for effete palates or the occasional blow-the-diet treat. It is emphasized over and over in presentations and

---

[3]Midcoasters' native term for a lobster is, in fact, "bug," as in "Come around on Sunday and we'll cook up some bugs."

[4]Factoid: Lobster traps are usually baited with dead herring.

pamphlets at the festival that lobster meat has fewer calories, less cholesterol, and less saturated fat than chicken.[5] And in the Main Eating Tent, you can get a "quarter" (industry shorthand for a 1¼-pound lobster), a four-ounce cup of melted butter, a bag of chips, and a soft roll w/butter-pat for around $12.00, which is only slightly more expensive than supper at McDonald's.

Be apprised, though, that the Maine Lobster Festival's democratization of lobster comes with all the massed inconvenience and aesthetic compromise of real democracy. See, for example, the aforementioned Main Eating Tent, for which there is a constant Disneyland-grade queue, and which turns out to be a square quarter mile of awning-shaded cafeteria lines and rows of long institutional tables at which friend and stranger alike sit cheek by jowl, cracking and chewing and dribbling. It's hot, and the sagged roof traps the steam and the smells, which latter are strong and only partly food-related. It is also loud, and a good percentage of the total noise is masticatory. The suppers come in Styrofoam trays, and the soft drinks are iceless and flat, and the coffee is convenience-store coffee in more Styrofoam, and the utensils are plastic (there are none of the special long skinny forks for pushing out the tail meat, though a few savvy diners bring their own). Nor do they give you near enough napkins considering how messy lobster is to eat, especially when you're squeezed onto benches alongside children of various ages and vastly different levels of fine-motor development—not to mention the people who've somehow smuggled in their own beer in enormous aisle-blocking coolers, or who all of a sudden produce their own plastic tablecloths and spread them over large portions of tables to try to reserve them (the tables) for their own little groups. And so on. Any one example is no more than a petty inconvenience, of course, but the MLF turns out to be full of irksome little downers like this—see for instance the Main Stage's headliner shows, where it turns out that you have to pay $20 extra for a folding chair if you want to sit down; or the North Tent's mad scramble for the Nyquil-cup-sized samples of finalists' entries handed out after the Cooking Competition; or the much-touted Maine Sea Goddess pageant finals, which turn out to be excruciatingly long and to consist mainly of endless thanks and tributes to local sponsors. Let's not even talk about the grossly inadequate Port-A-San facilities or the fact that there's nowhere to wash your hands before or after eating. What the Maine Lobster Festival really is a midlevel county fair with a culinary hook, and in this respect it's not unlike Tidewater crab festivals, Midwest corn festivals,

---

[5]Of course, the common practice of dipping the lobster meat in melted butter torpedoes all these happy fat-specs, which none or the council's promotional stuff ever mentions, any more than potato industry PR talks about sour cream and bacon bits.

Texas chili festivals, etc., and shares with these venues the core paradox of all teeming commercial demotic events: It's not for everyone.[6] Nothing against the euphoric senior editor of *Food & Wine*, but I'd be surprised if she'd ever actually been here in Harbor Park, amid crowds of people slapping canal-zone mosquitoes as they eat deep-fried Twinkies and watch Professor Paddywhack, on six-foot stilts in a raincoat with plastic lobsters protruding from all directions on springs, terrify their children.

Lobster is essentially a summer food. This is because we now prefer our lobsters fresh, which means they have to be recently caught, which for both tactical and economic reasons takes place at depths less than 25 fathoms. Lobsters tend to be hungriest and most active (i.e., most trappable) at summer water temperatures of 45–50 degrees. In the autumn, most Maine lobsters migrate out into deeper water, either for warmth or to avoid the heavy waves that pound New England's coast all winter. Some burrow into the bottom. They might hibernate; nobody's sure. Summer is also lobsters' molting season—specifically early- to mid-July. Chitinous arthropods grow by molting, rather

---

[6]In truth, there's a great deal to be said about the differences between working-class Rockland and the heavily populist flavor of its festival versus comfortable and elitist Camden with its expensive view and shops given entirely over to $200 sweaters and great rows of Victorian homes converted to upscale B&Bs. And about these differences as two sides of the great coin that is US tourism. Very little of which will be said here, except to amplify the above-mentioned paradox and to reveal your assigned correspondent's own preferences. I confess that I have never understood why so many people's idea of a fun vacation is to don flip-flops and sunglasses and crawl through maddening traffic to loud, hot, crowded tourist venues in order to sample a "local flavor" that is by definition ruined by the presence of tourists. This may (as my festival companions keep pointing out) all be a matter of personality and hardwired taste: the fact that I do not like tourist venues means that I'll never understand their appeal and so am probably not the one to talk about it (the supposed appeal). But, since this FN will almost surely not survive magazine-editing anyway, here goes:

As I see it, it probably really is good for the soul to be a tourist, even if it's only once in a while. Not good for the soul in a refreshing or enlivening way, though, but rather in a grim, steely-eyed, let's-look-honestly-at-the-facts-and-find-some-way-to-deal-with-them way. My personal experience has not been that traveling around the country is broadening or relaxing, or that radical changes in place and context have a salutary effect, but rather that intranational tourism is radically constricting, and humbling in the hardest way—hostile to my fantasy of being a true individual, of living somehow outside and above it all. (Coming up is the part that my companions find especially unhappy and repellent, a sure way to spoil the fun of vacation travel:) To be a mass tourist, for me, is to become a pure late-date American: alien, ignorant, greedy for something you cannot ever have, disappointed in a way you can never admit. It is to spoil, by way of sheer ontology, the very unspoiledness you are there to experience. It is to impose yourself on places that in all non-economic ways would be better, realer, without you. It is, in lines and gridlock and transaction after transaction, to confront a dimension of yourself that is as inescapable as it is painful: As a tourist, you become economically significant but existentially loathsome, an insect on a dead thing.

the way people have to buy bigger clothes as they age and gain weight. Since lobsters can live to be over 100, they can also get to be quite large, as in 30 pounds or more—though truly senior lobsters are rare now because New England 's waters are so heavily trapped.[7] Anyway, hence the culinary distinction between hard- and soft-shell lobsters, the latter sometimes a.k.a. shedders. A soft-shell lobster is one that has recently molted. In midcoast restaurants, the summer menu often offers both kinds, with shedders being slightly cheaper even though they're easier to dismantle and the meat is allegedly sweeter. The reason for the discount is that a molting lobster uses a layer of seawater for insulation while its new shell is hardening, so there's slightly less actual meat when you crack open a shedder, plus a redolent gout of water that gets all over everything and can sometimes jet out lemon like and catch a tablemate right in the eye. If it's winter or you're buying lobster someplace far from New England, on the other hand, you can almost bet that the lobster is a hard-shell, which for obvious reasons travel better.

As an à la carte entrée, lobster can be baked, broiled, steamed, grilled, sauteed, stir-fried, or microwaved. The most common method, though, is boiling. If you're someone who enjoys having lobster at home, this is probably the way you do it, since boiling is so easy. You need a large kettle w/cover, which you fill about half full with water (the standard advice is that you wane 2.5 quarts of water per lobster). Seawater is optimal or you can add two tbsp salt per quart from the tap. It also helps to know how much your lobsters weigh. You get the water boiling, put in the lobsters one at a time, cover the kettle, and bring it back up to a boil. Then you bank the heat and let the kettle simmer—ten minutes for the first pound of lobster, then three minutes for each pound after that. (This is assuming you've got hard-shell lobsters, which, again, if you don't live between Boston and Halifax is probably what you've got. For shedders, you're supposed to subtract three minutes from the total.) The reason the kettle's lobsters turn scarlet is that boiling somehow suppresses every pigment in their chitin but one. If you want an easy test of whether the lobsters are done, you try pulling on one of their antennae—if it comes out of the head with minimal effort, you're ready to eat.

A detail so obvious that most recipes don't even bother to mention it is that each lobster is supposed to be alive when you put it in the kettle. This is part of lobster's modem appeal: It's the freshest food there is. There's no decomposition between harvesting and eating. And not only do lobsters require no cleaning or dressing or plucking, they're relatively easy for vendors to keep alive.

---

[7]Datum: In a good year, the US industry produces around 80,000,000 pounds of lobster, and Maine accounts for more than half that total.

They come up alive in the traps, are placed in containers of seawater, and can—so long as the water's aerated and the animals' claws are pegged or banded to keep them from tearing one another up under the stresses of captivity,[8] survive right up until they're boiled. Most of us have been in supermarkets or restaurants that feature tanks of live lobsters, from which you can pick out your supper while it watches you point. And part of the overall spectacle of the Maine Lobster Festival is that you can see actual lobstermen's vessels docking at the wharves along the northeast grounds and unloading fresh-caught product, which is transferred by hand or cart 150 yards to the great clear tanks stacked up around the festival's cooker—which is, as mentioned, billed as the World's Largest Lobster Cooker and can process over 100 lobsters at a time for the Main Eating Tent.

So then here is a question that's all but unavoidable at the World's Largest Lobster Cooker, and may arise in kitchens across the US: Is it all right to boil a sentient creature alive just for our gustatory pleasure? A related set of concerns: Is the previous question irksomely PC or sentimental? What does "all right" even mean in this context? Is the whole thing just a matter of personal choice?

As you may or may not know, a certain well-known group called People for the Ethical Treatment of Animals thinks that the morality of lobster-boiling is not just a matter of individual conscience. In fact, one of the very first things we hear about the MLF . . . well, to set the scene: We're coming in by cab from the almost indescribably odd and rustic Knox County Airport[9] very late on the night before the festival opens, sharing the cab with a wealthy political consultant who lives on Vinalhaven Island in the bay half the year (he's headed for the island ferry in Rockland). The consultant and cabdriver are responding to informal journalistic probes about how people who live in the midcoast region actually view the MLF, as in is the festival just a big-dollar tourist thing or is it something local residents look forward to attending, take genuine civic pride in, etc. The cabdriver (who's in his seventies, one of apparently a whole platoon of

---

[8]N.B. Similar reasoning underlies the practice of what's termed "debeaking" broiler chickens and brood hens in modern factory farms. Maximum commercial efficiency requires that enormous poultry populations be confined in unnaturally close quarters, under which conditions many birds go crazy and peck one another to death. As a purely observational sidenote, be apprised that debeaking is usually an automated process and that the chickens receive no anesthetic. It's not clear to me whether most *Gourmet* readers know about debeaking or about related practices like dehorning cattle in commercial feed lots, cropping swine's tails in factory hog farms to keep psychotically bored neighbors from chewing them off, and so forth. It so happens that your assigned correspondent knew almost nothing about standard meat-industry operations before starting work on this article.

[9]The terminal used to be somebody's house, for example, and the lost-luggage-reporting room was clearly once a pantry.

retirees the cab company puts on to help with the summer rush, and wears a US-flag lapel pin, and drives in what can only be called a very deliberate way) assures us that locals do endorse and enjoy the MLF, although he himself hasn't gone in years, and now come to think of it no one he and his wife know has, either. However, the demilocal consultant's been to recent festivals a couple times (one gets the impression it was at his wife's behest), of which his most vivid impression was that "you have to line up for an ungodly long time to get your lobsters, and meanwhile there are all these ex-flower children coming up and down along the line handing out pamphlets that say the lobsters die in terrible pain and you shouldn't eat them."

And it turns out that the post-hippies of the consultant's recollection were activists from PETA. There were no PETA people in obvious view at the 2003 MLF,[10] but they've been conspicuous at many of the recent festivals. Since at least the mid-1990s, articles in everything from *The Camden Herald* to *The New York Times* have described PETA urging boycotts of the Maine Lobster Festival, often deploying celebrity spokesmen like Mary Tyler Moore for open letters and ads saying stuff like "Lobsters are extraordinarily sensitive" and "To me, eating a lobster is out of the question." More concrete is the oral testimony of Dick, our florid and extremely gregarious rental-car liaison, to the effect that PETA's been around so much during recent years that a kind of brittlely tolerant homeostasis now obtains between the activists and the festival's locals, e.g.: "We had some incidents a couple years ago. One lady took most of her clothes off and painted herself like a lobster, almost got herself arrested. But for the most part they're let alone. [Rapid series of small ambiguous laughs, which with Dick happens a lot.] They do their thing and we do our thing."

---

[10]It turned out that one Mr. William R. Rivas-Rivas, a high-ranking PETA official out of the group's Virginia headquarters, was indeed there this year, albeit solo, working the festival's main and side entrances on Saturday, 2 August, handing out pamphlets and adhesive stickers emblazoned with "Being Boiled Hurts," which is the tagline in most of PETA's published material about lobsters. I learned that he'd been there only later, when speaking with Mr. Rivas-Rivas on the phone. I'm not sure how we missed seeing him in situ at the festival, and I can't see much to do except apologize for the oversight—although it's also true that Saturday was the day of the big MLF parade through Rockland, which basic journalistic responsibility seemed to require going to (and which, with all due respect, meant that Saturday was maybe not the best day for PETA to work the Harbor Park grounds, especially if it was going to be just one person for one day, since a lot of diehard MLF partisans were off-site watching the parade (which, again with no offense intended, was in truth kind of cheesy and boring, consisting mostly of slow homemade floats and various midcoast people waving at one another, and with an extremely annoying man dressed as Blackbeard ranging up and down the length of the crowd saying "Arrr" over and over and brandishing a plastic sword at people, etc.; plus it rained)).

This whole interchange takes place on Route 1, 30 July, during a four-mile, 50-minute ride from the airport[11] to the dealership to sign car-rental papers. Several irreproducible segues down the road from the PETA anecdotes, Dick—whose son-in-law happens to be a professional lobsterman and one of the Main Eating Tent's regular suppliers—explains what he and his family feel is the crucial mitigating factor in the whole morality-of-boiling-lobsters-alive issue: "There's a part of the brain in people and animals that lets us feel pain, and lobsters' brains don't have this part."

Besides the fact that it's incorrect in about nine different ways, the main reason Dick's statement is interesting is that its thesis is more or less echoed by the festival's own pronouncement on lobsters and pain, which is part of a Test Your Lobster IQ quiz that appears in the 2003 MLF program courtesy of the Maine Lobster Promotion Council:

> The nervous system of a lobster is very simple and is in fact most similar to the nervous system of the grasshopper. It is decentralized with no brain. There is no cerebral cortex, which in humans is the area of the brain that gives the experience of pain.

Though it sounds more sophisticated, a lot of the neurology in this latter claim is still either false or fuzzy. The human cerebral cortex is the brain-part that deals with higher faculties like reason, metaphysical self-awareness, language, etc. Pain reception is known to be part of a much older and more primitive system of nociceptors and prostaglandins that are managed by the brain stem and thalamus[12]. On the other hand, it is true that the cerebral cortex is involved in what's variously called suffering, distress, or the emotional experience of pain—i.e., experiencing painful stimuli as unpleasant, very unpleasant, unbearable, and so on.

Before we go any further, let's acknowledge that the questions of whether and how different kinds of animals feel pain, and of whether and why it might be justifiable to inflict pain on them in order to eat them, turn out to be

---

[11]The short version regarding why we were back at the airport after already arriving the previous night involves lost luggage and a miscommunication about where and what the midcoast's National franchise was—Dick came out personally to the airport and got us, out of no evident motive but kindness. (He also talked nonstop the entire way, with a very distinctive speaking style that can be described only as manically laconic; the truth is that I now know more about this man than I do about some members of my own family.)

[12]To elaborate by way of example: The common experience of accidentally touching a hot stove and yanking your hand back before you're even aware that anything's going on is explained by the fact that many of the processes by which we detect and avoid painful stimuli do not involve the cortex. In the case of the hand and stove, the brain is bypassed altogether; all the important neurochemical action takes place in the spine.

extremely complex and difficult. And comparative neuroanatomy is only part of the problem. Since pain is a totally subjective mental experience, we do not have direct access to anyone or anything's pain but our own; and even just the principles by which we can infer that other human beings experience pain and have a legitimate interest in not feeling pain involve hard-core philosophy—metaphysics, epistemology, value theory, ethics. The fact that even the most highly evolved nonhuman mammals can't use language to communicate with us about their subjective mental experience is only the first layer of additional complication in trying to extend our reasoning about pain and morality to animals. And everything gets progressively more abstract and convoluted as we move farther and farther out from the higher-type mammals into cattle and swine and dogs and cats and rodents, and then birds and fish, and finally invertebrates like lobsters.

The more important point here, though, is that the whole animal-cruelty-and-eating issue is not just complex, it's also uncomfortable. It is, at any rate, uncomfortable for me, and for just about everyone I know who enjoys a variety of foods and yet does not want to see herself as cruel or unfeeling. As far as I can tell, my own main way of dealing with this conflict has been to avoid thinking about the whole unpleasant thing. I should add that it appears to me unlikely that many readers of *Gourmet* wish to think about it, either, or to be queried about the morality of their eating habits in the pages of a culinary monthly. Since, however, the assigned subject of this article is what it was like to attend the 2003 MLF, and thus to spend several days in the midst of a great mass of Americans all eating lobster, and thus to be more or less impelled to think hard about lobster and the experience of buying and eating lobster, it turns out that there is no honest way to avoid certain moral questions

There are several reasons for this. For one thing, it's not just that lobsters get boiled alive, it's that you do it yourself or at least it's done specifically for you, on-site.[13] As mentioned, the World's Largest Lobster Cooker, which is highlighted

---

[13]Morality-wise, let's concede that this cuts both ways. Lobster-eating is at least not abetted by the system of corporate factory farms that produces most beef, pork, and chicken. Because, if nothing else, of the way they're marketed and packaged for sale, we eat these latter meats without having to consider that they were once conscious, sentient creatures to whom horrible things were done. (N.B. "Horrible" here meaning really, really horrible. Write off to PETA or peta.org for their free "Meet Your Meat" video, narrated by Mr. Alec Baldwin, if you want to see just about everything meat-related you don't want to see or think about. (N.B.2 Not that PETA's any sort of font of unspun truth. Like many partisans in complex moral disputes, the PETA people are fanatics, and a lot of their rhetoric seems simplistic and self-righteous. But this particular video, replete with actual factory-farm and corporate-slaughterhouse footage, is both credible and traumatizing.))

as an attraction in the festival's program, is right out there on the MLF's north grounds for everyone to see. Try to imagine a Nebraska Beef Festival[14] at which part of the festivities is watching trucks pull up and the live cattle get driven down the ramp and slaughtered right there on the World's Largest Killing Floor or something—there's no way.

The intimacy of the whole thing is maximized at home, which of course is where most lobster gets prepared and eaten (although note already the semiconscious euphemism "prepared," which in the case of lobsters really means killing them right there in our kitchens). The basic scenario is that we come in from the store and make our little preparations like getting the kettle filled and boiling, and then we lift the lobsters out of the bag or whatever retail container they came home in . . . whereupon some uncomfortable things start to happen. However stuporous a lobster is from the trip home, for instance, it tends to come alarmingly to life when placed in boiling water. If you're tilting it from a container into the steaming kettle, the lobster will sometimes try to cling to the container's sides or even to hook its claws over the kettle's rim like a person trying to keep from going over the edge of a roof. And worse is when the lobster's fully immersed. Even if you cover the kettle and turn away, you can usually hear the cover rattling and clanking as the lobster tries to push it off. Or the creature's claws scraping the sides of the kettle as it thrashes around. The lobster, in other words, behaves very much as you or I would behave if we were plunged into boiling water (with the obvious exception of screaming[15]). A blunter way to say this is that the lobster acts as if it's in terrible pain, causing some cooks to leave the kitchen altogether and to take one of those little lightweight plastic oven-timers with them into another room and wait until the whole process is over.

---

[14]Is it significant that "lobster," "fish," and "chicken" are our culture's words for both the animal and the meat, whereas most mammals seem to require euphemisms like "beef" and "pork" that help us separate the meat we eat from the living creature the meat once was? Is this evidence that some kind of deep unease about eating higher animals is endemic enough to show up in English usage, but that the unease diminishes as we move out of the mammalian order? (And is "lamb"/"lamb" the counterexample that sinks the whole theory, or are there special, biblico-historical reasons for that equivalence?)

[15]There's a relevant populist myth about the high-pitched whistling sound that sometimes issues from a pot of boiling lobster. The sound is really vented steam from the layer of seawater between the lobster's flesh and its carapace (this is why shedders whistle more than hard-shells), but the pop version has it that the sound is the lobster's rabbit-like death-scream. Lobsters communicate via pheromones in their urine and don't have anything close to the vocal equipment for screaming, but the myth's very persistent—which might, once again, point to a low-level cultural unease about the boiling thing.

There happen to be two main criteria that most ethicists agree on for determining whether a living creature has the capacity to suffer and so has genuine interests that it may or may not be our moral duty to consider.[16] One is how much of the neurological hardware required for pain-experience the animal comes equipped with—nociceptors, prostaglandins, neuronal opioid receptors, etc. The other criterion is whether the animal demonstrates behavior associated with pain. And it takes a lot of intellectual gymnastics and behaviorist hairsplitting not to see struggling, thrashing, and lid-clattering as just such pain-behavior. According to marine zoologists, it usually takes lobsters between 35 and 45 seconds to die in boiling water. (No source I could find talks about how long it takes them to die in superheated steam; one rather hopes it's faster.)

There are, of course, other ways to kill your lobster on-site and so achieve maximum freshness. Some cooks' practice is to drive a sharp heavy knife point-first into a spot just above the midpoint between the lobster's eyestalks (more or less where the Third Eye is in human foreheads). This is alleged either to kill the lobster instantly or to render it insensate, and is said at least to eliminate some of the cowardice involved in throwing a creature into boiling water and then fleeing the room. As far as I can tell from talking to proponents of the knife-in-head method, the idea is that it's more violent but ultimately more merciful, plus that a willingness to exert personal agency and accept responsibility for stabbing the lobster's head honors the lobster somehow and entitles one to eat it (there's often a vague sort of Native American spirituality-of-the-hunt flavor to pro-knife arguments). But the problem with the knife method is basic biology: Lobsters' nervous systems operate off not one but several ganglia, a.k.a. nerve bundles, which are sort of wired in series and distributed all along the lobster's underside, from stem to stern. And disabling only the frontal ganglion does not normally result in quick death or unconsciousness.

Another alternative is to put the lobster in cold salty water and then very slowly bring it up to a full boil. Cooks who advocate this method are going on the analogy to a frog, which can supposedly be kept from jumping out of a boiling pot by heating the water incrementally. In order to save a lot of research-summarizing, I'll simply assure you that the analogy between frogs and lobsters turns out not to hold—plus, if the kettle's water isn't aerated seawater, the immersed lobster suffers from slow suffocation, although usually not decisive enough suffocation to keep it

---

[16]"Interests" basically means strong and legitimate preferences, which obviously require some degree of consciousness, responsiveness to stimuli, etc. See, for instance, the utilitarian philosopher Peter Singer, whose 1974 Animal Liberation is more or less the bible of the modern animal-rights movement:

It would be nonsense to say that it was not in the interests of a stone to be kicked along the road by a schoolboy. A stone does not have interests because it cannot suffer. Nothing that we can do to it could possibly make any difference to its welfare. A mouse, on the other hand, does have an interest in not being kicked along the road, because it will suffer if it is.

from still thrashing and clattering when the water gets hot enough to kill it. In fact, lobsters boiled incrementally often display a whole bonus set of gruesome, convulsion like reactions that you don't see in regular boiling.

Ultimately, the only certain virtues of the home-lobotomy and slow-heating methods are comparative, because there are even worse/crueler ways people prepare lobster. Time-thrifty cooks sometimes microwave them alive (usually after poking several vent-holes in the carapace, which is a precaution most shellfish-microwavers learn about the hard way). Live dismemberment, on the other hand, is big in Europe—some chefs cut the lobster in half before cooking; others like to tear off the claws and tail and toss only these parts into the pot.

And there's more unhappy news respecting suffering-criterion number one. Lobsters don't have much in the way of eyesight or hearing, but they do have an exquisite tactile sense, one facilitated by hundreds of thousands of tiny hairs that protrude through their carapace. "Thus it is," in the words of T. M. Prudden's industry classic *About Lobster*, "that although encased in what seems a solid, impenetrable armor, the lobster can receive stimuli and impressions from without as readily as if it possessed a soft and delicate skin." And lobsters do have nociceptors,[17] as well as invertebrate versions of the prostaglandins and major neurotransmitters via which our own brains register pain.

Lobsters do not, on the other hand, appear to have the equipment for making or absorbing natural opioids like endorphins and enkephalins, which are what more advanced nervous systems use to try to handle intense pain. From this fact, though, one could conclude either that lobsters are maybe even more vulnerable to pain, since they lack mammalian nervous systems' built-in analgesia, or, instead, that the absence of natural opioids implies an absence of the really intense pain-sensations that natural opioids are designed to mitigate. I for one can detect a marked upswing in mood as I contemplate this latter possibility. It could be that their lack of endorphin/enkephalin hardware means that lobsters' raw subjective experience of pain is so radically different from mammals' that it may not even deserve the term "pain." Perhaps lobsters are more like those frontal-lobotomy patients one reads about who report experiencing pain in a totally different way than you and I. These patients evidently do feel physical pain, neurologically speaking, but don't dislike it—though neither do they like it; it's more that they feel it but don't feel anything *about* it—the point being that the pain is not distressing to them or something they want to get away from. Maybe lobsters, who are also without frontal lobes, are detached from the neurological-registration-of-injury-

---

[17]This is the neurological term for special pain-receptors that are "sensitive to potentially damaging extremes of temperature, to mechanical forces, and to chemical substances which are released when body tissues are damaged."

or-hazard we call pain in just the same way. There is, after all, a difference between (1) pain as a purely neurological event, and (2) actual suffering, which seems crucially to involve an emotional component, an awareness of pain as unpleasant, as something to fear/dislike/want to avoid.

Still, after all the abstract intellection, there remain the facts of the frantically clanking lid, the pathetic clinging to the edge of the pot. Standing at the stove, it is hard to deny in any meaningful way that this is a living creature experiencing pain and wishing to avoid/escape the painful experience. To my lay mind, the lobster's behavior in the kettle appears to be the expression of a preference; and it may well be that an ability to form preferences is the decisive criterion for real suffering.[18] The logic of this (preference → relation may be easiest to see in the negative case. If you cut certain kinds of worms in half, the halves will often keep crawling around and going about their vermiform business as if nothing had happened. When we assert, based on their post-op behavior, that these worms appear not to be suffering, what we're really saying is that there's no sign the worms know anything bad has happened or would prefer not to have gotten cut in half.

Lobsters, though, are known to exhibit preferences. Experiments have shown that they can detect changes of only a degree or two in water temperature; one reason for their complex migratory cycles (which can often cover 100-plus miles a year) is to pursue the temperatures they like best.[19] And, as mentioned, they're bottom-dwellers and do not like bright light—if a tank of food lobsters is out in the sunlight or a store's fluorescence, the lobsters will always congregate in whatever part is darkest. Fairly solitary in the ocean, they also clearly dislike the crowding that's part of their captivity in tanks, since (as also mentioned) one

---

[18]"Preference" is maybe roughly synonymous with "interests," but it is a better term for our purposes because it's less abstractly philosophical—"preference" seems more personal, and it's the whole idea of a living creature's personal experience that's at issue.

[19]Of course, the most common sort of counterargument here would begin by objecting that "like best" is really just a metaphor, and a misleadingly anthropomorphic one at that. The counterarguer would posit that the lobster seeks to maintain a certain optimal ambient temperature out of nothing but unconscious instinct (with a similar explanation for the low-light affinities upcoming in the main text). The thrust of such a counterargument will be that the lobster's thrashings and clankings in the kettle express not unpreferred pain but involuntary reflexes, like your leg shooting out when the doctor hits your knee. Be advised that there are professional scientists, including many researchers who use animals in experiments, who hold to the view that nonhuman creatures have no real feelings at all, merely "behaviors." Be further advised that this view has a long history that goes all the way back to Descartes, although its modern support comes mostly from behaviorist psychology.

To these what-looks-like-pain-is-really-just-reflexes counterarguments, however, there happen to be all sorts of scientific and pro–animal rights counter-counterarguments. And then further attempted rebuttals and redirects, and so on. Suffice it to say that both the scientific and the philosophical arguments on either side of the animal-suffering issue are involved, abstruse, technical, often informed by self-interest or ideology, and in the end so totally inconclusive that as a practical matter, in the kitchen or restaurant, it all still seems to come down to individual conscience, going with (no pun) your gut.

reason why lobsters' claws are banded on capture is to keep them from attacking one another under the stress of close-quarter storage.

In any event, at the MLF, standing by the bubbling tanks outside the World's Largest Lobster Cooker, watching the fresh-caught lobsters pile over one another, wave their hobbled claws impotently, huddle in the rear corners, or scrabble frantically back from the glass as you approach, it is difficult not to sense that they're unhappy, or frightened, even if it's some rudimentary version of these feelings . . . and, again, why does rudimentariness even enter into it? Why is a primitive, inarticulate form of suffering less urgent or uncomfortable for the person who's helping to inflict it by paying for the food it results in? I'm not trying to give you a PETA-like screed here—at least I don't think so. I'm trying, rather, to work out and articulate some of the troubling questions that arise amid all the laughter and saltation and community pride of the Maine Lobster Festival. The truth is that if you, the festival attendee, permit yourself to think that lobsters can suffer and would rather not, the MLF begins to take on the aspect of something like a Roman circus or medieval torture-fest.

Does that comparison seem a bit much? If so, exactly why? Or what about this one: Is it possible that future generations will regard our present agribusiness and eating practices in much the same way we now view Nero's entertainments or Mengele's experiments? My own initial reaction is that such a comparison is hysterical, extreme—and yet the reason it seems extreme to me appears to be that I believe animals are less morally important than human beings;[20] and when it comes to defending such a belief, even to myself, I have to acknowledge that (a) I have an obvious selfish interest in this belief, since I like to eat certain kinds of animals and want to be able to keep doing it, and (b) I haven't succeeded in working out any sort of personal ethical system in which the belief is truly defensible instead of just selfishly convenient.

Given this article's venue and my own lack of culinary sophistication, I'm curious about whether the reader can identify with any of these reactions and acknowledgments and discomforts. I'm also concerned not to come off as shrill or preachy when what I really am is more like confused. For those Gourmet readers who enjoy well-prepared and -presented meals involving beef, veal, lamb, pork, chicken, lobster, etc.: Do you think much about the (possible) moral status and (probable) suffering of the animals involved? If you do, what ethical convictions have you worked out that permit you not just to eat but to savor and enjoy

---

[20]Meaning a *lot* less important, apparently, since the moral comparison here is not the value of one human's life vs. the value of one animal's life, but rather the value of one animal's life vs. the value of one human's taste for a particular kind of protein. Even the most diehard carniphile will acknowledge that it's possible to live and eat well without consuming animals.

flesh-based viands (since of course refined *enjoyment*, rather than mere ingestion, is the whole point of gastronomy)? If, on the other hand, you'll have no truck with confusions or convictions and regard stuff like the previous paragraph as just so much fatuous navel-gazing, what makes it feel truly okay, inside, to just dismiss the whole thing out of hand? That is, is your refusal to think about any of this the product of actual thought, or is it just that you don't want to think about it? And if the latter, then why not? Do you ever think, even idly, about the possible reasons for your reluctance to think about it? I am not trying to bait anyone here—I'm genuinely curious. After all, isn't being extra aware and attentive and thoughtful about one's food and its overall context part of what distinguishes a real gourmet? Or is all the gourmet's extra attention and sensibility just supposed to be sensuous? Is it really all just a matter of taste and presentation?

These last few queries, though, while sincere, obviously involve much larger and more abstract questions about the connections (if any) between aesthetics and morality—about what the adjective in a phrase like "The Magazine of Good Living" is really supposed to mean—and these questions lead straightaway into such deep and treacherous waters that it's probably best to stop the public discussion right here. There are limits to what even interested persons can ask of each other.

FOR INFORMAL WRITING

What do you think is Wallace's main point in this essay? How do you know?

FOR DISCUSSION

1. How does the context of the Maine Lobster Festival inspire Wallace's argument? What is the effect of the juxtaposition of the Festival with his claims?
2. What do you think of the interdisciplinary nature of this essay? What lenses or perspectives does Wallace use to support his claims? How effective are they?
3. How does Wallace attempt to elicit the reader's sympathies? How effective are these strategies?

FOR WRITING

Scientific understandings of lobster anatomy aside, what ethical considerations are evoked by Wallace's article? What is the tension between being a gourmet (or a "foodie") and the ethics of certain types of eating? How might Wallace argue that we weigh human pleasure against the ethical realities of certain types of eating?

1918 Influenza: The Mother of All Pandemics (2006)

Jeffrey K. Taubenberger and David M. Morens

Dr. Jeffrey Taubenberger is chair of the Department of Molecular Pathology at the Armed Forces Institute of Pathology, Rockville, Maryland. His research interests include the molecular pathophysiology and evolution of influenza viruses. Dr. David Morens is an epidemiologist with a long-standing interest in emerging infectious diseases, virology, tropical medicine, and medical history. Since 1999, he has worked at the National Institute of Allergy and Infectious Diseases.

> "Curiouser and curiouser!" cried Alice.
> —Lewis Carroll, *Alice's Adventures in Wonderland*, 1865

An estimated one third of the world's population (or 500 million persons) were infected and had clinically apparent illnesses (1,2) during the 1918–1919 influenza pandemic. The disease was exceptionally severe. Case-fatality rates were >2.5%, compared to <0.1% in other influenza pandemics (3,4). Total deaths were estimated at 50 million (5–7) and were arguably as high as 100 million (7).

The impact of this pandemic was not limited to 1918–1919. All influenza A pandemics since that time, and indeed almost all cases of influenza A worldwide (excepting human infections from avian viruses such as H5N1 and H7N7), have been caused by descendants of the 1918 virus, including "drifted" H1N1 viruses and reassorted H2N2 and H3N2 viruses. The latter are composed of key genes from the 1918 virus, updated by subsequently incorporated avian influenza genes that code for novel surface proteins, making the 1918 virus indeed the "mother" of all pandemics.

Jeffrey K. Taubenberger and David M. Morens 1918 Influenza: the Mother of All Pandemics (2006).

In 1918, the cause of human influenza and its links to avian and swine influenza were unknown. Despite clinical and epidemiologic similarities to influenza pandemics of 1889, 1847, and even earlier, many questioned whether such an explosively fatal disease could be influenza at all. That question did not begin to be resolved until the 1930s, when closely related influenza viruses (now known to be H1N1 viruses) were isolated, first from pigs and shortly thereafter from humans. Seroepidemiologic studies soon linked both of these viruses to the 1918 pandemic (8). Subsequent research indicates that descendants of the 1918 virus still persists enzootically in pigs. They probably also circulated continuously in humans, undergoing gradual antigenic drift and causing annual epidemics, until the 1950s. With the appearance of a new H2N2 pandemic strain in 1957 ("Asian flu"), the direct H1N1 viral descendants of the 1918 pandemic strain disappeared from human circulation entirely, although the related lineage persisted enzootically in pigs. But in 1977, human H1N1 viruses suddenly "reemerged" from a laboratory freezer (9). They continue to circulate endemically and epidemically.

Thus in 2006, 2 major descendant lineages of the 1918 H1N1 virus, as well as 2 additional reassortant lineages, persist naturally: a human epidemic/endemic H1N1 lineage, a porcine enzootic H1N1 lineage (so-called classic swine flu), and the reassorted human H3N2 virus lineage, which like the human H1N1 virus, has led to a porcine H3N2 lineage. None of these viral descendants, however, approaches the pathogenicity of the 1918 parent virus. Apparently, the porcine H1N1 and H3N2 lineages uncommonly infect humans, and the human H1N1 and H3N2 lineages have both been associated with substantially lower rates of illness and death than the virus of 1918. In fact, current H1N1 death rates are even lower than those for H3N2 lineage strains (prevalent from 1968 until the present). H1N1 viruses descended from the 1918 strain, as well as H3N2 viruses, have now been cocirculating worldwide for 29 years and show little evidence of imminent extinction.

TRYING TO UNDERSTAND WHAT HAPPENED

By the early 1990s, 75 years of research had failed to answer a most basic question about the 1918 pandemic: why was it so fatal? No virus from 1918 had been isolated, but all of its apparent descendants caused substantially milder human disease. Moreover, examination of mortality data from the 1920s suggests that within a few years after 1918, influenza epidemics had settled into a pattern of annual epidemicity associated with strain drifting and substantially lowered death rates. Did some critical viral genetic event produce a 1918 virus of remarkable pathogenicity and then another critical genetic event occur soon after the 1918 pandemic to produce an attenuated H1N1 virus?

In 1995, a scientific team identified archival influenza autopsy materials collected in the autumn of 1918 and began the slow process of sequencing small viral RNA fragments to determine the genomic structure of the causative influenza virus (10). These efforts have now determined the complete genomic sequence of 1 virus and partial sequences from 4 others. The primary data from the above studies (11–17) and a number of reviews covering different aspects of the 1918 pandemic have recently been published (18–20) and confirm that the 1918 virus is the likely ancestor of all 4 of the human and swine H1N1 and H3N2 lineages, as well as the "extinct" H2N2 lineage. No known mutations correlated with high pathogenicity in other human or animal influenza viruses have been found in the 1918 genome, but ongoing studies to map virulence factors are yielding interesting results. The 1918 sequence data, however, leave unanswered questions about the origin of the virus (19) and about the epidemiology of the pandemic.

WHEN AND WHERE DID THE 1918 INFLUENZA PANDEMIC ARISE?

Before and after 1918, most influenza pandemics developed in Asia and spread from there to the rest of the world. Confounding definite assignment of a geographic point of origin, the 1918 pandemic spread more or less simultaneously in 3 distinct waves during a 12-month period in 1918–1919, in Europe, Asia, and North America (the first wave was best described in the United States in March 1918). Historical and epidemiologic data are inadequate to identify the geographic origin of the virus (21), and recent phylogenetic analysis of the 1918 viral genome does not place the virus in any geographic context (19).

Although in 1918 influenza was not a nationally reportable disease and diagnostic criteria for influenza and pneumonia were vague, death rates from influenza and pneumonia in the United States had risen sharply in 1915 and 1916 because of a major respiratory disease epidemic beginning in December 1915 (22). Death rates then dipped slightly in 1917. The first pandemic influenza wave appeared in the spring of 1918, followed in rapid succession by much more fatal second and third waves in the fall and winter of 1918–1919, respectively. Is it possible that a poorly adapted H1N1 virus was already beginning to spread in 1915, causing some serious illnesses but not yet sufficiently fit to initiate a pandemic? Data consistent with this possibility were reported at the time from European military camps (23), but a counter argument is that if a strain with a new hemagglutinin (HA) was causing enough illness to affect the US national death rates from pneumonia and influenza, it should have caused a pandemic sooner, and when it eventually did, in 1918, many people should have been immune or at least partially immunoprotected. "Herald" events in 1915, 1916, and possibly even in early 1918, if they occurred, would be difficult to identify.

The 1918 influenza pandemic had another unique feature, the simultaneous (or nearly simultaneous) infection of humans and swine. The virus of the 1918 pandemic likely expressed an antigenically novel subtype to which most humans and swine were immunologically naive in 1918 (12,20). Recently published sequence and phylogenetic analyses suggest that the genes encoding the HA and neuraminidase (NA) surface proteins of the 1918 virus were derived from an avianlike influenza virus shortly before the start of the pandemic and that the precursor virus had not circulated widely in humans or swine in the few decades before (12,15,24). More recent analyses of the other gene segments of the virus also support this conclusion. Regression analyses of human and swine influenza sequences obtained from 1930 to the present place the initial circulation of the 1918 precursor virus in humans at approximately 1915–1918 (20). Thus, the precursor was probably not circulating widely in humans until shortly before 1918, nor did it appear to have jumped directly from any species of bird studied to date (19). In summary, its origin remains puzzling.

WERE THE 3 WAVES IN 1918–1919 CAUSED BY THE SAME VIRUS? IF SO, HOW AND WHY?

Historical records since the 16th century suggest that new influenza pandemics may appear at any time of year, not necessarily in the familiar annual winter patterns of interpandemic years, presumably because newly shifted influenza viruses behave differently when they find a universal or highly susceptible human population. Thereafter, confronted by the selection pressures of population immunity, these pandemic viruses begin to drift genetically and eventually settle into a pattern of annual epidemic recurrences caused by the drifted virus variants.

In the 1918–1919 pandemic, a first or spring wave began in March 1918 and spread unevenly through the United States, Europe, and possibly Asia over the next 6 months. Illness rates were high, but death rates in most locales were not appreciably above normal. A second or fall wave spread globally from September to November 1918 and was highly fatal. In many nations, a third wave occurred in early 1919 (21). Clinical similarities led contemporary observers to conclude initially that they were observing the same disease in the successive waves. The milder forms of illness in all 3 waves were identical and typical of influenza seen in the 1889 pandemic and in prior interpandemic years. In retrospect, even the rapid progressions from uncomplicated influenza infections to fatal pneumonia, a hallmark of the 1918–1919 fall and winter waves, had been noted in the relatively few severe spring wave cases. The differences between the waves thus seemed to be primarily in the much higher frequency of complicated, severe, and fatal cases in the last 2 waves.

But 3 extensive pandemic waves of influenza within 1 year, occurring in rapid succession, with only the briefest of quiescent intervals between them, was unprecedented. The occurrence, and to some extent the severity, of recurrent annual outbreaks, are driven by viral antigenic drift, with an antigenic variant virus emerging to become dominant approximately every 2 to 3 years. Without such drift, circulating human influenza viruses would presumably disappear once herd immunity had reached a critical threshold at which further virus spread was sufficiently limited. The timing and spacing of influenza epidemics in interpandemic years have been subjects of speculation for decades. Factors believed to be responsible include partial herd immunity limiting virus spread in all but the most favorable circumstances, which include lower environmental temperatures and human nasal temperatures (beneficial to thermolabile viruses such as influenza), optimal humidity, increased crowding indoors, and imperfect ventilation due to closed windows and suboptimal airflow.

However, such factors cannot explain the 3 pandemic waves of 1918–1919, which occurred in the spring-summer, summer-fall, and winter (of the Northern Hemisphere), respectively. The first 2 waves occurred at a time of year normally unfavorable to influenza virus spread. The second wave caused simultaneous outbreaks in the Northern and Southern Hemispheres from September to November. Furthermore, the interwave periods were so brief as to be almost undetectable in some locales. Reconciling epidemiologically the steep drop in cases in the first and second waves with the sharp rises in cases of the second and third waves is difficult. Assuming even transient postinfection immunity, how could susceptible persons be too few to sustain transmission at 1 point, and yet enough to start a new explosive pandemic wave a few weeks later? Could the virus have mutated profoundly and almost simultaneously around the world, in the short periods between the successive waves? Acquiring viral drift sufficient to produce new influenza strains capable of escaping population immunity is believed to take years of global circulation, not weeks of local circulation. And having occurred, such mutated viruses normally take months to spread around the world.

At the beginning of other "off season" influenza pandemics, successive distinct waves within a year have not been reported. The 1889 pandemic, for example, began in the late spring of 1889 and took several months to spread throughout the world, peaking in northern Europe and the United States late in 1889 or early in 1890. The second recurrence peaked in late spring 1891 (more than a year after the first pandemic appearance) and the third in early 1892 (21). As was true for the 1918 pandemic, the second 1891 recurrence produced of the most deaths. The 3 recurrences in 1889–1892, however, were spread over >3 years, in contrast to 1918–1919, when the sequential waves seen in individual countries were typically compressed into 8–9 months.

What gave the 1918 virus the unprecedented ability to generate rapidly successive pandemic waves is unclear. Because the only 1918 pandemic virus samples we have yet identified are from second-wave patients (16), nothing can yet be said about whether the first (spring) wave, or for that matter, the third wave, represented circulation of the same virus or variants of it. Data from 1918 suggest that persons infected in the second wave may have been protected from influenza in the third wave. But the few data bearing on protection during the second and third waves after infection in the first wave are inconclusive and do little to resolve the question of whether the first wave was caused by the same virus or whether major genetic evolutionary events were occurring even as the pandemic exploded and progressed. Only influenza RNA–positive human samples from before 1918, and from all 3 waves, can answer this question.

WHAT WAS THE ANIMAL HOST ORIGIN OF THE PANDEMIC VIRUS?

Viral sequence data now suggest that the entire 1918 virus was novel to humans in, or shortly before, 1918, and that it thus was not a reassortant virus produced from old existing strains that acquired 1 or more new genes, such as those causing the 1957 and 1968 pandemics. On the contrary, the 1918 virus appears to be an avianlike influenza virus derived in toto from an unknown source (17,19), as its 8 genome segments are substantially different from contemporary avian influenza genes. Influenza virus gene sequences from a number of fixed specimens of wild birds collected circa 1918 show little difference from avian viruses isolated today, indicating that avian viruses likely undergo little antigenic change in their natural hosts even over long periods (24,25).

For example, the 1918 nucleoprotein (NP) gene sequence is similar to that of viruses found in wild birds at the amino acid level but very divergent at the nucleotide level, which suggests considerable evolutionary distance between the sources of the 1918 NP and of currently sequenced NP genes in wild bird strains (13,19). One way of looking at the evolutionary distance of genes is to compare ratios of synonymous to nonsynonymous nucleotide substitutions. A synonymous substitution represents a silent change, a nucleotide change in a codon that does not result in an amino acid replacement. A nonsynonymous substitution is a nucleotide change in a codon that results in an amino acid replacement. Generally, a viral gene subjected to immunologic drift pressure or adapting to a new host exhibits a greater percentage of nonsynonymous mutations, while a virus under little selective pressure accumulates mainly synonymous changes. Since little or no selection pressure is exerted on synonymous changes, they are thought to reflect evolutionary distance.

Because the 1918 gene segments have more synonymous changes from known sequences of wild bird strains than expected, they are unlikely to have emerged directly from an avian influenza virus similar to those that have been sequenced so far. This is especially apparent when one examines the differences at 4-fold degenerate codons, the subset of synonymous changes in which, at the third codon position, any of the 4 possible nucleotides can be substituted without changing the resulting amino acid. At the same time, the 1918 sequences have too few amino acid differences from those of wild-bird strains to have spent many years adapting only in a human or swine intermediate host. One possible explanation is that these unusual gene segments were acquired from a reservoir of influenza virus that has not yet been identified or sampled. All of these findings beg the question: where did the 1918 virus come from?

In contrast to the genetic makeup of the 1918 pandemic virus, the novel gene segments of the reassorted 1957 and 1968 pandemic viruses all originated in Eurasian avian viruses (26); both human viruses arose by the same mechanism—reassortment of a Eurasian wild waterfowl strain with the previously circulating human H1N1 strain. Proving the hypothesis that the virus responsible for the 1918 pandemic had a markedly different origin requires samples of human influenza strains circulating before 1918 and samples of influenza strains in the wild that more closely resemble the 1918 sequences.

WHAT WAS THE BIOLOGICAL BASIS FOR 1918 PANDEMIC VIRUS PATHOGENICITY?

Sequence analysis alone does not offer clues to the pathogenicity of the 1918 virus. A series of experiments are under way to model virulence in vitro and in animal models by using viral constructs containing 1918 genes produced by reverse genetics.

Influenza virus infection requires binding of the HA protein to sialic acid receptors on host cell surface. The HA receptor-binding site configuration is different for those influenza viruses adapted to infect birds and those adapted to infect humans. Influenza virus strains adapted to birds preferentially bind sialic acid receptors with α(2–3) linked sugars (27–29). Human-adapted influenza viruses are thought to preferentially bind receptors with α(2–6) linkages. The switch from this avian receptor configuration requires of the virus only 1 amino acid change (30), and the HAs of all 5 sequenced 1918 viruses have this change, which suggests that it could be a critical step in human host adaptation. A second change that greatly augments virus binding to the human receptor may also occur, but only 3 of 5 1918 HA sequences have it (16).

This means that at least 2 H1N1 receptor-binding variants cocirculated in 1918: 1 with high-affinity binding to the human receptor and 1 with mixed-affinity binding to both avian and human receptors. No geographic or chronologic indication exists to suggest that one of these variants was the precursor of the other, nor are there consistent differences between the case histories or histopathologic features of the 5 patients infected with them. Whether the viruses were equally transmissible in 1918, whether they had identical patterns of replication in the respiratory tree, and whether one or both also circulated in the first and third pandemic waves, are unknown.

In a series of in vivo experiments, recombinant influenza viruses containing between 1 and 5 gene segments of the 1918 virus have been produced. Those constructs bearing the 1918 HA and NA are all highly pathogenic in mice (31). Furthermore, expression microarray analysis performed on whole lung tissue of mice infected with the 1918 HA/NA recombinant showed increased upregulation of genes involved in apoptosis, tissue injury, and oxidative damage (32). These findings are unexpected because the viruses with the 1918 genes had not been adapted to mice; control experiments in which mice were infected with modern human viruses showed little disease and limited viral replication. The lungs of animals infected with the 1918 HA/NA construct showed bronchial and alveolar epithelial necrosis and a marked inflammatory infiltrate, which suggests that the 1918 HA (and possibly the NA) contain virulence factors for mice. The viral genotypic basis of this pathogenicity is not yet mapped. Whether pathogenicity in mice effectively models pathogenicity in humans is unclear. The potential role of the other 1918 proteins, singularly and in combination, is also unknown. Experiments to map further the genetic basis of virulence of the 1918 virus in various animal models are planned. These experiments may help define the viral component to the unusual pathogenicity of the 1918 virus but cannot address whether specific host factors in 1918 accounted for unique influenza mortality patterns.

WHY DID THE 1918 VIRUS KILL SO MANY HEALTHY YOUNG ADULTS?

The curve of influenza deaths by age at death has historically, for at least 150 years, been U-shaped, exhibiting mortality peaks in the very young and the very old, with a comparatively low frequency of deaths at all ages in between. In contrast, age-specific death rates in the 1918 pandemic exhibited a distinct pattern that has not been documented before or since: a "W-shaped" curve, similar to the familiar U-shaped curve but with the addition of a third (middle) distinct peak of deaths in young adults 20–40 years of age. Influenza and pneumonia death rates for those 15–34 years of age in 1918–1919, for example, were >20 times higher than in previous years (35). Overall, nearly half of the influenza-related deaths in the 1918 pandemic were in young adults 20–40 years of age, a phenomenon unique to that pandemic year. The 1918 pandemic is also unique among influenza pandemics in that absolute risk of influenza death was higher in those <65 years of age than in those >65; persons <65 years of age accounted for >99% of all excess influenza-related deaths in 1918–1919. In comparison, the <65-year age group accounted for 36% of all excess influenza-related deaths in the 1957 H2N2 pandemic and 48% in the 1968 H3N2 pandemic (33).

A sharper perspective emerges when 1918 age-specific influenza morbidity rates (21) are used to adjust the W-shaped mortality curve. Persons <35 years of age in 1918 had a disproportionately high influenza incidence. But even after adjusting age-specific deaths by age-specific clinical attack rates, a W-shaped curve with a case-fatality peak in young adults remains and is significantly different from U-shaped age-specific case-fatality curves typically seen in other influenza years, e.g., 1928–1929. Also, in 1918 those 5 to 14 years of age accounted for a disproportionate number of influenza cases, but had a much lower death rate from influenza and pneumonia than other age groups. To explain this pattern, we must look beyond properties of the virus to host and environmental factors, possibly including immunopathology (e.g., antibody-dependent infection enhancement associated with prior virus exposures [38]) and exposure to risk cofactors such as coinfecting agents, medications, and environmental agents.

One theory that may partially explain these findings is that the 1918 virus had an intrinsically high virulence, tempered only in those patients who had been born before 1889, e.g., because of exposure to a then-circulating virus capable of providing partial immunoprotection against the 1918 virus strain only in persons old enough (>35 years) to have been infected during that prior era (35). But this theory would present an additional paradox: an obscure precursor virus that left no detectable trace today would have had to have appeared and disappeared before 1889 and then reappeared more than 3 decades later.

Epidemiologic data on rates of clinical influenza by age, collected between 1900 and 1918, provide good evidence for the emergence of an antigenically novel influenza virus in 1918 (21). Jordan showed that from 1900 to 1917, the 5- to 15-year age group accounted for 11% of total influenza cases, while the >65-year age group accounted for 6% of influenza cases. But in 1918, cases in the 5- to 15-year-old group jumped to 25% of influenza cases (compatible with exposure to an antigenically novel virus strain), while the >65-year age group only accounted for 0.6% of the influenza cases, findings consistent with previously acquired protective immunity caused by an identical or closely related viral protein to which older persons had once been exposed. Mortality data are in accord. In 1918, persons >75 years had lower influenza and pneumonia case-fatality rates than they had during the prepandemic period of 1911–1917. At the other end of the age spectrum, a high proportion of deaths in infancy and early childhood in 1918 mimics the age pattern, if not the mortality rate, of other influenza pandemics.

COULD A 1918-LIKE PANDEMIC APPEAR AGAIN? IF SO, WHAT COULD WE DO ABOUT IT?

In its disease course and pathologic features, the 1918 pandemic was different in degree, but not in kind, from previous and subsequent pandemics. Despite the extraordinary number of global deaths, most influenza cases in 1918 (>95% in most locales in industrialized nations) were mild and essentially indistinguishable from influenza cases today. Furthermore, laboratory experiments with recombinant influenza viruses containing genes from the 1918 virus suggest that the 1918 and 1918-like viruses would be as sensitive as other typical virus strains to the Food and Drug Administration–approved antiinfluenza drugs rimantadine and oseltamivir.

However, some characteristics of the 1918 pandemic appear unique: most notably, death rates were 5–20 times higher than expected. Clinically and pathologically, these high death rates appear to be the result of several factors, including a higher proportion of severe and complicated infections of the respiratory tract, rather than involvement of organ systems outside the normal range of the influenza virus. Also, the deaths were concentrated in an unusually young age group. Finally, in 1918, 3 separate recurrences of influenza followed each other with unusual rapidity, resulting in 3 explosive pandemic waves within a year's time. Each of these unique characteristics may reflect genetic features of the 1918 virus, but understanding them will also require examination of host and environmental factors.

Until we can ascertain which of these factors gave rise to the mortality patterns observed and learn more about the formation of the pandemic, predictions are only educated guesses. We can only conclude that since it happened once, analogous conditions could lead to an equally devastating pandemic.

Like the 1918 virus, H5N1 is an avian virus (39), though a distantly related one. The evolutionary path that led to pandemic emergence in 1918 is entirely unknown, but it appears to be different in many respects from the current situation with H5N1. There are no historical data, either in 1918 or in any other pandemic, for establishing that a pandemic "precursor" virus caused a highly pathogenic outbreak in domestic poultry, and no highly pathogenic avian influenza (HPAI) virus, including H5N1 and a number of others, has ever been known to cause a major human epidemic, let alone a pandemic. While data bearing on influenza virus human cell adaptation (e.g., receptor binding) are beginning to be understood at the molecular level, the basis for viral adaptation to efficient human-to-human spread, the chief prerequisite for pandemic emergence, is unknown for any influenza virus. The 1918 virus acquired this trait, but we do not know how, and we currently have no way of knowing whether H5N1 viruses are now in a parallel process of acquiring human-to-human transmissibility. Despite an explosion of data on the 1918 virus during the past decade, we are not much closer to understanding pandemic emergence in 2006 than we were in understanding the risk of H1N1 "swine flu" emergence in 1976.

Even with modern antiviral and antibacterial drugs, vaccines, and prevention knowledge, the return of a pandemic virus equivalent in pathogenicity to the virus of 1918 would likely kill >100 million people worldwide. A pandemic virus with the (alleged) pathogenic potential of some recent H5N1 outbreaks could cause substantially more deaths.

Whether because of viral, host or environmental factors, the 1918 virus causing the first or "spring" wave was not associated with the exceptional pathogenicity of the second (fall) and third (winter) waves. Identification of an influenza RNA-positive case from the first wave could point to a genetic basis for virulence by allowing differences in viral sequences to be highlighted. Identification of pre-1918 human influenza RNA samples would help us understand the timing of emergence of the 1918 virus. Surveillance and genomic sequencing of large numbers of animal influenza viruses will help us understand the genetic basis of host adaptation and the extent of the natural reservoir of influenza viruses. Understanding influenza pandemics in general requires understanding the 1918 pandemic in all its historical, epidemiologic, and biologic aspects.

FOR INFORMAL WRITING

"Until we can ascertain which of these factors gave rise to the mortality patterns observed and learn more about the formation of the pandemic, predictions are only educated guesses. We can only conclude that since it happened once, analogous conditions could lead to an equally devastating pandemic." What do the authors think had been learned from the epidemic of 1918?

FOR DISCUSSION

1. What is your experience reading what is notably a science- and data-heavy article? What can you assume about the intended audience based on this language?
2. What aspects of the article are most useful to us as general readers to help us understand the overall point of the article?
3. Have we learned the lessons of 1918? Why or why not?

FOR WRITING

What other information can you find about the Spanish Influenza—published in newspapers, magazines, etc.—at the time of the 1918 pandemic? What, if any, connections, or common perspectives can you find among them? What new perspective or context is provided by this analysis, published in 2006?

WHAT'S NEW IS OLD

Consider this essay along with the more recent article by Charles C. Mann, "Pandemics Leave Us Forever Altered." The disciplinary "lens" for each is quite different—one is a more scientific analysis while the other is more a cultural response. Nonetheless, one can't help but note the ironies when reading each within the other's context. What similarities or differences strike you, and to what effect?

Is Google Making Us Stupid? (2008)
Nicholas Carr (1959–)

A well-known writer whose work focuses on the intersection between technology and culture, Nicholas Carr has been a columnist for nearly twenty years. His name, however, came into prominence in 2008 when "Is Google Making Us Stupid?" was published by The Atlantic. *Carr further developed the argument in this well-known piece in his book,* The Shallows: What the Internet is Doing to Our Brains *(2010), which was a finalist for the 2011 Pulitzer Prize. He teaches sociology at Williams College in Massachusetts, and he was previously the editor of the* Harvard Business Review. *What follows is one of the first pieces to sound the alarm about our obsessions with being online; remember that when this article was published, the iPhone had been out for only one year.*

"Dave, stop. Stop, will you? Stop, Dave. Will you stop, Dave?" So the supercomputer HAL pleads with the implacable astronaut Dave Bowman in a famous and weirdly poignant scene toward the end of Stanley Kubrick's *2001: A Space Odyssey*. Bowman, having nearly been sent to a deep-space death by the malfunctioning machine, is calmly, coldly disconnecting the memory circuits that control its artificial brain. "Dave, my mind is going," HAL says, forlornly. "I can feel it. I can feel it."

I can feel it, too. Over the past few years I've had an uncomfortable sense that someone, or something, has been tinkering with my brain, remapping the neural circuitry, reprogramming the memory. My mind isn't going—so far as I can tell—but it's changing. I'm not thinking the way I used to think. I can feel it most strongly when I'm reading. Immersing myself in a book or a lengthy article used to be easy. My mind would get caught up in the narrative or the turns of the argument, and I'd

---

From The Atlantic. © 2008 The Atlantic Monthly Group, LLC. All rights reserved. Used under license.

spend hours strolling through long stretches of prose. That's rarely the case anymore. Now my concentration often starts to drift after two or three pages. I get fidgety, lose the thread, begin looking for something else to do. I feel as if I'm always dragging my wayward brain back to the text. The deep reading that used to come naturally has become a struggle.

I think I know what's going on. For more than a decade now, I've been spending a lot of time online, searching and surfing and sometimes adding to the great databases of the Internet. The Web has been a godsend to me as a writer. Research that once required days in the stacks or periodical rooms of libraries can now be done in minutes. A few Google searches, some quick clicks on hyperlinks, and I've got the telltale fact or pithy quote I was after. Even when I'm not working, I'm as likely as not to be foraging in the Web's info-thickets—reading and writing e-mails, scanning headlines and blog posts, watching videos and listening to podcasts, or just tripping from link to link to link. (Unlike footnotes, to which they're sometimes likened, hyperlinks don't merely point to related works; they propel you toward them.)

For me, as for others, the Net is becoming a universal medium, the conduit for most of the information that flows through my eyes and ears and into my mind. The advantages of having immediate access to such an incredibly rich store of information are many, and they've been widely described and duly applauded. "The perfect recall of silicon memory," *Wired*'s Clive Thompson has written, "can be an enormous boon to thinking." But that boon comes at a price. As the media theorist Marshall McLuhan pointed out in the 1960s, media are not just passive channels of information. They supply the stuff of thought, but they also shape the process of thought. And what the Net seems to be doing is chipping away my capacity for concentration and contemplation. My mind now expects to take in information the way the Net distributes it: in a swiftly moving stream of particles. Once I was a scuba diver in the sea of words. Now I zip along the surface like a guy on a Jet Ski.

I'm not the only one. When I mention my troubles with reading to friends and acquaintances—literary types, most of them—many say they're having similar experiences. The more they use the Web, the more they have to fight to stay focused on long pieces of writing. Some of the bloggers I follow have also begun mentioning the phenomenon. Scott Karp, who writes a blog about online media, recently confessed that he has stopped reading books altogether. "I was a lit major in college, and used to be [a] voracious book reader," he wrote. "What happened?" He speculates on the answer: "What if I do all my reading on the web not so much because the way I read has changed, i.e. I'm just seeking convenience, but because the way I THINK has changed?"

Bruce Friedman, who blogs regularly about the use of computers in medicine, also has described how the Internet has altered his mental habits. "I now have almost totally lost the ability to read and absorb a longish article on the Web or in print," he wrote earlier this year. A pathologist who has long been on the faculty of the University of Michigan Medical School, Friedman elaborated on his comment in a telephone conversation with me. His thinking, he said, has taken on a "staccato" quality, reflecting the way he quickly scans short passages of text from many sources online. "I can't read *War and Peace* anymore," he admitted. "I've lost the ability to do that. Even a blog post of more than three or four paragraphs is too much to absorb. I skim it."

Anecdotes alone don't prove much. And we still await the long-term neurological and psychological experiments that will provide a definitive picture of how Internet use affects cognition. But a recently published study of online research habits, conducted by scholars from University College London, suggests that we may well be in the midst of a sea change in the way we read and think. As part of the five-year research program, the scholars examined computer logs documenting the behavior of visitors to two popular research sites, one operated by the British Library and one by a UK educational consortium, that provide access to journal articles, e-books, and other sources of written information. They found that people using the sites exhibited "a form of skimming activity," hopping from one source to another and rarely returning to any source they'd already visited. They typically read no more than one or two pages of an article or book before they would "bounce" out to another site. Sometimes they'd save a long article, but there's no evidence that they ever went back and actually read it. The authors of the study report:

> It is clear that users are not reading online in the traditional sense; indeed there are signs that new forms of "reading" are emerging as users "power browse" horizontally through titles, contents pages and abstracts going for quick wins. It almost seems that they go online to avoid reading in the traditional sense.

Thanks to the ubiquity of text on the Internet, not to mention the popularity of text-messaging on cell phones, we may well be reading more today than we did in the 1970s or 1980s, when television was our medium of choice. But it's a different kind of reading, and behind it lies a different kind of thinking—perhaps even a new sense of the self. "We are not only *what* we read," says Maryanne Wolf, a developmental psychologist at Tufts University and the author of *Proust and the Squid: The Story and Science of the Reading Brain*. "We are *how* we read." Wolf worries that the style of reading promoted by the Net, a style that puts "efficiency" and "immediacy" above all else, may be weakening our capacity for the kind of deep reading that emerged when an earlier technology, the printing press, made long and complex works of prose commonplace. When we read online, she says, we tend to become "mere decoders of information." Our ability to interpret text, to make the rich mental connections that form when we read deeply and without distraction, remains largely disengaged.

Reading, explains Wolf, is not an instinctive skill for human beings. It's not etched into our genes the way speech is. We have to teach our minds how to translate the symbolic characters we see into the language we understand. And the media or other technologies we use in learning and practicing the craft of reading play an important part in shaping the neural circuits inside our brains. Experiments demonstrate that readers of ideograms, such as the Chinese, develop a mental circuitry for reading that is very different from the circuitry found in those of us whose written language employs an alphabet. The variations extend across many regions of the brain, including those that govern such essential cognitive functions as memory and the interpretation of visual and auditory stimuli. We can expect as well that the circuits woven by our use of the Net will be different from those woven by our reading of books and other printed works.

Sometime in 1882, Friedrich Nietzsche bought a typewriter—a Malling-Hansen Writing Ball, to be precise. His vision was failing, and keeping his eyes focused on a page had become exhausting and painful, often bringing on crushing headaches. He had been forced to curtail his writing, and he feared that he would soon have to give it up. The typewriter rescued him, at least for a time. Once he had mastered touch-typing, he was able to write with his eyes closed, using only the tips of his fingers. Words could once again flow from his mind to the page.

But the machine had a subtler effect on his work. One of Nietzsche's friends, a composer, noticed a change in the style of his writing. His already terse prose had become even tighter, more telegraphic. "Perhaps you will through this instrument even take to a new idiom," the friend wrote in a letter, noting that, in his own work, his "'thoughts' in music and language often depend on the quality of pen and paper."

"You are right," Nietzsche replied, "our writing equipment takes part in the forming of our thoughts." Under the sway of the machine, writes the German media scholar Friedrich A. Kittler, Nietzsche's prose "changed from arguments to aphorisms, from thoughts to puns, from rhetoric to telegram style."

The human brain is almost infinitely malleable. People used to think that our mental meshwork, the dense connections formed among the 100 billion or so neurons inside our skulls, was largely fixed by the time we reached adulthood. But brain researchers have discovered that that's not the case. James Olds, a professor of neuroscience who directs the Krasnow Institute for Advanced Study at George Mason University, says that even the adult mind "is very plastic." Nerve cells routinely break old connections and form new ones. "The brain," according to Olds, "has the ability to reprogram itself on the fly, altering the way it functions."

As we use what the sociologist Daniel Bell has called our "intellectual technologies"—the tools that extend our mental rather than our physical capacities—we inevitably begin to take on the qualities of those technologies. The mechanical clock, which came into common use in the 14th century, provides a compelling example. In *Technics and Civilization*, the historian and cultural critic Lewis Mumford described how the clock "disassociated time from human events and helped create the belief in an independent world of mathematically measurable sequences." The "abstract framework of divided time" became "the point of reference for both action and thought."

The clock's methodical ticking helped bring into being the scientific mind and the scientific man. But it also took something away. As the late MIT computer scientist Joseph Weizenbaum observed in his 1976 book, *Computer Power and Human Reason: From Judgment to Calculation*, the conception of the world that emerged from the widespread use of timekeeping instruments "remains an impoverished version of the older one, for it rests on a rejection of those direct experiences that formed the basis for, and indeed constituted, the old reality." In deciding when to eat, to work, to sleep, to rise, we stopped listening to our senses and started obeying the clock.

The process of adapting to new intellectual technologies is reflected in the changing metaphors we use to explain ourselves to ourselves. When the mechanical clock arrived, people began thinking of their brains as operating "like clockwork." Today, in the age of software, we have come to think of them as operating "like computers." But the changes, neuroscience tells us, go much deeper than metaphor. Thanks to our brain's plasticity, the adaptation occurs also at a biological level.

The Internet promises to have particularly far-reaching effects on cognition. In a paper published in 1936, the British mathematician Alan Turing proved that a digital computer, which at the time existed only as a theoretical machine, could be programmed to perform the function of any other information-processing device. And that's what we're seeing today. The Internet, an immeasurably powerful computing system, is subsuming most of our other intellectual technologies. It's becoming our map and our clock, our printing press and our typewriter, our calculator and our telephone, and our radio and TV.

When the Net absorbs a medium, that medium is re-created in the Net's image. It injects the medium's content with hyperlinks, blinking ads, and other digital gewgaws, and it surrounds the content with the content of all the other media it has absorbed. A new e-mail message, for instance, may announce its arrival as we're glancing over the latest headlines at a newspaper's site. The result is to scatter our attention and diffuse our concentration.

The Net's influence doesn't end at the edges of a computer screen, either. As people's minds become attuned to the crazy quilt of Internet media, traditional media have to adapt to the audience's new expectations. Television programs add text crawls and pop-up ads, and magazines and newspapers shorten their articles, introduce capsule summaries, and crowd their pages with easy-to-browse info-snippets. When, in March of this year, *The New York Times* decided to devote the second and third pages of every edition to article abstracts, its design director, Tom Bodkin, explained that the "shortcuts" would give harried readers a quick "taste" of the day's news, sparing them the "less efficient" method of actually turning the pages and reading the articles. Old media have little choice but to play by the new-media rules.

Never has a communications system played so many roles in our lives—or exerted such broad influence over our thoughts—as the Internet does today. Yet, for all that's been written about the Net, there's been little consideration of how, exactly, it's reprogramming us. The Net's intellectual ethic remains obscure.

About the same time that Nietzsche started using his typewriter, an earnest young man named Frederick Winslow Taylor carried a stopwatch into the Midvale Steel plant in Philadelphia and began a historic series of experiments aimed at improving the efficiency of the plant's machinists. With the approval of Midvale's owners, he recruited a group of factory hands, set them to work on various metalworking machines, and recorded and timed their every movement as well as the operations of the machines. By breaking down every job into a sequence of small, discrete steps and then testing different ways of performing each one, Taylor created a set of precise instructions—an "algorithm," we might say today—for how each worker should work. Midvale's employees grumbled about the strict new regime, claiming that it turned them into little more than automatons, but the factory's productivity soared.

More than a hundred years after the invention of the steam engine, the Industrial Revolution had at last found its philosophy and its philosopher. Taylor's tight industrial choreography—his "system," as he liked to call it—was embraced by manufacturers throughout the country and, in time, around the world. Seeking maximum speed, maximum efficiency, and maximum output, factory owners used time-and-motion studies to organize their work and configure the jobs of their workers. The goal, as Taylor defined it in his celebrated 1911 treatise, *The Principles of Scientific Management*, was to identify and adopt, for every job, the "one best method" of work and thereby to effect "the gradual substitution of science for rule of thumb throughout the mechanic arts." Once his system was applied to all acts of manual labor, Taylor assured his followers, it would bring about a restructuring not only of industry but of society, creating a utopia of perfect efficiency. "In the past the man has been first," he declared; "in the future the system must be first."

Taylor's system is still very much with us; it remains the ethic of industrial manufacturing. And now, thanks to the growing power that computer engineers and software coders wield over our intellectual lives, Taylor's ethic is beginning to govern the realm of the mind as well. The Internet is a machine designed for the efficient and automated collection, transmission, and manipulation of information, and its legions of programmers are intent on finding the "one best method"—the perfect algorithm—to carry out every mental movement of what we've come to describe as "knowledge work."

Google's headquarters, in Mountain View, California—the Googleplex—is the Internet's high church, and the religion practiced inside its walls is Taylorism. Google, says its chief executive, Eric Schmidt, is "a company that's founded around the science of measurement," and it is striving to "systematize everything" it does. Drawing on the terabytes of behavioral data it collects through its search engine and other sites, it carries out thousands of experiments a day, according to the *Harvard Business Review*, and it uses the results to refine the algorithms that increasingly control how people find information and extract meaning from it. What Taylor did for the work of the hand, Google is doing for the work of the mind.

The company has declared that its mission is "to organize the world's information and make it universally accessible and useful." It seeks to develop "the perfect search engine," which it defines as something that "understands exactly what you mean and gives you back exactly what you want." In Google's view, information is a kind of commodity, a utilitarian resource that can be mined and processed with industrial efficiency. The more pieces of information we can "access" and the faster we can extract their gist, the more productive we become as thinkers.

Where does it end? Sergey Brin and Larry Page, the gifted young men who founded Google while pursuing doctoral degrees in computer science at Stanford, speak frequently of their desire to turn their search engine into an artificial intelligence, a HAL-like machine that might be connected directly to our brains. "The ultimate search engine is something as smart as people—or smarter," Page said in a speech a few years back. "For us, working on search is a way to work on artificial intelligence." In a 2004 interview with *Newsweek*, Brin said, "Certainly if you had all the world's information directly attached to your brain, or an artificial brain that was smarter than your brain, you'd be better off." Last year, Page told a convention of scientists that Google is "really trying to build artificial intelligence and to do it on a large scale."

Such an ambition is a natural one, even an admirable one, for a pair of math whizzes with vast quantities of cash at their disposal and a small army of computer scientists in their employ. A fundamentally scientific enterprise, Google is motivated by a desire to use technology, in Eric Schmidt's words, "to solve problems that have never been solved before," and artificial intelligence is the hardest problem out there. Why wouldn't Brin and Page want to be the ones to crack it?

Still, their easy assumption that we'd all "be better off" if our brains were supplemented, or even replaced, by an artificial intelligence is unsettling. It suggests a belief that intelligence is the output of a mechanical process, a series of discrete steps that can be isolated, measured, and optimized. In Google's world, the world we enter when we go online, there's little place for the fuzziness of contemplation. Ambiguity is not an opening for insight but a bug to be fixed. The human brain is just an outdated computer that needs a faster processor and a bigger hard drive.

The idea that our minds should operate as high-speed data-processing machines is not only built into the workings of the Internet, it is the network's reigning business model as well. The faster we surf across the Web—the more links we click and pages we view—the more opportunities Google and other companies gain to collect information about us and to feed us advertisements. Most of the proprietors of the commercial Internet have a financial stake in collecting the crumbs of data we leave behind as we flit from link to link—the more crumbs, the better. The last thing these companies want is to encourage leisurely reading or slow, concentrated thought. It's in their economic interest to drive us to distraction.

Maybe I'm just a worrywart. Just as there's a tendency to glorify technological progress, there's a countertendency to expect the worst of every new tool or machine. In Plato's *Phaedrus*, Socrates bemoaned the development of writing. He feared that, as people came to rely on the written word as a substitute for the knowledge they used to carry inside their heads, they would, in the words of one of the dialogue's characters, "cease to exercise their memory and become forgetful." And because they would be able to "receive a quantity of information without proper instruction," they would "be thought very knowledgeable when they are for the most part quite ignorant." They would be "filled with the conceit of wisdom instead of real wisdom." Socrates wasn't wrong—the new technology did often have the effects he feared—but he was shortsighted. He couldn't foresee the many ways that writing and reading would serve to spread information, spur fresh ideas, and expand human knowledge (if not wisdom).

The arrival of Gutenberg's printing press, in the 15th century, set off another round of teeth gnashing. The Italian humanist Hieronimo Squarciafico worried that the easy availability of books would lead to intellectual laziness, making men "less studious" and weakening their minds. Others argued that cheaply printed books and broadsheets would undermine religious authority, demean the work of scholars and scribes, and spread sedition and debauchery. As New York University professor Clay Shirky notes, "Most of the arguments made against the printing press were correct, even prescient." But, again, the doomsayers were unable to imagine the myriad blessings that the printed word would deliver.

So, yes, you should be skeptical of my skepticism. Perhaps those who dismiss critics of the Internet as Luddites or nostalgists will be proved correct, and from our hyperactive, data-stoked minds will spring a golden age of intellectual discovery and universal wisdom. Then again, the Net isn't the alphabet, and although it may replace the printing press, it produces something altogether different. The kind of deep reading that a sequence of printed pages promotes is valuable not just for the knowledge we acquire from the author's words but for the intellectual vibrations those words set off within our own minds. In the quiet spaces opened up by the sustained, undistracted reading of a book, or by any other act of contemplation, for that matter, we make our own associations, draw our own inferences and analogies, foster our own ideas. Deep reading, as Maryanne Wolf argues, is indistinguishable from deep thinking.

If we lose those quiet spaces, or fill them up with "content," we will sacrifice something important not only in our selves but in our culture. In a recent essay, the playwright Richard Foreman eloquently described what's at stake:

> I come from a tradition of Western culture, in which the ideal (my ideal) was the complex, dense and "cathedral-like" structure of the highly educated and articulate personality—a man or woman who carried inside themselves a personally constructed and unique version of the entire heritage of the West. [But now] I see within us all (myself included) the replacement of complex inner density with a new kind of self—evolving under the pressure of information overload and the technology of the "instantly available."

As we are drained of our "inner repertory of dense cultural inheritance," Foreman concluded, we risk turning into "'pancake people'—spread wide and thin as we connect with that vast network of information accessed by the mere touch of a button."

I'm haunted by that scene in *2001*. What makes it so poignant, and so weird, is the computer's emotional response to the disassembly of its mind: its despair as one circuit after another goes dark, its childlike pleading with the astronaut—"I can feel it. I can feel it. I'm afraid"—and its final reversion to what can only be called a state of innocence. HAL's outpouring of feeling contrasts with the emotionlessness that characterizes the human figures in the film, who go about their business with an almost robotic efficiency. Their thoughts and actions feel scripted, as if they're following the steps of an algorithm. In the world of *2001*, people have become so machinelike that the most human character turns out to be a machine. That's the essence of Kubrick's dark prophecy: as we come to rely on computers to mediate our understanding of the world, it is our own intelligence that flattens into artificial intelligence.

FOR INFORMAL WRITING

Nicholas Carr details the myriad ways his own brain has deteriorated, in his view, since his dependence on the internet and Google. Most notably, he now struggles to read long passages, preferring instead to skim and consult only short "sound bites," as the Internet apparently has trained us all to do. You likely have had access to the Internet for as long as you can remember. While you may not be able to discern differences between then and now, how, specifically, do you identify with Carr's concern? (Can you imagine what it might have been like to experience pre-internet reading and gathering of information?)

FOR DISCUSSION

1. How do you find the answers to questions you might have? How has your own reliance on the internet changed the way you engage with information?
2. Carr's argument goes so far as to suggest that our brains are physically changing because of our engagement with the Internet. Do you agree? Why or why not?
3. Carr writes that Richard Foreman concluded, "We risk turning into 'pancake people'—spread wide and thin, as we connect with that vast network of information accessed by a mere touch of a button." What do you think Foreman means by "pancake people?" Explore this metaphor.

FOR WRITING

Nicholas Carr talks about older inventions that caused many to fear that the end of literacy and civilization (not to mention, some forms of employment) were near. Research some of those inventions—for instance, the typewriter, the telephone, the printing press, and so forth. What were the cultural and other responses at the time? How have sociologists and others measured the impact of these inventions? Is there a downside to convenience? (We are also thinking of current ads on commercial television. Should we really be able to say, "Alexa, start my Buick?")

The Matthew Effect (2008)
Malcolm Gladwell (1963–)

Malcolm Gladwell is a well-known writer of nonfiction and journalism who helped to make types of data "hip." His work often intersects history, popular culture, and economics. The author of a number of successful books and articles, Gladwell's first book, The Tipping Point *(2000), was named as "one of the best books of the decade" by* The New York Times. *Many of Gladwell's books and articles start with a simple premise: "What Makes People Successful," as in* Outliers: The Story of Success *(2008), for instance, or "How Does Culture Inform Communication (or Miscommunication)," as in* Talking to Strangers *(2019). While sometimes controversial, Gladwell is seen as genre-bending and "the most original American journalist since the young Tom Wolfe," according to* The Baltimore Sun. *"The Matthew Effect" is the opening chapter of* Outliers.

> For unto everyone that hath shall be given, and he shall have abundance. But from him that hath not shall be taken away even that which he hath.
> —Matthew 25:29

1

One warm, spring day in May of 2007, the Medicine Hat Tigers and the Vancouver Giants met for the Memorial Cup hockey championship in Vancouver, British Columbia. The Tigers and the Giants were the two finest teams in the Canadian Hockey League, which in turn is the finest junior hockey league in the world. These were the future stars of the sport—seventeen-, eighteen-, and nineteen-year-olds who had been skating and shooting pucks since they were barely more than toddlers.

From Outliers by Malcolm Gladwell, copyright © 2008. Reprinted by permission of Little, Brown, an imprint of Hachette Book Group, Inc.

The game was broadcast on Canadian national television. Up and down the streets of downtown Vancouver, Memorial Cup banners hung from the lampposts. The arena was packed. A long red carpet was rolled out on the ice, and the announcer introduced the game's dignitaries. First came the premier of British Columbia, Gordon Campbell. Then, amid tumultuous applause, out walked Gordie Howe, one of the legends of the game. "Ladies and gentlemen," the announcer boomed. "Mr. Hockey!"

For the next sixty minutes, the two teams played spirited, aggressive hockey. Vancouver scored first, early in the second period, on a rebound by Mario Bliznak. Late in the second period, it was Medicine Hat's turn, as the team's scoring leader, Darren Helm, fired a quick shot past Vancouver's goalie, Tyson Sexsmith. Vancouver answered in the third period, scoring the game's deciding goal, and then, when Medicine Hat pulled its goalie in desperation, Vancouver scored a third time.

In the aftermath of the game, the players and their families and sports reporters from across the country crammed into the winning team's locker room. The air was filled with cigar smoke and the smell of champagne and sweat-soaked hockey gear. On the wall was a hand-painted banner: "Embrace the Struggle." In the center of the room the Giants' coach, Don Hay, stood misty-eyed. "I'm just so proud of these guys," he said. "Just look around the locker room. There isn't one guy who didn't buy in wholeheartedly."

Canadian hockey is a meritocracy. Thousands of Canadian boys begin to play the sport at the "novice" level, before they are even in kindergarten. From that point on, there are leagues for every age class, and at each of those levels, the players are sifted and sorted and evaluated, with the most talented separated out and groomed for the next level. By the time players reach their midteens, the very best of the best have been channeled into an elite league known as Major Junior A, which is the top of the pyramid. And if your Major Junior A team plays for the Memorial Cup, that means you are at the very top of the top of the pyramid.

This is the way most sports pick their future stars. It's the way soccer is organized in Europe and South America, and it's the way Olympic athletes are chosen. For that matter, it is not all that different from the way the world of classical music picks its future virtuosos, or the way the world of ballet picks its future ballerinas, or the way our elite educational system picks its future scientists and intellectuals.

You can't buy your way into Major Junior A hockey. It doesn't matter who your father or mother is, or who your grandfather was, or what business your family is in. Nor does it matter if you live in the most remote corner of the most northerly province in Canada. If you have ability, the vast network of hockey scouts and talent spotters will find you, and if you are willing to work to develop that ability, the system will reward you. Success in hockey is based on *individual merit*—and both of those words are important. Players are judged on their own performance, not on anyone else's, and on the basis of their ability, not on some other arbitrary fact.

Or are they?

2

This is a book about outliers, about men and women who do things that are out of the ordinary. Over the course of the chapters ahead, I'm going to introduce you to one kind of outlier after another: to geniuses, business tycoons, rock stars, and software programmers. We're going to uncover the secrets of a remarkable lawyer, look at what separates the very best pilots from pilots who have crashed planes, and try to figure out why Asians are so good at math. And in examining the lives of the remarkable among us—the skilled, the talented, and the driven— I will argue that there is something profoundly wrong with the way we make sense of success.

What is the question we always ask about the successful? We want to know what they're *like*—what kind of personalities they have, or how intelligent they are, or what kind of lifestyles they have, or what special talents they might have been born with. And we assume that it is those personal qualities that explain how that individual reached the top.

In the autobiographies published every year by the billionaire/entrepreneur/rock star/celebrity, the story line is always the same: our hero is born in modest circumstances and by virtue of his own grit and talent fights his way to greatness. In the Bible, Joseph is cast out by his brothers and sold into slavery and then rises to become the pharaoh's right-hand man on the strength of his own brilliance and insight. In the famous nineteenth-century novels of Horatio Alger, young boys born into poverty rise to riches through a combination of pluck and initiative. "I think overall it's a disadvantage," Jeb Bush once said of what it meant for his business career that he was the son of an American president and the brother of an American president and the grandson of a wealthy Wall Street banker and US senator. When he ran for governor of Florida, he repeatedly referred to himself as a "self-made man," and it is a measure of how deeply we associate success with the efforts of the individual that few batted an eye at the description.

"Lift up your heads," Robert Winthrop told the crowd many years ago at the unveiling of a statue of that great hero of American independence Benjamin Franklin, "and look at the image of a man who rose from nothing, who owed nothing to parentage or patronage, who enjoyed no advantages of early education which are not open—a hundredfold open—to yourselves, who performed the most menial services in the businesses in which his early life was employed, but who lived to stand before Kings, and died to leave a name which the world will never forget."

In *Outliers*, I want to convince you that these kinds of personal explanations of success don't work. People don't rise from nothing. We do owe something to parentage and patronage. The people who stand before kings may look like they did it all by themselves. But in fact they are invariably the beneficiaries of hidden advantages and extraordinary opportunities and cultural legacies that allow them to learn and work hard and make sense of the world in ways others cannot. It makes a difference where and when we grew up. The culture we belong to and the legacies passed down by our forebears shape the patterns of our achievement in ways we cannot begin to imagine. It's not enough to ask what successful people are like, in other words. It is only by asking where they are *from* that we can unravel the logic behind who succeeds and who doesn't.

Biologists often talk about the "ecology" of an organism: the tallest oak in the forest is the tallest not just because it grew from the hardiest acorn; it is the tallest also because no other trees blocked its sunlight, the soil around it was deep and rich, no rabbit chewed through its bark as a sapling, and no lumberjack cut it down before it matured. We all know that successful people come from hardy seeds. But do we know enough about the sunlight that warmed them, the soil in which they put down the roots, and the rabbits and lumberjacks they were lucky enough to avoid? This is not a book about tall trees. It's a book about forests – and hockey is a good place to start because the explanation for who gets to the top of the hockey world is a lot more interesting and complicated than it looks. In fact, it's downright peculiar.

3

Here is the player roster of the 2007 Medicine Hat Tigers. Take a close look and see if you can spot anything strange about it.

NO.	NAME	POS.	L/R	HEIGHT	WEIGHT	BIRTH DATE	HOMETOWN
9	Brennan Bosch	C	R	5'8"	173	Feb. 14, 1988	Martensville, SK
11	Scott Wasden	C	R	6'1"	188	Jan. 4, 1988	Westbank, BC
12	Colton Grant	LW	L	5'9"	177	Mar. 20, 1989	Standard, AB
14	Darren Helm	LW	L	6'0"	182	Jan. 21, 1987	St. Andrews, MB
15	Derek Dorsett	RW	L	5'11"	178	Dec. 20, 1986	Kindersley, SK
16	Daine Todd	C	R	5'10"	173	Jan. 10, 1987	Red Deer, AB
17	Tyler Swystun	RW	R	5'11"	185	Jan. 15, 1988	Cochrane, AB
19	Matt Lowry	C	R	6'0"	186	Mar. 2, 1988	Neepawa, MB

NO.	NAME	POS.	L/R	HEIGHT	WEIGHT	BIRTH DATE	HOMETOWN
20	Kevin Undershute	LW	L	6'0"	178	Apr. 12, 1987	Medicine Hat, AB
21	Jerrid Sauer	RW	R	5'10"	196	Sept. 12, 1987	Medicine Hat, AB
22	Tyler Ennis	C	L	5'9"	160	Oct. 6, 1989	Edmonton, AB
23	Jordan Hickmott	C	R	6'0"	183	Apr. 11, 1990	Mission, BC
25	Jakob Rumpel	RW	R	5'8"	166	Jan. 27, 1987	Hrnciarovce, SLO
28	Bretton Cameron	C	R	5'11"	168	Jan. 26, 1987	Didsbury, AB
36	Chris Stevens	LW	L	5'10"	197	Aug. 20, 1986	Dawson Creek, BC
3	Gord Baldwin	D	L	6'5"	205	Mar. 1, 1987	Winnipeg, MB
4	David Schlemko	D	L	6'1"	195	May 7, 1987	Edmonton, AB
5	Trever Glass	D	L	6'0"	190	Jan. 22, 1998	Cochrane, AB
10	Kris Russell	D	L	5'10"	177	May 2, 1987	Caroline, AB
18	Michael Sauer	D	R	6'3"	205	Aug. 7, 1987	Sartell, MN
24	Mark Isherwood	D	R	6'0"	183	Jan. 31, 1989	Abbotsford, BC
27	Shayne Brown	D	L	6'1"	198	Feb. 20, 1989	Stony Plain, AB
29	Jordan Bendfeld	D	R	6'3"	230	Feb. 9, 1988	Leduc, AB
31	Ryan Holfeld	G	L	5'11"	166	Jun. 29, 1989	LeRoy, SK
33	Matt Keetley	G	R	6'2"	189	Apr. 27, 1986	Medicine Hat, AB

Do you see it? Don't feel bad if you don't, because for many years in the hockey world no one did. It wasn't until the mid-1980s, in fact, that a Canadian psychologist named Roger Barnsley first drew attention to the phenomenon of relative age.

Barnsley was at a Lethbridge Broncos hockey game in southern Alberta, a team that played in the same Major Junior A league as the Vancouver Giants and the Medicine Hat Tigers. He was there with his wife, Paula, and their two boys, and his wife was reading the program, when she ran across a roster list just like the one above that you just looked at.

"Roger," she said, "do you know when these young men were born?"

Barnsley said yes. "They're all between sixteen and twenty, so they'd be born in the late sixties."

"No, no," Paula went on. "What *month*."

"I thought she was crazy," Barnsley remembers. "But I looked through it, and what she was saying just jumped out at me. For some reason, there were an incredible number of January, February, and March birth dates."

Barnsley went home that night and looked up the birth dates of as many professional hockey players as he could find. He saw the same pattern. Barnsley, his wife, and a colleague, A. H. Thompson, then gathered statistics on every player in the Ontario Junior Hockey League. The story was the same. More players were born in January than in any other month, and by an overwhelming margin. The second most frequent birth month? February. The third? March. Barnsley found that there were nearly five and a half times as many Ontario Junior Hockey League players born in January as were born in November. He looked at the all-star teams of eleven-year-olds and thirteen-year-olds—the young players selected for elite traveling squads. Same story. He looked at the composition of the National Hockey League. Same story. The more he looked, the more Barnsley came to believe that what he was seeing was not a chance occurrence but an iron law of Canadian hockey: in *any* elite group of hockey players—the very best of the best—40 percent of the players will have been born between January and March, 30 percent between April and June, 20 percent between October and December.

"In all my years in psychology, I have never run into an effect this large," Barnsley says. "You don't even need to do any statistical analysis. You just look at it."

Look back at the Medicine Hat roster. Do you see it now? Seventeen out of the twenty-five players on the team were born in January, February, March, or April.

Here is the play-by-play for the first two goals in the Memorial Cup final, only this time I've substituted the players' birthdays for their names. It no longer sounds like the championship of Canadian junior hockey. It now sounds like a strange sporting ritual for teenage boys born under the astrological signs Capricorn, Aquarius, and Pisces.

> March 11 starts around one side of the Tigers' net, leaving the puck for his teammate January 4, who passes it to January 22, who flips it back to March 12, who shoots point-blank at the Tigers' goalie, April 27. April 27 blocks the shot, but it's rebounded by Vancouver's March 6. He shoots! Medicine Hat defensemen February 9 and February 14 dive to block the puck while January 10 looks on helplessly. March 6 scores!

Let's go to the second period now.

> Medicine Hat's turn. The Tigers' scoring leader, January 21, charges down the right side of the ice. He stops and circles, eluding the Vancouver defenseman February 15. January 21 then deftly passes the puck to his teammate December 20—wow! what's *he* doing out there?!—who shrugs off the onrushing defender May 17 and slides a cross-crease pass back to January 21. He shoots! Vancouver defenseman March 12 dives, trying to block the shot. Vancouver's goalie, March 19, lunges helplessly. January 21 scores! He raises his hands in triumph. His teammate May 2 jumps on his back with joy.

4

The explanation for this is quite simple. It has nothing to do with astrology, nor is there anything magical about the first three months of the year. It's simply that in Canada the eligibility cutoff for age-class hockey is January 1. A boy who turns ten on January 2, then, could be playing alongside someone who doesn't turn ten until the end of the year—and at that age, in preadolescence, a twelve-month gap in age represents an enormous difference in physical maturity.

This being Canada, the most hockey-crazed country on Earth, coaches start to select players for the traveling "rep" squad—the all-star teams—at the age of nine or ten, and of course they are more likely to view as talented the bigger and more coordinated players, who have had the benefit of critical extra months of maturity.

And what happens when a player gets chosen for a rep squad? He gets better coaching, and his teammates are better, and he plays fifty or seventy-five games a season instead of twenty games a season like those left behind in the "house" league, and he practices twice as much as, or even three times more than, he would have otherwise. In the beginning, his advantage isn't so much that he is inherently better but only that he is a little older. But by the age of thirteen or fourteen, with the benefit of better coaching and all that extra practice under his belt, he really *is* better, so he's the one more likely to make it to the Major Junior A league, and from there into the big leagues.*

Barnsley argues that these kinds of skewed age distributions exist whenever three things happen: selection, streaming, and differentiated experience. If you make a decision about who is good and who is not good at an early age; if you separate the "talented" from the "untalented"; and if you provide the "talented" with a superior experience, then you're going to end up giving a huge advantage to that small group of people born closest to the cutoff date.

In the United States, football and basketball don't select, stream, and differentiate quite as dramatically. As a result, a child can be a bit behind physically in those sports and still play as much as his or her more mature peers.*

---

*The way Canadians select hockey players is a beautiful example of what the sociologist Robert Merton famously called a "self-fulfilling prophecy"—a situation where "a false definition, in the beginning... evokes a new behavior which makes the original false conception come true." Canadians start with a false definition of who the best nine- and ten-year-old hockey players are. They're just picking the oldest every year. But the way they treat those "all-stars" ends up making their original false judgment look correct. As Merton puts it: "This specious validity of the self-fulfilling prophecy perpetuates a reign of error. For the prophet will cite the actual course of events as proof that he was right from the very beginning."

A physically immature basketball player in an American city can probably play as many hours of basketball in a given year as a relatively older child because there are so many basketball courts and so many people willing to play. It's not like ice hockey, where you need a rink. Basketball is saved by its accessibility and ubiquity.

But baseball does. The cutoff date for almost all nonschool baseball leagues in the United States is July 31, with the result that more major league players are born in August than in any other month. (The numbers are striking: in 2005, among Americans playing major league baseball 505 were born in August versus 313 born in July.)

European soccer, similarly, is organized like hockey and baseball—and the birth-date distributions in that sport are heavily skewed as well. In England, the eligibility date is September 1, and in the football association's premier league at one point in the 1990s, there were 288 players born between September and November and only 136 players born between June and August. In international soccer, the cutoff date used to be August 1, and in one recent junior world championship tournament, 135 players were born in the 3 months after August 1, while just 22 were born in May, June, and July. Today the cutoff date for international junior soccer is January 1. Take a look at the roster of the 2007 Czechoslovakian National Junior soccer team, which made the Junior World Cup finals.

Here we go again:

NO.	PLAYER	BIRTH DATE	POSITION
1	Marcel Gecov	Jan. 1, 1988	MF
2	Ludek Frydrych	Jan. 3, 1987	GK
3	Petr Janda	Jan. 5, 1987	MF
4	Jakub Dohnalek	Jan. 12, 1988	DF
5	Jakub Mares	Jan. 26, 1987	MF
6	Michal Held	Jan. 27, 1987	DF
7	Marek Strestik	Feb. 1, 1987	FW
8	Jiri Valenta	Feb. 14, 1988	MF
9	Jan Simunek	Feb. 20, 1987	DF
10	Tomas Oklestek	Feb. 21, 1987	MF
11	Lubos Kalouda	Feb. 21, 1987	MF
12	Radek Petr	Feb. 24, 1987	GK
13	Ondrej Mazuch	Mar. 15, 1989	DF
14	Ondrej Kudela	Mar. 26, 1987	MF
15	Marek Suchy	Mar. 29, 1988	DF
16	Martin Fenin	Apr. 16, 1987	FW
17	Tomas Pekhart	May 26, 1989	FW
18	Lukas Kuban	Jun. 22, 1987	DF
19	Tomas Cihlar	Jun. 24, 1987	DF
20	Tomas Frystak	Aug. 18, 1987	GK
21	Tomas Micola	Sep. 26, 1988	MF

At the national team tryouts, the Czech soccer coaches might as well have told everyone born after midsummer that they should pack their bags and go home.

Hockey and soccer are just games, of course, involving a select few. But these exact same biases also show up in areas of much more consequence, like education. Parents with a child born at the end of the calendar year often think about holding their child back before the start of kindergarten: it's hard for a five-year-old to keep up with a child born many months earlier. But most parents, one suspects, think that whatever disadvantage a younger child faces in kindergarten eventually goes away. *But it doesn't.* It's just like hockey. The small initial advantage that the child born in the early part of the year has over the child born at the end of the year persists. It locks children into patterns of achievement and underachievement, encouragement and discouragement, that stretch on and on for years.

Recently, two economists—Kelly Bedard and Elizabeth Dhuey—looked at the relationship between scores on what is called the Trends in International Mathematics and Science Study, or TIMSS (math and science tests given every four years to children in many countries around the world), and month of birth. They found that among fourth graders, the oldest children scored somewhere between four and twelve percentile points better than the youngest children. That, as Dhucy explains, is a "huge effect." It means that if you take two intellectually equivalent fourth graders with birthdays at opposite ends of the cutoff date, the older student could score in the eightieth percentile, while the younger child could score in the sixty-eighth percentile. That's the difference between qualifying for a gifted program and not.

"It's just like sports," Dhuey said. "We do ability grouping early on in childhood. We have advanced reading groups and advanced math groups. So, early on, if we look at young kids, in kindergarten and first grade, the teachers are confusing maturity with ability. And they put the older kids in the advanced stream, where they learn better skills; and the next year, because they are in the higher groups, they do even better; and the next year, the same things happen, and they do even better again. The only country we don't see doing this is Denmark. They have a national policy where they have no ability grouping until the age of ten." Denmark waits to make selection decisions until maturity differences by age have evened out.

Dhuey and Bedard subsequently did the same analysis, only this time looking at college. What did they find? At four-year colleges in the United States—the highest stream of postsecondary education—students belonging to the relatively youngest group in their class are underrepresented by about 11.6 percent. That initial difference in maturity doesn't go away with time. It persists. And for thousands of students, that initial disadvantage is the difference between going to college—and having a real shot at the middle class—and not.*

"I mean, it's ridiculous," Dhuey says. "It's outlandish that our arbitrary choice of cutoff dates is causing these long-lasting effects, and no one seems to care about them."

5

Think for a moment about what the story of hockey and early birthdays says about success.

It tells us that our notion that it is the best and the brightest who effortlessly rise to the top is much too simplistic. Yes, the hockey players who make it to the professional level are more talented than you or me. But they also got a big head start, an opportunity that they neither deserved nor earned. And that opportunity played a critical role in their success.

The sociologist Robert Merton famously called this phenomenon the "Matthew Effect" after the New Testament verse in the Gospel of Matthew: "For unto everyone that hath shall be given, and he shall have abundance. But from him that hath not shall be taken away even that which he hath." It is those who are successful, in other words, who are most likely to be given the kinds of special opportunities that lead to further success. It's the rich who get the biggest tax breaks. It's the best students who get the best teaching and most attention. And it's the biggest nine- and ten-year-olds who get the most coaching and practice. Success is the result of what sociologists like to call "accumulative advantage." The professional hockey player starts out a little bit better than his peers. And that little difference leads to an opportunity that makes that difference a bit bigger, and that edge in turn leads to another opportunity, which makes the initially small difference bigger still—and on and on until the hockey player is a genuine outlier. But he didn't start out an outlier. He started out just a little bit better.

The second implication of the hockey example is that the systems we set up to determine who gets ahead aren't particularly efficient. We think that starting all-star leagues and gifted programs as early as possible is the best way of ensuring that no talent slips through the cracks. But take a look again at that roster for the Czech Republic soccer team. There are no players born in July, October, November, or December, and only one each in August and September. Those

---

*Even more social phenomena can be linked to relative age. Barnsley and two colleagues, for instance, once found that students who attempt suicide are also more likely to be born in the second half of the school year. Their explanation is that poorer school performance can lead to depression. The connection between relative age and suicide, however, isn't nearly as pronounced as the correlation between birth date and athletic success.

born in the last half of the year have all been discouraged, or overlooked, or pushed out of the spot. *The talent of essentially half of the Czech athletic population has been squandered.*

So what do you do if you're an athletic young Czech with the misfortune to have been born in the last part of the year? You *can't* play soccer. The deck is stacked against you. So maybe you could play the other sport that Czechs are obsessed with—hockey. But wait. (I think you know what's coming.) Here's the roster of the 2007 Czech junior jockey team that finished fifth at the world championships.

NO.	PLAYER	BIRTH DATE	POSITION
1	David Kveton	Jan. 3, 1988	Forward
2	Jiri Suchy	Jan. 3, 1988	Defense
3	Michael Kolarz	Jan. 12, 1987	Defense
4	Jakub Vojita	Feb. 8, 1987	Defense
5	Jakub Kindl	Feb. 10, 1987	Defense
6	Michael Frolik	Feb 17, 1987	Forward
7	Martin Hanzal	Feb. 20, 1987	Forward
8	Tomas Svoboda	Feb. 24, 1987	Forward
9	Jakub Cerny	Mar. 5, 1987	Forward
10	Tomas Kudelka	Mar. 10, 1987	Defense
11	Jaroslav Barton	Mar. 26, 1987	Defense
12	H.O. Pozivil	Apr. 22, 1987	Defense
13	Daniel Rakos	May 25, 1987	Forward
14	David Kuchejda	Jun. 12, 1987	Forward
15	Vladimir Sobotka	Jul. 2, 1987	Forward
16	Jakub Kovar	Jul. 19, 1988	Goalie
17	Lukas Vantuch	Jul. 20, 1987	Forward
18	Jakub Voracek	Aug. 15, 1989	Forward
19	Tomas Pospisil	Aug. 25, 1987	Forward
20	Ondrej Pavelec	Aug. 31, 1987	Goalie
21	Tomas Kana	Nov. 29, 1987	Forward
22	Michael Repik	Dec. 31, 1988	Forward

Those born in the last quarter of the year might as well give up hockey too.

Do you see the consequences of the way we have chosen to think about success? Because we so profoundly personalize success, we miss opportunities to lift others onto the top rung. We make rules that frustrate achievement. We prematurely write off people as failures. We are too much in awe of those who succeed and far too dismissive of those who fail. And, most of all, we become much too passive. We overlook just how large a role we all play—and by "we" I mean society—in determining who makes it and who doesn't.

If we chose to, we could acknowledge that cutoff dates matter. We could set up two or even three hockey leagues, divided up by month of birth. Let the players develop on separate tracks and then pick all-star teams. If all the Czech and Canadian athletes born at the end of the year had a fair chance, then the Czech and the Canadian national teams suddenly would have twice as many athletes to choose from.

Schools could do the same thing. Elementary and middle schools could put the January through April–born students in one class, the May through August–born students in another class, and those born in September through December in the third class. They could let students learn with and compete against other students of the same maturity level. It would be a little bit more complicated administratively. But it wouldn't necessarily cost that much more money and it would level the playing field for those who—through no fault of their own—have been dealt a big disadvantage by the educational system. We could easily take control of the machinery of achievement, in other words—not just in sports but, as we will see, in other more consequential areas as well. But we don't. And why? Because we cling to the idea that success is a simple function of individual merit and the world in which we all grow up and the rules we choose to write as a society don't matter at all.

6

Before the Memorial Cup final, Gord Wasden—the father of one of the Medicine Hat Tigers—stood by the side of the ice, talking about his son Scott. He was wearing a Medicine Hat baseball cap and a black Medicine Hat T-shit. "When he was four and five years old," Wasden remembered, "his little brother was in a walker, and he would shove a hockey stick in his hand and they would play hockey on the floor in the kitchen, morning till night. Scott *always* had a passion for it. He played rep hockey throughout his minor-league hockey career. He always made the Triple A teams. As a first-year peewee or a first-year bantam, he always played on the [top] rep team." Wasden was clearly nervous: his son was about to play in the biggest game of his life. "He's had to work very hard for whatever he's got. I'm very proud of him."

Those were the ingredients of success at the highest level: passion, talent, and hard work. But there was another element. When did Wasden first get the sense that his son was something special? "You know, he was always a bigger kid for his age. He was strong, and he had a knack for scoring goals at an early age. And he was always kind of a standout for his age, a captain of his team. ..."

Bigger kid for his age? Of course he was. Scott Wasden was born on January 4, within three days of the absolute perfect birthday for an elite hockey player. He was one of the lucky ones. If the eligibility date for Canadian hockey were later in the year, he might have been watching the Memorial Cup championship from the stands instead of playing on the ice.

FOR INFORMAL WRITING

What is "The Matthew Effect?" In this chapter, Gladwell introduces the concern that he will explore for the rest of *Outliers*—why some people are successful and some are not. As you likely gleaned, Gladwell rejects the concept of meritocracy, in which everyone can be credited with his/her/their own success. How does the Matthew Effect help Gladwell refute the notion of a meritocracy?

FOR DISCUSSION

1. To put it bluntly, what's up with the Canadian hockey team? When researching the rosters of Canada's National Hockey League, what does Gladwell notice? What are his conclusions?
2. Gladwell pivots from writing about hockey to writing about education. How are these connected?
3. The title of the chapter comes from the Bible verse "For unto everyone that hath shall be given, and he shall have abundance. But from him that hath not shall be taken away even that which he heath" (Matthew 25:29) What is the connection between this Biblical verse and Gladwell's argument?

FOR WRITING

The Matthew Effect introduces the concept of an "accumulative advantage." Define this term; what does it mean? In the context of this chapter, Gladwell applies this concept to education and hockey. Briefly review his argument. To what other context(s) might this concept (and perhaps Gladwell's argument) be applied?

Go Gentle Into That Good Night (2009)
Roger Ebert (1942–2013)

One of the most celebrated film critics of his or any other era, Roger Ebert was born in Champaign, Illinois, and was the film critic of the Chicago Sun-Times. *He was also the first to win a Pulitzer Prize for film criticism. Alongside* Chicago Tribune *critic Gene Siskel (1946–1999), Ebert co-hosted* Sneak Previews, *a long-running program during which Siskel and Ebert would debate (sometimes hotly) the merits of particular, newly released films. In 2002, Ebert was diagnosed with thyroid cancer, necessitating the removal of his lower jaw. However, he continued writing until his death, and "Go Gentle Into That Good Night" reveals Ebert's views about life and death.*

I know it is coming, and I do not fear it, because I believe there is nothing on the other side of death to fear. I hope to be spared as much pain as possible on the approach path. I was perfectly content before I was born, and I think of death as the same state. What I am grateful for is the gift of intelligence, and for life, love, wonder, and laughter. You can't say it wasn't interesting. My lifetime's memories are what I have brought home from the trip. I will require them for eternity no more than that little souvenir of the Eiffel Tower I brought home from Paris.

I don't expect to die anytime soon. But it could happen this moment, while I am writing. I was talking the other day with Jim Toback, a friend of 35 years, and the conversation turned to our deaths, as it always does. "Ask someone how they feel about death," he said, "and they'll tell you *everyone's gonna die*. Ask them, In the next 30 seconds? *No, no, no, that's not gonna happen.* How about this afternoon? *No.* What you're really asking them to admit is, *Oh my God, I don't really exist and I might be gone at any given second.*"

Licensed with permission from The Ebert Company.

Me too, but I hope not. I have plans. Still, this blog has led me resolutely toward the contemplation of death. In the beginning I found myself drawn toward writing about my life. Everyone's life story is awaiting only the final page. Then I began writing on the subject of evolution, that most consoling of all the sciences, and was engulfed in an unforeseen discussion about God, the afterlife, and religion.

When I began this blog I thought if there was one thing I'd never write about, it would be religion. But you, my readers, have wanted to write about it. In thousands of messages. Half a million words. Life, science, belief, gods, evolution, intelligent design, the afterlife, reincarnation, the nature of reality, what came before the Big Bang, what waits after final entropy, the nature of intelligence, the reality of the self, death, death, death. This dialog still continues. The thread beneath the evolution entry, posted Dec. 3, has drawn nearly 1,900 comments, some of them longer than the entry, and it is still active. How did I find a group of readers with so many metaphysicians?

This has been an education for me. No one will read all the comments except me, but if you did, you could learn all a layman should be expected to understand about the quantum level. You would discover a defender of Intelligent Design so articulate that when he was away for a couple of days, the Darwinians began to fret and miss him. You would have the mathematical theory of infinity explained so that, while you will still be unable to conceive of infinity, you will understand the thinking involved.

My opinions have been challenged. I had to defend what I believed. I did some more reading. I discovered fractals and Strange Attractors. I wrote an entry about the way I believe in God, which is to say that I do not. Not, at least, in the God that most people mean when they say God. I grant you that if the universe was Caused, there might have been a Causer. But that entity, or force, must by definition be outside space and time; beyond all categories of thought, or non-thought; transcending existence, or non-existence. What is the utility of arguing our "beliefs" about it? What about the awesome possibility that there was no Cause? *What if everything ... just happened?*

I was told that I was an atheist. Or an agnostic. Or a deist. I refused all labels. It is too easy for others to pin one on me, and believe they understand me. I am still working on understanding myself.

To explain myself, I turn to Walt Whitman:

So do we all. How sad if our freedom to think about the immensity of time and space could be defined by what someone informs us that we believe.

But certainly, some readers have informed me, it is a tragic and dreary business to go into death without faith. I don't feel that way. "Faith" is neutral. All depends on what is believed in. I have no desire to live forever. The concept frightens me. I relate it to the horror of the hero of Poe's *The Premature Burial*. To be in your grave and know it! Ah, but I am told, the afterlife does not involve time at all. In that case, how can it be eternal? Eternity is only thinkable in a universe that contains time. If I had but world enough, and time, I could spend time pondering a world without end.

That whole discussion has been forging ahead on one hand. On the other hand, we have been puzzling over quantum mechanics, which suggests the possibility of instantaneous communication between two entangled particles, even if they are at opposite ends of the universe (not that the universe has ends). This happens independently of time and space. They've proven it in their labs! If the scientists are correct, everything everywhere is, in some sense, the same thing, in the same place—or it might as well be. That, too, is small consolation.

All I can do is think with my mind. All I can be is who I seem to myself. I can only be where it seems that I am. Time seems to move quickly or slowly, but it is time all the same; my wristwatch proves it. I believe my wristwatch exists, and even when I am unconscious, it is ticking all the same. You have to start somewhere. It is within these assumptions that I must live. Even if everything everywhere is the same, I must eat an orange or I will die of scurvy.

So within that reality, someday I will certainly die. I am 66, have had cancer, will die sooner than most of those reading this. That is in the nature of things. When I read about the nature of life from Camus, the odds were that he would die sooner than me. Thomas Wolfe, who wrote about a wind-grieved ghost, was already dead. Cormac McCarthy will probably live longer than me. And there is Shakespeare, who came as close as any man to immortality. In my plans for life after death, I say, again with Whitman:

And with Will, the brother in Saul Bellow's *Herzog*, I say: *Look for me in the weather reports.*

Raised as a Roman Catholic, I internalized the social values of that faith and still hold most of them, even though its theology no longer persuades me. I wrote about that, too. I have no quarrel with what anyone else subscribes to; everyone deals with these things in his own way, and I have no truths to impart. All I require of a religion is that it not insist I believe in it. I know a priest, a lovely man, whose eyes twinkle when he says, "You go about God's work in your way, and I'll go about it in His."

What I expect will most probably happen is that my body will fail, my mind will cease to function, and that will be that. My genes will not live on, because I have had no children. Perhaps I have been infertile. If I discover that somewhere along the way I conceived a child, let that child step forward and he or she will behold a happy man. Through my wife, I have had stepchildren and grandchildren, and I love them unconditionally, which is the only kind of love worth bothering with.

I am comforted by Richard Dawkins' theory of memes. Those are mental units: thoughts, ideas, gestures, notions, songs, beliefs, rhymes, ideals, teachings, sayings, phrases, clichés, that move from mind to mind as genes move from body to body. After a lifetime of writing, teaching, broadcasting and happily torturing people with my jokes, I will leave behind more memes than many. They will all eventually die as well, but so it goes.

I drank for many years in a tavern that had a photograph of Brendan Behan on the wall, and under it this quotation, which I memorized:

> I respect kindness in human beings first of all, and kindness to animals. I don't respect the law; I have a total irreverence for anything connected with society except that which makes the roads safer, the beer stronger, the food cheaper and the old men and old women warmer in the winter and happier in the summer.

For 57 words, that does a pretty good job of summing it up.

"Kindness" covers all of my political beliefs. No need to spell them out. I believe that if, at the end of it all, according to our abilities, we have done something to make others a little happier, and something to make ourselves a little happier, that is about the best we can do. To make others less happy is a crime. To make ourselves unhappy is where all crime starts. We must try to contribute joy to the world. That is true no matter what our problems, our health, our circumstances. We must try. I didn't always know this, and am happy I lived long enough to find it out.

In a moment or a few years, maybe several, I will encounter what Henry James called, on his deathbed, "the Distinguished Thing." I may not be conscious of the moment of passing. I have already been declared dead. It wasn't so bad. After a ruptured artery following my first cancer surgery, the doctors thought I was finished. My wife Chaz said she sensed that I was still alive, and communicating to her that I wasn't finished yet. She said hearts were beating in unison, although my heartbeat couldn't be discovered. She told the doctors I was alive, they did what doctors do, and here I am, alive.

Do I believe her? Absolutely. I believe her literally—not symbolically, figuratively or spiritually. I believe she was actually aware of my call, and that she sensed my heartbeat. I believe she did it in the real, physical world I have described, the one I live in with my wristwatch. I see no reason why such communication could not take place. I'm not talking about telepathy, psychic phenomenon or a miracle. The only miracle is that she was there when it happened, as she was for many long days and nights. I'm talking about her standing there and knowing something. Haven't many of us experienced that? Come on, haven't you? I admire *Skeptic* magazine, but I'm not interested in their explanation or debunking of this event. What goes on happens at a level not accessible to scientists, theologians, mystics, physicists, philosophers or psychiatrists. It's a human kind of a thing.

Someday I will no longer call out, and there will be no heartbeat. What happens then? From my point of view, nothing. Absolutely nothing. Still, as I wrote today to a woman I have known since she was six: "You'd better cry at my memorial service."

I have been corresponding with a dear friend, the wise and gentle Australian director Paul Cox. Our subject sometimes turns to death. In 1988 he made a luminous documentary named *Vincent: The Life and Death of Vincent Van Gogh*. Today Paul wrote me that in his Arles days, van Gogh called himself "a simple worshiper of the external Buddha." Paul told me that in those days, Vincent wrote:

> Thank you, good Paul. I think that is a lovely thing to read, and a relief to find I will probably not have to go on foot. Or, as the little dog Milou says whenever Tintin proposes a journey, *pas à pied, j'espère!*

FOR INFORMAL WRITING

Although this was written four years before his death, this essay is, in many ways, Ebert's good-bye, akin to a kind of "last lecture." What parting wisdom do you take from the essay? Why does this particular wisdom stand out for you? With what effect?

FOR DISCUSSION

1. The title of the essay is an allusion to the Welsh poet Dylan Thomas's poem for his father, "Do Not Go Gentle Into That Good Night." The poem reiterates the following line: "Rage, rage against the dying of the light." How does this relate—or not—to the wisdom Ebert imparts?
2. Ebert writes "In the beginning I found myself drawn to writing about my life. Everyone's life story is awaiting only the final page. Then I began writing on the subject of evolution …" What effect does this have? What type of evolution is he referring to? What are the "contents" of this evolution?
3. Roger Ebert talks a good deal about his own faith. How does he reconcile his Roman Catholic upbringing with his atheism?

FOR WRITING

Ebert evokes the names of a number of important writers: Poe, Whitman, Thomas, Camus, Wolfe, McCarthy, Shakespeare, Bellow, among other notables. Research two of these writers, noting their important themes and works. What do you learn about them that sheds additional light on Ebert's use of them? What about their work seems to have resonated with Ebert? Why would he choose them?

Assassins of the Mind (2009)
Christopher Hitchens (1949–2011)

Social-political commentator, essayist, and journalist, Christopher Hitchens was a self-described "contrarian," with a book titled, in fact, Letters to a Young Contrarian *(2001). He was a well-known critic of religion, identity politics, and anything else he considered to be "dogma." In his most popular books, Hitchens admonished all institutions: religious, political—and otherwise. His books include* God Is Not Great: How Religion Poisons Everything *(2007),* The Portable Atheist: Essential Readings for the Non-Believer *(2007), and* Mortality *(published posthumously, in 2012). The following piece was published in* Vanity Fair, *and it was a response to the* fatwa *placed on the head of author Salman Rushdie.*

At a dinner party that will forever be green in the memory of those who attended it, somebody was complaining not just about the epic badness of the novels of Robert Ludlum but also about the badness of their *titles*. (You know the sort of pretentiousness: *The Bourne Supremacy, The Aquitaine Progression, The Ludlum Impersonation,* and so forth.) Then it happily occurred to another guest to wonder aloud what a Shakespeare play might be called if named in the Ludlum manner. At which point Salman Rushdie perked up and started to sniff the air like a retriever. "O.K. then, Salman, what would *Hamlet*'s title be if submitted to the Ludlum treatment?" "*The Elsinore Vacillation,*" he replied—and I find I must stress this—in no more time than I have given you. Think it was a fluke? *Macbeth*? "*The Dunsinane Reforestation.*" To persist and to come up with *The Rialto Sanction* and *The Kerchief Implication* was the work of not too many more moments.

This is the way, when discussing Rushdie and his work, that I like to start. He is sublimely funny, and his humor is based on a relationship with language that is more like a musical than a literary one. (I here admit to my own worst

---

© Christopher Hitchens

plagiarism: invited to write the introduction to *Vanity Fair*'s "Black & White Issue" some years ago, I took advantage of Salman's presence in my house to ask him to riff on the two keywords for a bit. He free-associated about everything from photogravure to the Taj Mahal, without a prompt, for about 30 minutes, and my piece was essentially done.) And this is a man whose first language was Urdu! Toward the end of the Second World War, George Orwell wrote to his friend Mulk Raj Anand to predict that one day there would be a whole category of English literature written by Indians. Today, no literate person has not absorbed a novel by Vikram Seth or Arundhati Roy or R. K. Narayan or Rohinton Mistry, and for most European and North American readers the breakthrough moment came when Salman Rushdie published *Midnight's Children,* in 1981. Here was someone born as a British colonial subject who had annexed the proudest part of the Raj's dominion—the English language itself—and made it his own. The novel is still the only one to have won the Booker Prize twice, but really that's the least of it.

His later novels have maintained the standard: I specially recommend *The Moor's Last Sigh,* which contains a marvelous portrait of the city of Bombay before the religious sectarians changed its name to Mumbai. "Those who hated India," wrote Salman with awful prescience, "those who sought to ruin it, would need to ruin Bombay." His fictional genius to one side, Rushdie also chronicled the new age of migration and the contradictory synthesis of cultures.

How often have I been able to speak and write about my friend in this way? Not that often. For example, when he was staying in my house back at Thanksgiving of 1993, so were about a dozen heavily armed members of the United States' finest anti-terrorist forces. And you all know at least some of the backstory. On Valentine's Day 1989, the Ayatollah Khomeini of Iran gave Salman's book *The Satanic Verses* the single worst review any novelist has ever had, calling in frenzied tones for his death and also for the killing of all those "involved in its publication." This was the first time that most people outside the Muslim world had heard the word *fatwa,* or religious edict. So if you have missed the humorous and ironic side of Mr. Rushdie, this could conceivably be the reason why. Just to re-state the situation before I go any farther: two decades ago the theocratic head of a foreign state offered a large sum of money, in his own name, *in public,* to suborn the murder of a writer of fiction who was not himself an Iranian. In the event that some would-be assassin died in the attempt and failed to pick up the dough, an immediate passage to paradise was assured. (Again, this was the first time that many in the West found out about this now notorious Koranic promise.) I thought then, and I think now, that this was not just a warning of what was to come. It was *the* warning. The civil war in the Muslim world, between those who believed in jihad and Shari'a and those who did not, was coming to our streets and cities. Within a short time, Hitoshi Igarashi, the Japanese translator of *The Satanic Verses,* was stabbed to death on the campus where he taught literature, and the Italian translator Ettore Capriolo was knifed in his apartment in Milan. William Nygaard, the novel's Norwegian publisher, was shot three times in the back and left for dead outside his Oslo home. Several very serious bids, often backed by Iranian Embassies, were made on the life of Salman himself. And all this because the senile Khomeini, who had publicly promised that he would never make a deal with Saddam Hussein because god was on the Iranian side, had had to swallow the poison (as he put it) of signing a treaty after all, and was urgently in need of a crowd-pleasing "issue" that would restore his purist religious credentials.

I nonetheless maintain that language and not politics was the crucial question here. Salman Rushdie, raised a Muslim, concluded that the Koran was a book made by the hands of men and was thus a fit subject for literary criticism and fictional borrowing. (Almost every historic battle for free expression, from Socrates to Galileo, has begun as a struggle over what is and is not "blasphemy.") In contrast, the very definition of a "fundamentalist" is someone who believes that "holy writ" is instead the fixed and unalterable word of god. For our time and generation, the great conflict between the ironic mind and the literal mind, the experimental and the dogmatic, the tolerant and the fanatical, is the argument that was kindled by *The Satanic Verses.*

Not everybody agreed with me about the nature of this confrontation. President George H. W. Bush, asked for a comment, said that no American interest was involved. I doubt he would have said this if the chairman of Texaco had been hit by a *fatwa,* but even if Salman's wife of the time (who had to go with him into hiding) had not been an American, it could be argued that the United States has an interest in opposing state-sponsored terrorism against novelists. Various intellectualoids, from John Berger on the left to Norman Podhoretz on the right, argued that Rushdie got what he deserved for insulting a great religion. (Like the Ayatollah Khomeini, they had not put themselves to the trouble of reading the novel, in which the only passage that can possibly be complained of occurs in the course of a nightmare suffered by a madman.) Some of this was a hasty bribe paid to the crude enforcer of fear: if Susan Sontag had not been the president of PEN in 1989, there might have been many who joined Arthur Miller in his initial panicky refusal to sign a protest against the ayatollah's invocation of Murder Incorporated. "I'm Jewish," said the author of *The Crucible.* "I'd only help them change the subject." But Susan would have none of that, and shamed many more pants wetters whose names I still cannot reveal. Others remarked darkly that Rushdie "knew what he was doing," as if that itself was something creepy or mercenary on its face. By the way, he certainly did know what he was doing. He had studied Islamic scripture at Cambridge University, and I well remember one evening, at the apartment of Professor Edward Said near Columbia, when the advance manuscript of *The Satanic Verses* was delivered to Edward by the Andrew Wylie agency. In a covering note, Salman asked America's best-known Palestinian for his learned advice, given the probability that the book might upset "the faithful." So, yes, he "knew" all right, but in a highly responsible way. In any case, it is not the job of writers and thinkers to appease the faithful. And the faithful, if in fact upset or offended, are quite able and entitled to explore all forms of protest. Short of violence.

Those last three words are not a proper sentence, but they summon to mind the various "sentences" that have since been pronounced by the faithful in their periodic fits of rage. The Dutch filmmaker Theo van Gogh, descendant of the painter, shot down and then ritually butchered on an Amsterdam street after making a short film about the maltreatment of Muslim women in Holland. His colleague Ayaan Hirsi Ali, an elected member of the Dutch parliament, forced into hiding and ultimately into exile by incessant threats of death. Another small (and unusually open and multicultural) European democracy, that of Denmark, its embassies burned and its exports boycotted and its citizens threatened, because of a few cartoons of the prophet Muhammad published in a morning newspaper in Copenhagen. Daniel Pearl, of *The Wall Street Journal,* taunted on video for being a Jew and then foully beheaded. Riots and burnings and killings all across the Muslim world, some of them clearly incited by the authorities, in response to some ill-judged words about Islam from the Pope.

These are among the things that have happened, and have become depressingly taken for granted, since the *fatwa* of the ayatollah. We live now in a climate where every publisher and editor and politician has to weigh *in advance* the possibility of violent Muslim reprisal. In consequence, there are a number of things that have *not* happened. Let me give a recent and trivial example that isn't altogether lacking in symbolic importance. Last October, Sony PlayStation abruptly delayed the release of its biggest video game in 2008, *LittleBigPlanet,* because an accompanying track by the Malian singer Toumani Diabaté included two expressions that, according to the Press Association report, "can be found in the Koran." Following the lead of the American press—which refused to show its readers the Danish cartoons and thus permit them to judge for themselves—the report did not care to say which "expressions" these were. It was a textbook instance of self-censorship or, if you prefer, of crying before you are hurt. There was one American magazine (the secular *Free Inquiry,* for which I write) that did print those Danish cartoons—Borders Books pulled that issue from the shelves.

But that you can be hurt, let nobody doubt. A few weeks before Sony PlayStation capitulated in advance, so to speak, a firebomb was thrown into a private home in North London that is also the office of a small publisher named Gibson Square Books. The director, Martin Rynja, was chosen for this atrocity because he had decided to publish a romantic novel called *The Jewel of Medina*, by the American writer Sherry Jones, which told the tale of the prophet Muhammad's youngest and favorite wife, the nine-year-old Aisha (aged six at the time of her betrothal). The novel had originally been commissioned by Random House in New York. How did such a small London press acquire the honor of becoming its British publisher? Because Random House dumped the book on receiving a threat from a single reader that it might have another "Rushdie affair" on its hands. The date of the subsequent firebombing, 26 September last, was the 20th anniversary of the publication of *The Satanic Verses*.

So there is now a hidden partner in our cultural and academic and publishing and broadcasting world: a shadowy figure that has, uninvited, drawn up a chair to the table. He never speaks. He doesn't have to. But he is very well understood. The late playwright Simon Gray was alluding to him when he said that Nicholas Hytner, the head of London's National Theatre, might put on a play mocking Christianity but never one that questioned Islam. I brushed up against the unacknowledged censor myself when I went on CNN to defend the Danish cartoons and found that, though the network would show the relevant page of the newspaper, it had pixelated the cartoons themselves. And this in an age when the image is everything. The lady anchor did not blush to tell me that the network was obliterating its very stock-in-trade (newsworthy pictures) out of sheer fear.

Sometimes this fear—and this blackmail—comes dressed up in the guise of good manners and multiculturalism. One must not wound the religious feelings of others, many of whom are poor immigrants in our own societies. To this I would respond by pointing to a book published in 1994. It is entitled *For Rushdie: Essays by Arab and Muslim Writers in Defense of Free Speech*. Among its contributors is almost every writer worthy of the name in the Arab and Muslim world, ranging from the Syrian poet Adonis to the Syrian-Kurdish author Salim Barakat, to the late national bard of the Palestinians, Mahmoud Darwish, to the celebrated Turkish writers Murat Belge and Orhan Pamuk. Especially impressive and courageous was the list of 127 Iranian writers, artists, and intellectuals who, from the prison house that is the Islamic Republic, signed their names to a letter which said: "We underline the intolerable character of the decree of death that the Fatwah is, and we insist on the fact that aesthetic criteria are the only proper ones for judging works of art. . . . To the extent that the systematic denial of the rights of man in Iran is tolerated, this can only further encourage the export outside the Islamic Republic of its terrorist methods which destroy freedom." In other words, the situation is the exact reverse of what the condescending multiculturalists say it is. To indulge the idea of religious censorship by the threat of violence is to insult and undermine precisely those in the Muslim world who are its intellectual cream, and who want to testify for their own liberty—and for ours. It is also to make the patronizing assumption that the leaders of mobs and the inciters of goons are the authentic representatives of Muslim opinion. What could be more "offensive" than that?

In the hot days immediately after the *fatwa*, with Salman himself on the run and the TV screens filled with images of burning books and writhing mustaches, I was stopped by a female Muslim interviewer and her camera crew and asked an ancient question: "Is nothing sacred?" I can't remember quite what I answered then, but I know what I would say now. "No, nothing is sacred. And even if there were to be something called sacred, we mere primates wouldn't be able to decide which book or which idol or which city was the truly holy one. Thus, the only thing that should be upheld at all costs and without qualification is the right of free expression, because if that goes, then so do all other claims of right as well." I also think that human life has its sacrosanct aspect, and though I can think of many circumstances in which I would take a life, the crime of writing a work of fiction is not a justification (even in the case of Ludlum) that I could ever entertain. Two decades on, Salman himself is thriving mightily and living again like a free man. But the culture that sustains him, and that he helps sustain, has twisted itself into a posture of prior restraint and self-censorship in which the grim, mad edict of a dead theocrat still exerts its chilling force. And, by the way, the next time that Khomeini's lovely children want to make themselves felt, they will be armed not just with *fatwa*s but with nuclear weapons.

FOR INFORMAL WRITING

This essay is commentary on media self-censorship that followed in the decades after the *fatwa* on Salman Rushdie. We recognize the relevance of Hitchens's argument, even now. How is this article still relevant? Does media self-censorship still exist? How? If so, how does it have an impact on our current cultural climate?

FOR DISCUSSION

1. What kinds of language does Hitchens use to describe Rushdie? What effect does this have on your view of him?

2. "For our time and generation, the great conflict between the ironic mind and the literal mind, the experimental and the dogmatic, the tolerant and the fanatical, is the argument that was kindled by *The Satanic Verses*." Comment on the meaning of this quote, both in terms of the essay itself and your own views about the ways in which we witness these issues now.
3. Hitchens was known as a critic of organized religion and spoke widely against it. What does this essay reveal about his perceptions about intolerance as it relates to diversity of religious beliefs?

FOR WRITING

Consider this quote from the essay, the way Hitchens wishes he'd responded to a Muslim reporter: "No, nothing is sacred. And even if there were to be something called sacred, we mere primates wouldn't be able to decide which book or which idol or which city was the truly holy one. Thus, the only thing that should be upheld at all costs and without qualification is the right of free expression, because if that goes, then so do all other claims of right as well." Research other times in recent history where religious freedom has encroached on freedom of expression—where the intersection of the two has made the news and been the subject of public interest. How do these compare? Do things change—or not? Craft a point of view with which you argue whether "nothing is sacred."

Reprieve (2009)
Tim Kreider (1967–)

Tim Kreider got his start with his cartoon entitled "The Pain—When Will It End?", which ran for twelve years in the Baltimore City Paper. *He later became an essayist and has contributed to such publications as* The New Yorker, The New York Times, *and* Vox; *he is now a regular columnist for* Medium. *He is known for his wit and his dark approach to his subjects, both of which form the basis for his two essay collections,* We Learn Nothing *(2012) and* I Wrote This Book Because I Love You *(2018). Originally published in the Opinion pages of* The New York Times, *"Reprieve" also serves as the prologue to* We Learn Nothing.

Fourteen years ago, I was stabbed in the throat. This is kind of a long story and less interesting than it sounds. A lot of people have told me about their own near-death experiences over the years, often in harrowing medical detail, imagining that those details—how many times they rolled the car, how many vertebrae shattered, how many months spent in traction—will somehow convey the subjective psychic force of the experience, the way some people will relate the whole narrative of a dream in a futile attempt to evoke its ambient feeling. Except for the ten or fifteen minutes during which it looked like I was about to die, which I would prefer not to relive, getting stabbed wasn't even among the worst experiences of my life. In fact it was one of the best things that ever happened to me.

After my unsuccessful murder I wasn't unhappy for an entire year. Winston Churchill's aphorism about the exhilaration of being shot at without result is verifiably true. I was reminded of an old Ray Bradbury story, "The Lost City of Mars," in which a man finds a miraculous machine that enables him to experience

---

From WE LEARN NOTHING: Essays and Cartoons by Tim Kreider. Copyright © 2012 by Tim Kreider. Reprinted with the permission of The Free Press, a division of Simon & Schuster, Inc. All rights reserved.

his own violent death over and over again, as many times as he likes—in locomotive collisions, race car crashes, exploding rocket ships—until he emerges flayed of all his Christian guilt and unconscious longing for death, forgiven and free, finally alive.

I can't claim to have been continuously euphoric the whole time; it's just that, during that grace period, nothing much could bother me or get me down. The horrible thing that I'd always dreaded was going to happen to me had finally happened. I figured I was off the hook for a while. In a parallel universe only two millimeters away—the distance between my carotid and the stiletto—I had been flown home in the cargo hold instead of in coach. As far as I was concerned everything in this life was what Raymond Carver, in writing of his own second chance, called "gravy."

My friends immediately mocked me out of my self-consciousness about the nerve damage that had left me with a lopsided smile. I started brewing my own dandelion wine in a big Amish crock. I listened to old one-hit wonders much too stupid to name in print. And I developed a strange new laugh that's stayed with me to this day—a raucous, barking thing that comes from deep in the diaphragm, the laugh of a much larger man, that makes people in bars or restaurants look over for a second to make sure I'm not about to open up on the crowd with a weapon. I don't laugh this way all the time—certainly not when I'm just being polite. The last time it happened was when I told my friend Harold, "You don't understand me," in mock-wounded protest at some unjust charge of sleazery, and he retorted: "No, sir, I understand you very well—it is you who do not understand yourself." The laugh always seems to be in response to the same elusive joke, some dark, hilarious universal truth.

Not for one passing moment did it occur to me to imagine that God Must Have Spared My Life for Some Purpose. Even if I'd been the type who was prone to such silly notions, I would've been rudely disabused of it by the heavy-handed coincidence of the Oklahoma City bombing occurring on the same day I spent in a coma. If there is some divine plan that requires my survival and the deaths of all those children in day care, I respectfully decline to participate. What I had been was not blessed or chosen but lucky. Not to turn up my nose at luck; it's better to be lucky than just about anything else in life. And if you're reading this now you're among the lucky, too.

I wish I could recommend the experience of not being killed to everyone. It's a truism that this is why people enjoy thrill-seeking pastimes, ranging from harmless adrenaline fixes like horror movies and roller coasters to what are essentially suicide attempts with safety nets, like bungee jumping and skydiving. The trick is that to get the full effect you have to be genuinely uncertain that you're going to survive. The best approximation would be to hire an incompetent, Clouseauesque hit man to assassinate you.

It's one of the maddening perversities of human psychology that we only notice we're alive when we're reminded we're going to die, the same way some of us appreciate our girlfriends only after they've become exes. I saw the same thing happen, in a more profound and lasting way, to my father when he was terminally ill: a lightening, an amused indifference to the nonsense that the rest of us think of as the serious business of the world. A neighbor was suing my father over some property dispute during his illness, but if you tried to talk to him about such practical matters he'd just sing you old songs like "A Bird in a Gilded Cage" in a silly, quavering falsetto until you gave up. He cared less about things that didn't matter and more about the things that did. It was during his illness that he gave me the talk that all my artist friends have envied, in which he told me that he and my mother believed in my talent and I shouldn't worry about getting "some dumb job."

Maybe people who have lived with the reality of their own mortality for months or years are permanently changed by it, but getting stabbed was more like getting struck by lightning, over almost as soon as it happened, and the illumination didn't last. You can't feel crazily grateful to be alive your whole life any more than you can stay passionately in love forever—or grieve forever, for that matter. Time makes us all betray ourselves and get back to the busywork of living. Before a year had gone by, the same everyday anxieties and frustrations began creeping back. I was disgusted to catch myself yelling in traffic, pounding on my computer, lying awake at night worrying about what was to become of me. I can't recapture that feeling of euphoric gratitude any more than I can really remember the mortal terror I felt when I was pretty sure I had about four minutes to live. But I know that it really happened, that that state of grace is accessible to us, even if I only blundered across it once and never find my way back. At my cabin on the Chesapeake Bay I'll see bald eagles swoop up from the water with wriggling little fish in their talons, and whenever they accidentally drop their catch, I like to imagine that fish trying to tell his friends about his own near-death experience, a perspective so unprecedented there are no words in the fish language to describe it: for a short time he was outside the world, he could see forever, there's so much more than they knew, but he's glad to be back.

Once a year on my stabbiversary, I remind myself that this is still my bonus life, a round on the house. But now that I'm back in the slog of everyday life, I have to struggle to keep things in what I still insist is their true perspective. I know intellectually that all the urgently pressing items on our mental lists— our careers, car repairs, the daily headlines, the goddamned taxes—are just so much noise, that what matters is spending time with the people you love. It's just hard to bear in mind when the hard drive crashes or the shower drain clogs first thing in the day. Apparently I can only ever attain that God's-eye view in the grip of the talons.

I was not cheered to read about psychological studies suggesting that most people inevitably return to a certain emotional baseline after circumstantial highs and lows. How happy we can hope to be may be as inalterable and unfair as our height or metabolism or the age at which we'll lose our hair. This is reassuring news if you've undergone some trauma, but less so if your own emotional thermostat is set so low it makes you want to phone up the landlord and yell at him. You'd like to think that nearly getting killed would be a permanently life-altering experience, but in truth it was less painful, and occasioned less serious reflection, than certain breakups I've gone through. I've demonstrated an impressive resilience in the face of valuable life lessons, and the main thing I seem to have learned from this one is that I am capable of learning nothing from almost any experience, no matter how profound. If anything, the whole episode only confirmed my solipsistic suspicion that in the story of Me only supporting characters would die, while I, its first-person narrator and star, was immortal. It gave me much more of an existential turn when my vision started to blur.

I don't know why we take our worst moods so much more seriously than our best, crediting depression with more clarity than euphoria. We dismiss peak moments and passionate love affairs as an ephemeral chemical buzz, just endorphins or hormones, but accept those 3 AM bouts of despair as unsentimental insights into the truth about our lives. It's easy now to dismiss that year as nothing more than the same sort of shaky, hysterical high you'd feel after getting clipped by a taxi. But you could also try to think of it as a glimpse of reality, being jolted out of a lifelong stupor. It's like the revelation I had the first time I ever flew in an airplane as a kid: when you break through the cloud cover you realize that above the passing squalls and doldrums there is a realm of eternal sunlight, so keen and brilliant you have to squint against it, a vision to hold on to when you descend once again beneath the clouds, under the oppressive, petty jurisdiction of the local weather.

FOR INFORMAL WRITING

How does Kreider's "near-death experience" influence his world view? What are the limitations of that experience? What in Kreider's essay leads you to these conclusions?

FOR DISCUSSION

1. What is the tone of this essay? Kreider uses such phrases as "after my unsuccessful murder," for instance. What is the effect of this tone? What do you think of the matter-of-factness and other types of tone with which he discusses this episode?

2. "I don't know why we take our worst moods so much more seriously than our best ones, crediting depression with more clarity than euphoria." What does Kreider mean? Do you agree? Why or why not?
3. How does Kreider's experience ring true to you? We hope you haven't had a near-death experience, but nonetheless, what aspects of Kreider's philosophy or worldview resonate with you? Why? How might they help you think differently about life?

FOR WRITING

Early in the essay, Kreider cites well-known, prominent figures Winston Churchill and Ray Bradbury for comparative purposes. Research one of these references. Why and how would Kreider select them? What do you believe is his purpose in selecting these particular men? How does what you find confirm or refute Kreider's "God's-eye view?" Be specific in defending your point of view.

A Tale of Three Coming Out Stories (2012)

Roxane Gay (1974–)

Roxane Gay is a well-known writer of articles and books, with an emphasis on social commentary. Gay was recently a visiting professor of English at Yale University, where she had completed her own undergraduate studies. Holding the PhD in Rhetoric and Technical Communications from Michigan Technological University, Gay's debut novel, An Untamed State *(2014), explores the story of a Haitian-American woman who is kidnapped for ransom. The novel reveals the many themes Gay often treats in her essays and news editorials, including race, class, and gender. "A Tale of Three Coming Out Stories" was first published in the online magazine* The Rumpus.

We are still in that time in our history where public figures come out of invisible closets largely built by a public insatiable in its desire to know all the intimate details of the private lives of very public people.

We want to know everything. In this information age, we are inundated with information, to which at times we feel entitled. We also like taxonomy, classification, definition. Are you a man or a woman? Are you a Democrat or Republican? Are you married or single? Are you gay or straight? We don't seem to know what to do when we don't know the answers to these questions, or worse, when the answers to these questions do not fall neatly into a category.

When public figures don't provide outward evidence of their sexuality, our desire to classify intensifies. Any number of celebrities are dogged by "gay rumors," because we cannot quite place them into a given category. We act like placing these people in categories will have some impact on our lives, or that it is our responsibility, when, most of the time, it won't change anything at all. There is nothing in my life that is impacted by knowing Ricky Martin, for example, is gay. The only thing satisfied by that information is my curiosity.

By permission of Roxane Gay

Sometimes, this zeal to classify has resulted in public figures being outed against their will. In particular, politicians who have gone on record for legislation that suppresses civil rights have found themselves in the glare of the spotlight. Congressman Edward Schrock was outed in 2004 because he voted for the Marriage Protection Act. There have been many others. When people have been forcibly outed, those doing the outing have said they were acting for the greater good or working to reveal hypocrisy as if the right to privacy and the right to determine if and when to come out is only afforded to those who are infallible.

This is, in part, a matter of privacy. What information do we have the right to keep to ourselves? What boundaries are we allowed to maintain in our personal lives? What do we have a right to know about the lives of others? When do we have a right to breach the boundaries others have set for themselves?

People with high public profiles are allowed very few boundaries. In exchange for the erosion of privacy, they receive fame and/or fortune and/or power. Is this a fair price? Are famous people aware of how they are sacrificing privacy when they ascend to a position of cultural prominence? Only they know but we do take it for granted that privacy for fame, fortune and power is a fair exchange.

There are many ways we have surrendered our privacy in the information age. Many people willingly disclose what they've eaten for breakfast, where they spent last night and with whom, and all manner of trivial information. We surrender personal information when registering for social media accounts and when making purchases online. We often surrender this information without question or reflection. These disclosures come so freely because we've long been conditioned to share too much with too many.

In his book *Privacy* (Picador), Garret Keizer explores privacy through a series of essays that consider privacy legally, from the feminist perspective, through the lens of class, and more. He demonstrates a real concern for how little privacy we have, how cavalier we sometimes are with our privacy, and how unthinkingly we might infringe on the privacy of others. He says, "We speak of privacy as a right but we might also think of it as a test, as a canary in the mine of our civilization. It lives or dies to the extent that we remain willing to believe that the human person, body and soul—our blood relatives in his or her flesh, and beyond reduction in his or her grandeur and nobility—is sacred, endowed with inalienable rights and a microcosm of us all."

We tend to forget that culturally prominent figures are as sacred as the people closest to us. We tend to forget that they are flesh and blood. We assume that as they rise to prominence, they shed their inalienable rights. We do this without question.

One of the most striking arguments Keizer makes is that privacy and class are intrinsically bound together. He asserts that people with privilege have more access to privacy than people who don't. Keizer notes, "Social class is defined in large part by the degree of freedom one has to move from private space to public space, and by the amount of time one spends in relative privacy."

I would also argue that this relationship between privacy and privilege extends to race, gender and sexuality. When a woman is pregnant, for example, there's increasingly less privacy because, as she reaches full term, her condition becomes more and more visible. Keizer remarks, with regard to pregnant women, that, "Her condition is an unequivocally public statement of a very private experience, begun in circumstances of intimacy and continued within the sanctum of her own body—yet there is no hiding it for her, nor any denying the feeling we have that somehow she belongs to us, that she embodies our collective future and represents our individual pasts."

Anytime your body represents some kind of difference your privacy is compromised to some degree. A surfeit of privacy is just one more benefit the privileged class gets to enjoy and often takes for granted; to the same extent, heterosexual people take the privacy of their sexuality for granted. They can date, marry and love whom they choose without needing to disclose much of anything about themselves. If they do choose to disclose, there are rarely negative consequences.

In recent years, celebrities have started coming out with little fanfare by way, perhaps, of an interview where a man might casually mention his male partner or refer to himself as a gay man, or a woman might thank her partner in an award acceptance speech. The public reacts when celebrities come out quietly but the spectacle is somewhat muted. When celebrities come out in this manner, they are generally saying, "This is simply one more thing you now know about me."

In July 2012, popular journalist Anderson Cooper came out of one of those invisible closets built by someone else's hands, in an email to *The Daily Beast*'s Andrew Sullivan, who then published that email on his blog.

Cooper wrote:

The fact is, I'm gay, always have been, always will be, and I couldn't be any more happy, comfortable with myself, and proud.

I have always been very open and honest about this part of my life with my friends, my family, and my colleagues. In a perfect world, I don't think it's anyone else's business, but I do think there is value in standing up and being counted.

There was a range of responses to Cooper's email and his coming out. Many people shrugged and said Cooper's sexuality was presumed, an open secret.

Others remarked it was important and even necessary for Cooper to come out and to, as he puts it, stand up and be counted.

This is often what is said when public figures do or do not come out: there is a greater obligation that must be met beyond what that person might ordinarily choose to meet. We make these demands, though, without considering how much less privacy that person might have not only because they are a public figure but also because they are part of an underrepresented group. I am not suggesting that we cry for the celebrity who enjoys a lush lifestyle; I am saying we should give thought to the celebrity who would prefer to keep his marriage to a man private for whatever reason, but isn't allowed that right, a right that is, for heterosexuals, inalienable.

In *Privacy,* Keizer notes that, "The public obligations of prominently powerful people can also constrain their private lives." We see these constraints time and again when celebrities and other prominent figures sidestep questions about their personal lives they are unwilling to answer. They may be hesitant for any number of reasons—protecting their privacy, protecting their careers and social standing, protecting loved ones. The public rarely seems to care about those reasons. They—we—need to know.

At the same time, we live in a complex cultural climate. Things are improving and we are inching slowly, ever closer, to equal rights for all.

But.

Prominent gay people need to stand up and be counted, because the word "gay" is still used as a slur. Nine out of ten LGBT teenagers report being bullied at school. LGBT youth are two to three times more likely to commit suicide. The bullying and harassment of LGBT youth was so pervasive that, in 2010, Dan Savage and his partner Terry Miller created a YouTube video to show LGBT youth how life can, indeed, get better beyond the torments of adolescence. That video spawned countless other videos and a foundation dedicated to continuing this project of showing LGBT youth there is a light at the end of an often very dark tunnel.

Gay celebrities like Cooper also need to stand up and be counted because there are only six states where gay marriage is legal. Those marriages are only recognized at the state level because the Defense of Marriage Act, passed in 1996, does not recognize gay marriage—or what it really is, marriage—federally. This act denies gay couples 1,138 federally preserved rights afforded to heterosexual couples. Twenty-nine states have constitutional provisions explicitly defining marriage as a union between a man and a woman. There are states where LGBT people cannot adopt children. Depending on where they live, members of the LGBT community may lose their jobs because of their sexual orientation. They may face ostracism from family, friends and community.

LGBT people are the victims of hate crimes. There is the young lesbian couple in Texas, Kristine Chapa and Mollie Olgin, who were both shot in the head by an unknown assailant and left to die. In Lincoln, Nebraska, a lesbian was attacked in her own home by three men who carved the word "dyke" and other slurs into her body. A gay couple in northeast DC were attacked two blocks from their apartment by three assailants who were shouting homophobic slurs. One, Michael Hall, remains in the hospital. He has no health insurance and has a fractured jaw. In Edmond, Oklahoma, a gay man's car was vandalized with a homophobic slur and set on fire. In Indianapolis, Indiana, there was a drive-by shooting of a gay bar.

These incidents have taken place within the past month. Hate is everywhere.

It gets better, sort of. It gets better unless you're in the wrong place at the wrong time. Sometimes the wrong place is your very home, which is the one place where you should be able to feel safe no matter what the world is like.

Sally Ride, the first woman astronaut, who died in July 2012 at the age of 61, is survived by her female partner of 27 years. Her widow will not be able to receive her federal benefits that would normally be given to a surviving spouse. Sally Ride was able to fly into space and reach the stars but, here on earth, her long-term relationship will go largely unrecognized. Republican presidential candidate Mitt Romney tweeted, "Sally Ride ranks among the greatest pioneers. I count myself among the millions of Americans she inspired with her travel to space." Music group The Mountain Goats replied, "Kind of despicable and grotesque that her partner of 27 years will be denied her federal benefits, don't you think?"

Despicable and grotesque, indeed; but in her death, Sally Ride stood up and was counted. She became even more of a hero than she already was.

The world we live in is not as progressive as we need it to be. When a celebrity comes out, it is still news. The coming out is still culturally significant. When a man like Anderson Cooper comes out, people feel like it's a step forward in achieving civil rights for everyone. At the very least, it is one more person saying, I am here. I matter. I demand to be recognized. Cooper is, by many standards, the "right kind of gay"—white, handsome, successful, masculine. Many celebrities who have successfully come out in recent years fit that profile—Neil Patrick Harris, Matt Bomer, Zachary Quinto and so on. These men are held up as examples—not too flamboyant, not *too* gay.

It's a problem, though, that there's a right kind of gay, that there are LGBT people who are warmly encouraged to step out of the closet while others who don't fit certain parameters go largely ignored. It's easy enough for a man like Anderson Cooper, living in fairly liberal New York City, to come out. He will likely continue to be very successful. He has a supportive family and a welcoming community to embrace him. Coming out stories for everyday people are often far different, complicated and difficult. We lose sight of that. We forget what it's like to come out in the so-called *flyover states*. It's not easy.

In July 2012, musician Frank Ocean, a celebrity with a lower profile than Cooper but with, perhaps, more to lose, came out as having once loved a man via Tumblr by sharing some of the liner notes for his critically acclaimed album *Channel Orange*. Once again, cultural observers noted that Ocean's coming out was important and significant.

For a black man to come out as gay or bisexual, particularly as part of the notoriously homophobic R&B and Hip Hop community, Ocean was taking a bold step, a risk. He was trusting that his music would transcend the prejudices, if any, of his audience. So far, that risk seems to have paid off. Many celebrities have vocalized their support of Ocean including Russell Simmons, Beyoncé, Fifty Cent and others. He is standing up to be counted. His album has been well received and continues to sell well.

Of course, Ocean is also part of the Odd Future collective. His friend and collaborator Tyler, the Creator's debut album, *Goblin*, contains 213 gay slurs. Tyler, the Creator continues to assert that he's not homophobic with that old canard of having gay friends. He stepped up his defense by also claiming his gay fans were totally fine with his use of the term "faggot" over and over and over—immunity by association. I do not know the man. Maybe he is homophobic, maybe he isn't. I do know he doesn't think about language very carefully. He believes that just because you can say something, you should. He is not shamed by using slurs 213 times on one album, no matter how that frequency reflects a lack of imagination.

For every step forward, there is some asshole shoving progress back.

Despite our complex cultural climate and what needs to be done for the greater good, it is still an unreasonable burden that someone who is marginalized must bear an extra set of responsibilities. It is unfair that prominent cultural figures who come out have to forge these inroads on our behalf, to satisfy our desperate desire to know. These figures carry the hopes of so many on their shoulders. They stand up and are counted so that someday things might actually be better for everyone, everywhere, not just the camera or radio-ready celebrities for whom coming out is far easier than most.

I am reminded of the Iowa lesbian couple whose son Zach Wahls testified in 2011 before the Iowa House Judiciary community about how a child raised by two women turns out. He spoke in support of gay marriage in Iowa. He was passionate and eloquent and a real credit to his parents. The video clip of his testimony was shared across the Internet. Every time I saw it I was both thrilled and angry—angry because queer people always have to fight so much harder for a fraction of the recognition. No one ever asks heterosexual parents to ensure that their children are models of citizenry. The bar for queer parents is unfairly, unnecessarily high, but young men like this one keep vaulting that bar nonetheless.

Perhaps, we expect gay public figures and other prominent queer people to come out, to stand and be counted so they can do the work we're unwilling to do to change the world, to carry the burdens we are unwilling to shoulder, to take the stands we are unwilling to make. As individuals, we may not be able to do much, but when we're silent when someone uses the word "gay" as an insult, we are falling short. When we don't vote to support equal marriage rights for all, we are falling short. When we support musicians like Tyler, the Creator, we are falling short. We are failing our communities. We are failing civil rights. There are injustices great and small and even if we can only fight the small ones, we're still doing something.

Too often, we fail to ask ourselves, what sacrifices will we make for the greater good? What stands will we take? We expect *role models* to model the behaviors we are perfectly capable of modeling ourselves. We know things are getting better. We know we have far to go. In *Privacy*, Keizer also says that, "The plurality of intrusions on our privacy has the cumulative effect of inducing a sense of helplessness." We are willing—even anxious—to see prominent figures in a state of helplessness as they sacrifice their privacy for the greater good. How helpless are *we* willing to be for the greater good? That's the question that interests me most.

FOR INFORMAL WRITING

How do you feel about "public figures being outed against their will"? What responsibility, if any, do famous figures have to the marginalized communities to which they may belong? Why or why not?

FOR DISCUSSION

1. "Anytime your body represents some kind of difference, your privacy is compromised to some degree. In the context of this article, why is this the case? To what effect?
2. Is Roxane Gay defending public figures' right to privacy? Why or why not? What do you think her position is? What in the article tells you so?
3. Gay writes, "In exchange for the erosion of privacy, [public figures] receive fame and/or fortune and/or power. Is this a fair price?" What do you think?

FOR WRITING

Research another celebrity coming out story, and compare, contrast, and analyze their experience through the lens of Gay's argument. How is the experience you've researched similar or different than the ones about which Gay writes? What do these experiences tell us about the issues of privacy and privilege?

My President Was Black (2017)
Ta-Nehisi Coates (1975–)

Ta-Nehisi Coates has become something of a national cultural icon. Coates attended Howard University, an historically Black institution, but left before completing his degree. He has ascended the cultural and literary ladder, however, beginning as a well-known blogger and becoming senior editor at The Atlantic *and writing a* New York Times *best-seller,* Between the World and Me *(2015). Coates has also received a prestigious MacArthur Fellowship and has written for* Black Panther *and* Captain America *from Marvel Comics. In "My President Was Black," Coates reflects on his experience as a Black man living through the terms of the first Black President in the United States.*

> "They're a rotten crowd," I shouted across the lawn. "You're worth the whole damn bunch put together."
> — F. Scott Fitzgerald, *The Great Gatsby*

I. "LOVE WILL MAKE YOU DO WRONG"

In the waning days of President Barack Obama's administration, he and his wife, Michelle, hosted a farewell party, the full import of which no one could then grasp. It was late October, Friday the 21st, and the president had spent many of the previous weeks, as he would spend the two subsequent weeks, campaigning for the Democratic presidential nominee, Hillary Clinton. Things were looking up. Polls in the crucial states of Virginia and Pennsylvania showed Clinton with solid advantages. The formidable GOP strongholds of Georgia and Texas were said to be under threat. The moment seemed to buoy Obama. He had been light

---

From The Atlantic. © 2017 The Atlantic Monthly Group, LLC. All rights reserved. Used under license."

on his feet in these last few weeks, cracking jokes at the expense of Republican opponents and laughing off hecklers. At a rally in Orlando on October 28, he greeted a student who would be introducing him by dancing toward her and then noting that the song playing over the loudspeakers—the Gap Band's "Outstanding"—was older than she was. "This is classic!" he said. Then he flashed the smile that had launched America's first black presidency, and started dancing again. Three months still remained before Inauguration Day, but staffers had already begun to count down the days. They did this with a mix of pride and longing—like college seniors in early May. They had no sense of the world they were graduating into. None of us did.

The farewell party, presented by BET (Black Entertainment Television), was the last in a series of concerts the first couple had hosted at the White House. Guests were asked to arrive at 5:30 p.m. By 6, two long lines stretched behind the Treasury Building, where the Secret Service was checking names. The people in these lines were, in the main, black, and their humor reflected it. The brisker queue was dubbed the "good-hair line" by one guest, and there was laughter at the prospect of the Secret Service subjecting us all to a "brown-paper-bag test." This did not come to pass, but security was tight. Several guests were told to stand in a makeshift pen and wait to have their backgrounds checked a second time.

Dave Chappelle was there. He coolly explained the peril and promise of comedy in what was then still only a remotely potential Donald Trump presidency: "I mean, we never had a guy have his own pussygate scandal." Everyone laughed. A few weeks later, he would be roundly criticized for telling a crowd at the Cutting Room, in New York, that he had voted for Clinton but did not feel good about it. "She's going to be on a coin someday," Chappelle said. "And her behavior has not been coinworthy." But on this crisp October night, everything felt inevitable and grand. There was a slight wind. It had been in the 80s for much of that week. Now, as the sun set, the season remembered its name. Women shivered in their cocktail dresses. Gentlemen chivalrously handed over their suit coats. But when Naomi Campbell strolled past the security pen in a sleeveless number, she seemed as invulnerable as ever.

Cellphones were confiscated to prevent surreptitious recordings from leaking out. (This effort was unsuccessful. The next day, a partygoer would tweet a video of the leader of the free world dancing to Drake's "Hotline Bling.") After withstanding the barrage of security, guests were welcomed into the East Wing of the White House, and then ushered back out into the night, where they boarded a succession of orange-and-green trolleys. The singer and actress Janelle Monáe, her famous and fantastic pompadour preceding her, stepped on board and joked with a companion about the historical import of "sitting in the back of the bus."

She took a seat three rows from the front and hummed into the night. The trolley dropped the guests on the South Lawn, in front of a giant tent. The South Lawn's fountain was lit up with blue lights. The White House proper loomed like a ghost in the distance. I heard the band, inside, beginning to play Al Green's "Let's Stay Together."

"Well, you can tell what type of night this is," Obama said from the stage, opening the event. "Not the usual ruffles and flourishes!"

The crowd roared.

"This must be a BET event!"

The crowd roared louder still.

Obama placed the concert in the White House's musical tradition, noting that guests of the Kennedys had once done the twist at the residence—"the twerking of their time," he said, before adding, "There will be no twerking tonight. At least not by me."

The Obamas are fervent and eclectic music fans. In the past eight years, they have hosted performances at the White House by everyone from Mavis Staples to Bob Dylan to Tony Bennett to the Blind Boys of Alabama. After the rapper Common was invited to perform in 2011, a small fracas ensued in the right-wing media. He performed anyway—and was invited back again this glorious fall evening and almost stole the show. The crowd sang along to the hook for his hit ballad "The Light." And when he brought on the gospel singer Yolanda Adams to fill in for John Legend on the Oscar-winning song "Glory," glee turned to rapture.

De La Soul was there. The hip-hop trio had come of age as boyish B-boys with Gumby-style high-top fades. Now they moved across the stage with a lovely mix of lethargy and grace, like your favorite uncle making his way down the *Soul Train* line, wary of throwing out a hip. I felt a sense of victory watching them rock the crowd, all while keeping it in the pocket. The victory belonged to hip-hop—an art form birthed in the burning Bronx and now standing full grown, at the White House, unbroken and unedited. Usher led the crowd in a call-and-response: "Say it loud, I'm black and I'm proud." Jill Scott showed off her operatic chops. Bell Biv DeVoe, contemporaries of De La, made history with their performance by surely becoming the first group to suggest to a presidential audience that one should "never trust a big butt and a smile."

The ties between the Obama White House and the hip-hop community are genuine. The Obamas are social with Beyoncé and Jay-Z. They hosted Chance the Rapper and Frank Ocean at a state dinner, and last year invited Swizz Beatz, Busta Rhymes, and Ludacris, among others, to discuss criminal-justice reform and other initiatives. Obama once stood in the Rose Garden passing large flash cards to the *Hamilton* creator and rapper Lin-Manuel Miranda, who then freestyled using each word on the cards. "Drop the beat," Obama said, inaugurating the session. At 55, Obama is younger than pioneering hip-hop artists like Afrika Bambaataa, DJ Kool Herc, and Kurtis Blow. If Obama's enormous symbolic power draws primarily from being the country's first black president, it also draws from his membership in hip-hop's foundational generation.

That night, the men were sharp in their gray or black suits and optional ties. Those who were not in suits had chosen to make a statement, like the dark-skinned young man who strolled in, sockless, with blue jeans cuffed so as to accentuate his gorgeous black-suede loafers. Everything in his ensemble seemed to say, "My fellow Americans, do not try this at home." There were women in fur jackets and high heels; others with sculpted naturals, the sides shaved close, the tops blooming into curls; others still in gold bamboo earrings and long blond dreads. When the actor Jesse Williams took the stage, seemingly awed before such black excellence, before such black opulence, assembled just feet from where slaves had once toiled, he simply said, "Look where we are. Look where we are right now."

This would not happen again, and everyone knew it. It was not just that there might never be another African American president of the United States. It was the feeling that this particular black family, the Obamas, represented the best of black people, the ultimate credit to the race, incomparable in elegance and bearing. "There are no more," the comedian Sinbad joked back in 2010. "There are no black men raised in Kansas and Hawaii. That's the last one. Y'all better treat this one right. The next one gonna be from Cleveland. He gonna wear a perm. Then you gonna see what it's really like." Throughout their residency, the Obamas had refrained from showing America "what it's really like," and had instead followed the first lady's motto, "When they go low, we go high." This was the ideal—black and graceful under fire—saluted that evening. The president was lionized as "our crown jewel." The first lady was praised as the woman "who put the O in *Obama*."

Barack Obama's victories in 2008 and 2012 were dismissed by some of his critics as merely symbolic for African Americans. But there is nothing "mere" about symbols. The power embedded in the word *nigger* is also symbolic. Burning crosses do not literally raise the black poverty rate, and the Confederate flag does not directly expand the wealth gap.

Much as the unbroken ranks of 43 white male presidents communicated that the highest office of government in the country—indeed, the most powerful political offices in the world—was off-limits to black individuals, the election of Barack Obama communicated that the prohibition had been lifted. It communicated much more. Before Obama triumphed in 2008, the most-famous depictions of black success tended to be entertainers or athletes. But Obama had shown that it was "possible to be smart and cool at the same damn time," as Jesse Williams put it at the BET party. Moreover, he had not embarrassed his people with a string of scandals. Against the specter of black pathology, against the narrow images of welfare moms and deadbeat dads, his time in the White House had been an eight-year showcase of a healthy and successful black family spanning three generations, with two dogs to boot. In short, he became a symbol of black people's everyday, extraordinary Americanness.

Whiteness in America is a different symbol—a badge of advantage. In a country of professed meritocratic competition, this badge has long ensured an unerring privilege, represented in a 220-year monopoly on the highest office in the land. For some not-insubstantial sector of the country, the elevation of Barack Obama communicated that the power of the badge had diminished. For eight long years, the badge-holders watched him. They saw footage of the president throwing bounce passes and shooting jumpers. They saw him enter a locker room, give a businesslike handshake to a white staffer, and then greet Kevin Durant with something more soulful. They saw his wife dancing with Jimmy Fallon and posing, resplendent, on the covers of magazines that had, only a decade earlier, been almost exclusively, if unofficially, reserved for ladies imbued with the great power of the badge.

For the preservation of the badge, insidious rumors were concocted to denigrate the first black White House. Obama gave free cellphones to disheveled welfare recipients. Obama went to Europe and complained that "ordinary men and women are too small-minded to govern their own affairs." Obama had inscribed an Arabic saying on his wedding ring, then stopped wearing the ring, in observance of Ramadan. He canceled the National Day of Prayer; refused to sign certificates for Eagle Scouts; faked his attendance at Columbia University; and used a teleprompter to address a group of elementary-school students. The badge-holders fumed. They wanted their country back. And, though no one at the farewell party knew it, in a couple of weeks they would have it.

On this October night, though, the stage belonged to another America. At the end of the party, Obama looked out into the crowd, searching for Dave Chappelle. "Where's Dave?" he cried. And then, finding him, the president referenced Chappelle's legendary Brooklyn concert. "You got your block party. I got my block party." Then the band struck up Al Green's "Love and Happiness"—the evening's theme. The president danced in a line next to Ronnie DeVoe. Together they mouthed the lyrics: "Make you do right. Love will make you do wrong."

II. HE WALKED ON ICE BUT NEVER FELL

Last spring, I went to the White House to meet the president for lunch. I arrived slightly early and sat in the waiting area. I was introduced to a deaf woman who worked as the president's receptionist, a black woman who worked in the press office, a Muslim woman in a head scarf who worked on the National Security Council, and an Iranian American woman who worked as a personal aide to the president. This receiving party represented a healthy cross section of the people Donald Trump had been mocking, and would continue to spend his campaign mocking. At the time, the president seemed untroubled by Trump. When I told Obama that I thought Trump's candidacy was an explicit reaction to the fact of a black president, he said he could see that, but then enumerated other explanations. When assessing Trump's chances, he was direct: He couldn't win.

This assessment was born out of the president's innate optimism and unwavering faith in the ultimate wisdom of the American people—the same traits that had propelled his unlikely five-year ascent from assemblyman in the Illinois state legislature to US senator to leader of the free world. The speech that launched his rise, the keynote address at the 2004 Democratic National Convention, emerged right from this logic. He addressed himself to his "fellow Americans, Democrats, Republicans, independents," all of whom, he insisted, were more united than they had been led to believe. America was home to devout worshippers and Little League coaches in blue states, civil libertarians and "gay friends" in red states. The presumably white "counties around Chicago" did not want their taxes burned on welfare, but they didn't want them wasted on a bloated Pentagon budget either. Inner-city black families, no matter their perils, understood "that government alone can't teach our kids to learn … that children can't achieve unless we raise their expectations and turn off the television sets and eradicate the slander that says a black youth with a book is acting white."

Perceived differences were the work of "spinmasters and negative-ad peddlers who embrace the politics of 'anything goes.'" Real America had no use for such categorizations. By Obama's lights, there was no liberal America, no conservative America, no black America, no white America, no Latino America, no Asian America, only "the United States of America." All these disparate strands of the American experience were bound together by a common hope:

> It's the hope of slaves sitting around a fire singing freedom songs; the hope of immigrants setting out for distant shores; the hope of a young naval lieutenant bravely patrolling the Mekong Delta; the hope of a mill worker's son who dares to defy the odds; the hope of a skinny kid with a funny name who believes that America has a place for him, too.

This speech ran counter to the history of the people it sought to address. Some of those same immigrants had firebombed the homes of the children of those same slaves. That young naval lieutenant was an imperial agent for a failed, immoral war. American division was real. In 2004, John Kerry did not win a single southern state. But Obama appealed to a belief in innocence—in particular a white innocence—that ascribed the country's historical errors more to misunderstanding and the work of a small cabal than to any deliberate malevolence or widespread racism. America was good. America was great.

Over the next 12 years, I came to regard Obama as a skilled politician, a deeply moral human being, and one of the greatest presidents in American history. He was phenomenal—the most agile interpreter and navigator of the color line I had ever seen. He had an ability to emote a deep and sincere connection to the hearts of black people, while never doubting the hearts of white people. This was the core of his 2004 keynote, and it marked his historic race speech during the 2008 campaign at Philadelphia's National Constitution Center—and blinded him to the appeal of Trump. ("As a general proposition, it's hard to run for president by telling people how terrible things are," Obama once said to me.)

But if the president's inability to cement his legacy in the form of Hillary Clinton proved the limits of his optimism, it also revealed the exceptional nature of his presidential victories. For eight years Barack Obama walked on ice and never fell. Nothing in that time suggested that straight talk on the facts of racism in American life would have given him surer footing.

I had met the president a few times before. In his second term, I'd written articles criticizing him for his overriding trust in color-blind policy and his embrace of "personal responsibility" rhetoric when speaking to African Americans. I saw him as playing both sides. He would invoke his identity as a president of all people to decline to advocate for black policy—and then invoke his black identity to lecture black people for continuing to "make bad choices." In response, Obama had invited me, along with other journalists, to the White House for off-the-record conversations. I attempted to press my points in these sessions. My efforts were laughable and ineffective. I was always inappropriately dressed, and inappropriately calibrated in tone: In one instance, I was too deferential; in another, too bellicose. I was discombobulated by fear—not by fear of the power of his office (though that is a fearsome and impressive thing) but by fear of his obvious brilliance. It is said that Obama speaks "professorially," a fact that understates the quickness and agility of his mind. These were not like press conferences—the president would speak in depth and with great familiarity about a range of subjects. Once, I watched him effortlessly reply to queries covering everything from electoral politics to the American economy to environmental policy. And then he turned to me. I thought of George Foreman, who once booked an exhibition with multiple opponents in which he pounded five straight journeymen—and I suddenly had some idea of how it felt to be the last of them.

Last spring, we had a light lunch. We talked casually and candidly. He talked about the brilliance of LeBron James and Stephen Curry—not as basketball talents but as grounded individuals. I asked him whether he was angry at his father, who had abandoned him at a young age to move back to Kenya, and whether that motivated any of his rhetoric. He said it did not, and he credited the attitude of his mother and grandparents for this. Then it was my turn to be autobiographical. I told him that I had heard the kind of "straighten up" talk he had been giving to black youth, for instance in his 2013 Morehouse commencement address, all my life. I told him that I thought it was not sensitive to the inner turmoil that can be obscured by the hardness kids often evince. I told him I thought this because I had once been one of those kids. He seemed to concede this point, but I couldn't tell whether it mattered to him. Nonetheless, he agreed to a series of more formal conversations on this and other topics.

The improbability of a black president had once been so strong that its most vivid representations were comedic. Witness Dave Chappelle's profane Black Bush from the early 2000s ("This nigger very possibly has weapons of mass destruction! I can't sleep on that!") or Richard Pryor's black president in the 1970s promising black astronauts and black quarterbacks ("Ever since the Rams got rid of James Harris, my jaw's been uptight!"). In this model, so potent is the force of blackness that the presidency is forced to conform to it. But once the notion advanced out of comedy and into reality, the opposite proved to be true.

Obama's DNC speech is the key. It does not belong to the literature of "the struggle"; it belongs to the literature of prospective presidents—men (as it turns out) who speak not to gravity and reality, but to aspirations and dreams. When Lincoln invoked the dream of a nation "conceived in liberty" and pledged to the ideal that "all men are created equal," he erased the near-extermination of one people and the enslavement of another. When Roosevelt told the country that "the only thing we have to fear is fear itself," he invoked the dream of American omnipotence and boundless capability. But black people, then living under a campaign of terror for more than half a century, had quite a bit to fear, and Roosevelt could not save them. The dream Ronald Reagan invoked in 1984—that "it's morning again in America"—meant nothing to the inner cities, besieged as they were by decades of redlining policies, not to mention crack and Saturday-night specials. Likewise, Obama's keynote address conflated the slave and the nation of immigrants who profited from him. To reinforce the majoritarian dream, the nightmare endured by the minority is erased. That is the tradition to which the "skinny kid with a funny name" who would be president belonged. It is also the only tradition in existence that could have possibly put a black person in the White House.

Obama's embrace of white innocence was demonstrably necessary as a matter of political survival. Whenever he attempted to buck this directive, he was disciplined. His mild objection to the arrest of Henry Louis Gates Jr. in 2009 contributed to his declining favorability numbers among whites—still a majority of voters. His comments after the killing of Trayvon Martin—"If I had a son, he'd look like Trayvon"—helped make that tragedy a rallying point for people who did not care about Martin's killer as much as they cared about finding ways to oppose the president. Michael Tesler, a political-science professor at UC Irvine, has studied the effect of Obama's race on the American electorate. "No other factor, in fact, came close to dividing the Democratic primary electorate as powerfully as their feelings about African Americans," he and his co-author, David O. Sears, concluded in their book, *Obama's Race: The 2008 Election and the Dream of a Post-Racial America*. "The impact of racial attitudes on individual vote decisions ... was so strong that it appears to have even outstripped the substantive impact of racial attitudes on Jesse Jackson's more racially charged campaign for the nomination in 1988." When Tesler looked at the 2012 campaign in his second book, *Post-Racial or Most-Racial? Race and Politics in the Obama Era*, very little had improved. Analyzing the extent to which racial attitudes affected people associated with Obama during the 2012 election, Tesler concluded that "racial attitudes spilled over from Barack Obama into mass assessments of Mitt Romney, Joe Biden, Hillary Clinton, Charlie Crist, and even the Obama family's dog Bo."

Yet despite this entrenched racial resentment, and in the face of complete resistance by congressional Republicans, overtly launched from the moment Obama arrived in the White House, the president accomplished major feats. He remade the nation's health-care system. He revitalized a Justice Department that vigorously investigated police brutality and discrimination, and he began dismantling the private-prison system for federal inmates. Obama nominated the first Latina justice to the Supreme Court, gave presidential support to marriage equality, and ended the US military's Don't Ask, Don't Tell policy, thus honoring the civil-rights tradition that had inspired him. And if his very existence inflamed America's racist conscience, it also expanded the country's anti-racist imagination. Millions of young people now know their only president to have been an African American. Writing for *The New Yorker*, Jelani Cobb once noted that "until there was a black Presidency it was impossible to conceive of the limitations of one." This is just as true of the possibilities. In 2014, the Obama administration committed itself to reversing the War on Drugs through the power of presidential commutation. The administration said that it could commute the sentences of as many as 10,000 prisoners. As of November, the president had commuted only 944 sentences. By any measure, Obama's effort fell woefully short, except for this small one: the measure of almost every other modern president who preceded him. Obama's 944 commutations are the most in nearly a century—and more than the past 11 presidents' combined.

Obama was born into a country where laws barring his very conception—let alone his ascendancy to the presidency—had long stood in force. A black president would always be a contradiction for a government that, throughout most of its history, had oppressed black people. The attempt to resolve this contradiction through Obama—a black man with deep roots in the white world—was remarkable. The price it exacted, incredible. The world it gave way to, unthinkable.

III. "I DECIDED TO BECOME PART OF THAT WORLD"

When Barack Obama was 10, his father gave him a basketball, a gift that connected the two directly. Obama was born in 1961 in Hawaii and raised by his mother, Ann Dunham, who was white, and her parents, Stanley and Madelyn. They loved him ferociously, supported him emotionally, and encouraged him intellectually. They also told him he was black. Ann gave him books to read about famous black people. When Obama's mother had begun dating his father, the news had not been greeted with the threat of lynching (as it might have been in various parts of the continental United States), and Obama's grandparents always spoke positively of his father. This biography makes Obama nearly unique among black people of his era.

In the president's memoir, *Dreams From My Father*, he says he was not an especially talented basketball player, but he played with a consuming passion. That passion was directed at something more than just the mastering of the pick-and-roll or the perfecting of his jump shot. Obama came of age during the time of the University of Hawaii basketball team's "Fabulous Five"—a name given to its all-black starting five, two decades before it would be resurrected at the University of Michigan by the likes of Chris Webber and Jalen Rose. In his memoir, Obama writes that he would watch the University of Hawaii players laughing at "some inside joke," winking "at the girls on the sidelines," or "casually flipping lay-ups." What Obama saw in the Fabulous Five was not just game, but a culture he found attractive:

> By the time I reached high school, I was playing on Punahou's teams, and could take my game to the university courts, where a handful of black men, mostly gym rats and has-beens, would teach me an attitude that didn't just have to do with the sport. That respect came from what you did and not who your daddy was. That you could talk stuff to rattle an opponent, but that you should shut the hell up if you couldn't back it up. That you didn't let anyone sneak up behind you to see emotions—like hurt or fear—you didn't want them to see.

These are lessons, particularly the last one, that for black people apply as much on the street as they do on the court. Basketball was a link for Obama, a medium for downloading black culture from the mainland that birthed the

Fabulous Five. Assessing his own thought process at the time, Obama writes, "I decided to become part of that world." This is one of the most incredible sentences ever written in the long, decorated history of black memoir, if only because very few black people have ever enjoyed enough power to write it.

Historically, in black autobiography, to be remanded into the black race has meant exposure to a myriad of traumas, often commencing in childhood. Frederick Douglass is separated from his grandmother. The enslaved Harriet Ann Jacobs must constantly cope with the threat of rape before she escapes. After telling his teacher he wants to be a lawyer, Malcolm X is told that the job isn't for "niggers." Black culture often serves as the balm for such traumas, or even the means to resist them. Douglass finds the courage to face the "slave-breaker" Edward Covey after being given an allegedly enchanted root by "a genuine African" possessing powers from "the eastern nations." Malcolm X's dancing connects him to his "long-suppressed African instincts." If black racial identity speaks to all the things done to people of recent African ancestry, black cultural identity was created in response to them. The division is not neat; the two are linked, and it is incredibly hard to be a full participant in the world of cultural identity without experiencing the trauma of racial identity.

Obama is somewhat different. He writes of bloodying the nose of a white kid who called him a "coon," and of chafing at racist remarks from a tennis coach, and of feeling offended after a white woman in his apartment building told the manager that he was following her. But the kinds of traumas that marked African Americans of his generation—beatings at the hands of racist police, being herded into poor schools, grinding out a life in a tenement building—were mostly abstract for him. Moreover, the kind of spatial restriction that most black people feel at an early age—having rocks thrown at you for being on the wrong side of the tracks, for instance—was largely absent from his life. In its place, Obama was gifted with a well-stamped passport and admittance to elite private schools—all of which spoke of other identities, other lives and other worlds where the color line was neither determinative nor especially relevant. Obama could have grown into a raceless cosmopolitan. Surely he would have lived in a world of problems, but problems not embodied by him.

Instead, he decided to enter this world.

"I always felt as if being black was cool," Obama told me while traveling to a campaign event. He was sitting on *Air Force One*, his tie loosened, his shirtsleeves rolled up. "[Being black] was not something to run away from but something to embrace. Why that is, I think, is complicated. Part of it is I think that my mother thought black folks were cool, and if your mother loves you and is praising you—and says you look good, are smart—as you are, then you don't kind of think in terms of *How can I avoid this?* You feel pretty good about it."

As a child, Obama's embrace of blackness was facilitated, not impeded, by white people. Obama's mother pointed him toward the history and culture of African Americans. Stanley, his grandfather, who came originally from Kansas, took him to basketball games at the University of Hawaii, as well as to black bars. Stanley introduced him to the black writer Frank Marshall Davis. The facilitation was as much indirect as direct. Obama recalls watching his grandfather at those black bars and understanding that "most of the people in the bar weren't there out of choice," and that "our presence there felt forced." From his mother's life of extensive travel, he learned to value the significance of having a home.

That suspicion of rootlessness extends throughout *Dreams From My Father*. He describes integration as a "one-way street" on which black people are asked to abandon themselves to fully experience America's benefits. Confronted with a woman named Joyce, a mixed-race, green-eyed college classmate who insists that she is not "black" but "multiracial," Obama is scornful. "That was the problem with people like Joyce," he writes. "They talked about the richness of their multicultural heritage and it sounded real good, until you noticed that they avoided black people." Later in the memoir, Obama tells the story of falling in love with a white woman. During a visit to her family's country house, he found himself in the library, which was filled with pictures of the woman's illustrious relations. But instead of being in awe, Obama realized that he and the woman lived in different worlds. "And I knew that if we stayed together, I'd eventually live in hers," he writes. "Between the two of us, I was the one who knew how to live as an outsider."

After college, Obama found a home, as well as a sense of himself, working on the South Side of Chicago as a community organizer. "When I started doing that work, my story merges with a larger story. That happens naturally for a John Lewis," he told me, referring to the civil-rights hero and Democratic congressman. "That happens more naturally for you. It was less obvious to me. *How do I pull all these different strains together: Kenya and Hawaii and Kansas, and white and black and Asian—how does that fit?* And through action, through work, I suddenly see myself as part of the bigger process for, yes, delivering justice for the [African American community] and specifically the South Side community, the low-income people—justice on behalf of the African American community. But also thereby promoting my ideas of justice and equality and empathy that my mother taught me were universal. So I'm in a position to understand those essential parts of me not as separate and apart from any particular community but connected to every community. And I can fit the African American struggle for freedom and justice in the context of the universal aspiration for freedom and justice."

Throughout Obama's 2008 campaign and into his presidency, this attitude proved key to his deep support in the black community. African Americans, weary of high achievers who distanced themselves from their black roots, understood that Obama had paid a price for checking "black" on his census form, and for living black, for hosting Common, for brushing dirt off his shoulder during the primaries, for marrying a woman who looked like Michelle Obama. If women, as a gender, must suffer the constant evaluations and denigrations of men, black women must suffer that, plus a broad dismissal from the realm of what American society deems to be beautiful. But Michelle Obama is beautiful in the way that black people know themselves to be. Her prominence as first lady directly attacks a poison that diminishes black girls from the moment they are capable of opening a magazine or turning on a television.

The South Side of Chicago, where Obama began his political career, is home to arguably the most prominent and storied black political establishment in the country. In addition to Oscar Stanton De Priest, the first African American elected to Congress in the 20th century, the South Side produced the city's first black mayor, Harold Washington; Jesse Jackson, who twice ran for president; and Carol Moseley Braun, the first African American woman to win a Senate race. These victories helped give rise to Obama's own. Harold Washington served as an inspiration to Obama and looms heavily over the Chicago section of *Dreams From My Father*.

Washington forged the kind of broad coalition that Obama would later assemble nationally. But Washington did this in the mid-1980s in segregated Chicago, and he had not had the luxury, as Obama did, of becoming black with minimal trauma. "There was an edge to Harold that frightened some white voters," David Axelrod, who worked for both Washington and Obama, told me recently. Axelrod recalled sitting around a conference table with Washington after he had won the Democratic primary for his reelection in 1987, just as the mayor was about to hold a press conference. Washington asked what percentage of Chicago's white vote he'd received. "And someone said, 'Well, you got 21 percent. And that's really good because last time'"—in his successful 1983 mayoral campaign—"'you only got 8,'" Axelrod recalled. "And he kind of smiled, sadly, and said, 'You know, I probably spent 70 percent of my time in those white neighborhoods, and I think I've been a good mayor for everybody, and I got 21 percent of the white vote and we think it's good.' And he just kind of shook his head and said, 'Ain't it a bitch to be a black man in the land of the free and the home of the brave?'

"That was Harold. He felt those things. He had fought in an all-black unit in World War II. He had come up in times—and that and the sort of indignities of what you had to do to come up through the machine really seared him." During his 1983 mayoral campaign, Washington was loudly booed outside a church in northwest Chicago by middle-class Poles, Italians, and Irish, who feared blacks would uproot them. "It was as vicious and ugly as anything you would have seen in the old South," Axelrod said.

Obama's ties to the South Side tradition that Washington represented were complicated. Like Washington, Obama attempted to forge a coalition between black South Siders and the broader community. But Obama, despite his adherence to black cultural mores, was, with his roots in Kansas and Hawaii, his Ivy League pedigree, and his ties to the University of Chicago, still an exotic out-of-towner. "They were a bit skeptical of him," says Salim Muwakkil, a journalist who has covered Obama since before his days in the Illinois state Senate. "Chicago is a very insular community, and he came from nowhere, seemingly."

Obama compounded people's suspicions by refusing to humble himself and go along with the political currents of the South Side. "A lot of the politicians, especially the black ones, were just leery of him," Kaye Wilson, the godmother to Obama's children and one of the president's earliest political supporters, told me recently.

But even as many in the black political community were skeptical of Obama, others encouraged him—sometimes when they voted against him. When Obama lost the 2000 Democratic-primary race against Bobby Rush, the African American incumbent congressman representing Illinois' First Congressional District, the then-still-obscure future president experienced the defeat as having to do more with his age than his exoticism. "I'd go meet people and I'd knock on doors and stuff, and some of the grandmothers who were the folks I'd been organizing and working with doing community stuff, they weren't parroting back some notion of 'You're too Harvard,' or 'You're too Hyde Park,' or what have you," Obama told me. "They'd say, 'You're a wonderful young man, you're going to do great things. You just have to be patient.' So I didn't feel the loss as a rejection by black people. I felt the loss as 'politics anywhere is tough.' Politics in Chicago is especially tough. And being able to break through in the African American community is difficult because of the enormous loyalty that people feel towards anybody who has been around awhile."

There was no one around to compete for loyalty when Obama ran for Senate in 2004, or for president in 2008. He was no longer competing against other African Americans; he was representing them. "He had that hybridity which told the 'do-gooders'—in Chicago they call the reformers the do-gooders—that he was acceptable," Muwakkil told me.

Obama ran for the Senate two decades after the death of Harold Washington. Axelrod checked in on the precinct where Washington had been so loudly booed by white Chicagoans. "Obama carried, against seven candidates for the

Senate, almost the entire northwest side and that precinct," he said. "And I told him, 'Harold's smiling down on us tonight.'"

Obama believes that his statewide victory for the Illinois Senate seat held particular portent for the events of 2008. "Illinois is the most demographically representative state in the country," he told me. "If you took all the percentages of black, white, Latino; rural, urban; agricultural, manufacturing—[if] you took that cross section across the country and you shrank it, it would be Illinois."

Illinois effectively allowed Obama to play a scrimmage before the big national game in 2008. "When I ran for the Senate I had to go into southern Illinois, downstate Illinois, farming communities—some with very tough racial histories, some areas where there just were no African Americans of any number," Obama told me. "And when we won that race, not just an African American from Chicago, but an African American with an exotic history and [the] name Barack Hussein Obama, [it showed that I] could connect with and appeal to a much broader audience."

The mix of Obama's "hybridity" and the changing times allowed him to extend his appeal beyond the white ethnic corners of Chicago, past the downstate portions of Illinois, and out into the country at large. "Ben Nelson, one of the most conservative Democrats in the Senate, from Nebraska, would only bring in one national Democrat to campaign for him," Obama recalls. "And it was me. And so part of the reason I was willing to run [for president in 2008] was that I had had two years in which we were generating enormous crowds all across the country—and the majority of those crowds were not African American; and they were in pretty remote places, or unlikely places. They weren't just big cities or they weren't just liberal enclaves. So what that told me was, it was possible."

What those crowds saw was a black candidate unlike any other before him. To simply point to Obama's white mother, or to his African father, or even to his rearing in Hawaii, is to miss the point. For most African Americans, white people exist either as a direct or an indirect force for bad in their lives. Biraciality is no shield against this; often it just intensifies the problem. What proved key for Barack Obama was not that he was born to a black man and a white woman, but that his white family approved of the union, and approved of the child who came from it. They did this in 1961—a time when sex between black men and white women, in large swaths of the country, was not just illegal but fraught with mortal danger. But that danger is not part of Obama's story. The first white people he ever knew, the ones who raised him, were decent in a way that very few black people of that era experienced.

I asked Obama what he made of his grandparents' impressively civilized reception of his father. "It wasn't Harry Belafonte," Obama said laughingly of his father. "This was like an *African* African. And he was like a blue-black brother. Nilotic. And so, yeah, I will always give my grandparents credit for that. I'm not saying they were happy about it. I'm not saying that they were not, after the guy leaves, looking at each other like, 'What the heck?' But whatever misgivings they had, they never expressed to me, never spilled over into how they interacted with me.

"Now, part of it, as I say in my book, was we were in this unique environment in Hawaii where I think it was much easier. I don't know if it would have been as easy for them if they were living in Chicago at the time, because the lines just weren't as sharply drawn in Hawaii as they were on the mainland."

Obama's early positive interactions with his white family members gave him a fundamentally different outlook toward the wider world than most blacks of the 1960s had. Obama told me he rarely had "the working assumption of discrimination, the working assumption that white people would not treat me right or give me an opportunity or judge me [other than] on the basis of merit." He continued, "The kind of working assumption" that white people would discriminate against him or treat him poorly "is less embedded in my psyche than it is, say, with Michelle."

In this, the first lady is more representative of black America than her husband is. African Americans typically raise their children to protect themselves against a presumed hostility from white teachers, white police officers, white supervisors, and white co-workers. The need for that defense is, more often than not, reinforced either directly by actual encounters or indirectly by observing the vast differences between one's own experience and those across the color line. Marty Nesbitt, the president's longtime best friend, who, like Obama, had positive interactions with whites at a relatively early age, told me that when he and his wife went to buy their first car, she was insistent on buying from a black salesperson. "I'm like, 'We've got to find a salesman,'" Nesbitt said. "She's like, 'No, no, no. We're waiting for the brother.' And I'm like, 'He's with a customer.' They were filling out documents and she was like, 'We're going to stay around.' And a white guy came up to us. 'Can I help you?' 'Nope.'" Nesbitt was not out to condemn anyone with this story. He was asserting that "the willingness of African Americans [in Chicago] to help lift each other up is powerful."

But that willingness to help is also a defense, produced by decades of discrimination. Obama sees race through a different lens, Kaye Wilson told me. "It's just very different from ours," she explained. "He's got buddies that are white, and they're his buddies, and they love him. And I don't think they love him just because he's the president. They love him because they're his friends from Hawaii, some from college and all.

"So I think he's got that, whereas I think growing up in the racist United States, we enter this thing with, you know, 'I'm looking at you. I'm not trusting you to be one hundred with me.' And I think he grew up in a way that he had to trust [white people]—how can you live under the roof with people and think that they don't love you? He needs that frame of reference. He needs that lens. If he didn't have it, it would be ... a Jesse Jackson, you know? Or Al Sharpton. Different lens."

That lens, born of literally relating to whites, allowed Obama to imagine that he could be the country's first black president. "If I walked into a room and it's a bunch of white farmers, trade unionists, middle age—I'm not walking in thinking, *Man, I've got to show them that I'm normal*," Obama explained. "I walk in there, I think, with a set of assumptions: like, these people look just like my grandparents. And I see the same Jell-O mold that my grandmother served, and they've got the same, you know, little stuff on their mantelpieces. And so I am maybe disarming them by just assuming that we're okay."

What Obama was able to offer white America is something very few African Americans could—trust. The vast majority of us are, necessarily, too crippled by our defenses to ever consider such a proposition. But Obama, through a mixture of ancestral connections and distance from the poisons of Jim Crow, can credibly and sincerely trust the majority population of this country. That trust is reinforced, not contradicted, by his blackness. Obama isn't shuffling before white power (Herman Cain's "shucky ducky" act) or flattering white ego (O. J. Simpson's listing not being seen as black as a great accomplishment). That, too, is defensive, and deep down, I suspect, white people know it. He stands firm in his own cultural traditions and says to the country something virtually no black person can, but every president must: "I believe you."

IV. "YOU STILL GOTTA GO BACK TO THE HOOD"

Just after Columbus Day, I accompanied the president and his formidable entourage on a visit to North Carolina A&T State University, in Greensboro. Four days earlier, *The Washington Post* had published an old audio clip that featured Donald Trump lamenting a failed sexual conquest and exhorting the virtues of sexual assault. The next day, Trump claimed that this was "locker room" talk. As we flew to North Carolina, the president was in a state of bemused disbelief. He plopped down in a chair in the staff cabin of *Air Force One* and said, "I've been in a lot of locker rooms. I don't think I've ever heard that one before." He was casual and relaxed. A feeling of cautious inevitability emanated from his staff, and why not? Every day seemed to bring a new, more shocking revelation or piece of evidence showing Trump to be unfit for the presidency: He had lost nearly $1 billion in a single year. He had likely not paid taxes in 18 years. He was running a "university," for which he was under formal legal investigation. He had trampled on his own campaign's messaging by engaging in a Twitter crusade against a former beauty-pageant contestant. He had been denounced by leadership in his own party, and the trickle of prominent Republicans—both in and out of office—who had publicly repudiated him threatened to become a geyser. At this moment, the idea that a campaign so saturated in open bigotry, misogyny, chaos, and possible corruption could win a national election was ludicrous. This was America.

The president was going to North Carolina to keynote a campaign rally for Clinton, but first he was scheduled for a conversation about My Brother's Keeper, his initiative on behalf of disadvantaged youth. Announcing My Brother's Keeper—or MBK, as it's come to be called—in 2014, the president had sought to avoid giving the program a partisan valence, noting that it was "not some big new government program." Instead, it would involve the government in concert with the nonprofit and business sectors to intervene in the lives of young men of color who were "at risk." MBK serves as a kind of network for those elements of federal, state, and local government that might already have a presence in the lives of these young men. It is a quintessentially Obama program—conservative in scope, with impacts that are measurable.

"It comes right out of his own life," Broderick Johnson, the Cabinet secretary and an assistant to the president, who heads MBK, told me recently. "I have heard him say, 'I don't want us to have a bunch of forums on race.' He reminds people, 'Yeah, we can talk about this. But what are we going to *do*?'" On this afternoon in North Carolina, what Obama did was sit with a group of young men who'd turned their lives around in part because of MBK. They told stories of being in the street, of choosing quick money over school, of their homes being shot up, and—through the help of mentoring or job programs brokered by MBK—transitioning into college or a job. Obama listened solemnly and empathetically to each of them. "It doesn't take that much," he told them. "It just takes someone laying hands on you and saying, 'Hey, man, you count.'"

When he asked the young men whether they had a message he should take back to policy makers in Washington, DC, one observed that despite their best individual efforts, they still had to go back to the very same deprived neighborhoods that had been the sources of trouble for them. "It's your environment," the young man said. "You can do what you want, but you still gotta go back to the hood."

He was correct. The ghettos of America are the direct result of decades of public-policy decisions: the redlining of real-estate zoning maps, the expanded authority given to prosecutors, the increased funding given to prisons. And all of this was done on the backs of people still reeling from the 250-year legacy of slavery. The results of this negative investment are clear—African Americans rank at the bottom of nearly every major socioeconomic measure in the country.

Obama's formula for closing this chasm between black and white America, like that of many progressive politicians today, proceeded from policy designed for all of America. Blacks disproportionately benefit from this effort, since they are disproportionately in need. The Affordable Care Act, which cut the uninsured rate in the black community by at least a third, was Obama's most prominent example. Its full benefit has yet to be felt by African Americans, because several states in the South have declined to expand Medicaid. But when the president and I were meeting, the ACA's advocates believed that pressure on state budgets would force expansion, and there was evidence to support this: Louisiana had expanded Medicaid earlier in 2016, and advocates were gearing up for wars to be waged in Georgia and Virginia.

Obama also emphasized the need for a strong Justice Department with a deep commitment to nondiscrimination. When Obama moved into the White House in 2009, the Justice Department's Civil Rights Division "was in shambles," former Attorney General Eric Holder told me recently. "I mean, I had been there for 12 years as a line guy. I started out in '76, so I served under Republicans and Democrats. And what the [George W.] Bush administration, what the Bush DOJ did, was unlike anything that had ever happened before in terms of politicized hiring." The career civil servants below the political appointees, Holder said, were not even invited to the meetings in which the key hiring and policy decisions were made. After Obama's inauguration, Holder told me, "I remember going to tell all the folks at the Civil Rights Division, 'The Civil Rights Division is open for business again.' The president gave me additional funds to hire people."

The political press developed a narrative that because Obama felt he had to modulate his rhetoric on race, Holder was the administration's true, and thus blacker, conscience. Holder is certainly blunter, and this worried some of the White House staff. Early in Obama's first term, Holder gave a speech on race in which he said the United States had been a "nation of cowards" on the subject. But positioning the two men as opposites elides an important fact: Holder was appointed by the president, and went only as far as the president allowed. I asked Holder whether he had toned down his rhetoric after that controversial speech. "Nope," he said. Reflecting on his relationship with the president, Holder said, "We were also kind of different people, you know? He is the Zen guy. And I'm kind of the hot-blooded West Indian. And I thought we made a good team, but there's nothing that I ever did or said that I don't think he would have said, 'I support him 100 percent.'

"Now, the 'nation of cowards' speech, the president might have used a different phrase—maybe, probably. But he and I share a worldview, you know? And when I hear people say, 'Well, you are blacker than him' or something like that, I think, *What are you all talking about?*"

For much of his presidency, a standard portion of Obama's speeches about race riffed on black people's need to turn off the television, stop eating junk food, and stop blaming white people for their problems. Obama would deliver this lecture to any black audience, regardless of context. It was bizarre, for instance, to see the president warning young men who'd just graduated from Morehouse College, one of the most storied black colleges in the country, about making "excuses" and blaming whites.

This part of the Obama formula is the most troubling, and least thought-out. This judgment emerges from my own biography. I am the product of black parents who encouraged me to read, of black teachers who felt my work ethic did not match my potential, of black college professors who taught me intellectual rigor. And they did this in a world that every day insulted their humanity. It was not so much that the black layabouts and deadbeats Obama invoked in his speeches were unrecognizable. I had seen those people too. But I'd also seen the same among white people. If black men were overrepresented among drug dealers and absentee dads of the world, it was directly related to their being underrepresented among the Bernie Madoffs and Kenneth Lays of the world. Power was what mattered, and what characterized the differences between black and white America was not a difference in work ethic, but a system engineered to place one on top of the other.

The mark of that system is visible at every level of American society, regardless of the quality of one's choices. For instance, the unemployment rate among black college graduates (4.1 percent) is almost the same as the unemployment rate among white high-school graduates (4.6 percent). But that college degree is generally purchased at a higher price by blacks than by whites. According to research by the Brookings Institution, African Americans tend to carry more student debt four years after graduation ($53,000 versus $28,000) and suffer from a higher default rate on their loans (7.6 percent versus 2.4 percent) than white Americans. This is both the result and the perpetuator of a sprawling wealth gap between the races. White households, on average, hold seven times as much wealth as black households—a difference so large as to make comparing the "black middle class" and "white middle class" meaningless; they're simply not comparable. According to Patrick Sharkey, a sociologist at New York University who studies economic mobility, black families making $100,000 a year or more live in more-disadvantaged neighborhoods than white families making less than $30,000. This gap didn't just appear by magic; it's the result of the government's effort over many decades to create a pigmentocracy—one that will continue without explicit intervention.

Obama had been on the record as opposing reparations. But now, late in his presidency, he seemed more open to the idea—in theory, at least, if not in practice.

"Theoretically, you can make obviously a powerful argument that centuries of slavery, Jim Crow, discrimination are the primary cause for all those gaps," Obama said, referencing the gulf in education, wealth, and employment that separates black and white America. "That those were wrongs to the black community as a whole, and black families specifically, and that in order to close that gap, a society has a moral obligation to make a large, aggressive investment, even if it's not in the form of individual reparations checks but in the form of a Marshall Plan."

The political problems with turning the argument for reparations into reality are manifold, Obama said. "If you look at countries like South Africa, where you had a black majority, there have been efforts to tax and help that black majority, but it hasn't come in the form of a formal reparations program. You have countries like India that have tried to help untouchables, with essentially affirmative-action programs, but it hasn't fundamentally changed the structure of their societies. So the bottom line is that it's hard to find a model in which you can practically administer and sustain political support for those kinds of efforts."

Obama went on to say that it would be better, and more realistic, to get the country to rally behind a robust liberal agenda and build on the enormous progress that's been made toward getting white Americans to accept nondiscrimination as a basic operating premise. But the progress toward nondiscrimination did not appear overnight. It was achieved by people willing to make an unpopular argument and live on the frontier of public opinion. I asked him whether it wasn't—despite the practical obstacles—worth arguing that the state has a collective responsibility not only for its achievements but for its sins.

"I want my children—I want Malia and Sasha—to understand that they've got responsibilities beyond just what they themselves have done," Obama said. "That they have a responsibility to the larger community and the larger nation, that they should be sensitive to and extra thoughtful about the plight of people who have been oppressed in the past, are oppressed currently. So that's a wisdom that I want to transmit to my kids ... But I would say that's a high level of enlightenment that you're looking to have from a majority of the society. And it may be something that future generations are more open to, but I am pretty confident that for the foreseeable future, using the argument of nondiscrimination, and 'Let's get it right for the kids who are here right now,' and giving them the best chance possible, is going to be a more persuasive argument."

Obama is unfailingly optimistic about the empathy and capabilities of the American people. His job necessitates this: "At some level what the people want to feel is that the person leading them sees the best in them," he told me. But I found it interesting that that optimism does not extend to the possibility of the public's accepting wisdoms—such as the moral logic of reparations—that the president, by his own account, has accepted for himself and is willing to teach his children. Obama says he always tells his staff that "better is good." The notion that a president would attempt to achieve change within the boundaries of the accepted consensus is appropriate. But Obama is almost constitutionally skeptical of those who seek to achieve change outside that consensus.

Early in 2016, Obama invited a group of African American leaders to meet with him at the White House. When some of the activists affiliated with Black Lives Matter refused to attend, Obama began calling them out in speeches. "You can't refuse to meet because that might compromise the purity of your position," he said. "The value of social movements and activism is to get you at the table, get you in the room, and then start trying to figure out how is this problem going to be solved. You then have a responsibility to prepare an agenda that is achievable—that can institutionalize the changes you seek—and to engage the other side."

Opal Tometi, a Nigerian American community activist who is one of the three founders of Black Lives Matter, explained to me that the group has a more diffuse structure than most civil-rights organizations. One reason for this is to avoid the cult of personality that has plagued black organizations in the past. So the founders asked its membership in Chicago, the president's hometown, whether they should meet with Obama. "They felt—and I think many of our members felt—there wouldn't be the depth of discussion that they wanted to have," Tometi told me. "And if there wasn't that space to have a real heart-to-heart, and if it was just surface level, that it would be more of a disservice to the movement."

Tometi noted that some other activists allied with Black Lives Matter had been planning to attend the meeting, so they felt their views would be represented. Nevertheless, Black Lives Matter sees itself as engaged in a protest against the treatment of black people by the American state, and so Tometi and much of the group's leadership, concerned about being used for a photo op by the very body they were protesting, opted not to go.

When I asked Obama about this perspective, he fluctuated between understanding where the activists were coming from and being hurt by such brushoffs. "I think that where I've gotten frustrated during the course of my presidency has never been because I was getting pushed too hard by activists to see the justness of a cause or the essence of an issue," he said. "I think where I got frustrated at times was the belief that the president can do anything if he just decides he wants to do it. And that sort of lack of awareness on the part of an activist about the constraints of our political system and the constraints on this office, I think, sometimes would leave me to mutter under my breath. Very rarely did I lose it publicly. Usually I'd just smile."

He laughed, then continued, "The reason I say that is because those are the times where sometimes you feel actually a little bit hurt. Because you feel like saying to these folks, '[Don't] you think if I could do it, I [would] have just done it? Do you think that the only problem is that I don't care enough about the plight of poor people, or gay people?'"

I asked Obama whether he thought that perhaps protesters' distrust of the powers that be could ultimately be healthy. "Yes," he said. "Which is why I don't get too hurt. I mean, I think there is a benefit to wanting to hold power's feet to the fire until you actually see the goods. I get that. And I think it is important. And frankly, sometimes it's useful for activists just to be out there to keep you mindful and not get complacent, even if ultimately you think some of their criticism is misguided."

Obama himself was an activist and a community organizer, albeit for only two years—but he is not, by temperament, a protester. He is a consensus-builder; consensus, he believes, ultimately drives what gets done. He understands the emotional power of protest, the need to vent before authority—but that kind of approach does not come naturally to him. Regarding reparations, he said, "Sometimes I wonder how much of these debates have to do with the desire, the legitimate desire, for that history to be recognized. Because there is a psychic power to the recognition that is not satisfied with a universal program; it's not satisfied by the Affordable Care Act, or an expansion of Pell Grants, or an expansion of the earned-income tax credit." These kinds of programs, effective and disproportionately beneficial to black people though they may be, don't "speak to the hurt, and the sense of injustice, and the self-doubt that arises out of the fact that [African Americans] are behind now, and it makes us sometimes feel as if there must be something wrong with us—unless you're able to see the history and say, 'It's amazing we got this far given what we went through.'

"So in part, I think the argument sometimes that I've had with folks who are much more interested in sort of race-specific programs is less an argument about what is practically achievable and sometimes maybe more an argument of 'We want society to see what's happened and internalize it and answer it in demonstrable ways.' And those impulses I very much understand—but my hope would be that as we're moving through the world right now, we're able to get that psychological or emotional peace by seeing very concretely our kids doing better and being more hopeful and having greater opportunities."

Obama saw—at least at that moment, before the election of Donald Trump—a straight path to that world. "Just play this out as a thought experiment," he said.

"Imagine if you had genuine, high-quality early-childhood education for every child, and suddenly every black child in America—but also every poor white child or Latino [child], but just stick with every black child in America—is getting a really good education. And they're graduating from high school at the same rates that whites are, and they are going to college at the same rates that whites are, and they are able to afford college at the same rates because the government has universal programs that say that you're not going to be barred from school just because of how much money your parents have.

"So now they're all graduating. And let's also say that the Justice Department and the courts are making sure, as I've said in a speech before, that when Jamal sends his résumé in, he's getting treated the same as when Johnny sends his résumé in. Now, are we going to have suddenly the same number of CEOs, billionaires, etc., as the white community? In 10 years? Probably not, maybe not even in 20 years.

"But I guarantee you that we would be thriving, we would be succeeding. We wouldn't have huge numbers of young African American men in jail. We'd have more family formation as college-graduated girls are meeting boys who are their peers, which then in turn means the next generation of kids are growing up that much better. And suddenly you've got a whole generation that's in a position to start using the incredible creativity that we see in music, and sports, and frankly even on the streets, channeled into starting all kinds of businesses. I feel pretty good about our odds in that situation."

The thought experiment doesn't hold up. The programs Obama favored would advance white America too—and without a specific commitment to equality, there is no guarantee that the programs would eschew discrimination. Obama's solution relies on a goodwill that his own personal history tells him exists in the larger country. My own history tells me something different. The large numbers of black men in jail, for instance, are not just the result of poor policy, but of not seeing those men as human.

When President Obama and I had this conversation, the target he was aiming to reach seemed to me to be many generations away, and now—as President-Elect Trump prepares for office—seems even many more generations off. Obama's accomplishments were real: a $1 billion settlement on behalf of black farmers, a Justice Department that exposed Ferguson's municipal plunder, the increased availability of Pell Grants (and their availability to some prisoners), and the slashing of the crack/cocaine disparity in sentencing guidelines, to name just a few. Obama was also the first sitting president to visit a federal prison. There was a feeling that he'd erected a foundation upon which further progressive policy could be built. It's tempting to say that foundation is now endangered. The truth is, it was never safe.

V. "THEY RODE THE TIGER"

Obama's greatest misstep was born directly out of his greatest insight. Only Obama, a black man who emerged from the best of white America, and thus could sincerely trust white America, could be so certain that he could achieve broad national appeal. And yet only a black man with that same biography could underestimate his opposition's resolve to destroy him. In some sense an Obama presidency could never have succeeded along the normal presidential lines; he needed a partner, or partners, in Congress who could put governance above party. But he struggled to win over even some of his own allies. Ben Nelson, the Democratic senator from Nebraska whom Obama helped elect, became an obstacle to healthcare reform. Joe Lieberman, whom Obama saved from retribution at the hands of Senate Democrats after Lieberman campaigned for Obama's 2008 opponent, John McCain, similarly obstructed Obamacare. Among Republicans, senators who had seemed amenable to Obama's agenda—Chuck Grassley, Susan Collins, Richard Lugar, Olympia Snowe—rebuffed him repeatedly.

The obstruction grew out of narrow political incentives. "If Republicans didn't cooperate," Obama told me, "and there was not a portrait of bipartisan cooperation and a functional federal government, then the party in power would pay the price and they could win back the Senate and/or the House. That wasn't an inaccurate political calculation."

Obama is not sure of the degree to which individual racism played into this calculation. "I do remember watching Bill Clinton get impeached and Hillary Clinton being accused of killing Vince Foster," he said. "And if you ask them, I'm sure they would say, 'No, actually what you're experiencing is not because you're black, it's because you're a Democrat.'"

But personal animus is just one manifestation of racism; arguably the more profound animosity occurs at the level of interests. The most recent Congress boasted 138 members from the states that comprised the old Confederacy. Of the 101 Republicans in that group, 96 are white and one is black. Of the 37 Democrats, 18 are black and 15 are white. There are no white congressional Democrats in the Deep South. Exit polls in Mississippi in 2008 found that 96 percent of voters who described themselves as Republicans were white. The Republican Party is not simply the party of whites, but the preferred party of whites who identify their interest as defending the historical privileges of whiteness. The researchers Josh Pasek, Jon A. Krosnick, and Trevor Tompson found that in 2012, 32 percent of Democrats held antiblack views, while 79 percent of Republicans did. These attitudes could even spill over to white Democratic politicians, because they are seen as representing the party of blacks. Studying the 2016 election, the political scientist Philip Klinkner found that the most predictive question for understanding whether a voter favored Hillary Clinton or Donald Trump was "Is Barack Obama a Muslim?"

In our conversations, Obama said he didn't doubt that there was a sincerely nonracist states'-rights contingent of the GOP. And yet he suspected that there might be more to it. "A rudimentary knowledge of American history tells you that the relationship between the federal government and the states was very much mixed up with attitudes towards slavery, attitudes towards Jim Crow, attitudes towards antipoverty programs and who benefited and who didn't," he said.

"And so I'm careful not to attribute any particular resistance or slight or opposition to race. But what I do believe is that if somebody didn't have a problem with their daddy being employed by the federal government, and didn't have a problem with the Tennessee Valley Authority electrifying certain communities, and didn't have a problem with the interstate highway system being built, and didn't have a problem with the GI Bill, and didn't have a problem with the [Federal Housing Administration] subsidizing the suburbanization of America, and that all helped you build wealth and create a middle class—and then suddenly as soon as African Americans or Latinos are interested in availing themselves of those same mechanisms as ladders into the middle class, you now have a violent opposition to them—then I think you at least have to ask yourself the question of how consistent you are, and what's different, and what's changed."

Racism greeted Obama in both his primary and general-election campaigns in 2008. Photos were circulated of him in Somali garb. Rush Limbaugh dubbed him "Barack the Magic Negro." Roger Stone, who would go on to advise the Trump campaign, claimed that Michelle Obama could be heard on tape yelling "Whitey." Detractors circulated emails claiming that the future first lady had written a racist senior thesis while at Princeton. A fifth of all West Virginia Democratic-primary voters in 2008 openly admitted that race had influenced their vote. Hillary Clinton trounced him 67 to 26 percent.

After Obama won the presidency in defiance of these racial headwinds, traffic to the white-supremacist website Stormfront increased sixfold. Before the election, in August, just before the Democratic National Convention, the FBI uncovered an assassination plot hatched by white supremacists in Denver. Mainstream conservative publications floated the notion that Obama's memoir was too "stylish and penetrating" to have been written by the candidate, and found a plausible ghostwriter in the radical (and white) former Weatherman Bill Ayers. A Republican women's club in California dispensed "Obama Bucks" featuring slices of watermelon, ribs, and fried chicken. At the Values Voter Summit that year, conventioneers hawked "Obama Waffles," a waffle mix whose box featured a bug-eyed caricature of the candidate. Fake hip-hop lyrics were scrawled on the side ("Barry's Bling Bling Waffle Ring") and on the top, the same caricature was granted a turban and tagged with the instructions "Point box toward Mecca for tastier waffles." The display was denounced by the summit's sponsor, the Family Research Council. One would be forgiven for meeting this denunciation with guffaws: The council's president, Tony Perkins, had once addressed the white-supremacist Council of Conservative Citizens with a Confederate flag draped behind him. By 2015, Perkins had deemed the debate over Obama's birth certificate "legitimate" and was saying that it "makes sense" to conclude that Obama was actually a Muslim.

By then, birtherism—inflamed in large part by a real-estate mogul and reality-TV star named Donald Trump—had overtaken the Republican rank and file. In 2015, one poll found that 54 percent of GOP voters thought Obama was a Muslim. Only 29 percent believed he'd been born in America.

Still, in 2008, Obama had been elected. His supporters rejoiced. As Jay-Z commemorated the occasion:

My president is black, in fact he's half-white,
So even in a racist mind, he's half-right.

Not quite. A month after Obama entered the White House, a CNBC personality named Rick Santelli took to the trading floor of the Chicago Mercantile Exchange and denounced the president's efforts to help homeowners endangered by the housing crisis. "How many of you people want to pay for your neighbor's mortgage that has an extra bathroom and can't pay their bills?" Santelli asked the assembled traders. He asserted that Obama should "reward people that could carry the water" as opposed to those who "drink the water," and denounced those in danger of foreclosure as "losers." Race was implicit in Santelli's harangue—the housing crisis and predatory lending had devastated black communities and expanded the wealth gap—and it culminated with a call for a "Tea Party" to resist the Obama presidency. In fact, right-wing ideologues had been planning just such a resistance for decades. They would eagerly answer Santelli's call.

One of the intellectual forerunners of the Tea Party is said to be Ron Paul, the heterodox two-time Republican presidential candidate, who opposed the war in Iraq and championed civil liberties. On other matters, Paul was more traditional. Throughout the '90s, he published a series of racist newsletters that referred to New York City as "Welfaria," called Martin Luther King Jr. Day "Hate Whitey Day," and asserted that 95 percent of black males in Washington, DC, were either "semi-criminal or entirely criminal." Paul's apologists have claimed that he had no real connection to the newsletters, even though virtually all of them were published in his name ("The Ron Paul Survival Report," "Ron Paul Political Report," "Dr. Ron Paul's Freedom Report") and written in his voice. Either way, the views of the newsletters have found their expression in his ideological comrades. Throughout Obama's first term, Tea Party activists voiced their complaints in racist terms. Activists brandished signs warning that Obama would implement "white slavery," waved the Confederate flag, depicted Obama as a witch doctor, and issued calls for him to "go back to Kenya." Tea Party supporters wrote "satirical" letters in the name of "We Colored People" and stoked the flames of birtherism. One of the Tea Party's most prominent sympathizers, the radio host Laura Ingraham, wrote a racist tract depicting Michelle Obama gorging herself on ribs, while Glenn Beck said the president was a "racist" with a "deep-seated hatred for white people." The Tea Party's leading exponent, Andrew Breitbart, engineered the smearing of Shirley Sherrod, the US Department of Agriculture's director of rural development for Georgia, publishing egregiously misleading videos that wrongly made her appear to be engaging in antiwhite racist invective, which led to her dismissal. (In a rare act of cowardice, the Obama administration cravenly submitted to this effort.)

In those rare moments when Obama made any sort of comment attacking racism, firestorms threatened to consume his governing agenda. When, in July 2009, the president objected to the arrest of the eminent Harvard professor Henry Louis Gates Jr. while he was trying to get into his own house, pointing out that the officer had "acted stupidly," a third of whites said the remark made them feel less favorably toward the president, and nearly two-thirds claimed that Obama had "acted stupidly" by commenting. A chastened Obama then determined to make sure his public statements on race were no longer mere riffs but designed to have an achievable effect. This was smart, but still the invective came. During Obama's 2009 address on health care before a joint session of Congress, Joe Wilson, a Republican congressman from South Carolina, incredibly, and in defiance of precedent and decorum, disrupted the proceedings by crying out "You lie!" A Missouri congressman equated Obama with a monkey. A California GOP official took up the theme and emailed her friends an image depicting Obama as a chimp, with the accompanying text explaining, "Now you know why [there's] no birth certificate!" Former vice-presidential candidate Sarah Palin assessed the president's foreign policy as a "shuck and jive shtick." Newt Gingrich dubbed him the "food-stamp president." The rhetorical attacks on Obama were matched by a very real attack on his political base—in 2011 and 2012, 19 states enacted voting restrictions that made it harder for African Americans to vote.

Yet in 2012, as in 2008, Obama won anyway. Prior to the election, Obama, ever the optimist, had claimed that intransigent Republicans would decide to work with him to advance the country. No such collaboration was in the offing. Instead, legislation ground to a halt and familiar themes resurfaced. An Idaho GOP official posted a photo on Facebook depicting a trap waiting for Obama. The bait was a slice of watermelon. The caption read, "Breaking: The secret service just uncovered a plot to kidnap the president. More details as we get them...." In 2014, conservatives assembled in support of Cliven Bundy's armed protest against federal grazing fees. As reporters descended on the Bundy ranch in Nevada, Bundy offered his opinions on "the Negro." "They abort their young children, they put their young men in jail, because they never learned how to pick cotton," Bundy explained. "And I've often wondered, are they better off as slaves, picking cotton and having a family life and doing things, or are they better off under government subsidy? They didn't get no more freedom. They got less freedom."

That same year, in the wake of Michael Brown's death, the Justice Department opened an investigation into the police department in Ferguson, Missouri. It found a city that, through racial profiling, arbitrary fines, and wanton harassment, had exploited law enforcement for the purposes of municipal plunder. The plunder was sanctified by racist humor dispensed via internal emails among the police that later came to light. The president of the United States, who during his first year in office had reportedly received three times the number of death threats of any of his predecessors, was a repeat target.

Much ink has been spilled in an attempt to understand the Tea Party protests, and the 2016 presidential candidacy of Donald Trump, which ultimately emerged out of them. One theory popular among (primarily) white intellectuals of varying political persuasions held that this response was largely the discontented rumblings of a white working class threatened by the menace of globalization and crony capitalism. Dismissing these rumblings as racism was said to condescend to this proletariat, which had long suffered the slings and arrows of coastal elites, heartless technocrats, and reformist snobs. Racism was not something to be coolly and empirically assessed but a slander upon the working man. Deindustrialization, globalization, and broad income inequality are real. And they have landed with at least as great a force upon black and Latino people in our country as upon white people. And yet these groups were strangely unrepresented in this new populism.

Christopher S. Parker and Matt A. Barreto, political scientists at the University of Washington and UCLA, respectively, have found a relatively strong relationship between racism and Tea Party membership. "Whites are less likely to be drawn to the Tea Party for material reasons, suggesting that, relative to other groups, it's really more about social prestige," they say. The notion that the Tea Party represented the righteous, if unfocused, anger of an aggrieved class allowed everyone from leftists to neoliberals to white nationalists to avoid a horrifying and simple reality: A significant swath of this country did not like the fact that their president was black, and that swath was not composed of those most damaged by an unquestioned faith in the markets. Far better to imagine the grievance put upon the president as the ghost of shambling factories and defunct union halls, as opposed to what it really was—a movement inaugurated by ardent and frightened white capitalists, raging from the commodities-trading floor of one of the great financial centers of the world.

That movement came into full bloom in the summer of 2015, with the candidacy of Donald Trump, a man who'd risen to political prominence by peddling the racist myth that the president was not American. It was birtherism—not trade, not jobs, not isolationism—that launched Trump's foray into electoral politics. Having risen unexpectedly on this basis into the stratosphere of Republican politics, Trump spent the campaign freely and liberally trafficking in misogyny, Islamophobia, and xenophobia. And on November 8, 2016, he won election to the presidency. Historians will spend the next century analyzing how a country with such allegedly grand democratic traditions was, so swiftly and so easily, brought to the brink of fascism. But one needn't stretch too far to conclude that an eight-year campaign of consistent and open racism aimed at the leader of the free world helped clear the way.

"They rode the tiger. And now the tiger is eating them," David Axelrod, speaking of the Republican Party, told me. That was in October. His words proved too optimistic. The tiger would devour us all.

VI. "WHEN YOU LEFT, YOU TOOK ALL OF ME WITH YOU"

One Saturday morning last May, I joined the presidential motorcade as it slipped out of the southern gate of the White House. A mostly white crowd had assembled. As the motorcade drove by, people cheered, held up their smartphones to record the procession, and waved American flags. To be within feet of the president seemed like the thrill of their lives. I was astounded. An old euphoria, which I could not immediately place, gathered up in me. And then I remembered, it was what I felt through much of 2008, as I watched Barack Obama's star shoot across the political sky. I had never seen so many white people cheer on a black man who was neither an athlete nor an entertainer. And it seemed that they loved him for this, and I thought in those days, which now feel so long ago, that they might then love me, too, and love my wife, and love my child, and love us all in the manner that the God they so fervently cited had commanded. I had been raised amid a people who wanted badly to believe in the possibility of a Barack Obama, even as their very lives argued against that possibility. So they would praise Martin Luther King Jr. in one breath and curse the white man, "the Great Deceiver," in the next. Then came Obama and the Obama family, and they were black and beautiful in all the ways we aspired to be, and all that love was showered upon them. But as Obama's motorcade approached its destination—Howard University, where he would give the commencement address—the complexion of the crowd darkened, and I understood that the love was specific, that even if it allowed Barack Obama, even if it allowed the luckiest of us, to defy the boundaries, then the masses of us, in cities like this one, would still enjoy no such feat.

These were our fitful, spasmodic years.

We were launched into the Obama era with no notion of what to expect, if only because a black presidency had seemed such a dubious proposition. There was no preparation, because it would have meant preparing for the impossible. There were few assessments of its potential import, because such assessments were regarded as speculative fiction. In retrospect it all makes sense, and one can see a jagged but real political lineage running through black Chicago. It originates in Oscar Stanton De Priest; continues through Congressman William Dawson, who, under Roosevelt, switched from the Republican to the Democratic Party; crescendos with the legendary Harold Washington; rises still with Jesse Jackson's 1988 victory in Michigan's Democratic caucuses; rises again with Carol Moseley Braun's triumph; and reaches its recent apex with the election of Barack Obama. If the lineage is apparent in hindsight, so are the limits of presidential power. For a century after emancipation, quasi-slavery haunted the South. And more than half a century after *Brown v. Board of Education*, schools throughout much of this country remain segregated.

There are no clean victories for black people, nor, perhaps, for any people. The presidency of Barack Obama is no different. One can now say that an African American individual can rise to the same level as a white individual, and yet also say that the number of black individuals who actually qualify for that status will be small. One thinks of Serena Williams, whose dominance and stunning achievements can't, in and of themselves, ensure equal access to tennis facilities for young black girls. The gate is open and yet so very far away.

I felt a mix of pride and amazement walking onto Howard's campus that day. Howard alumni, of which I am one, are an obnoxious fraternity, known for yelling the school chant across city blocks, sneering at other historically black colleges and universities, and condescending to black graduates of predominantly white institutions. I like to think I am more reserved, but I felt an immense satisfaction in being in the library where I had once found my history, and now found myself with the first black president of the United States. It seemed providential that he would give the commencement address here in his last year. The same pride I felt radiated out across the Yard, the large green patch in the main area of the campus where the ceremony would take place. When Obama walked out, the audience exploded, and when the time came for the color guard to present arms, a chant arose: "O-Ba-Ma! O-Ba-Ma! O-Ba-Ma!"

He gave a good speech that day, paying heed to Howard's rituals, calling out its famous alumni, shouting out the university's various dormitories, and urging young people to vote. (His usual riff on respectability politics was missing.) But I think he could have stood before that crowd, smiled, and said "Good luck," and they would have loved him anyway. He was their champion, and this was evident in the smallest of things. The national anthem was played first, but then came the black national anthem, "Lift Every Voice and Sing." As the lyrics rang out over the crowd, the students held up the black-power fist—a symbol of defiance before power. And yet here, in the face of a black man in his last year in power, it scanned not as a protest, but as a salute.

Six months later the awful price of a black presidency would be known to those students, even as the country seemed determined not to acknowledge it. In the days after Donald Trump's victory, there would be an insistence that something as "simple" as racism could not explain it. As if enslavement had nothing to do with global economics, or as if lynchings said nothing about the idea of women as property. As though the past 400 years could be reduced to the irrational resentment of full lips. No. Racism is never simple. And there was nothing simple about what was coming, or about Obama, the man who had unwittingly summoned this future into being.

It was said that the Americans who'd supported Trump were victims of liberal condescension. The word *racist* would be dismissed as a profane slur put upon the common man, as opposed to an accurate description of actual men. "We simply don't yet know how much racism or misogyny motivated Trump voters," David Brooks would write in *The New York Times*. "If you were stuck in a jobless town, watching your friends OD on opiates, scrambling every month to pay the electric bill, and then along came a guy who seemed able to fix your problems and hear your voice, maybe you would stomach some ugliness, too." This strikes me as perfectly logical. Indeed, it could apply just as well to Louis Farrakhan's appeal to the black poor and working class. But whereas the followers of an Islamophobic white nationalist enjoy the sympathy that must always greet the salt of the earth, the followers of an anti-Semitic black nationalist endure the scorn that must ever greet the children of the enslaved.

Much would be made of blue-collar voters in Wisconsin, Pennsylvania, and Michigan who'd pulled the lever for Obama in 2008 and 2012 and then for Trump in 2016. Surely these voters disproved racism as an explanatory force. It's still not clear how many individual voters actually flipped. But the underlying presumption—that Hillary Clinton and Barack Obama could be swapped in for each other—exhibited a problem. Clinton was a candidate who'd won one competitive political race in her life, whose political instincts were questioned by her own advisers, who took more than half a million dollars in speaking fees from an investment bank because it was "what they offered," who proposed to bring back to the White House a former president dogged by allegations of rape and sexual harassment. Obama was a candidate who'd become only the third black senator in the modern era; who'd twice been elected president, each time flipping red and purple states; who'd run one of the most scandal-free administrations in recent memory. Imagine an African American facsimile of Hillary Clinton: She would never be the nominee of a major political party and likely would not be in national politics at all.

Pointing to citizens who voted for both Obama and Trump does not disprove racism; it evinces it. To secure the White House, Obama needed to be a Harvard-trained lawyer with a decade of political experience and an incredible gift for speaking to cross sections of the country; Donald Trump needed only money and white bluster.

In the week after the election, I was a mess. I had not seen my wife in two weeks. I was on deadline for this article. My son was struggling in school. The house was in disarray. I played Marvin Gaye endlessly—"When you left, you took all of me with you." Friends began to darkly recall the ghosts of post-Reconstruction. The election of Donald Trump confirmed everything I knew of my country and none of what I could accept. The idea that America would follow its first black president with Donald Trump accorded with its history. I was shocked at my own shock. I had wanted Obama to be right.

I still want Obama to be right. I still would like to fold myself into the dream. This will not be possible.

By some cosmic coincidence, a week after the election I received a portion of my father's FBI file. My father had grown up poor in Philadelphia. His father was struck dead on the street. His grandfather was crushed to death in a meatpacking plant. He'd served his country in Vietnam, gotten radicalized there, and joined the Black Panther Party, which brought him to the attention of J. Edgar Hoover. A memo written to the FBI director was "submitted aimed at discrediting WILLIAM PAUL COATES, Acting Captain of the BPP, Baltimore." The memo proposed that a fake letter be sent to the Panthers' co-founder Huey P. Newton. The fake letter accused my father of being an informant and concluded, "I want somethin done with this bootlikin facist pig nigger and I want it done now." The words *somethin done* need little interpretation. The Panthers were eventually consumed by an internecine war instigated by the FBI, one in which being labeled a police informant was a death sentence.

A few hours after I saw this file, I had my last conversation with the president. I asked him how his optimism was holding up, given Trump's victory. He confessed to being surprised at the outcome but said that it was tough to "draw a grand theory from it, because there were some very unusual circumstances."

He pointed to both candidates' high negatives, the media coverage, and a "dispirited" electorate. But he said that his general optimism about the shape of American history remained unchanged. "To be optimistic about the long-term trends of the United States doesn't mean that everything is going to go in a smooth, direct, straight line," he said. "It goes forward sometimes, sometimes it goes back, sometimes it goes sideways, sometimes it zigs and zags."

I thought of Hoover's FBI, which harassed three generations of black activists, from Marcus Garvey's black nationalists to Martin Luther King Jr.'s integrationists to Huey Newton's Black Panthers, including my father. And I thought of the enormous power accrued to the presidency in the post-9/11 era—the power to obtain American citizens' phone records en masse, to access their emails, to detain them indefinitely. I asked the president whether it was all worth it. Whether this generation of black activists and their allies should be afraid.

"Keep in mind that the capacity of the NSA, or other surveillance tools, are specifically prohibited from being applied to US citizens or US persons without specific evidence of links to terrorist activity or, you know, other foreign-related activity," he said. "So, you know, I think this whole story line that somehow Big Brother has massively expanded and now that a new president is in place it's this loaded gun ready to be used on domestic dissent is just not accurate."

He counseled vigilance, "because the possibility of abuse by government officials always exists. The issue is not going to be that there are new tools available; the issue is making sure that the incoming administration, like my administration, takes the constraints on how we deal with US citizens and persons seriously." This answer did not fill me with confidence. The next day, President-Elect Trump offered Lieutenant General Michael Flynn the post of national-security adviser and picked Senator Jeff Sessions of Alabama as his nominee for attorney general. Last February, Flynn tweeted, "Fear of Muslims is RATIONAL" and linked to a YouTube video that declared followers of Islam want "80 percent of humanity enslaved or exterminated." Sessions had once been accused of calling a black lawyer "boy," claiming that a white lawyer who represented black clients was a disgrace to his race, and joking that he thought the Ku Klux Klan "was okay until I found out they smoked pot." I felt then that I knew what was coming—more Freddie Grays, more Rekia Boyds, more informants and undercover officers sent to infiltrate mosques.

And I also knew that the man who could not countenance such a thing in his America had been responsible for the only time in my life when I felt, as the first lady had once said, proud of my country, and I knew that it was his very lack of countenance, his incredible faith, his improbable trust in his countrymen, that had made that feeling possible. The feeling was that little black boy touching the president's hair. It was watching Obama on the campaign trail, always expecting the worst and amazed that the worst never happened. It was how I'd felt seeing Barack and Michelle during the inauguration, the car slow-dragging down Pennsylvania Avenue, the crowd cheering, and then the two of them rising up out of the limo, rising up from fear, smiling, waving, defying despair, defying history, defying gravity.

FOR INFORMAL WRITING

This essay examines Coates's own experience of a Black presidency as a Black man. What do you remember of the Obama presidency? Have there been any political figures who have left a particularly transformative impression on you, or whose candidacy has been equally important to you? How and why?

FOR DISCUSSION

1. Reflect on the contexts that Coates provides in the article regarding Barack Obama's first election. What, according to Coates, are some of the cultural and political factors that contributed to it?
2. How is the article organized? Why do you think Coates chose to organize it that way? How are the structure, tone, and point of view effective? Why? Look specifically at points in the article.
3. "There are no clean victories for Black people, nor, perhaps, for any people. The presidency of Barack Obama is no different." What does Coates mean by "clean victory?" How does he explain his point? What do you think, and why?

FOR WRITING

Coates spends some of the essay talking about his father, an early member of the Black Panthers, considered at the time to be a radical political group. In an attempt to situate the Obama presidency with the larger civil rights movement in America, do some research about the civil rights movement (or different aspects of the movement) to better answer the question, "What is the political and social relevance of the first Black American president?"

Going It Alone (2017)
Rahawa Haile (1985–)

Rahawa Haile is an environmentalist writer whose commitment to hiking the Appalachian Trail in 2016 gave way to her book, In Open Country *(2021). Her work has appeared in* The New York Times, The Atlantic, *and* The New Yorker. *A self-described "queer, black woman," she writes and speaks about climate change. On a panel discussion she moderated for the Zocallo Natural History Museum of Los Angeles County, she asked the question, "Is nature only for white people?" This is a question she more fully explores in "Going It Alone."*

> What happens when an African American woman decides to solo-hike the Appalachian Trail from Georgia to Maine during a summer of bitter political upheaval? Everything you can imagine, from scary moments of racism to new friendships to soaring epiphanies about the timeless value of America's most storied trekking route.

It's the spring of 2016, and I'm ten miles south of Damascus, Virginia, where an annual celebration called Trail Days has just wrapped up. Last night, temperatures plummeted into the thirties. Today, long-distance Appalachian Trail hikers who'd slept in hammocks and mailed their underquilts home too soon were groaning into their morning coffee. A few small fires shot woodsmoke at the sun as thousands of tent stakes were dislodged. Over the next 24 hours, most of the hikers in attendance would pack up and hit the 554-mile stretch of the AT that runs north through Virginia.

I've used the Trail Days layover as an opportunity to stash most of my belongings with friends and complete a short section of the AT I'd missed, near

From Outside Magazine, May 2017

the Tennessee-Virginia border. As I'm moving along, a day hiker heading in the opposite direction stops me for a chat. He's affable and inquisitive. He asks what many have asked before: "Where are you from?" I tell him Miami.

He laughs and says, "No, but really. Where are you from from?" He mentions something about my features, my thin nose, and then trails off. I tell him my family is from Eritrea, a country in the Horn of Africa, next to Ethiopia. He looks relieved.

"I knew it," he says. "You're not black."

I say that of course I am. "None more black," I weakly joke.

"Not really," he says. "You're African, not black-black. Blacks don't hike."

I'm tired of this man. His from-froms and black-blacks. He wishes me good luck and leaves. He means it, too; he isn't malicious. To him there's nothing abnormal about our conversation. He has categorized me, and the world makes sense again. Not black-black. I hike the remaining miles back to my tent and don't emerge for hours.

Heading north from Springer Mountain in Georgia, the Appalachian Trail class of 2017 would have to walk 670 miles before reaching the first county that did not vote for Donald Trump. The average percentage of voters who did vote for Trump—a xenophobic candidate who was supported by David Duke—in those miles? Seventy-six. Approximately 30 miles farther away, they'd come to a hiker hostel that proudly flies a Confederate flag. Later they would reach the Lewis Mountain campground in Shenandoah National Park—created in Virginia in 1935, during the Jim Crow era—and read plaques acknowledging its former history as the segregated Lewis Mountain Negro Area. The campground was swarming with RVs flying Confederate flags when I hiked through. This flag would haunt the hikers all the way to Mount Katahdin, the trail's end point, in northern Maine. They would see it in every state, feeling the tendrils of hatred that rooted it to the land they walked upon.

During the early part of my through-hike, I arrive in Gatlinburg, Tennessee, one afternoon, a little later than I planned. I was one of many thirtysomethings who'd ended their relationships, quit their jobs, left their pets with best friends, and flown to Georgia. By this point, I'm 200 miles into my arduous, rain-soaked trek. Everything aches. The bluets and wildflowers have emerged, and I've taken a break in town to resupply, midway through my biggest challenge thus far, the Smokies.

It isn't until I'm about to leave town that I see it: blackface soap, a joke item that supposedly will turn a white person black if you can trick them into using it. I'm in a general store opposite the Nantahala Outdoor Center. The soap is in a discount bin next to the cash register. I'd popped in to buy chocolate milk and was instead reminded of a line from Claudia Rankine's book *Citizen*: "The past is a life sentence, a blunt instrument aimed at tomorrow."

There's a shuttle back to the trail at Newfound Gap leaving in 15 minutes. I fumble to take a photograph of the cartoon white woman on the packaging, standing in front of her bathroom sink. She can't believe it. How could this happen? Her face and hands are black. She scrubs to no avail.

I leave. Cars honk. I'm standing at an intersection and straining to return to the world. The shuttle arrives to take us from town to trailhead. The van leads us up, up into the mountains. It's a clear day. Hikers are laughing, rejuvenated. "Did you have fun in town?" a friend I met on the trail asks. "This visibility is unreal," says another, nose against the window. He thinks he has spotted a bear. The sun has lifted spirits. The van spills us out, but I can barely see a thing.

Two days later, a stream of texts hit my phone. Prince has died. I feel my vision blur, sit down on the first rock I see, and don't move for a while. The hikers who walk past ask if I'm hurt. "I'm sorry to tell you this," I'll hear myself say. "Prince just died." No one knows who I'm talking about. I will see variations of the same vacant expression for the rest of the day. "The Prince of Wales?" one hiker asks.

I'm losing light. I have to get to the next shelter. The afternoon has been a learning experience: the trail is no place to share black grief. Later, when Beyoncé releases *Lemonade*, an album that speaks powerfully to black women, I won't permit myself to hear it out here. I'm lonely enough as it is, without feeling additional isolation. I keep it from myself, and I follow the blazes north. I tell the trees the truth of it: some days I feel like breaking.

The National Park Service celebrated its centennial last year. In one brochure, a white man stands boldly, precariously, in Rocky Mountain National Park, gazing at a massive rock face. He wears a full pack. He is ready to tackle the impossible. The poster salutes "100 years of getting away from it all." The parenthetical is implied if not obvious: for some.

In a *Backpacker* interview from 2000, a black man named Robert Taylor was asked about the hardest things he faced during his through-hike of the Appalachian Trail. He'd recently completed both the AT and the Pacific Crest Trail. "My problems were mainly with people," he said. "In towns, people yelled racist threats at me in just about every state I went through. They'd say, 'We don't like you,' and 'You're a nigger.' Once when I stopped at a mail drop, the postmaster said, 'Boy, get out of here. We got no mail drop for you.'"

It will be several months before I realize that most AT hikers in 2016 are unaware of the clear division that exists between what hikers of color experience on the trail (generally positive) and in town (not so much). While fellow through-hikers and trail angels are some of the kindest and most generous people I'll ever encounter, many trail towns have no idea what to make of people who look like me. They say they don't see much of "my kind" around here and leave the rest hanging in the air.

The rule is you don't talk about politics on the trail. The truth is you can't talk about diversity in the outdoors without talking about politics, since politics is a big reason why the outdoors look the way they do. From the park system's inception, Jim Crow laws and Native American removal campaigns limited access to recreation by race. From the mountains to the beaches, outdoor leisure was often accompanied by the words whites only. The repercussions for disobedience were grave.

"For me, the fear is like a heartbeat, always present, while at the same time, intangible, elusive, and difficult to define," Evelyn C. White wrote in her 1999 essay "Black Women and the Wilderness." In it she explains why the thought of hiking in Oregon, which some writer friends invited her to do, fills her with dread. In wilderness, White does not see freedom but a portal to the past. It is a trigger. The history of suffering is too much for her to overcome. This fear has conjured a similar paralysis nationwide. It says to the minority: Be in this place and someone might seize the opportunity to end you. Nature itself is the least of White's concerns. Bear paws have harmed fewer black bodies in the wild than human hands. She does not wish to be the only one who looks like her in a place with history like this.

Perspective is everything.

There are 11 cats at Bob Peoples's Kincora Hiking Hostel in Hampton, Tennessee. When I ask Peoples how he keeps track of them, he responds, "They keep track of me." We talk about the places he's hiked and the people he's met. "Germans have the best hiking culture of any country," he says. "If there was a trail to hell, Germans would be on it." The chance of precipitation the next day is 100 percent. When it drizzles the rain plays me, producing different sounds as it strikes hat, jacket, and pack cover. Of the many reasons to pause while hiking, this remains my favorite. The smell and sound of the dampening forest is a sensory gift, a time for reflection.

The first bumper sticker I see in Hot Springs, North Carolina, says that April is Confederate History Month. A week later, I stay in a hostel near Roan Mountain, Tennessee, next to a house that's flying a Confederate flag. Hikers who've hitched into town tell me that the rides they got were all from drunk white men. Be careful, they warn.

I reconsider going into town at all. It's near freezing. Two days ago, I woke up on Roan Mountain itself in a field of frozen mayapples. Today I wear my

Buff headband like a head scarf under my fleece hat. When I walk a third of a mile back to the trailhead alone the next morning, I look at the neighbor's flag and wonder if someone will assume I'm Muslim, whether I'm putting myself at risk. I lower the Buff to my neck and worry that I'm being paranoid. Six months later, the *San Francisco Chronicle* will report on a woman of color who was hiking in Fremont, California, while wearing a Buff like a bandana and returned to find her car's rear window smashed, along with a note. "Hijab wearing bitch," it said. "This is our nation now get the fuck out." She wasn't Muslim, but that's not the point. The point is the ease with which a person becomes a "them" in the woods.

Two weeks later, at Trail Days, there's a parade celebrating current and past hikers. A black man with the trail name Exterminator aims a water gun at a white crowd as he moves along. He shoots their white children. They laugh and shoot back with their own water guns. This goes on for 30 yards. I pause to corral my galloping anxiety. He is safe, I tell myself. This event is one of the few places in America where I don't fear for a black man with a toy gun in a public setting.

The Southern Poverty Law Center tracked more than 1,000 hate crimes and bias incidents that occurred in the month after the election. On November 16, 2016, the Appalachian Trail Conservancy posted information about racist trail graffiti on its Facebook page. It showed up along the trail corridor in Pennsylvania. The group was encouraging anyone who encountered "offensive graffiti or vandalism" to report it via e-mail.

Starting in 1936, amid the violence of Jim Crow, a publication known as the *Green Book* functioned as a guide for getting black motorists from point A to point B safely. It told you which gas stations would fill your tank, which restaurants would seat you, and where you could lay your head at night without fear. It remained in print for 30 years. As recently as 50 years ago, black families needed a guide just to travel through America unharmed.

There is nothing approximating a *Green Book* for minorities navigating the American wilderness. How could there be? You simply step outside and hope for the best. One of the first questions asked of many women who solo-hike the Appalachian Trail is whether they brought a gun. Some find it preposterous. But one hiker of color I spoke to insisted on carrying a machete, an unnecessarily heavy piece of gear. "You can never be too sure," he told me.

As a queer black woman, I'm among the last people anyone expects to see on a through-hike. But nature is a place I've always belonged. My home in South Florida spanned the swamp, the Keys, and the dredged land in between. My father and I explored them all, waving at everything from egrets to purple gallinules and paddling by the bowed roots of mangroves. This was before Burmese pythons overran the Everglades, when the rustling of leaves in the canopy above our canoe still veered mammalian.

Throughout my youth, my grandmother and I took walks in Miami, where I'd hear her say the words *tuum nifas*. It meant a delicious wind, a nourishing wind. These experiences shaped how I viewed movement throughout the natural world. How I view it still. The elements, I thought, could end my hunger.

Little has changed since. Now the rocks gnaw at my shins. I thud against the ground, my tongue coated in dirt. I pick myself back up and start again.

Every day I eat the mountains, and the mountains, they eat me. "Less to carry," I tell the others: this skin, America, the weight of that past self. My hiking partners are concerned and unconvinced. There is a weight to you still, they tell me. They are not wrong. My footing has been off for days. There were things I had braced for at the beginning of this journey that have finally started to undo me. We were all hurtling through the unfamiliar, aching, choppy, destroyed by weather, trying not to tear apart. But some of us were looking around as well. By the time I made it through Maryland, it was hard not to think of the Appalachian Trail as a 2,190-mile trek through Trump lawn signs. In July, I read the names of more black men killed by police: Philando Castile, Alton Sterling. Never did I imagine that the constant of the woods would be my friends urging, pleading, that I never return home.

That was then. Back home in Oakland, California, now, my knees hurt. I struggle with the stairs. I wonder if it's Lyme disease from an unseen tick bite. The weight I lost has come back. My arms, the blackest I ever saw them after weeks in the summer sun, have faded to their usual dark brown. The bruises on my collarbones from my pack straps are no more. My legs aren't oozing blood. My feet haven't throbbed in four months. I am once again soft and unblemished and pleading with my anxiety every day for a few hours of peace. My timing couldn't be worse. The news is relentless. Facts mean nothing. The truth is, I don't know how to move through the world these days. Everything feels like it needs saving. I can barely keep up.

Who is wilderness for? It depends on who you ask. In 2013, Trail Life USA, a faith-based organization, was established as a direct response to the Boy Scouts of America's decision to allow openly gay kids into their program. A statement by the group made the rules clear: Trail Life USA "will not admit youth who are open or avowed about their homosexuality, and it will not admit boys who are not 'biologically male' or boys who wish to dress and act like girls."

Roughly two years later, news outlets profiled the Radical Monarchs, a group for children of color between the ages of eight and twelve, intended as a Girl Scouts for social activists. Headlines like "Radical Brownies Are Yelling 'Black

Lives Matter,' Not Hawking Girl Scout Cookies" highlighted what an intersectional approach to youth activism could look like. Organizations such as Trail Life USA and Radical Monarchs show opposite ends of the outdoor spectrum. For conservative Christian men, religion is used as a means of tying exclusionary practices to outdoor participation. For people of color, the wilderness is everywhere they look. They don't need mountains. Wilderness lives outside their front doors. Orienteering skills mean navigating white anxiety about them. They are belaying to effect change. And even then, their efforts might not be enough.

"People on the trail, overwhelmingly, are good people, but it isn't advertised for us," says Bryan Winckler, a black AT through-hiker who went by the trail name Boomer. "If you see a commercial for anything outdoor related, it's always a white person on it. I think if people saw someone who looked like them they would be interested. It's not advertised, so people think, That's not for me."

Brittany Leavitt, an Outdoor Afro trip leader based in Washington, DC, echoed this sentiment. "You don't see it in the media," she told me recently. "You don't see it advertised when you go into outdoor stores. When I do a hike, I talk about what's historically in the area. Nature has always been part of black history."

She's right. Outdoor skills were a matter of survival for black people before they became a form of exclusion. Harriet Tubman is rarely celebrated as one of the most important outdoor figures in American history, despite traversing thousands of miles over the same mountains I walked this year.

"How can we make being in the outdoors a conduit for helping people realize, understand, and become comfortable with the space they occupy in the world?" says Krystal Williams, a black woman who through-hiked the AT in 2011. The change is happening slowly, in large part because of public figures bringing attention to the outdoors. Barack Obama designated more national monuments than any president before him. Oprah has called 2017 her year of adventure. "My favorite thing on earth is a tree," she told ranger Shelton Johnson, an advocate for diversity in the national parks, when she met him in Yosemite in 2010. A recent photo of Oprah at the Grand Canyon shows her carrying a full pack. "Hiking requires no particular skill, only two feet and a sturdy pair of shoes," she said. "You set the pace. You choose the trail. You lock into a certain rhythm with the road, and that rhythm becomes your clarion song."

Halfway through the descent into Daleville, Virginia, I found myself lying on the trail floor, wincing up at the canopy. I had taken a sudden tumble and was dazed. My right ankle ached badly, though my trekking poles had saved me from a truly nasty sprain. It was not a difficult stretch of trail—some packed dirt, a few small rocks, plenty of switchbacks. I felt betrayed and then ashamed. I could feel my confidence evaporating. If I couldn't walk a well-groomed trail, what in the world was I going to do with the boulder scrambles awaiting me in the north? Falls could be fatal. At worst this one was a slight embarrassment, but it marked the first time I needed to forgive myself for what I could not control.

Every inch of my being by that point had been shaped by an explicit choice. In pursuit of Katahdin—which I reached on October 1, after six months of hiking—I had wept and chopped off the long, natural hair, so politicized in America, that my grandmother had told me to always treasure. My afro was no more. I had left my skin to ash, my lips to crack. I wore my transmission-tower-print bandana like an electric prayer. The Appalachian Trail was the longest conversation I'd ever had with my body, both where I fit in it and where it fits in the world.

One of the popular Appalachian Trail books I read while preparing for my trek asked readers to make a short list of reasons why they wanted to do it. The author suggested we understand these reasons, down to our core, before embarking, coming up with something deeper than "I like nature." I took out this document often when things felt overwhelming on the AT, when the enormity of the pursuit threatened to swallow me whole. Looking back, the list is a series of unrealized hopes. One line reads: "I have always been the token in a group; I have never chosen how I want to lead." Another says: "It will be the first time I get to discover not whether I will succeed but who I am becoming." The last line is a declaration: "I want to be a role model to black women who are interested in the outdoors, including myself."

There were days when the only thing that kept me going was knowing that each step was one toward progress, a boot to the granite face of white supremacy. I belong here, I told the trail. It rewarded me in lasting ways. The weight I carried as a black woman paled in comparison with the joy I felt daily among my peers in that wilderness. They shaped my heart into what it will be for the rest of my life.

One of the most common sentiments one hears about the Appalachian Trail is how it restores a person's faith in humanity. It is no understatement to say that the friends I made, and the experiences I had with strangers who, at times, literally gave me the shirt off their back, saved my life. I owe a great debt to the through-hiking community that welcomed me with open arms, that showed me what I could be and helped me when I faltered. There is no impossible, they taught me: only good ideas of extraordinary magnitude.

FOR INFORMAL WRITING

"Heading north from Springer Mountain in Georgia, the Appalachian Trail class of 2017 would have to walk 670 miles before reaching the first county that did not vote for Donald Trump." What is the intersection in this article of the environment and politics?

FOR DISCUSSION

1. In an interview, Haile has said, "There's a great deal of privilege that goes into through-hiking." What might she mean by this?
2. The epigraph of the article says this: "What happens when an African American woman decides to solo-hike the Appalachian Trail from Georgia to Maine during a summer of bitter political upheaval?" After you read the article, discuss what, indeed, does happen?
3. How might Haile characterize her hiking the Appalachian Trail as an act of political resistance? How do you know?

FOR WRITING

Rahawa Haile credits organizations like Outdoor Afro, Fat Girls Hiking, and others with helping connect new and more diverse communities to the outdoors. What might these organizations be reacting to? Look at advertisements or marketing for well-known outdoor brands—Patagonia, REI, even off-road vehicles (Subaru, etc.), and magazines (such as *Backpacker*). What are the assumptions behind the marketing and advertisements you find? How do these relate to Haile's points? How do the missions of the organizations dedicated to outdoor adventures work to challenge these marketing assumptions? Do they?

To Be, or Not to Be (2018)
Masha Gessen (1967–)

Masha Gessen, whose birth name is Maria Alexandrovna Gessen, writes extensively about queer and trans rights and identifies as nonbinary, preferring the pronouns they *and* them. *They are a leading voice championing gay and LBGTQT rights in Russia. They are the author of* The Future is History: How Totalitarianism Reclaimed Russia, *which won the National Book Award for Nonfiction in 2017, and have had their battles with the Russian government. Gessen moved to New York from Russia in 2013 because of a threat by the government to take children away from gay parents. This essay was originally delivered as a lecture at the New York Public Library in 2017 and was published in* The New York Review of Books *in 2018.*

1. FETUS

The topic of my talk was determined by today's date. Thirty-nine years ago my parents took a package of documents to an office in Moscow. This was our application for an exit visa to leave the Soviet Union. More than two years would pass before the visa was granted, but from that day on I have felt a sense of precariousness wherever I have been, along with a sense of opportunity. They are a pair.

I have emigrated again as an adult. I was even named a "great immigrant" in 2016, which I took to be an affirmation of my skill, attained through practice—though this was hardly what the honor was meant to convey. I have also raised kids of my own. If anything, with every new step I have taken, I have marveled more at the courage it would have required for my parents to step into the abyss. I remember seeing them in the kitchen, poring over a copy of an atlas of the

---

Original title: The Stories of a Life. By permission of Masha Gessen

world. For them, America was an outline on a page, a web of thin purplish lines. They'd read a few American books, had seen a handful of Hollywood movies. A friend was fond of asking them, jokingly, whether they could really be sure that the West even existed.

Truthfully, they couldn't know. They did know that if they left the Soviet Union, they would never be able to return (like many things we accept as rare certainties, this one turned out to be wrong). They would have to make a home elsewhere. I think that worked for them: as Jews, they never felt at home in the Soviet Union—and when home is not where you are born, nothing is predetermined. Anything can be. So my parents always maintained that they viewed their leap into the unknown as an adventure.

I wasn't so sure. After all, no one had asked me.

2. VULNERABLE

As a thirteen-year-old, I found myself in a clearing in a wood outside of Moscow, at a secret—one might say underground, though it was out in the open—gathering of Jewish cultural activists. People went up in front of the crowd, one, two, or several at a time, with guitars and without, and sang from a limited repertoire of Hebrew and Yiddish songs. That is, they sang the same three or four songs over and over. The tunes scraped something inside of me, making an organ I didn't know I had—located just above the breastbone—tingle with a sense of belonging. I was surrounded by strangers, sitting, as we were, on logs laid across the grass, and I remember their faces to this day. I looked at them and thought, *This is who I am.* The "this" in this was "Jewish." From my perch thirty-seven years later, I'd add "in a secular cultural community" and "in the Soviet Union," but back then space was too small to require elaboration. Everything about it seemed self-evident—once I knew what I was, I would just be it. In fact, the people in front of me, singing those songs, were trying to figure out how to be Jewish in a country that had erased Jewishness. Now I'd like to think that it was watching people learning to inhabit an identity that made me tingle.

Some months later, we left the Soviet Union.

In autobiographical books written by exiles, the moment of emigration is often addressed in the first few pages—regardless of where it fell in a writer's life. I went to Vladimir Nabokov's *Speak, Memory* to look for the relevant quote in its familiar place. This took a while because the phrase was actually on page 250 out of 310. Here it is: "The break in my own destiny affords me in retrospect a syncopal kick that I would not have missed for worlds."

This is an often-quoted phrase in a book full of quotable sentences. The cultural critic and my late friend Svetlana Boym analyzed Nabokov's application of the word "syncope," which has three distinct uses: in linguistics it's the shortening of a word by omission of a sound or syllable from its middle; in music it is a change of rhythm and shift of accent when a normally weak beat is stressed; and in medicine it is a brief loss of consciousness. "Syncope," wrote Svetlana, "is the opposite of symbol and synthesis."

Suketu Mehta, in his *Maximum City*, wrote:

> Each person's life is dominated by a central event, which shapes and distorts everything that comes after it and, in retrospect, everything that came before. For me, it was going to live in America at the age of fourteen. It's a difficult age at which to change countries. You haven't quite finished growing up where you were and you're never well in your skin in the one you're moving to.

Mehta didn't let me down: this assertion appears in the very first pages of his magnificent book; also, he moved to America at the same age that I did. And while I think he might be wrong about *everyone*, I am certain he is right about émigrés: the break colors everything that came before and after.

Svetlana Boym had a private theory: an émigré's life continues in the land left behind. It's a parallel story. In an unpublished piece, she tried to imagine the parallel lives her Soviet/Russian/Jewish left-behind self was leading. Toward the end of her life, this retracing and reimagining became something of an obsession. She also had a theory about me: that I had gone back to reclaim a life that had been interrupted. In any case, there are many stories to be told about a single life.

3. DIVERSITY

On Valentine's Day in 1982—I was fifteen—I went to a gay dance at Yale. This was a great time for gay dances. It was no longer terrifying to be queer on campus, but gay life was still half-hidden in a way that was thrilling. I do not remember, in fact, dancing, and I don't even remember catching anyone's eye. In other words, I'm pretty sure that no one noticed me. Strangely, that wasn't crushing. Because what I do remember is standing somewhere dark, leaning against something, and feeling like I was surrounded by community. I remember thinking, *This is who I could be.*

What the syncope of emigration had meant for me was the difference between discovering who I was—the experience I had in the woods outside of Moscow—and discovering who I could be—the experience I had at that dance. It was a moment of choice and, thanks to the "break in my destiny," I was aware of it.

4. ENTITLEMENT

In this sense my personal narrative splits from that of the American gay and lesbian movement. The latter was based on choicelessness. A choice may have to be defended—certainly, one has to be prepared to defend one's right to make a choice—while arguing that you were born this way appeals to people's sympathy or at least a sense of decency. It also serves to quell one's own doubts and to foreclose future options. We are, mostly, comfortable with less choice—much as I would have felt safer if my parents had not set out on their great emigration adventure.

After I left Moscow, one of my grandmothers was compelled to hide the fact of our emigration—we had committed an act of treason that could have threatened those left behind. So in the little town where she lived and where I had spent summers as a child, she continued to update my friends on the life I wasn't leading. In that Soviet life, I applied to colleges and failed to get in. In the end, I settled for some mediocre-sounding technical route.

I was hurt by the predictability of the story my grandmother chose for me. In the United States, I was living an imaginative and risky life—I dropped out of high school, ran away from home, lived in the East Village, worked as a bicycle messenger, dropped out of college, worked in the gay press, became the editor of a magazine at twenty-one, got arrested at ACT UP protests, experimented sexually and romantically, behaved abhorrently, was a good friend, or tried to be—but in the mirror held up by my grandmother, it wasn't just my location that was different: it was the presence of choice in my life.

After ten years in this country, I went back to Moscow as a journalist, on assignment. I felt so unexpectedly comfortable in a country that I had expected to feel foreign—as though my body relaxed into a space that had stayed open for it—that I also felt resentful about not having had a choice in leaving. I kept going back and eventually stayed, refashioning myself as a Russian-language journalist. I pretended that this was the life I would have had if I had never left, but deep inside I believed that my grandmother had been right: there was some parallel me, toiling miserably on some dead-end engineering task. This made me a double impostor in the life I was living.

I'm not sure when I made the choice to stay in Russia, but I remember hearing the statement come out of my mouth, surprising me, as it sometimes happens when a decision makes itself known. I had been living there a year, and I was talking to a close friend, an American graduate student who had also been there a year and was now going back. "I think I'm going to stay," I said. "Of course you are," he responded, as though it weren't a choice at all.

Around the same time, I was interviewed by a young Russian journalist: having chosen to return to Russia made me exotic enough to be written about. He asked me which I liked better: being a Russian in America or an American in Russia. I was furious—I believed myself to be a Russian in Russia and an American in America. It took me many years to come around to liking being an outsider wherever I go.

I remet my two grandmothers, whom I hadn't seen since I was a teenager, and started interviewing them. This project became a book about the choices they had made. The one who disapproved of our emigration had become a censor, which, she told me, was a moral choice. She had been educated to be a history teacher, but by the time she had completed her studies she was convinced that becoming a history teacher in the Soviet Union would require her to lie to children every day. Censoring, on the other hand, seemed to her a job that could have been done by a robot: any other person would have crossed out the same lines or confiscated the same mail (her first job was as a censor of printed material in incoming international mail), whereas every history teacher uses a different kind of charm and persuasion to distort children's understanding of the past.

My other grandmother I knew as a rebel and a dissident, someone who never compromised. But as I interviewed her I learned that when she was offered a job with the secret police (as a translator), she had agreed to take it. This was during Stalin's so-called anti-cosmopolitan campaign, when Jews were purged from all kinds of Soviet institutions. She could not get a job to save her life, or, more to the point, her toddler son's life. It had been no choice at all, she told me: she had to feed her child. She never started the job because she failed the medical exam.

The central figure in the book, however, was her father, who was killed in Majdanek. I had always known that he had participated in the rebellion in the Bialystok Ghetto. But then I also found out that he had served in the Judenrat (Jewish council) before choosing to help the rebels.

As I studied the archives—a remarkable number of documents from the Bialystok Ghetto have been preserved—I realized that my great-grandfather had been one of the de facto leaders of the Judenrat. He had been responsible for food deliveries to and garbage removal from the ghetto, and I saw strong evidence that he took part in putting together the lists of names for extermination. I also found a memoir written by a member of the resistance in which she recalled my great-grandfather's efforts to stop the resistance. Later he apparently changed his position and started helping the resistance to smuggle weapons into the ghetto. Before the war, he had been an elected official, a member of both the city council and the Jewish council, so it was clear to me that he had seen his duties in the Judenrat as the logical outgrowth of his elected service. I could see the trajectory of my great-grandfather's choices.

My grandmother didn't want me to publish the part about the Judenrat, and we had a protracted battle over whose story it was to tell—hers or mine, or both of ours. In the end, she had only one demand: that I omit a quote from Hannah Arendt's *Eichmann in Jerusalem*. This is the infamous quote in which Arendt says that the Holocaust would not have been possible without the help of the Jewish councils.

I saw it as a story of impossible, anguished choices that he nonetheless insisted on making. Totalitarian regimes aim to make choice impossible, and this was what interested me at the time. I was awed by the gap between my capacity for judgment and the unbearably limited options faced by my grandparents. I fixated on the ideas of "impossible choice" and of having "no choice." But what interests me now is that I think resistance can take the shape of insisting on making a choice, even when the choice is framed as one between unacceptable options.

5. SCIENCE-BASED

Back in the United States, my parents' adventure came to a halt, eleven years after we landed in America. My mother died of cancer in the summer of 1992. Another eleven years later, I returned for a yearlong fellowship—to be a Russian in America for a year. During that year I took a test that showed I had the genetic mutation that had caused the cancer that killed my mother and her aunt before that. I was "born this way"—born to develop cancer of the breasts or ovaries, or both. The genetic counselors and doctors asked me what I wanted to do. It was a choice, framed as one between "aggressive monitoring"—for the first signs of cancer, which the doctors were certain would appear—and preventive surgery.

I ended up writing, first, a series of articles and then a book on making choices in the age of genetic testing. I talked to people who had faced far more drastic choices than the one before me. These people had chosen to live without such essential organs as the stomach or pancreas, whereas all the doctors were suggesting to me was the removal of breasts and ovaries. I chose to remove my breasts and reconstruct them. I was choosing my breast size and my fate!

The doctors, incidentally, didn't think this was the right choice: they advocated for the removal of the ovaries rather than, or more importantly than, the breasts. I found more compelling evidence in favor of keeping the ovaries for a while, but two and a half years ago I had those removed as well. Around that time, my doctor was strongly suggesting I really no longer had a choice.

6. TRANSGENDER

Two decades after moving back to Russia, I left again. It was one of those impossible choices that don't feel like much of a choice: I was one of many people pushed out of the country during the crackdown that followed the protests of 2011–2012. Some were given the choice between emigrating or going to prison. My options were emigrating or seeing social services go after my kids, on the grounds that I am queer.

What had happened to the life my discontinuous self was leading back in America while I was in Russia? My writing life had been proceeding apace, more or less—I was publishing in the United States while living in Russia. Socially, who was I? Who were my people? Where did I belong? I had lost some friends and gained others. Some friends had become couples, split up, recoupled, had children. I had coupled and recoupled and had children too.

Also, some of the women I had known had become men. That's not the way most transgender people phrase it; the default language is one of choicelessness: people say they have always been men or women and now their authentic selves are emerging. This is the same "born this way" approach that the gay and lesbian movement had put to such good political use in the time that I'd been gone: it had gotten queer people access to such institutions as the military and marriage.

The standard story goes something like this: as a child I always felt like a boy, or never felt like a girl, and then I tried to be a lesbian, but the issue wasn't sexual orientation—it was gender, specifically, "true gender," which could now be claimed through transitioning. I found myself feeling resentful at hearing these stories. I too had always felt like a boy! It had taken some work for me to enjoy being a woman (whatever that means)—I'd succeeded, I had learned *how to be* one. But still: here I was, faced with the possibility that in the parallel life that my left-behind self was leading in the United States while I was in Russia, I would have transitioned. True gender (whatever that means) didn't have much to do with it, but choice did. Somehow, I'd missed the fact that it was there.

I had written an entire book on making choices that had to do with removing the parts of the body that would appear to have made me female: the breasts, the ovaries, the uterus. And I had not questioned the assumptions that after a mastectomy one considers one's options for reconstruction, and after a radical hysterectomy one considers whether to receive hormone "replacement" in the form of estrogen. Indeed, I had had reconstruction and was taking estrogen. I had failed, miserably, at seeing my choices, made as they were under some duress, as an opportunity for adventure. I had failed to think about inhabiting a different body the way one would think about inhabiting a different country. How do I invent the person I am now?

I quit estrogen and started testosterone. I had some trouble with the evidence part of the science, because, as I have found, all published papers on the use of testosterone in people who start out as women fall into one of two categories: articles that aim to show that people taking testosterone will experience all of the masculinizing changes that they wish for, and ones that aim to show that women will have none of the masculinizing changes that they fear. I am taking a low dose, and I have no idea how it's going to affect me. My voice has become lower. My body is changing.

But then again, bodies change all the time. In her book *The Argonauts* Maggie Nelson quotes her partner, the artist Harry Dodge, as saying that he is not going anywhere—not transitioning but being himself. I recognize the sentiment, though I'd probably say the opposite: for thirty-nine years, ever since my parents took those documents to the visa office, I have felt so precarious that I lay no claim to someone I "really am." That someone is a sequence of choices, and the question is: Will my next choice be conscious, and will my ability to make it be unfettered?

7. EVIDENCE-BASED

It took little effort to organize the notes I jotted down for this talk around the seven words that the Trump administration was reported to have banned the Centers for Disease Control from using. All seven words—from "fetus" to "evidence-based"—are words that reflect on our understanding of choice.

Choice is a great burden. The call to invent one's life, and to do it continuously, can sound unendurable. Totalitarian regimes aim to stamp out the possibility of choice, but what aspiring autocrats do is promise to relieve one of the need to choose. This is the promise of "Make America Great Again"—it conjures the allure of an imaginary past in which one was free not to choose.

I've been surprised, in the last year, that the resurgence of interest in some of the classic books on totalitarianism has not brought back Erich Fromm's wonderful *Escape from Freedom* (though Fromm, who was a psychoanalyst and social psychologist, has been rediscovered by many people in the mental health profession because he introduced the idea of "malignant narcissism"). In the introduction, Fromm apologizes for what he perceives as sloppiness, which he says stems from the need to write the book in a hurry: he felt that the world was on the verge of catastrophe. He was writing this in 1940.

In the book, Fromm proposes that there are two kinds of freedom: "freedom from," which we all want—we all want our parents to stop telling us what to do—and "freedom to," which can be difficult or even unbearable. This is the freedom to invent one's future, the freedom to choose. Fromm suggests that at certain times in human history the burden of "freedom to" becomes too painful for a critical mass of people to bear, and they take the opportunity to cede their agency—whether it's to Martin Luther, Adolf Hitler, or Donald Trump.

No wonder Trump appears to be obsessed with people who embody choice. Immigrants are his most frightening imaginary enemy, the ones who need to be "extremely vetted," blocked out with a wall, whose crimes need to be reported to a special hotline and whose families need to be kept out of this country. It puts me in mind of the "aggressive monitoring" for the cancer that's sure to come. Transgender people have been another target of Trump's apparently spontaneous lashing out—witness the transgender ban in the military, the rescinding of protections for transgender students, and now the ban on the very word "transgender."

But in speaking about immigrants we tend to privilege choicelessness much as we do when we are speaking about queer people or transgender people. We focus on the distinction between refugees and "economic migrants," without asking why the fear of hunger and destitution qualifies as a lesser reason for migration than the fear of imprisonment or death by gunshot wound—and then only if that wound is inflicted for political or religious reasons. But even more than that, why do we assume that the more restricted a person's choices have been, the more qualified they are to enter a country that proclaims freedom of personal choice to be one of its ideals?

Immigrants make a choice. The valor is not in remaining at risk for catching a bullet but in making the choice to avoid it. In the Soviet Union, most dissidents believed that if one were faced with the impossible choice between leaving the country and going to prison, one ought to choose exile. Less dramatically, the valor is in being able to experience your move less as an escape and more as an adventure. It is in serving as living reminders of the choicefulness of life—something that immigrants and most trans people do, whether their personal narratives are ones of choice or not.

I wish I could finish on a hopeful note, by saying something like: If only we insist on making choices, we will succeed in keeping darkness at bay. I'm not convinced that's the case. But I do think that making choices and, more important, imagining other, better choices, will give us the best chance possible of coming out of the darkness better than we were when we went in. It's a bit like emigrating that way: the choice to leave rarely feels free, but choices we make about inhabiting new landscapes (or changed bodies) demand an imagination.

FOR INFORMAL WRITING

What do you think of the headings of each section of the article—for instance, "Fetus" and "Vulnerable?" Why would Gessen choose these headings? To what effect? What might they mean?

FOR DISCUSSION

1. How does Gessen evoke the immigrant experience? What about the article particularly catches your attention?
2. What do they mean when they say, "the before and the after?"

3. In many ways, Gessen's article is a coming-of-age story in that it explores Gessen's own identity but also their identity as a member of several communities. When they write, "This is who I am," how does this simple sentence belie great complexity? What is that complexity?

FOR WRITING

Research the sociological concept of "intersecting identities." What does the concept mean in light of this particular article? What aspects of the article indicate that this is the case? Explore the concept of intersecting identities broadly, and more specifically, with what particular identities Gessen grapples.

WHAT'S NEW IS OLD

Many of the readings in this anthology grapple with the notion of "intersecting identities," such as Adrienne Rich's "Split at the Root," Jaquira Díaz's "Carrying Histories of Protest," and Gloria Anzaldúa's "How to Tame a Wild Tongue." Choose one or two of these readings and analyze the ways in which each author evokes this sense of identity and challenges to one's identity.

You Owe Me an Apology (2018)
Brittany Packnett Cunningham (1984–)

Perhaps the only person in this anthology to have graced the cover of British Vogue *(September 2020), Brittany Packnett Cunningham was also named as one of* Time *magazine's twelve new faces of Black leadership, and one of* Marie Claire's *most influential women. Packnett is an educator, social organizer, and writer; she was a 2020 fellow at the Harvard Institute of Politics and is an NBC and MSNBC News contributor. Her 2019 Ted Talk on "Confidence" has gone viral and has over five million views. Her upcoming book,* We Are Like Those Who Dream: Black Women Speak, *will be published by One World Press. "You Owe Me an Apology" appeared in* Elle *magazine in September 2018.*

Serena Williams is the GOAT by all athletic standards. LeBron James has proclaimed it. Colin Kaepernick declared it. I'm very sure her daughter Olympia believes it. There is no modern athlete as awarded and credentialed as her, and if she never stepped foot on a court again, her status as the greatest of all time is, for many of us, set in stone, cast in gold, and permanently irrefutable.

This is why it was fascinating to watch as the validity of Williams' reaction to being accused of cheating by umpire Carlos Ramos during the Women's Final of this year's US Open was debated, and debated, and debated some more. Some self-proclaimed tennis aficionados have argued that Serena's reaction was nothing more than the display of a sore, entitled loser. Others—including several professional male tennis stars and Billie Jean King, the grand matron of women's tennis—have called out the sexist double standard in both the umpire's calls and the public response to Serena's words. And just when we thought the conversation had quieted, an Australian cartoonist resurrected the trend in uninspired, boringly racist fashion, depicting Serena as an oversized brute, and Naomi Osaka,

---

As seen on elle.com, September 12, 2018. Written by Brittany Packnett.

the new and powerful US Open champion of Haitian and Japanese descent, as a blonde-haired white woman.

But I'm not here to relitigate the incident. Because the most striking lesson I derived from all of this was a profound life lesson: demand the apologies you deserve.

Williams uttered the phrase with clarity, without irony or apology. Her feet were firm and her voice was steady.

"You owe me an apology."

In that instant, it occurred to me that I have never spoken this phrase. To anyone. Not a lover, not a friend. Not a bad boss or a vindictive colleague. This is not for lack of opportunity. I'm a black woman in America. I have been owed plenty of apologies.

I just never believed I deserved to demand one.

In the instant that I watched Serena's firm command, I anxiously searched my consciousness to determine why, in my 33 years of living, I had never demanded an apology I believed I was owed. I have certainly expressed personal and professional grievances; I have given voice to hurt feelings and frustrated moments with greater intention as I've grown in confidence—a confidence which is hard earned.

But the idea that someone would need to affirm responsibility for their actions and impact on me had just never occurred to me. I have quietly carried the scars of apologies desired but never received, seething with resentment but never questioning why I didn't demand an apology in the first place. I have always known, as seemingly all Black mothers say, that "closed mouths don't get fed," and that it is rare that anyone receives that which they do not ask for. Still, I had not formed my lips to utter the words: you owe me an apology.

The cycle of my socialization was centered on the archetype of the Strong Black Woman. I met her early and often. She was the long-suffering mother in films, and the sturdy women of my church. They held everything together—and I do mean everything—with little thanks, acknowledgment or applause. They suffered quietly and labored intensely. When they were wronged by men, they chalked it up. When they were abused by systems and institutions, they kept pushing. That's a Black woman's life. Take a licking, keep on ticking, because if you don't, your family won't eat, the church won't run, and the school can't function. The weight of the world sits on our bosom, simply leaving no time to argue with the people who have harmed you. That's a Black woman's life.

And if we ever did muster the audacity to push back, to demand, to respond? That did not come without punishment. As each of us are socialized, we develop survival mechanisms based on what we observe. When our proverbial hands get slapped, we learn to silence our instincts until that silence becomes habit.

I was an early and vocal leader at my predominately white, affluent, private Midwestern high school. I spoke up in class, made speeches in school-wide assembly, and co-founded our school's first diversity organization back in 1998, long before the concept died an unceremonious death from overuse.

Despite some people's discomfort with the topics we broached, our club was highly regarded and well-attended. There was one student, however, whose privileged existence saw my work as an existential threat to his way of life and inflated ego. I ignored him for several weeks as he harassed me between classes, walking closely behind me and asking me if his "whiteness" or "maleness" was "offending" me today. One day, though, I had had enough. Standing in front of the girls' locker room, I finally turned and confronted him.

Then? He spit at me.

I now know this to be the classic fragility of patriarchal white supremacy. Back then, I was stunned.

I turned and entered the locker room. As I sat on the hard bench and stared into an empty locker, I somehow instinctively knew this was the quiet plight I had to carry. It was the same spit I'd seen hurled at Elizabeth Eckford, one of the Little Rock Nine, as I watched her silently integrate Little Rock's Central High School in the documentaries my parents had us watch. It was the same spit Diane Nash felt as she sat at segregated lunch counters in Nashville, TN. My adolescent pursuits toward social awareness were undoubtedly humble and incredibly minor by comparison, but the hate for the audacity of black womanhood was the same.

After a week, I finally told someone—one of the two black teachers I had in my entire secondary experience. I told him only because I couldn't carry the emotional stain anymore, the shame that shouldn't have been mine to carry, but made me feel dirty all the same. But as I sat on his office couch, I knew the confession was futile. At just 15 years old, life had taught me enough for me to know nothing real would be done. The student who assaulted me was a rich white boy, the son of a trustee who was well-connected and well-respected. I was little black girl, a scholarship kid and the daughter of a hard-working widow. I knew how that story ended.

My prediction was correct. After my teacher made me tell our head of school, I received a forced, clenched-mouth apology—and further retribution from a student who was now even more angry. I never told anyone about the harassment that continued. I never asked for another apology.

On that day, I learned with abundant clarity that black girls don't demand apologies. As a Black woman, speaking up about the needs of others would win me applause; speaking up for myself would earn me punishment. I'd be vilified for even thinking I deserve dignity, and as I try to pursue justice for the rest of the world, I simply don't have that kind of time. For black girls, demanding the apologies we deserve is usually just wasted energy in a world where we can't afford to waste anything.

I didn't tell that story again until I was 29 years old. By then, I was working daily in the Ferguson Uprising, and my high school asked me to return to that same assembly hall that had once earned me abuse and discuss our protest, power and plan. Before my speech I called that same trusted teacher and confided I was at an uncharacteristic loss for words. "The words will come to you," he said. And that story is what came out.

Even as I write this, tears are welling in my eyes, a salty mix of shame that I don't deserve and grief of a trauma unhealed. Consider, for a moment, all the apologies the women in your life, on your teams and in your family have never requested but were owed. Consider all the times they were given apologies and responded, "it's ok," even though it wasn't. Consider all the times they themselves apologized for asking for an apology. Consider that the umpire may be any one of us who have harmed someone socialized to believe they must stomach the harm they receive.

Women are socialized to prioritize the comfort of others over self, no matter how shameful or painful the moment. This responsibility increases for women of color, who are often the mules of a society determined to pin domestic and social labor on Black, Latinx, Asian and Indigenous women who suffer in silence for fear of punishment and degradation.

Serena's declaration was an instantaneous declaration of freedom. Freedom for every woman who deserves an apology from the boss who gave her a #MeToo story to tell. Liberation for every black woman who was spoken over by a white woman in the erroneous name of unity in feminism. Deliverance for every little girl who's been socialized to believe she must sacrifice her dignity for your comfort.

You owe us an apology. And thanks to Serena, I'm no longer ashamed to demand it.

FOR INFORMAL WRITING

How does this article explore what some tennis stars call a "sexist double standard in both the umpire's calls and the public response to Serena's words?" What realization does Packnett Cunningham have about her own response?

FOR DISCUSSION

1. What does the author mean when she says, "I have been owed plenty of apologies. I just never believed I deserved to demand one"?

2. In what ways does the author reflect on her own upbringing in reaction to this incident? How does it enhance her argument?
3. "I now know this to be the classic fragility of patriarchal white supremacy." Who are the victims of this "classic fragility?" Why is it "fragile," however?

FOR WRITING

Packnett Cunningham writes as follows: "Women are socialized to prioritize the comfort of others over self, no matter how shameful or painful the moment. This responsibility increases for women of color, who are often the mules of a society determined to pin domestic and social labor on Black, Latinx, Asian and Indigenous women who suffer in silence for fear of punishment and degradation." What other examples of women—especially prominent women and women of color, prominent or not—can you find who have faced and documented similar treatment? How was that treatment overcome if it was?

Origin Story: Carrying Histories of Protest (2019)

Jaquira Díaz

A Puerto Rican American writer of fiction, Jaquira Díaz also describes herself as an essayist and journalist. She was raised in Miami and is a former visiting professor of creative writing at the University of Wisconsin-Madison. Diaz has served as consulting editor for the prestigious Kenyon Review. *She has won numerous awards, including the Barnes and Noble Discover Great New Writers Collection for her debut book,* Ordinary Girls: A Memoir *(2019). Her second book,* I Am Deliberate: A Novel, *is forthcoming from Algonquin Books. The following piece is an excerpt from* Ordinary Girls.

Puerto Rico, 1985

Papi and I waited in the town square of Ciales, across from Nuestra Señora del Rosario, the Catholic church. He was quiet, stern-faced, his picked-out Afro shining in the sun, his white polo shirt drenched in sweat. Papi was tall and lean-muscled, with a broad back. He'd grown up boxing and playing basketball, had a thick mustache he groomed every morning in front of the bathroom mirror. Squinting in the sun, one hand tightened around his ring finger, I pulled off Papi's ring, slipped it onto my thumb. I was six years old and restless: I'd never seen a dead body.

My father's hero, Puerto Rican poet and activist Juan Antonio Corretjer, had just died. People had come from all over the island and gathered outside the parish to hear his poetry while his remains were transported from San Juan. Mami and Anthony, my older brother, were lost somewhere in the crowd.

During the drive from Humacao to Ciales, I'd listened from the backseat while Papi told the story: how Corretjer had been raised in a family of indepen-

---

From ORDINARY GIRLS by Jaquira Díaz ©2019 by Jaquira Díaz. Reprinted by permission of Algonquin Books of Chapel Hill. All rights reserved.

dentistas, how he'd spent his entire life fighting for el pueblo, for the working class, for Puerto Rico's freedom. How he'd been a friend of Pedro Albizu Campos, "El Maestro," who my father adored, the Puerto Rican Nationalist Party leader who'd spent more than twenty-six years in prison for attempting to overthrow the US government. How he had spent a year in "La Princesa," the prison where Albizu Campos was tortured with radiation. After his release, Corretjer became one of Puerto Rico's most prominent activist writers.

In the car, Mami had lit a cigarette and rolled down her window, her cropped, blond waves blowing in the wind. She took a long pull from her cigarette, then let the smoke out, her red fingernails shining. My mother smoked like the whole world was watching, like she was Marilyn Monroe in some old movie, or Michelle Pfeiffer in *Scarface*. Every time we left the house, my mother was made up from head to red-pedicured toes, her hair colored, her eyes dramatically set in eye shadow and a thick coat of mascara, with lipstick to match her nail polish.

While my mother smoked, not paying attention to my father's story, Anthony slept beside me in the back, his mouth half open. My brother had no interest in stories, but I lived for Papi's tales of magic and Boricua Robin Hoods, imagined myself as a character in them, riding a black horse into battle, slicing conquistadores in half with my razor-sharp machete.

It was my father who'd taught me to tie my shoelaces like rabbit ears, to catch fireflies at dusk, to eat ensalada de pulpo bought from chinchorros on the side of the road in Naguabo and Luquillo, to play chess. He'd told me stories of coconut palms that bowed to the sun, of jíbaros like his uncles and grandfather, who got up before daylight to cut cane in the cañaverales. Stories of machetes, sweat, and sugar, before paved roads and indoor plumbing and English. Stories of women: Lucecita Benítez, one of Puerto Rico's most famous singers, who sang about race and liberation; Lolita Lebrón, who fought among men, taking up arms after La Masacre de Ponce; Yuíza, a Taíno cacica who would be resurrected, rising from ash and clay and blood to avenge the death of her people. His tales were spun of history and wind and poetry.

The funeral procession approached, a caravan of cars led by a white hearse—every car flying a Puerto Rican flag—moving slowly uphill toward the plaza, closer to the church, where arrangements of roses and lirios and carnations already waited. The crowd grew, hundreds of people approaching the square, some of them waving Puerto Rican flags. Papi watched them, never looked away, even when I yanked his hand this way and that way or when I tugged on the hem of his shirt, even as I picked up pebbles and flung them across the plaza at the pigeons. Not even to wipe the tears from his eyes. I wanted to ask about his tears, to remind him of what I'd heard Mami say while Anthony, during one of his tantrums, thrust himself against the walls of our apartment, then the floor: Los hombres no lloran.

Papi and I moved through the crowd, the two of us zigzagging in between couples and families and students in their school uniforms, all of them waiting for their turn in front of the open casket. When we'd finally made our way to the front, I saw the man in the casket for the first time: in his seventies, balding, patches of white hair on the sides, pale, white mustache. I tried to memorize the lines around Corretjer's mouth, the shape of his forehead, the arch of his eyebrows. I wanted to trace my fingers along the creases of his unmoving face, commit them to memory.

I don't know how long Papi and I stood there in front of that open casket, as if in a trance, as if waiting for the rise and fall of Corretjer's chest, my father voiceless, sweat trickling down his face. But I was sure of one thing: that I wanted everything my father wanted, and if he loved this man, then I would love him, too.

Months after Alaina was born, Anthony in the second grade, Mami working at a factory in Las Piedras, I spent my days at home with Papi. Abuela took care of Alaina while Mami worked, so I had Papi all to myself. He'd sit up in bed, reading to me from Juan Antonio Corretjer's *Yerba bruja* or Hugo Margenat's *Obras completas* or Julia de Burgos's *El mar y tú*, a mug of café con leche in his hand. My father, who'd been a student at the University of Puerto Rico, had spent his college days writing protest poems and studying literature and the work of independentistas and activists.

I loved books because Papi loved books, and his were the first I tried to read. I was a kid trying to learn my father's secrets, whatever mysteries he'd found in those pages that kept him from me for so many hours each day. Imagine my disappointment when I discovered that Manuel Puig's *El beso de la mujer araña* didn't involve a masked superhero using her spider powers to save innocent people from muggers or mad scientists. Or that Mario Vargas Llosa's *La ciudad y los perros* was not about a society made up entirely of dogs.

In my father's books, I got lost in stories: children who sprouted eagles' wings, a baby born with the curled tail of a pig, a man who spent a hundred years on an island prison mourning the loss of his lover but never aged a day, a woman who carried a pistol into a government building and opened fire.

One morning, I woke to find Papi in the bedroom I shared with Anthony, sitting at my desk, his back to me. He pulled dollar bills, wrinkled and folded, from a black garbage bag, unfolding them, lining them up in stacks. Our bedroom was cramped with our twin beds, Alaina's crib, stacks of Papi's books in a corner, our toys littering the floor. From my bed, under a nautical bedspread sewn by my mother, I watched him counting and bundling and fastening them with rubber bands, until the desk was covered with money.

There was another morning, and another, and another, and I learned not to ask questions, not to let slip what I knew about the money, about Papi's hiding places: the top shelf in our closet, which Anthony and I couldn't reach, the small suitcase under my parents' bed, my father's toolbox.

Every afternoon when my mother came home from the factory, my father left and went to the little plaza in El Caserío. And every afternoon I begged him to take me along, but he refused. I could play outside, but la plaza, he said, was no place for a girl.

"How come Anthony *always* gets to go?" I would ask Mami, yelling, slamming my fists on the kitchen counter. Anthony was never banned from any place, always got what he wanted because he was a boy.

But Mami, she didn't take no shit. She'd pull me by the arm, the half-moons of her sharp fingernails biting into my skin, and shut me right up. She'd leave me sobbing, longing for something to lift this burden of girlhood.

One afternoon, outside our apartment building, I kicked off my chancletas and ran around on the front lawn, barefoot, looking for morivivi. It grew all over the neighborhood, a small plant with leaves that closed like tiny fists when you touched them, faking their own death, reopening when left undisturbed. I leaned down to touch it, running my fingers over it, until my friend Eggy, who lived two blocks over, showed up on his bike.

"Wanna go for a ride?" he called from the street. Eggy was my best friend, always wandering the streets because his mom didn't pay him or his brother Pito any mind. He was brown, a dash of freckles across his nose and cheeks, his Afro always unkempt, his T-shirts always either too small or too big, with holes on the front. Eggy was too smart for his own good, always knew everybody's business: whose husband crashed their car into a barbershop, who kissed who behind the elementary school, which boys got caught looking up the girls' skirts on the playground.

I glanced back at our building, our balcony, our apartment's open windows. Mami had told me to stay where she could keep an eye on me, but Papi was in the plaza, and I was dying to see what he did there, why girls weren't allowed. So I climbed up on Eggy's handlebars.

"Don't drop me!" I said.

Eggy pedaled hard, making a left toward the building across the street, then past his building. We rode around to the back, the wind slapping my head, my curls blowing in my face. I held on to the handlebars, my bare feet in the air.

When we finally got to la plaza, a small square surrounded by two-story buildings, shaded by ceiba trees and flamboyanes, I hopped off the bike.

Next to one of the buildings, children's clothes were drying on a clothesline. A homeless man slept on a discarded sofa, baking under the sun. Four hustlers, three men and one woman, played dominoes around a makeshift card table made from a large paint bucket and four milk crates used as chairs. Papi was standing among his stone-faced friends. Tecatos walked up to Papi, said something I couldn't hear, handed him money, then disappeared behind the buildings.

"You know what they're doing, right?" Eggy asked.

"What are they doing?"

"Your dad is selling them perico."

I knew what perico was, just like I knew what tecatos were—Eggy had told me. His mother, he'd said, had sold all her jewelry and their TV to get perico. She would've sold the food in their fridge, if they'd had any.

Eggy got off his bike, leaned it against the building.

I looked for my brother among the men, feeling betrayed, wondering how much he knew, if this was a secret he and Papi shared, something else they kept from me. But Anthony was not around.

My face hot, upper lip sweaty, I turned and started walking back home.

"Where you going?" Eggy called after me.

I kept walking, ignoring his question. Bare feet on the grass, then the sidewalk, on tiptoes, trying not to step on broken glass while crossing the street. As I reached the front of my building, I found one chancleta there, right where I'd left it. The other one gone. I leaned down and ran my fingers over all the moriviví. They each shriveled, leaf by leaf, dying their fake deaths. And me, pretending I'd been there all along, in case Mami looked out the window, stepped out on the balcony, asked where I'd been.

During the warm nights in El Caserío, I lay in the hammock on our first-floor balcony, listening to the coquís' songs as they echoed through the whole neighborhood. Every night, at all hours, Papi's friends came asking for him. I fetched my father when I saw them approaching, watched as he took their balled-up dollar bills and handed them their baggies over the railing. Some of them came by every day. Some of them, a few times a day.

I was rocking myself in the hammock when one of them strolled right up to our balcony, a man with a curved, jagged scar on his face extending from the corner of his lips all the way up to his eye.

"Is your father home?" he asked.

"No," I said, even though my father *was* home. I lied without hesitating, without knowing why. Maybe I thought I was protecting my father. Maybe I sensed that something about this man was dangerous.

"Do you want to see what I'm holding?" the man asked, stepping closer. He looked past me, through the door into our living room. "I have something for you."

I got up out of the hammock and walked over, thinking that maybe he'd hand me a few crumpled dollar bills to give my father. I wanted so much to believe him. But when I looked at his pants, down below his waist, he pulled out his dick.

It wasn't like the ones I'd seen before—my brother's, a baby cousin's, or Eggy's, which I saw once when he pulled it out and started pissing on a dead toad. Eggy's had been no big deal. I'd been more interested in the toad, its carcass torn open and full of live maggots. Those other ones had been small, shriveled-up things. But this was something else. This was a grown man's dick, swollen and thick and veiny. Horrifying.

At first I thought it was a mistake, that he'd meant to pull something out of his pocket and it somehow slipped out. But then, the smile on his face, the serrated edges of his sickle feather scar. I stumbled back.

"Papi!" I screamed at the top of my lungs. The man tore past the side of our building toward the cañaverales behind El Caserío.

Papi came out to the balcony, barefoot, wiping sleep from his eyes. But how could I explain what had just happened? From my mother, I'd learned that a girl's body was special, that I should stay away from men, who were not to be trusted, that I should not let boys see my private parts, or let them show me theirs. How could I explain what the man had done without admitting that I'd stupidly let him? Years later I'd remember this moment, how I'd thought it was my own fault. How, ashamed, I thought of it like a secret that needed to be kept.

Standing there, heart pounding in my chest, I said nothing as my father rushed over, as he wrapped his arms around me, as he asked, "What's wrong?"

I held my stomach, willing the tears to come, as Papi asked again and again, "What's wrong? Where does it hurt?"

But I kept it to myself, just cried and cried, wilting like moriviví in his arms. I adored my father. He was the center of my universe, and I wanted, more than anything else, to be the center of his. That whole year, I had Papi mostly to myself during the day. But when I didn't, at least I had his books.

In my father's books, I would learn about the genocide of the Taínos, about our island's Taíno name, Boríken, which then became Borínquen, and later, Puerto Rico. About Africans who were brought through the Transatlantic slave trade, including part of our black family, although most of my father's side came from Haiti right after the Haitian Revolution, and settled in Naguabo. In my father's books, and in my father's own stories, I would find our history:

Ponce, 1937

After Pedro Albizu Campos' first imprisonment in La Princesa, members of the Puerto Rican Nationalist Party and civilians organized a march in protest. Puerto Ricans wanted independence from the United States, and from Blanton Winship, the US-appointed governor, who had not been elected by the people. They secured all the necessary permits, invited a marching band, gathered with their families after church. Men, women, and children headed toward the parade, where they would celebrate Palm Sunday with music and palm fronds.

Hundreds of people marched as the band played "La Borinqueña." They were met by hundreds of police officers in riot gear who shot their Tommy Guns directly at the crowd of unarmed civilians. Under Winship's orders, the cops surrounded the demonstrators, leaving them no route for escape.

The shooting lasted about thirteen minutes, some people say. Others insist it was fifteen.

The police murdered nineteen people, and wounded about 235, including a seven-year-old girl, a man shielding his young son, and an eighteen-year-old boy looking out his window.

Witnesses said that as the cops walked by the dead or dying, they beat them with their clubs. Most of the victims who lay dead on the street, the evidence showed, were shot in their backs while running away from the gunfire.

Although an investigation by the US Commission on Civil Rights found that Governor Winship had ordered the massacre, none of the murderers were ever convicted, or even prosecuted.

This was our history, I would eventually learn. We'd come from uprisings against colonial rule, slavery, massacres, erasure. We'd carried histories of resistance, of protest.

And I would also learn that my father, even though he spent his days selling perico, was imagining some other life. All that time lost in his books, all those nights writing poetry and painting, every single dollar he stashed away—Papi dreaming of another place, where his kids could play outside, where he didn't have to sell dope anymore. One day, he would tell me all his secrets, all the stories not meant for children: the other woman he'd loved, the baby who died before I was born, the army days. And I would write it all down, determined to remember.

Prohibido olvidar.

FOR INFORMAL WRITING

"One day, he would tell me all his secrets, all the stories not meant for children: the other woman he'd loved, the baby who died before I was born, the army days. And I would write it all down, determined to remember. Prohibido olvidar." What responsibility does Díaz have to her family's history?

FOR DISCUSSION

1. Comment on the language of the article. How does the language evoke your sense of Díaz's father? Of her mother?
2. How does "prohibido olvidar" resonate with the article by Elie Wiesel included in this volume? What does this tell us about the importance of remembrance?
3. Look carefully at the two sections of this article—Puerto Rico, 1985; and Ponce, 1937. What effect does this have on your reading? Why do you think Díaz chose to structure the piece in this way? To what effect?

FOR WRITING

"This was our history, I would eventually learn. We'd come from uprisings against colonial rule, slavery, massacres, erasure. We'd carried histories of resistance, of protest." In addition to Diaz's own words in this article, research an aspect of Puerto Rican history that further explains this quotation. To what conclusion do you come about this history, based on the facts you read?

The American Nightmare (2020)
Ibram X. Kendi (1982–)

Award-winning scholar, professor, and antiracist activist, Ibram X. Kendi was born Ibram Henry Rogers. He is the founding director of the Boston University Center for Antiracist Research and also serves as Andrew Mellon Professor of the Humanities. This professorship has been held by only one other person in the history of Boston University—Elie Wiesel, whose work appears elsewhere in this volume. Kendi has written three New York Times best-selling books: Stamped from the Beginning: The Definitive History of Racist Ideas in America *(2016, which won the National Book Award);* How to Be an Antiracist *(2019); and* Antiracist Baby *(2020). Kendi was awarded a Guggenheim Fellowship in 2019. "The American Nightmare," published in June of 2020, went viral at the height of unrest in the wake of ongoing police brutality.*

It happened three months before the lynching of Isadora Moreley in Selma, Alabama, and two months before the lynching of Sidney Randolph near Rockville, Maryland.

On May 19, 1896, *The New York Times* allocated a single sentence on page three to reporting the US Supreme Court's *Plessy v. Ferguson* decision. Constitutionalizing Jim Crow hardly made news in 1896. There was no there there. Americans already knew that equal rights had been lynched; *Plessy* was just the silently staged funeral.

Another racial text—published by the nation's premier social-science organization, the American Economic Association, and classified by the historian Evelynn Hammonds as "one of the most influential documents in social science at the turn of the 20th century"—elicited more shock in 1896.

From The Atlantic. © 2020 The Atlantic Monthly Group, LLC. All rights reserved. Used under license.

"Nothing is more clearly shown from this investigation than that the southern black man at the time of emancipation was healthy in body and cheerful in mind," Frederick Hoffman wrote in *Race Traits and Tendencies of the American Negro*. "What are the conditions thirty years after?" Hoffman concluded from "the plain language of the facts" that black Americans were better off enslaved. They are now "on the downward grade," he wrote, headed toward "gradual extinction."

Hoffman's *Race Traits* helped legitimize two nascent fields that are now converging on black lives: public health and criminology.

Hoffman knew his work was "a most severe condemnation of moderate attempts of superior races to lift inferior races to their elevated positions." He rejected that sort of assimilationist racism, in favor of his own segregationist racism. The data "speak for themselves," he wrote. White Americans had been naturally selected for health, life, and evolution. Black Americans had been naturally selected for disease, death, and extinction. "Gradual extinction," the book concluded, "is only a question of time."

Let them die, Hoffman seemed to be saying. That thought has echoed through time, down to our deadly moment in time, when police officers in Minneapolis let George Floyd die.

With its pages and pages of statistical charts, *Race Traits* helped catapult Hoffman into national and international prominence as the "dean" of American statisticians. In his day, Hoffman "achieved greatness," assessed his biographer. "His career illustrates the fulfillment of the 'American dream.'"

Actually, his career illustrates the fulfillment of the American nightmare—a nightmare still being experienced 124 years later from Minneapolis to Louisville, from Central Park to untold numbers of black coronavirus patients parked in hospitals, on unemployment lines, and in graves.

"We don't see any American dream," Malcolm X said in 1964. "We've experienced only the American nightmare."

A nightmare is essentially a horror story of danger, but it is not wholly a horror story. Black people experience joy, love, peace, safety. But as in any horror story, those unforgettable moments of toil, terror, and trauma have made danger essential to the black experience in racist America. What one black American experiences, many black Americans experience. Black Americans are constantly stepping into the toil and terror and trauma of other black Americans. Black Americans are constantly stepping into the souls of the dead. Because they know: They could have been them; they *are* them. Because they know it is dangerous to be black in America, because racist Americans see blacks as dangerous.

To be black and conscious of anti-black racism is to stare into the mirror of your own extinction. Ask the souls of the 10,000 black victims of COVID-19 who might still be living if they had been white. Ask the souls of those who were told the pandemic was the "great equalizer." Ask the souls of those forced to choose between their low-wage jobs and their treasured life. Ask the souls of those blamed for their own death. Ask the souls of those who disproportionately lost their jobs and then their life as others disproportionately raged about losing their freedom to infect us all. Ask the souls of those ignored by the governors reopening their states.

The American nightmare has everything and nothing to do with the pandemic. Ask the souls of Breonna Taylor, Ahmaud Arbery, and George Floyd. *Step into their souls.*

No-knocking police officers rushed into your Louisville home and shot you to death, but your black boyfriend immediately got charged, and not the officers who killed you. Three white men hunted you, cornered you, and killed you on a Georgia road, but it took a cellphone video and national outrage for them to finally be charged. In Minneapolis, you did not hurt anyone, but when the police arrived, you found yourself pinned to the pavement, knee on your neck, crying out, "I can't breathe."

History ignored you. Hoffman ignored you. Racist America ignored you. The state did not want you to breathe. But your loved ones did not ignore you. They did not ignore your nightmare. They share the same nightmare.

Enraged, they took to the streets and nonviolently rallied. Some violently rebelled, burning and snatching property that the state protected instead of your life. And then they heard over America's loudspeaker, "When the looting starts, the shooting starts."

Your loved ones are protesting your murder, and the president calls for *their* murder, calls them "THUGS," calls them "OUT OF STATE" agitators. Others call the violence against property senseless—but not the police violence against you that drove them to violence. Others call both senseless but take no immediate steps to stem police violence against you, only to stem the violence against property and police.

Mayors issue curfews. Governors rattle their sabers. The National Guard arrives to protect property and police. Where was the National Guard when you faced violent police officers, violent white terrorists, the violence of racial health disparities, the violence of COVID-19—all the racist power and policy and ideas that kept the black experience in the American nightmare for 400 years?

Too many Americans have been waiting for black extinction since Hoffman. *Let them die.*

The National Guard lines up alongside state and local police. But they—your loved ones mourning you and mourning justice—are not going home, since you are not at home. They don't back down, because they will never forget what happened to them, what happened to you!

You! You! You! The murdered black life that matters.

You are them. They are you. You are all the same person—all the murdered, all the living, all the infected, all the resisting—because racist America treats the whole black community and all of its anti-racist allies as dangerous, just as Hoffman did. What a nightmare. But perhaps the worst of the nightmare is knowing that racist Americans will never end it. Anti-racism is on you, and only you. Racist Americans deny your nightmare, deny their racism, claim you have a dream like a King, when even his dream in 1967 "turned into a nightmare."

In 1896, Frederick Hoffman deployed data to substantiate racist ideas that are still building caskets for black bodies today. Black people are supposed to be feared by all, murdered by police officers, lynched by citizens, and killed by COVID-19 and other lethal diseases. It has been proved. No there there. Black life is the "hopeless problem," as Hoffman wrote.

Black life is danger. Black life is death.

Hoffman's *Race Traits* was "arguably the most influential race and crime study of the first half of the twentieth century," wrote the historian Khalil Gibran Muhammad in *The Condemnation of Blackness*. It was also arguably the most influential race and public-health study of the period.

In the first nationwide compilation of racial crime data, Hoffman used the higher arrest and incarceration rates of black Americans to argue that they are, by their very nature and behavior, a dangerous and violent people—as racist Americans still say today. Hoffman compiled racial health disparities to argue that black Americans are, by their very nature and behavior, a diseased and dying people. Hoffman cataloged higher black mortality rates and showed that black Americans were more likely to suffer from syphilis, tuberculosis, and other infectious diseases than white Americans. The same disparities are visible today, as black Americans die of COVID-19 at a rate nearly two times their share of the national population, according to the COVID Racial Data Tracker.

Now step back into their souls.

You are sick and tired of the nightmare. And you are "sick and tired of being sick and tired," as Fannie Lou Hamer once said. But racist America stares at your sickness and tiredness, approaches you, looks past the jagged clothes of your history, looks past the scars of your trauma, and asks: *How does it feel to be the American nightmare?*

While black Americans view their experience as the American nightmare, racist Americans view black Americans as the American nightmare. Racist Americans, especially those racists who are white, view themselves as the embodiment of the American dream. All that makes America great. All that will make America great again. All that will keep America great.

But only the lies of racist Americans are great. Their American dream—that this is a land of equal opportunity, committed to freedom and equality, where police officers protect and serve—is a lie. Their American dream—that they have more because they are more, that when black people have more, they were given more—is a lie. Their American dream—that they have the civil right to kill black Americans with impunity and that black Americans do not have the human right to live—is a lie.

From the beginning, racist Americans have been perfectly content with turning nightmares into dreams, and dreams into nightmares; perfectly content with the law of racial killing, and the order of racial disparities. They can't fathom that racism is America's nightmare. There can be no American dream amid the American nightmare of anti-black racism—or of anti-Native, anti-Latino, anti-Asian racism—a racism that causes even white people to become fragile and die of whiteness.

Take Minneapolis. Black residents are more likely than white residents to be pulled over, arrested, and victimized by its police force. Even as black residents account for 20 percent of the city's population, they make up 64 percent of the people Minneapolis police restrained by the neck since 2018, and more than 60 percent of the victims of Minneapolis police shootings from late 2009 to May 2019. According to Samuel Sinyangwe of Mapping Police Violence, Minneapolis police are 13 times more likely to kill black residents than to kill white residents, one of the largest racial disparities in the nation. And these police officers rarely get prosecuted.

A typical black family in Minneapolis earns less than half as much as a typical white family—a $47,000 annual difference that is one of the largest racial disparities in the nation. Statewide, black residents are 6 percent of the Minnesota population, but 30 percent of the coronavirus cases as of Saturday, one of the largest black case disparities in the nation, according to the COVID Racial Data Tracker.

This is the racial pandemic within the viral pandemic—older than 1896, but as new as COVID-19 and the murder of George Floyd. But why is there such a pandemic of racial disparities in Minneapolis and beyond? "The pages of this work give but one answer," Hoffman concluded in 1896. "It is not in the conditions of life, but in race and hereditary that we find the explanation of the fact to be observed in all parts of the globe, in all times and among all peoples, namely, the superiority of one race over another, and of the Aryan race over all."

The two explanations available to Hoffman more than a century ago remain the two options for explaining racial disparities today, from COVID-19 to police violence: the anti-racist explanation or the racist explanation. Either there is something superior or inferior about the races, something dangerous and deathly about black people, and black people are the American nightmare; or there is something wrong with society, something dangerous and deathly about racist policy, and black people are experiencing the American nightmare.

Hoffman popularized the racist explanation. Many Americans probably believe both explanations—and live the contradiction of the American dream and nightmare. Many Americans struggle to be anti-racist, to see the racism in racial disparities, to cease blaming black people for disproportionate black disease and death, to instead blame racist power and policy and racist ideas for normalizing all the carnage. They struggle to focus on securing anti-racist policies that will lead to life, health, equity, and justice for all, and to act from anti-racist ideas that value black lives, that equalize all the racial groups in all their aesthetic and cultural differences.

In April, many Americans chose the racist explanation: saying black people were not taking the coronavirus as seriously as white people, until challenged by survey data and majority-white demonstrations demanding that states reopen. Then they argued that black Americans were disproportionately dying from COVID-19 because they have more preexisting conditions, due to their uniquely unhealthy behaviors. But according to the Foundation for AIDS Research, structural factors such as employment, access to health insurance and medical care, and the air and water quality in neighborhoods are drivers of black infections and deaths, and not "intrinsic characteristics of black communities or individual-level factors."

There's also no clear relationship between violent-crime rates and police-violence rates. And there's no direct relationship between violent-crime rates and black people. If there were, higher-income black neighborhoods would have the same levels of violent crime as lower-income black neighborhoods. But that is hardly the case.

Americans should be asking: Why are so many unarmed black people being killed by police while armed white people are simply arrested? Why are officials addressing violent crime in poorer neighborhoods by adding more police instead of more jobs? Why are black (and Latino) people during this pandemic less likely to be working from home; less likely to be insured; more likely to live in trauma-care deserts, lacking access to advanced emergency care; and more likely to live in polluted neighborhoods? The answer is what the Frederick Hoffmans of today refuse to believe: racism.

Instead, they say, like Donald Trump—like all those raging against the destruction of property and not black life—that they are "not racist." Hoffman introduced *Race Traits* by declaring that he was "free from the taint of prejudice or sentimentality . . . free from a personal bias." He was merely offering a "statement of the facts." In fact, the racial disparities he recorded documented America's racist policies.

Hoffman advanced the American nightmare. What will we advance? Hoffman implied we should *let them die*. Will we fight for black people to live?

History is calling the future from the streets of protest. What choice will we make? What world will we create? What will we be?

There are only two choices: racist or anti-racist.

FOR INFORMAL WRITING

"To be black and conscious of anti-black racism is to stare into the mirror of your own extinction." This is the epigraph to the original publication of the online article. What does Kendi argue here, in your view? Although we recognize the gravity and density of this quote, use evidence from the article itself to support what you believe is Kendi's point.

FOR DISCUSSION

1. What is the "nightmare?" How does it relate to a generally held "ideal" of the "American dream"?
2. What events, of which you are aware, inform your reading of this article? How and why?
3. "But only the lies of racist Americans are great." What does Kendi mean by this? How do the previous statements before this quote lead up to this contention?

FOR WRITING

Research several of the many analyses and responses to the book that Kendi refers to, *Race Traits and Tendencies of the American Negro* (1896) by Frederick Hoffman. The book characterizes African Americans as exceptionally disease-prone, and this is one excuse for inequities, for instance, in insurance costs. Examine a contemporary issue such as gaps in health outcomes, police brutality, or another, similar issue through the context of Hoffman's contentions and Kendi's refutations.

Pandemics Leave Us Forever Altered (2020)

Charles C. Mann (1955–)

A journalist specializing in scientific topics, Charles C. Mann's book 1491: New Revelations of the Americas Before Columbus *(2005) won the National Academies Communication Award in 2006. Mann is a regular contributor to* Science, The Atlantic, *and* Wired. *Interestingly, he has also written for the television series* Law and Order. *He also writes about population and the environment, most notably in his 2018 book* The Wizard and the Prophet. *The following was published in* The Atlantic *in the summer of 2020.*

In 2008 a young economist named Craig Garthwaite went looking for sick people. He found them in the National Health Interview Survey. Conducted annually by the US Census Bureau since 1957, the NHIS is the oldest and biggest continuing effort to track Americans' health. The survey asks a large sample of the citizenry whether it has a variety of ailments, including diabetes, kidney disorders, and several types of heart disease. Garthwaite sought out a particular subset of respondents: people born between October 1918 and June 1919.

Those months were the height and immediate aftermath of the world's worst-ever influenza pandemic. Although medical data from the time are too scant to be definitive, its first attack is generally said to have occurred in Kansas in March 1918, as the US was stepping up its involvement in the First World War. In a flurry of wartime propaganda, American and European governments downplayed the epidemic, which helped it spread. Estimates of the final death toll range from 17 million to 100 million, depending on assumptions about the number of uncounted victims. Almost 700,000 people are thought to have died in the United States—as a proportion of the population, equivalent to more than 2 million people today.

From The Atlantic. © 2020 The Atlantic Monthly Group, LLC. All rights reserved. Used under license.

Remarkably, the calamity left few visible traces in American culture. Hemingway, Faulkner, Fitzgerald, and Dos Passos saw its terrible effects firsthand, but almost never mentioned it in their work. Nor did the flu affect US policies—Congress didn't even allocate extra money for flu research afterward.

Just a few decades after the pandemic, American-history textbooks by the distinguished likes of Arthur M. Schlesinger Jr., Richard Hofstadter, Henry Steele Commager, and Samuel Eliot Morison said not a word about it. The first history of the 1918 flu wasn't published until 1976—I drew some of the above from it. Written by the late Alfred W. Crosby, the book is called *America's Forgotten Pandemic*.

Americans may have forgotten the 1918 pandemic, but it did not forget them. Garthwaite matched NHIS respondents' health conditions to the dates when their mothers were probably exposed to the flu. Mothers who got sick in the first months of pregnancy, he discovered, had babies who, 60 or 70 years later, were unusually likely to have diabetes; mothers afflicted at the end of pregnancy tended to bear children prone to kidney disease. The middle months were associated with heart disease.

Other studies showed different consequences. Children born during the pandemic grew into shorter, poorer, less educated adults with higher rates of physical disability than one would expect. Chances are that none of Garthwaite's flu babies ever knew about the shadow the pandemic cast over their lives. But they were living testaments to a brutal truth: Pandemics—even forgotten ones—have long-term, powerful aftereffects.

The distinguished historians can be forgiven for passing over this truth. Most modern people assume that our species controls its own destiny. *We're in charge!* we think. *After all, isn't this the Anthropocene?* Being modern people, historians have had trouble, as a profession, truly accepting that brainless packets of RNA and DNA can capsize the human enterprise in a few weeks or months.

The convulsive social changes of the 1920s—the frenzy of financial speculation, the resurgence of the Ku Klux Klan, the explosion of Dionysian popular culture (jazz, flappers, speakeasies)—were easily attributed to the war, an initiative directed and conducted by humans, rather than to the blind actions of microorganisms. But the microorganisms likely killed more people than the war did. And their effects weren't confined to European battlefields, but spread across the globe, emptying city streets and filling cemeteries on six continents.

Unlike the war, the flu was incomprehensible—the influenza virus wasn't even identified until 1931. It inspired fear of immigrants and foreigners, and anger toward the politicians who played down the virus. Like the war, influenza (and tuberculosis, which subsequently hit many flu sufferers) killed more men than women, skewing sex ratios for years afterward. Can one be sure that the ensuing, abrupt changes in gender roles had nothing to do with the virus?

We will probably never disentangle the war and the flu. But one way to summarize the impact of the pandemic is to say that its magnitude was in the same neighborhood as that of the "war to end all wars."

Nobody can predict the consequences of today's coronavirus pandemic. But history can tell us a little about what kind of landscape we're approaching.

Consider the Black Death. Sweeping through Europe from about 1347 to 1350, the plague killed somewhere between a third and half of all Europeans. In England, so many people died that the population didn't climb back to its pre-plague level for almost 400 years.

With the supply of European workers suddenly reduced and the demand for labor relatively unchanged, medieval landowners found themselves in a pickle: They could leave their grain to rot in the fields, or they could abandon all sense of right and wrong and raise wages enough to attract scarce workers. In northern Italy, landlords tended to raise wages, which fostered the development of a middle class. In southern Italy, the nobility enacted decrees to prevent peasants from leaving to take better offers. Some historians date the separation in fortunes of the two halves of Italy—the rich north, the poor south—to these decisions.

When the Black Death began, the English Plantagenets were in the middle of a long, brutal campaign to conquer France. The population losses meant such a rise in the cost of infantrymen that the whole enterprise foundered. English nobles did not occupy French châteaus. Instead they stayed home and tried to force their farmhands to accept lower wages. The result, the Peasants' Revolt of 1381, nearly toppled the English crown. King Richard II narrowly won out, but the monarchy's ability to impose taxes, and thus its will, was permanently weakened.

Nobody thinks the coronavirus will kill anywhere near as many people as the Black Death did. A shortage of labor due to corpses piling up in the streets will not cause wages to rise. Even so, the new virus has been a shock to society. The plague struck a Europe that was used to widespread death from contagious disease, especially among children. The coronavirus is hitting societies that regarded deadly epidemics as things of the past, like whalebone corsets and bowler hats.

When I went to college, in the 1970s, premed students carried around a fat textbook co-written by the Nobel Prize–winning virologist Macfarlane Burnet. "The most likely forecast about the future of infectious disease," it sunnily concluded, "is that it will be very dull." Such optimism was not exceptional. A few years later, Robert G. Petersdorf, a future president of the Association of American Medical Colleges, contemplated the current crop of MDs seeking certification in infectious disease and said, "I cannot conceive of a need for 309 more infectious-disease experts unless they spend their time culturing each other."

When AIDS came into the world, disease researchers reconsidered, loudly warning of new pandemics. Journalists wrote books with titles such as

The Coming Plague and *Spillover: Animal Infections and the Next Human Pandemic*. But not many nonscientists took these warnings to heart. The American public has not enjoyed its surprise reentry into the world of contagion and quarantine—and this unhappiness seems likely to have consequences.

Scholars have long posited that the shattering of norms by the Black Death was the first step on the path that led to the Renaissance and the Reformation. Neither government nor Church could explain the plague or provide a cure, the theory goes, leading to a crisis in belief. Secular and religious leaders died just like common people—the Black Death killed the archbishop of Canterbury, Thomas Bradwardine, a mere 40 days after he assumed office. People sought new sources of authority, finding them through direct personal experience with the world and with God.

To some extent, all of this is surely true. The plague came in waves, and after each wave doctors, clerics, and chroniclers speculated about the causes and described the treatments they'd seen deployed. As the University of Glasgow historian Samuel K. Cohn Jr. has shown, the early claims about the plague's origin invoked "floods of snakes and toads, snows that melted mountains, black smoke, venomous fumes, deafening thunder, lightning bolts, hailstones, and eight-legged worms that killed with their stench." Some writers blamed the poor: their fecundity, their improvidence, their sinfulness. Others pointed fingers at that ever-ready European bogeyman, the Jew.

To save themselves from the disease, scared Europeans sought favor from the heavens, most famously taking off their clothes in groups and striking one another with whips and sticks. Images of half-nude flagellants have, since Monty Python, become a comic staple. Far less comical was the accompanying flood of anti-Semitic violence. As it spread through Germany, Switzerland, France, Spain, and the Low Countries, it left behind a trail of beaten cadavers and burned homes.

Within a few decades, Cohn wrote, hysteria gave way to sober observation. Medical tracts stopped referring to conjunctions of Saturn and prescribed more earthly cures: ointments, herbs, methods for lancing boils. Even priestly writings focused on the empirical. "God was not mentioned," Cohn noted. The massacres of Jews mostly stopped.

It's easy to see this as a comforting parable of rationality winning out over the engines of rumor, prejudice, and superstition, ultimately leading to the Renaissance and the Enlightenment. But the lesson seems more that humans confronting unexpected disaster engage in a contest for explanation—and the outcome can have consequences that ripple for decades or centuries.

As I write, the contest for explanation is well under way—Donald Trump is to blame, or Barack Obama, or the Centers for Disease Control and Prevention, or China, or the US military's biowarfare experiments, or Bill Gates. Nobody has yet invoked eight-legged worms. But in our age of social media, the engines of rumor, prejudice, and superstition may have even greater power than they did in the era of the Black Death.

Christopher Columbus's journey to the Americas set off the worst demographic catastrophe in history. The indigenous societies of the Americas had few communicable diseases—no smallpox, no measles, no cholera, no typhoid, no malaria, no bubonic plague. When Europeans imported these diseases into the Western Hemisphere, it was as if all the suffering and death these ailments had caused in Europe during the previous millennia were compressed into about 150 years.

Somewhere between two-thirds and nine-tenths of the people in the Americas died. Many later European settlers, like my umpteen-great-grandparents, believed they were coming to a vacant wilderness. But the land was not empty; it had been *emptied*—a world of loss encompassed in a shift of tense.

Absent the diseases, it is difficult to imagine how small groups of poorly equipped Europeans at the end of very long supply chains could have survived and even thrived in the alien ecosystems of the Americas. "I fully support banning travel from Europe to prevent the spread of infectious disease," the Cherokee journalist Rebecca Nagle remarked after President Trump announced his plan to do this. "I just think it's 528 years too late."

For Native Americans, the epidemic era lasted for centuries, as did its repercussions. Isolated Hawaii had almost no bacterial or viral disease until 1778, when the islands were "discovered" by Captain James Cook. Islanders learned the cruel facts of contagion so rapidly that by 1806, local leaders were refusing to allow European ships to dock if they had sick people on board. Nonetheless, Hawaii's king and queen traveled from their clean islands to London, that cesspool of disease, arriving in May 1824. By July they were dead—measles.

Kamehameha II and Kamāmalu had gone to Britain to negotiate an alliance against the United States, which they correctly believed had designs on their nation. Their deaths scuttled the talks, and their successor, 12-year-old King Kamehameha III, could not resume them. The results changed the islands' political destiny. Undeterred by the British navy, the US annexed Hawaii in 1898. Historians have seldom noted the connection between measles and the presidency of Barack Obama.

As a rule, epidemics create what researchers call a "U-shaped curve" of mortality—high death rates among the very young and very old, lower rates among working-age adults. (The 1918 flu was an exception; a disproportionate number of 20-somethings perished.) For Native peoples, the U-shaped curve was as devastating as the sheer loss of life. As an indigenous archaeologist once put it to me, the epidemics simultaneously robbed his nation of its future and its past:

the former, by killing all the children; the latter, by killing all the elders, who were its storehouses of wisdom and experience.

For reasons as yet unknown, the U-shaped curve does not apply to today's coronavirus. This virus largely (but not entirely) spares the young and targets the old. Terrible stories of it sweeping through nursing homes reinforce this impression, especially if, like me, you've lost a relative in one. The result will be, among other things, a test of how much contemporary US society values the elderly.

So far, the evidence suggests: not much. The speed with which pundits emerged to propose that the US could more easily tolerate a raft of dead oldsters than an economic contraction indicates that the reservoir of appreciation for today's elders is not as deep as it once was. This change may reflect another: Today's old are typically older than the old of the past, when life spans were shorter, and more likely to be retired.

Past societies mourned the loss of collective memory caused by epidemics. Ours may not, at least at first.

I have no idea what the ultimate effects of the coronavirus will be in this country, but I hope that they will be like those of the 2003 SARS epidemic in Hong Kong. That epidemic, which killed about 300 people, was stopped only by heroic communal efforts. (As a percentage of the population, the equivalent US death toll would be about 15,000.)

Everyone in Hong Kong knows the city dodged a bullet. Or, at any rate, it seems that way when I visit. My work has taken me there, off and on, since 1992. In a city that once resounded with smokers' coughs, people now don hospital masks at the first sign of a cold. Omnipresent signs—in hotel elevators, on convenience-store doors, in office waiting rooms—describe how often their locations are disinfected. An amazing number of people wear hospital gloves to serve food, handle papers, even push elevator buttons. During my stays, the TV news seems always to be covering disease outbreaks in remote places, as if trying to keep viewers on alert.

These measures may suggest a community in the grip of fear. But the masks and signs and gloves seem more like the "victory gardens" in families' front yards during the Second World War—cheerful public notices of people doing their part. Most important, Hong Kong may have contained COVID-19 faster than any other place in the world.

The last time I went there was during last fall's democracy protests. At one point, I found myself near a university at the center of the unrest. Almost nobody was outside and the shops were closed. There was a lot of trash on the ground and smoke in the air. As I stood there, befuddled, a man ran out of a convenience store and pulled me inside. "The police are coming," he said. "Very dangerous!" Inside was a cross section of Hong Kong citizens—young and old, sneakers and salaryman shoes, quite a few in makeshift masks. I thanked the proprietor for rescuing me from what could have been an unpleasant encounter. "We are all here together," someone said.

Later it occurred to me that a possible legacy of Hong Kong's success with SARS is that its citizens seem to put more faith in collective action than they used to. I've met plenty of people there who believe that the members of their community can work together for the greater good—as they did in suppressing SARS and will, with luck, keep doing with COVID-19. It's probably naive of me to hope that successfully containing the coronavirus would impart some of the same faith in the United States, but I do anyway.

FOR INFORMAL WRITING

How would you explain the context that motivated Mann and within which he wrote this article? What about the article tells you this?

FOR DISCUSSION

1. How do pandemics "leave us forever altered?"
2. Why does Mann end on a hopeful note? Will history bear him out? What do you think, and why?
3. Why might Mann's response to the pandemic about which he's writing include a deep dive into the history of both epidemics and pandemics worldwide? What does he learn?

FOR WRITING

In the article, Mann references well-known epidemics and pandemics such as the AIDS crisis, the Black Death, the measles, and SARS. Explore further the social responses to one or two of these crises. What were these responses? How did they reveal themselves? What were their effects? What parallels, if any, can you draw to current, similar health crises?

WHAT'S NEW IS OLD

Read this essay along with Martin Luther King, Jr.'s "Letter from a Birmingham Jail." How are they similar in structure? In purpose? How do you know? In what ways do both selections address an audience of the advantaged towards ameliorating the situation of the disadvantaged?

Facebook Is a Doomsday Machine (2020)
Adrienne LaFrance (1982–)

Executive Editor of The Atlantic *and former reporter for a variety of publications, Adrienne LaFrance earned the BA in Journalism from Michigan State University and the MS in Journalism from Boston University. A journalist of varied interests, she has worked as a staff writer at the Nieman Journalism Lab and as a reporter in the Washington bureau of Honolulu Civil Beat. LaFrance has also worked as reporter and news anchor for Hawaii Public Radio and as a news writer for Boston's WBUR, a National Public Radio affiliate.*

The doomsday machine was never supposed to exist. It was meant to be a thought experiment that went like this: Imagine a device built with the sole purpose of destroying all human life. Now suppose that machine is buried deep underground, but connected to a computer, which is in turn hooked up to sensors in cities and towns across the United States.

The sensors are designed to sniff out signs of the impending apocalypse—not to prevent the end of the world, but to complete it. If radiation levels suggest nuclear explosions in, say, three American cities simultaneously, the sensors notify the Doomsday Machine, which is programmed to detonate several nuclear warheads in response. At that point, there is no going back. The fission chain reaction that produces an atomic explosion is initiated enough times over to extinguish all life on Earth. There is a terrible flash of light, a great booming sound, then a sustained roar. We have a word for the scale of destruction that the Doomsday Machine would unleash: megadeath.

Nobody is pining for megadeath. But megadeath is not the only thing that makes the Doomsday Machine petrifying. The real terror is in its autonomy, this idea that it would be programmed to detect a series of environmental inputs, then

---

From The Atlantic. © 2020 The Atlantic Monthly Group, LLC. All rights reserved. Used under license.

to act, without human interference. "There is no chance of human intervention, control, and final decision," wrote the military strategist Herman Kahn in his 1960 book, *On Thermonuclear War*, which laid out the hypothetical for a Doomsday Machine. The concept was to render nuclear war unwinnable, and therefore unthinkable.

Kahn concluded that automating the extinction of all life on Earth would be immoral. Even an infinitesimal risk of error is too great to justify the Doomsday Machine's existence. "And even if we give up the computer and make the Doomsday Machine reliably controllable by decision makers," Kahn wrote, "it is still not controllable enough." No machine should be that powerful by itself—but no one person should be either.

The Soviets really did make a version of the Doomsday Machine during the Cold War. They nicknamed it "Dead Hand." But so far, somewhat miraculously, we have figured out how to live with the bomb. Now we need to learn how to survive the social web.

People tend to complain about Facebook as if something recently curdled. There's a notion that the social web was once useful, or at least that it could have been good, if only we had pulled a few levers: some moderation and fact-checking here, a bit of regulation there, perhaps a federal antitrust lawsuit. But that's far too sunny and shortsighted a view. Today's social networks, Facebook chief among them, were built to encourage the things that make them so harmful. It is in their very architecture.

I've been thinking for years about what it would take to make the social web magical in all the right ways—less extreme, less toxic, more true—and I realized only recently that I've been thinking far too narrowly about the problem. I've long wanted Mark Zuckerberg to admit that Facebook is a media company, to take responsibility for the informational environment he created in the same way that the editor of a magazine would. (I pressed him on this once and he laughed.) In recent years, as Facebook's mistakes have compounded and its reputation has tanked, it has become clear that negligence is only part of the problem. No one, not even Mark Zuckerberg, can control the product he made. I've come to realize that Facebook is not a media company. It's a Doomsday Machine.

The social web is doing exactly what it was built for. Facebook does not exist to seek truth and report it, or to improve civic health, or to hold the powerful to account, or to represent the interests of its users, though these phenomena may be occasional by-products of its existence. The company's early mission was to "give people the power to share and make the world more open and connected." Instead, it took the concept of "community" and sapped it of all moral meaning. The rise of QAnon, for example, is one of the social web's logical conclusions. That's because Facebook—along with Google and YouTube—is perfect for amplifying and spreading disinformation at lightning speed to global audiences. Facebook is an agent of government propaganda, targeted harassment, terrorist recruitment, emotional manipulation, and genocide—a world-historic weapon that lives not underground, but in a Disneyland-inspired campus in Menlo Park, California.

The giants of the social web—Facebook and its subsidiary Instagram; Google and its subsidiary YouTube; and, to a lesser extent, Twitter—have achieved success by being dogmatically value-neutral in their pursuit of what I'll call *megascale*. Somewhere along the way, Facebook decided that it needed not just a very large user base, but a tremendous one, unprecedented in size. That decision set Facebook on a path to escape velocity, to a tipping point where it can harm society just by existing.

Limitations to the Doomsday Machine comparison are obvious: Facebook cannot in an instant reduce a city to ruins the way a nuclear bomb can. And whereas the Doomsday Machine was conceived of as a world-ending device so as to forestall the end of the world, Facebook started because a semi-inebriated Harvard undergrad was bored one night. But the stakes are still life-and-death. Megascale is nearly the existential threat that megadeath is. No single machine should be able to control the fate of the world's population—and that's what both the Doomsday Machine and Facebook are built to do.

The cycle of harm perpetuated by Facebook's scale-at-any-cost business model is plain to see. Scale and engagement are valuable to Facebook because they're valuable to advertisers. These incentives lead to design choices such as reaction buttons that encourage users to engage easily and often, which in turn encourage users to share ideas that will provoke a strong response. Every time you click a reaction button on Facebook, an algorithm records it, and sharpens its portrait of who you are. The hyper-targeting of users, made possible by reams of their personal data, creates the perfect environment for manipulation—by advertisers, by political campaigns, by emissaries of disinformation, and of course by Facebook itself, which ultimately controls what you see and what you don't see on the site. Facebook has enlisted a corps of approximately 15,000 moderators, people paid to watch unspeakable things—murder, gang rape, and other depictions of graphic violence that wind up on the platform. Even as Facebook has insisted that it is a value-neutral vessel for the material its users choose to publish, moderation is a lever the company has tried to pull again and again. But there aren't enough moderators speaking enough languages, working enough hours, to stop the biblical flood of shit that Facebook unleashes on the world, because 10 times out of 10, the algorithm is faster and more powerful than a person. At megascale, this algorithmically warped personalized informational environment is extraordinarily difficult to moderate in a meaningful way, and extraordinarily dangerous as a result.

These dangers are not theoretical, and they're exacerbated by megascale, which makes the platform a tantalizing place to experiment on people. Facebook has conducted social-contagion experiments on its users without telling them. Facebook has acted as a force for digital colonialism, attempting to become the de facto (and only) experience of the internet for people all over the world. Facebook has bragged about its ability to influence the outcome of elections. Unlawful militant groups use Facebook to organize. Government officials use Facebook to mislead their own citizens, and to tamper with elections. Military officials have exploited Facebook's complacency to carry out genocide. Facebook inadvertently auto-generated jaunty recruitment videos for the Islamic State featuring anti-Semitic messages and burning American flags.

Even after U.S. intelligence agencies identified Facebook as a main battleground for information warfare and foreign interference in the 2016 election, the company has failed to stop the spread of extremism, hate speech, propaganda, disinformation, and conspiracy theories on its site. Neo-Nazis stayed active on Facebook by taking out ads even after they were formally banned. And it wasn't until October of this year, for instance, that Facebook announced it would remove groups, pages, and Instagram accounts devoted to QAnon, as well as any posts denying the Holocaust. (Previously Zuckerberg had defended Facebook's decision not to remove disinformation about the Holocaust, saying of Holocaust deniers, "I don't think that they're *intentionally* getting it wrong." He later clarified that he didn't mean to defend Holocaust deniers.) Even so, Facebook routinely sends emails to users recommending the newest QAnon groups. White supremacists and deplatformed MAGA trolls may flock to smaller social platforms such as Gab and Parler, but these platforms offer little aside from a narrative of martyrdom without megascale.

In the days after the 2020 presidential election, Zuckerberg authorized a tweak to the Facebook algorithm so that high-accuracy news sources such as NPR would receive preferential visibility in people's feeds, and hyper-partisan pages such as *Breitbart News*'s and Occupy Democrats' would be buried, according to *The New York Times*, offering proof that Facebook could, if it wanted to, turn a dial to reduce disinformation—and offering a reminder that Facebook has the power to flip a switch and change what billions of people see online.

The decision to touch the dial was highly unusual for Facebook. Think about it this way: The Doomsday Machine's sensors detected something harmful in the environment and chose not to let its algorithms automatically blow it up across the web as usual. This time a human intervened to mitigate harm. The only problem is that reducing the prevalence of content that Facebook calls "bad for the world" also reduces people's engagement with the site. In its experiments with human intervention, the *Times* reported, Facebook calibrated the dial so that *just enough* harmful content stayed in users' news feeds to keep them coming back for more.

Facebook's stated mission—to make the world more open and connected—has always seemed, to me, phony at best, and imperialist at worst. After all, today's empires are born on the web. Facebook is a borderless nation-state, with a population of users nearly as big as China and India combined, and it is governed largely by secret algorithms. Hillary Clinton told me earlier this year that talking to Zuckerberg feels like negotiating with the authoritarian head of a foreign state. "This is a global company that has huge influence in ways that we're only beginning to understand," she said.

I recalled Clinton's warning a few weeks ago, when Zuckerberg defended the decision not to suspend Steve Bannon from Facebook after he argued, in essence, for the beheading of two senior US officials, the infectious-disease doctor Anthony Fauci and FBI Director Christopher Wray. The episode got me thinking about a question that's unanswerable but that I keep asking people anyway: How much real-world violence would never have happened if Facebook didn't exist? One of the people I've asked is Joshua Geltzer, a former White House counterterrorism official who is now teaching at Georgetown Law. In counterterrorism circles, he told me, people are fond of pointing out how good the United States has been at keeping terrorists out since 9/11. That's wrong, he said. In fact, "terrorists are entering every single day, every single hour, every single minute" through Facebook.

The website that's perhaps best known for encouraging mass violence is the image board 4chan—which was followed by 8chan, which then became 8kun. These boards are infamous for being the sites where multiple mass-shooting suspects have shared manifestos before homicide sprees. The few people who are willing to defend these sites unconditionally do so from a position of free-speech absolutism. That argument is worthy of consideration. But there's something architectural about the site that merits attention, too: There are no algorithms on 8kun, only a community of users who post what they want. People use 8kun to publish abhorrent ideas, but at least the community isn't pretending to be something it's not. The biggest social platforms claim to be similarly neutral and pro–free speech when in fact no two people see the same feed. Algorithmically tweaked environments feed on user data and manipulate user experience, and not ultimately for the purpose of serving the user. Evidence of real-world violence can be easily traced back to both Facebook and 8kun. But 8kun doesn't manipulate its users or the informational environment they're in. Both sites are harmful. But Facebook might actually be worse for humanity.

"What a dreadful set of choices when you frame it that way," Geltzer told me when I put this question to him in another conversation. "The idea of a free-for-all sounds really bad until you see what the purportedly moderated and curated set of platforms is yielding . . . It may not be blood onscreen, but it can really do a lot of damage."

In previous eras, US officials could at least study, say, Nazi propaganda during World War II, and fully grasp what the Nazis wanted people to believe. Today, "it's not a filter bubble; it's a filter shroud," Geltzer said. "I don't even know what others with personalized experiences are seeing." Another expert in this realm, Mary McCord, the legal director at the Institute for Constitutional Advocacy and Protection at Georgetown Law, told me that she thinks 8kun may be more blatant in terms of promoting violence but that Facebook is "in some ways way worse" because of its reach. "There's no barrier to entry with Facebook," she said. "In every situation of extremist violence we've looked into, we've found Facebook postings. And that reaches *tons* of people. The broad reach is what brings people into the fold and normalizes extremism and makes it mainstream." In other words, it's the megascale that makes Facebook so dangerous.

Looking back, it can seem like Zuckerberg's path to world domination was inevitable. There's the computerized version of Risk he coded in ninth grade; his longstanding interest in the Roman empire; his obsession with information flow and human psychology. There's the story of his first bona fide internet scandal, when he hacked into Harvard's directory and lifted photos of students without their permission to make the hot-or-not- style website FaceMash. ("Child's play" was how Zuckerberg later described the ease with which he broke into Harvard's system.) There's the disconnect between his lip service to privacy and the way Facebook actually works. (Here's Zuckerberg in a private chat with a friend years ago, on the mountain of data he'd obtained from Facebook's early users: "I have over 4,000 emails, pictures, addresses . . . People just submitted it. I don't know why. They 'trust me.' Dumb fucks.") At various points over the years, he's listed the following interests in his Facebook profile: Eliminating Desire, Minimalism, Making Things, Breaking Things, Revolutions, Openness, Exponential Growth, Social Dynamics, Domination.

Facebook's megascale gives Zuckerberg an unprecedented degree of influence over the global population. If he isn't the most powerful person on the planet, he's very near the top. "It's insane to have that much speechifying, silencing, and permitting power, not to mention being the ultimate holder of algorithms that determine the virality of anything on the internet," Geltzer told me.

"The thing he oversees has such an effect on cognition and people's beliefs, which can change what they do with their nuclear weapons or their dollars."

Facebook's new oversight board, formed in response to backlash against the platform and tasked with making decisions concerning moderation and free expression, is an extension of that power. "The first 10 decisions they make will have more effect on speech in the country and the world than the next 10 decisions rendered by the US Supreme Court," Geltzer said. "That's power. That's real power."

In 2005, the year I joined Facebook, the site still billed itself as an online directory to "Look up people at your school. See how people know each other. Find people in your classes and groups." That summer, in Palo Alto, Zuckerberg gave an interview to a young filmmaker, who later posted the clip to YouTube. In it, you can see Zuckerberg still figuring out what Facebook is destined to be. The conversation is a reminder of the improbability of Zuckerberg's youth when he launched Facebook. (It starts with him asking, "Should I put the beer down?" He's holding a red Solo cup.) Yet, at 21 years old, Zuckerberg articulated something about his company that has held true, to dangerous effect: Facebook is not a single place on the web, but rather, "a lot of different individual communities."

Today that includes QAnon and other extremist groups. Back then, it meant mostly juvenile expressions of identity in groups such as "I Went to a Public School... Bitch" and, at Harvard, referencing the neoclassical main library, "The We Need to Have Sex in Widener Before We Graduate Interest Group." In that 2005 interview, Zuckerberg is asked about the future of Facebook, and his response feels, in retrospect, like a tragedy: "I mean, there doesn't necessarily have to be more. Like, a lot of people are focused on taking over the world, or doing the biggest thing, getting the most users. I think, like, part of making a difference and doing something cool is focusing intensely... I mean, I really just want to see everyone focus on college and create a really cool college-directory product that just, like, is very relevant for students and has a lot of information that people care about when they're in college."

The funny thing is: This localized approach is part of what made megascale possible. Early constraints around membership—the requirement at first that users attended Harvard, and then that they attended any Ivy League school, and then that they had an email address ending in .edu—offered a sense of cohesiveness and community. It made people feel more comfortable sharing more of themselves. And more sharing among clearly defined demographics was good for business. In 2004, Zuckerberg said Facebook ran advertisements only to cover server costs.

But over the next two years Facebook completely upended and redefined the entire advertising industry. The pre-social web destroyed classified ads, but the one-two punch of Facebook and Google decimated local news and most of the magazine industry—publications fought in earnest for digital pennies, which had replaced print dollars, and social giants scooped them all up anyway. No news organization can compete with the megascale of the social web. It's just too massive.

The on-again, off-again Facebook executive Chris Cox once talked about the "magic number" for start-ups, and how after a company surpasses 150 employees, things go sideways. "I've talked to so many start-up CEOs that after they pass this number, weird stuff starts to happen," he said at a conference in 2016. This idea comes from the anthropologist Robin Dunbar, who argued that 148 is the maximum number of stable social connections a person can maintain. If we were to apply that same logic to the stability of a social platform, what number would we find?

"I think the sweet spot is 20 to 20,000 people," the writer and internet scholar Ethan Zuckerman, who has spent much of his adult life thinking about how to build a better web, told me. "It's hard to have any degree of real connectivity after that."

In other words, if the Dunbar number for running a company or maintaining a cohesive social life is 150 people; the magic number for a functional social platform is maybe 20,000 people. Facebook now has *2.7 billion* monthly users.

On the precipice of Facebook's exponential growth, in 2007, Zuckerberg said something in an interview with the *Los Angeles Times* that now takes on a much darker meaning: "The things that are most powerful aren't the things that people would have done otherwise if they didn't do them on Facebook. Instead, it's the things that would never have happened otherwise."

Of the many things humans are consistently terrible at doing, seeing the future is somewhere near the top of the list. This flaw became a preoccupation among Megadeath Intellectuals such as Herman Kahn and his fellow economists, mathematicians, and former military officers at the Rand Corporation in the 1960s.

Kahn and his colleagues helped invent modern futurism, which was born of the existential dread that the bomb ushered in, and hardened by the understanding that most innovation is horizontal in nature—a copy of what already exists, rather than wholly new. Real invention is extraordinarily rare, and far more disruptive.

The logician and philosopher Olaf Helmer-Hirschberg, who overlapped with Kahn at Rand and would later co-found the Institute for the Future, arrived in California after having fled the Nazis, an experience that gave his desire to peer into the future a particular kind of urgency. He argued that the acceleration of technological change had established the need for a new epistemological approach to fields such as engineering, medicine, the social sciences, and so on. "No longer does it take generations for a new pattern of living conditions to evolve," he wrote, "but we are going through several major adjustments in our lives, and our children will have to adopt continual adaptation as a way of life." In 1965, he wrote a book called *Social Technology* that aimed to create a scientific methodology for predicting the future.

In those same years, Kahn was dreaming up his own hypothetical machine to provide a philosophical framework for the new threats humanity faced. He called it the Doomsday Machine, and also the Doomsday-in-a-Hurry Machine, and also the Homicide Pact Machine. Stanley Kubrick famously borrowed the concept for the 1964 film *Dr. Strangelove*, the cinematic apotheosis of the fatalism that came with living on hair-trigger alert for nuclear annihilation.

Today's fatalism about the brokenness of the internet feels similar. We're still in the infancy of this century's triple digital revolution of the internet, smartphones, and the social web, and we find ourselves in a dangerous and unstable informational environment, powerless to resist forces of manipulation and exploitation that we know are exerted on us but remain mostly invisible. The Doomsday Machine offers a lesson: We should not accept this current arrangement. No single machine should be able to control so many people.

If the age of reason was, in part, a reaction to the existence of the printing press, and 1960s futurism was a reaction to the atomic bomb, we need a new philosophical and moral framework for living with the social web—a new Enlightenment for the information age, and one that will carry us back to shared reality and empiricism.

Andrew Bosworth, one of Facebook's longtime executives, has compared Facebook to sugar—in that it is "delicious" but best enjoyed in moderation. In a memo originally posted to Facebook's internal network last year, he argued for a philosophy of personal responsibility. "My grandfather took such a stance towards bacon and I admired him for it," Bosworth wrote. "And social media is likely much less fatal than bacon." But viewing Facebook merely as a vehicle for individual consumption ignores the fact of what it is—a network. Facebook is also a business, and a place where people spend time with one another. Put it this way: If you owned a store and someone walked in and started shouting Nazi propaganda or recruiting terrorists near the cash register, would you, as the shop owner, tell all of the other customers you couldn't possibly intervene?

Anyone who is serious about mitigating the damage done to humankind by the social web should, of course, consider quitting Facebook and Instagram and Twitter and any other algorithmically distorted informational environments that manipulate people. But we need to adopt a broader view of what it will take to fix the brokenness of the social web. That will require challenging the logic of today's platforms—and first and foremost challenging the very concept of megascale as a way that humans gather. If megascale is what gives Facebook its power, and what makes it dangerous, collective action against the web as it is today is necessary for change. The web's existing logic tells us that social platforms are free in exchange for a feast of user data; that major networks are necessarily global and centralized; that moderators make the rules. None of that need be the case. We need people who dismantle these notions by building alternatives. And we need enough people to care about these other alternatives to break the spell of venture capital and mass attention that fuels megascale and creates fatalism about the web as it is now.

I still believe the internet is good for humanity, but that's despite the social web, not because of it. We must also find ways to repair the aspects of our society and culture that the social web has badly damaged. This will require intellectual independence, respectful debate, and the same rebellious streak that helped establish Enlightenment values centuries ago.

We may not be able to predict the future, but we do know how it is made: through flashes of rare and genuine invention, sustained by people's time and attention. Right now, too many people are allowing algorithms and tech giants to manipulate them, and reality is slipping from our grasp as a result. This century's Doomsday Machine is here, and humming along.

It does not have to be this way.

FOR INFORMAL WRITING

How might you reconcile your own engagement with social media with LaFrance's article?

FOR DISCUSSION

1. What is LaFrance's central argument? How does she prove her points? Is this proof effective? (Why or why not?)
2. How are the strategies of Facebook, as articulated by the author, deliberate and insidious as a business model and as a media platform?
3. What have been the political ramifications of Facebook's prevalence? How would you apply these ramifications to other social media? (And what are we all to do about it?)

FOR WRITING

Research a number of articles—from credible sources—about the comparative upsides, downsides, and downright concerns about the prevalence of social media. To what conclusion do you come? How do the authors of these pieces (choose at least two) articulate their arguments? How do those arguments either credibly confirm or refute LaFrance's central claims?

WHAT'S NEW IS OLD

Consider this piece alongside Nicholas Carr's "Is Google Making Us Stupid?" Although more than a decade separates these articles—which may seem like many or very few, depending on one's perspective—examine whether LaFrance's piece seems to be the inevitable outcome of Carr's warnings. What do you think, and why?

Index

abolition/abolitionists, 23–43, 37–38, 45, 61, 224. *See also* slaves/slavery guilt of American churches, 37–38
speech by Frederick Douglass, 23–43
abortions, 10, 289
activism
Black Lives Matter movement, 436
civil rights movement, 107, 125, 139–140, 145–149
do-nothingism *vs.*, 132
nonviolent activism, 125–128, 125–137, 132–133, 136–137, 155
youth activism, 457
Affordable Care Act, 433, 437
African Americans, 107–124. *See also* Obama, Barack; *Race Traits* (Hoffman); slaves/slavery
Black ghettos, 115, 121–122, 151, 220
Black nationalism, 132, 145–146, 150–155, 446, 448
civil rights struggles, 139, 141–142, 145–149, 153, 229
fear experienced by black men, 231–235
fear of black men in public places, 231–232
jailing of, 125–137, 438, 443
King, Jr.'s letter from jail, 125–137
lynchings, 424, 446, 485
reasons for demanding apologies, 471–474
solo hike of the Appalachian Trail by a woman, 451–458
student debt data, 434
urge for freedom of, 132
women of color, 228
AIDS (acquired immunodeficiency syndrome), 490, 495–496, 499
Alabama Christian Movement for Human Rights, 126–127

American Equal Rights Association for Women, 45
America's Forgotten Pandemic (Crosby), 494
Amontillado wine, 17–20
animals, communication with, 238–240
anti-business mindset, 61
anti-Semitism, 219–220, 223, 225–229, 446, 496, 504
anti-slavery speech, by Frederick Douglass, 23–43
apartheid, South Africa, 296, 314
apologies, reasons for demanding, 471–474
artificial intelligence (AI), 369–371
Asian youth, 319–326
Auden, W. H., 219, 270
Australia gold rush, 66–67

back-to-nature mindset, 61
Barnes, Albert, 37–38
bedtime/sleeping advice, by Twain, 78
Beecher, Henry Ward, 38
beggars, 9–12, 15
Bible, 30, 36–38, 66, 222, 272–273, 300, 314, 375
Biden, Joe, 423
bigotry, 55, 69, 200, 222, 432
Birmingham, Alabama, 125–137
Black Death, 495–497
Black Entertainment Television (BET), 416–419
Black Lives Matter movement, 436
blogging, 364–365, 388, 409, 415
bombings
in Birmingham, Alabama, 126–127
in Oklahoma, 402
in Vietnam War, 159–161, 164–166, 171, 176, 186–191, 198, 201
A Book of Common Prayer (Didion), 216–217
book selection advice, by Twain, 79–80
Brin, Sergey, 369
Buber, Martin, 130

513

Buddhism, 89–90, 164, 184, 311–313, 317
Burma (present day Myanmar), 89–95
Bush, George H. W., 395
Bush, George W., 433
Bush, Jeb, 375

California gold rush, 66–67
Canada, 251–264
capitalism, 165, 303, 443
cave allegory, 1–7
cave wall drawings, 1–2
cellphones, 416, 419, 487
Cheyenne Mountain Air Force Station, 299–300, 304
Chicana Spanish, 243–249
children
    age-related saleability of, 10–12
    Asian youth, 319–326
    breeding of, for food, 11, 13–14
    cooking and eating of, 11, 13
    cost of nursing by beggar mothers, 11–12
    fear of a father, 109
    of mothers begging for alms, 9–10
    profitability of breeding, 13
    Twain's advice to youth, 77–80
Christianity, 35, 37, 39–40, 127, 130–136, 135, 150, 220–223
civil-disobedience mindset, 61
"Civil Disobedience" (Thoreau), 61
civil rights, 128, 147
    Black Civil Rights struggles, 145, 148, 229
    Black nationalism and, 132, 145–146, 150–155, 446, 448
    civil rights movement (activism), 107, 125, 139–140, 145–149
    legislation, 141–142, 423
Clinton, Bill, 211, 293, 311, 439
Clinton, Hillary, 293–295, 415–416, 421, 423, 439–440, 446–447, 505
Cohen, Leonard, 271
Colonial America (American colonies), 25–26, 28
coming out/outing of gay people, 407–414. *See also* gay people
communication/conversation. *See also* social media
    with animals, 238–240
    Chicana Spanish, 243–249
    First Amendment and, 244
    linguistic terrorism, 247–249
    ordinary/surface conversation, 70
    overcoming ordinary/surface conversation, 70
    role of the Internet, 368
    speaking Chicana Spanish, 243–249
Congress (United States), 35, 63, 74, 143–144, 208–209, 305, 427, 439, 442, 494
Constitutional Convention, 210

Constitution (New York State), 48, 59
Constitution (United States), 40–41, 130, 141, 143–144, 207–211, 244, 327
Continental Congress (1776), 26
coolies, 91, 95
Cooper, Anderson, 409–410, 409–411
COVID-19 pandemic, 486–490, 498–499
crime, 31–32, 35, 46, 48–51, 115
crimes against humanity, 296
    hate crimes, 410–411, 455
    high crimes and misdemeanors, 208–209
    racial crime data, 488
    violent crime rates, 490
    war crimes, 160, 197
Crosby, Alfred W., 494
cultural assimilation, 225–226, 228, 279–291

dances/dancing, 84, 98
darkness *vs.* light, 2–5
Dawkins, Richard, 390
death
    contemplation of/preparing for, 387–391
    near-death experience, 401–404
Declaration of Independence, 26–27, 29, 41, 135, 190
deep reading, 364–365, 371
Defense of Marriage Act (1996), 410
deindustrialization, 443
Democratic Party, 142–144, 155, 195, 327–328, 407, 420, 423, 426–429, 439–440, 445
despotism, 32–33
diamond necklace, 84
divine contemplations, 4
dogs
    owning/taking care of, 319–325
    police dogs, 136, 146–147
    racism and, 233–234
Don't Ask, Don't Tell policy, 423
Doomsday Machine, 501–511. *See also* Facebook
Dr. Strangelove film (Kubrick), 509
drunkenness, 17–18
Dylan, Bob, 271, 391, 417

education, Plato's vision of, 5
elephants, 70, 89–95
Emerson, Ralph Waldo, 61, 316, 317
employment
    of an efficient/valuable man, 64
    of children, 10
    women's rights and, 51
equal rights/equal rights movement
    for colored people, 131
    for gay people, 410
    Plessy v. Ferguson and, 485
    for women, 45, 58–59

Facebook, 442, 455, 501–511
fashion, 81–84, 98
fast food, history of, 299–307
fatwa on Salman Rushdie, 393–398
Federalist Papers (Hamilton), 208
feminism/feminist perspective, 228–229, 247–248, 301, 408, 474
Fillmore, Millard, 23, 36
firearms. *See* guns
firearms advice, by Twain, 78–79
First Amendment (US Constitution), 130, 244, 327
food
    children as, 11, 13–14
    history of fast food, 299–307
    racial discrimination and, 136
    traveling and, 310
    Vietnam War shortages, 190
Foreman, Richard, 371
Fortunato, 17–20
free men (post-slavery), 108
Fugitive Slave Law (U.S.), 35–36
funeral homes, 303
funerals of a father, 107–108, 118–121
    of a husband, 53
    of a mother, 325

Garrison, William Lloyd, 42–43
Garthwaite, Craig, 493–494
gay marriage, 410, 412
gay people
    coming out/outing of, 407–414
    discrimination against, 456
    lesbians, 219–229, 411–412, 463, 467
    LGBT people, 410–411, 461–469
    Odd Future collective, 412
    transgender people, 466–469
genocide, 482, 503–504
ghettos
    Black ghettos, 115, 121–122, 151, 220, 232
    Jewish ghettos, 222, 226, 295, 465
    politics and, 432
globalization, 443
golden rule, 56–57
gold rush, 66–67
Google, 361–372
GOP. *See* Republican Party
Graham, Billy, 152
gratitude
    for the Declaration of Independence, 26, 29
    of Douglass, 24
    expressed in love songs, 276
    of Wiesel, 294
graveyards, robbing of, 68
Great Britain, 24–26, 28, 90, 497
Greek philosophy, 1–7
Greene, Graham, 314

grieving, management of, 251–264
guns, 78–79, 327–332, 469, 483

habitation, 3–4, 7
Hamilton, Alexander, 207, 208
Hanoi, Vietnam, 157–205
Harlem, New York City, 107, 115, 119, 121–122, 175
hatred, 39, 107, 114–116, 121–123, 132, 225, 227, 295, 442, 452
Hitler, Adolf, 131, 295–296, 468
Ho Chi Minh, 167–168, 184–188, 192, 195
Hoffman, Frederick, 486–491
Holocaust, 223–224, 293, 465, 504. *See also* Nazi Germany, concentration camps
Howitt, William, 67–68
human rights, 47, 126–127, 147–148, 157

impeachment, 207–211
imperialism, 90, 165
income inequality, 443
Independence Day (July 4th), 24, 32
influenza pandemic (1918), 351–362
    age-related curve of deaths, 358–360
    background, 352–353
    cause of, 352
    global impact, 351
    H1N1 virus strain, 351–353, 357–358, 361
    H2N2 virus strain, 351–353, 359
    H3N2 virus strain, 351–353, 359
    identification of the animal host, 356–357
    origins of, 353–354
    pathogenicity's biological basis, 357–358
    potential for reappearance, 360–361
    sequential waves (1918–1919), 353–356, 358, 360–361
    virus lineages, 352
Instagram, 503–504, 509–510
Internet, 310, 363–372, 412–413, 506–507, 509–510. *See also* social media
irony, 16, 30, 32, 43, 88, 170, 179, 187, 234, 264
Isherwood, Christopher, 313
Island of the Color Blind (Sacks), 316
Islands of the Blessed, 6

Jackson, Michael, 311
jailing of African Americans, 125–137, 438, 443
Jefferson, Thomas, 39, 135
Jesus Christ, 37–38, 126, 133, 223, 270
Jim Crow discrimination, 112, 431, 435, 440, 452, 454–455, 485
Judaism/Jewish people, 14, 29, 130, 131, 168, 186, 219–229, 295, 465. *See also* Holocaust

Kahn, Herman, 502, 508–509
Keizer, Garret, 408–409
Kennedy, John F., 209
Khomeini, Ayatollah, 394–395, 398
King, Martin Luther, Jr., 125–137, 294, 441, 444, 448, 468
Kosovo genocide, 294, 296–297
Kubrick, Stanley, 363, 371, 509
Ku Klux Klan, 131, 448, 494

Latinx women, 243, 474, 475
Lawrence, D. H., 314
lesbian people, 219–229, 411–412, 463, 467
LGBT (lesbian, gay, bisexual, transgender) people, 410–411, 461–469
Lincoln, Abraham, 133, 422
linguistic terrorism, 247–249
lotteries, 66–67, 97–105
love songs, 269–277
Luther, Martin, 133, 468
luxurious living, thoughts of, 81–82
lying advice to youth, by Twain, 78
lynchings, 424, 446, 485

Madison, James, 209–211
Madonna, 314
Maine Lobster Festival (MLF), 335–350
marriage
    American men, non-English-speaking women, 239
    Douglass's comparison of hunter's rights to, 353
    dowry expectations, 81
    gay marriage, 410, 412
    impact of poverty, 82–83
    raising/selling of children for food and, 14
    Stanton on related laws, 49–50
    state-level definition of, 410
Marriage Protection Act (US), 408
Mathiessen, Peter, 316
"The Matthew Effect" (Gladwell), 373–385
May, Samuel J., 38
meme theory (Dawkins), 390
memories of a dead parent, 107–109
Meredith, James, 136
Midnight's Children (Rushdie), 394
Miller, Henry, 314
Miller, Terry, 410
Minogue, Kylie, 273–274
monarchies, 32
money
    borrowing money, 86
    money-making/hoarding, 62–65
Montresor family, 17–20
The Moor's Last Sigh (Rushdie), 394

Muhammad, Elijah, 132
murder
    of an elephant, 89–95
    attempted, of Kreider, 401–402
    of a friend, 17–20
    by mothers, of bastard children, 10
    by stoning, 97–104
Muslim movement, 132
"My Negro Problem-And Ours" (Podhoretz), 232, 234
My Other Life (Theroux), 316

Naipaul, V. S., 316
naming of things/objects, 2
National Association for the Advancement of Colored People (NAACP), 150, 152
National Health Interview Survey, 493
National Rifle Association, 327, 332
Native Americans, 346, 454, 497
Nazi Germany, concentration camps, 223, 293–296
near-death experiences, 401
New Orleans, Louisiana, 33–34, 108–109
newspapers, 70–71, 75
New York Times, 159–160, 342, 368, 446, 485, 504
Nietzsche, Friedrich, 366, 368
Nixon, Richard, 209, 305
nonviolent activism, 125–128, 125–137, 132–133, 136–137, 155

Obama, Barack (Obama administration), 415–449, 457, 496–497
Occidentals, 66
Ocean, Frank, 412
On Thermonuclear War (Kahn), 502
Orientals, 65–66
Orwell, George, 213, 394
outing of gay people, 408
Outliers (Gladwell), 373–385

Page, Larry, 369
Paine, Thomas, 223
pandemics, 493–499. *See also* influenza pandemic (1918)
    AIDS crisis, 490, 495–496, 499
    Black Death, 495–497
    COVID-19, 486–490, 498–499
    SARS epidemic, 498–499
patriotism, 26, 28
philosophy, 1–7, 62, 66, 69, 132, 145–146, 150–152, 294, 344, 509
"The Philosophy of Travel" (Santayana), 309
Plato, 1–7, 65–66, 370

Plessy v. Ferguson, 485
Podhoretz, Norman, 232, 234
politics. *See also* Democratic Party; Republican Party
  belief in kindness and, 390
  family disagreements about, 328
  food and, 305
  ghettos and, 432
  impeachment of a president, 207–211
  slavery/slave-trade and, 33, 39
  Thoreau on the superficiality of, 75
  women's rights and, 57
poverty, ramifications of, 81–87
principled living, 61–76
printing press, 365, 367, 370–372, 509
prisoners, 1–7, 90, 294, 423, 438
privacy
  body difference/compromising of, 409
  coming out and, 409–410
  Keizer's argument on, 408–410
Privacy (Keizer), 408–409
protests
  ACT UP protests, 464
  anti-Vietnam War, 201–202
  Black Lives Matter movement, 436
  by Bundy against federal grazing fees, 443
  First Amendment and, 130
  in Hong Kong, 498
  Montgomery, Alabama bus protest, 134
  nonviolent protests, 132
  Puerto Rican history, 477–484
  Russia, 2011-2012, 466
  Tea Party protests, 443
Psalm 137, 272–273
Puerto Rican history, 477–484

Race Traits (Hoffman), 486–491
racism, 128, 227–228, 410, 421, 439–444, 446–447, 451, 486–491. *See also* white supremacy
Raymond, R. R., 38
reality *vs.* shadows of artificial objects, 2–4
Reed, Lou, 271–272
Republican Party, 31–32, 141–144, 325, 327, 407, 411, 416, 420, 423, 432–433, 439–440
respectful behavior, 77–78
revenge, 17–18, 273
Ride, Sally, 411
right, 493
riots
  Detroit race riots, 107
  Harlem race riots, 107, 121–122
  protest riots, 483
  in Puerto Rico, 483

  race riots, 107, 121–122
  throughout the Muslim world, 396
Romney, Mitt, 423
Roosevelt, Franklin D., 295–296
Rushdie, Salman, 393–398
Russia, LGBTQ+ rights, 461–469

Sacks, Oliver, 316
saleability of children, 10–12
Santayana, George, 309, 317
SARS epidemic, Hong Kong, 498–499
The Satanic Verses (Rushdie), 394–397
Savage, Dan, 410
Schmidt, Eric, 369
Schrock, Edward, 408
segregation, 128–130, 132–134, 136, 143–147, 153
self-hatred, 225, 227
self-reflection, 3
sexist double standards, 471
Sikhs, 252, 255, 258, 261
slaves/slavery
  anti-slavery speech by Douglass, 23–43
  Bible and, 36–37
  capture/torture of, 35
  Christianity and, 35, 37, 39–40
  comparison of women's rights, 55–56
  crimes punishable by death in Virginia, 31
  description of plight of the slaves, 34–35
  escaping from, 23–24
  King, Jr. on, 135
  meaninglessness of Independence Day for, 32
  profitability of the slave trade, 33–34
  raising of white children by black women, 239
  Stanton's comparison of women's rights, 50
  Thoreau's comment on, 61
  U.S. Constitution and, 40–41
  U.S. nationalization of, 35
The Snow Leopard (Mathiessen), 316
social activism, 125, 436
social media, 408, 497, 509–511. *See also* blogging; Facebook; Instagram; Twitter; YouTube
societal obligations, 64–65
"Song of Solomon," 272
souls
  ascension of, 4
  indwelling powers/virtues of, 5
  perturbation of, 4–5
Southern Christian Leadership Conference, 126
Southern Poverty Law Center, 455

Star Spangled Banner, 35
stoning to death, 97–104
stupidity, 36, 78, 83, 256, 289, 402, 442, 482
Supreme Court
    comment of Malcolm X, 153
    comparisons of Facebook's decisions, 507
    1954 segregation ruling, 129–130, 146
    Obama's nomination of Sotomayor, 423
    Plessy v. Ferguson decision, 485
    role in impeachment ruling, 423

Taylor, Frederick Winslow, 368–369
teenagers, 98, 100, 107, 165, 174, 223–224, 233, 238, 251–252, 256, 301, 320, 327, 410
text-messaging, 365, 367, 370–372, 509
Theroux, Paul, 316
Thoreau, Henry David, 316, 317
transgender people, 466–469
traveling, reasons for, 309–317
Trump, Donald (Trump administration), 211, 416, 420–421, 431–432, 437–438, 440–441, 443–444, 446–448, 452, 456, 468–469, 490–491, 496–497
Twitter, 432, 503, 509, 510
2001: A Space Odyssey film, 363, 371

United Nations (UN), 147–148
United States (U.S.)
    anti-slavery speech of Douglass, 23–43
    bombings in Vietnam War, 159–161, 164–166, 171, 176, 186–191, 198, 201
    California gold rush, 66–67
    Continental Congress, 26
    countrywide racial tension, 115
    Fugitive Slave Law, 35–36
    history as British subjects, 24–25
    Independence Day (July 4th), 24, 32
    nationalization of slavery, 35
    profitability of the Southern slave trade, 33
    Stanton's demands for women's rights, 45–59
    Vietnam War, 157–205
    work ethic in, 62–63

Van Morrison, 271
vaults, for wine, 18–19

Vietnam War, 157–205, 159–161, 164–166, 171, 176, 186–191, 198, 201

Wahls, Zach, 412–413
Waits, Tom, 271
Walden (Thoreau), 61
walking in the woods, 62
war crimes, 107, 160
Washington, George, 207
A Way in the World (Naipaul), 316
whiteness, 123, 222, 419, 473, 488
white supremacy, 440–441, 458, 473, 475, 504
Williams, Serena, 445, 471–472, 474
Wilson, Woodrow, 208–209
wine, 17–20
Wolf, Maryanne, 365–366, 371
Wolfe, Thomas, 389
The Woman's Bible (Stanton), 45
Woman's Loyal National League, 45
women's rights
    comparison of U.S. and England, 47
    comparison to men's rights, 49–51
    comparison to slave rights, 55–56
    in Constitution of N.Y., 48
    in England, 47, 51
    impact of right to property law, 51–52
    New York State laws (1848, 1849), 58–59
    rights of mothers and children, 54–55
    rights of widows, 52–54
    speech by Stanton, 45–59
    women's suffrage, 45, 58, 59
work ethic in the United States, 62–64
World War I, 493
World War II, 167, 199, 279, 294, 394, 427–428, 498, 506
writing
    love songs, 269–277
    reasons for, 213–218
    sh**** first drafts, 265–268

Young, Neil, 271
youth, Twain's advice to, 77–80
YouTube, 410, 448, 502–503, 507

Zuckerberg, Mark, 502, 504–508